York Deeds Volume bk.4

You are holding a reproduction of an original work that is in the public domain in the United States of America, and possibly other countries. You may freely copy and distribute this work as no entity (individual or corporate) has a copyright on the body of the work. This book may contain prior copyright references, and library stamps (as most of these works were scanned from library copies). These have been scanned and retained as part of the historical artifact.

This book may have occasional imperfections such as missing or blurred pages, poor pictures, errant marks, etc. that were either part of the original artifact, or were introduced by the scanning process. We believe this work is culturally important, and despite the imperfections, have elected to bring it back into print as part of our continuing commitment to the preservation of printed works worldwide. We appreciate your understanding of the imperfections in the preservation process, and hope you enjoy this valuable book.

YORK DEEDS.

BOOK IV.

1684 – 1697

PORTLAND:
JOHN T. HULL AND B. THURSTON & CO.
1888.

PRINTED BY B. THURSTON & CO.

1128628

CONTENTS.

PREFACE	Pages	5—17
REGISTER'S CERTIFICATE,	Page	19
ERRATA	Page	20
YORK DEEDS	Folios	1—162
INDEX	Pages	1—158
I. Grantors	Pages	1— 57
II. Grantees	Pages	58—115
III. Other Persons	Pages	116—127
IV. Places	Pages	128—134
V. General	Pages	135—158

PREFACE.

On the 5th of February, 1684, Edward Rishworth made the first record in the volume which he marked on a fly leaf, "The fourth Book of Records for Deeds &c in the County of York." The last record, in the regular series, was made by Joseph Hammond, July 25, 1699. Four conveyances were afterward recorded, in 1700 and 1702, on pages previously left blank[1]; and three supplementary records were affixed to the proper documents in 1700, 1718 and 1719[2]; but the regular series ended in July, 1699. The book was in use for fifteen years.

During five of these years, New England was the scene of intense political excitement, which culminated in revolution. The charter of the Massachusetts Bay company was annulled by a decree in chancery in 1684; but the reorganization which would naturally have followed, was delayed nearly two years by the death of Charles II, the accession of James II, and the rebellion of the Duke of Monmouth. During this interval, the government under the charter continued by its own momentum. In May, 1686, Joseph Dudley was proclaimed president of the council of Massachusetts, New Hampshire, Maine and Narraganset, and in December Sir Edmund Andros arrived at Boston in the character of captain-general and governor-general of the same territory and also of Plymouth. There was no provision in the new government for a general assembly of representatives of the people. Public affairs were to be administered with the advice of the council appointed by the king; but the commonalty could be heard only by petition. Thomas Danforth had been president of Maine under the Massachusetts charter, but his authority now ceased. Edward Tyng of Falmouth, Francis Champernon of Kittery and Bartholomew Gedney of Salem, were appointed councillors for Maine.[3] The county of Cornwall, east of the Kennebec river, was still a part of New York; and thither, in 1686,

---
[1] Fol. 161, 150, 69. [2] Fol. 151, 158, 128.
[3] 1 Williamson's Maine, 584 n. Gedney had large interests in Maine, and sometimes resided at York. Champernon did not take his seat in the council.

Governor Dongan of New York sent John Palmer, a member of his council, with John West as deputy secretary, to reestablish the land titles and especially to provide for the regular collection of quit-rents and customs. Edward Randolph, member of the New England council and secretary of the board, was charged with similar duties. His deputy secretary and register for Maine, appointed in 1686, was Thomas Scottow, son of Joshua Scottow of Scarborough.[1] Probate business was administered by the governor or through his deputies, and appeals might be taken to the governor in person.[2] In 1687 Joshua Scottow was appointed surrogate for Maine, and his son was designated for register of the new probate court.[3] A member of the council always presided at the county courts, and was assisted by resident justices of the peace. Appeals were heard in Boston by a superior court consisting of a majority of the council. Dudley, as president of the council, became chief justice of the superior court. It was ordered that all public records of the former governments should be brought to Boston.

Before the end of the year 1687, Governor Andros had secured the submission of Rhode Island and Connecticut to his authority. In April, 1688, he was commissioned governor of the Dominion of New England, meaning all the English territory north of the 40th parallel of latitude, including of course New York and the Jerseys, and extending eastward to the river St. Croix. Under the new commission he had 42 councillors — John Palmer among the rest, but five constituted a quorum, and the governor's authority was practically absolute. Legislative, judicial and executive powers were all vested in his will. The people chafed under this arbitrary government. They resented the exaction of fees for new patents and quit-rents for the enjoyment of their lands. So far as they could, they evaded the acts of trade and navigation, which obstructed their commerce. They watched with keen interest the ferment in the mother country. They suspected Andros of a plan to hold New England for King James in any case, even if the sceptre should be wrested from the king. They thought he was negotiating for this purpose with the French and their Indian allies. At last, on the 4th of April, 1689, they heard

---

[1] In 3 Palfrey's New England, 503 n., the name is printed incorrectly Sutton It was sometimes written Scottoway, and appears in the form Skottowe, on the title-page of Mr. B C Skottowe's Short History of Parliament, published in 1886 or 1887.

[2] 3 Palfrey's New England, 522   [3] Willis's Law, Courts and Lawyers of Maine, 55.

that William of Orange had landed in England. On the 18th of April they rose, seized and imprisoned Andros and 25 of his principal officers,— Randolph, Palmer, West, Dudley and others,— and reëstablished the governments which had been dissolved in 1686 and 1687.

In Maine, Danforth was restored to the office of president and Charles Frost, Francis Hooke, Edward Tyng, John Davis, Joshua Scottow, Samuel Wheelwright and John Wincoll were reappointed councillors. These temporary arrangements were approved by King William, and continued until the charter of 1691 passed the seals. By that instrument Maine, Cornwall, Massachusetts and Plymouth were consolidated in one royal province, called the province of Massachusetts Bay. The governor, lieutenant governor and secretary were to be appointed by the king. The council was to be chosen annually by the general court. The house of representatives was to be chosen by the people in their towns. Maine was to have three councillors, and Job Alcock and Samuel Donnell of York and Samuel Heyman of Berwick were named in the charter for the first council. These names were proposed by the Rev. Increase Mather, who was the agent of Massachusetts in London when the charter was granted. His acquaintance in Maine appears to have been limited. At the first election, Alcock and Heyman were dropped and Francis Hooke and Charles Frost were elected to their places. Sylvanus Davis was designated for Cornwall. He lived at Falmouth, but owned lands on the eastern side of the Kennebec and was consequently qualified though not a resident of the territory which he was to represent. The charter was brought over by Sir William Phips, the first governor, and the provincial government was inaugurated May 14, 1692. Sir William died in London, Feb. 18, 1695. The administration was continued by the lieutenant governor, William Stoughton. Richard, earl of Bellomont, was appointed governor in November, 1697, but did not arrive in Boston until May 20, 1699.

During the ten years from 1689 until 1699, the war known as King William's war had raged in Maine. James Stuart arrived on the coast of Ireland in March, 1689, with a French fleet and French troops, to recover the crown which William of Orange had accepted from the Westminster convention a month before. War between England and France was proclaimed in Boston on

8   PREFACE.

the 7th of December, 1689, but the declaration lagged more than a year behind the fact. The French resented the intrusion of New England fishermen upon the Acadian fishing grounds and the meddling of New York buyers with the fur trade on the great lakes. The dispute about the fur trade had ended in hostilities between the French and the western Indians, and in 1688 Canada was invaded by the fierce Iroquois. At the same time, the eastern tribes, encouraged by the French, drove out the English planters on the Sheepscot and the Kennebec, and broke up the settlement at North Yarmouth. In 1689 the stockade at Pemaquid was burned and the country east of Falmouth was abandoned to the savage enemy. In 1690 the French themselves took part in the conflict. Parties of French and Indians destroyed the plantation at Salmon Falls, in Berwick, and burned Fort Loyal in Falmouth, leaving the town desolate. The people of Scarborough, Saco and Cape Porpoise fled to Wells, which became the frontier town. Troops were sent from Massachusetts and Plymouth, and Major Robert Pike, of Salisbury, then 74 years old, was appointed commander-in-chief of all the English forces east of the Merrimac. Major Elisha Hutchinson, of Boston, was associated with Pike in November, for the negotiation of a truce with the Indians, which was accomplished, but hostilities were renewed in the spring of 1691. Wells was beset; the settlement at Cape Neddick was laid in ashes. Major Pike, worn out with anxiety and responsibility, fell ill in September, and Major Hutchinson succeeded him in the chief command, which he held until Governor Phips became *ex officio* commander of all the provincial forces in May, 1692.[1] In February of that year, a great part of York was burned, and in June Wells was attacked but was successfully defended. In August the governor proceeded in person to Pemaquid, where he ordered a stone fort to be built. The work was finished in a few months, and in 1693 a fortress, also of stone, was erected on the right bank of the Saco, near the falls. The Indians were now closely pressed by the rangers, and professed to be tired of the war, but in 1694 they rallied and penetrated to Kittery, the last town in Maine. There were no operations in 1695 on a large scale, but the whole country was infested by prowling savages and about 40 English people were killed or

[1] 1 N. E. Hist. and Gen. Register, 301. 2 Hutchinson's Massachusetts, 66. Pike's New Puritan, 120, 128, 145.

carried into captivity. Among the captives, Major Joseph Hammond of Kittery was perhaps the most distinguished. In 1696 the new fort at Pemaquid was taken and demolished. Peace was concluded between the French and English in 1697; but the Indian war continued during the year 1698, and was ended at last by the treaty signed at Mare Point in Casco bay, Jan. 7, 1699.

The confusion of the times is reflected in the records now printed. Although the fourth book was in use from 1684 till 1699, it was not in continuous use. From 1687 until 1689, the register used the book now numbered sixth. From 1690 until 1696, the records were continued in what is now the fifth book, and from 1696 till 1699 the register returned to the fourth book. The records of the fifteen years are thus scattered through three volumes. The registers during this period were Edward Rishworth, from 1684 to 1686; Thomas Scottow, from 1686 to 1689; John Wincoll, from 1689 to 1694; and Joseph Hammond, senior, from 1694 to 1699.

When Rishworth wrote his last official line in June, 1686, he had been recorder of the province for nearly 33 years. He was first appointed in October, 1651, and had held the office continuously, except in 1668 and 1669, when Peter Weare occupied the place. He was now an old man. His wife's name appears for the last time in the volumes now printed, under the date 1675.[1] She doubtless died before 1682, when he conveyed his dwelling and lands in York to his son-in-law, John Sayward, for £60, to be devoted mainly to the payment of his debts, receiving also Sayword's bond for an annuity of £6 and free use of a lower room in the house with "comfortable diet," fire wood and keeping for a horse.[2] Sayward married Rishworth's daughter Mary. After her husband's death she married again and was Mrs Mary Hall when she filed the inventory of her father's estate, Feb. 25, 1691.[3] The estate was valued by Abraham Preble and Matthew Austin, at £39. It was a year after Rishworth's death, when York was burned by the French and Indians in February, 1692. His son-in-law, Mr. Dummer, the minister of York, was slain, and his daughter, Mrs. Lydia Dummer, was borne away to captivity and death. This horror, Rishworth was mercifully spared.

Thomas Scottow, son of Joshua Scottow, merchant, was born in Boston, June 30, 1659, and named for an uncle who once lived on the City hall lot in School street, and sold it to the town in

[1] 2 York Deeds, 180.   [2] 3 York Deeds, 121.   [3] 5 York Deeds.

1645.[1] Thomas the younger was graduated at Harvard college in 1677, at the foot of a class of six. His father had bought Abraham Jocelyn's farm on Black Point river in Scarborough, in 1660, and in 1663 had advanced £310 to Henry Jocelyn, taking a mortgage on lands, buildings and other property, at Black Point. In 1666 the debt had increased to £484, and was secured by a new mortgage covering specifically the Cammock patent of 1500 acres at Black Point with 750 acres adjacent granted directly to Jocelyn by Sir Ferdinando Gorges, and the neighboring islands called Stratton's islands It appears that an extensive fishing business was carried on at Black Point, in which Scottow had become interested, probably by furnishing supplies, and in the course of time Jocelyn had fallen heavily in debt to the merchant. Possession of the mortgaged property was given to Scottow in July, 1668, and in 1670, or about that time, he came to Scarborough to live.[2] In 1671 he was licensed to sell wines and liquors to his fishermen and others. When the first Indian war began, in 1675, Captain Scottow succeeded in obtaining a detachment of troops from Boston to defend his property at Black Point. Captain John Wincoll also came to the relief of Scarborough with the Kittery company of 60 men. In the fall of 1676, the place was deserted by the English inhabitants, but was speedily reoccupied. When the government of Maine was reorganized in 1680, Captain Scottow was appointed one of Governor Danforth's councillors, and in 1681 he gave a lot of a hundred acres on the plains near the great pond for the site of a fort and of dwellings which might be occupied in safety near the fortification. The fort was built by the town. Captain Scottow was also one of the trustees to whom Governor Danforth, in 1684, confirmed the land within the town of Scarborough for the benefit and use of the inhabitants and their successors.[3] In July, 1686, his son Thomas became deputy clerk and register of deeds for Maine under Edward Randolph who, as has been stated, had a royal commission as sole register in New England, by himself or his deputies.[4] In September, 1687, Joshua Scottow received from Governor Andros his commission as deputy judge of probate for Maine, and his son was appointed register of probate. Thomas was also admitted attorney of the inferior

[1] 2 Memorial Hist of Boston, xxxiii
[2] 1 York Deeds, I, 92, 137, 163 2 York Deeds, 6, 98.
[3] 3 Maine Hist. Collections, 115 &c
[4] The commission is printed in 27 Mass. Hist. Coll. 161.

PREFACE.   11

court of common pleas in Maine about the same time.[1] His last record as register of deeds is dated April 14, 1689, four days before the revolution in Boston. During the remainder of the year he remained at Scarborough, in command of the fort on the plains ; but in May, 1690, Fort Loyal at Falmouth fell, and thereupon the garrison at Black Point drew off to Wells. It was a dozen years before the settlement at Scarborough was revived, and in the interval both Scottows passed away. The father died January 20, 1698, leaving his estate to his wife during her life, then a double portion to his son Thomas, and the rest equally to his daughters Elizabeth, Rebecca and Mary. What became of Thomas was unknown, until his will was recently discovered in England. It is described as follows :

Will of Thomas Scottow, of Boston in New England, now bound forth on a voyage to sea in the ship Gerrard of London, Captain William Dennis commander, 14 Nov. 1698, proved 4 Sept. 1699. To my loving sister Elizabeth Savage of New England aforesaid, all my real and personal estate in New England of what kind soever. To my loving friend Margaret Softly, of the parish of St. Paul, Shadwell, in the county of Middlesex, widow, all and singular such moneys, salaries and wages whatsoever as is and shall become due to me for my service in said ship, to her own use in satisfaction of what I shall owe and be indebted unto her at my death, and I appoint her my executrix.[2]

Elizabeth Scottow, to whom her brother thus left his estate in New England, had married Thomas Savage in 1664. Their daughter, Lydia, married Timothy Prout, bringing to him her share of the Cammock patent. Her husband afterward bought the rest of the patent from the other heirs and removed to Scarborough, and Black Point thus became and remains Prout's Neck.[3]

After the revolution of April, 1689, John Wincoll of Kittery was chosen clerk of the courts and recorder of the province of Maine, at York, on the 20th of December. Captain Wincoll was then about 67 years old. He came from Watertown, Massachusetts, to Kittery, while still a young man, and was one of the signers of the submission to the government of Massachusetts in 1652.[4] The first representative of Kittery in the general court at Boston, in 1653, he was reëlected in 1654 and 1655, and was also one of the selectmen of the town in 1654, and many times afterward. After his service as deputy in 1655, he appears to have returned

[1] 4 Maine Hist. and Gen. Recorder, 292.   [2] 39 N. E. Hist. and Gen. Register, 169.
[3] 3 Maine Hist. Coll. 221.   [4] Sullivan's Maine, 343.

to Watertown for a time. At any rate he sat for Watertown in the general court for 1658, and in an extensive timber grant from the town of Kittery in 1659, he is described as John Wincoll of Watertown.[1] This grant conveyed to him the right to cut timber above Salmon falls on the great Newgewanac river to the northern boundary of the town and three miles from the river eastward into the woods. Having secured this privilege he built two saw mills at Salmon falls, where he lived for many years. He was aided in this enterprise by Thomas Broughton, a Boston merchant, who had previously been interested in a mill at Sturgeon creek, where Wincoll bought a house and land in 1651.[2] In 1676, a fourth part of the property and rights at Salmon falls was conveyed to George and John Broughton, sons of Thomas, to satisfy their claim. Appointed a justice of the peace by John Archdale in behalf of Ferdinando Gorges, in 1663, Wincoll was reappointed to the same dignity by the royal commissioners who in 1665 overthrew the short-lived Gorges government. After the authority of Massachusetts was restored, in 1668, Wincoll remained in private life for a season in consequence of his acceptance of office from the obnoxious royal commissioners; but from 1671 to 1686 he was continuously in the magistracy — associate of York county from 1671 to 1680, justice of the peace in Governor Danforth's council from 1680 till 1686. He was again deputy for Kittery to the general court in 1675, 1677 and 1678. He was also for many years town surveyor; a large part of the real estate in Berwick was platted by him, and he was often employed as referee in the division of important properties, such as the Lewis and Bonython patent at Saco in 1680 and the Shapleigh estate in Kittery in 1684. As early as 1670, he was captain of the Kittery company. In October, 1675, while he was with his company at Scarborough, which was beset by Indians, his house at Salmon falls was burned by the enemy. In the second Indian war when the greater part of the settlement at Salmon falls was burned by a party of French and Indians in March, 1690, Captain Wincoll's house was twice assaulted but the enemy were beaten off by six or seven men who were within.[3] On the 1st of November, 1692, Wincoll was reappointed clerk of York county under the new Massachusetts charter, and in 1693, when the probate court was reorganized, he was appointed register. He continued to serve as clerk of courts and

[1] Infra, fol. 8.   [2] 2 York Deeds, 161.
[3] Mass. Archives cited in Hull's Fort Loyall, 56.

PREFACE. 13

register of deeds and of probate until October 22, 1694, when he was killed by a fall from his horse.[1]

Joseph Hammond of Kittery was appointed clerk and register to succeed Wincoll, Dec. 4, 1694. He was born in Wells, in 1647 or 1648, the second son of William Hammond, who died in 1702 at the extraordinary age of 105.[2] His son Joseph was born in 1678. Joseph Hammond, senior, settled in Kittery. He was a carpenter,[3] but as skilful with a pen as with the tools of his trade. In 1692 he was chosen town clerk, and the Kittery records show a marked improvement after they came into his hands. He was interested in military matters too, and in 1695 had risen to the rank of major. In July of that year, he was captured by Indians near Saco fort and taken to Canada. Count Frontenac, the French governor, respecting the prisoner's rank, it is said, treated him with great kindness, and he was exchanged and sent home, arriving in Maine after an absence somewhat less than six months.[4] From 1698 till 1703, and again in 1705, he was a member of the governor's council.[5] In June, 1700, he was appointed a judge of the county court of common pleas, to fill a vacancy caused by the death of Samuel Wheelwright. It appears to have been the practice at that time to select one of the four judges of common pleas for judge of probate. At any rate Francis Hooke and Samuel Wheelwright had filled both offices simultaneously and Hammond succeeded Wheelwright in both capacities. In 1707 he was appointed commissioner of oyer and terminer to try Joseph Gunnison for murder. He died Feb. 24, 1710. Joseph Hammond, junior, was 22 years old in 1700, and was then appointed clerk and register, succeeding in after life to others of his father's dignities.[6] Both were men of good repute, esteemed by all who knew them.

John Newmarch, whose name figures in the records as clerk and register in September, October and November, 1695, was a young minister at Kittery, temporarily appointed to fill Hammond's place during the major's involuntary journey to Canada. Newmarch

---

[1] See Savage's Genealogical Dictionary and indexes to York Deeds, s. v. Wincoll.
[2] 9 N. E. Hist. and Gen. Register, 312. [3] Infra, fol. 3.
[4] 2 Hutchinson's Massachusetts, 85.
[5] 4 Palfrey's New England, 600. Williamson (2 Maine, 75) says he was a councillor nine years, but gives no dates. Palfrey is undoubtedly right.
[6] It has been supposed, by reason of the identity of the names, that the elder Hammond was register of deeds until 1710, when he died; but a careful examination of the records shows that he retired from the office in 1701, soon after his appointment to the bench. The writing of father and son is much alike, and the signature remains "Joseph Hammond, register," instead of "Joseph Hammond, Jr.," as might have been expected.

belonged to an Ipswich family and was a graduate of Harvard college in 1690.[1]

With these facts and dates in mind, it becomes possible to unravel the snarl in which the York records between 1684 and 1700 were left. Those records are scattered through three volumes, the fourth, fifth and sixth in the registry of deeds. The fourth was opened by Rishworth in 1684 and continued by him regularly till June, 1686. The fifth had been opened by Rishworth in July, 1680, as a special record of probate business, which had not before been separated from the ordinary proceedings of the courts and records of conveyances. In this book he not only recorded current probate business but transcribed earlier records from time to time, so that finally he had completed a record of probate proceedings for ten years, from 1676 to 1686. Scottow, beginning in July, 1686, continued the record of deeds in the fourth book and added an inventory to the probate record in the fifth book. But in February, 1687, Scottow opened a new volume for deeds, now the sixth, and in September of the same year, opened what is now the first book of probate records. The fourth and sixth books of deeds were in Scottow's keeping, probably at Scarborough. The fifth, a probate record, for which Scottow had no further use, appears to have remained at York. It has been supposed that Scottow perhaps resided and kept his records in Boston during his term of office[2]; but that is doubtful. After he left college in 1677, he often witnessed deeds executed at Scarborough, and the probability is, that he lived there constantly with his father.[3] The earlier records were removed to Boston, in pursuance of the order issued by Governor Andros in May, 1687, but the current volumes remained with the deputy register at Scarborough, and the forgotten fifth book with Rishworth at York. Thomas Scottow, as has been stated, commanded the fort at Black Point in 1689. When the garrison withdrew in 1690, the Scarborough records were carried to Boston for safety,[4] and Scottow's Maine records of course went with the town books. Meanwhile Wincoll had been appointed clerk and register, and he, searching for a record book, came upon Rishworth's fifth volume. He continued the probate record as a general record of deeds; and turning the book upside down, began at the other end a court record. Having this double character,

[1] Savage's Genealogical Dictionary, s. v. Newmarch.
[2] 1 York Deeds, Introduction, 70 and note. [3] See folios 23, 38 and 74, in this volume.
[4] 3 Maine Hist. Coll. 165.

the volume may be claimed with equal reason by the register of deeds, or by the clerk of courts, who in fact had possession of it for a long time, as appears by the following passage from a schedule prepared by Jeremiah Goodwin, register, in 1816, when the records were carried to Alfred:

On the following day [May 4, 1816] received ninety-two Books of Records, & the Alphabets belonging to the same, numbered from one to ninety-three, excepting number five, which is in the Clerk's Office, as also, numerous files of deeds &c. all of which were removed to Alfred.

Among Wincoll's records, are three orders of the county court with regard to the records which had been carried away to Boston. At a court of sessions at York, Nov. 1, 1692,—

This Court orders Jn° Wincoll y° Clarke to take the records of this County into his Custody that are with Mr Hutchinson in Boston and to pervse them as occasion may require.

This Mr. Hutchinson is probably Major Elisha Hutchinson, who had recently been commander-in-chief of the troops serving in Maine. He was the grandson of the celebrated Ann Hutchinson, and the grandfather of Governor Hutchinson, the historian of Massachusetts. His wife was a daughter of Mrs. Bridget Sanford, afterward Bridget Phillips, of Saco; and Hutchinson was one of the number to whom Major Phillips in 1676 granted the famous nineteen thousand acres in the township now called Sanford. He was a member of the Massachusetts council after the revolution of 1689 until he died in 1717, serving two years, 1708 and 1709, as a representative of Maine in that board.[1] With his special interest in Maine, it is not unlikely that he may have taken possession of the Maine records in Boston after Andros was deposed. They were not immediately returned, however. The court at Wells, Oct. 3, 1693, passed this order:

Vpon Complaint of Dyuers persons for want of the records It is ordered that the Clarke of the court shall goe to Boston for the records that are with Mr Hutchinson and with Captain Scottow, takeing the aprobation of his Exclency and Councill.

The clerk's mission appears to have been successful, for on the 2d of January following, 1694, the following order was adopted:

[1] 1 Williamson's Maine, 680.

16   Preface.

Whereas there is great Complaint for want of the records this Court with the advice of the grand Jury doe order that the records of this County which are at Boston shall be speedily sent for and brought to Leuit William Fernald's House vppon his Island and kept till further order and y[e] Clarke of this Court to fetch them as soone as may be and the Sheriff to Deliver him thirty shillings to pay for the bookes in Cap· Scottows hands which are a part of the County records.

Lieutenant Fernald was a son of Reginald Fernald, surgeon, who was sent over to Piscataqua in 1631 by John Mason. The war was still raging in 1694, and the books were probably left on Fernald's island for greater security. In October following, Wincoll died. His successor continued the court record in the fifth book to 1699, and the deeds until January, 1696. Then he went back to the fourth book, which had been returned from Boston, and filled the blank pages with deeds until July, 1699, skipping in August to the blank pages of the sixth book, opened by Scottow. The record of deeds is continued in the sixth book by the younger Hammond, to February, 1702.

The volume now printed is the last of the four brought out by the aid of the State under the resolve of March 15, 1883. It has been shown that in order to complete the printing of the 17th century records in the York registry of deeds, the fifth and sixth books should be included in the series. It has also been proved by actual experiment, that the cost of printing these useful documents cannot be met by private subscriptions. It is hoped, therefore, that the State will provide at least for the printing of the two volumes described above.

This fourth book, like its predecessors, contains much interesting historical matter,— some circumstances of the last days of George Cleeve's only child, Mrs. Elizabeth Harvey, a dozen pages about Richard Wharton's title at Pejepscot, derived from Thomas Purchase and others; Danforth's commission to George Pearson and others to lay out North Yarmouth and assign lots to the inhabitants; testimony concerning Robert Jordan's suit in 1645 against Richard Vines, and his attachment of Saco Neck and judgment thereon; testimony concerning Robert Nanny's suit against Gorges in 1647, and attachment of Gorges point in York, and the manner in which Nanny's title was set aside by President Danforth nearly forty years afterward[1]; a trace of Henry Joce-

---

[1] See Sargent's note on this affair, 3 Maine Recorder, 53.

lyn's life at Pemaquid, in 1680; a conveyance by Robert Tufton Mason in 1687, of 500 acres in Kittery, under the title conveyed by Gorges to John Mason in 1635, in the deed discovered by Wm. M Sargent, Esq., and printed in his introduction to the second book of York Deeds. All these documents will be readily found by the help of the indexes.

Acknowledgment must again be made to Mr. Sargent for his valuable services in copying the text of the records and preparing the indexes. The contractions in the text are explained in the preface to the first book.

H. W. RICHARDSON.

REGISTER'S CERTIFICATE.

State of Maine.

COUNTY OF YORK, ss:

This may certify that the following printed volume is a true copy of the fourth book of records of the Registry of Deeds for this County; that I have read and compared the same with the original records; and that all accidental variations that have been detected are noted in the table of errata on the following page.

Attest:

Justin M. Leavitt

Register of Deeds for York County.

ERRATA.

☞ The sign — is used below, when the line indicated is numbered backward from the end of the folio

Folio	72	line	24	*for*	Jun^r_e	*read*	Junr
	74		49	"	Rep^t	"	Dep^t
	88		35	*erase*	considerations me hereunto mouing, but more Especially for the		
	100	margin		*for*	60^b	*read*	60^{bb}
	109		—1	"	Testimong	"	Testimony.

YORK DEEDS.

[pa : 1 :] Know all men by these Presents, that I Elihew Crookett of Kittery in the Prouince of Mayne fisherman, with the Consent of Ann Geffrey formerly the wife of Thomas Crockett deceased, & now the wife of Dygory Jefferys, & with the Consent of my brother Ephraim Crockett, for & in Consideration of the sume of Twenty three pounds, of Current pay of New England in hand payd & receiued, before ye Ensealeing & deliuery of these Presents,

Elihu Crocket
To
Aaron Ferris

the receipt w^rof sd Elihew Crockett doth acknowledg, & him selfe to bee fully satisfyd, Content & payd, & y^rof & of euery part & Prcell thereof doth acquitt, exonerate & discharge Aron ferris, his heyres, executors, Administrators & Assignes for euer, p these Presents: As also for diuerse other good Causes, & Considerations him ye sayd Elihew Crockett y^runto espetially moueing, hath given, granted barganed & sould, aliend Enfeoffed, released, deliuered & Confirmed, & by these Presents do giue grant bargane, & sell aliene release, deliuer & Confirme unto the sd Aron fferris, his heyers, executors, Administrators & Assignes, uidz^t Aron fferris of the great Ysland, In ye Prouince of New Hampshyre fisherman, Twenty Acres of Land lijng scituate & being in Spruse Cricke, something Neare the mouth of the sd Cricke, in the Township of Kittery in the prouince of Mayne aforesd, and begins about foure foot from Joseph Crocketts West Corner of his fejld, runns about Twenty nine rodds by the Cricke, West & by North, or there about to a stake driuen down in the ground, leaueing out one whoole rodd & an halfe, the whoole breadth of sd Land, along by the Cricke for an high way, for people to pass & repass, and runns from the stake at the Westward end of the Twenty nine rodds or there abouts, next the high way, on a North & by East poynt, ouer to another Cricke,

Book IV, Fol. 1.

on the North end of the Land, and vp that Cricke from a small spruse marked on the banke side, & runns vp the sd Cricke about ffiuety foure rodds, to a Hemlocke marked on the Banke side, and is the North Nore East, Corner bounds, and runns from that sd bounds, on a South South West poynt, neare Ninety six rodds or there abouts, to the place where It began, togeather with ye priuiledges profitts & aduantages, belonging & appertaineing to both the sd Crickes, as also with all Contayned with in the sd boundary whatsoeuer/

To haue and to hould, the before given granted & barganed Premises to the sayd Aron fferris his heyres, executors, Administrators and Assignes for euer, and the sayd Elihew Crockett, for him selfe his heyres, executors, Administrators & Assignes, doth Couenant promiss & grant to and with the sayd Aron fferris, his heyres executors Administrators & Assignes, & with euery of them by these Presents, that all and singular the sd Premisses, with all the profitts priuiledges & Aduantages, in & by these Presents given granted barganed & sould, & euery part & Parcell thereof at the tyme of the Ensealeing & deliuery of these Presents, are and bee at all tymes hereafter, shall bee remaine and Continew, clearely acquitted, exonerated & discharged, & keept harmeless of & from all & all manner of former & other barganes, sales Gyfts, grants, leases, charges Dowers, titles troubles, & incomberances whatsoeuer, had made Committed suffered done or to bee had made, committed suffered or done, by the sayd Elihew Crockett his heyrs executors, Administrators or Assignes or any of them, or any other Person or Prsons whatsoever, by his or thejr meanes acts, titles, Consent or procurement: as also to keepe harmeless from the abousd Ann Jeffery & Ephraim Crockett. It is further to bee vnderstood, that the aboue sayd Land is sould to the aboue sayd Aron fferris his heyres executors administrators & Assignes, togeather with all the trees Woods underwoods & priuiledges whatsoeuer/ as wit-

ness my hand & scale, this Thirteenth of June, one thousand six hundred eighty & three/ the Persons abouesayd do Ingage to the sayd fferris priuilidg to Land on the Westerne side of the Cricke/ Elihew Crockett ($^{his}_{seale}$)
Signed & Deliuered
  in the Presence of us
  The marke of Ephraim   Elihew Crockett owned this In-
  Crockett   strument to bee his Act &
                            Deede to Aron Ferris, &
  Elizabeth Hill/   moreouer Ann Jeffery, &
                            Ephraim Crockett ownes as is
                            aboue expressed, that It is by
                            y^r Consent, all which acknowl-
                            edged this fourth day of August 1683 : before mee
                            ffran^s Hooke Jus : pe :
A true Coppy of this Instrument transcribed out of the originall & there with Compared this 5th day of ffebrua : 1683 :
            p Edw : Rishworth Re :Cor :

                Bee It known unto all men by these Presents,
Ste. Batson   that I Stephen Batson of Wells, in the County
  To
his Son John of yorke, & Colloney of the Massatusetts, in
                New England, haue barganed & sould, & by these Presents do fully & absolutely bargan & sell unto my sonn John Batson of Cape Porpus a Parcell of vpland being eighteen acres more or less, & Twenty fiue acres of Marsh, more or less lijng & being in Cape Porpus, & bounded as followeth, On the North East side with the Little Riuer, & on the North West side with branch of the little Riuer, that runnes vp to the beauer pond, on the West side, a little aboue the stepping stoones; and so to runn vpon a streight lyne South East Eastwardly, till It come to the head of a Cricke Comanly Called by the name of Middle

Cricke, & so to runn till it Come till It cometh to the Mayne Riuer which is the Southerne bounds: To haue & to hould, y⁰ abouesd Marsh, [2] & vpland to the aforesd John Batson, his heyres, executors, Administrators & Assignes, to his & yʳ own proper vsses & behoofes for euer/ & I the sayd Stephen Batson, my heyres, executors Administrators, do Assign the aforesd Tract of Land unto the aforesd John Batson, his executors or Administrators shall & will from any Person or Persons by from or under mee, warrant, acquitt, & for euer defend/ In witness whereof I haue here unto sett my hand & seale this eigh day of ffebru: 1672/3

Signed sealed & deliuered,   Steuen Batson (his seale)
  In Presence of us   ffebru: the: 8ᵗʰ 1672:
  Samell Wheelewright/   This Instrument acknowledged
  John Trott/   the day yeare aboue written
           by Stephen Batson to bee his
           Act, & Deede, before us
           Commissioⁿ Ezekell Knight
           Senjoʳ, & William Hamonds/

A true Coppy of this Instrumeᵗ transcribed out of the Originall & yʳwith Compared this 6th day of ffebru: 1683:
         p Edw: Rishworth Re: Cor:

Wee Aylce Shapleigh & John Shapleigh do mutually agree, & make Choyce of Capᵗ ffrancis Champernown & Majoʳ Dauess to lay out Mʳˢ Shapleighs Thirds, & what they do in the Premisses, Wee the sd Ailce & John Shapleigh, do bind our selues in the full sume of one hundred pounds Sterling, each to other, to rest oʳselues satisfyd, & Contented, & hereafter to giue each to other a full discharge, wⁿ all things shall bee Compleated, which is to bee done

BOOK IV, FOL. 2.

with all Convenient speede/ In witness hereto wee haue each to other Interchangably sett o[r] hands, This one & Twenteth day of August 1683 :   Alice Shapleigh/
In Pursewance of the abouesd obli-   John Shapleigh/
gation, Wee ffran[s] Champernown & John Dauess, haue layd out M[is] Alice Shapleigh her thirds/ Inp[m]
Too peyre of Dowlass sheetes/ too peyre of Cotton sheetes/ Three dozen of Napkines/ Three peyre of pillow beares/ three table Cloaths, one Cubbard Cloath, Six Towells/ Three bedds with what belongeth to y[m] besids y[e] bed in her owne Rowme, with the furniture belonging to the rowme/ Three Cows out of the stocke, & Mis Shapleigh is to acquitt Mr Shapleigh of a fatt Cow was killed of Mis Shapleighs formerly Two Trunkes or Chests/ The 3d of the swine w[n] they come home/ Too Calfes, one of which shee then gaue to Allexand[r]/ Two yearelings shee to pay Mr John Shapleigh 10s/ Three oxen, & 3d of an oxe/ The 3d part of an horse to bee payd in money one pounds Six shillings 8d/ The 3d part of a steare, & one steare of three yeares ould, one third part of too fatt oxen, & one 3d part of too fatt Cows/ an horse left for y[e] vss of them both ; The 3d part of y[e] Corne on the ground, shee paijng one 3d part of the Labour, which comes to more then her mans labour, & the third part of the hay on y[e] same tearmes/ Item shee is to haue the third part of the Corne, now In y[e] house or Mill, & the third part of the produce of all the Mills, shee paying the 3d part of the Charge, the Third part of y[e] Mills to bee accompted for, since the Twelth of June 1683 : foure sheepe & one 3d part of a sheepe/ the copper Kettle/   ffran[s] : Champernown
    John Dauess/
M[is] Alyce Shapleigh, & Mr John Shapleigh came before mee this fifth of ffebru : 1683 : & did own this Inventory to bee y[r] act & Deed by mutuall agreement/
    Edw Rishworth Jus : pe :

BOOK IV, FOL. 2.

A true Coppy of this Instrume^t or Inventory aboue written, transcribed out of the originall & y^r with Compared this 8th day of ffebru : 1683/ p Edw : Rishworth Re : Cor :

A mutuall agreement made by Mis Alyce Shapleigh, & Mr John Shapleigh, this fifth of Febru : 1683 :

1 : first that the sd AlyCe shapleigh, doth Lett & sett out unto her kinesman John Shapleigh her right of thirds due from the saw Mills at Spruse Cricke, for his own Perticular uss & Aduantage dureing the Tyme & tearme of her naturall life

2 : It is further agreed between the partys abouesd, the sd John Shapleigh shall deliuer & Cause to bee deliuered unto his Aunt Shapleigh the full quantity of Twelue thousand foote of M^rchātable pine boards yearely, the one halfe at the spring, & ye other halfe at the ffall, at ye sd Mills w^r a boate can Conueniently take them in/

3 : Wee do agree y^t this rent shall bee payd to Mis Shapleigh as aboue specifyd dureing her life, vnless by any accidentall prouidence, the Mills should bee burned : And w^t shall appeare iustly due to Mis Shapleigh vpon Accompts for her thirds since June last till this Present date, they to bee made vp & satisfyd by sd John Shapleigh, shee allowing the thirds of the Charge, as witness our hands/

Mis Aylce Shapleigh & Mr John Shapleigh came before mee this fifth of ffebru : 1683 : & acknowledged this writeing to bee y^r Act & Deede/

Alice Shapleigh & John Shapleigh/

Edw : Rishworth Jus : pe :

A true Coppy of this agreement aboue written transcribed & with originall Compared this 8th day of ffebru : 1683 :

p Edw : Rishworth ReCor :

BOOK IV, FOL. 2, 3.

These are to giue notice vnto all whome they may Concerne, that I Alice Shapleigh doth giue & bequeath unto Nicholas Shapleigh sonn unto Mr John Shapleigh, the bedding, pewter & lining, that properly belongs to her Estate for her diuission as a Widdow, according to Prticulars on record mentioned, vpon the Inventory returned into the Court, if not worne out in ye meane tyme, & In Case of ye decease of ye sd Nicholas, Mrs Shapleigh giueth & disposeth of the sd Prticulars aboue mentioned, unto one or more of sd Mr John Shapleighs children, as shee shall see meete/ as witness her hand at ye date here of, ffeb : 6 : 1683 :

   Mis Alyce Shapleigh came before mee Febru : 6 :
   1683, & acknowledged this Instrument to bee
   her Act & Deede/ Edw : Rishworth Jus : pe :
This was acknowledged,
 Major Dauess & Mr Samuell
Wheelewright being both Present/
A true Coppy of this Ingageme^t transcribed out of the originall, & y^{r}with Compared this 8th day of ffebru : 1683 :
     p Edw : Rishworth ReCor :

[3] This witnesseth, y^t I Joseph Bolles of Wells, In the County of yorke, In the Colony of the Massatusetts, In New England Gentle͠ : & Mary his wife for & in Consideration of Twenty fiue pounds Sterling, to them in hand payd before ye sealeing & deliuery here of, by John Batson of Cape Porpus in the County aforesd, haue given, granted, barganed, sould, Enfeoffed, & Confirmed, & do by these Prsents for them selues, theire heyres, executors & Administrators, Giue grant bargan sell, Infeoffe & Confirme unto the aforesd John Batson, a Certen Tract of vpland, & Meddow, scituate & being in the Town of Cape Porpus aforesd Contajneing by Estimation about fiuety Acres, being part of y^t hundred acres granted by Mr Thomas Gorges, unto Morgan Howell, as by Deed beareing date the eighteenth of

BOOK IV, FOL. 3.

July 1643: doth more amply appeare; The sd Tract of vpland Meddow or Marsh, lijng on the North West of y^t Necke of Land, on w^{c}h the aforesd Morgan liued bounded on the South East with a streight lyne between ye heads of ye too Coues y^t diuided the aforesd Tract of land from the aforesd Necke of Land & from thence runeing into the Woods towards the Northwest, according to the bounds y^t was layd out by John Dauis & William Hammonds Which sd Tract of vpland, of Meddow or Marsh, was lately belonging to the aforesd Morgan Howell, deceased, by his last Will & testament, bequeathed unto the sd Mary the wife of the sayd Joseph Bolls, & now by the aforesd Joseph Bolls, & Mary his wife sould vnto the aforesayd John Batson.

To haue & to hould, the aboue bargained Premisses, with all the appurtenances, & priuiledges there to belonging to him the sayd John Batson his heyres executors, Administrators, or Assignes for euer, the same to defend against all Prsons whatsoeuer claimeing any lawfull right title or Interest, in any of the aboue barganed Premisses, or any part or Parcell thereof, by from or under the sayd Joseph Bolls, or Mary his wife or either of theire heyres, executors, or Administrators; the sayd John Batson yeilding & paijng unto the heyres or Assignes of Sir ffardinando Gorges the one halfe of six shillings eight peence, p Annū: If Legally due/ & for Confirmation of the Premisses, the aforesd Joseph Bolls, & Mary his wife, haue sett to theire hands & seales, this Ninth day of July, In the yeare of o^r Lord one thousand six hundred seauenty foure/

Signed sealed & Deliuered   Joseph Bolles   (his seale)
  In the Presence of/   The marke of
  John Dauess/   Mary Bolles MB (her seale)
  Charles ffrost/

                    The aboue written deed of sale was acknowledged by ye with in named Joseph Bolles, & Mary his wife, to bee y^r act & Deed this ninth day of July 1674: before mee John Wincoll Assotiate/

BOOK IV, FOL. 3.

A true Coppy of this Instrum[t] aboue written, transcribed, & with Originall Compard this 9[th] day of ffebru : 1683 :
p Edw : Rishworth Re : Cor :

To all Christean people, before whome 'all these Presents shall Come/ Know yee y[t] I William Goodhue Senior, of Ipswich In New England in the County of Essex M[r]chant for diuerse good Causes, & Considerations mee y[r]unto espetially moueing, haue made ordayned Constituted, & in my place & steade put, & authorized, my well beloued frejnd Joseph Hammonds of Kittery, In the Prouince of Mayne Carpenter, to bee my true sufficient & lawfull Atturney, for mee & in my name, & for the uss of mee the sd William Goodhue to Enter into all y[t] house & Land, that came unto mee by way of Morgage, from William Oliuer of the ysles of shoales, scituate, & lijng & being in the prouince of Mayne in Kittery aforesayd, at a place called Tompsons Poynt, abbutting vpon Pischataqua Riuer, & into euery part & parcell thereof, for mee & in my name to uew, & suruay, & by these Presents do giue full pouer & authority unto y[e] aforesd Jos : Hammonds to bee my stuard, for mee my in name to bargane & sell the aboue named Parcell of Land, as hee shall thinke meete & requisitt to the uttmost & best Commodity, & profitt of mee the sd William Goodhue, & the Deed of the same so to bee made for mee, & in my name to seale & Deliuer, in my stead to the party & partys, to whom y[e] same shall bee sould, giueing & by these Presents granting to my sd lawfull Atturney, my full pouer & lawfull authority in & about the Premisses, ratifijng & allowing all y[t] my sd Atturney shall do in and about y[e] Premisses, according to the true Intent & meaning of these Presents/ In witness hereof I the aboue named William

Book IV, Fol. 3.

Goodhue haue here unto set my hand & seal this 3ᵈ day of
Decemb' 1683 :   William Goodhue (his scale)
Signed sealed & Deliuer̄d/ William Goodhue did acknowl-
In yᵉ Presents of us/   edg this writeing aboue writ-
Thomas Wade/   ten, this 6th of Decemb'
Thomas Sparke/   1683 : before mee
                    Sam̄ell Appleton Assistant :
A true Coppy of this Instrum' aboue written, transcribed
& with originall Compared this 5th day of March 168¾
            p Edw : Rishworth Re :Cor :

These Presents do testify, yᵗ I Abraham Conley of Kittery
in Sturgion Cricke Planter, vpon diuerse good Considerations there vnto mee moueing, & more espetially for the
some of fiue pounds receiued of Peter Wittum of the sd
Town & place in Mʳchatble pipe staues being full satisfaction for a parcell of swampe by mee sould unto him, that I
the sd Conley do hereby sell giue, grant, aliene, bargan &
Confirme, & with mee my heyres executors, Administrators,
& Assignes haue sould, granted, giuen, aliend, & Confirmed
unto yᵉ aforesd Peter Wittum, his heyres, executors, Administrators & Assignes, the full & just quantity of three Acres
& an halfe of Land or swampe & sixteen poole lijng & being,
& next Adioyneing unto the sd Conleys Marsh being between the sd Conleys Marsh, & Kittery high way, part wʳof
hath been already Cleard & Mowne by the sd Wittum &
brought to Meddow, with all the rightts, proprietys, priuiledges, & appurtenances belonging to the sayd swampe or
Meddow : I the sd Conley do hereby Confirme, vnto the sd
Wittum him selfe, & his heyres for euer, this sd Land or
Swampe as bounded, on the southerne side with Abra :
Conlys Marsh, on the Western side with Abra . Conleys
swamp, & seuerall pine trees, & on the Northermost side, or
end, It is bounded with Kittery high way, which Land or

swamp bounded as aforesd, with [4] all the priuiledges, benefitts & Immunitys app^r^tajneing y^r^unto hee the sd Peter Wittum is to haue & to hould, to & for him selfe his heyres, & Assignes for euer, for his own proper vss & behoufe, & further ye sd Abra: Conley doth by these Presents, Ingage him selfe his heyres & Assignes, to defend & make good the Title there of, against all Titles, claimes, Demands, or Incomberances w^t^soeuer, against all Persons clajmeing any Title y^r^unto, unto the sd Peter Wittum his heyres & Assigns for euer/ And further it is to bee understood, that Abra: Conley doth hereby grant for him selfe & his heyres for euer, that Peter Wittum & his heyrs shall haue free Egress & regress for a sufficient high way, from y^e^ head of the sd Swamp of Kittery high way with out any lett Molestation or incomberance/ In Confirmation of the soole Premisses as aboue written, I haue here unto affixed my hand & seale this foureteenth day of March 167$\frac{2}{3}$ one thousand six hundred seauenty too seauenty three/

Abraham Conley

his marke ⚔ (his seale.)

Abraham Conley owned this Instrument aboue written to bee his act & Deede, & that seuerall years Peter Wittum by his free Consent had, & hath possession of the Premisses before mee   Edw: Rishworth Assoti^te^

A true Coppy of this Instrum^t^ transcribed out of the ReCords & y^r^with Compared this fifth day of March 168$\frac{2}{3}$

p Edw: Rishworth Re: Cor:

Bee it known vnto all men by these Presents, that I Thomas Baston formerly of the Town of Wells in the County of yorke, now of Ipswich In the County of Essex, for an in consideration of ualewable satisfaction in hand receiued, haue barganed sould, aliend, Enfeoffed Confirmed,

BOOK IV, FOL. 4.

& made ouer unto Thomas Wells of the Town of Amesbury In the County of Norfocke, all my right title & Interest unto & in one hundred acres of vpland, & Tenn Acres of Meddow, scituate & lijng in the Town of Wells at a place comanly called Maryland, according as It is expressed in the Deed of the sd Land, made unto the sd Baston from ffran^s Littlefejld & Peter Cloyce; ffor the sd Wells, to haue & to hould the Premisses quietly, & peaceably to the proper vss bchoofe & benefitt, of him selfe his heyres, executors, Administrators or Assignes with out any lett sujte, hinderance, or Molestation from mee ye sd Baston, or any Prson or Prsons, in by from or under mee; declareing the Premisses at the Date of these Presents, to bee free & cleare, from all former alienations, Incomberances, or Molestations whatsoeuer: & do hereby warrantize the saile thereof, & do acknowledg to haue Deliuered them into the possession of the sd Wells/ In Confirmation where of I haue here unto subscribed my hand & seale, this eighteenth day of ffebru: Anno Dom: one thousand six hundred seauenty eight, seauenty nine/   Thomas Baston (his seale)

Signed sealed & Deliuerd   Thomas Baston ackowledged the
  In the Presence of us/   aboue written, to bee his Act
  The marke of Thomas   & Deede, this 2cund of Octob^r
  Colebie   A   1683: before mee Bartholmew
Samuell Hardy/   Gydney Assistant:

vera Copia of this Instrume^t aboue written transcribed out of the originall & y^{r}with Compared this 8th day March 168¾ p Edw: Rishworth Re: Cor:

This Indenture made the third day of Nouember one thousand six hundred eighty two, & In the thirty fourth yeare of the Reign of o^r Soueraign Lord King Charles ye secund, by the grace of god, of England Scotland ffrance & Ireland Defend^r of ye faith, between John Smyth Senjo^r

BOOK IV, FOL. 4.

of Cape Nuttacke in the Prouince of Mayn in New England in America Planter, & Mary his wife on the one part, & William Sawyer of Wells on the other part Planter in the prouince of Mayne/

Wittesseth that yᵉ sayd John Smyth & Mary his wife, for & in consideration of yᵉ sume of Thyrty pounds of Current pay of new England in hand before the sealeing & deluery of these Presents, well & truely payd, the receipt whereof the sayd Joⁿ Smyth & Mary his wife doth hereby acknowledg to bee fully satisfyd & payd, & there of & of euery part & Parcell, & penny there of acquitt, exonerate & discharge the sayd William Sawyer his heyres, executors, administrators & Assignes, & euery of them for euer by these Presents, hath barganed granted sould aliend Enfeoffed Convayed released, assured Deliuered & Confirmed, & these Presents doth grant bargane & sell aliene Enfeoff conuay release Assure deliuer & Confirme unto the sayd William Sawyer his heyres & Assignes part of that Tract or Percell of vpland, and sault Marsh & fresh which fell to my wife Mary, by the death of her naturall father, George ffarrow, scituate, lijng & being in Wells aforesayd Contajneing eighty Acres of vpland being sixteene pooles broad/ and eight Acres of sault & ffresh Meddow, togeather with all trees Woods, underwoods, easements profitts, Commoditys Aduantages emoliments hæriditaments, & appurtenances whatsoeuer : The sayd eighty Acres of vpland being bounded by the Land of Beniam: Curtis on the South side, & William Sawyers on the North side, And the eight acres of Meddow bounded vidzᵗ Too Acres & an halfe Joyneing to the sd Land, & one acre at the little Riuer ffalls, & three acres lijng by the side of the little Riuer bounded by the woods on the north side and one acre and halfe an acre on the Easterne side of the little Riuer on the Eastern branch bounded by William Sawyers Meddow, on the South East End, & on the West side by the Riuer, & also all yᵉ right

Book IV, Fol. 4, 5.

Title Clajme, possession uss reuersion remajnder & Demand w'soeuer, of him ye sayd John Smyth Senjor, & Mary his wife, & unto the sd Premisses, & of & in & unto euery, or any part or Parcell thereof: To haue & to hould, the sayd Tract of vpland & Meddow, & all and singuler before, hereby barganed & granted Premisses, & euery part & Parcell there of, with thejr & euery of thejr appurtenances & the reuertion & reuertions, remajnder & remajnders thereof unto the sd William Sawyer, his heyres & Assigns for euer, to the soole & onely proper vss and behoofe of the sayd William Sawyer his heyres & Assigns for euer, & to and for no other uss Intent & purpose whatsoeuer; And the sayd John Smyth Senior & Mary his wife, for them selues thejr heyres executors Administrators & Assignes & for all & euery of them do hereby Coucnant promiss & grant to & [5] with the sayd William Sawyer his heyres, executors, administrators, & Assignes, & to & with euery of them, by these Presents, that the sayd William Sawyer his heyres and Assignes & euery of them shall & lawfully may from tyme to tyme & at all tymes hereafter, lawfully, peaceably & quietly haue hould vss occupy possess and inioy, to his & thejre own proper vss & behoofe all & singular the before hereby granted & barganed Premisses, & euery part & parcell there of with the appu'tenances freed acquitted & discharged, or otherwise well & sufficiently saued & keept hameless of & from all & all manner of former, & other barganes sales, Gifts, grants, leases, Joynters, Dowers, & Titles of Dowers, of Mary now wife of the sayd John Smyth Senjo', Judgments, executions, titles, troubles, Charges, & Incomberances whatsoeuer, heretofore had made, Committed suffered or done, or to bee had Committed suffered by the sayd John Smyth Senjor, & Mary his wife, & thejr heyres executors, Administrators or any or either of them; In witness where of the Partys first aboue named to these Presents Indenturs, haue set too thejr hands & Seales, the day & yeare first aboue written/

Sealed & deliuered, & quiett & peaceable possession & seizin of the Lands aboue granted was given & deliuered by the aboue named John Smyth vnto sd William Sawyer, vpon the day of the Date aboue written, in name of possession & seizen of all Lands in the deed aboue expressed, to haue & to hould unto the sd William Sawyer, his heyres & Assignes for euer/ according to ye Tenour & true meaneing of ye Deed aboue written/

John Wheelewright/
George Pearson/

The marke of John Smyth (his seale)
Senio^r *F*
The Marke of Mary Smyth (her seale)
M

John Smyth Senjor, & Mary his wife, appeared before mee this 3^d day of Novemb^r 1682 : & owned this Instrument to bee thejr act & deed/
Samell Wheelewright Jus : pe :

vera Copia of this Instrument aboue written, transcribed out of ye originall & there with Compared this 9th of March 168¾ p Edw: Rishworth Re : Cor :

Know all men by these Presents, that I Thomas Withers of Kittery In the County of Yorke Gentlemā : for an in Consideration of foure pounds already payd in hand before the Insealeing & deliuery of these Presents, well & truely payd receip^t of the same Thomas Withers acknowledgeth, & him selfe to bee fully satisfyd Contented, & payd, & y^rof, & of euery part & Parcell thereof, doth acquitt exonerate & discharge Rowland Williams of the same Town & County, his heyres executors Administrators & Assignes, for euer, as

' BOOK IV, FOL. 5.

also diuerse other good Causes & Considerations him there
unto espetially moueing, haue given granted barganed &
sould alien'd released Confirmed, & deliuered, & by these
Presents, doth giue grant bargan & sell, aliene, release,
deliuer & Confirme, vnto the sd Rowland Williams his heyres
executors, Administrators & Assignes, a Tract of Land lijng
& being in Kittery, butting vpon a lott of Land of Nicholas
weekes In spruse Cricke, bounded vpon the South side with
Enocke Houchings, & vpon the North side of John Phillips
his Land Millwright, being seauenty fiue pooles in length,
& by a Northern line In breadth, & also all profitts priuiledges to & with in the sd boundary belonging & appertajneing : To haue & to hould the before hereby granted, & barganed Premisses, & euery part & Parcell hereof, unto the
sayd Rowland Williams his heyres, executors, Administrators & Assignes for euer, & the sayd Thomas Withers for
him selfe his heyres, executors, administrators & Assignes
doth Couenant promiss & grant to & with the sayd Rowland
Williams, his heyres executors, administrators & Assignes,
to & with euery of them, by these Presents, that all and
singlar the aforesayd Premisses with the profitts Priuiledges, & aduantages, by these Presents, given granted &
sould & euery part & parcell at the tyme of the sealeing &
deliuery of these Presents are & to bee at all tymes hereafter,
shall remajne & Continew, Clearely acquitted, exonerated
discharged and kept harmeless from all manner of former,
& other barganes sales gyfts grants leases, Charges, Titles,
Dowers, troubles or Incomberances whatsoeuer, made Committed suffered or done, or be made Comitted, suffered or
done, by ye sayd Thomas Withers his heyres, executors,
administrators or Assignes, or by any of them, or any other
Persons whatsoeuer, by his or y^r meanes, acts titles Consents
or procurements, to the treuth of which, I haue sett my

hand & seale, this Twenty fifth of November, one thousand six hundred seauenty nine 1679 :

Signed sealed & Deliuered/   Thomas Withers (his seale)
in the Presence of/   Mr Thomas Withers came & owned
Elizabeth Withers/   this abouesd Deed of sale to bee
The Marke of Mary   his Act & Deede unto Rowland
Palmer/   Williams this sixteenth day of
Janvary one thousand six hundred seauenty nine before mee
Fran : Hooke Comissior/

A true Coppy of this Instrumet transcribed out of the originall & yrwith Compared this 12th day of March 168¾

       p Edw : Rishworth Re : Cor :

This Twenty fifth of March one thousand six hundred seaventy one, William Eueritt freely Consents to aboue barganed Premisses, & rendered vp all his right Title & Interest there unto, before mee Elyas Styleman Comissior/

Nathan Lawd & Martha his wife, the daughter of the with in named Margery Nash, & heyre & by her husband Administrator to the Estate of William Eueritt deceased, appeared before mee this Three & Twenteth day of November one thousand six hundred seaventy foure, & acknowledged yr free Consent unto the within barganed Premisses, & did uolentarily giue vp thejr whoole right, title, & Interest, to or in any of the with in barganed Premisses, or any part or parcell either as heyre to the aforesd Margery, or as Administrators to ye aforesd William Eueritt/

       John Wincoll Assōte/

A true Coppy of the Consents of William Eueritt, Nathan Lawd, & Martha his wife as aboue written owned before authority relateing to a Certen Deed made by Isaac Nash & Margery his wife standing now vpon the ould ReCords pa :

Book IV, Fol. 5, 6.

76: transcribed out of ye originall & there with compared this 14th of March 1684:   p Edw: Rishworth Re: Cor

A Deede of Gyft made by mee William Freathy, unto my too sonns Samuell Freathy & John ffreathy, this fourth day of December, one thousand six hundred eighty & three as followeth/

Inp^rs I do freely giue unto my sonn Samell ffreathy all the Land on the South East [6] side of my now planted fejld, which is now Inclosed to him the sd Samuell ffreathy & his heyres for euer: And likewise I giue vnto my sonn Samuell ffreathy, the whool propriety of my house & Oarchard, to him & his heyres for euer, after my decease & his Mothers, for all the Land aboue mentioned, aboue on the South East side of the planting fejld to bee Inioyed for ye Present/

2ly I giue unto my sonn John Freathy, the North West side of my now planting fejld, to him & his heyres for euer, & after my decease & my wifes, all my land Inclosed to my sd too sonns, Samell & John for euer, to bee æqually diuided between them, to them, to them & thejr heyers for euer (except the house & the Oarchard aboue express'd)

And this is the free gyft of mee, the abouesd William ffreathy given under my hand, & seale, the day & yeare aboue written/

Signed Sealed Deliuered   The marke of 2⌒
  In Presence of,   William Freathy (his sealo)
  William Lewice his   Elizabeth Freathy (her seale)

  Marke ⋏| her marke ✓

  The marke of Mary   William Freathy & Elizabeth
  Dauess ⋀⊇   ffreathy, came before mee, this
                            4th of December 1683: & did
                            acknowledg the aboue Instru-
                            ment to bee thejr act & Deede/
                                John Dauess Jus: pe:

BOOK IV, FOL. 6.

A true Coppy of this Instrument transcribed out of the originall & theire with Compared this 5th day of Aprill 1684 : p Edw : Rishworth Re : Cor :

Receiued Janvary 18th 1681 : of Joseph Rajne of the Great ysland M^rchant Goods to the ualew of sixteen pounds one shilling, seauen peence, which sayd some of sixteen pounds one shilling & 7d Wee both Joyntly & scuerally, whose names are here subscribed, do promiss & oblidg, to pay unto the sd Joseph Rajne or order, the ualew of the sd sume of sixteen pounds one shilling & 7d in good spring beauer, at or before the first day of May next Insewing, at seauen shillings p ld William ffurbush
 Witness James Harbert/
 Elizabeth Cranch/ his marke
  Thomas Rodes/

James Harbert deposed this 8th day of Octob^r 1683 : that William ffurbush & Thomas Rodes signed the with in written, & deliuered it as y^r act & Deeds to Jos : Rayne
  Sworne before mee Natha^ll ffryer Jus . pe :
Elizabeth Cranch deposed this 21th March 168¾ that William Furbush & Thomas Rodes, signed the with in Wiitten, & delueied it as thejr Acts & Deeds, to Joseph Rajne/
 Taken vpon oath this one & Twenteth day of March 168¾
  before mee Robert Mason/

A true Coppy of this bill as Attested transcribed & with originall Compared this 10th of Aprill 1684 :
  p Edw . Rishworth ReCor :

This Indenture made the 11th day of June, In the yeare of o^r Lord one thousand six hundred eighty three, between Elihew Gunnisson In the Town of Kittery In the prouince

Book IV, Fol. 6.

of Mayne, & John Pickerin of the Town of Portsmouth of the prouince of New Hampshire on the other party, Witnesseth that the sd Elihew Gunnisson, for & In Consideration of the full & iust sume of one hundred pounds In money & other goods payd in hand, by the sd John Pickerin the receipt whereof the sd Gunnisson doth hereby acknowledge, & him selfe to bee fully satisfyed, Content & payd, and of euery part & penny there of, do cleerly acquitt discharge the sayd John Pickerin his heyres & Assignes: And for diuerse other good Causes & Considerations, him the sayd Elihew Gunnisson there unto moueing, haue giuen granted barganed & sould, and by these Presents do giue grant bargane and Confirme, unto the sayd John Pickerin his heyres, executors, Administrators & Assignes, all that dwelling house & barne, with all the Necke of Land y^{r}unto belonging, Where the sayd Gunnisson now liueth, In the Town of Kittery in the Prouince of Mayn abouesayd, which house & barne and Land, standeth & lyeth at the Entering in of Spruse Cricke so Called, & known by that name, and lyeth on the West or North West side of the Entering in of the sayd Cricke, togeather with foure Acres of Land vp the Cricke, next Adioyneing to a Prcell of Land of Ephraim Crocketts, which foure Acres I bought of William Addams (excepting out of all the Land onely tenn Acres or there abouts adioyneing the house where Mr Cowell now liueth, & Adioyneing to ffrancis Trickeys Land) To haue & to hould, the before hereby granted and barganed Premisses, with all the priuiledges & appurtenances, there unto belonging or any wise appertajneing with all the trees woods, underwoods, Corne standing, growing, & lijng (excepting onely ye tenn Acres or y^{r}abouts before excepted) unto the sayd John Pickerin his heyres & Assigns executors or Administrators, to haue, hould & Inioy from the day of the date hereof, & thence forward, untill the full end & tearme of Ninety nine yeares bee Computed, compleated & ended, to the soole uss benefitt & behoofe, of ye sd John Pickerin, his heyres executors,

administrators or Assignes, dureing the whoole tyme or Tearme of ninety nine yeares, as abouesd, with out the Lawfull Lett, sujte or Interruption of him ye sd Elihew Gunnisson, his heyres, executors, administrators or assignes, free & Cleare from all, & all manner of Gyfts, grants bargans Morgages sajles, or any other Incomberances whatsoeuer, suffered or done by them or either of them prouided always It is neuertheless agreed & Concluded by & between the sd Partys to this Presents, & It is the true Intent and meaneing thereof, that If the sd Gunnisson his heyres executors administrators & Assignes or either of them, shall well & truely pay or cause to bee payd unto the sd Pickerin, his heyres executors, Administrators or Assignes or any of them at the now dwelling house of the sd John Pickerin in Portsmouth abouesd the full & Intire sume of one hundred pounds, In good sound fish, & other good goods at the price y^t I can buy for fish at price Current, at or before the last day of July which will bee In the yeare of o^r Ld one one thousand six hundred eighty & eight, that then this Present Indenture, bargane & grant, & euery Clawse & article there in contajned, shall Cease, determine, & bee utterly uoyd, & of none æffect, to all Intents, & purposes w^{t}soeuer, any thing in these Presents Contajned to the Contrary Notwithstanding; other wise to bee in full pouer & force: In Confirmation of all above written, I the sd Elihew Gunnisson haue put to my hand & scale the day & yeare first aboue written/ Elihew Gunnisson ($^{his}_{seale}$)
Signed sealed & Deliuer'd
  In Presence of us/ Mary Stanion/
  The marke of Saraih O Reed/

Elihew Gunnisson came & acknowledged this Instrum^t to bee his act & Deede, this 12th day of June 1683 before meo
ffran^s · Hooke Jus · pe ·

A true Coppy of this Instrument with in written transcribed out of the originall & there with Compared the 16th day of Aprill 1684: p Edw: Rishworth Re: Cor:

BOOK IV, FOL. 7.

[7] Let all men know by these Presents, y^t I Patience Spencer of Barwicke, In the Town of Kittery Widdow, for & in Consideration of ye naturall loue & affection that I haue for, & do beare unto my Youngest sonn Moses Spencer of the Town & place aforesd, which is In the Prouince of Mayne, haue given granted, & by these Presents do giue grant & Confirme, unto him the sd Moses Spencer my sd sonn, all y^t land vidz^t that is to say all the Residue & remajnder of y^t Two hundred Acres given unto my late husband Thom^s Spencer by the sd Town of Kittery, of which two hundred Acres Danniell Goodine, Thomas Etherinton, John Gattensby, & my secuñd sonn Humphrey Spencer & others, haue had each of them a part layd out, to them, which part purpoty & portion of sd Too hundred Acres, lyeth & is beyond the aforesd foure Lotts, of Dan^{ll} Goodings, Tho: Etherintons deceased, & John Gattensby deceased, & Humphrey Spencer, & It lyeth to the East & South, from ye aforesd Lotts, of them foure partys aforesd, & bounded on ye East or y^{r}abouts, by Dañell Goodings Land, Called & Comanly known by the name of Slutts Corner, & on the South or y^{r}abouts, by the Lands of Rıchd Nason, & to runne East wards or y^{r}abouts, into the Woods as fare as the extent of the sd Two hundred Acres goeth, untill It bee Compleated:

Also I do further giue him ye sd Moses my sonn, all y^t Thyrty Acres of vpland, & halfe the Meddow ground Adıoyneing to It, & now belonging to It, & lyeth neare ye Land of George Gray, & Adioyneing to Richd Nasons Meddow/ & also all y^t my third part of them too logg swamps, ye one Called by the name of Tom Tinkers Swampe, & the other Called by the name of ye Great Swampe, both lijng & being by the little Riuers side, y^t Cometh down to ye great Mill workes, or Mr Hutchinsons Mill, or Saw Mill: To haue & to hould, the sd part purpoty, & Portion of that Two hundred Acres not disposed off, before this tyme, Neither by mee nor by deceased husband, & also y^t thirty Acres of vpland & halfe the sd Meddow groūd as aforesd, & all the

third part of the Too swamps of Tymber, for to Cutt loggs
or otherwise (always excepting & reseruceing unto mee
Patience Spencer absolute pouer) to Cutt fell load & Carry
away, Wood & fewell, for my uss & sceruice, dureing my
life tyme, In as absolute & free manner, & Gyft from &
after my death & decease for euer: as I the sd Patience Can
or may grant giue or Estate the same, so large & ample to
all Constructions, intents & purposes (except before exceptd)
unto him the sd Moses Spencer & his heyrs for euer, hee
ye sd Moses paijng doing & Prformeing, all such due dutys
& taxes for ye tyme hee & his heyrs shall possess it, after
my decease, as shall grow due, or Impos^d of or from y^e
Premisses, or any part or Parcell y^{r}of, Whither It bee to y^e
King Proprieto^r, or any other Town or Countrey Tax; And
I the sd Patience Spencer, for mee my heyres, executors, &
Administrators, the sd Moeity of Land Meddow & Swampe,
with y^r & euery of y^r app^{r}tenances, do hereby Confirme &
warrant unto the sd Moses & his heyres as abouesd for euer,
against all Prson & Prsons w^{t}soeuer, lawfully Clajmeing the
sd Lands or any part y^{r}of (the King & proprietor onely
excepted) & foreprised/ In Witness w^{r}of I the sd Patience
Spencer, haue here unto set my hand & seale, euon the last
day of June, In y^e Thirty fourth Yeare of y^e Reigne, of o^r
Soueraign Ld Charls the secund, Now King of England
Scotland, ffrance, & Ireland, Annoq, Dom : 1682 :

Sealed & Deliuer'd In y^e Patience Spencer ($^{her}_{Seale}$)
  Presence of us/
    William Playstead/ ⎫
    Abra: Lawde/   ⎬ Witneses
    Samll Lorde/   ⎭
                              Patience Spencer owned this y^e
                              with written deed of Gyft to
                              her sonn Moses Spencer, to
                              bee her free Act & deede, in
                              ye yeare 1682: before mee
                                John Wincoll Jus: pe:

Book IV, Fol. 7.

A true Coppy of this Instrume^t transcribed, & with originall Compared this first of May 1684:

p Edw: Rishworth ReCor:

Witnesseth these Presents y^t I Thomas Curtis In the Town of yorke In the Prouince of Mayne, In New England In America Planter, for diuerse good Causes & Considerations y^runto mee moueing, & more epetially for & in Consideration of the Just & full sume of Tenn pounds, fourty shillings In money, & Eight pounds In Goods to mee In hand payd at the sealeing & deliuery of these presents, vpon the receipt whereof I do acknowledg my selfe to bee fully satisfyd & payd, & there of & euery part & Parcell y^rof, I the sd Curtis do acquit & discharge Hene Lamprill of Yorke aforesd, Cooper, his heyres executors Administrators & Assignes for euer by these Presents, & haue hereby giuen, granted bargained sould Infeoffed Conuayed, Assured deliuered & Confirmed And by these Presents do giue grant, bargane sell Infeoff & Conuay, Assure deliuer & Confirme, unto the aforesd Hene: Lamprell, from mee my heyres executors administrators & Assigns, unto the sd Lamprill, his heyres, executors, Administrators, & Assigns, a Certen Tract, or Parcell of vpland, Contaying the quantity of Tenn Acres, bee It more or less formerly granted to mee by the Town of yorke, as by ye Town ReCords will more fully appeare, the bounds of which Lands are as followeth, vidz^t bounded by the Land of John Brawn, on the South East side which lyeth adioyneing unto the North West side of Bass Coue, Abutting vpon ye high way North East at the hyer end which leadeth to Scottland, And fronting vpon yorke Riuer on the South West, and the Land of William Wormewood on the North West, Which land was formerly bought of Richd Bankes; Which Land as thus bounded, with all Tymber trees, woods, underwoods, pfitts, priuiledges, Com-

BOOK IV, FOL. 7, 8.

moditys, & all other appurtenances whatsoeuer, & all the right Title, Clajme, Interest vss possession, w'soeuer, doth or did euer belong to mee the sayd Thomas Curtis, with all & euery part of the singular before mentioned Premisses/ To haue & to hould the aboue mentioned Tract of vpland, as aboue bounded with all the appurtenances there unto belonging, from mee my heyrs executors Administrators, & Assignes, unto ye sd Hene: Lamprill, his heyres Executors, Administrators, & Assignes for euer; And further I the sd Thomas Curtis in behalfe of my selfe my heyres, executors, Administrators, & Assignes, do Couena^t & promiss to & with the sd Henerrie Lamprill, his heyres executors, Administrators, & Assignes, that the sd Land is free & Cleare from all former Gifts, grants, barganes, sailes, leases Joynters, Dowers, 3d of Dowers Titles, Judgmts executions, & all other troubles & Incomberances whatsoeuer, had made Com-
[8]mitted, or done, or to bee made, Committed, or suffered to bee done, by the sayd Thomas Curtis his heyres, executors, & Assignes, & by him selfe & them to bee sufficiently saued, & keept harmeless from all manner of Person or Persons w'soeuer, from by or under him or them or any others by thejr procurement, w^{r}by the sayd Lamprill is peaceably & quietly to Inioy the aboue barganed Premisses, to him selfe, his heyres, administrators, & Assigns for euer: In witness where of I haue here unto afixed my hand & seale, this eighteenth day of March one thousand six hundred eighty three foure, In the Thirty fifth or sixt yeare of y^e Reigne of our Souciaigne Ld Charles of Greate Biittajne France & Ireland, King, fidej Defenso^{rs} Anno Dom: 168¾

Signed Sealed & Deliuer̃d/   Thomas Curtis ($^{his}_{seale}$)
   In Presence of/   Thomas Curtis came before mee this
   John Sayword/   29th day of Aprill 1684: And owned
   Mary Sayword/   this Instrument aboue written, to
                   Hene: Lamprell to bee his Act &
                   Deede/ Edw: Rishworth Jus: pe:

Book IV, Fol. 8.

vera Copia of this Instrument aboue written, transcribed out of ye originall, & y^{r}with Compared, this first day of May 1684: p Edw: Rishworth ReCor:

To all whome these Presents may Concerne/ W^{r}as the Town of Kittery In the County of yorke In New England by thejr Select men, did giue & grant unto John Wincoll of Water Town Yeamon, & his heyres for euer, all the accomodations of Tymber, from the Sallmon ffalls & vpwards, on great Newgewanacke riuer, so fare as ye sayd Town of Kittery goeth, & three miles from ye sd Riuer into the Woods so fare as It is ye Precincts of sd Kittery, as by thejr grant dated the fiueteenth day of Decemb^r sixteen hundred fiuety & nine more amply appeares. And w^{r}as the sd John Wincoll hath bujlt two Saw Mills, vpon or neare unto the Salmon ffalls, vpon the sd Riuer, Now know all men by these Prsents, that the sayd John Wincoll for & In consideration of saueing & keepeing harmeless of John Hull of Boston M^{r}chant & Roger Playstead of Kittery Planter, from any Damage by y^r Entering into bonds to Capt Thos Clarke & others, & for the secureing other payments, that the sd John Hull, Roger Playstead or either of them may or shall make in the behalfe of the sd Wincoll: Hath absolutely given granted sould Assignd, & by these Presents doth absolutely giue grant sell Assigne & set ouer, & Confirme unto the sd John Hull & Rog^r Playstead all his right Title & Interest in the sd Mills, Tymber grant with priuiledges & appurtenances to them belonging, Dam, Running gears utinsells, free Egress & regress by land & water, Rowme to lay ye Tymber & boards in & on for the uss of the sd Mills, to haue & to hould the before bargained Premisses, to the sd John Hull & Roger Playstead, & to thejr heyres for euer, & to his & thejr onely vss from the day of the date hereof, & the sayd John Wincoll doth for him selfe his heyres, & Assignes,

Conenant promiss & grant to & with the sd John Hull & Roger Playstead, thejr heyrs & Assignes, y^t the sd John Wincoll is the true & proper owner of all the aboue granted Premisses, according to ye grant before sd made by Kittery, & his Charges bestowed since In bujlding the sd Mills, & Dame, & stands Seized of a good Estate of Inhearitance, infee symple there in/ And also hath In him selfe good right free pouer & lawfull authority, the same to Sell & dispose in manner & forme as abouesd/ And y^t the aboue granted Premisses, now bee & shall bee from tyme to tyme to the sd John Hull & Rog^r Playstead, & y^r heyres as y^r Proper Inheritance, free & Cleare, & freely & clearly acquitted & discharged, from all manner of former, & other Gyfts grants, Morgages Joynters, Wills, Judgments, extents, executions, Dowers & Title of Dowers, & all other Incomberances whatsoeuer, had made done, or suffered to bee done by him ye sd John Wincoll or any other Person Claimeing from by or under him, whereby the sd John Hull Roger Playstead y^r heyres or Assignes shall or may bee molested, Euicted, or Eiected out of the possession, of the aboue granted Premisses, or any part y^{r}of; And the sd John Wincoll doth hereby warrant, & defend all the aboue granted Premisses against all men makeing any lawfull Clajme y^{r}to or to any part y^{r}of; Prouided always y^t It is agreed by, & between the partys to these Presents, that It is true Intent & meaneing of the aboue mentioned Deede, & euery of the Clawses y^{r}in, that If ye aboue mentioned John Wincoll, by him selfe heyres, executors, Administrators or Assignes, shall well & truely pay or cause to bee payd & fully discharge a bond of Twenty Two hundred pounds sterling, Which sd Hull & Playstead stand bound in to Capt Thomas Clarke of Boston, It beareing date the sixth of Aprill, sixteene hundred seauenty one/ The Condition of Which bond is as follows: The sd John & Roger are to pay or Cause to bee payd to the sd Capt Clarke or his order, the sume of Two hundred & three pounds, fiue shillings in good M^{r}chtble pine boards full inch deliuered at Quamphegyne rafting place, at the price of three shillings six peence p hundid foote, at or before the Twenteth of August Next Insewing, as the sd Clarke shall send for them by small Parcells, Three hundred & sixteen pounds at or before the Twetenth of August sixteen hundred seauenty too, in boards as afore sd for price & place/ one huudred pounds, at or before the Twenteth of Augst which shall bee in the yeare 1673: in boards as aforesd, in the place, & at the price abouesd, one hundred pounds at or before ye Twenteth of August, which shall bee in the yeare 1674: in boards in the place & at the price aforesd, one hundred pounds at or before the Twenteth of August 1675: as aforesd, in the place & price aforesd, & one hundred pounds, at or before the Twenteth of Augst 1676 as aforesd, in ye place, & at the prise aforesd, one hundred pounds at or before ye Twenteth of August 1677: as aforesayd in ye place, & at ye price aforesd, & one hundred pounds at or before the Twenteth of August, which shall bee in the yeare One thousand six hundred seauenty & eight, & abouesd in ye place, & at the price aforesd: On which [9] Conditions Performed the sd Hull & Playsteads bond for Twenty too hundred pounds is made voyd to Capt Thom^s Clarke, & a debt of fiue hundred fiuety eight pounds shall bee truely satisfyd. to ye fore mentioned John Hull his heyres or Assigns, & a debt of Two hundred pounds, or what else shall bee due, If any eror shall bee found on Accop^t shall bee duely payd to Capt Thom^s Lake, as also the remajneing debt of Majo^r John Leueiett, being about fiuety thousand foote of boards, & w^t is remajneing due to Mr John Cutt, At this day all which Ingagem^{ts} being payd, then this Present Deede of Morgage, & Sale to bee voyd, as to the sd Hulls & Playsteads Interest there in/

It is to bee understood as to the Premisses y^t the partys obleigd Mr Hull & Mr Playstead are to pay the Mills Anuall ient to ye Town of Kittery/ In witness w^{r}of the sd John Wincoll doth here unto sett his hand & seale, this sixth day

of Aprill, one thousand six hundred seauenty one, In the Twenty third yeare of the Reign of o^r Soueraign Ld King Charles the secund/ John Wincoll (Locus Sig.ill)
Signed sealed, & Deluerd in the Presence of us/
Jabez Fox/
Thos Lake/
Geo: Broughton

Geo: Broughton testifyd vpon oath y^t hee was Present & did see John Wincoll, signe seale & deliuer this Instrume^t as his Act & Deede In Boston, 16th Janvary 1679·
before us/ Edw: Tynge
Humphrey Daiue/

ffeb 19·
79.80

Mr Jabez ffox Minister appeared, & made oath y^t hee was Present, & saw John Wincoll signe seale & Deliuer y^s Iustrum^t as his Act & Deede, before us
S: Bradstreet Gouer

Tho: Damforth Dep^{ty} Gouer/

Kittery in the Prouince of Mayne/ 2 May 1684: Capt John Wincoll came & acknowledged the aboue written Instrume^t to bee Act & Deede, before mee Charles ffrost
Just: pe·

A true Coppy of this Deede as attested & acknowledged, transcribed out of the originall & y^{r}with Compared this 3d of May 1684: p Edw: Rishworth ReCor:

Know all men by these Presents, y^t In Consideration of Capt John Hull his fully acquitting John Wincoll, William Playstead & James Playstead, Administrators to Roger Playsteads Estate, from any obligation to pay a bond of Twenty & two hundred pounds, for default of seasonable paijng eleuen hundred & nineteene pounds fiue shillings which ye sd Roger Playstead with John Hull stood bound in Joytly & seuerally to pay to Thom^s Clarke M^{r}chant which bond beareth date Aprill sixth 1671: I William Plaistead haueing full pouer Committed to mee by a letter of Atturney made July 26th 1679: by the sd John Wincoll & James Playstead, ioynt Administrators with mee ye sd William

Playstead, to yᵉ sd Roger Playsteads Estate; do by these Presents fully & absolutely Assigne, & set ouer both in mine own, & in the sd John Wincolls & sayd James Playsteads behalfe, all oʳ right & Title to yᵉ Saw Mills & appʳtenancēs mentioned in the Adioyneing deed of sale & Morgage Which John Hull & Roger Playstead tooke for thejr Joynt security against all Damāges by entering into the aforesd bonds, to the sd Clarke, to bee sooly security to the sd John Hull his heyrs executors & Administrators, to all Intents & purposes In Law, of wᵗ kind or nature soeuer, as witness my hand & seale this fourth of August 1679:

Signed sealed & Deluerd,   William Playstead (his seale)
 In Presence of/   William Playstead Prsonally appeare-
 Eᵐ Hutchinson/   ing, acknowledged the aboue Instru-
 Mathew Atkines/   ment to bee his Act & Deede, to
        which his hand & seale is afixed,
        this 2 : May 1684 : before mee
         John Wincoll
        Jus · pe : of Prouince of Mayne/

Mr Eliakime Hutchinson & Mr Mathew Attkines, appeared & made oath yᵗ they were Present, & saw William Playstead signe seale & Deliuer the Instrumᵗ aboue as his Act & Deede, March : the :   : 167$\frac{9}{80}$ before us Peter Buckley
          Hum : Dauie/

The before written Deede of Morgage & testimonys there unto annexed, with the aboue written Assigneᵗ & Its testimonys stand reCorded, In yᵉ 220 · 221 : 222 : pagˢ of yᵉ sixth booke of ReCords of the Notary publique, of yᵉ Massatusetts Coloney of New England, as Attests John Hayward Notoʳˢ Publqˢ/

vera Copia of this obligation aboue written, as acknowledged & Attested, transcribed & with originall Compard this 3d of May 1684 :   p Edw : Rishworth

BOOK IV, FOL. 9, 10.

Know all men by these Presents, y^t I George Jefferay of Portsmouth, In the prouince of New Hampshire, In New England, M^{r}chant Haue Assigned ordained & made, & In my stead & place by these Presents, do put, & Constitute my trusty frejnd John Macgowen now rescident neare Pischataq, Riuer, in new England my true & lawfull Atturney, for mee, & in my name & to my uss to aske Demand, sue for, leauy, require recouer, & receiue of all & euery Person, & Persons w^{t}soeuer Inhabitting, or resciding in New England aforesd, in either of the Prouinces or Colonys therein, all & euery such debt & debts sume & somes of Money Goods Wares & M^{r}chandize, & other Estate w^{t}soeuer which is are or hereafter shall bee due, owing, belonging, or app^{r}tajneing unto mee by any manner of meanes, or ways w^{t}soeuer, & for default of payment ye sd Debto^{rs} or any of them to sue arrest, Attatch, Implead Imprison & Condemne, his & y^r bodys, Lands, tenaments Goods, & Chattles, In execution to take, & out of execution to deliuer, & vpon the receipt of any such debts, som̃ of Money or other Estate due to mee as aforesd, acquittances, or other discharges for mee & in my name to make seale, & Deliuer Atturney or Atturneys under him my sayd Atturney to make, & substitute, & at pleasur to reuoake, Giueing & by these Presents Granting, unto my sd Atturney full & full & whoole pouer strength & authority, to do say, & Conclude, Performe & finish all & euery Act & Acts, thing & things Deuise & deuises, whatsoeuer in the law Needfull to bee done, in & about, & Concerneing the Premisses, In as full large & ample manner, & forme, as I might or could do, if I were Per- [10] sonally Present, ratifijng Allowing & houlding firme, & stable all, & whatsoeuer my sd Atturney or his substitute shall lawfully do, or cause to bee done In & about the Premisses, by uertue of these Presents/ In witness Whereof I the sd

George Jefferay haue here vnto sett my hand & seale the
Twenty eight of Aprill 1684. George Jeffray ($\genfrac{}{}{0pt}{}{\text{locus}}{\text{sigilli}}$)
Signed sealed & deliuered/

  In the Presence of us/ Boston In New England Aprill
  ffrancis Hammond/   29th 1684 ffrancis Hamond &
  John Denness   John Denness did testify vpon
                         oath, that they did see George
                         Jefferay, signe seale & Deliuer
                         the aboue written Instrum^t to
                         which y^r hands are subscribed,
                         as witnesses/
                                S : Bradstreet Gouer

vera Copia of this Instrum^t aboue written transcribed out
of the originall, & there with Compared this fiueteenth day
of May 1684 :   .   p Edw : Rishworth ReCor :

Know all men by these Presents, that I Samull Snow of
Boston In New England Cordwaino^r, soole executor, to the
last will & Testament of Margerett Mountegue the Relict,
& Administratrix of Griffine Mountegue formerly of Cape
Porpus In the County of yorke, In ye Prouince of Mayne,
In new England in America deceased : ffor & In consideration of the sume of sixty pounds in Current money In New
England to mee In hand payd by Tymothy Dwight of Boston In New England aforesd, GouldSmith, before ye sealeing & deliuery here of, w^{r}of I the sayd Samull Snow do
acknowledg the receipt & do hereby fully Clearely & absolutely release, acquitt, & discharge the sd Tymothy Dwight,
his heyres executors, Administrators & Assignes, & euery
of them, Haue giuen granted barganed & sould, & by these
Presents, giue, grant, bargane & sell, unto the sd Tymothy
Dwight his heyres, & Assigns for euer : One Tract of Land
Contameing one hundred Acres, with appurtenances lijng &
being in Cape Porpus, aforesd, & is bounded by Certen

BOOK IV, FOL. 10.

Marked trees, begining at Morgan Howells Land, & from thence to take in the remajnder of the Necke, unto the East Coue, & for makeing vp & fully Compleateing the hundred Acres is to go ouer the Coue, & to begine at a small Gutt next to Ambrose Berrys vpland, & to runne vp the Coue to a Long small Cricke y^t runnes into the woods, & so along the wood side to the end of the Cricke, to make vp fully the hundred Acres; And also one hundred Acres of Land more lijng & being at Kenebunke Riuer. In the County of yorke aforesd, with the app^{r}tenances, & is bounded South westwardly by the Land of John Renalds, & measureth fiuety pooles by the Riuer abouesd, & to runne back into the woods South & by East, untill the hundred Acres bee fully made vp butting vpon the Comans, & likewise one hundred Acres of Land more lijng & being at ye Dezart Marshes, between the lott of John Millers, & the land of Thomas Mussy, butting vpon the aforesd Marsh, & also w^t land that shall bee made to appeare is or was belonging, & app^{r}tajneing unto the sd Samell Snow In Cape Porpus, and Kenebunke Riuer, or the Dezart Marshes abouesd, togeather will all the woods underwoods, Commans, Meddows, Pastures, feedings Comoditys, Immunitys, hereditaments houseing fenceing & priuiledges, belonging & app^{r}tajneing to any of the premises aboue specifyd, & all the Deeds writeings & euidences, of for & concerneing the same to haue & to hould the sd Tract of Land & all the Premisses, aboue mentioned with the appurtenances before by these barganed, & sould or mentioned, or Intended to bee hereby barganed, & sould, & euery part & Parcell y^{r}of unto the sd Tymothy Dwight his heyres & Assignes for euer: And I the sd Samull Snow for my selfe my heyrs executors & Administrators, the sd Tracts of Land, houseing & all the Premisses, with ye app^r- tenances hereby specifyd, to bee barganed & sould. mentioned or intended, to bee hereby barganed & sould unto the sd Tymothy Dwight his heyres, & Assigns, shall & will warrant, & defend against all Persons for euer, by these

Presents: And Saraih wife of the sd Samell Snow, doth by these Presents, surrender & yeild vp all her right of Dowry, & Title of Thirds, wch shee hath, might or out to haue had of in & to the Premisses, before specifyd to ye sd Tymothy Dwight his heyres & Assigns for euer: Prouided always & It is Couenanted, Concluded & agreed by & between the sd partys to these Presents: that if the sd Samell Snow his heyres executors Administrators & Assignes, or any of them do well & truely Content & pay or Cause to bee contented & payd to the sd Tymothy, his heyres, Executors, Administrators or Assigns at the now dwelling house of him the sd Timothy Twight, the full some of sixty foure pounds fiueteen shillings of Current Money of New England, at or before the eight day of September next Inswing the date here of with out fraude, or gyle, then this Present bargan & sajle, & all & euery Couenant, grant, article, & thing here in Contajned shall to all æffects & purpo ses & Constructions bee utterly frustrate & of none æffect: But If default of payment In ye day of payment aforesd, In part or in all, that then this Present bargane & saile, & all euery Couenant, article, & thing y^rin contayned, shall to all æffects & purposes stand, remaine & abide, in full force & strength, any there in before expressed to ye Contrar y thereof in any wise Notwithstanding; In witness where of the sd Samll Snow & Sarah his wife, haue here vnto set thejr hands & seals, this eight day Septem^br one thousand six hundred eighty & two/ 1682:

Signed sealed & Deliuered/   Samuell Snow (his seale)
 In the Presence of/   Saraih Snow her
 Moses Collier Junjo^r/   marke/
 Samuell Nanny/

  Samuell Snow acknowledged this Instrum^t
  to bee his Act & Deed, & also testifyd
  vpon oath that his wife signd & Deliu-

ered the same, togeather with him selfe, as her Act & Deed this 30th of Aprill 1683 : before mee Samell Nowell
Assistant :

A true Coppy of this Instrum^t transcribed out of the originall, & y^rwith Compard this 23th day of May 1684 :

p Edw : Rishworth Re : Cor :

Know all men by these Presents, that I Joseph Cross of Wells, In the prouince of Mayne In New England, yeomon, with the free Consent of Mary my wife, & seuerall good Causes & Considerations y^rvnto mee moueing, & more especially for & In Consideration of tenn pounds to mee In hand payd by Samuell Austine of the abouesd Town, with which I the abouesd Cross, do acknowledg my selfe to bee fully payd, satisfyd & Contented, haue given granted Enfeoffed & Confirmed & by these Presents do giue, grant Infeoff & Confirme freely fully & absolutely unto Samuell Austine, from mee my heyres, executors, Administrators & Assignes, my soole right title, & Interest of one halfe of the Ysland, Comanly known by the name of Drakes Ysland, togeather with one halfe of ye Marsh, which was formerly my father Crosses Marsh, the March lijng on the North side on the sd Ysland, begining [11] at a Rocke, a little distance from the Ysland, & so to runne from sd Ysland, by that rocke down to the Cricke, & so by the Ysland & the Cricke, to runne till it come to a Prcell of Marsh, which was formerly Mr John Gouches Marsh, with all the profitts & priuiledges there unto belonging, freely & peaceably to haue & to hould with out any matter of Challenge, claime or demand of mee the sd Jos : Cross, or anie Person or Persons w^tsoeuer, either from by or under mee, my heyres, executors Administrators for euer : Hee the sd Samell Austine & his heyres executors, Administrators & Assignes, I do hereby declare to bee the true & rightly possessed of each & euery part of the aboue mentioned Premisses; And that hee the sayd Samell Austine, his heyres executors, Administrators & Assignes, shall quietly & peaceably Inioy all & euery part & parcell of the Premisses granted, & sould to them for euer: And I do hereby promiss & Couenant to & with the sd Samuell Austine, that yᵉ Ysland & Marsh & euery part of It, are free & Cleare from all Gyfts Grants, barganes, leases, Legacys, Dowrys Judgmts, executions, Morgages, & all other Incomberances wᵗsoeuer, & do promiss to warrant, & defend the title & Interest of the Premisses, from mee my heyres executors, & Assignes, & from all Person or Persons under mee, or by my meanes, or any other by my procurement: In testimony wʳof, I haue here vnto set my hand & seale, this nine & Twenteth day of May, one thousand six hundred eighty foure   Joseph Cross (his seale)

Signed sealed & Deliueřd

   In the Presence of us/   Joseph Cross, & Mary Cross the
   John Barrett/   wife of Joseph Cross, came
   Jonathan Hamonds/   before mee this 29ᵗʰ day of
                             May & acknowledged this aboue
                             written Instrumeᵗ to bee yʳ Act
                             & Deed
                      p Samuell Wheelewright
                                     Jus: pe:

A true Coppy of this Instrument aboue written transcribed out of the originall & there with Compared this 9th day of June 1684: p Edw: Rishworth ReCor:

Know all men by these Presents, yᵗ I William Spencer of Barwicke, In the Prouince of Mayne, In New England, Yeoman, for & In Consideration of Tenn pounds in Money, or pay æquiuolent, which I am Ingaged by the last Will & testament of my father, Thomas Spencer late of Barwicke aforesd, deceased, to pay unto Susanna his daughter, & my sister, shee being now ye wife of Ephraim Joy, of the same Town & prouince, Carpenter, do by these Presents, for my selfe, my heyrs, executors, & Administrators, Giue, grant, bargan, sell, Infeoff, & Confirme unto the aforesayd Ephraim Joy & Susanna his wife, a Certajn Parcell of Land being, & scituate In Barwicke, Contajneing three Acres & a quarter, more or less, as It is now bounded out on the North side of the house lott of my late deceased father aforesd, & is about fourty pooles In length & about thirteen pooles In breadth, & bounded on the North, with ye Land Called Parkers fejld, & on the West & South with the rest of own Land, & on the East high way, leading to Mr Hutchinsons Saw Mill, & is pait of y^t Land which my late deceased father aforesd, gaue mee by will: And now vpon the Consideration aforesayd, & in Perticular in lue, & stead of the payment of six pounds, & tenn shillings of the aforesayd Tenn pounds, that the sayd Three Acres & a quarter of Land is by mee the sd William Spencer sould unto the aforesayd Ephraim Joy, & Susanna his wife, To haue & to hould all & singular the app^{r}tenances & Premisses, with all priuiledges y^{r}unto belonging, unto him the sd Ephraim Joy, & Susanna his wife their heyres, executors Administrators, or Assignes, for euer as Witness my hand & Seale, this three & Twenteth day of May 1684:   William Spencer (his seale)

Signed Sealed & deliuered   William Spencer acknowledged
   In the Presence of us/   the aboue written Deede of
   John Shapleigh/   Sayle, to bee his free act &
   John Wincoll/   Deede, May 23: 1684: before
                                mee John Wincoll Just: pe:

A true Coppy of this Instrument transcribed out of ye originall, & y^{r}with Compared this 13th day of June 1684:
                     p Edw: Rishworth Re: Cor:

Book IV, Fol. 11.

The Deposition of John Cossons aged about 88 yeares/
Being Sworne Sayth, y^t John Mayne, had possession seuerall yeares y^t hee made vss of, a certajn Parcell of Marsh, contayning about fiue or six Acres of Bastard Meddow, lijng on the head of the Eastermost branch of the Cricke Called Sysquissett, next aboue ye head of this deponents Marsh, being bounded by the vpland on the one side, & on ye Riuer on ye other, & further sayth not/ Dated 15th of May 1684: Taken vpon oath this 15th day of May 1684· before mee   Edw: Rishworth Jus: pe/

Richard Carter about 40 yeares of age/
Came before mee this 9th day of June 1684: & did Attest vpon his oath, that this testimony aboue written of John Cossons, his referring to John Mayns Marsh, is the treuth according to his own knowledg/ taken at ye date here of vpon his oath/ Edw: Rishworth Jus: pe:

A true Coppy of these testimonys transcribed out of ye originall, & y^{r}with Compared this 20th day of June 1684:
p Edw: Rishworth Re: Cor:

To all whome these Presents may come/ that I Thomas Withers of the Prouince of Mayne, In New England In Pischataqua, In the Town of Kittery yeamon, do & haue barganed, granted sould & Confirmed, & by these Presents do bargane Sell & Confirme vnto Joseph Berry Mariner belonging to Pischataqua, to him his heyres & Assignes, one halfe Acre of Land, lijng being In the sd Prouince; next Adiacent to the Eastern bounds of the sayd Withers his Land, where his dwelling house now stands, the bounds runns eight rod along the fence Northward, from a little Cricke or coue by the water side, w^r stands a little Stumpe, & so It runns vp the Riuer vpon a streight Lyne Tenn Rodds, which lyne stretcheth one rodd by the Riuer side

Westward, of a little red oake stumpe, or bush y{t} is now growing, & so runns from y{t} Corner paralell to the fence that now is Northward eight rodd, & from y{t} Corner Eastward agajne to the fence/ This land for & In consideration of six pounds In money receiued In hand, w{r}of three pounds fiueteen shillings is receiued already, & the remajnd{r} shall bee payd at the signeing & sealing here of; This Land I the sd Withers do sell & make ouer from mee & my successors, vnto the sd Joseph Berry & his successors, to haue & to hould for euer, with out lett Molestation or deniall, or Interrvption, of mee, the sd Thomas Withers my heyres or Assignes, or any other Person lawfully Clajmeing the same, from by or under mee, or any part or Parcell there of : And also the sd Berry to haue free Egress & regress, through the sd Withers his Land to the Commans or high way to the Town of Kittery, to bee appoynted by the sd Withers or his successors, with [12] all rights & priuiledges belonging there vnto, vnto all which I do here unto set my hand & seale, this ninth day of January one thousand six hundred Eighty Three/   Thomas Withers (his seale)

Signed sealed & deliuered   This Instrument was acknowl-
  In this Presence of us/   edged by Mr Thomas Withers,
  Mary Hooke/   to bee his act & Deede, unto
  The Marke of Mary   Jos : Berry this Ninth of Jan-
  Broosy/ ƲƲ .   vary 1683 : before mee
                            ffrancis Hooke Jus : pe :
vera Copia of this Instrume{t} tran-   Witness my hand
  scribed out of y{e} originall & y{r}-   Robert Fisher/
  with Compared this 24th day of   Elizabeth Withers
  June 1684 :

    p Edw : Rishworth ReCor :

Know all men these Presents, that I Thomas Bracket now of Greenlād neare Pischataqua River Planter, do acknowledg my selfe to ow, & stand Justly indebted unto Mis Elizabeth Harvey of Falmouth the full & Just some of one hundred pounds Sterling, to y° which payment Well & truely to bee made, I the sd Thomas Bracket bind mee, my heyres executors, Administrators unto the sayd Elizabeth Harvy her heyres executors, administrators & Assigns firmely by these Presents/

The Condition of y° obligation is such, that In Case the sd Thomas Brackett shall faithfully Performe, & fullfill what is mentioned in a deed of Gyft I gaue him of my house & Land, & Goods, In y° prouideing for mee, as is there expressed dureing my life, Which Deed beareth date with these Presents, to say to prouide for mee meate drinke Lodging, apparell washing & all other Conuenient Necessarys dureing my life, then this obligation to bee noyd, & of none æffect, otherwise to stand In full pouer force strength & uertue, as witness my hand & seale, this 2cund of June 1671:   Thomas Brackett (his seale)

Signed sealed & Deliuered/   Leef^t George Ingersall appeared
In the Presence of us/   before mee the 29th of Novemb^r
George Munioy/   1682: & made oath y^t hee see
George Ingersall/   Thos Bracket signe seale &
   Deliuer this Instrum^t as his
   Act & Deede & y^t Mr Geo:
   Munioy did signe as a witness,
   at ye same Tyme/ Taken vpon
   oath this 29th of Nouemb^r 1682:
   before mee Edw: Tynge
                    Jus: pe:

A true Coppy transcribed & Compard y^s 28: June 1684:
                    p Edward Rishworth ReCor:

Cascoe In ffalmouth the eight of July 1680/
Mis Elizabeth Haruy did declare the Condition of the aboue written obligation not to bee P^{r}formed, & deliuered It vp, with all her right & Interest y^{r}unto to her sonn In law

Taddeous Clarke, & did Intreat us to witness It, & did acknowledg It before mee

 John Palmer   Walter Gyndall Comissio^r/
 Joseph Hodgsden vera Copia Edw · Rishworth ReCor:

    5th Septemb^r 1683:

I Elizabeth Haruy widdow, do Assigne this bond on the other side, for good & ualewable Considerations In hand receiued to all its Intents purposes & Improuem^{ts}, & to my beloued Sunn Taddeous Clarke, of Falmouth/ In witness of ye Premisses I haue sign'd the day & yeare aboue written, my hand/   Elizabeth Haruys
Read signed & Deliuered,   marke C
 In Presence of us/
 Edw: Tynge/   This Assigme^t aboue was made before
 George Burroghs/ mee & owned by ye sd Elizabeth
       Haruy the day & yeare aboue writ-
       ten/ Joshua Scottow Jus. pe:
vera Copia transcribed & Compard y^s 28: June 84:
     p Edw: Rishworth

Know all men by these Presents, that I Nicholas Coole of Cape Porpus, In the County of yorke, for & In consideration of two pounds, Twenty shillings w^{r}of is already in hand receiued, the other Twenty shillings to bee left in the hands of John Barrett, at his house in Wells for ye vss of the sd Coole, in good & M^{r}chantble Goods, do bargan with, sell grant, & make ouer vnto Thom^s Wells, his heyres, executors, administrators, & Assignes, all my right, titile, & Interest unto, & in a Percell of Marsh & Thatch, scituate & lijng between the sea Wall, & Webhannett River, towards ye mouth of ye sd River, which was formerly granted to Edmund Littlefejld Senjo^r, Jos: Bolls, John Littlefejld, & Nichol^s Coole, as also unto a Parcell of vpland, which I formerly purchased of Francis Littlefejld, Senjo^r, always prouided ye sd Wells, or his Assignes, shall allow the sd Nicholas Coole, the priuiledg of a burijng place, for his generation, & to fence in a place, w^r the Dead Corps are already buried: unto him the sd Wells his heyres or Assignes, to haue, & to hould, for y^r soole uss, behowfe, & benefitt for euer: And for the good Performance here of, I haue by these Presents bound my selfe, my heyres, executors, Administrators, & Assignes, unto Thomas Wells his heyres, executors, Administrators, & Assignes; In witness whereof I haue here unto subscribed my hand & seale/ Dated this Twenty fifth of June Anno Dom: one thousand six hundred sixty nine/ 1669:   Nicho^s Coole (his seale)

Subscribed, Sealed, &   Nicolas Coole Senjor, acknowl-
Deliuerd In Presence of   edged this Instrument to bee
John Barrett/   his Act & Deede this 29th of
Elizabeth Barret/   Aprill 1684: before mee/
                        Samuell Wheelewright Jus: pe:
her ◯ Marke

A true Coppy of this Instrument aboue written, transcribed out of the originall, & y^rwith Compared this 8th day of July: 1684:   p Edw: Rishworth ReCor:

There being a difference, or dispute about a Tract of Land, or Percell, now & long in the possession of Capt Raynes, which is Claimed by Capt Champernown/ & both partys haueing mutually agreed to referr the matter of difference to Mr Samuell Nowell, Capt Josua Scottow, & Capt Edw: Tynge, who were mette at yorke, June 28: 84: These are to satisfy all whom it may Concerne, that ye Partys aboue named, vidz^t Capt Champernown, & Capt Raynes did mutually agree that for a finall Issew of this difference, the Land In Controuersy should continew & remajne in the occupation, & quiett fruition of ye sd Capt

BOOK IV, FOL. 12, 13.

Raynes, & his wife dureing thejre naturall lifes, & after y^r decease the sd Land to descend to the heyre In law, of the sd Capt Raynes, according to the Coman law of England, to bee Inioyed by him & his heyres for euer : which sayd agreement by Consent of both partys, is to stand vpon record : And also the sd Capt Champerown doth obleige to make a Deede for a more full Confirmation of all his claimes, & Titles, to the sayd Capt Raynes, & his heyre or Elldest sonn : The Land lijng in braueboat Harbour neare Pischataq, Riuer/ In witness whereof the sd partys haue subscribed y^r names/

This writeing was subscribed by   Francis Champernown
  both partys In the Presence   ffran^s Raynes/
  of us/

Samuell Nowell/ Joshua Scottow/ Edw · Tynge/ yorke June 28 : 1684 : Capt Fran^s Champernown, & Capt Raynes came before mee & owned this Instrument to bee y^r Act & Deede/   Edw : Rishworth Jus . pe :

vera Copia of this agreement aboue written, transcribed & with originall Compared this 8th day of July 1684 :

                       p Edw : Rishworth ReCor :

These may Certify whome It may Concerne, that I Francis Champernoown of Kittery in the prouince of Mayne In New England, do vpon diuerse good Causes, & Considerations, there unto mee moueing, & espetially for ye tender affections y^t I beare unto my well beloued wife, & do freely giue unto my well beloued wife Mary Champernown, all my whoole part of ye Ysland & houses, & all & euery thing be-
[13] longing to that part of the Ysland that I now liue vpon after my decease, to bee her proper Inheritance, & after my sd wifes decease, the one halfe to bee my daughter in laws Elizabeth Cutts, & If shee dyeth before her Mother, my sd wife, then to wholly at the disposall of my beloued wife,

Book IV, Fol. 13.

Mary Champernoown as abouesd/ witness my hand this eight day of July : 1684 ·   ffran^s Champnowne/

ffran^s Champernowne came before mee the 8th of July 84 & acknowledged this aboue Instrume^t to bee his Act & Deede/   John Dauess Deputy President/

vera Copia, of this Instrume^t aboue written transcribed, & with originall Compared, this 19th day July 1684 :
        Edw : Rishworth Re : Cor :

Know all men by these Presents, that I Rowland young of the Ysles of shoals fisherman, haue bargaaned sould & set ouer, vnto Edward Martine of sayd Yslands his heyres, Administrators, executors, & Assignes, all y^t my dwelling house scituate & being on Smuttinose Ysland, neare to the flakes of Samuell Mathews, with the priuiledges y^{r}vnto belonging, as of setting & placeing wood &c : I say I haue hereby sould & alliend, vnto the sd Edw · Martyne, his heyres, executors, administrators & Assignes, all my right, title, Interest, In the Premisses, & do hereby promiss for my selfe, heyres, executors, Administrators, & Assignes, to defend the Title, & the Sayle from all manner of Prsons w^{t}soeuer : It being for a valewable consideration/ In witness w^{r}of I haue hereunto set my hand & seale, this sixteenth day of Octob^r 1683, one thousand six hundred Eighty three/

Sign'd Sealed & deliuered/   Rowland young (his seale)

In the Presence of us/
Phillip Odihorne/   his marke R
Samell Mathews/   Susanna young (her seale)

A true Coppy of this Deede aboue written transcribed out of the originall & y^{r}with Compard this 19th day of July 1684 :   p Edw : Rishworth ReCor :

Book IV, Fol. 13.

To all Christian people, to whome this Present writeing shall Come/ Know yee that I Richard Downes Senjo^r of the Ysels of shoales fisherman, In Consideration of the full & iust some of eighty pounds, to mee In hand payd by ffrancis Waneright of Ipswich, haue given granted sould, alienated & by these Presents, do giue grant sell alienate Confirme & set ouer, all that Messueg or Tenement of one dwelling house, Contajning too lowers Rowmes & one Chamber, with one baite house & one stage, with what is belonging to it, & all my flake Rowme, & fiue flakes which are now vpon it, & my shallop with all her Tackelling, & appurtenances, & Sailes Masts, yards, roads grappers, porrige pott, oares, with my moreing place, my moreing Cable, & standing part, with all the priuiledges & appurtenances belonging to the sd houses stage, flakes, flakerowm, boate & moreing place, wch houses stage flake flakerowme & moreing place are scituate ljng & being vpon Hog Ysland in the Ysles of shoales, In the Prouince of Mayne, & are sould, alienated & set ouer to ffrancis Wanewright of Ipswich, & is now in the Tenure & occupation of mee ye sd Downes, all which sd houses stages flakes & flake rowm boate & moreing place, with all thejr singular priuiledges, & appurtenances, I do hereby declare to bee the proper Estate, right & Interest of the sayd Francis Wanewright, & for him his heyres, executors, Administrators, & Assignes, to hould euery part & Parcell thereof as his & there own for euer; And they shall quietly & peaceably inioy & possess ye sd Premisses by mee granted, without ye lett, hinderance, or molestation or Trouble of mee, or of any of my heyres, executors, administrators, or assigns, or any other Pison or Persons w^{t}soeuer; Always prouided the abouesd Richd Downes Senjo^r do & shall well & truly pay, or Cause to bee payd the full & iust sume of eighty pounds, In good M^{r}chtble dry Codd fish at or before the fifth day July: 1686: then this Instrument to bee uoyd,

& of none æffect, or else to stand & bee in full force & vertue/
Dated 16 : July : 1684 :   Richard Downs
Signed Sealed & deliuer'd   Senjo^r his marke ($^{his}_{seale}$)
  In the Presence of us/
  John Wanewright/   Richard Downs Senjo^r, came before
  Simon Wanewright/   mee this 16th day of July 1684 :
              & acknowledged this Instrume^t
              to bee his free act & Deede/
              Edw : Rishworth Jus : pe :
A true Coppy of this Instrument aboue written, transcribed & with the originall Compared this 19th day of July
1684 :   p Edw . Rishworth ReCor :

        July : 7th 1684 :

  These Presents witnesseth, that w^{r}as Capt William Lang, & John Lane about two years past, left In the Custody of Mr Roger Kelley Inhabitant on Smuttinoss Yslands at the Yslands of shoales, one Certen Cable & Anker to bee sould & disposd of by the sd Kelly & James Blagdon, of starr Ysland, & for which sayd Roger Kelly & James Blagdon gaue a receipt for : I William Goodhew of Ipswich, by order & desire of Mr Humphrey Dauie M^{r}chant In Boston, being Intrusted to demand, & receiue payment for the sd Anker, & Cable do hereby acquitt & discharge the sd Roger Kelly & James Blagdon from all manner of Demands on Accomp^t of the anker & Cable, I haueing receiued full satisfaction for the same/   William Goodhew Seno^r

  July 7th 1684 : Receiued of Mr Roger Kelly & James Blagdon on the Accomp^t of Mr Humphrey Dauie, sixty quin^{tls} of M^{r}ch^{t}ble Codd fish for the anker & Cable aboue mentioned, by mee receiued   John Wilde/
  A true Coppy of this order, & receipts as aboue written transcribed & with the originall Compared this 19th of July 1684 : p Edw : Rishworth ReCor .

Book IV, Fol. 13, 14.

In the name of God Amen/ It may euidently appeare & bee known unto all people to whom this Present writeing or procuration shall come, to bee seene read, or heard, that on thursday the fourth day of March, In the yeare of o^r Lord God according to the Accompt of England, one thousand six hundred seauenty & foure, at the Citty of Bristoll In the Kingdome of England, there came Personally unto mee the Notary publique here under named, being then in my shopp scituate in Corne streete, [14] with in the sd Citty of Brystoll, Robert Vickers, Richard Bickeham, & William Williams, all of the same Citty M^{r}chants, who then & there of there own deliberate minds, & uolentary accords, euery of them seuerally & respectiuely, did before mee the sd Notary publique, & the witnesses here under named, make nominate ordaye Constitute, & appoynt & Depute their trusty & well beloued frejnd ffrancis Tucker, M^{r}chant now rescident in or about Pischataqua, in New England, although hee bee absent as If hee were here Personally Present (their true & lawfull Atturney procurator, actor & doer, of thejre business, here under mentioned/ And the sd Constituents haue euery of them seuerally, & a part, given & granted, & by these Presents do giue & grant vnto thejr sd Procrurator, full pouer, lawfull authority, & speciall Command for them ye sd Constituants, & In thejr names, & steade, & to & for y^r onely proper usses & behoofes, do aske, Demand, sue for, leauy recouer & receiue, of William Bickeham M^{r}cha^t now rescident In New England, & of all & euery other Person, & P^{r}sons w^{t}soeuer, whom it shall or may by any means Concerne, inhabiting, resciding, or abideing in New England, All such sume or sumes of money, debts goods, wares, Marchandizes, Aduenturs & Demands, w^{t}soeuer which are due or owing vnto, or detained from the sayd Constituants, Joyntly or to either of them seuerally by the sd William Bickeham, or any other of the sd P^{r}son or Persons, either vpon Accompt or by any other ways or meanes howsoeuer, or for any matter or Cause whatsoeuer/ & also the sd Constituants, ioyntly & seuerally, & a part, haue given, & granted unto the sd Procurator, full pouer & Authority for them & In theire names & steads, to require, take, receiue, & place, all euery or any Accompt or Reckonings, of him the sd William Bickeham, & all other Person, or Persons touching, & Concerneing the Premisses/ And If neede require, the same to resist & reject & also to make any agreement touching the Premisses, & to moue, try bring & prosecute, any Action, or Actions, suites, striffes & busnises, for the recouery of the sd moneys, debts, goods, Aduentures & Premisses, In any Court or Courts w^{t}soeuer, before any Judges, Just^s Deligates, subdeligates, stuards, officers, & other Ministers w^{t}souer; as well against the sd William Bickeham, & all euery other Person & Persons concerned y^{r}in, & to against his, or thejr moneys, goods, or M^{r}chandizes & him & them & his & thejr moneys goods & M^{r}chandize to arrest Attatch, Imprison, & cause to bee keept in safe Costody, & the same agajne to release, & to declare, obiect, & Alledge, any thing or things, concerneing the Premisses, definatiue sentence, or other finall decrees, concerning the same, to heare & see, to bee given & done & also to Compound, with him them or any of them concerning the Premisses, & after the receipt y^{r}of, or composition made, accquittances, or other lawfull discharges to make for the same to make Seale & deliuer procurator, & procurators, one or more under him to make, & substitute, & at his pleasure the same agajne to reuoake, & generally to do, execute, Performe fullfill & finish all & w^{t}soeuer else shall bee needfull, or requisite to bee done in & about ye Premisses, In as large & ample manner & forme as the sd Constituants, or any of them might do the same if they were there Prsoually Present, Promissing & the sd Constituants, haue promissed that they will ratify, Confirme & allow all w^{t}soeuer thejr sd Procurator, shall do, cause or procure to bee done, in or about ye Premises And that they will not Contradict the same vnder the obligation of all thejre goods, & they do

Book IV, Fol. 14.

also promiss, & obligue them selues to pay & discharge all such money as shall bee expended, & disbursed in the Comenceing & prosecuting of any Sujte or businesses concerneing the Premisses, & also to saue their procurator, harmeless Concerneing the same, & In that behalfe, haue put down thejr cawtion by these Presents/ All these things were Acted, & done as they are before recited, the day yeare & place aforesd, thejr being then & there Present Phillip Knill of Charles Town In New England Mariner, George Gooding of North petherton In the County of Sumers^{tt} yeoman, & Thomas Ryder of the sd Citty of Bristoll Seaman, witnesses requested to testify the Premisses/ And for the better Creditt & treuth of the Premisses, the sd Constituants haue Confirmed these Presents with y^r own hands & seales/

Witnesses requested   Robert Vickris (locus sigilli)
  Phillip Knill/   Richd Bickham (his seale)
  George Gooding/   William Williams (his seale)

  The marke of   And I Thomas Hartwell Notary
  Thom^s Rider   publique lawfully authorized,
         Cittizen & Burgess of the sd
         Citty of Brystoll, because I
         was Present, & did see heare
         & know, all the sayd things to
         bee acted, & done as they are
         before recited, the day yeare
         & place aforesd haue y^{r}fore
         here unto subscribed my name,
         & set too my wonted and ac-
         coustomed firme, & the Seale
         of my office, being requested
         to testify and certify the Premisses/

(Locus Sigilli)   Thomas Hartwell
         Noto^{rius} Publi^{cus}

~ || ~ Iustitiæ Oculis ~ || ~ || ~

Book IV, Fol. 14, 15.

These may Certify all whome It may concerne, that on the sayd 4th day of March 1674 : the aboue named Robert Vickers, Richard Bickham, & William Williams came Personally before mee Ralph Olliffe, Esqr, Major of the sd Citty of Bristoll, & seuerally seale & Deliuer as thejr acts &

Ralph Olliffe Major] Deedes, the writeing aboue written, & In Testimony y^{r}of vpon request I haue subscribed my name, & caused ye seale of my office of Mayrollty to bee here unto afixed, the day & yeare aboue written 1674 :

Phillip Knill aged about thirty eight years/ & George Gooding, testifyeth vpon oath that they were Present at the day of the date of this Instrum^t & did see Mr Robert Vickers, Mr Richd Bickham, & W : Williams, signe seale & Deliuer the same as thejr Act & Deede/

Taken vpon oath before mee the 20th of May 1675 :

Edw : Tynge Assist^t

vera Copia of this Instrume^t of Atturney or Procuration, as Confirmed & Attested aboue written, transcribed out of the originall, & there with Compared this 25th day of July 1684 as Attests Edw : Rishworth Re : Cor :

·

To all people to whome these Presents shall come/ Know yee that w^{t}as neare three scoore years since, Mr Thomas Purchase deceased, came into this Countrey as Wee haue been well Informed, & did as well by pouer, or Pattent deriued from the King of England, as by Consent, Contract, & agreement, with Sagamores & proprietors of all the Lands lijng on the Easterly side of Casco Bay, & on the both sides of Androscogan Riuer, & Kenebecke Riuer, enter vpon & take possession of all [15] the Lands, lijng foure Miles Westward from the uppermost falls, In sayd Androscoggan riuer, to Mayquoit In Casco bay, & on the Lands on the other side Androscoggan Riuer, from aboue sd falls down to Pegipscott & Merry meeteing bay, to bee bounded by a South West & North East lyne, to runne from the vpper part of sd falls to Kenebecke Riuer, & all the Land from Maqcooit to Pegipscott, & to hould the same breadth where ye Land will beare it, down to a place called Atkines his Bay, Neare to Sagadehock are the Westerly side, of Kenebecke Riuer, & all the Yslands In the sayd Kenebecke Riuer & land between the sd Atkines his bay, & small poynt Harbour, the Land & riuer & ponds interiacent, Contajneing y^{r}in breadth, about three English Miles more or less; And w^{r}as wee are well Assured, that Majo^r Nicho^s Shapleigh In his life tyme, was both by purchase from the Indeans Sagamores, our Ancestors, & Consent of Mr Gorg^e Comissio^r possessed, & dyed seized of the remajnder of all ye Lands, lijng & Adioyneing vpon the Mayne, & all the Yslands between the sd small Poynt Harbour, & Mayquoit aforesd, & Prticularly of a Necke of land called Mereconeeg, & an ysland Called Sebascoa Diggin, & w^{r}as the relicts & heyres of sd Mr Purchase, & Majo^r Nichol^s Shapleigh haue reserved accomodations for thejr seuerall familys, sould all the remainder of the aforesd Land, & Ysland, to Richard Wharton of Boston M^{r}chant & for as much as the sd Mr Purchase did Personally possess, Improue, & Inhabitt, at Pegipscott aforesd, neare the Center or middle of all the Lands aforesd, for neare fiuety yeares before the late unhappy warr, And w^{r}as the sd Richard Wharton hath desired an Inlargement vpon, & between the sd Androscoggan & Kenebecke riuer, & to Incorage the sd Richard Wharton to Settle an English Town, & promote the Salmon & Sturgeon fishing, by which wee promiss o^{r}selues great supplies, & releife : Therefore & for other good Causes, & considerations, & especially for & In consideration of a ualewable sume receiued from the sd Wharton In M^{r}chandize, Wee Warumbee Durumkine, Wihikermett Weedon, Domhegon Neonongasett, & Nimbanewett, Cheife Sagamores of all the aforesd & other Riuers, & land Adiacent, haue in Confirmation of the sd Richd Whartons

Book IV, Fol. 15.

Title, & propriety, fully freely & absolutely giuen granted ratify'd, & Confirmed to him the sd Richd Wharton all the aforesd Land, from the vppermost part of Androscoggan falls foure Miles Westward & so down to Maquoitt & by sd Riuer of Pegypscott, & from the other side of Androsscoggan Falls, all the Land from the ffalls to Pegypscott, & Merrimeeting Bay to Kenebecke, & towards the Willderness to bee bounded by a South West & North East lyne to extend from the vpper part of the sd Androscoggan vppermost ffalls, to the sayd River of Kenebecke, And all the Land from Maquoit to Pejepscott, & to runne & hould the same breadth w^r the Land will beare it, vnto Atkines his Bay In Kenebecke Riuer, & Small poynt Harbo^r In Cascoe Bay, & all Yslands In Kenebecke, & Pejepscott Riuers, & merrimeeteing Bay and with in ye aforesd bounds, espetially the aforesd Necke of Land called Merecaneeg And Ysland Called Sebascoa Diggine, togeather, with all Riuers Riueletts, brookes ponds, poules, waters water Courses, all wood trees of Tymber, or other trees, & all mines, Minneralls, quaries, & espetially the soole & absolute uss and benefitt of Salmon & Sturgeon fishing, in all the Riuers, riuerletts or Bays aforesayd, and in all Riuers brookes, Crickes, or pond with in any of the bounds aforesd, & also wee the sd Sagamors haue vpon the Considerations aforesd, giuen granted barganed & sould, enfeoffed & Confirmed, And do by these Presents, giue grant bargan & Sell, alliene, Infeoff & Confirme to him the sd Richd Warton all the Land lijng fiue Miles aboue the vppermost of the sayd Androscoggan ffalls, In breadth & lengh houlden the same breadth from Androscoggin falls to Kenebecke riuer, & to bee bounded, by the aforesd south west & North East lyne, & a Parcell of lands at fiue Miles distance to runn from Androscoggin to Kenebecke Riuer as aforesd/ togeather with all the profetts priuiledges, Commoditys, benefitts, & Aduantages, & Perticularly the soole propriety, benefitt & aduantage of the salmon & Sturgion fishing with in bounds & lymitts aforesd/ To haue & to hould to him the sd Rich'd Wharton, his heyrs and Assignes for euer, all the aforenamed land prineleges & piiuiledges & Premisses, with all benefitts rights, appurtenances, or Aduantages, y^t now do, or hereafter shall or may belong unto any part or Parcell of the Premisses, fully freely & absolutely accquitted & discharg from all former & other Gyfts grants bargans Sailes, Morgages, & incombeiances whatsoeuer/ And wee the sd Warrumbee Derumkine Whihkermett Wedon, Domhegon, Neonongassett & Nimbanuett, do couenant & grant to & with the sd Richard Wharton, that wee haue in our selues good right, & full pouer thus to Confirme & conuay the premisses and that wee our heyres & successors shall & will warrant, & Defend the sd Rich'd Wharton, his heyres & Assignes for euer, In the peaceable inioyment of the premisses, and euery part thereof, against all & euery Person or persons, that may legally Clajme any right, title, Interest or propriety in the premisses, by from or under us the aboue named Sagamores, or any of o^r Ancetors, or Predecessors/ Prouided neuertheless that nothing in this Deede, bee Construed to depriue us the sd Sagamores, successors or people, from Improueing o^r Antient planting, grounds, nor from hunting in any of the sayd Land, being not Inclosed, nor from fishing for our own prouission, so long as no damage shall bee to the English ffishery/ prouided alsoe that nothing here in contajned, shall Preiudice any of the Inglish Inhabitants or planters, being at Present Actually possessed, of any part of ye Premisses, & legally deriueing right from sd Mr Purchase, & o^r Ancestors; In witness hereof Wee the afore named Sagamores, well understanding the puiport here of, do set to o^r hands & seales, at Pejepscott the Seuenth day of July, In the thirty fifth yeare of the Reign of our souergane Ld King Charles the secund one thousand six hundred eighty foure/

The marke of Warumbee/   The Marke ✛ of Darumkine

W (his seal)   (his seal)

of Weeden Domhegon/ ◯

The marke of (his seal) Mihikermett of Nehonongassett

The marke of Numbanuett/   his marke & (his seal)

[16] Sealed & Deliuered   Memorandum that vpon the day
in the Presence of,   of the date with in written
John Blany/   Deede, the severall Sagamores
James Andrews/   whose names are subscribed
Henery Walters/   y^rto & Inserted therein, did at
John Parker/   the Fort of Pejepscott, deliuer
Geo: ffellt/   quiett & peaceable possession
of the Premisses, with Liuery & Ceizing, to Mr John Blany & his wife; & the sayd Mr John Blany & his wife, In thejr own right, as shee is Administratrix to the Estate of Mr Thom^s Purchase, Deceased, & In right of his children, also the sd Mr Blany as Atturney to Mr Eliazer Way, did the same day Deliuer quiett & peaceable possession, with Liuery & Ceizing, of the Premisses to Mr Richard Wharton, the quantity of seaven hundred Acres of Land being Excepted, according to a former agreement/

Henery Walters/   Taken vpon oath this 19th of July
John Parker/   1684: this was sworne too by John
Parker before mee
          Edw: Tynge Jus: pe:

James Andrews aged about fourty nine yeares, testifyeth vpon oath, that hee saw this Deed or Instrument, Sealed & Deliuered by the six Sagamores, with in named, to Mr Richd Wharton, & saw John Parker, & Geo: ffelt the other

witnesses subscribe as witnesses, as now they are on the Indorseme^t aboue Sworne before mee this 21th of July 1684 :
Edw : Tynge Just^s pe .

Falmouth In Cascoe Bay July 21th 1684 :
Warumbee the Sagamore with in named, this day appeared before mee, & in behalfe of him selfe & other Sagamores, that sealed & Deliuerd the with in written Instrument, Acknowledged the same to bee his & y^r free & uolentary act & deede/   Edw : Tynge Just : pe :

John Parker of Kenebecke aged about fiuety yeares, deposeth that hee saw this Deede signed, Sealed & Deliuered by the seuerall Sagamores with in named, & y^t hee saw possession togeather with liuery & seizine of the Premisses, given as is expressed in the other Indorseme^t on this deede, & in Presence of the seuerall witnesses thereto subscribing : And further the Deponent sayth, y^t vpon the Eleauenth of this Instant Moenth, hee with Mr Hene : Walters was Present & saw Warumbee deliuer possession & Liuery & seizine by a Turffe & Twigg & bottle of Water taken by him selfe off the Land, & out of the Majne Riuer, aboue Androscoggin Falls, to Richard Wharton In full Compliance with a conueyance of the Premises with in granted & Confirmed/ Taken vpon oath 9th July 1684 : before mee
Edw : Tynge Jus : pe :
A true Coppy of this Deede or Instrument with in written, Subscribed by the seuerall Sagamors to Mr Richd Wharton, acknowledg'd by warumbee & Attested as by diuerse wittnesses aboue written, transcribed out of ye originall, & y^r with Compared this 26th day of July 1684
p Edw : Rishworth ReCor :

Book IV, Fol. 16.

To all Christian people to whom this Present Deede of sale shall Come, John Blany of Lynn In the Coloney of the Massatusetts, In New England & Elizabeth his wife, the late relict & Administratrix of Thomas Purchase of Pejepscott In the prouince of Mayne In New England, aforesd, do send greeting &c : Know yee y' w'as, by a Pattent from y' Councill of Plymoth, with in the kingdome of England, the Lands at Pejepscot aforesd, togeather with the Land adiacent, lyng vpon & between the River of Kenebecke, Ambroscoggan & Cascoe bay, with the priuiledges y'unto belonging, were long since granted to George Way of Dorchester, in the Kingdome of England deceased, & w'as the sayd Tho' Purchase euer since the third yeare of the reigne of King Charles the first of blessed memory, actually possessed, planted, & Improued the sayd Lands till y' late warr, And for as much as Eliazer Way, the sonn & heyre of y' sd George Way, hath granted & sould unto Richard Wharton of Boston in sayd Coloney In New England aforesayd, M'chant all his Moeyty, part or share in the sayd Pattent, or land granted & possessed as aforesd, with all priuiledges, Royaltys & app'tenances there unto belonging as by his Deed beareing date this tenth day of y' Instant Octob' more fully may appeare : Now bee it further known, that the sd John Blany, & Elizabeth his wife, with the free & full Consent of all the children of the sd Thomas Purchase, & In order to some further settlement, & prouission for y' subsistance, & liuelihood, & for & in consideration of the some of one hundred & fiuety pounds, of Current money of New England, payd, & secured to bee payd by the sd Richd Wharton, & seauen lotts, & shares of Land reserved & secured by articles signed by the sd Wharton, beareing date with these Presents, w'with they do hereby acknowledg y'"selfes now to bee fully satisfyd, & contented & thereof & euery part y'of, do acquit, exonerate & discharge the sd Richd Wharton his heyres, executors, & Administrators for euer by these presents, haueing given granted, barganed, sould, allien'd, Enfeoffed, & Confirmed unto him the sd Richd Wharton his heyres & Assigns for euer, all y^t Moyety halfe deale & remajneing share w^{t}soeuer the same is or may bee of the sd Lands late belonging to the sd Thomas Purchase, by uertue of ye sd Pattent, or any other right In partneishipp with ye sd George, or Eliazer Way, & all the right & Title, propriety & Interest which the sayd Thomas Purchase dyed seized of, or y^t hee might should or out to haue had In the sd prouince of Mayne: togeather with all & singular the vplands, Arable Lands, Meddow lands, Marshes, swamps, trees, woods, vnderwoods, waters, water courses, riuers, fishing, fowling, Mines, Mineralls, Royaltys profitts, priuiledges, beach, flatts, rights, Comoditys, hæriditame^ts emoluments, & appurtenances w^{t}soeuer, to the sd Premisses, or any part or Parcell y^{r}of belonging or any wise app^{r}tajneing, or there with now, heretofore ussed occupyed, or inioyed: To haue & to hould all & singular ye aboue granted premisses, [17] with there appurtenances, & euery part & Parcell y^{r}of, unto him the sd Richard Wharton his heyres, & assignes, and to y^r onely proper vss, benefitt & behowfe, of him the sd Richard Wharton, his heyres & assignes for euer; & the sd John Blany, & Elizabeth his wife for y^{m}selues, thejre heyres, executors & Administrators, do hereby Couenant, promiss, & grant, to & with the sd Richd Wharton his heyres & Assignes in manner & forme following, y^t is to say, that ye sayd Richd Wharton his heyres, & Assigns shall & may by force & uertue of these Presents, from tyme to tyme, & at all tymes, for euer hereafter lawfully, peaceably, & quietly haue hould, vse occupy, possess, & inioy the aboue granted premisses, with there appurtenances, & euery part & parcell thereof, as a good Prfect & absolute Estate of inheritance of fee simple, with out any manner of Contradiction, reuersion, or lymitation w^{t}soeuer, so as to alter Change defeate, or make noyd the same, free, & cleare, & clearly acquitted & discharged of & from & all manner of former & other Gyfts, grants, bargans, sales, leases Morgages, ioynturs, Dowers Judgm^ts executions, Intailes, forfitures, & of & from all other Titles, charges, & Incoumberances w'soeuer, had made Committed done, or suffered to bee done by them the sd John Blany, & Elizabeth his wife, or by the sd Thomas Purchase, or either of them, or either or any of thejr heyres, or Assigns at any tyme or tymes before ye Ensealeing hereof: And further that the sd John Blany, & Elizabeth his wife, thejr heyres, executors, & Administrators, shall well tiuely from tyme to tyme & at all tymes hereafter warrant & Defend, the aboue granted Premisses, with y^r appurtenances, & euery part & parcell y^rof, unto the sd Rich'd Wharton his heyres & Assignes, against all Persons whatsoeuer, any wise lawfully Claimeing, or demanding the same or any part y^rof, by from or under ye sd Thomas Purchase deceased or by or from or under them, the sd John Blany & Elizabeth his wife, or either of them y^r heyres or Assigns; And lastly that ye sd John Blany & Elizabeth his wife, y^r heyres & Assignes, shall & will giue unto ye sayd Richd Wharton his heyres & Assignes vpon resonable request such further & ample Assurance, of all the aforesd barganed Premisses, as the sd Wharton his heyres or Assignes, or by his, or y^r Councill, learned in the law, shall bee reasonably, deuised, aduised, or required, according to ye true Intent & meaneing of these Presents; In witness w^rof the sd John Blany & Elizabeth his wife, haue here vnto set y^r hands & seales, the 25th day of Octob^r Anno Dom̃: 1683: Annoq̨ Regni Regis Charolj secundi &c: tricescimo quinto/ John Blany his seale (his seale)

Sealed & Deliuered Elizabeth Blany her seale (her seat)

In the Presence of John Blany & his wife Personally
John Whitte/ appeared before mee, & acknowl-
William Haynes/ edged the with in written Instrume^t to bee y^r Act & Deede/
Thomas Damforth
ꝑsident of ye prouince of Mayn

Book IV, Fol. 17.

Elizabeth Purchase the relict of Thomas Purchase Junjoʳ deceased, & Oliuer Ellkine & Jane his wife, the daughter of Thomas Purchase Senjoʳ Deceased, & Elizabeth Blany daughter of yᵉ sd Thoˢ Purchase Senjoʳ, do all freely Consent to this deed & alianation of the Lands with in written, & in testimony set to thejr hands yᵉ tenth day of Janvary 1683 : & haue acknowledged the same before/

    Elizabeth Purchase   William Brown ⸺ Assis-
    her marke   Samll Appleton ⸺ tants
    Oliver Ellkines his
    marke
    Jane Ellkines/
    Elizabeth Blany her marke

vera Copia of this Deede aboue written as Attested & acknowledged, transcribed, & with originall Compared this 27ᵗʰ July 1684 :   p Edw : Rishworth ReCor :

This Indenture made the fifteenth day of July in the thirty sixt yeare of the Reigne of our Soueraigne Lord King Charles the secund, annoq Dom⁻ one thousand six hundred eighty foure, between Richard Wharton of Boston In New England Mʳchant on the one part, & John Parker of Kenebecke In the prouince of Mayn In New England aforesayd fisherman, on the other part ; Witnesseth that forasmuch as the sayd John Parker hath for vpwards of Twenty six yeares last past beene possessed of Certen Lands, lijng between Knenebecke aforesd, & Cascoe Bay extending in length about six Miles, & bounded at the vpper end of Winnigance Cricke, as by an Indean Deed made to the sayd John Parker, & acknowledged before Hene Jocelin Esqʳ, Jus : pe : & Entered in the ReCords of yᵉ sd Prouince ; And for as much as the sayd John Parker, was the fiʳst of the English Nation that began to subdue the sayd tract of

Lands, & undertake In the fishing trade, and hath since alienated sundrey parcells of the sd Land to seuerall Persons, who haue made Improuement y^{r}on, & promoted the fishery, And where as the aforesd Tract did of right belong unto and was included In an Antient Pattent, granted by the great Councill of Plymoth to Mr Thomas Purchase, and Mr George Way deceased/ And now the soole Interest & propriety of sd Thomas Purchase, & George Way, In the aforesd Land, & all other the land between the sd Kenebecke & Cascoe bay, being inuested in, & became the propriety of sd Richard Wharton: Therefore & for other good Causes, & Considerations, but espetially to Incorage fishery, & husbandry in the places aforesd, the sayd Richard Wharton hath given granted & Confirmed, & doth by these Presents, giue grant & Confirme. to the sd John Parker his heyres & Assignes, all the first mentioned tract of Land, lijng between Kenebecke & Cascoe bay, being in length about six Miles bounded as aforesd, togeather with all woods trees waters water Courses, passages, priuiledges, profitts, Comoditys, & aduantages to the Premisses or any part y^r of, belonging, or any wise app^{r}tajneing, And to haue & to hould the Premisses, & euery part & Prcill there of, togeather with all priuiledges, profitts, Commoditys & Aduantages to the Premisses, or any part thereof belonging, or any wise app^{r}tajneing, And the sd Wharton doth Couenant & grant to & with the sayd John Parker, his heyres, & Assignes, & euery of them, y^t hee & they & each of them respectiuely, shall & may peaceably & quietly possess & inioy thejr seuerall & respectiue parts, & portions In the Premisses, with out the let trouble & Molestation Clajme or Clajmes, or demand, except w^t is hereafter reserued, of him the sayd Richd Wharton, his heyres, executors, Administrators or Assignes, or any other Person or Persons legally Clajmcing by from or under him, them or any of them The sayd John Parker his heyres, or sume of them yeilding, & paijng yearely vid^t vpon each tenth day of June too dry Cuske, or too dry Cod fish, if demanded, to him the sd Richard Wharton, his heyres & Assigns for euer; And the sd John Parker [18] And the sayd John Parker doth for him selfe, his heyres, & Assignes for euer, Couenant promiss & grant, to and with the sayd Richd Wharton his heyres, & Assignes, to Incorage settlement of a Town vpon the Premisses, that when tenn familys Besids what are already settled shall agree to settle vpon the Premisses, vpon thejr request or notice given by the sayd Richard Wharton, his heyers, or Assignes, to sd John Parker, his heyres or Assigns, hee & they shall & will affoard æquall Accommodation of Lands, with them selues to each family, & will In lew y^{r}of accept the like quantity or Valew of Land, & In Case of difference, the sd Wharton his heyres & Assignes Consenting, referr ye same to the Estimation, or apprisall to such Persons as his Majestys Just^s shall at the quarter sessions appoynt, vpon oath to apprise the same, & submit the regulation of such Town, & affayrs thereof, to such Persons as shall bee Annually chosen by the Major uoate of free houlders, or Inhabitants there of: In witness whereof, the partys haue hereunto Interchangably set thejr hands & seales the day & yeare first aboue written/

Sealed & Deliuered/   John Parker his marke (his seale)

In the Presence of/

Elias Whitte/   I P

Edw: Hannet/   This Deede was acknowledged by John Parker to bee his Act & Deed to Mr Richard Wharton/ & owned this 19th of July 1684:

before mee Edw: Tynge Jus: pe:

A true Coppy of this Instrum^t transcribed out of ye originall & there with Compared this 27th day of July 1684:

p Edw: Rishworth ReCor:

Book IV, Fol. 18.

To all Christian people, to whome this Present Deede of Sale shall come/ Eliazer Way of Hartford In the Coloney of Conneeticott In New England M^rchant sonn & heyre of George Way of Dorchester, In the County of Dorcett, within in the Kingdome of England sendeth Greeteing. Know yee that sd Eliazer Way, for & in Consideration of the some of one hundred pounds of Current money of New England to him in hand payd, at or before the sealeing & Deliuery of these Presents, by Richard Wharton of Boston In the Coloney of the Massatusetts/ In New England aforesd/ M^rchant well & truely payd, the receipt w^rof hee doth hereby acknowledge, & him selfe fully & throughly satisfyd, & Contented & y^rof & euery part there of doth hereby acquitt, exonerate, & discharge the sayd Richd Wharton his heyres, executors, Administrators & euery of them for euer by these Presents; Hath granted, barganed, sould, alienated, Enfeoffed & Confirmed & p these Presents, doth fully freely, clearely, & absolutely giue, grant, bargan, sell, aliene, Enfeoffe & Confirme, unto him the sd Richard Wharton his heyres & Assignes for euer, one Moeity or halfe part, or w^tsoeur share, part or proportion, bee the same more or less, hee the sayd Eliazer Way, now hath may might should, or in any wise out to haue, or Clajme of in or too, a Certen Tract or Percell of Land, Commanly Called & known by the name of Pejeepscott, scituate, lijng & being within the prouince of Mayne, in New England aforesd, togeather with one Moiety or halfe part of w^tsoeuer other shayre part or portion, bee the same more or less, which her the sd Eliazer Way now hath, may might should, or in any wise out to haue, or Clajme of in or to, all & singular the vplands, Meddows lands, arable lands Marshes swamps trees, woods underwoods, waters, water Courses, Riuers, fishing, fowling, Mines, Mineralls, Royaltys, profitts priuiledges, beaches, flatts rights, Commoditys hæriditaments, Emoluments, & appurtenances, w^tsoeuer, to the Premisses or any part or Parcell there of, belonging or any wise app^rtajneing, which sd Tract of Land, & Premisses, for the space of fourty years, or yrabouts, before the late warr with the Indeans was in actuall possession & Improuement of Mr Thomas Purchase deceased, & was Antiently given & granted, by Pattent from the Councill of Plymouth, with in the sayd kingdome of England, to the sayd George Way & Thomas Purchase, deceased, To haue, & to hould all & singular, the aboue granted Premisses, with thejr & euery of thejr rights hæridaments, & appurtenances, & euery part & Parcell yrof, unto the sd Richard Wharton his heyres for euer, & to the onely proper vss, benefitt & behoofe of him the sayd Richard Wharton, his heyres & Assigns for euer/ And the sd Eliazer Way, for him selfe his heyres, executors, & Administrats doth hereby Couenant, & promiss, & grant to & with the sayd Richard Wharton, his heyres, & Assignes In manner & forme following (that is to say that the sd Richd Wharton, his heyres & Assigns, shall & may by force & uertue of these Presents, from tyme to tyme & at all tymes for euer hereafter, lawfully quietly & peaceably haue, hould vsse, occupy possess & Inioy the aboue granted Premisses, with thejr appurtenances, & euery part & parcell thereof, as a good Perfect, & absolute Estate, of Inheritance In fee simple, with out any manner of Condition, Reuersion, or lymitation wtsoeuer, so as to Alter Chang defeat, or make uoyd the same, full & clearly acquitted & dischargd off & from all manner of former & other Gyfts, grants, bargans, leases, sales, Morgages, Dowers, Jountyres, Judgmts executions, Entailes forfeturs, & of & from all other titles, troubles, Charges, wtsoeuer, had made or Committed, done or suffered to bee done, by him the sd Eliazer Way, his heyres, or Assignes at any tyme or tymes, before the enscaleing here of, & further that the sd Eliazer Way his heyres, executors & Administrators, shall & will from tyme to tyme & at all tymes for euer hereafter, warrant & Defend the aboue named Premisses, with yr & euery of yr rights, hæriditaments, & appurtenances, & euery part & Parcell y^rof, unto ye sd Richd Wharton his heyrs & Assigns, against all & euery Prson or Persons w'soeuer, any wise lawfully Clajmeing or demanding the same; or any part thereof, by or from und^r him his heyres or Assigns, & lastly y^t hee the sd Eliazer Way, his heyrs & assigns shall & will giue vnto the sd Richd Wharton his heyrs & Assignes, or by his & y^r Councill learned in ye law, shall bee reasonably deuised, Aduised or required according to ye true Intent, & meaneing of these Presents/ In witness w'of ye sd Eliazer Way, hath here unto set his hand & seale the tenth day of October, Año Dom: one thousand six hundred Eighty three/ Annoq regni regis Charolj secundj, tricessimo quinto/

Signed Sealed & Deliuered,   Eliazer Way (his seale)
  in the Presence of John   The with in written Deed was
  Hayword Noto^s Puplic^s/   acknowledged by Mr John
  Eliazer Moody serua^t   Hayword notary publique, &
                             Atturney to the with in named
                             Eliazer Way, being espetially
                             Impoured to acknowledg y^e
                             Deed in forme of law, in be-
                             halfe of sd way as p pouer
                             produced, dated Octob^r 10 ·
                             1683: this was thus acknowl-
                             edged Octob^r 23: 1683: be-
                             fore Thomas Damforth Presid^t
                             of ye Prouince of Mayn

vera Copia of this Deede aboue written, transcribed out of ye originall, & there with Compared this 30th day of July 1684: p Edw: Rishworth ReCor:

[19] Thomas Haynes, & Joyce Haynes his wife, & Sampson Penley haueing all been antient Inhabitants In Cascoe Bay, do testify vpon oath, that aboue Twenty years last past, they haue vnderstood by coman report, that y^e

Book IV, Fol. 19.

Indeans had sould to ffrancis Smale, an Indea Trader the Ysland of Sebascoe Diggin lijng In Casco Bay aforesd, & haue since been Informed, that ye sd Franc^s Smale bought ye sd Ysland for Maj^r Nicholas' Shapleigh, & the Deponents say after sd Purchase, there was Improuem^t made by ye English on sd ysland which was Called by the name of Smales Ysland, & this Deponents say that they neuer heard y^t any other Person layd Clajme to ye sd ysland/ & further say not/ Taken vpon oath this 21th of July 1684: before mee Edw: Tynge Just pe/

.vera Copia transcribed & with originall Compard this 31th of July p Edw: Rishworth

Elias White aged about fiuety six yeares, & Edw: Skinner aged about sixty yeares/ Testify vpon oath, that vpon the eighteenth day of this Instant July, they were Present & saw Mr Richard Wharton, deliver possession with Lyuery & seizine, of the ysland Called Sebasqua Diggin lijng in Cascoe Bay to John Parker of Kenebecke the sd Wharton declareing, that hee did possess the sd Parker of the sd ysland for uss, & In the behalfe of Mr William Wharton his sonn/ & further these Deponents say not/

Taken vpon oath this 21th of July 1684: before mee
Edw. Tynge Jus: pe:
vera Copia transcribed & with originall Compar'd this 31: July, 1684: p Edw: Rishworth Re: Cor:

W^as I John Smith Senio^r of Cape Nuttacke, In the Townshipp of Yorke In the prouince of Mayne Planter, haue for seuerall years past vpon good Considerations, y^runto mee moueing, given granted sould made ouer & Confirmed, vnto my beloued son John Smyth of Cape Nuttacke aforesd, & more espetially In Consideration of my affection to him, & of his Settleing down by mee vpon a peece of Land which

Book IV, Fol. 19.

I formerly gaue him, w'by hee might bee the more helpfull to mee In fenceing & planting part of my land, as in my other Occasions; Do by these Presents, giue grant & Confirme, the former Deed of Sale or Gyft, made by mee & Joane my former wife his mother, beareing date the Twenty third day of May 1674: acknowledged & ReCorded, with all the houseing vplands Meddows, pastures, oarchards gardens, & all other Imunitys & app'tenances y'unto belonging, as Prticularly expressed In the abouesd record; At & after my decease, to the aforesd Jo^n Smith my sonn & to his heyres & Assigns for euer; Always prouided this to bee the true meaneing & intent of these Presents; That w'as my son John Smith hath not hitherto fullfilled the Conditions of planting my Land to the halfes, & fenceing the same with worke besids &c: as obleig'd by y^t Instrument: ffor the makeing good w^{r}of, It is mutually agreed between us, that If my sd sonn John Smith do pay or cause to bee payd by him selfe or his heyres or Assignes to mee my heyres & Assignes, the iust sume of Thirty younds, Twenty shillings In Current money, & the other Twenty nine pounds in goods M^{r}chãble & prouissions sutable to supply my necessity at Current prises, to bee payd In twelue years tyme at fiuety shillings p Annũ: the one halfe at the spring, the other halfe at the fall yearely, On the Performance hereof, I the sayd John Smith Senjor, do absolutely & Totally reuerse all those Conditions expressd In the former Deed, aboue mentioned, of Planting, worke &c: & by these Presents do freely & absolutely ratify, & Confirme my soole Interest & Title, of all my houses & Lands, as expressed In the former Deede of sale or gift, from mee my heyres & Assigns, to the sayd John Smith my sonn his heyres & assignes for euer/ In testimony whereof I haue here unto afixed my hand & Seale this first day August 1684: I do further giue unto my sd sonn John Smith, that peece of sault March lijng between the Riuer & the Cricke, adioyneing vpon the vpland, Contajneing the quantity of one Acre more or less, prouided

hee keepe it seasonably fenced : & do Confirme & like wise
I grant to him for his Present uss & benefitt, one halfe of
y^t fruite, which that little orchard produceth, which lyeth
aboue his house, next unto that Land which was belonging
to James Jackeson/   John Smith Senjo^r ($^{his}_{seale}$)
Signed Sealed & Deliuered/
 In the Presence of/   his marke 𐆅
  Edw : Rishworth/   John Smith Senjor, & John Smith
  George Spencer/   Junjor, came before mee this first
  his marke/ ╼   day of August 1684 : & did ac-
             knowledg this Instrument to bee
             y^r act & Deede/
             Edw : Rishworth Jus : pe :
 A true Coppy of this Instrum^t aboue written, transcribed
out of the Originall & y^{r}with Compared this 5th day of
August 1684 : p Edw : Rishworth Re : Cor :

 To all people to whome this writeing, or deede of Saile
shall come/ I Thomas Haynes once of Maquoyt, now of
Lynn, both In New England, husbandman, & I Joyce his
wife send Greeteing : Know yee, that for & in Consideration
of seauenteen pounds Eleauen shillings & too peence, in
money, to Content to him in hand payd, by Edw : Cricke of
Boston In New England Taylo^r, w^{t}with wee do acknowledg
o^{r}selues to bee fully satisfyd, contented & payd : & thereof
do acquitt and discharge, him, & his heyres, executors,
Administrators & Assignes, p these Presents : Haue giuen,
granted, barganed & sould : And do by these Presents, fully
freely, & absolutely, giue, grant bargan for, & sell, vnto
him the sayd Edward Cricke, & his heyres, executors,
Administrators, & Assignes for euer ; Too hundred Acres of
vpland & fiue acres of Marsh or more, commanly Called the
beareberry Marsh, lijng in the head of Cascoe bay, In the
Town of Westgostuggoe at Maycoyt being butted & bounded

In manner & forme following: By a Cricke adioyneing to Allexander Thawits land, or once In his tenour & Occupation, North West, & by a Cricke Adioyneing to Thomas Haynes his land, North West, fronting by the bay, or into the Bay South East & y[e] bareberry Marsh butting vpon the Bay North West, & bounded by one Cricke South East, adioyneing to the sayd vpland South East/ and alsoe the dwelling house & houseing vpon the Premisses; & arable Land, and all other Marsh, there unto belonging: & all Tymber trees, profitts priuiledges emoluments & commoditys thereunto belonging To haue and to hould, the sd vpland & Meddows or Marsh togeather, with all the houseings, Woods, Tymbers, under woods, mines Mineralls, priuiledges, easements & appurtenances, there unto belonging, or that hereafter shall there to belong, or appertajne; And all the Estate, right, title, Interest, [20] vss propriety, possession claime, and demand w'soeuer, of mee the sayd Thomas Haynes, & Joyce his wife, of in or too the sayd vpland, Meddows houseing and appurtenances, unto him the sd Edw: Cricke, & to the onely proper uss, & benefitt & behoofe of him & his heyres, executors, Administrators or Assignes, or the Assignes of either of them, from the day of the Date hereof, for euer; And the sayd Thomas Haynes, doth hereby for him selfe & his heyres, executors, & Administrators, Couenant, promiss, & grant, to & with the sayd Edward Cricke & his heyres, executors, Administrators and Assignes, In manner & forme following; That hee the sayd Thomas Haynes at the tyme of the signeing hereof, & untill the deliuery hereof, is the true soole & proper owner of the aboue mentioned vpland, and Meddow, or Marsh/ and of euery part y[r]of, in fee symple, & hath in him selfe, good right, full power & lawfull authority to bargan for, & sell the same, in manner & forme abouesd/ And that the Premisses & euery part there of, is fiee and Cleare, & freely & Clearely acquitted, & discharged of, and from all former grants Gifts barganes, sales, Morgages, Titles, &

Book IV, Fol. 20.

Incomberances whatsoeuer; And the same to warrant & defend, against euery Person & Persons, Clajmeing, & that shall Clajme any right, title or Interest in or unto the Premisses, or any part y^{r}of, from by or under him, Thomas Haynes & Joyce his wife, or his heyres executors, Administrators, or Assignes, or any of thejr procurement, w^{r}by hee the sayd Edw: Cricke, or his heyres executors Administrators or Assignes, or the Assignes of either of them, may bee Enected, or Euicted out of, or molested, or interrupted, In the quiett & peaceable inioyment & Improuement of the Premisses, or any part thereof; In witness whereof the sayd Thomas Haynes, and Joyce his wife, haue here unto put their hands & seals this secund day of August, In the yeare of o^r Ld one thousand Six hundred Seauenty eight, & In the Thirteth yeare of o^r Soueraign Ld, Charles the secund by the grace of god, of great Brittane, France, & Ireland King, Defender of the faith &c: Thomas Hayns ($^{his}_{seal}$)
Sealed & deliuered/ Joyce Haynes ($^{her}_{seale}$)
  In y^e Presence of us/   her marke
  George Purkis/   Acknowledged by Thom^s Haynes &
  Thomas Pembbarton/   Joyce his wife, to bee y^r ioynt
  Re: Goulding/   act & Deede/ 3: 6: 78:
                    Thom^s Damforth Asistant:

Liber 6: pa: 276: 277: Entered & reCorded with the ReCords of y^e Notary Publique, for ye Coloney of the Massatusetts In New England/ June: 17: 84: As Atests John Howard Noto^s Publicus/

vera Copia of this Instrum^t aboue written transcribed out of ye originall, & y^{r}with Compared this 8th day of August 1684: p Edw: Rishworth Re: Cor:

Mi^s Bridgitt Phillips executrix to the last will & testament of her husband Maior William Phillips lately deceased, for the saueing of the Interest & Title of those Mills built

BOOK IV, FOL. 20.

at Sacoe falls & those lands yrunto belonging, app'rtajneing to the Estate of Major Phillips aforesd/ Entereth Caution against the acknowledment or reCording of any deeds or Intruments vpon those ReCords of this prouince of Mayne, in behalfe of Capt Walter Barefoote any Person or Persons wtsouer, which under any Pretence of title shall make any Clajme unto the lands or Mills aforesd/

This Cawtion Entred by order from Mis Bridgitt Phillips, receiued about the 9th or 10th of August: 1684 : & vpon the the Eleaventh of August Entered into these ReCords : 84 :

p Edw : Rishworth Re : Cor :

I George Burdett do hereby bind my selfe heyres, executors or Assignes to pay unto Ann Messant Widdow, one hundred & Twelue pounds Of lawfull money the last of March which shall bee in yeare 1641 : for the true payment whereof, I bind ouer to the sd Widdow, my six steares, & three Cows togeather with the farme I now haue in possession of John Allcocke/ witness my hand this Eighteenth day of March, one thousand six hundred thirty nine/

In the Presence of us/   George Burdett/
 William Hooke/   A true Coppy of this writeing aboue
 Ralph Blasdell/   written transcribed & Compar'd
        with the originall this 13th day of
        August 1684 :

p Edw : Rishworth Re : Cor :

To all whome these Presents shall Come/ I Ailce Shapleigh Widdow, & Inhabitant in Kittery In the prouince of Mayne New England send greetıng/ Know yee yt I the sayd Ailce Shapleigh for & in Consideration of Three hundred & sixty pounds, Current money of New England, to mee in hand payd, by Francis Raynes, & Nathāell Raynes of Yorke, In the Prouince of Mayne aforesd, Gentlē: before the Insealing & deliuery hereof, the receipt w^{r}of I the sayd Alice Shapleigh do hereby acknowledg, & my selfe there with to bee fully satisfyd, Contented & payd, & y^{r}of & euery part & Parcell there of, do acquitt exonerate & discharge the sayd Francis Raynes, & Nathan^{ll} Raynes, thejr heyres, executors, Administrators & Assignes, & euery of them for euer by these Presents, haue for my selfe my heyres, executors, administrators, & Assignes, & euery of them for euer, by these Presents; Haue for my selfe, my heyres, executors, Administrators & Assignes given, granted, barganed, sould, aliend, Enfeoffed, deliuered, & Confirmed, & by these Presents do giue, grant, bargane, & sell, aliene, Enfeoffe, Convay, release, Assure, deliuer, & Confirme, vnto the sd Francis Raynes, & Natha^{ll} Raynes, thejr heyres, executors, Administrators, & Assignes, all that tract peece, parcell of Land, scituate, lijng & being, with in the Territoryes, & Presincts of yorke aforesd: where the sayd Ann Godfrey formerly dwelt, & inhabited, togeather with all the dwelling house, barnes, stables, out houses, & Linnys vpon the sayd Tract, peece or Parcell of Land, & farme, belonging, or in any wise app^{r}tajncing, and also all the Marsh, or Meddow, to the sd Farme belonging, to & with ye same . now or here to fore used, occupied, or Inioyed, as part Parcell or Member thereof or of any part y^{r}of, and also all trees, underwoods, comānes, easements, profitts, Emoluments, hæriditaments, [21] & appurtenances whatsoeuer, to the sayd Farme belonging, or in any wise appertaineing, & also all the right Title, Clajme, Interest, uss, possession reuersion remajnder, & demānd w^{t}soeuer, of her the sayd Alice Shapleig, her heyres executors, Administrators, & Assignes, of in & to the Premisses, or of in or vnto euery or of any part or Parcell thereof/ To haue & to hould the sayd Tract, peece, Parcell of Land or farme, houses Edificeses, & bujldings, vplands, & Marshes, trees woods & underwoods, Comānes, easements, profitts, Comoditys, aduantages, Emoluments, hæriditaments, & appurtenances whatsoeuer, vnto the sayd ffrancis Rayns, & Nathañell Raynes, thejr heyres, executors, administrators, & Assignes for euer; & to both them, & y^r own proper uss for euer more; And I the sd Aylce Shapleigh for my selfe, & heyres, executors, Administrators, & Assignes, & for all & euery of them, do Couenant, promiss, & grant, to & with the sd Francis Raynes & Nathaniell Raynes, there heyres, executors, Administrators, & Assignes, & euery of them by these Presents, that the sayd Aylce Shapleigh, on the day of the date hereof, & at the tyme of the sealeing & Deliuery of these Presents, haue in my selfe full pouer, good right, & lawfull authority, to giue grant bargan, sell, deliuer & Confirme the sayd Tract, peece, parcell of Land, & farme & Premisses, hereby barganed, & sould, vnto the sayd ffrancis Raynes, & Nathaniell Raynes, thejr heyres, executors, Administrators, & Assignes for euermore in manner & forme aforesayd: & also that the aforesd Francis Raynes, & Nathãll Rayns thejr heyers, executors, Administrators, & Assignes, or any of them shall & lawfully may from tyme to tyme, & at all tymes hereafter, peaceably & quietly haue hould, vss, & Inioy the sayd Tract, peece, Parcell of Land, & farme, & Premises, hereby barganed, & sould, with out any manner of Lett, Sujte, trouble euiction, eiection, Molestation, disturbance, Challenge, Claime, Deniall, or demand w^{t}soeuer of or by mee ye sd Aylce Shapleigh, my heyres executors, Administrators & Assignes, or any of them, or of or by any other Person or Prsons w^{t}soeuer lawfully Clajmeing or do Clajme from by or und^r mee, my act or Title/ In witness w^{r}of, I haue hereunto putt my hand & seale, this eight day of July 1684/

Signed sealed & Deliuered/   Alice Shapleigh
  In the Presence of us/   (her seale)
  John Dauess/   Mis Alice Shapleigh came before mee
  Francis Hooke/   this foureteenth day of July 1684:
          & did acknowledg this Instrument
          aboue written to bee her Act &
          Deed/ Edw: Rishworth Jus: pe:

Book IV, Fol. 21.

A true Coppy of this Deede or Instrument aboue written, transcribed. & with the originall Compared this 13th day of August 1684. p Edward Rishworth Re : Cor :

To all Christian people, whome It may Concerne, this is to certify that Capt Francis Raynes, & his wife Elnier Raynes do of y^r own free will, & uolentary Consent, loue, & affection, towards y^r sonn Nathaell Raynes, haue freely given the house y^t hee now liueth in, & the Farme wholly after the decease of them selues, to his sonn Nat$\overline{\text{ll}}$ Raynes; And y^e sd Francis Ra$\overline{\text{ye}}$s Elldest sonn of the sayd Nathaniell Raynes, thejr grandchild, after the decease of my son Nathaell Raynes/ & for the Performance of this, these partys haue set two y^r hands, this 8th day of July 1684 :
Francis Raynes/
Elner Raynes/

I underwritten Francis Champernown, do acknowledg to giue all my right, & Title & Interest, unto the sd Natha^{ll} Raynes, of that Land as aboue mentioned, & Meddow y^t falls with in my diuident, belonging to y^t ffarme, & do acquit Mr Francis Raynes of all Claimes of right, & Title, In my Diuident/ as witness my hand, the date & day aboue mentioned/ ffrancis Champernoown/

The Partys within mentioned, came before mee this eight of July 1684 : & acknowledged this to bee y^r Act & Deede/
John Dauess Dep^{ty} Presid^t/

A true Coppy of these obligations aboue written, transcribed, & with ye originall Compared this 13th day of August 1684 : p Edw : Rishworth ReCor :

BOOK IV, FOL. 21.

These Presents bindeth mee Isacke Parker my heyres & Assignes, to pay or Cause to bee payd, to John Wentworth his heyres & Assignes, the iust some of fourty pounds to bee payd In M^rchable staues, Three thousand of whitte pipe staues to bee Deliuered at some conueniett Landing place in yorke, by the water side, at three pounds p thousand, & the rest to bee payd In red oake pipe staues at fourty shillings p thousand, & Hodged staues at thirty shillings p ^M, to bee deliuered as abouesd Namely at yorke, between this & winter the whitte oake staues are to bee Deliuered, & the other staues to bee payd so many as to make vp the full some of Twenty pounds between this & the next spring, & the other Twenty pounds to bee payd in red oake staues at the same prises the next fall & spring following, for security of Which payment I do bind ouer y^t house & Land bought of John Wentworth as by bill of sajle appears beareing date the 28th of August 1679 : from mee my heyrs, & Assignes, vnto the sd John Wentworth, his heyres & Assignes, as witness my hand this 29th day of August 1679 :
Testes Mary White/   Icaac Parker/
     Icacac Parker ownes this bill written,
      to bee his Act & Deede, the 29th of
      August 1679 : before mee
        Edw : Rishworth Assote
vera Copia transcribed & with ye originall Compared this 27th August 1684 : p Edw : Rishworth Re : Cor :

·

To all Christian People to whome these Presents may come/ Know yee y^t I Daniell Gooddine Senjo^r of Barwicke, In the Town of Kittery & Prouince of Mayne, In New England Planter, for diuerse good Causes & Considerations mee moueing y^runto, espetially for the naturall relation & loue I beare to my sonns Thomas Goddin & James Godine

BOOK IV, FOL. 21, 22.

of the same town & Prouince, haue freely & uolentarily given, granted, alienated & Confirmed, & do by these Presents for my selfe, my heyres, executors, & Administrators, absolutely & freely pass ouer, giue grant, alienate, Enfeoff & Confirme, vnto my aforesd Two sonns Thomas Goddine & James Gooddine, a Certen Tract or Parcell of Land, scituate & being in ye parish of Barwicke, & Town of Kittery aforesd, Contajneing Thirty Acres of vpland, with swampe & Marsh belonging there unto, as It was formerly bought of James Grant late of Kittery, as by deede of sajle may more fully appeare, under his hand & seale beareing date the 16th day of May 1662 : onely & & always referring to my selfe, & to my heyres & Assigns for euer, all y^t Marsh & swampe, that I haue already fenced in, togeather with one halfe Acre of land ioyneing tow yorke high way, & liberty of cutting fyre wood In any part of the the foregiuen Premisses/ The rest of the fore mentioned Premisses of Land I the aforesd Daniell Goodin Senior do hereby freely I giue unto my too aforesd sonns/ To haue & to hould [22] with all & singular the appurtenances, & priuiledges in any wise, y^runto appertajneing & belonging, freely & Clearely exonerated, from all former Gyfts grants, Morgages Incomberances whatsoeuer/ In Confirmation of the treuth hereof, I the aforesayd Daniell Goodine Senjo^r, haue here unto set my hand & seale this foureteenth day of July one thousand six hundred eighty & three/ 1683 :   Daniell Goddine (his seale)

Signed sealed, & Deliuered/   his marke
In the Presence of us/   Daniell Goddine Senjo^r owned the
John Broughton/   aboue written deede of Gyft, to
William Spencer/   bee his free Act & Deede this
                        foureteenth day of July 1683 :
                        before mee
                                John Wincoll Jus : pe :

A true Coppy of this Instrum^t aboue written, transcribed out of the Originall & y^rwith Compared this 5th day of Septemb^r 1684 : p Edw : Rishworth Re : Cor :

Book IV, Fol. 22.

To all Christean people Greeting, W^{r}as there hath been some transactions between mee John Bonighton of Sacoe, & Beniamen Blackeman rescident in the sd in behalfe of some men of Andiuer, In order to thejr remouall, & being willing to Incorage them did Promiss to thejr agent abouesd a Tract of Land now therefore, Know all men by these Presentts, y^t I John Bonighton of Sacoe In the Prouince of Mayne, for a ualewable Consideration to mee In hand payd, the receipt w^{r}of and my selfe y^{r}with Content, I do acknowledg by these Presents, haue given granted barganed sould, Enfeoffed & Confirmed unto Benjam: Blakeman his heyres & Assignes by these Presents one Tract of Land, lijng & being vpon the East side of Sacoe riuer, bounded by a smal brooke Northward, which parts my pattent deuission, from the deuission of James Gibbons, Westward, with the sd riuer Eastward, with Two Miles distant from the Riuer Southward, with a Small Brooke to the Northward of Nicolls his house, to haue & to hould all the sd Land, with all its rights, priuiledges & appurtenanc^s appertajneing to the same, or any part y^{r}of, as fully freely absolutely as I my selfe may & can do to him the sd Blackeman his heyres or Assignes by these Presents, And hee the sd Bonighton doth Couenant for him selfe his heyres executors, & Administrators y^t hee ye sd Bonighton stands lawfully seized of the Premisses, of euery part & Parcell y^{r}of, & hath in him selfe full pouer, & lawfull Authority to giue grant & Sell the Premisses & singular part y^{r}of, & doth Couenant to & with the sd Blackeman his heyres & Assignes, from all Prson or Persons, Clajmes, Deeds, morgages, or any other incomberances whatsoeuer, had made or done by or under him, or any other Person tending to Molestation, or euicting of peaceable possession, him or them by these Presents for euer will defend/ And lastly the sd Bonighton will do all further acts deeds, thing, or things, for the full Confirmation of euery & singular ye Premisses, according to ye laws of this prouince, & true Intent of this Deede/ In witness whereof

Book IV, Fol. 22.

I haue set two my hand & seale, this Twlth day of December In the yeare of our Lord one thousand six hundred eighty three/ 1683 : The marke of
John Hills
the marke of John Bonighton ⟩ 6 (his seale)
William W Martine This Instrum^t owned by John Bonighton to bee his act & Deede, this fiueteenth of July one thousand six hundred eighty foure before mee
Joshu : Scottow Just pe :

A true Coppy of this Instrument aboue written, transcribed out of ye originall, & y^{r}with Compared this 6th day of Septemb^r 1684 : p Edw : Rishworth ReCor :

W^{r}as there hath been some motions by seuerall men of the Westward, to remoue them selues to Sacoe Riuer, & settle vpon the Easterne side, & in order y^{r}unto haue by Beniamen Blackeman beene Incoraged, by disburseing moneys in part payment of a purchase of land of James Gibbons, now y^{r}fore for the full & firme Conuayance of the sayd Land/ Know all men by these Presentts, that I James Gibbons of Sacoe, In the Prouince of Mayne yeoman, with Assent & Consent of my wife Judeth, for & in Consideration of a ualewable sume to mee In hand payd, at sealeing hereof, the receipt w^{r}of, I do hereby acknowledg, & my selfe y^{r}with fully satisfyed, Haue giuen, granted, barganed sould Enfeoffed & Confirmed unto Benja͞ : Blackeman Clerke in the same Town rescident; a Tract of land ljng & being vpon the sd Riuer of Sacoe begineing at a Small runne, on the North of Mr Bonightons ould Plantation extending it selfe vp the sd Riuer three Miles & an halfe & eighteen pooles, & backe from the Riuer Two Miles, being the whoole secund diuission of Pattent Land layd out to mee the sd James : To haue &

to hould the sd Tract of Land, with all & singular the apprtenances yrunto belonging, growing, lijng or being vpon the same, with all rights, priuiledges & Conueniences, as I my selfe do or may possess any manner of ways unto him ye sayd Blackeman, his onely uss & behoofe his heyres & Assignes, & hee the sd Gibbons for him selfe his heyres, executors, Administrators doth Couenant to & with the sd Blackeman, his heyres & Assigns by his Presents, that hee the sd Gibbones Standeth lawfully seized of the Premisses, & euery pa1t yrof, & hath in him selfe full pouer & lawfull right to sell & Insure the Premisses, aforesd, & that hee the sd Blackmā his heyres & Assigns shall Inioy the Premisses, free & Clerely acquitted & discharged, of & from all manner of Acts deeds, incomberances wtsoeuer, made Committed or done, by him the sd Gibbons his heyres or Assignes, Wrby the sayd Blackeman, his heyres & Assignes, may bee Molested, or lawfully Euicted out of possession, by any Prson or Persons wtsoeuer, & further that the sd Gibbons will & shall do or Cause to bee done other or further thing, or things, for Assuring of the Premisses to the sd Blackeman, according to ye laws of this Prouince/ In witness to the Premisses the sd James Gibbons & Judeth his wife haue sett two thejre hands & seales, this Twelth of December one thousand six hundred Eighty three/

Signed sealed & deliuered/
  in Presence of us/   The Marke of *G* (his seale)
Hubertus Matton/
The marke of   James Gibbons

John Sharpe   The marke of (her seale)
     Judeth Gibbons

   July 15 : 1684 :
   This Instrumet owned by James & Judeth
   Gibbones to bee yr act & Deede before
   mee Josh : Scottow Jus : pe :

Book IV, Fol. 22, 23.

A true Coppy of this Instrument aboue written transcribed out of ye originall & there with Compared this eight day of Septemb^r 1684 :   p Edw : Rishworth Re : Cor :

Know all men by these Presents that I Joshua Scottow of Boston M^{r}cha^t for & In consideration of the affection I beare vnto my sonn Benja: Blackeman, & of ye naturall loue to Rebeccah, my daughter his wife, haue given, granted, Enfeoffed & Confirme & by these Presents do giue grant, Enfeoffe, & Confirme vnto them & y^r heyres foreuer, Tenn Acres of Land vidz^t vpland & swampe, lijng neare the Ferry place, being in Bla: poynt, alias the Town of Scarborrōgh : In the Prouince of Mayne, & also a Prcell of Marsh, lijng in the sd Town Called Crooked Layne Marsh, bounded in that part with ye River running vp to Dunstannce, in part with y^e [23] comeing vp to Milles, & In part, with the Marsh now in the possession of Joseph Whinnicke, & is part of a Tract of Land bought of Hene : Joclein Esqr ; To haue & to hould the sayd Tenn Acres of Land, with ye Marsh aboue mentioned, unto the sd Benjam: Blakeman & Rebeccah his wife, dureing thejr naturall life, to y^r own proper vss & behoofe for euer, & do hereby release all Clajme, right, & title y^{r}unto, & that they shall Inioy the same quietly & peaceably without any let molestation or Interruption, from any Person or Persons vidz^t heyres, exeutors, administrators, or assignes, of mee the sd Scottow, or from any other by or under mee, or them : Alsoe the sd Blakeman, & partys aboue mentioned shall haue liberty to keepe tenn head of neate Cattle, or y^r proportion in sheepe on the Plaines, although they bee fenced in, prouided hee or they shall make & mantajne such a proportion of the fence, as Scottow or his heyres, according to ye Number of Cattle, which the sd Scottow or his heyres shall putt vpon the Plaines/ also the sayd Scottow shall haue lyberty to cutt w^t pines hee shall haue Occasion

for, out of his swampe, & the sd Blackeman building Tymber for his vss, out of the sd Scottows swampes/ In witness w^{r}of I haue here vnto sett my hand & seale, the first of Janvary one thousand six hundred & eighty/
Witness/ Thomas Scottow/   Joshua Scottow (his seale)
   John Starts ⨏ Marke/
   A true Coppy of this Instrum^t transcribed out of the originall, & y^r with Compared this 10th day of Sepber 1684 :
            p Edw: Rishworth ReCor:

   Know all men by these Presents, that I Joshua Scottow of Boston M^{r}chant haue for, & In Consideration of the affection I beare to my sonn Benja: Blakman, & the naturall loue to Rebeccah my daughter, his now wife, haue giuen granted, & Enfeoffed & Confirmed, & by these Presents do giue grant Enfeoff & Confirme vnto them both & y^r heyres for euer, Tenn Acres of Land lijng & being in bla: Poynt In the Prouince of Mayne, the sayd land bounded Southwardly, with tenn Acres of land formerly given unto the sd Benja: & Rebeccah & so to bee layd out square adioyneing to the aforesd Tenn Acres, & being bounded Eastwardly, Westwardly & Northwardly, with ye Land of the sayd Scottow; To haue & to hould the sd Tenn Acres of Land, & to bee unto the sd Benja: & Rebeccah, dureing her naturall life, & to thejr heyres, unto thejr proper uss & behoofe for euer/ And do hereby release all Clajme right & title y^{r}unto, & that they inioy the same quietly & peaceably with out any lett molestation, from mee the sd Scottow, my heyres or Assignes, or from any other by or from mee or vnder them/ In Witness hereof I haue here vnto sett my hand & Seale/ Made at Blacke Poynt this eighteenth day of Janvary one thousand six hundred eighty one 1681:
Witness Thomas   Joshua Scottow (his seale)
   Scottow/

BOOK IV, FOL. 23.

A true Coppy of this Instrument aboue written transcribed, & with the originall Compared this 10th day of September 1684 : p Edw : Rishworth ReCor :

At a Generall Court held at Boston the 7th of Nouembr 1683 : In answere to the petition of Mr Richd Wharton, to ye end that ye petitioners former grant of one Thousand Acres of Land granted to him may bee made æffectuall, this Court doth order that Capt Edw : Tyng, Mr James Andrews, Mr George Pearson, Capt Brackett & Mr Syluanus Dauess, or any three of them lay out sd Land & make returne &c : That this is a true Coppy taken out of the Courts booke of reCords/
     Attests Edw : Rawson Secrety

In Pursuance of the aboue written order, Wee whose names are underwritten, haue layd out on the ysland of Chabeage, six hundred & fiuety Acres of Land, which is ye halfe of the sd ysland, there being Improuement made on the Easterne part of ye sayd ysland ; Wee haue layd out the Westerne halfe for Mr Richard Wharton, & haue layd out Three hundred & fiuety Acres, at the Westward of Macoyte begining at the Mouth of Pogamqua River, & runns eight scoore poole East, & by South to the uttermost end of a great Rocke, on the Edg of the shoare, & from thence North, Three hundred & fiuety pooles, to a great spruse tree marked on foure sides, which stands on a Hill in a spruce swampe & from thence West eight scoore pooles/ as witness or hands this Twenty fifth of July 1684 :
      Edw : Tyng/
      Anthony Brackett/
      James Andrews/

BOOK IV, FOL. 23.

This order of the Generall Court aboue written, & the bounding of this Land underwritten, & the returne made according to sd order, Entred into the fourth booke of ReCords for ye Prouince of Mayn, pa : 24 : this 23th day of Octob^r 1684 :
    p Edw : Rishworth ReCor :

Know all men by these Presents, that w^{ras} Eliakime Hutchinson of Boston hath given & granted unto Mr John Eemerson by Deede tenn Acers of land in the pai ish of Barwicke in the Town of Kittery, vidz^t foure Acres next the Ministey Land, & six Acres next Daniell Goddings Land, for ye accomodation & settleing of sd Mr Emerson, Minister of sd place, Now know yee y^t wee the Selectmen of the parish of Barwicke, in the Town of Kittery, do obleidg o^r selues heyres & successors, in the behalfe of sd Town vnto the sayd Eliakime Hutchinson his heyres, executors, & Administrators, to Continew the sd Mr Emerson in the Ministrey, for the benefitt of the sd Town for ye tearme & space of Tenn yeares, from the Date here of, or in his absence some other able Minister, or else to make full satisfaction to ye sd Hutchinson, his heyers, executors, & Administrators for ye ualew y^rof, as there in indifferent Prsons shall Judg, & to returne the Land agajne with out respect to the Improuement/ In witness w^rof Wee haue here unto sett o^r hands & seales, this eighteenth day of Septe^br 1684 :
Signed sealed & Deliuered   John Wincoll (locus sigilli)
  In the Presence of/   James Emery (his seale)
  Henery Benning/   Thomas Abbott (his seale)
  William Henderson/ Capt John Wincoll, James Emery &
  James Playstead/   Thomas Abett came before mee, &

BOOK IV, FOL. 23, 24.

acknowledged this Instrume^t to bee y^r Act & Deede this 28th of October 1684:

Edw . Rishworth Jus: pe:

vera Copia of this Instrument aboue written transcribed out of the originall & y^{r}with Compared this Twenty ninth day of Octob^r 1684 : p Edw: Rishworth ReCor:

yorke In ye prouince of Mayne June 30th 1684 :
Hono^{ble} Sir//

Wee are by sundrey of the Inhabitants Settled in this his Majesty^s Prouince, Informed, that the officers of yor prouince of New Hampshire do from tyme to tyme obstruct all y^r vessells, as well Constant fishermen, & small vessells, as others of greater burthen in thejr passage into Pischataqua Harbour, leading into the River of Newgewanacke; & that they are Compelled to y^r great Damage to trauell into your Prouince, & pay such moneys as are y^r demanded of them, before they can bee Permitted to haue Ingress, & regress into y^e [24] sd harbour, all which is Contrary to the grant made them by his Majesty^s Ro . . . Charter, & haueing beene debated by the Generall Assembly now mett: Haue Judged it necessary to acquant yor Hono^r there with, expecting that you will take order so to gouerne yor officers, that for the future there may bee no Cause for any of his Majestys subjects to Complayne of so greate an abuse putt vpon his Majestys authority, & his good subjects here settled in thejr lawfall Callings, & Imployments, or otherwise wee shall bee Compelled to make o^r humble address to his Majesty: And in the meane tyme shall Consider of some mette way for secureing the iust Lybertys, & for ye protection of his Majesty^s subjects in y^r iust rights, according to the trust reposed in us, & is required of us/

BOOK IV, FOL. 24.

In y{e} meane tyme wee take leaue to subscribe o'selues
Hono{ble} Sir/ your humble Seruants/
p order of y{e} Generall Assembly
These for the hono{ble} Edw: Edw: Rishworth Secr{ty}
Cranefejld Esqr, Gouer of
his Majestys Prouince of
Hampshire in New England/
vera Copia transcribed & with the originall Compared,
this 24{th} of Octob{r} 1684:   p Edw: Rishworth Re: Cor:

The Deposition of Edw: Stephens aged 56 years or y{r} abouts/ Testifyeth y{t} many yeares agoe this Deponent being at John Cossons his house in Cascoe bay did see & heare read a Deed of Saile, which sd John Cossons had from Mr Richd Vines, as hee was agent to Sir ffardinando Gorges, In which Deede was specifyd, that the sd Mr Richard Viues had sould unto John Cossons & his heyres for euer Two Yslands lijng, & being in the sd Cascoe Bay, neare to the place Called Westcostuggoh which too Yslands were then Called hogg Yslands but since is Called Cossons Ysland, togeather with all the libertys, priuiledg{s}, & appurtenances to the sd Islands belonging ; In which Deede It was specifyd, that y{e} Two Yslands, w{ch} sd Vines sould to y{e} sd Cossins, did Contajne fiue hunderd Acres of land, bee they more or lesse/ & further sayth not/

Sworne this 22{th} day of Septem{br} 1684 : before mee Robert Pike Assistant/

The abouesd Deponent Edw: Stephens further sayth, that bp vertue of the Deede aboue mentioned, John Cossons had possession of y{e} Yslands as aboue sd, & hath keept it euer since by him selfe & order/ & further sayth not/ This testimony aboue written was taken vpon oath referring to the possession this 12{th} day of Octob{r} 1684 : before mee Edw: Rishworth Jus: pe:

BOOK IV, FOL. 24.

A true Coppy transcribed & with ye originall Compared this 24th day of Octob^r 1684 : p Edw : Rishworth Re : Cor :

The testimony of John Webber aged about 28 yeares/
Being examined maketh oath, that about ye latter end of June last being at Wells, & desireing my passage with John Cloyce who was then bound for Boston, which sayd Cloyce gaue him/

September first 1683 :
Measured & layd out to William Sanders his Town grant of Thirty Acres of Land Dated June 24 : 1682 : foure scoore poole In lengh East & West, & sixty poole in breadth, North & South, bounded on the West with ffrancis Blachfords land in part & bounded on the South in part with Capt ffrosts land, & the North & East, & part of the South bounded with Present Comans/   John Wincoll Surv^r
vera Copia transcribed out of the originall & y^rwith Compard, this 19 day of October 1684 :
p Edw : Rishworth Re : Cor : *

Know all men by these Presents, that Wee Francis Raynes, & Natha^{ll} Raynes, Inhabiters in yorke in the Prouince of Mayne, New England &c : do by these Presents owne & acknowledg our selues to bee iustly Indebted unto Mis Aylce Shapleigh Widdow, The full iust sume of three hundred & sixty pounds, Current Money of new England, it being for & in consideration of a farme bought of Mis Ailce Shapleigh according to the Deede of Sajle given under her hand beareing date ye eight of July 1684 : & for ye true payment of the aboue sd Three hundred & sixty pounds money, Wee the sd Francis Raynes & Nathan^{ll} Raynes, do by these Presents bind o^r selues, our heyrs, executors, administrators, & assignes vnto the sd Alice Shapleigh her heyres, executors, Administrators & assignes, to bee payd in manher & forme following, that is to say eighteen pounds in money Annually, at or before the Twenty ninth of Julie yearely, being from the date here of, & so to make pay from yeare to yeare, & euery yeare at or before the 10th of July untill the Three hundred & sixty pounds money bee payd, It being to bee payd eighteene pounds in money annually, as aboue specifyd, which will bee Computed in the yeare one thousand seaven hundred & foure, & for the true Prfor mance of each & singular of euery part, & Parcell of Money payable according to tyme Wee the abouesd ffrancis Raynes, & Nathaniell Raynes, do bind o^r selues, o^r heyres, executors, Administrators, & Assignes, & also the sayd farme unto the sd Alice Shapleigh, her heyres, executors, Administrators, & Assignes, that vpon non payment of any part or Parcell of money according to tyme as aboue expressed, It shall bee lawfull then for the sd Mis Alice Shapley, her heyrs executors, Administrators, & Assignes, to haue full pouer to make reentry vpon the sd farme & for the true Prformance of euery part & tittle here of, wee haue for. o^r selues o^r heyres, executors, Administrators, & Assignes, fixed our hands & seales, this tenth day of July 1684 :

Sealed signed & Deliuered/ Francis Raynes (his seale)
In the Presence of us/ Nathaniell Raynes (his seale)
John Dauess/ before^l the signeing hereof it is
ffrancis Hooke/ mutually agreed that this money shall bee payd at Kittery house, being formerly the house of Majo^r Nicho : Shapleigh deceased, to Mis Alice Shapleigh or her order/

BOOK IV, FOL. 24.

Capt Francis Raynes, & Nathaniell Raynes his sonn came before mee this foureteenth day of July 1684: & acknowledged this Instrum^t to bee y^r act & deede/ Edw: Rishworth Jus: pe:

vera Copia of this Instrume^t or agreement, transcribed out of the originall, & y^{r}with Compared this 6th day of Novemb^r 1684:   p Edw: Rishworth Re: Cor:

Wee whose names are underwritten being appoyted a Commitee, by the Honord Generall Assembly of this prouince, for the settleing of Mis Alice Shapleighs thirds, of the Estate of her deceased husband, Majo^r Nicho^s Shapleigh, as appeareth by y^r order beareing date the 25th of June 1684: wee accordingly went vpon the place & surueaed, & Measured the whoole Tract, & Sett out her thirds thereof, on ye North west side y^r of & Joyneing to ye dwelling house, & Contaynes about Too hundred fiuety & three Acres, bounded with Mr Mauericks land on the North West, & on the South East with ye rest of the Land, belonging to ye sd house, & ffrom the Riuer on the South West, runnes North East & by east, the whoole length of the sd Tract fiue hundred & Eighty pooles, as by ye marked trees may appeare, as also a Third part of there marsh at Sturgeon Cricke, Which third is nine Acres, as also a third part of the househould Goods, & Cattle, with all the western parts of the Dwelling house, where her lodging Chamber is, with ye parlour opposite on the East side, & two sellers one of them vnder ye lodging Rowme, & the other by the Hall Chimney, & to haue liberty in the in the Hall Kitchen & brew house, for her necessary Occasions, with the 3d part of the barne, on the West End y^{r}of, & a third part of the Too Mills, allowing to the Administrators the too thirds of the ould Oarchard, with a Convenient Garden pott, & yaids with the

Book IV, Fol. 24, 25.

liberty of the land unfenced, y ᵗ lyes about the house & barnes, & out houses for the vss of them selues, & yʳ Cattle, with liberty of Convenient high way or ways, to & from the aforesd houses & Mills, the land on which part of yʳ houses stands, to belong unto them, with liberty about yᵉ houseing to repayre &c: as Occasion may call for/ Dated this 6th day of Septembʳ 1684: John Wincoll/
  A true Coppy of this Act of the   John Penwill/
  Comĩtee transcribed & with yᵉ   Joseph Hamonds/
  Originall Compared this 6th
  day of Novebʳ 1684:
    p Edw: Rishworth ReCor:

[25] Know all men by these Presents that I Henery Bodg of Kittery, in the prouince of Mayn for & in Consideration of fiue pounds, & Eleauen shillings Sterling, in hand receiued before yᵉ Ensealeing & dehuery of these Presents, of Joseph Curtis of Kittery aforesd, wʳof & of euery part yʳof, I the sd Henery Bodg do acquitt, exonerate & discharge yᵉ sd Jos: Curtis his heyres executors & Administrators, yᵐ & euery one of them; & for other Good Considerations mee moueing yʳunto: haue given granted, barganed, sould, Enfeoffed & Confirmed, & do by these Presents for my selfe, my heyres, executors & Administrators, giue, grant, bargane, sell Enfeoff & Confirme unto the aforsd Joseph Curtis, Tenn Acres of Land scituate & being in the Town of Kittery, & lijng in too distinct Parcells, the one wʳof is fiue Acres & lyes bounded by yᵉ Northerne side of a Certen sault water Cricke, Called the Easterne Cricke, Neare to the head yʳof, bounded on yᵉ East with an high way, by Joseph Willsons land, & bounded on the North West, with Land of Edmund Hamons, & on the South West with yᵉ Land of Thomˢ Withers; And the other fiue Acres of Land

being in a place, Called Pudding hoole, bounded on the South with the Land of Bennonje Hodgeden, & Edm^d Hamons, & on the East, North, & West, bounded with ye Present Comans, the whoole Tenn Acres of Land being Granted to mee, by the Town of Kittery, & now by mee the sd Henery Bodg, sould unto the sd Joseph Curtis: To haue & to hould, to him the sd Jos: Curtis his heyres, executors, Administrators or Assignes for euer: with all & singular ye app^{r}tenances, priuiledges y^{r}unto belonging, or in any wise appertaineing; fully & Clearely acquitted exonerated, & discharged of & from all former Gyfts, Grants, sales Morgages, or any other incomberance, had made, or done by mee, or any other Person or Prsons, by from or under mee; Always warranting & defending the same against all or any Person or Persons Clajmeing any lawfull right, title or Interest in any of ye Premisses; or any part or Prcell y^{r}of, by or from vnder in the sd Hene: Bodg; for Confirmation of ye Premisses, I the sd Hene: Bodg haue Sett too my hand & seale, this seauenth day of Novemb^r In the yeare of o^r Lord, one thousand six hundred Eighty & too/

Signed sealed & Deliuered in   Henery Bodg HB (his seale)
   the Presence of us/
   John Hoole/   his marke
   John Wincoll/   Hene: Bodg acknowledged the aboue
                          written deed of Sale, to bee his
                          free act & Deed this 7th of Noveb^r
                          1682: before mee
                                John Wincoll Jus: pe:

vera Copia of this Deede aboue written transcribed, & with ye originall Compared this 6th: day of November 1684:   p Edw: Rishworth ReCor:

Book IV, Fol. 25.

Know all men by these Presents, y^t I Thomas Withers of Kittery for & in Consideration of eighty pounds Sterlg, in hand receiued, before the Ensealeing & Deliuery of these Presents, well & truely payd the receipt of & y^{r}with, I do acknowledg, & y^{r}with too bee fully satisfyd & payd, & y^{r}of, & euery part & penny y^{r}of doth acquitt, exonerate & discharge Jos : Curtis of Kittery aboue sd, his heyres executors, Administrators & Assignes, & euery of them for euer by these Presents, as alsoe for diuerse other good Considerations, mee moueing there unto, haue given, granted, barganed & sould, alien'd Enfeoffed, released & deliuered, & by these Presents do giue grant, bargan, & sell, & Confirme unto the sd Joseph Curtis, his heyres, executors Administrators & Assigns a Certen Tract of Land in spruse Cricke neare the head of the sd Cricke on the Easterne side of the sd Cricke, Contayneing Eighty Acres of vpland, begiining at the head of the little Cricke, that is between John Hools house & the sd Curtis & from thence to runn South West & p West fiuety poole the Cricke to bee bound & then to runn from the Mouth of the little Cricke, North West & by West, Ninety seauen poole, to a marked pine tree, In which lyne the Marsh from the first marked tree unto the little Cricke where formerly Mr Hooles sparrs layd, to belong unto the sd Curtis, which little Cricke, is the bounds of sayd Marsh, & the sayd Curtis is to sett his fence on the vpland ioyneing to the Marsh from the little Cricke vp along the Mane Cricke, & so to runn till I meete with my own, & the sayd Curtis his fence, & from thence as the fence runneth, vp to the marked tree aforesayd, & so from thence North, seaventy six poole, by the Marked trees, & from thence East by the Marked trees, one one hundred & fiuety pooles, & from thence South & by East, seaventy two poole, and from thence South, Twenty eight poole, and from thence West Thirty seaven pooles runneing to the head of the little Cricke, between Mr Hooles & sd Curtisis, which bounds is to bee, as it was layd out by Capt John Wincoll: To haue & to hould, the aforesayd Land, as also all the profitts & priuiledges y^{r}unto belonging, to the sayd Curtis, his heyres, executors, Administrators & Assignes for euer: And moreouer I the sd Thomas Withers, for my selfe my heyres, executors, & Administrators, do Couenant, promiss, & Grant to & with the sayd Curtis, his heyres, executors, Administrators & Assigns, to & with euery of them by these Presents, that all & singular the sd Premisses, with all the profitts and uantages in & by these Presents, before given, granted, barganed, & sould, & euery part & Parcell there of at the tyme of the Ensealeing and deliuery of these Presents, are & at all tymes shall remajne and Continew Clearly acquitted, exonerated discharged & keept harmeless, of & from all manner of former and other barganes, sales, Gyfts, Grants, leases, dowrys, title, troubles, and Incomberances whatsoeur, made Comitted or suffered to bee done, by mee Thomas Withers my heyres, executors, Administrators, & Assignes; And y^t the sayd Thomas Withers the sd Premisses hereby given, granted, & sould, euery part & Parcell thereof, with the appurtenances, against him selfe or any other Person or Persons w^{t}soeuer, Clajmeing any right vnto the Premisses; shall & will warrant & for euer defend according to the true Intent & meaneing of these Presents, & to no other Intent vss & purpose whatsoeuer/ In witness whereof I haue here vnto sett my hand & seale, this Twelfth day of June, one thousand six hundred Eighty two/   Thomas Withers (locus li)

Signed, Sealed, & Deliuered,   Mr Thomas withers came &
   In the Presence of us/   owned this Instrme^t aboue
   Roger Deareing,   written to bee his Act &
   The marke of ᐯ   Deed to Jos: Curtis the 12th
                                    day of June 1682, before
   Thomas Dear/   mee
                                    ffrancis Hooke Jus. pe:

Book IV, Fol. 25, 26.

vera Copia of this Instrume^t aboue written, transcribed & with the originall Compared this 7th day of Noveb^r 1684:
p Edw: Rishworth Re: Cor:

[26] This Indenture made the 29th day of October, In the yeare of o^r Lord one thousand six hundred eighty foure, Witnesseth y^t John Parrett of Cape Elizabeth, In New England fisherman, for & in Consideration of the full sume of one hundred sixty three pounds one shilling & six peence, of Current pay of New England, In hand receiued before the ensealing & deliuery of these Presents; w^r with hee doth acknowledg him selfe to bee fully satisfyd Contented & payd, by these Presents hath barganed, & sould, & by these Presents doth bargane, & sell, aliene, Enfeoffe, Convay, release Confirme & Deliuer vnto Nathall Fryer Senjor, sometymes of Portsmouth In New England, Now of ye prouince of Mayne In New England, aforesd, M^rchant: All that my now dwelling house, out housen, stage, flakes & flake Rowme, moreing place with mooreing Cable, Anker & Aukers, for moreing of boates togeather, with his Two boates with all y^r furniture, & all priuilidges & appurtenances to all & euery part belonging, & app^rtayneing all which the before barganed Premisses, to bee to the onely vss, behoofe, & benefitt of sd Nathall Fryer, his heyres, & Assigns for euer, all which sd Premisses are Scituate, lijng & being & Cape Elizabeth aforesd; To haue & to hould, the before barganed Premisses, with thejr appurtenances to him the sd Nathaull Fryer, his heyres & Assigns for euer, as now being on the East side of the Coue, next to the stage of ye sd Nath^ll Fryer, always prouided It is the full Intent, & meaning of these Presents & Premisses, y^t if the aboue named John Parrett, his heyres, executors, Administrators, or Assignes do pay, or Cause to bee payd vnto the sd

BOOK IV, FOL. 26.

Nath̃all Fryer, his heyres, executors, Administrators or Assignes, the full sum̃e of one hundred sixty three pounds, one shilling & six peence, at three Intyre payments vidz^t 63 : 01 : 06, at or before ye Twenteth day of June now next Insewing, the date here of, in good sound well Cured dry Cod fish, M^{r}chtable to bee Deliuered at Cape Elizabeth aforesd, to the sd ffryer his heyres or Assigns, at two Ryalls uuder price Current, as ye markett shall then bee, at ye ysles of shoales, & If In case the sd Parret shall pay the sd sume in M^{r}chatble fish as aboue, at ye dwelling house of ye sd Fryer on ye great Ysland in Pischataq, riuer, at by or before the aforesd day, y^t then ye sd Fryer is to allow the sd Parret the price Current as then it shall bee at the aforesd Yslands of shoales, as also fiuety pounds in like well Cured dry M^{r}chanble Cod fish at or before the 20th day of June, which will bee in ye yeare one thousand six hundred eighty six, at price & place as beforesd, as also fiuety pounds In M^{r}chan^{t}ble well cured Cod ffish at or before the 20th of June, which will bee In ye yeare 1687 : at price & places aboue mentioned; furthermore It is Couenanted, & Indented, by & between ye sd Partys y^t if ye sd Parret his heyrs, & Assigns, shall fajle to make payment of any of the sd Sum̃s, at euery season as they happen, to bee due from tyme to tyme, or in any part of ye sd sum̃es, according as is aboue mentioned, y^t then It shall bee lawfull for ye sd Nath̃ll Fryer his heyres or Assignes to sue for, Enter vpon all, or any part of ye aboue bargand Premisses, at his or y^r pleasure to haue hould, possess keepe & Inioy, as his & y^r proper right & Inheritance for euer, but if ye sd Parret pay or Cause to bee payd the abouesd sum̃s according as is aboue agreed, vpon tyme place, & speties, that then this Indenture, Morgage, or writeing to bee voyd, & of none æffect, otherwise to stand In full force pouer & vertue, & hereunto ye sd John Parret binds him selfe his heyres, executors, & Administrators togeather, with w^t is aboue bounden unto y^e sd Nat̃ll

Fryer his heyres, executors, Administrators & Assigns/ In witness w^{r}of the sd John Parret hath to these Presents set too his hand & seale, the day & year aboue written 1684/

Signed, sealed, & Deliuer̃d   The signe of John ($_{seal}^{his}$)
  In the Presence of us/   Parrett ℣
  Elyas Styleman/ ffran^s Hooke/

               John Parret came & owned this Instrum^t to bee his act & Deed to Mr Nath^n ffryer this 30th of Ooctob^r 1684 : before mee   ffran^s Hooke Jus : pe :

A true Coppy of this Instrument on the other side of Parretts to Mr Fryer, transcribed out of the originall & y^r with Compared this 20th of Nouemb^r 1684 :

               p Edw : Rishworth ReCor :

Wee whose names are underwritten being appoynted a Committee by the Honord Generall Assembly of this Prouince, for the setting out of Mis Alice Shapleighs thirds of the Estate of her deceased husband, Majo^r Nicholas Shapleigh as appeareth by y^r order, beareing Date the 25th of June 1684 : Wee accordingly went vpon the place, & surueighted & measured the whoole Tract, & set out her thirds y^r of on the North west side, & Joyneing to the dwelling house, & Contajneth about Two hundred fiuety & three acres, bounded with Mr Mauericks land on the North West, & on ye South West, with ye rest of ye Land belonging to the aforesd house, & from ye Riuer on the South West, runnes North East & by East, the whoole Length of the sd Tract of fiue hundred Acres Eighty poole, as by ye marked Trees may appeare; As also the third part of thejr Marsh at Sturgeon Cricke, Which third is Nine Acres, as also a Third part of ye househould Goods, & Cattle, with all y^t westerne part of ye dwelling house where her lodging Chamber is,

with the parlour opposite on the East side, & two Cellars, one of y^m under her lodging rowme, & the other by the Hall Chymney, to haue Lyberty In the Hall, Kitchine, & brew house, for her Necessary Occasions, with the third part of the barne on the West End y^rof, & a third part of ye too Mills, allowing to the Administrators the too thirds of the ould Oarchard with a Couenjent Garding plott, & yards, with ye liberty of the Land vnfenced, y^t lyeth about the house & barnes, & out houses, for y^r vss of them selues, & y^r Cattle, with lyberty of Conuenjent high way or ways, to & from the aforesd houses, & Mills; the land on which thejr part of the houses stands, to belong to them, with lyberty about any of the houseing to repayre &c: as Occasion may Call for/   John Wincoll/
 Dated the 6th of   John Penwill/
 Septemb^r 1684:   Jos: Hamonds/

A true Coppy of this diuission transcribed & with ye originall Compared this 25th day of November 1684:
       p Edw: Rishworth ReCor:

     Kittery the 23 of July 1684:

At a Meeteing of a Comittee appoynted, by order of the Court at yorke beareing Date the 25th of June 1684: to approue of all inst Clajms to the Estate of Majo^r Nichol^s Shapleigh, late deceased, vpon heareing & examining of the sd Clajms, the Committee finds due from the sd Estate as followeth/

Mr Samuell Shrympton Money...	37 11. 06
Mr Eliakime Hutchinson 5902 foote of boards & 494 ffoote of redd Oake pipe staues	
It John Purringtons Accop^t	15 00 00
It John Penwills Accop^t	08 02 8
It Mr Nathanll Fryers Accop^t	03 14 5
It Mr Edw Rishworths	00 14 f0
	59 11 01

The seuerall sumes as aboue written are
 approued by us/ John Wincoll/
 John Penwill/ John Pickerin/

vera Copia of this Accop^t as by the Comittee approued, & testifyd under thejr own hands, transcribed & with ye originall Compared this 26th of Novemb^r 1684:

p Edw : Rishworth Re : Cor :

[27] Know all men by these Presents, that I Arther Wormestall of the Town of Sacoe fisherman, In the prouince of Mayne, for diuerse good Causes, & Considerations mee y^{r}unto moueing, & more espetially for & In Consideration of that loue & affection wch I do unfaynedly beare unto my sonn In law William Daggett, Carpenter, now dwelling in the sd Town, as a part of y^t filiall portion which I giue unto my daughter, now wife of the sd Daggett, In Consideration w^{r}of I do acknowledg my selfe to bee fully Contented & satisfyd for the Premisses : Haue given, granted barganed, sould, Enfeoffed, & Confirmed, & by these Presents do giue grant bargane, sell, Enfeoffe & Confirme unto the aforesd William Daggett, from mee my heyres, executors, Administrators, & Assignes, unto y^t sd Dagget his heyres, executors, Administrators, & Assignes for euer, which are or shall bee begotten on the body of Rebeccah Daggett his now wife, a Certen Tract or small Tracts of Lands, vplands & Meddow bounded as followeth Inp^{rs} a New fejld fenced in, & ye most part of it broake vp lijng aboue my planting ground 4 or 5 Acres bee it more or less, & a Certen Parcell of vpland, lijng at the end of the fejld of John Abbetts, & one Moeity & halfe of y^t land, wch I bought formerly of Mr Thos Williams which land euer since hath lyen vndiuided, & further haue given & granted unto my sd sonn William Dugget two Acres of vpland, on ye lower side of ye same fejld, & also a certen Tract of sault Meddow, Contajneing about foure Acres, bee It more or less, lijng under y^t fejld formerly Richd Hitchcocks, between y^t & ye water side/ To

haue & to hould, ye vplands & Meddow, as aboue bounded, with all y^r rightts, priuiledges, Comanages, Imunitys, profitts, Aduantages, with all other app^{r}tenances of Tymber Trees or fyre Wood y^{r}unto belonging, or in any wise appertajneing, from mee ye sd Arther Wormestall my heyres, executors, Administrators, & Assigns, vnto ye aforesd William Daggett, his heyres, Administrators, & Assigns for euer: And I do further Couenant & agree to & with y^t sd William Daggett, y^t the sd Lands are free & Cleare, from all other Titles, Clajmes, sales, Morgages, Dowers Title of Dowers, Judgm^{ts}, executions, & all other Incomberances w^{t}soeuer, & I do hereby stand Ingagd in the behalfe of my selfe my heyres, executors Administrators, & Assignes, to mantayne & defend ye Interest, & Title of ye sd Lands, from all Prson or Person^r w^{t}soeuer, Clajmeing or Pretending any Clajme from by or under mee, or any other by my procurement/ In testimony w^{r}of I haue here unto afixed my hand & seale this sixteenth day of Nouemb^r Año: Dom͠: one thousand six hundred Eighty foure/

Signed sealed & Deliuered/   Arther Woormestall (his seale)

In the Presence of/
John Sargeant his   his marke
  marke/
Ruth Sargeant   Arther Wormestall came before
 her marke   mee this 17th of Noveb^r 1684:
                          & own'd ye Instrum^t to bee his
                          act & Deed:
                          Edw: Rishworth Jus: pe:

vera Copia of this Instrume^t transcribed, out of the originall & y^{t}with Compared this 26thof Novemb^r 1684:
                p Edw: Rishworth Re: Cor:

To all Christian people, to whome this Present deede of sale shall come, greeteing: w^{c}as the Select men for the Town of Kittery, with in y̅ᵉ prouince of Mayne In New England, vpon the 3d of March 1651 : did lay out vnto Hene : Pounden, alias Pounding at Coole Harboʳ six acres of Land at his house to him his heyres or assignes for euer, as appeareth by yᵉ ReCord of yᵉ sd Town booke, & a Coppy from thence drawn, under the hand of Charles ffrost Town Clarke, the 10ᵗʰ of July 1684 : vpon which is vnderwritten Memorand : John Whitte next Hene : Pounding on the North, now In yᵉ hands of Robert Allene, & the Land formerly belonging to Anthony Emery, on yᵉ South, now In the possession of John Morrall ; Know yee yᵗ Elizabeth Pounding Relict, widdow, & soole Administratrix, of the Estate of yᵉ sd Henery Pownding late of Boston In the Massatusetts Coloney of New England, shopp keeper deceased, Jonathan Bridgham, & Elizabeth his wife, Mary Pounding, Saraih Pownding, & Daniell Pounding, Children & heyres, of yᵉ sd Hene : Pownding ; for & In Consideration of the sume of Tenn pounds Current money of new England to them In hand at or before yᵉ Ensealeing, & deliuery of these Presents, well & truely payd, by Jabez Jenkines of the Town of Kittery abouesd ; Haue given, granted, barganed, sould, & by these Presents do fully & absolutely giue, grant, bargan, sell, release, Enfeoff, & Confirme, vnto the sd Jabez Jenkins for yᵉ aforesd sume of money, which they yʳby acknowledg to haue receiued, all the aboue mentioned six Acres of Land & bounded as abouesd, or howeuer otherwise, all the Estate right title, Interest, vss, propriety, possession, Clajm, & demand wᵗsoeuer of yᵐ or either of them of in & to the sd Land, & euery part or parcell yʳof : To haue & to hould, the afore granted Premisses, with yᵉ libertys priuiledges, Comoditys, benefitts, & appurtenances yʳvnto belonging, in as large & ample manner & sort, unto yᵉ sd Jabez Jenkins his heyres & Assigns for euer, as the sd granters or either of them, euer did Could or might haue vsed, & inioyed the same, in the right of the sd deceased

Hen: Pownding by vertue of yᵉ abouesd recited Town grant, or laijng it out by the Towns men of Kittery, to bee to yᵉ onely proper vss, & benefitt, & behoofe, of yᵉ sd Jabez Jenkins his heyres & Assigns for euer; And yᵉ sd Elizabeth Pouning, Jonathan Bridgham, & Elizabeth his wife Mary Powning, Sarah Powning, & Danⁱⁱ Pounding for yᵐ selues, yʳ heyres, executors Administrators, & Assigns do hereby Couenᵗ & promiss with yᵉ sd Jabez Jenkins heyrs & assigns yᵗ yᵉ sd Jab: Jenkins his heyrs & Assigns shall & may at all tyme & tyms, for euer hereafter lawfully peaceably & quietly, haue, hould, vss, occupy, possess, & Inioy all yᵉ sd Parcell of Land, with yᵉ priuiledges, & appʳtenances yʳ of, with out yᵉ least let hinderanc Clajm, challenge or Euiction by or from yᵐ or either of yᵐ, or by or from all & or under euery or other Prsons & Prson or Prsons haueing or Clameing any right Title, or interest yⁿⁱⁿ, by or from yᵉ sd Hen: Pouning deceased In witness wʳof they haue here unto set yʳ hands & seales In Boston this thirteenth day of Octobʳ Anno Dom one thousand six hundred eighty foure, Annoqᵤ R: Regnis Caroli Secundj, Angliæ &c: Tricessimo sexto/

   Elizabeth Pouning (her senle) Elizabeth Powning (her seale)
   Jonath: Bridgham (his seale) Sarah Pouning (her seal)
   Elizabeth Bridgham (her seale) Danⁱⁱ Pouning (his seale)

Signed Sealed & Deliuerd
 in the Presence of
 Edw: Drinker/
 Isᵃ Addington/

  This Instrumᵗ was acknowledged by yᵉ six prsons subscribing to bee yʳ uolentary act & Deed Boston 15: of Octobʳ 1684: before Elisha Hutchinson Assistᵗ
A true Coppy of this Instrumᵗ transcribed & Compar'd this 4th day of Decembʳ 1684 p Edw: Rishworth Re: Cor/

BOOK IV, FOL. 28.

[28] To all Christian people to whome this Present deed of Sale shall Come, greeteing: Whereas ye Select men for the Town of Kittery, with in the prouince of Mayne In New England, vpon the 3d of March 1651: did lay out vnto Henery Pouning, alias Pounding at Coole Harbour, Six Acres of land at his house, to him his heyres, or Assignes for euer, as appeareth by ye ReCord of the sd Town booke, & a Coppy from thence drawn, vnder the hand of Charles Frost Town Clarke, the 10th of July 1684: vpon which is vnderwritten Memorand̃ John Whitte next Hene: Pouning on the North now In the hands of Robert Allene, & the Land formerly belonging to Anthony Emery on the South now In the possesison of John Morrall; Know yee y^t Elizabeth Pouning, Relict, widdow & soole Administratrix of the Estate of the sayd Henery Pounmg, late of Boston In the Massatusetts Coloney of New England, shopp keeper deceased, Jonathan Bridghā & Elizabeth his wife, Mary Pouning, Sarah Pouning, & Daniell Pouning children & heyres of the sd Hene: Pouning, for & In Consideration of the sum̃e of Tenn pounds, Current money of New England, to them in hand at or before the Ensealeing, & deliuery of these Presents, well & truely payd by Jabez Jenkins of the Town of Kittery, abouesd; haue given granted barganed, sould, '& by these Presents do fully & absolutely giue grant bargane, sell, release, Enfeoffe & Confirme, vnto the sd Jabez Jenkins for the aforesd sume of Money, which they hereby acknowledg to haue receiued, all the aboue mentioned six Acres of Land butted & bounded as abouesd, or how euer otherwise, all the Estate, right, title, Interest, vss, propriety, possession Claime, & Demand w^{t}soeuer, of them or either of them of in & to the sd land, & euery part & Parcell there of; To haue, & to hould the aforesd granted Premisse: with the lybertys, priuiledges Com̃oditys, benefitts & appurtenances y^{r}unto belonging, in as large & ample manner & sort

unto ye sd Jabez Jenkins his heyrs & Assigns for euer, as the sd Granters or either of them, euer did, could or might haue vsed & Inioyed the same, In the right of the sayd deceased Hene· Pouning, by vertue of the abouesd recited Town grant, or laijng it out by the Townsmen of Kittery, to bee to the onely proper vss & benefitt, & behoofe of the sd Jabez Jenkins, his heyrs & Assigns for euer; And the sd Elizabeth Pouning Jonathan Bridgham, & Elizabeth his wife, Mary Pouning, Sarah Pouning & Daniell Pounding for them selfes, y^r heyres, executors, Administrators & Assigns, do hereby Couenant & promiss, to & with the sd Jabez Jenkins his heyres & Assignes, that ye sd Jabez Jenkins his heyres & Assigns, shall & may at all tyme & tyms for euer here after, lawfully, peaceably & quietly haue hould, vss, occupy, possess & Inioy, all the sd Parcell of Land, with the priuiledges, & appurtenances there of, with out the least lett hinderance Clajme Challenge or euiction, by or from them or either of them, or by or from all, & euery other Person & Persons haueing or Clajmeing any right title or Interest y^rin, by from or under· the sd Hene: Pouning Deceased, In witness Where of they hane here unto sett y^r hands & scales, In Boston this thirteenth day of Octob^r Anno Dom: One thousand six hundred Eighty & foure, Annoq R: Regn^s Carolj secundj Angliæ, &c: tricesimo sexto/

      Mary Powning (her seale)   Elizabeth Pouning (her seale)
      Sarah Pouning (her seale)   Jonathan Bridgham (his seale)
      Daniell Pouning (his seale)   Elizabeth Bridgham (her seale)

Signed sealed & Deliuerd
  I Presence of/
  Edward Drinker/
  Is^a Addington/
   This Instrument was acknowledged by the six Persons subscribeing, to bee there uolentary Act & Deede/ Boston Octob^r 15: 1684:   Elisha Hutchinson Assist:

Book IV, Fol. 28.

A true Coppy of this Instrument aboue written, transcribed & with originall Compared this fourth day of Decemb^r 1684: p Edw: Rishworth Re: Cor:

In answere to the petition of John Mayne, formerly of Cascoe, now of yorke In the prouince of Mayne, to the Generall Assembly houlden for ye sayd prouince, the 25th day of June 1684:
Testimonys in the Case haueing beene by the Honord President Pervsed; who doth Judg meete to order & appoynt, that the petitionor do Inioy & 'possess all that Land by him possessed & Improued, as the law title possession doth Lymitt: & that ye same bee sett out to him, by the Select men of the sd Town, or such as they shall appoynt not exceeding sixty Acres/ 28: June: 1684:
Tho: Damforth President:
vera Copia of this answere transcribed & Compared with the originall this 13th day of Decemb^r 1684:
p Edw: Rishworth Re: Cor:

Wee the Select men of the Town of yorke, whose names are here vnderwritten, haue layd out unto Mr Edw: Rishworth a Tract of Land which was granted to him by the Select men of yorke aforesd, the 22th of Aprill one thousand six hundred sixty one, which grant was seauenty foure Acres, lijng & being on the North North East side of Nathae^{ll} Maystersons fence, Wee haue layd out & bounded as followeth/ Begining at a Red oake tree, standing att the North East Corner of Maystersons fence, marked foure squaie, & from thence North North East, one hundred Eighty & foure pools, to a pine tree marked foure square,

BOOK IV, FOL. 28, 29.

from thence from thence North West sixty seaven pooles, or pearch to a Redd Oake marked foure square; then South West to Maistersons fence, 176 pooles, & marked the trees along in ye lyne as Wee went, & is to runne South Eastward, along by Maistersons fence, to the redd oake Where wee first began, leaueing about one poole & an halfe, or two poole along by Maystersons fence for ye high way for ye passage of the Inhabitants y^t dwell y^rabouts/

Layd out this Twenty one of Decemb^r 1683:

         Mathew Austine
         Abraham Preble
A true Coppy of this Instrum^t Com- Select men of the
pared, & transcribed out of ye orig- Town of yorke/
inall this 13th day of Decemb^r 1684:
 p Edw: Rishworth ReCor:

[29] Know all men by these Presents, that I John Renalds of Kenebunke, In the Town of Cape Porpus fisherman, for & in Consideration of full & ample satisfaction to mee in hand payd before the signeing hereof, haue given granted, barganed, & sould, & by these Presents do give grant sell & make ouer vnto Peter Rendle, Marriner, his heyres, executors, Administrators & Assigns for euer, one hundred Acres of Land & Marsh which Land & Marsh is the ould Plantation, which was late in the possession of my father William Renalds, & is bounded as followeth: Begining at a Cricke, which runns vp between the Plantation wch was formerly Peter Turbetts, & the sd ould Plantation, & from y^t Cricke one hundred twenty & seaven rodd vp ye Riuer, & then one hundred twenty seaven rod backe into the woods, & so one hundred Twenty seaven rod square to make vp the one hundred acres of Land & Marsh, which Marsh is Included In the sd one hundred Acres of Land,

euen as much Marsh as lyeth with in the bounds of the sd Land, with all yᵉ appurtenances profitts priuiledges, of right yʳᵛnto belonging, or in any wise appertajneing, & for him & them to haue & to hould the same, & peaceably to Inioy it for euer, with out yᵉ lett hinderance, Molestation, or trouble, of mee yᵉ sd Renalds or any my heyres, executors, Administrators or Assignes, or any other Person or persons whatsoeuer/ In witness wʳof, I haue here vnto set my hand & seale, this fourth day of Nouembʳ one thousand six hundred Eighty & foure/

Signed Sealed & Deliuered/   John Renalds/ (his seale)
  In Presence of vs/
  William Seauy/   his Marke R
  James Leach/   John Renalds came & owned this Instrument to bee his act & Deede to Peter Rendle abouesd, this 4ᵗʰ day of Novembʳ 1684 : before mee
                    Francis Hooke Jus : pe :

A true Coppy of this Instrument aboue written transcribed out of the originall, & yʳwith compared this 23ᵗʰ day of Decembʳ 1684 as attests Edw : Rishworth ReCor :

To all Chriſtian people to whome this ρsent Deede of Sale shall come Arther Beale, & his wife Ann alias Agnes sendeth greeteing; Now know yee, yᵗ I yᵉ sd Arther Beale with Ann or Agnes my wife, for & in Consideration of a valewable some to mee In hand payd by William Craffts, the which payment, I the sd Arther Beale, with Ann or Agnes my wife do fully & Clearely acquitt & discharge & exonerate the sd Craffts him his heyres executors Administrˢ Assigˢ for euer, & by these Presents, in Consideration of yᵉ sayd summe, do freely, & fully & absolutely sell, Convay, Assigne Enfeoff, & Confirme unto the sd William Craffts, one peece or Parcell of Land lijng & being at braueboate Harbour, according to Estimation to yᵉ valew of Twenty one Acres more or less, scituate, & bounded according to a Town grant, granted vnto mee the sd Arther Beale, beareing date the 27ᵗʰ of Aprill 1675 : may more fully appeare, being by the sd granted in the Townshipp of yorke, & lijng on the North side of Brafiboate as aforesd, & neare the Bridg & Adioyneing to the land of William Moore on the North side, & so lyeth Nore West Twenty foure Rod, or pooles In breadth, & so runneth into the Woods, or Wast, North East one hundred & fiuety pooles, or iodd Contajueing Twenty one Acres ; To haue & to hould the sd sume of Twenty one Acres, as aboue sd, to him the sd Craffts his heyres executors Administrators & assigns for euer, & further I the sd Arther Beale do promiss & Ingage, yᵗ at the signeing & sealeing of these Presents, I am the true owner & propretor of the aforesd Premisses, & haue with in my selfe full pouer, & lawfull authority the sd Premisses to sell, alliene, & Enfeoff, & do further promiss vnto the sd Crafft him, his heyres & Assigns, that the sd Land premised, is free & Cleare, & freely & Clearely acquitted from all former Grants Deeds Sales, Morgages, Entailes, forfiturs, seisurs arrests Attachments, Dowers, or pouer of thirds, or from any Incomberance w'soeuer : And that yᵉ sd Craffts may peaceably & quietly Inioy vse Occupy & possess the sd premised articles, him his heyres & Assigns for euer, without the Lett hinderance, Molestation, or resistance of mee the sd Arther Beale, or any my heyres, executors, or Assignes for for euer, & also do further promiss, for mee my heyres, executors, Administrators, & Assignes, vnto the sd Craffts his heyres, executors Administrators & Assigns, that yᵉ sd Premised articles I will warrant & Defend, to him the sayd Craffts, & to his Assigns for euer, from any person or Prsons w'soeuer, laijng iust & Legall Clajme yʳunto, from by or under mee, & also that I will Prforme & do, all other

Act or Acts that may bee, for the better & fuller Confirmation of the sd Premisses, as acknowledgme^t due In witness here of I haue here unto set my hand & scale, the sixth of Aprill, one thousand six hundred eighty three, Annoq, Regnj Regis, Charolus Secund^s xxxv :   The Marke of
Signed sealed & Deliuer̃d
  In the Presence of/   Arther Beale /B ($^{his}_{scale}$)
  Thimothy Yeales   Arther Beale came & acknowledged
  Sampson Whittes   this Deede or Instrument, to bee
  Signum/   his Act & Deede, unto Willia
                        Crafft this sixth day of Aprill,
                        1683 before mee
                        ffrancis Hooke Jus : pe :
vera Copia of this Instrum^t aboue written transcribed out of the originall, & there with Compared this 23th day of Decemb^r 1684 :   p Edw : Rishworth ReCor :

In answere to John Maynes petition to the last Generall Assembly for the province of Mayne, June 25 : 1684 :

Testimonys In the Case haueing beene Perused by the Honor^d President, who doth Judg mee to order & appoynt, that the petitioner do Inioy & possess all that Land by him possessed & Improued, as the Land title possession [**30**] doth Lymitt/ & that the same bee set out to him by the Select men of the sd Town, or such as they shall appoynt, not exceeding Sixty Acres/   Thomas Damforth
thers another Coppy of y, other side 29, Signed | E . R .   President :

To all to whome these Presents shall Come/ I John Dauess of yorke In the prouince of Mayne In New England, Gentle : send greeteing &c : Know yee y^t I the sd John Dauess, for & In Consideration of the sume of Tenn pounds,

Book IV, Fol. 30.

Current pay of New England to mee in hand payd, by James Freathy of yorke In New England, husbandman, before ye Ensealeing & Deliuery hereof, the Receipt w^rof I the sayd John Dauess, do hereby acknowledg my selfe, there with to bee fully satisfyd; Haue giuen, granted, barganed sould deliuered, & Confirmed, & by these Presents do fully, freely, & absolutely giue, grant, bargane sell deliuer & Confirme, vnto the sayd James ffreathy his heyres, executors, Administrators & Assignes, a Certen tract of vpland Contajneing twelue Acres & an halfe, ljng nere to the bounds of William Dixons Land, at Bass Coue vpon the North North East side, of the path goeing to the Marshes, the sd Lott extending from the sd Dixons Lott, twenty & fiue Pooles in breadth, & In length foure scoore poole, with all & singular the houses, woods, & vnder woods, & all priuiledges, & appurtenances w^tsocuer to the sd Land belonging; To haue & to hould the sayd Tract of vpland & Premisses, hereby barganed & sould, vnto the sayd James Freathy his heyres, executors, Administrators & Assignes, as his & thejr own proper Goods, & Chattles for euer, & to his, & for thejr own proper vsse for euermore : And I the sd John Dauess for my selfe, my heyres, executors, Administrators, & Assignes, & euery of them do Covenant, promiss & Grant to & with the sayd James Freathy, his heyres, executors Administrators & Assignes by these Presents; that I the sd John Dauess on the day ot the date hereof, & at the tyme of the Ensealeing & Deliuery hereof, haue In my selfe full pouer, good right & lawfull authority to give, grant, bargane, & sell, deliuer & Confirme, the sd Land & Premisses hereby barganed, & sould vnto the sd James Freathy, his heyres, executors Administrators & Assigns for euer more; In manner & forme aforesd, & also y^t hee ye sd James ffreathy, his heyres, executors, Administrators, & Assignes, or any of them, shall or may lawfully from tyme to tyme & at all tymes hereafter, peaceably & quietly haue hold vsse & Inioy the sd twelue acres & an halfe of upland & Premisses hereby barganed & sould, without any manner of lett suite trouble, euiction, Eiection, molestation, disturbance, challenge, Clajme Deniall, or demand w'soeuer, of or by mee ye sd Jo^n Dauess my heyres executors, administrators, & Assignes, or any of them, or of or by any other Person or Prsons w'soeuer, lawfully Claimeing, or to Clajme from by or under mee, my act or title/ In witness w^r of I haue here vnto sett my hand & Seale, this eight day of December: 1684:

Signed Sealed & Deliuered in the Presence of us/
John Penwill/
Arther Bragdon/

Before the signeing & sealeing & deliuery hereof, the meaneing of saueing harmeless from all others; Is to bee vnderstood as from Majo^r Clarke, & his sucessors/ John Dauess (locus sigilli)

Majo^r John Dauess came before mee this eight day of December 1684: & owned this Instrument to bee his Act & Deede/ Edw: Rishworth Jus: pe:

vera Copia of this Instrume^t aboue written, transcribed out of ye originall, & y^r with Compared this 6th day of Janvary 1684: p Edw: Rishworth Re: Cor.

Know all men by these Presents, that I Franc^s Champernowne, In the County of Yorke Gentlem: do ow & stand firmely Indebted vnto Capt Walter Barefoote of Douer In the River of Pischataqua Cheirgeon, the full & Just sume of fourty pounds of lawfull pay of New England due to bee payd vnto the sd Walter Barefoote, or his heyres, executors, administrators or Assignes, or to his lawfull Atturney, In New England, at or vpon the thirteth day of July which shall bee In the yeare of our Lord God, one thousand six hundred & seaventy, with out fraude or further delay, to the which payment Well & truely to bee made, I bind mee my heyres, executors Administrators, or Assignes, in the full some aboue specifyd/ as witness my hand & seale this Thirteth day of July 1669 :

Signed sealed & Deliuerd   ffran^s Champernowne (his seale)
  In the Presence of/   Mr Geo : Pearson maketh oath, that
  Henery Greeneland/   hee saw Capt Champernowne signe
  George Pearson/   & Deliuer this bill as his Act &
      Deede to Capt Barefoote, & y^t
      Hene : Greeneland was Present,
      & signed it also as a witness/
      July 26 . 1681 : before mee
          Francis Hooke Jus : pe :

I vnderwritten do Assigne, & set ouer vnto George Pearson of Boston M^{r}chant, all my right Title & Interest of the bill with in specifyd, as his own reall & proper debt, for him to aske demand, receiue & recouer the sd bill with all Costs, Interests & Damages w^{t}soeuer, y^{r}unto belonging, as witness my hand & seale this 31th day of July 1669 :

Signed sealed & Deliuered/   Walter Barefoote (his seale)
  in the Presence of/
  The Marke of John

Parker of   X   yorke

The marke of   *I B*   Joane Bray/
Hene : Greeneland/   Mis Joane Bray maketh oath, y^t
      shee saw Capt Barefoote signe
      seale & Deliuer the abouesd
      Assignation, vnto Mr Geo :
      Pearson, as his Act & Deed,
      this 26 : of July 1681 : before
      mee   Francis Hooke Jus : pe :

Book IV, Fol. 30.

vera Copia of this bill aboue written, & Capt Barefootes Assignem^t vnder written, transcribed out of ye originall & y^{r}with Compared this 7th of Janv: 1684:

p Edw: Rishworth ReCor:

Received of John Sayword the Thirteenth of Novemb^r 1683: eight quarters of beife, that is eight hundred three quarters & foure pounds, & fiue quin^{tls} of Cod fish receiued In the behalfe of my Cosson John Cutt for Accop^t of Mr Edw: Rishworth/ Rev: Hull/

vera Copia of this receipt transcribed out of the originall & y^{r}with Compared this Eleaueth day of Febru: 1684:

p Edw: Rishworth ReCor:

Receiued of Mr Tho: Holms the Twenty fifth day of May, one thousand six hundred eighty three, six thousand eight hundred foote of M^{r}chtable pine boards, which were deliuered to Mr Vahans order, & Receiued the Twenteth of June, one Thousand six hundred eighty Three, eight thousand seaven hundred foote of M^{r}chable pine boards, Deliuerd to my seruant John Wackum/ Receiued for Accopt of Mr Edw: Rishworth, & for ye vss of my Cosson Mr John Cutt, executor to the last Will & Testament of John Cutt Esqr deceased/ Receiūd p Reu: Hull/

A true Coppy of this receipt transcribed & with originall Compared this 11th of Febru: 1684:

p Edw: Rishworth ReCor:

BOOK IV, FOL. 30, 31.

To the Committee of the Militia of Boston, or any other Person whome It may Concerne, y^t wee whose names are here vnderwritten, do Certify y^t thejr was a fatt Cow of George Pearsons killd in Wells In May 1676: by order & Comand of Capt Charles ffrost, for the vss of the Countrey which Wee do Judg was Well worth In moneys foure pounds, fiue shillings & seauen peence in moneys which hee is not payd for/ as witness o^r hands this 26th day of Aprill 1678 : Sam^{ll} Wheelewright
   The Councill referrs this bill to William Symonds
   ye Treas^r of ye County of Jo^n Littlefejld
   yorke to examine & make
   satisfaction for ye same, out
   of the Treasury of that
   County/ 20th June 1678 : p
   ye Court Edw : Rawson Secr^{ty}

The note aboue mentioned is not payd/ neither haue I y^e æffects Sam^{ll} Wheelewright/

vera Copia of this ord^r transcribed & Compared 11 : ffeb : 84:   p Edw : Rishworth ReCor :

[31] Know all men by these Presents, that I Benjamen Curtis sometyms of yorke, in the prouince of Mayne, now of Wells Carpenter, for seuerall good Causes & Considerations, y^{r}vnto mee moueing, & more espetially for a ualewable sume of fiueteene pounds tenn shillings, in Current Money of New England to mee In hand payd, in yorke, w^{r}with I am fully Contented & satisfyd, by William young of yorke Glasier, do hereby giue, grant, bargan, sell, aliene, & Confirme. And haue hereby given, granted, barganed sould aliend, & Confirmed from mee the sd Curtis my heyres, executors, administrators, & Assignes vnto the aforesd William young his heyres executors Administrators & Assignes a Cer-

ten Tract or Parcell of Land Contajneing the full quantity of Twenty Acres, with a small house or Tenement Erected vpon it, which sd house & Land, lijeth on ye South West side, of the North West branch of yorke River, aboue yorke bridg, bounded with ye Lotts of Phillip Frost on the South West, & of John Hoys house & Land on ye North East/ To haue & to hould ye aforesd Tract & parcell of Land as aboue bounded, & the house built y^{r}on, with all the profitts, priuiledges, lybertys Comonages, Imunitys with all other appurtenances, y^{r}unto belonging, or any wise app^{r}tameing, from mee my heyres, executors, administrators & Assignes, vnto the sd William Young his heyres, executors, Administrators & Assignes, for euer, & I the sayd Benia : Curtis do further Covenant, & promiss, to & with the sayd William young, that ye sd house & Land is free & Cleare from all bargans, sales, Clames, Titles, Interests, Dowers, or Titles of Dowers & all other Incomberances w^{t}soeuer, & do promiss to warrant & Defend the same, vidz^t : the Title & Interest y^{r}of, from all Person or persons whatsoeuer, Clajmeing or pretending any Claimes y^{r}unto, from by or vnder mee, or in any wise by my procurement : In testimony w^{r}of I haue here vnto afixed my hand & seale, this Eleauenth day of February one thousand six hundred eighty foure/

 Testes   Benjamen Curtis (his seale)
Will : Gowen alias   Benja : Curtis came before mee this
 Smith/   11th day of February 1684 : &
Daniell Liueingstonn/   owned this Instrument aboue
        written to bee his Act & Deede/
        Edw : Rishworth Jus : pe :

A true Coppy of this Deede aboue written, transcribed out of the originall & y^{r}with Compared this : 12th day of Febru : 1684 :   p Edw Rishworth ReCor :

Book IV, Fol. 31.

The Deposition of John Mayne aged 70 yeares or y^{r}abouts/
Testifyeth & Sayth, that the Land which Richard Bray Senjor sould to George Pearson of Boston, that lyeth on the Mayne, Adioyneing to this Deponents Land in Cascoe bay, neare vnto Maynes Poynt, & did Contajne Sixty Acres of Land bee it more or less, hath beene possessed by building & other improuement, as planting &c : these Thirty six yeares, at least to my owne knowledg/
Witness John Sayword/ John Mayne/
John Mayne came before mee this 3d day of Janvary 1684 : & did Attest vpon his oath the treuth of this euidence aboue written/ Edw : Rishworth Jus : pe :

Elizabeth Mayne, about 61 : years of age or there abouts testifys, & giues in vpon her oath to the treuth aboue written, y^t her husband John Mayne doth declare, & that ye sd Land y^r mentioned hath beene possess'd about 35 years or more/
Taken vpon oath this 16th of Febru : 1684 : Before mee Edw : Rishworth Jus : pe :

vera Copia of these 2 depositions, of John Mayne & Elizabeth his wifes transcribed out of ye originall & Compared this 21th day of Febr : 1684 : p Edw : Rishworth Re : Cor :

Receiued July 9th 1672 : of John Batson of Cape Porpus foureteene quin^{tlls} of M^{r}chTble, & fiue & an halfe of Codd fish, & foure of refuge fish/ I say receiued by mee
ffrancis Tucker/
vera Copia of this receipt transcribed, & with the originall Compared this 24th of ffebru : 1684 :
p Edw : Rishworth ReCor :

BOOK IV, FOL. 31.

A true Draught of Mr Robert Elliets Land, lijng & adioyneing vnto Mr Phillip ffoxwells Land at Blew Poynt, Contents one hundred & Twenty fiue Acres, taken by us whose names are underwritten, the 15th day of August Anno: Chiistj, 1684:   John Wincoll/
And also another true Draught of Mr   John Penwill
Robert Elliets Marsh Land & at
Blew Poynt Contents fiuety one
Acres/ taken by sd Jon Wincoll &
John Pewill & given under yr
hands & layd out at the same as p
a Draught appeareth, wrof Mr Elliett hath both the Originalls subscribed by thejr owne hands/ as
Attests   Edw: Rishworth ReCor

          ·

This Instrument made the ninth day of March, In the yeare of our Lord one thousand six hundred Eighty foure, between Peter Glanfejld, of ye Town of Portsmouth in the prouince of New Hampshire taylour of the one parte; And Christopher Addams of the Town of Kittery in the prouince of Mayne Yeoman, of the other parte; Witnesseth, that the sayd Glanfeild, for & in Consideration of the sume of sixty pounds in hand receiued of the sayd Christopher Addams, the receipt where of I the sayd Peter Glanefeild do acknowledg and am fully satisfyd therewith, And do hereby acquitt & discharge the sd Addams, his heyres executors & Administrators thereof for euer: And also for diuerse Considerations mee there unto moueing, haue barganed sould, and do by these Presents, bargane, sell, aliene, Enfeoff, Confirme, & sett ouer, vnto the sayd Christopher Addams his heyres, executors Administratois & Assignes for euer, a Certen parcell, or Tract of Land lying & being in the Town of Kittery

Book IV, Fol. 31, 32.

aforesayd, containeing Twenty six Acres Certen, or Twenty eight Acres vncerten, which sayd Land I the sayd Glanefejld bought of William Palmer, Sixteene Acres thereof as appeares, with the butts & bounds thereof, by two Deeds of sale under the sd Palmers hand and seale one of them beareing date Aprill the one an Twenteth, In the yeare one thousand six hundred and seaventy, & the other beareing date the Twenty first of May, one thousand six hundred seaventy foure: And tenn Acres Certen, or twelue Acres unCerten, of the abouesd Land, I sayd Glanfejld bought of Samuell Knight, as appeares with ye butts & bounds thereof, by a Deed of Sayle under the hand & seale of the sd Kight beareing Date July eight one thousand six hundred eighty Two, with all ye priuiledges & appurtenances y^{r}unto belonging, or in any wise whatsoeuer app^{r}tajneing: To haue & to hould, to him the sayd Christopher Addams, his heyres, executors, Administrators, and Assignes for euer: All the aboue mentioned Premisses, togeather with all the priuiledg^s [32] and appurtenances there unto belonging; And I the sayd Glandfeild for my selfe, mine heyres, executors, & Administrators, do Couenant promiss & grant, to & with the sayd Christopher Addams, his heyres, executors Administrators, & Assignes, & euery of them by these Presents, that all & singular the Premisses, with all there profitts benefitts & Aduantages, in & by these Presents given granted, barganed & sould, & euery part & Parcell there of, at the tyme of the Ensealeing & deliuery of these Presents, are & bee and at all tymes hereafter shall bee, remaine, & Continew clearely acquitted exonerated & discharged, from all manner of former & other barganes sales Gyfts, Grants, leases, Dowers, titles, troubles & Incomberances whatsoeuer, made, Comitted, suffered, or done, or to bee made Comitted, suffered or done, by the sd Glanfeild, his heyres, executors, or administrators, or by any of them, or by any other Person or persons w^{t}soeuer, Clajmeing from by or und^r him them, or any of them, & shall defend the title of sd Land to him the sd Addams his heyres & Assignes for euer: In witness w'of I haue here unto set my hand & seale, the day & yeare aboue written, & in the thirty & seauenth yeare of the Reign of o' soueraign Lord, Charles the secund by the Grace of god, of England, Scotland, ffrance, & Ireland King/

Signed scaled & Deliuered/
In Prsence of us/
Humphrey Axell/
William Addams/
John Dyemont/

The marke of Peter)⟨ Glanfejld

The marke of /⟨|
Margerett
Glanefeild/

Peter Glanefejld came and acknowledged the aboue written Deed of saile, to bee his free act & Deede, this 10th March 1684:5 before mee

Charles ffrost Jus: pe:

A true Coppy of this Instrument aboue wrttten transcribed out of ye originall, & y^r with Compared this xi day of March 1684: p p Edw: Rishworth Re: Cor:

Received by mee John Smyth Senio^r of Cape Nuttacke of the Town of yorke of my sonn John Smyth Junjo^r rescident in ye same Town & place, the iust sume of seauen pounds six shillings 13^d in money the remajnder In Corne & worke vidz^t In worke accepted of Thos Everell, fiuety shillings, In Corne Twenty eight shillings, payd mee tenn shillings by my sd sonn John In worke, & fourty fiue shillings after wards; I say received of my sonn John Smith the iust sume of seauen pounds six shillings, in part of payment of y^t thirty pounds which was for ye Land that I sould him;

by mee his father John Smith as abouesd, this 21th day of Aprill 1685 : as Witness my hand or marke/

 Witness/   John Smith Senjo^r
 Edw : Rishworth/   his marke ⊥
 Mary Sayword Jujo^r/

vera Copia of this receate transcribed & with originall Compared this 29 : Aprill 1685 :

       p Edw : Rishworth Re : Cor :

August 24 : 1664 :

These are to Certify all whome It may or shall Concerne, that I Thomas Drake haue received of Richd Bray the full & iust sum̄e of Tenn pounds, for & Consideration of a plantation that I Thomas Drake haue sould vnto the sayd Bray, which plantation lyeth Adioyneing between Goodman Carters & John Maynes plantations/ In testimony here of I haue sett my hand, the Twenty fourth of August 1664 :

 Witness   Signum Thom^s
 John Phillips/   Drake   (his scale)
 Hene : Williams/

   Henery Williams testifyd vpon oath that hee was Present & saw Thomas Drake deliuer the with in written Instrume^t as his Act & Deed, & hee did then subscribe his name as a witness, & saw John Phillips do ye like/ Sworne at Boston Octob^r 6 : 1684 : Before Sam̄ell Nowell Assist^t

vera Copia of this Instrume^t aboue written as subscribed, & of the Attest vnderwritten as taken transcribed & with originall Compared, this 23 : of Febru : 1684 :

       p Edw : Rishworth ReCor :

Book IV, Fol. 32.

To all Christian people to whome these Present deed of Sale shall come/ Samuell Shrimpton of Boston with in the County of Suffocke, & Colony of the Massatusetts bay in New England, Merchant, & Elizabeth his wife send greeteing/ Know yee y^t w^{r}as Robert Cutt late of Kittery with In the prouince of Mayne in New England deceased in & by one obligation vnder his hand & seale, beareing date the eighteenth of March Año Dom͠ : 1671 : stood iustly indebted vnto the sd Samuell Shrimpton, in the full & iust sum͠e of one hundred finety too pounds sixteen shillings & vpon non payment y^{r}of, hee put the same in suite in his Majestys Court of pleas houlden at yorke, with in the aforesd sd Prouince of Mayne the Twenty ninth day of May 1683 : vpon which recouered Judgment again st the Estate of the sayd Robert Cutt to the ualew of Two hundred fourty fiue pounds fiueteen shillings, & tooke out execution the fifth day of July then next following & leuied the same, the Ninth day of July sd vpon the Estate of the sd Robert Cutt shewed him to bee his by his sonn Richard Cutt, executor to his deceased father, to the ualew of Two hundred fourty fiue pounds fiueteen shillings, money according to the apprisement of Christopher Addams & William Furnell, Inhabitants of the Town of Kittery aforesd, as by the ReCords of the sd Court on file in sd Yorke, reference y^{r}unto being had, more planely doth & may appeare, Now bee It further known, That the sd Sam͠ell Shrimpton & Elizabeth his wife, for & in Consideration of the sum͠e of one hundred fourty two pounds current money of New England, to them in hand payd before the Ensealeing & deliuery of these Presents, by the sd Richard Cutt of Kittery aforesd Yeoman, the receipt whereof they do hereby acknowledg, & them selues there with to bee fully satisfyd, & Contented, & there of & of euery part y^{r}of do acquitt, exonerate and discharge the sayd Richard Cutt, his heyres, executors, Administrators for euer, by these Presents : Haue given, granted, barganed, sould, Aliend, Enfeoffed & Confirmed by these Presents; do fully, freely Clearely, & absolutely giue grant, bargan, sell, aliene, Enfeoff, & Confirme unto him the sd Richad Cutt, his heyres, & Assigns for euer: All that thejr Tract peece or parcell of Land scituate, lijng & being within the Town, or Townshipp of Kittery aforesd, Contajneing by Estimation three hindred Acres, bee yᵉ same more or less, [33] being butted, & bounded by the Land of AMerideth, & Michaell Endell, on yᵉ East by the Land of William Diamond deceased, on the West, & so runns North East to Spruse Cricke, & on the South side by a branch of the riuer, Comanly Called or known by the name of Crooked lane, togeather with one Dwelling house, one barne, & sheepe shedd, standing yʳvpon, also two oxen, one steare, Two Cows, one Heffer, with all other profitts, priuiledges, rights Comoditys hæriditaments, & appʳteances whatsoeuer, to yᵉ sd parcell or Tract of Land belonging, or in any kind appʳtajneing, as the same was deliuered to him sd Samell Shrimpton by vertue of the abouesd Judgmᵗ & execution: To haue & to hould, the sd Tract or parcell of Land, butted bounded & containeing as aforesd, with all other yᵉ aboue granted Premisses & euery part & Parcell yʳof, vnto the sd Richard Cutt his heyres and Assignes for euer: To the onely proper vss benefitt, & behoofe of him the sd Richard Cutt his heyres & Assignes for euermore: And the sd Samuell Shrimpton & Elizabeth his wife for themselues, thejr heyres, executors & Administrators do hereby Couenant promiss, & grant, to & with the sd Richard Cutt his heyres, & Assignes in manner & forme following that is to say/ that at the time of the Ensealeing, & delivery of these Presents, they yᵉ sd Samll Shrimpton, & Elizabeth his wife, are yᵉ true soole & lawfull owners of all the afore barganed Premisses; & are lawfully Ceized of & in the same in thejr owne proper right: & that they haue in them selus full pouer, good right, & Lawfull authority, to grant, sell, conuay, & Assure the same unto the sd Richard Cutt, his heyres, & Assignes in manner & forme afforesayd : and y^t the sd Richd Cutt his heyres, & Assignes, shall & may by force & uertue of these Presents from time to tyme, & at all tyms for euer hereafter, lawfully, peaceably, & quietly, haue hould vss, occupy possess, & inioy the aboue barganed Premisses with thejr appurtenances, & euery part & Prcell there of, free & Cleare, & Clearly acquitted & discharged of & from all, & all manner of former & other gifts, grants, bargans Sales, leases, Morgages Joynters, Dowers, Judgm^ts executions, Wills, Intailes, forfiturs & of & from all other titles troubles, Charges, & incomberances w'soeuer, had, made, Comitted, done, or suffered to bee done, by them the sayd Samell Shrimpton & Elizabeth his wife, or y^m or either of them, thejr or either of thejr heyres or Assignes at any tyme, or tymes before the Ensealeing here of : And the abouesayd Premisses with thejr appurtenances, & euery part & parcell thereof, vnto him the sayd Richard Cutt his heyres & Assignes, against the sayd Samuell Shrimpton, & Elizabeth his wife thejr heyres, executors, & Administrators, & each & euery of them, & against all & euery other Person & Persons whatsoeuer any ways lawfully Clajmeing, or demanding the same, or any part there of, by from or under them, or either or any of them shall & will warrant, & for euer defend by these Presents. In witness w^rof the sayd Samell Shrimpton, and Elizabeth his wife, haue here unto Sett thejr hands & seales, the Eleaventh day of February Anno Dom; one thousand six hundred eighty foure/ Annoq, Regni Regis Carolj secundj Angliæ &c : xxxiijj/

    Samuell Shrimpton (locus) Elizabeth her (locus)
     his Seale (sigilli) Shrimpton seale(sigilli)

   Signed sealed & deliuered in Presence
      of us/
    Michaell Williams/
    John Hinkes/
    Edward Lyde/

BOOK IV, FOL. 33.

At Kittery In the Prouince of Mayne In New England ffebruary 19th 1684: Michaell Williams of Boston In New England M^rchant Atturney to the with in named Samuel Shrimpton according to his pouer to him deriued by letter of Atturney from the sd Samuell Shrimpton, Did give full & quiett & peaceable possession & Ceizin, of the with in mentioned Tract or Parcell of Land & other the Premisses contained in this Present Deede, by Turffe & Twigg, unto the with in named Richard Cutt, to haue & to hould the same unto him his heyres, & Assignes, according to ye forme, purpurt & true meaneing of the sd Deede/ this done in the Presence of the witnesses hereunto subscribed/

Ephraim Endell/
William Adams/

A true Coppy of this Instrument or deede of Sale aboue written transcribed out of the originall & y^rwith Compared this 28th day of Febru : 1684 :   p Edw : Rishworth ReCor :

This writeing witnesseth, y^t I John Parker of Kenebecke River in New England, for & in consideration of the ualew of tenn pounds to mee in hand payd, the receipt w^rof I do hereby acknowledg, & y^rwith to bee fully satisfyd, & do by these Presents with the free & full Consent of my wife Margery Parker, bargan, sell alliene Enfeoff Convay & make ouer vnto Syluanus Davess all my right title & Interest of & in a Tract of Land, as well vpland & Meddow lijng & being scituate in the Riuer of Kenebecke, aforesd togeather, with all Tymber & tymber trees swamps sault Marsh & fresh, & all other priuiledges both of fishing fowleing haukeing hunting & all other Imunitys whatsoeuer doth there vnto belong, with all thejr appurtenances w^tsoeuer : To haue & to hould, all & singular the afore deuised Premisses, & euery part & Parcell y^rof, to him the sd Siluanus Dauis, hee heyres & Assigns for euer, free & Cleare of & from all former & other bargancs Sales, Morgages, titles, troubles, & Incomberances w^{t}soeuer; And I the sd John Parker, do for my selfe my heyres, executors, & Administrators, Couenant promiss & agree to & with the sd Siluanus Dauess his heyres & Assigns, y^t they & euery of them, shall quietly possess & Inioy all the aforesd Premisses, which is butted & bounded, by a fresh runne or Riuerlett, on the one side, & another fresh riuer on the other side, both which Riuers runne, into the aforesd Riuer of Kenebecke, about 3 quarters of a mile or y^{r}abouts aboue or more vp the Riuer then ye house of the sayd Parker, and to runn from the sd Riuers vpon a Streight lyne ouer into Cascoe Bay, right ouer the land from ye riuer to ye sea on Cascoe side, & that the sd Parker his heyres executors & Administrators shall & will make vnto him the sd Siluanus Daus his heyres & Assigns any further & better Assurance of the Premisses w^n required or desired, there unto/ In witness w^{r}of I the sd John Parker, & his wife haue here unto set y^r hands & seales, the first day of June one thousand six hundred sixty one/

Signed sealed & deliuer͞d/   John Parker his ✝ P (his seale)
& quiett possession giuen   marke
in the Presence of/   This act & Deede was acknowl-
Thomas Kymble   edged in Court the 7th of Sep-
William Robbinson/   temb^r 1666 : before mee
                            Henry Joclein Jus Qo͞r :

A true Coppy of this Instrume^t transcribed & Compared with ye originall this 6th of Aprill 1685 :

                   p Edw : Rishworth Re : Cor :

[34] To all Christian people, vnto whom these Presents shall come/ John Parker of Kenebecke River In the Prouince of Mayne In New England fisherman Sendeth greete-

ing : Know yee that w'as I John Parker about Twenty fiue yeares since, for good & ualewable Considerations mee y'unto moueing did grant bargan & Sell vnto Capt Siluanus Dauvis of the same Riuer, a Certen Tract of vpland & Meddow scituate & lijng in Kenebecke abouesd, & gaue him a Deede of Sale of the same vnder my hand, & seale acknowledged before authority as may appeare by w^t is aboue written, being the first grant & Sale my by mee of any lands in Kenebecke, & which haue by the space of Twenty fiue yeares, last past or there abouts, been possessed & Occupied by the sd Dauis, or his assignes, I haueing since beene hyred & payd by him for mowing, & makeing his hay vpon the sd Meddow land, which sd grant & sale & all the lands there in mentioned, I do here by ratify & Confirme vnto the sd Silvanus Dauis, his heyres, & Assignes for ever, & haue vpon the day of the Date hereof runn & renewed the lynes & bounds, w^{r}by I formerly sould him the sd Lands, & a fresh marked the ould bound trees: the sd granted Land & Meddow, lijng on the westward side of the aforesd Riuer, the southward bounds begins at a runn or brooke of water, about halfe a mile to the Southward of the sd Dauis his house, at a greate Hemlocke tree marked, & vp the sd run or brooke, to the Southward side of a sprice swampe, & from thence to the Southward end of two fresh Meddows lijng to the westward or West Southwardly, from ye sd Dauis house, with Marked trees from the aforesd Hemlocke tree to the Southward end of the aforesd fresh Meddows, at the Meddows & vpland with in ye sd bounds; so fare as the carrjing place into Weñeganse Marshes, I did formerly grant, bargane, & sell vnto the sd Silvanus Dauis & haue ever since beene possessed by him which I do hereby Confirme according to the abouesd bounds/ To haue & to hould the same, with all the woods timber trees, fences buildings, & improuements made there on, & the rights libertys priuiledges, & appurtenauces, y^{r}unto belonging vnto him the sd

Book IV, Fol. 34.

Siluanus Dauis his heyrs & Assigns, to his & there onely proper vss, & behoofe for ever, & will warrant & defend the same & euery part & Parcell thereof, vnto him & them for euer, against the lawfull Clajms & Demand, of all Prsons whomesoeuer/ In witness where of I haue here vnto put my hand & seale/ Dated this thirteenth day of November Anno Dom. one thousand six hundred eighty foure/

Signed Sealed & delvered   John Parker (his seale)

  In the Presence of/   his signe *IP*
  Thomas Parker/

John Pane his   And the bounds renewed & from the
   signe *IP*   South end of the sayd fresh Med-
William Bacon   dows, vpon a streight line ouer to
his signe *WB*   Cascoe Bay/ owned In the Presence
     of these witnesses/
     Witness James Ingles/

A true Coppy of this Instrument transcribed out of the Originall & there with Compared this seauenth day of Aprill 1685 : .   p Edward Rishworth ReCor :

To all Christian people to whom these Present Instrument shall come, Elizabeth Haruie Widdow of Michaell Mittone of Cascoe, alias Falmouth In the County of yorke, alias y e prouince of Mayne In New England, sendeth greeting, In our Ld God Euerlasting : Know yee that the sd Elizabeth Haruy, for the naturall loue which I haue & do beare, vnto my sonn in law Thomas Brackett of Cascoe, In the prouince of Mayne who married my daughter, Mary Mitton, It being also part of the portion belonging to my aforesayd daughter, Haue, given, granted, Enfeoffed, & Confirmed, & by these Presents do freely, clearely & absolutely give, grant, aliene, Enfeoff & Confirme, vnto my sonn in law Thomas Brackett his heyres, & Assignes for ever, fifety Acres of Land lijng &

BOOK IV, FOL. 34.

being in Cascoe bay, bounded by the bounds hereafter expressed, vidz^t to begine at the Poynt which lyeth on the Easterne side of the mouth of the gutt ioyneing to the backe Coue which Issueth out from before the now dwelling house of the sayd Thomas Brackett, & so to rune fiuety pooles Cross the Necke right vp into the woods, & eight scoore pooles vp along ye Cricke, comanly called the ware Cricke, the same breadth till fiuety Acres bee ended, togeather with all the woods vnderwoods Meddowing, pasture & tillage land, with all & singular the profitts & priuiledges y^{r}to belonging/

To haue & to hould, all & singular the afore mentioned Premisses, to the onely proper vss & behoofe of him the sd Thomas Brackett, his heyrs & Assigns for euer, freely, peaceably & quietly, with out any manner of reclajme, Challenge or Contradiction, by mee my heyres, or executors, or any other Prson or Persons by my means or procurement, hee the sd Thomas Brackett his heyres, executors or Assigns, yeilding & paijng from the Date here of, so much rent as shall bee due unto the high Ld, when lawfully demanded; In witness where of I ye sayd Elizabeth Haruy, haue here vnto set my hand & seale the eight day of May In the yeare of o^r Lord one thousand six hundred sixty seaven/

Signed sealed & deliuered   Elizabeth Harvy (her seale)
   In the Presence of us/   her marke E
ffrancis Neale/
Nathaniell Mitton/

vera Copia of this Instrument abone written, transcribed of ye originall & y^r with Compared, this 7th day of Aprill 1685:   p Edw: Rishworth ReCor:

These Present witnesseth, that I Thomas Brackett with in mentioned, do by these Presents assigne sell & make ouer vnto Mr George Munioy of Casco Bay, all my right title &

Interest in the with in written Deede for euer, vnto the sayd Geo: Munioy, his heyres, executors, Administrators or Assignes, from mee my heyres executors & Administrators firmely by these Presents, & is for twenty pounds given under his hand, to pay mee for the same/ as witness my hand & seale this thirteenth day of Octob^r 1668 :
:13:

Signed sealed & Deliuered/ Thomas Brackett/ ($^{his}_{seale}$)

In the Presence of, vs

Thomas Wise Agnis Stevens
his marke/ her marke

Thomas Wise, & Agnes Stevens made oath they were Present & did see Thomas Brackett signe seale & deliuer y^s Assignment of this Deede vnto Mr George Munioy before mee, this 15th of Octob^r 1668 : ffran^s Neale Assöte

I the sd Thomas Bracket do appoynt Thos wise to deliuer the Premisses vnto ye sd Geo: Munioy as witness my hand this 13th of Octob^r 1668 : Thom^s Brackett/

Witness Agnis Stevens her marke

Susanna Lewis her marke

I haue given possession of the with in Premisses, vnto George Munioy this 13th of Octob^r 1668 : as Witness my hand/ the marke of Thom^s Wise

Thomas wise made oath of the deliuery of the Premisses to Mr Geo: Munioy, before mee Fran^s Neale Assotiat : 15 of Octob^r 1668 :

TheAssignment & deliuery of these Presents as within written transcribed out of the originall & y^{r}with Compared this 7th of Aprill 1685 : p Edw: Rishworth Re: Cor

[35] I Mary Brackett wife to Thomas Bracket, do giue my free & full Consent, to the bargan & Sale my husband Thomas Bracket hath made to Mr Geo: Munioy of the Premisses written on the other side, as witness this 21 : July 1670 :

Mary Brackett wife to Thoˢ Brackett acknowledged this aboue written to bee her act & deede, & set her hand there to this 21ᵗʰ July 1670 : before mee
    Francis Neale Assõte/

Mary Brackett/

I Robert Lawrrance & Mary my wife being Administratoʳ to Mr Geo : Munioy deceased, do for & in Consideration of thirty & fiue pounds, bargane & sell all that is with in expressd, which was formerly Thomˢ Bracketts vnto Dinis Maraugh, his heyres, executors, Administrators & Assignes for euer, as witness our hands this 26ᵗʰ day of Janv : 168¾ : Deliuered in the Presence of us/   Robert Lawrence/

Henery Horewood/ Mr Robert Lawrence, & Mʳˢ Mary
Matt : Paulling/   Lawrence Acknowledges the aboue Assignemᵗ to bee there act & Deede, this 24ᵗʰ day of March 168¾ before mee
                  Edw : Tyng Jus : pe :

A true Coppy of these two Assignᵗˢ with in written the one from Tho : Brackett to Mr Geo : Munioy, & the other from Mr Robert Lawrence & Mary his wife Administratrix to her former husband Geo : Munioy deceased, transcribed out of yᵉ originall & yʳ with Compared this 7th day of Aprill 1685 :   p Edw : Rishworth ReCõr :

BOOK IV, FOL. 35.

Know all men by these Presents y^t w^{r}as I Thomas Withers of Kittery being of great age, & finding my selfe weake of body & helpless, onely as yet of reasonable memory, & understanding, yet by reason also y^t my wife waxeth antient, & decaijng, our grat dependance being vpon o^r daughter Elizabeth, Wee y^{r}fore both father & Mother haue made ouer our Cows, namely too Cows, & foure Heffers fully & freely to her given & bequeathed to her as her owne to dispose of at her pleasure, as witness my hand this 22th day of Decemb^r in ye yeare of o^r Ld one thousand six hundred eighty & foure, as also the sheepe/ also before signeing, Wee withers aforesd haue given to her our daughter formerly three steares & a yoake of oxen & too Cows more/

  In Presence of   Thom^s Withers/
  William Heyns/   Jane Withers/
  Jonathan Mendum/
            marke/ }

Jonathan Mendum came & made oath to ye uerity of ye Instrum^t on the other side, vnto the which hee is a witness, & Mr Heynes was then Prsent & did likewise witness it/ March 30 : 1685 : as the sd Mendum doth affirme/ before mee ffran^s Hooke Jus : pe :

A true Coppy of this writeing, & this oath vnderwritten transcribed, & with ye originall Compared this 8th Aprill 1685 :   p Edw : Rishworth Re : Cor :

    This 13 day of Aprell Anno 1685

I Wm Heynes doe testifye and acknowledge that the contents of what was written by mee at the request of the sd m^r Thomas Withers deseased being but little before his death was Signed by him at his owne houss as appeares according to the contents upon the other side of this paper,

BOOK IV, FOL. 35.

as his act and deede, to his said daughter Elizabeth Withers
as witness my hand the day afores^d
William Heynes
Taken upon Oath before me this 13th of Aprell 1685.
Edward Rishworth Jus : pe.
vera Copia transcribed & Compard this 13th Aprill 1685 :
p Edw : Rishworth ReCor :

Noverint vniuersi p Presentis me Johanes Tomson fileā :
Guilielmi Tomsson deceasd in Kittery prouince of Mayne,
Carpenter, teneri &^t firmiter obligarj Johannes Wincoll, &
Jacobus Emery Quinqueginṫ . libris moneṫ Angliæ soluendis,
altē Johannes Wincoll autē : Jacobus Emery, aut eius Atturney, hæridibus, executors suis, ad quori quiden solution^s,
bene ett fideliter obligarie me heredi^s executors Administrators meis firmiter p Presentis sigillo mei sigillaṫ daṫ uices-
simo die July Anno Regni Dom̄ : dei gratiæ : Charoli,
Angliæ, Scotiæ frañ Et Hyberniæ, Regis fidei Defensoris,
Trigintie sexto, Anno Dom . 1684/
This Condition of this Prsent obligation is such, that If
the aboue bounden John Tomson his heyres, executors Administrators & Assignes, do well & truely obserue, Performe fullfill & keepe all, & euery of the couenants here
after & here in mentioned, & specifyd, Vidz^t That If hee do
from tyme to tyme, & at all tyms hereafter free & discharge
the Court for this prouince that granted pouer of Administration of his father William Tompsons Estate, vnto Capt
John Wincoll & James Emery abouesd, as also free & discharge the sd Administrators, of all Accompts y^t may bee
by the Court or any other demāded them, & also discharge
the Town of Kittery of & from all Charges y^t may come on
the sd Town by James Tompson his lame Impotent brother,
& giue the sd Administrators a Cleare discharge, for all &

euery thing they haue acted in & with the sd Estate, that then this Present obligation to bee voyd, & of none æffect, or else to remajne in force/ It is to bee understood that ye sd Administrators did take into y^r hands too Cows at seauen pounds price, one peyre coomes with stays & tackeling belonging to it, & one hand gunn. or Muskett, which the sd John Tompson abouesd, doth acknowledg that ye sd Administrators haue given him Accop^t how they haue disposed of it, & y^{r}of, & euery part & Parcell y^{r}of; The sd John, in behalfe, & in the name of all his brothers, doth acquitt ye sd John Wincoll & James Emery Administrators for euer by these Presents/

Sealed by him & Deliuered,   The signe of T (locus sigilli)

In ye Presence of us/   John Tompson

The signe of John Searle +

The signe of Mary Searle

In reference to this Administration, John Tompson ownes this obligation In Court to bee his Act & Deede, March the 31 : 1685 : as Attests Edw : Rishworth Re : Cor :

vera Copia of this obligation transcribed & with ye originall Compared y^s 15th of Aprill 1685 :

p Edw : Rishworth Re : Cor :

Know all men by these Presents, that Wee Namely William Furbush & Mary Forgisson haueing had frequent difference arise between us about the middle & diuiding lyne which out to regulate us in o^r home lotts; ffor Preuention of Trouble for ye future, Wee haue mutually Chosen, Capt John Wincoll, Capt Charles Frost, James Emrey & William Gowen alias Smyth, to runne out the sd Middle diuission order & marke the same, betweene us, y^t so it stand good, & bee of full force for vs, & o^r Successors, for euer, for Con-

BOOK IV, FOL. 35, 36.

firmation w{r}of, Wee bind o{r} selues & o{r} successors each to other in pœnall sume of fourty pounds sterlg : to bee forfeted to the party swerueing from the other party declining, as witness o{r} hands this 12{th} day of Aprill 1680 :

 Testes John   The signe of William
 Roberts Senjo{r}   Furbush/ W/
 Thom{s} Roberts
 Senjo{r} T R   The signe of Mary
          Forgisson/

A true Coppy of this obligation transcribed & Compared with the originall this : 15{th} of Aprill : 1685 :
        p Edw : Rishworth ReCor :

Wee whose names are here vnderwritten being mutually Chosen by William Furbush & Mary Forgisson, for y{e} ending of all Controuersys usually ariseing between them, about or touching the deuideing or Middle lyne of thejr home Lotts ; Wee do by these Presents declare, that Wee haue accordingly runne out the sd lyne, begining at the Edg of a little Coue of Marsh of Daniell Forgissons, & from thence to a Tall Stumpe of a Whitte oake neare to William Furbushes fence, & from thence to standing whitte [36] oake with in William Furbush his fejld, so backeward by an East & by north north lyne, till a full mile be Compleated, with allowance for the Countrey high way, & this wee giue under o{r} hands as a finall Conclusion, & Determination as touching the Premises, to which both Partys stand bound on the other side as witness o{r} hands, this 12{th} day of Aprill 1680 :

 A true Coppy of this determina-   John Wincoll/
 tion according to the bounds   Charles Frost/
 Concluded & measured out by   James Emery/
 y{e} arbitrators/ transcribed &   William Gowen
 Compared this 15{th} day of   alias Smyth/
 Aprill 1685 :
 p Edw : Rishworth Re : Cor :

BOOK IV, FOL. 36.

This writeing witnesseth, that I John Pritchett of Sagadehocke In the Prouince of Mayne do giue vnto my wife Jane Pritchett all my goods with out doores, (excepting halfe the Cattle, & halfe the house & Land) which shall bee æqually diuided between my sonn & daughter, after my decease, but if after my decease my wife shall not Marry to another man, If shee do shee shall not haue any thing of y^t aboue mentioned, or y^t was mine; Moreouer I giue vnto my brother Richard Pritchett that necke of land at the vpper end of the Marsh called by the name of the Ysland: But if my wife nor children, nor brother nor sister come to not mee, nor after I am dead to looke after ye aboue mentioned house, & Land, Goods & Chattles I do freely giue all ye sd house & lands, good & Chattles vnto John Burrell after my decease: Furthermore if in case my wife & children do come to mee that then I do freely give vnto the sd burrell, a Certen Tract of Land lijng & being on the Northerne side of the falls, begining at the Coue, right ouer against the sand banke, Closs to the great rocke, & from thence vp along by the brooke side to the vpper end of Allders, & then to go vpon a streight lyne to an heape of Rockes, Closs to the Marsh or Riuer side, commanly called Cannow poynt, with all ye Marsh on the South side of the sayd poynt, & runne along by the Mayne Cricke home along to the Falls, with all the priviledges & app^{r}tenances y^{r}vnto belonging; Furthermore I the sd John Pritchett shall & will secure, & keepe the sd John Burrell, his heyrs executors administrators or Assignes, harmeless from any Person, or Persons w^{t}soeuer, laijng any Claime right or Title to any part or percell thereof, furthermore the sd Burrell shall not sell lett nor giue ye sd Land nor Marsh to any Person or persons w^{t}soeuer, without the free Consent of the sd John Pritchett or his Assignes, & in witness here of I haue here vnto set my hand & seale, this

Book IV, Fol. 36.

foureteenth of Nouember, one thousand six hundred seaventy
foure/   John   (his seale)
Witness Robert Edmones/   Pritchett

Beniam͠: Mussy/   John Piitchett appeared before
Thomas Atkines   mee & acknowledged this Instru-
         ment to bee his act & Deede in
         Boston 28 : March 1685 : before
         mee Hum : Davie Assistant :

A true Coppy of this Instrume^t aboue written transcribed,
& with the originall Compared this . 16th day of Aprill : 1685 :
      p Edw : Rishworth Re . Cor :

   To all Christian people, to whom these Piesents shall Come ; Know yee y^t I ffran^s Champernoown of Kittery in the Prouince of Mayne In New England Esqr, do freely & absolutely giue, & acquitt Will : Moore his heyres, execu-tors, Administrators, & Assignes, from my heyres, execu-tors Administrators, & Assignes of Too Acres of sunken Marsh which the sd Moore bought of Mis Ann Godfrey, in case the sd Marsh is found in my Interest, or my deuission, the sd Marsh lijng on the North East side of Biaue boate Harbour, at the vpper end vsually Called ye Muddy Marsh, & by the Presence as aboue sd, do Assigne ouer all my right & Interest from mee, my heyres, executors, Administratois & Assignes, vnto the sd William Moore, his heyres, execu-tors, Administrators, & Assignes, with out any sujte trouble, Molestation, or disturbance w^{t}soeuer, from by or vnder mee, my heyres, executors, Administrators, & Assignes, as Wit-ness my hand this fiueteenth day of Aprill one thousand six hundred Eighty fiue/ 1685 :   ffrancis Champernown/

Testes/   Capt͠a ffrancis Champnown came before
  John Penwill/   mee this 15th of Aprill 1685 : & owned
  Rich͠d : Whitte/   the abouesd Instrument to bee his Act
  his marke ⊗   & Deede/ John Dauess Dep^{ty} Presid^t/

Book IV, Fol. 36.

vera Copia of this Instrum^t Compared, & transcribed, this 24th of Aprill 1685   p Edw: Rishworth ReCor:

Prouince of Mayne In the County of East yorke In New England; This Deede of Gyft by Mr Thomas Withers before his decease, according to his last Addition to his last approved written will, & testament to his youngest daughter Elizabeth vocally, & now y^{r}fore accordingly to too Certen sworne Euidences, before Capt Francis Hooke affirmed, & also now likewise further Confirmed, & by a secund acknowledgm^t by further & firmer giueing her thejr sayd daughter Elizabeth possession befoie too Certen witnesses more, Namely William Heynes, & Mary Ryce, by her Mother, Mis Jane Withers, on the day of this Instant Aprill the Twenty secund Anno: one thousand six hundred Eighty & fiue, both of the Now new dwelling house, w^{r}in they them selues not onely do dwell, but also did liue some yeares before the sd Withers decease, vndisposed off: And also at the same tyme accordingly of a Part of Land, at the Present given the sayd Daughter by the sd mother, In lew of the whoole verball Complem^t Intend & also bequeathed by the sd deceased father vpon his death bedd; Namely Twenty Aacres scitituated not onely round about the sd house, & the feild w^{r}in it now stands, but as fare forth vpon y^t part of the house lott, next vnto John Dyamotts lyne, or Tract of Land, at leasure, & in Conveniett tyme measured to the Compleate proportion & iust Number of the afore mentioned Acres, to hee marked out & bounded: To haue & to hould, & Inioy after the decease of her mother afoiesd, And till then dureing her sayd Mothers pleasure, but afterwards, & for euer hereafter to her sd lawfull heyres & Assignes for euer/ And in Confirmation of the abouesd Premisses, shee the sd Mother Jane

hath not onely sett too her hand as subscribed, but sealed & deliuered accordingly at the day & date forementioned/
n the Presence of/   The marke of
   Fran^s Hooke
   William Heynes/   Jane Withers 🖊 (her seale)

Mis Jane Withers came & acknowledged this Instrum^t to bee her act & Deed unto her daughter Elizabeth, Withers, this Twenty secund day of April: 1685 : Before mee Francis Hooke Jus : pe :

A true Coppy of this Instrument transcribed out of ye originall & y^{r}with Compared this 28th day of Aprill 1685 :
                p Edw : Rishworth Re : Cor :

Know all men by these Presents, y^t I John Smyth of Cape Nuttacke Senjo^r, for diuerse good causes & considerations y^{r}unto mee moueing, & more espetially for & in Conside. of the iust sume of Twenty pounds [37] & vpwards, to mee In hand payd, by John Sayword of yorke in behalfe of him selfe & others, do by these Presents giue, grant, sell bargane, Enfeoff & Confirme, & hereby haue given, granted, sould, barganed, Enfeoffed, & Confirmed, from mee, my heyres executors Administrators, & Assigns to the sd John Sayword his heyres executors Administrators & Assigns for euer for euer, All my soole right title & Interest which I had to ye sd Mill, & of foure acres of Land adioyneing to the Mills, vidz^t the Saw Mills at Cape Nuttacke, bee it more or less, with all that Tymber fit for sawing, pine or oake, according to a Town grant, given & granted to the sd Smith, by the Town of yorke, with all the priuiledges, Imunitys & app^{r}tenances y^{r}vnto belonging, which the sd John Smith, had, hath, or out to haue from ye sd Town, vnto the sd John Sayword of the sd Land & Tymber, to his heyres, executors, & Assignes for euer/

To haue, & to hould the sd Tract of Land, & tymber from mee my heyres & Assigns, to the sd John Sayword, his heyres & Assignes for euer, & I the sd Smith do Couenant, & agree y^t the sd Land & Tymber are free & Cleare from all Clajms, titles, Moigages, executions, & all other Intanglem^ts w^tsoeuer, & I do hereby stand bound to make good & Defend the Interest of the Premisses, from all Person or Persons w^tsouer, claimeing or p^rtending any claim from by or vnder mee, or any other by my procurement/ In witness w^rof I haue here vnto set my hand & seale, this third day of Decemb^r one thousand six hundred eighty foure 1684:

In the Presence of/   John Smith (his seale)
John Twisden/   his marke

John Smith came before mee this 3d day of Decemb^r 1684 : & owned this Instrum^t to bee his Act & Deede/

Edw : Rishworth Jus : pe :

A true Coppy of this Instrume^t transcribed out of ye originall, & therewith Compared this 5th day of May 1685 :

p Edw : Rishworth ReCor :

Know all men by these Presents, y^t I Benja : Whittney of yorke In the prouince of Mayne Taylo^r In New England, for seuerall good causes, & Considerations y^runto mee moueing (& more espetially) for a ualewable sume of Tenn pounds fourteen shillings in Current money, or M^rchañible pine boards at money price already receiued, & by mee secured, w^rwith I am fully contented, & satisfyd, by Jonathan Sayword of yorke liueing in the prouince aforesd, for ye which payment I the sd whittney do in the behalfe of myselfe & heyres, & Assignes fully acquitt, & discharge the sd Jonathan Sayword, his heyres executors & Assignes for euer ; And do hereby giue, grant, bargan, sell, aliene, Convay, & Confirme from mee Benja : Whittney my heyres, my executors, administrators, & Assignes, vnto the aforesd Jonathan Sayword his heyres executors, & Assignes, A Certen tract & Parcell of Land which I haue Improued possessed, haue bujlded a small tenement vpon, planted & liued vpon these seuerall yeares, granted, & layd out to mee by the select men of ye Town of york, Contajneing the quantity of tenn Acres as by Town grant appeareth beareing Date Septem^{br} 21 : 1680 : & also tenn Acres of Land of which I had a former promiss, & accordingly since granted : And Dated auswerable y^{r}vnto Aprill 13th 1674 : vnder the hands of the Select men of the Town of yorke, which house & houseing, Lands as bounded distinctly in the Perticular grants fiom ye Select men, hitherto I the sd Whittney haue quietly, & peaceably possessed, Jonathan Sayword aforesd is to haue & to hould, with all woods, vnderwoods pfitts, priuiledges, lybertys, Comonages, immunjtyes, with all other appurtenances y^{r}vnto belonging, or in any wise appertajning, from mee my heyres executors, administrators & Assignes vnto sd Jonathan Sayword his heyres Administrators executiors & Assignes for euer ; And y^t the sd Benja: Whitney do further couenant & promiss to & with the sd Jonathan Sayword, that ye house & Lands, & euery part & Parcell of them, are free & Cleare from all bargans, sales, Claims, titles, Interest, Dowers, & all other Incomberances w^{t}soeuer, & do hereby promiss to warrant & defend the Premisses, vidz^t the Title & Interest y^{r}of from all Person, or Persons w^{t}soeuer claimeing, or Pretending any legall Clajm y^{r}unto, from by or under mee, or in any wise by my procurement ; In testimony w^{r}of I I haue here vnto afixed my hand & seale, this Twenty fourth day of March in the Twenty seauenth yeare of o^r soueraign Lord Charles the secund of England, Scottland, France, & Ireland, King,

BOOK IV, FOL. 37.

one thousand six hundred eighty foure, eighty fiue/ 168¾:
Signed, sealed, & Deliuer̃d   Benjamen Whitney
   in the Presence of, us   his Seale (his/seale)
   John Sayword/   Jane whitney
   Mary Sayword/   her marke ◯
   the younger/   Benjamen Whittney came before mee
           this 24th of March 168¾ & owned this
           Instrument to bee his Act & Deede/
             Edw: Rishworth Jus. pe:

Jane whitney ye wife of Benja͠: Whitney came before mee this 4th of May 85: & ownd this Instrumt aboue written to bee her act & deede/   Edw: Rishworth Jus: pe:

A true Coppy of this Instrumt transcribed, & with originall Compared this 5th day of May 1685:
             p Edw: Rishworth ReCor:

     John Cossones aged eighty fiue years or there abouts, testifyeth & sayth/ That about twelue years since, that John Attwell purchased a Parcell of Land about sixty Acres more or less of Richard Bray, & payd the sayd Richd Bray for it, according to the condition & agreement, made betwixt the sd Atwell & ye sayd Bray, which sayd Land lyeth In Cascoe Bay in the Prouince of Mayne, scituate & being on the Westermost side of a Riuer there, formerly called Ryalls River, at Westquostuggo, bounded with a gutt of Water, on the west side of it, & with ye River on the East side of it, & so to runne North West vnto the Marked trees which was ye former bounds of it, & further sayth not/

     Taken vpon oath the 23th of March 168¾ before mee
             John Dauess Justs: pe:

     Henery Donell, & Richard Carter testify also to what is aboue written to bee ye treuth/ Taken vpon oath ye 24th of March 168¾ before mee   John Dauess Jus pe:

BOOK IV, FOL. 37, 38.

A true Coppy of these Depositions aboue written transcribed out of y⁰ originall & there with Compared this 25ᵗʰ day of May 1685 :

p Edw : Rishworth ReCor :

John Howleman aged about fourty eight yeares, testifyeth that y⁰ sd John yorke hath fenced in some of sayd John Attwells land that hee bought of the sd Ric : Bray & doth refuse to surrender it vp/ Taken vpon oath this 3ᵈ day of Aprill 1685 : before mee Walter Gyndall Comissioʳ/
vera Copia transcribed & Compared this 25 : May 1685 :

p Edw : Rishworth ReCor :

The testimony of William Leatherby aged about 27 yeares/ Testifyeth that hee knoweth yᵗ the Land yᵗ John yorke now liueth vpon, which lyeth in Cascoe Bay In North yarmouth now called, was once possessed by John Atwell who bought the same Land of Richard Bray Scujoʳ, & that y⁰ sd Land was possesed by the sayd Attwell, & children was borne yʳ to the sd Attwell, & there hee Inhabited till drouen out by the Heathen, & at Present sayth no more/

Taken vpon oath this 16ᵗʰ of May 1685 before mee John Dauess Depᵗʸ Presidᵗ

A true Coppy of this testimony transcribed, & with originall Compared this 25 : of May 1685 :

p Edw : Rishworth Re : Cor :

[38] Know all men by these Presents, that I Clement Swett of Cape Elizabeth ffisherman, In y⁰ Prouince of Mayne, haue barganed sould Enfeoffed & Confirmed, & by these Presents do bargan, sell, Enfeoff & Confirme unto

BOOK IV, FOL. 38.

Thomas Sparke now rescident at Cape Elizabeth, for & in Consideration of Twenty foure pounds, well & truely to mee in hand payd, before ye signeing & sealeing hereof, a tract of Land vidz^t vpland, ljing & being on Cape Elizabeth, to the valew of Twenty Acres more or less, according to the bounds y^{r}of, adioyneing to ye land of John Parrott, on ye North side of the sd Parrots land, takeing its begining neare a little Hill, w^r there is a parcell of firr trees growing, & is about sixteene poole from the sd Swetts house, & ye South West lyne nearest unto a tree marked on the foure sids, which is the bounds between ye sd Parrett & the sd Swett, & from y^t marked tree to runne into the Woods one hundred thirty too pooles on a North East & by East lyne, & from ye marked tree y^t is the bounds between John Parrett & Swett Northly, & from ye sd house of Swett to runne a West & by North lyne, sixteene pooles, & from thence to runne one hundred & twenty pooles into ye woods, on a North East & by East lyne, which is the full bounds, togeather with one single dwelling house standing & being on ye same, with all Tymber trees priuiledges, & app^{r}tenancs w^{t}souer y^{r}unto belonging; To haue & to hould the sd Tract according to ye limitts & bounds aboue expressed, to the soole & proper vss of Thom^s Sparks his heyres executors Administrators & Assignes for Euer/

And ye sd Clement Swett do for my selfe My heyres, executors & Administrators, do Couenant & grant unto Thomas Sparks his heyres, & Assignes, that I ye sd Swett do stand lawfully possessd to my own vss & behoofe of ye sd barganed Premisses, & appurtenances in a good Prfect & absolute Estate of inheritance of fee symple, & haue of my selfe full pouer & right to bargan sell & Convay away, & Assure the same, in manner & forme as aboue expressed, & y^t the sd Thomas Sparks his heyres & Assignes, & each & euery of them shall & may for euer here after peaceably & quietly haue & hould the sd barganed Premisses, with all the appurtenances, free from all dowers, Incomberances, intanglements, or Molestation w'soeuer, either from the sd Clement Swett my selfe, my heyres, executors, & Administrators, or from any Person by or from them or any of them, or of any other person or Prsons w'soeuer, Claimeing any right or Title y^runto/ In witness of ye treuth of w'soeuer is aboue, & Confirmation thereof, I the sd Clement Swett haue here vnto sett my hand & seale/ Made at Blacke Poynt In ye Town of Scarborough the 22th of May In ye yeare of our Ld 1685 : & in the first yeare of ye Reigne of our soueraigne Lord James the secund by the grace of God, King of England, Scottland, France, & Ireland, &c :

Witnesses/   Clement Swett
  Tho : Scottow/   his marke ⊗ (his seale)
  Richd Tarr   This Deed aboue acknowledged before mee
                 by Clement Swett, the day & yeare
                 aboue written/ Joshua Scottow Jus : pe :

A true Coppy of this Instrument aboue written transcribed & with the originall Compared this 27th day of May 1685 :   p Edw : Rishworth ReCor :

To all Christian people to whom these Presents may come : Know yee y^t I John Hoole of Kittery In the prouince of Mayne, for many good Causes & Considerations, mee moueing there unto, espetially in consideration of the full & iust some of fiuety pounds Ster̃lg : to mee In hand payd by Joseph Curtis of the same Town & prouince, In New England, w^rof & of euery part & Parcell y^rof, I do acquitt & discharge the sd Jos : Curtis, his heyres executors & Administrators, for euer : do by these Presents for my selfe, my heyres, executors & Administrators, absolutely giue grant bargane sell Enfeoffe & Confirme unto the aforesd Joseph Curtis a Certen Tract of Land, scituate & lijng in the Town of Kittery aforesd, & contajneing by Estimation a hundred thirty fiue Acres more or less, as It is now bounded, begining at ye west end of it at a little Cricke, neare spruse Cricke, fiuety foure poole East, halfe a poynt Southwardly, & from thence thirty one pooles North nor West, & on the North side bounded with a Cricke, & an East & West lyne, & the rest of ye sd land runns too hundred & twenty poole North and from thence a hundred & fiuety poole East, & then sixty poole South, & then is bounded on the South East, with a South west lyne a little Southwardly; W^ch tract of Land the sd Hoole bought part of Mr Thom^s Withers, & part was granted to him by the Town of Kittery, & now by the sd Jo^n Hoole sould unto ye sd Jos: Curtis, with all the appurtenances, & priuiledges y^runto belonging w^tsoeuer: To haue & to hould to him the sd Jos: Curtis, his heyres, executors, Administrators & assigns for euer, freely & Clearely exonerated & dischargd from all former Gyfts, grants, sales, Morgages, Dowers, & title of Dowers, the sd Curtis always paijng the due rents to the Cheefe Ld Proprietor; ffor confirmation w^rof, the sd John Hoole, & Elizabeth his wife, haue here unto sett their hands & seales, this twelfth day of Novemb^r Año: Dom: one thousand six hundred Eighty foure/ John Hoole (his seal)

Signed, sealed, & deliuered,   Elizabeth Hoole (her seale)
  In the Presence of us/   John Hoole, & Elizabeth his
  Henery /HB Bodg   wife, acknowledged the
    his marke/   aboue written Deed of Sale,
  John Wincoll   to bee y^r act & Deede, this
      12th day of November
      1684: before mee
      John Wincoll Jus: pe:

A true Coppy of this Instrum^t aboue written transcribed out of ye originall & y^rwith Compared this 4th of June 1685:
      p Edw: Rishworth ReCor

BOOK IV, FOL. 38, 39.

To all Christian people to whome these Presents shall come; Know yee y^t Joseph Cross of Wells yeoman, In the Prouince of Mayne In the County of yorke in New England In America, & Mary my wife sendeth greeteing/ Know yee y^t sd Joseph Cross & Mary my wife, for diuerse good Causes & Considerations mee y^runto moueing but more espetially for the unlewable some of Eighty pounds, In current & lawfull pay of New England, to mee in hand payd before the Ensealeing & deliuery of these Presents, by Franc^s Littlefejld Senjo^r of Wells yeoman In the prouince & County as abouesd, the receipt w^rof I do acknowledg, & do for my selfe, my heyres, executors, administrators, acquitt and discharge, the aboue named Fran^s Littlefejld Senio^r his heyres executors, Administrators from euery part & Parcell y^rof; Haue given, granted, & by these Presents do freely & absolutly Giue, grant, bargan, sell, aliene, Enfeoff, assigne & sett ouer & Confirme vnto Fran^s Littlefejld Senjo^r, his heyres, executors one hundred & fiuety ackers of vpland given mee by the select men of Wells, lijng between the Lott that was James Littlefeilds Senio^r, & the high way next vnto John Discoes lott, wch is in breadth thirty pooles more or less, & to runne that breadth as other lotts runne untill the one hundred & fiuety Acres of Land bee accomplished & fullfilld, & six [39] Acers of vpland more lijng vpon, or Adioyneing vnto Mr Samuell Wheelewright Senjo^r his Land, & neare to that Poynt of Land Comanly Called Crosses Poynt neare Ogunquett Riuer Falls, & eleuen Acres & halfe of Marsh bounded, too acres & a halfe vp in the Countrey more or less on the West Ogunquett River, & foure acres more or less on the East side Ogunquett River at the falls, & so down betweene the Riuer & ye vpland, unto it come to Leeft John Littlefejlds Senjo^r, his land or Marsh, & fiue Acres more or less between Mr Samell Wheelewrights Senio^r his Marsh, & Daniell Mannings Marsh, begining at the vpland, & so runne downeward to the River, with one dwelling house vpon the sayd vpland, togeather with all out houseings, tillage Land fences, Pastures, with all my right Title, & Interest I now haue, or out to haue, at the tyme of the sealeing of these Presents, In all the aforesayd houseings, Arrable Land, fences, vpland, or Meddows, with all Mines, Mineralls, Commanages, Tymber, & tymber trees, woods vnder woods profitts, priuiledges, & appurtenances, y^{r}unto belonging; To haue & to hould, all & singular the aboue granted barganed Premisses, to euery part & Parcell there of, with all my singular, & other priuiledges, and to euery part & parcell thereof unto mee belonging, with all my right Title & Interest, there of unto the sd Francis Littlefejld Senjo^r, his heyres executors Administrators, or Assignes, to his & y^r owne proper vss, benefitt & behoofe for euer: And I the sd Joseph Cross & Mary my now wife, do by these Presents Couenant & promiss, for my selfe, o^r heyres, executors & Administrators, that at and Immediately before the Insealeing of these Presents, was the true and lawfull owner of all & singular the afore barganed Premisses, and that I haue good right, & lawfull authority, in o^r own names to give grant, bargane sell, aliene, conuay, & Confirme the same as aforesd; And that the sayd Francis Littlefejld Senjo^r, his heyrs, executors, Administrators, shall & may by vertue and force of these Presents, from tyme to tyme, & at all tymes, for euer here after lawfully quietly & peaceably haue hould vss occupy, possess & Inioy the aboue granted, & barganed Premisses, with thejr appurtenances, free & Cleare, & freely and clearly discharged, acquitted of, & from all manner of former Gyfts, Grants barganes, sales, leases, Morgages, Joynters, Dowers, Judg^{ts} executions, forfiturs, troubles, Incomberances whatsoeuer, had made done, or suffered to bee done by mee Joseph Cross & Mary my wife, our heyres executors, Administrators, & Assignes, at any tyme or tyms before the sealeing & Deliuery of these Presents; And the sd Jos: Cross & Mary my wife our heyres executors Administrators, & Assignes, shall & will from tyme to tyme & at all tymes for euer hereafter warrant &

Book IV, Fol. 39.

Defend the aboue given & granted Premisses, with y^r app^rtenances, & euery part & parcell y^rof, unto ye aboue named Fran^s Littlefejld, Senjo^r his heyrs, executors, Administrators, against all, & euery Person or Persons laijng Clajme y^rto or any part there of for by or und^r us o^r heyrs executors, Admmistrators & Assignes ; In witness w^rof wee haue here unto sett o^r hands & seales, this secund day of Aprill one thousand six hundred eighty three, Annoq, Regni, Regis Charolj secundj, xxxv :   Joseph Cross (his seale)
Signed, sealed, & deliuerd,   Mary Cross (her seale)

In Presence of,   Joseph Cross & Mary his wife ap-
John Wheelewright/   peared before mee this seund day
George Pearson/   of Aprill 1683 : & owned this Instrum^t to bee y^r act & Deed, Samell Wheelewright Jus : pe :

vera Copia of this Instrum^t aboue written transcribed & with originall Compared, this 9th day of June 1685 :

p Edw : Rishworth Re : Cor :

To all christian People, to whome these Presents shall come : Know y^t Francis Littlefejld Senio^r of Wells yeoman, In the prouince of Mayn, & In the County of yorke In America sendeth Greeteing ; Know yee that Francis Littlefejld Senio^r, for diuerse good Causes & Considerations, mee y^runto Moueing, but more espetially for ye ualewable sume of Eighty pounds In Current pay of New England, to mee In hand payd before the Ensealing & deliuery of these Presents ; by my sonn In law John Elldredg of Wells yeoman, as aboue sayd, The receipt w^rof I do acknowledg, & do for my selfe my heyres, executors, Admistrators acquitt & discharge the aboue named John Elldridg, his heyres, executors, Administrators from euery part & Parcell there of ; Haue giuen, granted, And by these Presents do fully freely & absolutly giue, grant, bargan, sell, aliene, assigne

Book IV, Fol. 39.

and sett ouer, & Confirme unto John Elldridg my sonn In law, his heyres, executors, Administrators & Assignes, one hundred & fiuety Acres of vpland, with houseing there vpon, belonging, lijng In the Town shipp of Wells, butting vpon Ogunquett Riuer ffalls, next the Marsh & so runn vp into the Countrey, between the lott which was James Littlefejlds Senjo^r, and the high way next to John Driscos lott, which is in breadth Thirty pooles, more or less, & that to runn as other lotts rune untill one hundred fiuety & six Acres is compleated, & Eleauen Acres & an halfe of Marsh bounded Two Acres and halfe vp in the Countrey, on the West of Ogunquett Riuer, foure Acres more on the East side Ogunquett Riuer, at the ffalls, & so down between the Riuer & the vpland, untill It come to Leefte^t John Littlefejlds Marsh more or less, And fiue Acres between Mr Samll Wheelewright Senjo^{rs} Marsh, & Daniell Manning his Marsh, Begining at the vpland & to runne downeward to ye Riuer more or less, with all Tillidge Land with in and with out fence, pasture &c: with all my right title & Interest I now haue, or out to haue at the tyme of the sealeing, of these Presents: In all the afores^d Houseings, Arrable Land fences, Marsh vpland or Meddows: Houseing or out houseings Mines, Mineralls, Comonages, Tymber & Tymber trees, Woods, vnderwoods, profitts priuiledges, and appurtenances there vnto belonging: To haue & to hould, all and singular the aboue granted, & bargened Premisses, to euery part and parcell thereof, with all & singular & other priuiledges, to euery part or parcell there of, unto mee belonging with all my right title & Interest thereof, unto the sd John Elldridg my sonn in law, his heyres executors Administrators, to his or thejr own proper vss benefitt and behoofe for euer: And the sayd Francis Littlefejld Senio^r do by these Presents Couenant and promiss for my selfe my heyres executors Administrators & Assignes/ that at & Immediately before the Ensealeing of these Presents, was the true & lawfull owner of all & singular the afore barganed Premisses; And that I haue good right & lawfull authority in my own name to giue and grant, bargane, sell, aliene, Convay & Confirme the same as aforesayd, and the sayd John Elldridg my sonn In law, his heyres, executors, & Administrators shall & may, by vertue & force of these Presents, from him from tyme to tyme, & at all tymes for euer hereafter, lawfully quietly & peaceably, [40] Haue hould uss, Occupy, possess, & Inioy the aboue granted Premisses with thejr appurtenances free & Cleare, & freely clearely discharged, and acquitted of from all manner of former Gyfts grants barganes, sailes, leases, Morgages, Joyntures, Dowers, Judgm^{ts}, executions, forfiturs, troubles, Incomberances w^{t}soeuer, had made done, or suffered to bee done by mee, the sayd Francis Littlefejld Senjo^r, or my heyrs executors, Administrators or Assignes, at any tyme or tymes, before the sealing and deliuery of these Presents; And the sd Francis Littlefejld Senjo^r or my heyres executors, Administrators shall & will from tyme to tyme & at all tyms for euer here after warrant, & Defend the aboue giuen & granted Premisses, with ther appurtenances, & euery part & Parcell there of, vnto the aboue named John Elldridg my sonn in law, his heyres, executors Administrators, against all, & euery Person or Persons, lajjng Clayme thereto, or any part part thereof, for by or vnder mee, my heyres, executors, Administrators/ In witness wheare of, I haue here unto sett my hand & seale, this secund day of Aprill one thousand six hundred eighty three Annoq, Regni Regis Carolie Secundj xxxv:

Signed, sealed, & deliuered/ ffrancis Littlefejld Senj^{or} ($^{his}_{seale}$)

In y^e Presence of
Robert Hilton
George Pearson/

A true Coppy of this Instrument aboue written, transcribed out of the originall & there with Compared this 10th day of June 1685: p Edw: Rishworth Re: Cor

BOOK IV, FOL. 40.

Know all men by these Presents, that I Joshua Scottow of Boston, haue for & in Consideration, part of tenn pounds to mee In hand payd, & to bee payd, & part of Peter Hinxens relinquishing all Clajme from Scottows heyres or assignes, to any part of Marsh sould to him by Christopher Ellkines, or his father both of them, late of Scarbrough deceased, haue sould, & by these Presents do bargan & sell unto the sayd Peter Hinxen his heyres or Assignes, a Parcell of Marsh Land contajneing tenn Acres, more or less lijng in the sayd Scarbrough, neare pine tree Cricke, and is bounded westwardly with the Land of Richard Moore, Northerly with the Land of the late John Burren, Eastwardly with ye Land of John Lybby, Southwardly with the Cricke; The sayd barganed Premisses to haue & to hould for euer, paijng that rent due for the same unto Mr Henery Joclein or his Assigns according to its first grant, with lyberty of Passage, and to fall trees in the Swampe Joyneing unto it, for a way vnto It, I the sd Joshua Scottow do acknowledg the saile aforesayd, & do bind my selfe heyres, executors, & Administrators, to make the same good, against all Clajmes and demands what soeuer, from by or vnder mee, my heyrs executors, & Administrators, unto the sayd Peter Hinxen his heyres or Assignes/ In witness of the Premisses, I haue here vnto putt my hand & seale/ Blacke Poynt this Twenty fourth day of August: 1669:

Witness John   Joshua Scottow ($_\text{seale}^\text{his}$)
ffrancis Robinson

    Mr Joshua Scottow acknowledged this aboue written to bee his Act & Deed to Peter Hinkeson this 15th of June: 1671: before mee

          Francis Neale Assotiate/

A true Coppy of this Instrume^t aboue written transcribed, & with the Originall Compared this 12th of June 1685:

      p Edw: Rishworth ReCor:

Book IV, Fol. 40.

It is also agreed that it shall bee lawfull for ye sd Scottow his heyres or Assignes at all tymes to pass & repass throug any part of the sd Land with horse cart or slead except through his garden.

This Indenture made the first day of August 1668 : & In the 20th yeare of ye Reign of our Soueraign Lord Charles the secund, between Joshua Scottow of Boston on the one part, & Peter Hinkeson of Blacke Poynt ffisherman, on the other part Witnesseth, that ye sayd Josh · Scottow for him selfe, heyres, executors, & Administrators for in & vnder the Conditions & lymitations here vnder expressed, doth giue, grant, & Confirme, vnto the sayd Peter Hinkeson & his heyres for euer, Twenty three Acres of vpland lijng & being in blacke Poynt, & bounded on the West with Christipr Peckitts, & John Machannys line, on the North with a swampe, & also on the South with a swamp belonging to the sd Scottow, according to the runeing of Peter Hinkesons fence, unto a birch tree, which bounds Willia͞: Battene & him selfe on the East unto a Maple Tree marked on foure sides, & from thence to an ould pine Marked on 4 sides In ye swampe, seaven rodds from a Whitte Oake belonging to John Mechanny, & being his bounds prouided it runnes not vpon William Shelldens lyne : To haue & to hould, the sd twenty three Acres, of & fro͞ the sd Scottow, his heyres or Assignes, paijng his too days worke yearely for euer, at such tyme or tymes, as by the sd Scottow his heyres Or Assigns It shall bee lawfully demanded & for not Performance of the same It shall bee lawfull for the sd Scottow his heyres or Assignes, to Enter & distrajne vpon the Premisses, & the distress so taken to carry away & apprise by two sworne men, & pay him him selfe his heyres or Assignes the sd rent & Charges, valewing each day distrained for at three shillings money, & to deliuer the ouerplus of the distress unto ye owner, & In case that the sd Land shall bee discerted or left unocupyd, so as there shall not at any tyme bee found sufficient quicke stocke or house hould Implemts to satisfy ye rent & charge of distreining, that this Grant shall bee utterly uoyd, to all intents, & purposes w^{t}soeuer, any thing in this Deed expressed Notwithstanding; And It shall bee lawfull for the sd Scottow his heyres & Assignes, with out any sujte at law to possess him selfe, or them selues y^{r}of prouided it bee not ouer any corne growing & standing vpon the same: It is further agreed y^t It shall not bee lawfull for the sd Peter Hinkeson his heyres, executors, or Administrators, directly or Indirectly to cutt Carry away of any tree tymber or wood, except from the sd Twenty three Acres, not to put out or suffer to feede or grazse any sort of Cattle w^{t}soeuer, vpon any part of the sd Scottows Pattent: Except vpon the sd twenty three Acres with out leaue, first had or obtained from the sd Scottow, his heyres or assignes, vpon the pœnulty of pajjng of tenn tenn shillings in money for euery tree so fallne, cutt or caryed off, & foure shillings in money for euery head of Cattle, which shall bee found In Scottows Land, contrary to this agreement/ The sd pœnaltys to bee leauied by distress as aboue mentioned; finally y^t the sd Peter Hinkeson his heyres executors or administrators, shall not sell or let ye sd land, or any part y^{r}of, or any building y^t is or may bee erected vpon any part of the same, to any Person or Persons, but such as the sd Scottow his heyres or Assignes, shall allow of by writeing, under y^r hand vpon pœnulty of forfiting the sd Land, & building y^{r}vpon unto ye sd Scottow, his heyres or Assigns according to the true Intent & full purport of ye forfiture expressed in the secund Clawse aboue relateing to quicke stocke or househould Implem^{ts} not being found to satisfy rent; In Confirmation of all & euery of the aboue given & granted Premisses, under or vpon the seuerall Conditions & lymitations In this Deed declared, the partys aboue mentioned haue signed & sealed Interchangeably/

Read Signed sealed & deliuered,   Joshua Scottow (his scale)

   9th August Witness/
      1676.

In Presence of us, the subscribers Prudence Howell/

BOOK IV, FOL. 40, 41.

It being by the Consent of both partys Antedated, y^r rent ruñiug from y^t tyme/ It is also agreed y^t the sd Peter hath lyberty to cut down any of the Tymber trees or wood growing or being on the sd land for building, fireing fenceing or plow stuffe, or also vpon any swampe belonging to sd Scottow, In case y^r bee not tymber &c: left vpon ye sd Land for bujlding, & also y^t hee shall haue runne In ye Wast Land for tenn head of his own Cattle/

This Instrume^t was owned before mee by Capt Joshua Scottow to bee his act & Deede unto Peter Hincson this 9th of August: 1676:

Henery Jocelin, Comissio^r/

vera Copia of this Instrum^t aboue written transcribed out of ye originall & y^{r}with Compared this 12th of June 1685:

p Edw: Rishworth ReCor:

[41] Know all men by these Presents, that I Elizabeth seely of Kittery, In the County of yorke shyre, & In Massatusetts Coloney in New England alias Prouince of Mayne, Administratrix to the Estate of my late husband deceased William Seely, the one & twenteth of November 1671: for & in Consideration of Eleauen pounds In Current pay of New England, already receiued of William Screuen of the Towne aforesd, where with I do acknowledg my selfe fully satisfyd, & payd. & do here by exonerate acquitt & discharge, the sayd William Screuene of Euery part and Percell thereof· Haue Given granted, barganed sould Enfeoffed, and Confirmed, And do by these Presents for my selfe my heyres, executors and administrators, giue grant bargan sell Enfeoff & Confirme unto the aforesayd William Screuen one Messuage or tenement scituate and being in the Town of Kittery aforesd, and lijng against spruse Cricke, on the West side there off, & Comanly known by the name

Book IV, Fol. 41.

of Carles Poynt, Contajneing tenn Acres by Measure more or less, as It is bounded on the East, With the Land of Mis Mary Cutt, the South & West bounded with the aforesayd Spruse Cricke, And bounded on the North with other land belonging to mee, the sayd Elizabeth Seely/ the aforesayd tenn Acres of Land was bought of Ric: Carle of Kittery, as by his Deede beareing date the first day of March one thousand six sixty six, more amply appeareth, & now by mee the sd Elizabeth Seely sould unto the aforesayd William Screuen: To haue & to hould, all the aboue barganed Premisses, with all & singular the appurtenances, & priuiledges there to belonging, or in any wise app^{r}tajneing to him the sayd William Screuen his heyrs & Assignes for euer, the same to warrant & Defend against all Persons whatsoeuer, making any lawfull Clajme y^{r}to, or to any part or Parcell there of, by from or vnder me my heyres executors Administrators, or Assignes/ And for Confirmation of y^e treuth hereof I the aforesayd Elizabeth Seely haue sett too my hand & seale this fiueteenth day of November Anno Dom͞: one thousand six hundred seauenty & three/

Signed sealed & Deliuered/   Elizabeth Seely ($_{Sigill}^{locus}$)

  In the Presence of us   The aboue written Elizabeth Seely,
  Saraih Foxwell/   did acknowledg the aboue writ-
  John Wincoll/   ten Deed of Saile, to bee her
                                  free act & Deede, the 15th day
                                  of Novemb^r one thousand six
                                  hundred seauenty three, before
                                  mee John Wincoll Assotiate/

vera Copia, of this Instrum^t aboue written transcribed out of ye originall, & y^{r}with Compared this 15th day of June
1685:   p Edw: Rishworth ReCor:

BOOK IV, FOL. 41.

Thomas Kemble aged sixty three yeares or y'abouts, testifyeth, that about too & Twenty yeares agone hee being at ye house of Maj^or Nicho^s Shapleigh now deceased, was desired by the sd Maj^or Shapleigh to draw his will which this Deponent did then draw according to his Instructions, & in that Will hee did will & bequeath ye one halfe of all his Estate both reall & Personall to his Cozen John Shapleigh & ye other halfe to his wife Mis Aylce Shapleigh, which shee was to Inioy dureing ye tearme of her naturall life: And y^n ye sd John Shapleigh was to possess & Inioy ye whoole of the sd Estate, to him his heyres, & Assignes for euer; And this Deponent further testifyeth y^t hee hath seuerall tyms since, heard ye sd Maj^or Shapleigh say, that hee did intend his Cosson John Shapleigh should bee heyre to his whoole Estate, after his wifes decease: Taken vpon oath this 2: of Octob^r 1684: before Walter Barefoote Cheife Just^s

A true Coppy transcribed & with originall Compar'd this 18th June: 1685: p Edw: Rishworth ReCor:

Francis Smale Senjo^r aged fiuety six yeares or y^r abouts, testifyeth & Sayth/

That being in Company with Maj^or Nicholas Shapleigh, with in foure or fiue yeares before his decease, I this Deponent did then heare the aboue written, Nicho^s Shapleigh say, that hee had brought his Cosson John Shapleigh from his mother in England, & promised her, y^t If hee had no Child of his own, that John Shapleigh should bee the heyre to his whoole Estate, & If hee should haue any Children of his own y^t John Shapleigh aforesd, should haue as good a share in his Estate as any of them, & y^t hee should haue halfe of his Estate at his death, & his own wife Alice Shapleigh should haue ye other halfe dureing her naturall life, & after

BOOK IV, FOL. 41.

her death to bee & remajne to the sd John Shapleigh & his heyres for euer/

Prouince of Mayc: Taken vpon oath this 3ᵈ of Aprill 1685 before mee John Dauess Depᵗʸ Pʳsident

veɪa Copia of yᵉ testimony aboue written transcribed & Compared, this 18ᵗʰ day of June 1685:

p Edw: Rishworth ReCor:

Boston the 17ᵗʰ of 6: 1681:

ffor yᵉ furtherance of the settlement & planting of the Inhabitants of North yarmouth in Caso, Mr Geo: Pearson, Leefᵗ Anthony Brackett, & Geo: Ingerson Senjoʳ are appoynted a Comittee to Intertajne, & allow of inhabitants, & to grant such allotments, as shall bee meete for yʳ Incoragemᵗ: & meete accomodation being reserued for yᵉ settleing of a minister; Alsoe they are ordered so to lay out yᵉ Towne, yᵗ at least eighty familys may bee accommodated/

p Thomas Danforth Prsident

Memorand: of the prouince of Mayne/

This abouesd Committee are hereby desired & ordered, to lay out unto Isaac Cossons such a tract of Land, for his settlement within the abouesd Townshipp as may bee a meete accomodation, hee or his sonn, Ingageing to come & dwell yʳ, & to accomodate the inhabitants, by yᵉ worke of his Trade/ 17:6:81:   T: D:

vera Copia of this aboue written transcribed out of yᵉ originall & yʳwith Compared this 20ᵗʰ day of June 1685:

p Edw: Rishworth Re: Cor:

BOOK IV, FOL. 41, 42.

New Hampshire/
The testimony of Peter Coffine aged 54 yeares or y^r abouts/ Testifyeth & Sayth, that about seauen years past hee being in bed with Majo^r Nicho^s Shapleigh of Kittery now deceased, In the house of Arther Beñicke, at Lamprill River, did then & there heare Majo^r Nichol^s Shapleigh say that his kinesman John Shapleigh should bee his heyre, & that hee would giue unto him his sd kinesman John Shapleigh, the one halfe of his Estate at his decease, & after his wifes decease, hee should haue ye other halfe, In Consideration y^t hee was his brothers sonn, & that hee had liued with him all his dayes, from his Childhood, & that hee brought him from his Mother In England/

Peter Coffine/
Taken vpon oath this 19th of March 1684: before mee
Ric: Chamberlajn Jus: pe:
vera Copia transcribed, & with ye originall Compared this 23th of June 1685: p Edw: Rishworth ReCor:

Prouince of Mayn

The testimony of John Smyth Senjo^r aged about 73 yeares/ This Deponent maketh oath y^t about 40 yeares agone, being a Marshall under Mr Geo: Cleaues, who then carried on Colonell Rigbys authority in this Prouince, doth uery well remember Mr Robert Jordan had an Attatchment grãted vnder that authority, to attatch y^t Necke of Land at Saco, as ye Estate of [42] Mr Rich̃d Vines, for a debt due from him to sd Jordan, who recouered a Judgment of Court against him to the ualew of Twenty pounds or more as fare as I do remember between y^t some, & Thyrty pounds, vpon which Judgment execution was granted to mee as Marshall, namely this Deponent: who leuied the same vpon sd Necke of Land, & deliuered it to

BOOK IV, FOL. 42.

Mr Jordan as satisfaction for his sd debt/ & further sayth not/ Dated June 23 : 1685 :
 Taken vpon oath this 23 : June 1685 : before mee
      Edw : Rishworth Jus : pe :
A tiue Coppy of this testimony transcribed, & with originall Compared this 23th of June 1685 :
      p Edw : Rishworth ReCor :

 To all People, to whome this Present Deede of Sale shall come/ John Gifford of Boston In New England M^rchant & Margerett his wife, Know yce that John Giffard & Margerett his wife for & in Consideration of the sume of Sixty pounds, current money of New England uidz^t part y^rof to them in hand payd, before the Ensealeing & deliuery of these Presents, & part thereof secured In law to bee payd, by John Sargeant of Winter Harbour with in the prouince of Mayne in New England abouesd fisherman, where with they do thereby acknowledg them selues to bee fully satisfyd, & Contented, & y^rof and of euery part thereof, do acquit exonerate & discharge, the sd John Sargeant his heyrs executors, & Administrators for euer by these Presents/ Haue and do hereby fully freely Clearely, & absolutly giue, grant, bargan, Sell aliene Enfeoffe, & Confirme unto him the sd John Sargeant his heyres & Assigns for euer, a peece or Prcell of Land scituate, lijng & being with in the Townshipp of Sacoe, & Prouince of Mayne aforesd, Contayning by estimation Thirty Acres, bee the same more or less, being butted & bounded on the North East, with the Land of Thomas Williams, on the South West, with the Land of George Pearson, on the North West with the Coman Land, & on the South East with Winter Harbour aforesd ; also another Tract or parcell of Land to say vpland, being thirty Acres more or less, lijng in Sacoe aforesd, being but-

BOOK IV, FOL. 42.

ted & bounded on the North East, with the abouesd peece of Land on the South West, with a Cricke y^t goes to & with the land of the sd John Sargeant on the North West with the coman land, & on ye South East with Winter Harbour: with Six Acres of Meddow more or less, being butted with Robert Booths Mill, & a Cricke Northward, with ye Marsh land of Ralph Trustrums South West; Togeather with all houses edifisces, buildings trees, fences, woods, vnderwoods, ways, easements, profitts priuiledges, rights, Comoditys, & appurtenances, whatsoeuer to the sd Parcells of Land or either of them belonging, or in any kind appertajneing, or there with now ussed, occupyed or Inioyed, with all Deeds & euidences, & writeings touching or Concerneing the Premises; To haue & to hould all the aboue granted Premisses, with y^r appurtenances & euery part thereof, unto the sd John Sargeant his heyres & Assignes for euer, & ye sd John Giffard & Margerett his wife for y^{m}selues y^r heyres executors & Administrators do hereby Coucnant promiss & grant too & with the sayd John Sargeant, his heyres & Assigns in manner & forme following, that is to say, that at the tyme of then Ensealeing, & deliuery of these Presents, that they are the true soole & lawfull owners, of all the afore barganed Premisses, & are lawfully Seized of & in the same, & euery part y^{r}of In there own proper right, of a good Perfect and absolute state of inhæritance in fee symple, with out any manner of Condition reuersion or lymitation whatsoeuer, so as to alter, Change to defeate or make uoyd the same, and haue in them selues full pouer good right & lawfull authority to grant sell, conuay and Assure the same as abouesd, & that the sayd John Sargeant his heyres and Assigns shall & may, by force and uertue of these Presents, from tyme to tyme and at all tymes for euer hereafter, quietly, lawfully, & peaceably haue hould vss occupy possess & inioy the aboue granted Premisses, with there appurtenances, Free and Clearly acquitted & discharged of, and from all manner of former & other gifts grants bargans, sales, leases, Morgages, Joyntures, dowers, Judgm^{ts} executions entails forfitures, & of & from all other titles troubles Charges & Incumberances whatsoeuer, had made Comitted, done or suffered to bee done by them the sd John Giffard and Margeret his wife, or either of them or either of thejr heyrs, or Assigns, at any tyme or tyms, before the Ensealeing here of: And the sd bargained Premisses and euery part y^{r}of, unto him the sayd John Sargeant, his heyres & Assigns against them selues thejr heyrs, executors, & Administrators, & euery of them, & against all & euery other Person, & Persons w^{t}souer any ways lawfully Claimeing or demanding the same, or any part y^{r}of, in by from or under them, or either, or any of them, shall & will warrant & for euer Defend by these Presents; In Witness w^{r}of the sayd John Giffard & Margerett his wife, haue here unto sett y^r hands & Seales the Nineteenth day of May Anno: Dom: one thousand six hundred eighty fiue, Annoq, Rx Regnis Jacobj secundi Angliæ &c: primo/   John Giffard ($^{locus}_{sigilli}$)

Signed, sealed & Deliuered   Mr John Giffard acknowledged
  In Presence of us/   this Instrument to bee his act
  George Turfrey/   & Deede/ Boston May 19th
  George Pearson/   Anno Dom: 1685: before
  Eliazer Moody/   Samuell Nowell Assistant

    Mr George Turfrey as a witness to this Instrum^t doth Attest vpon his oath, that this is ye Act & Deede of John Giffard to John Sargeant Taken before mee this 25th of June Edw: Rishworth Jus: pe:

A true Coppy of this Instrum^t aboue written transcribed, & with the Originall Compared this 2: day of July 1685:
    p Edw: Rishworth ReCor:

BOOK IV, FOL. 42, 43.

The testimony of John Miller aged 45 years, testifys as followeth, yt wras there was a bill given under the hand of Capt Francis Champernown, to Mr Walter Barefoote to the iust some of fourty pounds, & from the sd Barefoote assignd ouer unto Mr Geo: Pearson of Boston, & from the sd pearson assign'd ouer to ye Deponent; Which bill of fourty pounds was fully satisfyd & payd by sd Capt Frans Champernoown unto mee ye Deponent: the reason of this my deposition is because yt the sd Capt Champernoown demands his bill being satisfyd, which bill belongs to him haueing made full satisfaction, which bill is now not to bee found, but by Information is in the hands of Mr George Pearson, & for Preuenting of future Damage the Deponent testifys ye uerity aboue/ Taken vpon oath before mee 26: June 1685: Edw: Tyng Jus: pe:

vera Copia Compared & transcribed July 2: 85:

p Edw Rishworth Re: Cor:

yorke June 25th 1685:

Formerly receiued of Capt Frans Champernoown the full & iust some of Thirty six pounds being towards the satisfaction & payment of a bill giuen by Capt Champernoown to Mr Walter Barefoote, & signed to Mr George Pearson from sd Barefoote, & from the sd Pearson to mee [43] the which some of Thirty six pounds, I receiued by uertue of the Assignemt to mee from Pearson, as witness my hand this 25th of June as aboue/

Testes/   The Marke of
            John ✠ Miller

John Miller came before mee this 25th of June, & owned the aforesd some was receiued by him which was thirty six 36: pounds/   Edw: Tyng Jus: pe:

vera Copia of ye receipt transcribed & Compared ye 2: of July 1685:   p Edw:

The Deposition of George Ingersall aged, aged Sixty seauen years or there abouts/

Testifyeth, & Sayth, that about Twenty eight years since Robert Corben Cleared a parcell of y^t Meddow, commanly Called Geo: Lewises March, about eight or tenn Acres or there abouts at the North end of the sd Marsh bounded as followeth, vidiz^t On the West side with a little spruse swamp, & so running ouer ye Marsh East, to a little small Coue where they did vsually stocke there hay : And sayd Corben quietly possessed the sayd Marsh, till hee was Slayne by ye Indeans In ye late warr, & further sayth not/

Taken vpon oath this 24th of June 1685 : before mee

Edw : Tyng, Jus : pe :

vera Copia transcribed & Compared this 2 : July 1685 :

p Edw : Rishworth Re : Cor :

The Deposition of Henery Watts aged 71 yeares/

Sworne sayth, y^t John Mills deceased, hath for thirty yeares since, or y^r abouts possessed by moueing a Parcell of Marsh y^t lyeth on both sides of a River, going vp toward Nonesuch, so fare as the dead roote of a tree lijng in a Cricke y^t usually was the path going toward None such, & adioyneing to ye Meddow Mr Robert Jordan Claimed, & so down y^t Riuer to ye Clay pitt, & did see the sd Mills Cutt sundrey years hay in that Marsh, on both sides ye Riuer, & did then w^n hee gaue in a list of his Estate putt in one hundred Acres, for the Town rate as by a list this Deponent still hath/ & further sayth not/

Taken vpon oath this 29th of June 1675 : before mee George Munioy Asso^{te}

A true Coppy transcribed & with originall Compared this 4th July 1685 :   p Edw : Rishworth ReCor :

Book IV, Fol. 43.

The Deposition of John Howell aged 48 years/
Sworne Sayth y^t John Mills deceased, hath for thirty yeares since or y^{r}abouts possessed by Mowing a Parcell of Marsh, y^t lyeth on both sids of a Riuer y^t goeth vp towards Nonesuch, so fare as a deed roote of a tree lijng in a Cricke y^t usually was the path going towards Nonesuch, & adioyneing to ye Meddow Mr Robert Jordan Clajmed, & so down y^t riuer to the Clay pitt, & did see the sd Mills cutt sundrey years hay In that Marsh on both sids of y^t Riuer/ this Deponent sayth, & further sayth not/ Sworne this 13 : July 1681 : before mee Bartholmew Gydney Assista^t

vera Copia transcribed & Compared wth originall ye 4th July 85 : p Edw : Rishworth ReCor :

The Deposition of William Burrage aged 33 years or y^r abouts, Sworne Sayth y^t hee did heare Anthony lybby say y^t hee did fetch hay with Connows out of Jo^n Mills his Marsh, y^t was given to Thomas Bickeford by the Town : & Jo^n Mills did forewarne Anthony Libby for cutting hay in his Marsh, Illegally, & further sayth not/ Taken vpon oath ye 25th July 1681 : before mee Walter Gyndall Comisso^r

vera Copia transcribed & Compayred this 4th July 1685 :
p Edw : Rishworth ReCor :

The Deposition of George Taylo^r aged 70 years or y^{r}abouts, being sworne sayth y^t hee heard Anthony Libby say, y^t hee did fetch hay with Connows out of John Mills his Marsh y^t was given to Thomas Bickeford, by ye Towne, & John Mills did forewarne Anthony Libby of Cutting hay in his Marsh illegally/ & further sayth not/

Taken vpon oath this 25th of July 1681 : before mee
Walter Gyndall Comissio^r

vera Copia transcribed & Compard ye 4th July 1685 :
Edw : Rishworth ReCor :

Book IV, Fol. 43.

Edw: Rishworth in behalfe of Mis Katterine Nanny, alias Nayler, executrix to ye Estate of her former husband, Mr Robert Nanny Deceased, Entereth Cawtion to saue harmeless the Interest of a poynt or Parcell of Land, Commanly called by name Mr Gorges Poynt lijng in yorke Prouince of Mayne, which Land was granted according to a Judgm^t of Court, beareing date October 18th 1647: by extent to ye sd Nanny, for a debt due to him from ye Lord Proprietor of Elueaven pounds Sterl̄ig; & deliuered into the possession of Edw: Rishworth in sd Nannys behalfe, wch sd Rishworth Inioyd some years; Namely the sd land taken from him & Detajned by Jere: Mowlton, ye right w^rof was afterwards restored to him by the Court of pleas May 30: 1682: & vpon an appeale, at ye next Court of appeals following, Thom^s Damforth Esqr, then President of y^t Court on y^t tryall Cast the sd Rishworth & tooke away y^t land from him, & sould It to sd Mowlton for Twenty pounds in siluer, ye halfe of wch money hee promised y^n to sd Rishworth, to Issue y^t difference, but now refuseth to do it, either to let the sd Katterine Nanny haue ye Land or satisfaction for it/
Entred into ye ReCords July 25: 1685:

•   p Edw. Rishworth Re: Cor:

To all Christian people to whome this Present Deede of Sale shall Come/ William Hilton of yorke Senjo^r In the prouince of Mayne, Sendeth greeteing; Now know yee y^t the sd I William Hilton for sundrey good Causes mee moueing y^runto, haue given & granted, & by these Presents do giue & grant to Tymothy Yeales of ye abouesd yorke in ye abouesd prouince, ye one halfe part or Mocity of a Tract of Land lijng on ye westermost side of yorke Riuer, & formerly called by the name of Inglebys Lott, Contajneing one hundred Acres bee it more or less, bounded & being by the Land of Andrew Eueret, on the North West, & by ye land of Mr Godfreys formerly on the South East, & also on the abouesd River to the North East, as also the halfe part of a peece of sault Marsh or Meddow to y̅e ualew of three Acres be It more or less, formerly called Inglesbys Meddow, lijng & being on the River of yorke, & neare y̅e being or habitation of Micū with all y̅e priuiledges & appurtenances y̅r̅to belonging, both of vpland & Meddow: The sayd Tract of Land & Meddow to haue & to hould, to him y̅e sd Yeales, his heyres, executors Administrators & Assignes, for euer, promissing, & couenanting for my selfe, heyres, executors Administrators & assignes, unto the sd yeales his heyres, executors, administrators & Assigns y̅t I am the true owner & proprietor of the abouesd Premisses, & y̅t I haue in my selfe full pouer, good right & lawfull authority, the aboue named Premisses to giue, grant aline & dispose, & y̅t y̅e sd yeales may y̅e same hould Occupy, uss & possess as his own proper right & Inheaṙitance of fee symple, with out y̅e let suite deniall or hinderance of any Person or Persons w̅t̅soeuer, laijng claime to all or any part of y̅e abouesd Premises from by or vnder mee/ further promissing & Ingageing for my selfe, heyres, & Assignes, to ye sd Yles his heyres, executors, & Administrators, y̅t the sd Land, & Meddow is free, & Cleare, & freely & clearely acquitted from all other & former Gifts, grants, sailes, Deeds, Morgages, arrests Attchments, Judgmts, Joyntures pouer of thirds, seizures, executions or any incomberances w̅t̅soeuer, & that I will for my selfe, heyrs, executors, & Assignes for euer, from tyme to tyme, & at all tymes against any Person or Prsons w̅t̅soeuer, claijng any iust Claime y̅r̅unto, & y̅t I will for further ratification of y̅e Premisses abouesd, do any act or Acts y̅t may bee needfull, or necessary, or y̅t law requireth, as acknowledgm̅t of Which may tend unto & bee for y̅e better cleareing of y̅e sd title/ In witness here of I haue here unto put my hand, & afixed my seale, this 18th

Book IV, Fol. 43, 44.

day of May 1682 : Annoq̨ Regni Regis Charoli Secundj xxxv/

signum

Signed Sealed, & Deliuered In Presence of,

William ◯ Hilton (locus sigilli)

William Delton
    signum/
Hester ℘ℋ Roanes

December 19th : 1682 :
William Hilton came before mee & acknowledged this Instrumet of Sale to bee his Act & Deed/
    John Dauess Jus : pe :

A true Coppy of this Instrume' aboue written, transcribed, & with the Originall Compared this 18th day of August 1685 :   p Edw : Rishworth Re : Cor :

Know all men by these Presents yt I Arther Wormestall of winter Harbour alias Sacoe In New England Prouince of Mayne with ye Consent of my wife Susanna Wormestall for diuerse good Causes, & Considerations here unto mee moueing, & more espetially for Twenty pounds in hand already payd, do giue, grant, sell, Enfeoffe & Confirme, [44] & by this Present deede of sale, hath given, granted, sould Enfeoffed, & Confirmed vnto John Abbett of the sd winter Harbour, alias Sacoe, a Certen Parcell of Land & sault marsh as followeth, vidzt to say fourty Acres of vpland, & six acres of sault Marsh, thirteen acres & an halfe of vpland, lijng neare the water side, next the house of sd Abbett, where in now hee dwelleth, & twenty six Acres & an halfe of vpland Adioyñ to Thomas Williams on the North side, being bounded with a great red oake tree, on ye South side Marked foure square, & from thence to runn vpon a West South west lyne eighty pooles to a red oake tree marked foure square, & from thence fiuety three pooles, North north West being his breadth a loft, & so down East North East, to a red oake tree, so yt it is to bee eighty pooles In length, & fiuety three pools in breadth, & for ye aforesd Six Acres

BOOK IV, FOL. 44.

of sault marsh hee is to haue too Acers of Marsh, at Winter Harbour, alias Sacoe, Mowable Marsh, which was formerly Thomas Williams, & foure Acres of sault Marsh at the little River, neare that house Richd Randall now liueth in, all which Parcells of vpland, & Marsh the sd John Abbett shall hereby haue hould with all the appurtenances & primiledges y^{r}unto belonging, to him his heyres, executors, Administrators or Assignes for euer, from mee the sd Arther Wormestall, my heyr. executors, Administrators or assignes for euermore, with out any disturbance or Molestation, w'soeuer, from mee my heyres, executors, Administrators, or assignes: And further more I the sd Arther Wormestall do warrant the sd vpland & Marsh to bee free of all Incomberances w'soeuer, the sd Abbett is to allow an high way if in case Neede do require/ In witness w^{r}of ye sayd Arther Wormestall, hath sett his hand & seale, in the behalfe of him selfe his heyres, executors, Administrators or Assignes, this Twenty third day of Septemb^r 1681:

Signed, sealed & deliuered,   The marke of Arther
  In Presence of us/   Wormestall (his seale)
  Abra: Preble/   The marke of Susanna (her seale)
  Edw: Sargent/   Wormestall
  John Penwill/

Arther Wormestall, & Susanna Wormestall came before mee this 23th day of September 1681: & acknowledged this Instrument of writeing to bee y^r Act & Deede/   John Wincoll Jus: pe:

A true Coppy of this Instrument, transcribed of ye Originall & there with Compard this first day of Septemb^r 1685:

p Edw: Rishworth ReCor:

BOOK IV, FOL. 44.

Know all men by these Presents, y^t Dominicus Jordan of Spurwinke In the Town of Falmouth, & prouince of Mayne, for & in Consideration of Eleauen pounds, & fiue shillings Sterling in hand payd to mee by John Sargeant, of Sacoe in the Prouince aforesd, In the behalfe of his sonn Edward Sargeant of y^t Town afore sayd, the receipt w^{r}of I the sd Dominicus Jordan do acknowledg, & am y^{r}with fully Content & satisfyd, & do hereby acquitt & discharge the sd Edw : Sargeant of euery part & Parcell therof : And do by these Presents with Consent of Hannah my wife & Dauid Trustrum her brother, Giue, grant, bargane, sell, Enfeoff & Confirme, vnto the aforesd Edw : Sargeant, a Certen house with vpland & Marsh belonging to it & lijng in the Town of Sacoe, which house & vpland lyeth between ye Land of ye late Ralph Trustrum, & John Sargeant aforesd, & the Marsh being fiue Acres is bounded & layd out between Robert Booths & Majo^r Pendletons Marsh, neare ye little River, & It was formerly the plantation of Richd Randall, & by seuerall sales & gyfts lawfully descended to the propriety of mee, the sd Dominicus Jordan, & now by mee vpon the Considerations aforesd, sould unto the abouesd Edw : Sargeant ; to Haue & to hould all ye aboue barganed Premisses, with all ye appurtenances, & priuiledges y^{r}to belonging, or appertajneing, to him the sd Edw : Sargeant, his heyres, executors, Administrators or or Assigns for euer, fully & Clearely exonerated, & discharged from & all manner of former gifts, grants, barganes, sales, Morgages, or any other Incomberance w^{t}soeuer, done or suffered to bee done by mee the sd Dominicus Jordan or any other Person or Persons w^{t}soeuer, by from or under mee, & for Confirmation of y^e Premisses, I the aforesd Dominicus Jordan with Hannah my wife, & Dauid Trustrum aforesd, haue hereto sett o^r hands &

Book IV, Fol. 44.

seales this seventeenth day of Octob{r} 1684 : In y{e} yeare of o{r} Ld one thousand six hundred eighty foure/

Signed sealed & Deliuered, Dominicus Jordan/ ($^{his}_{seale}$)
  in the Presence of us/ Hannah Jordan ($^{her}_{seale}$)
Jonathan Lamberd/ Dauid Trustrum ($^{his}_{seale}$)
John Wincoll/ his Marke 𐌕

    Dominicus Jordan, Hannah Jordan, & Dauid Trustrum, acknowledged the aboue written Deed of sale, to bee y{r} free Act & Deede, this 17{th} day of Octob{r} 1684 : before mee John Wincoll Jus : of pe :
A true Coppy of this bill of Sale transcribed out of the originall & y{r} Compared y{s} secund day of Septemb{r} 1685 :

        p Edw : Rishworth Re : Cor :

    To all to whome these Presents shall come/ I Richd Bray husbandman, Inhabitant in Cascoe In New England, send greeting &c : Know yee y{t} I the sd Richard Bray, for & in Consideration of the sume of Eleaven pounds, good & lawfull money of New England to mee In hand payd, by John Attwell fisherman, & Inhabitant of Casco, In New England before y{e} Ensealeing & deliuery hereof, the receipt w{r}of I the sd Richard Bray do hereby acknowledg, & my selfe y{r}with to bee fully satisfyd, haue for my selfe, my heyres executors, Administrators & Assignes, given, granted, bargaued, sould, deliuered & Confirmed, & by these Presents, do fully freely & absolutely giue, grant, bargan sell deliuer & Confirme, vnto the sd John Attwell his heyres, executors, Administrators & Assignes, a Certen Parcell or tract of Land Contajneing sixty Acres, bee It more or less which Land lyeth in Casco Bay, In the Prouince of Mayne scituate & being on the Westermost side of a River there, formerly called Ryalls Riuer, at Westgostuggoe bounded with a Gutt, of water on the West side of it, & with y{e} river on the East side of it, & so to runn North West vnto y{e} Marked trees,

Joyneing vpon Thomas Maynes, togeather with all the woods, vnderwoods, priuiledges & appurtenances, unto y° sd land belonging, or in any wise appertajneing; To haue & to hould the sd Tract & parcell of land & Premisses, hereby barganed & sould vnto the sd John Atwell his heyres executors, Administratois & assignes, as his & there own proper goods, & estate for euer, & to his & thejr own proper vss, & behoofe for euermore/ & I the sd Richd Bray for my selfe, my executors, & Administrators & euery of them, do Couenant promiss & grant, to & with John Attwell, his executors, administrators & Assignes by these Presents, that I Richd Bray on the day of the date here of, & at the tyme of y° Ensealeing & Deliuery hereof, haue in my selfe full pouer & good right & lawfull authority to give, grant, bargane, Sell deliuer & Confirme the sd Tract or Parcell of land, & Premisses, hereby barganed, & sould vnto the sayd John Attwell his executors, administrators & Assignes for euermore, in manner & forme aforesd, & at the sd John Attwell his executors, administrators or Assignes or any of them shall & lawfully may, from tyme to tyme, & at all tymes hereafter peaceably & quietly haue hould, & inioy the sd Tract or Parcell of sixty acres, bee It more or less, & Premisses hereby barganed, & sould with out any manner of lett suite trouble euiction, molestation, disturbance, Challenge, deniall & demand w'soeuer, of or by mee Richd Bray, my executors, Administrators, & Assignes, or any of [**45**] them, or of or by any other Person, or Persons w'soeuer, lawfully Clajmeing or to Clajme, from by or under mee, my act or title/ In witness where of I haue here unto put my hand & seale this fiueteenth day of August one thousand six hundred eighty fiue: In the yeare of o' Lord 1685:

Sealed & deliuered   The marke of
  In y° Presence of
   Thomas Pajne   Richard Bray (his seale)
    marke/
   Joseph Weare/   Richard Bray came before mee
          the 15th of August 1685 &

Book IV, Fol. 45.

      owned the abouesd Instrum[t] to
      bee his Act & Deede/
      John Dauess Dep[ty] President
vera Copia of this Instrument aboue written, transcribed
out out of the originall & y[r]with Compared this 5[th] day of
Septe[br] 1685 :   p Edw : Rishworth ReCor/

Know all men by these Presents, that I Pendleton ffetcher
of Saco of the Prouince of Mayne In New England, for &
in Consideration of eight pound tweluc shillings Sterling, to
mee In hand payd, by Edw : Sargeant of the same Town &
Prouince, before y[e] Insealeing & deliuery of these Presents,
to full Content & satisfaction, & of euery part & Parcell
y[r]of, do clearely acquitt, exonerate, discharge the sd Edw :
Sergeant, his heyrs, executors & administrators, foreuer;
Do by these Presents, giue, grant bargane, sell, Allienate,
Enfeoff, & Confirme unto the sd Edward Sergeant a Certen
Tract of vpland, & Marsh, scituate, & being, in y[e] Town of
Saco aforesd, It being y[t] Tract of vpland & Marsh, lately
occupied, Inhabited, & Improued by Symon Booth, & by
the sd Symon Booth, lately sould to Majo[r] Brian Pendleton,
as p Deed of sale vnder his hand & seale, may more fully
appeare; & by sd Brian Pendleton giuen to the abouesd
Pendletō : Fletcher, & deliuered to him by the Executors of
y[e] aforesd Bryan Pendleton & It lyeth in winter Harbour
neare the Ould Grist Mill, & bounded with y[e] sea Wall on
y[e] South, & y[e] land of y[e] widdow Ladbrooke (formerly the
relict of Robert Booth, on y[e] North, & on the west with
John Leighton, & on the East, with Walter Penwills, &
John Sargeants Lands, & is now by the aforesd Pendleton
Fletcher sould unto the aforesd Edw : Sargeant; To haue &
to hould, the sd Tract of vpland, & Marsh, with all & singular y[e] appurtenances, & priuilidges y[r]to belonging or in
any wise appertajneing, to him y[e] sd Edw : Sargeant, his

Book IV, Fol. 45.

heyres, executors, administrators, or Assignes for euer: fully & clearely exonerated, from all former other Gifts grants, sales, Morgages, or other incomberances w^tsoeuer, made done, or suffered to bee done, by mee Pendleton ffletcher of any other Person, or Persons by from or und^r mee, & for Confirmation of the Premisses, I the sd Pendleton ffletcher haue here sett unto my hand & seale, this six & twenteth day of May in ye yeare of o^r Lord, one thousand six hundred eighty & foure 1684 ·

Signed, sealed, & Deliuered/   Pendelton Fletcher (his seale)
  In the Presence of us/   Pendleton ffletcher acknowledged
  John Emerson/   the aboue written Deede of
  William Playstead/   Sale to bee his free Act &
                              Deede, this 26th day of May
                              1684 · before mee
                                   John Wincoll Jus : pe :

A true Coppy of this aboue written Instrum^t transcribed & Compared with the originall this 5th of Septemb^r 1685
                              p Edw : Rishworth ReCor

Wheare as y^r is a necessity lyeth vpon us as parence to prouide for o^r children both at Present & hereafter, so fare as wee are able, according to Christian & humajne obligations, & for as much as, prouidence calls us to remoue for o^r better Conveniency to the Premisses, w^rby wee shall bee put vpon it to settle some new plantation plant & build at yorke, w^rhy wee may bee the better able to bee in a capacity to prouide for selues, & such as do belong unto us; & for ye better effecting of our purpose here in; Wee Daniell Liueingstone, & Joanna Liueington, Husband & wife, do by these Presents mutually agree & Consent one with another, that In Case y^t Johanna my wife, come unto mee the sd Daniell her husband, & bring her too sonns & daughter with her to yorke, w^rby the sd Daniell Liueingstoone &

Johanna his wife, & her three youngest children do unanimously Joyne togeather, to bujld, plant, fence & Improue that fourty Acres of Land given him by the Town of yoike, or w^t other improuem^{ts} that shall make In the meane tyme, that then it is by these Presents further couenanted, & Concluded vpon, between the sd Damell Liueington & Johanna his wife, y^t If it shall happen by piouidence, that ye sd Joanna shall dy before her husband, Daniell Liueingston then w^tsoeuer Estate is y^r Improued of Lands (houseing excepted) with all the Estate of moueables, belonging to the sd Daniell & his wife, shall bee æqually diuided, between the sd Daniell, & the too sonns & daughter of the sd Joanna his wife, to remajne as y^r own pioper Estate of Inheritance, to them & y^r heyres for euer/ In witness w^rof wee haue here unto sett o^r hands, this ninth day of July 1685 ·   Daniell Liuemgstoone/

Signed In ye Presence of/   Daniell Liueingstone & Johanna
Allexand^r Maxwell/   his wife, came before mee this
his marke/   9th day of July 1685 : &
acknowledged this Instrument
Samuell Sayword/   to bee y^r Act & Deede/
Edw : Rishworth Jus : pe :

A True Coppy of this couenant, or agreement, transcribed out of the Originall & y^rwith Compared this 8th day Septemb^r 1685 :   p Edw : Rishworth Re : Cor :

Bee It known unto all men by these Presents, y^t I Robert Wadleigh Senjo^r of Ecceter, In the prouince of New Hampshire, New England Gentle : send Greeteing &c : Know yee, y^t I the sd Robert Wadleigh for a ualewable consideration to mee in hand payd, or sufficient Security y^rfore, by Wilham Sayer of Wells In the Prouince of Mayne In New England, aforesd Planter, do therewith acknowledg my selfe to bee fully satisfyd, contented & payd, & y^rof & euery part &

Prcell thereof, do exonerate acqutt and discharge the sd
William Sawyer, his heyres, executors, administrators and
assignes for euer, by these Presents; haue giuen, granted,
barganed, sould, aliend Enfeoffed & Confirmed, & by these
Present do giue, grant, bargan, sell aliene Enfeoff & confirme vnto the sd William Sawyer, his heyres, executors &
Administrators for euer a certen parcell of Meddow, & vpland, being ye sixth part of ye farme or Estate of my [**46**]
father John Wadleigh deceased, lijng & being in the Town
of Wells afore sayd, the sd Meddow or Marsh being to bee
mesured or layd out to the sd Sawyer, hee paijng for so
many acres as shall bee y^r found so much p acre, as by
another Contract may appeare, & ye same Meddow, & vpland being bounded on ye one side with ye Land which the
sd Sawyer lately bought of the sd John young, & on the
other side, with the Land which I lately sould unto Peter
ffolshum; To haue & to hould the sd sixth part of the Meddow & vpland with all & singular the wood, trees, Tymber,
houses, barnes, out houses, & all other ye appurtenances,
y^{r}unto in any wise app^{r}tayneing or belonging unto the sd
William Sawyer, his heyres, executors, Administrators &
Assignes for euer: Also I the sd Robert Wadleigh, do Couenant promiss & Ingage, to & with sd William Sawyer, y^t
the sd Robert Wadleigh am the true, proper & undoubted
owner, of ye sd barganed Premises, & y^t ye sd Premises
were full & Cleare, & freely & clearely exonerated & acquitted, & discharged off, & from all, & all manner of former
barganes, sales, Gyfts grants, titles Morgages suits, dow-
reys, & all other Incomberances w^{t}soeuer, from ye begining
of the world untill ye date here of, And further I ye sd
Robert Wadleigh do Couenant promiss & Ingage, to & with
ye sd Williā Sawyer, his heyrs executors, & Administrators,
all & singular ye app^{t}tenances, with the Premise y^{r}vnto belonging, to warrant, acquitt, & defend for euer, against all
Persons w^{t}soeuer, from by or vnder mee, Clajmemg any
right title or Interest of o^r into ye same, or any part or Par-

cell y^rof, & In testimony hereof, I the sd Robert Wadleigh, with Saraih Wadleigh my now wife, haue hereunto set o^r hands & seals this twelth day of August Anno Dom : 1685 : Annoq̃ Regni, Jacobi Regis secundi, primo/ John Wadleigh Elldest sonn of mee ye sd Robert Wadleigh, by his hand & seale doth allow of & Confirme ye Premises aboue written/

Signed, sealed, & deliuer̃d   Robert Wadleigh (his seale)
  in p̃sence of/   Saraih Wadleigh (her seale)
  Edw : Smith/   John Wadleigh (his seale)
  Peter Folshum   Mr Robert Wadleigh, & John Wad-
  his marke ℘   leigh, acknowledged this aboue In-
                   stiument to bee y^r act & Deed this
                   18th of Septeb^r 1685 · before mee
                   Samuell Wheelewright Jus : pe :

A true Coppy of this Instrument aboue written, transcribed out of the originall & y^rwith Compared this 6th of October 1685   p Edw : Rishworth Re : Cor :

The thirteenth of June one thousand six hundred eighty fiue/ Wee whose names are under written testify y^t the fiueteen Acres of Land which was layd out, & bounded vnto Mr Lewis Beane, resigned vp by William Johnson vnto the Towns men of yorke, before It was layd out unto ye sd Beane, vpon the Consideration y^t the sd Johnson should haue some Land for y^t Land which the sd Johnson had resigned vp to the Towns disposeing/

vpon Consideration of ye Land aforesd, the sd Johnson had given & layd out vpon the Northward side of the Ledg of Rockes, neare the way which goeth to Cape Nuddacke, which sd land the sd Johnson sould vnto Richd Woods, &

y̅ᵉ sd Woods sould yᵉ same vnto Joseph Preble, as vpon oʳ Information by seuerall Persons as Witness oʳ hands/
          Peter Weare/
Mr Peter Weare, & John Twisden came   John Twisden/
 before mee this 13ᵗʰ of June 1685. & made oath to yᵉ treuth aboue written/   Edw: Rishworth Jus: pe:
 A true Coppy of this Instrumeᵗ aboue written transcribed, & with originall Compared, this 10ᵗʰ day of October 1685:
      p Edw: Rishworth Re: Cor:

 To all to whome these shall come, greeteing; Know yee yᵗ I Thomas Gorges Esqr Depᵗʸ Gouer of the prouince of Mayne, by vertue of authority vnto mee given by Sir Fardinando Gorgˢ Kniᵗᵗᵉ Ld proprietor of sd Prouince, for diuerse good Causes, & Considerations, mee yʳunto especially moueing, haue given, granted barganed sould, Enfeoffed, & Confirmed, & by these Presents do give grant bargane sell Enfeoff & Confirme, unto the Majoʳ & Coality & yʳ successors vnto the Town of Gorgeana, In the County of Deauon, a Necke of Land lijng at the Harhours mouth of Gorgeana, aforesd, on the South side of the riuer there, to bee taken on a streight lyne from yᵉ sd sir Fardindᵒ Gorges house there, to the pond neare Mr Edw: Godfrey his farme house, & all the Marsh at Braue boate Harbour, lijng between yᵉ Marsh of Capᵗ Francis Champernown, & yᵉ sd Farme, saueing Twenty Acres heretofore granted to George Burdett Minister, togeather with all yᵉ Marsh & yslands, lijng on yᵉ South side of River of Gorgeana, from Poynt Ingleby to yᵉ Harbours mouth, reserueing onely unto Sir Fardi: Gorge his heyres, & Assigns, the Tymber growing on the sd Necke of Land, with free lyberty to sett vp houses for fishermen, by the water side there, if Occasion bee/ To haue & to hould the aforesd Premisses, with all & singular the Premisses with appurtenances, & euery part & Parcell yʳof unto the sd

Majo^r & Coality, & y^r successors for euer to ye onely vss & behoofe of ye sd Majo^r & Coality & y^r successors for euermore, yeilding & paijng for ye Premisses unto ye sd Sir Fardindo Gorg^e his heyrs & Assignes, fiue shillings yearely on the twenty ninth day of Septemb^r And I the sd Thomas Gorges do by these Presents, Constitute, ordajne & appoynt Fran^s Rayns Gentle͠ my true & lawfull Atturney, In my place & steade, in ye name of Sir Fard: Gorges, to Enter into ye sd Premisses, or any part or Parcell y^{r}of, in the name of the whoole, & y^{r}of take full & peaceable possession & seizine, & after such possession & seizine so had, & taken then for him & in his name, to deliuer full & peaceable possession & seazin of the same Land, & Premisses to ye sd Majo^r & Coality, or either of them or there successors, according to the Teano͠^{r} æffect, & true meaneing of these Presents/ In witness w^{r}of I the sd Thom^s Gorges haue hereunto sett my hand & seale this eighteenth day of July one thousand six hundred fourty three/

     Thomas Gorges Dep^{ty} Goñe$_1$ / (his seale)

vera Copia of this Instrument transcribed out of the originall & Compared this 16th Octob^r 1685

     p Edw: Rishworth Re: Cor:

To all Christian people to whome these Presents shall come/ greeteing, w^{s}as George Cleeues Gentle ͠: Dep^{ty} President of the Prouince of Lygonia, in new England, by order of Allexand^r Rigby Esqr surgiant at Law, & one of the Barrones of the Exchequ^r In the Kingdome of England did grant vnto Walter Merry of Boston In New England, all that small ysland lijng In Cascoe Bay in the sayd Prouince Com͠anly Called & known by the name of Chebage, & now by the name of Merrys Ysland, with ye rightts, priuiledges, & appurtenances y^{r}unto belonging, as by Deed under the hand & seale of the sd George Cleeue, beareing Date the

18th day of September Anno Domini 1650 : more fully may appeare ; And w'as the sd Yslands with the rights priuiledges & appurtenances hath many tymes beene granted, & Assigned from one to another, & now at this tyme is wholly & legally inuested in & of right doth app'tajne [47] vnto Edmund Whitte of the Citty of Londone, with in the sd Kingdome of England M'chant; Now know yee, yt I Thomas Danforth Esq', President of the Prouince of Mayne, At the Instant motion & request of Humphrey Dauie of sd Boston Esq' in the name & behalfe & for y* Account of y* sayd Edmund Whitte, do hereby Confirme unto y* sd Edmund Whitte, & to his heyres & Assigns for euer, all the aboue mentioned Ysland, with y* rights priuiledges lybertys & app'tenances y' unto belonging, to haue & to hould y* same vnto him the sd Edmund Whitte his heyres & Assignes for euer/ Hee or they paijng onely y' quitt rent Annually to y* Cheefe Ld Proprietor, as is due by agreement made by y* Generall Assembly for y* sayd Prouince, at thejr Sessions held at yorke in March Anno Dom: 1681 : Giuen under my hand & seale of sd Prouince the Twenty Six day of June Anno Dom: 1685 : Annoq, Rex Regis Jacobj Secundi Angliæ primo &c :   Thomas Damforth
   President :

A true Coppy of this Instrume'
transcribed & with originall
Compared this 24th day of
Octob' 1685 :

p Edw : Rishworth ReCor :

Yorke in the Prouince of Mayne In New England, In the yeare of our Lord God one thousand six hundred sixty & six/
Bee It known unto all men by these Presents whom it may Concerne that I James Dixon of the aboue mentioned Prouince being my father William Dixons lawfull heyre, do here by giue & bequeath unto my brother John Brawn, &

do Impoure him to Inioy my whoole right & title of my fathers will to his own proper uss, to his heyrs executors, Administrators or Assignes, prouided that I the sayd James Dixon do not returne from sea, nor send my order, but if it please god, that I do returne or send my order, then this Deed of Gyft is of no æffect, but it is at my own disposeing; It is likewise mutually agreed vpon, by both Partys, that John Brawn is to pay out of this Gyft fiue pounds Sterling, to my Cosson Dorothy Moore, If I do not returne, nor send my order, to the Contrary/ I haue here vnto sett my hand & seale, this 9th of Janvary : 1666 :

Sealed signed & deliuered/   James Dixon (his seale)
  in yᵉ Presence of us/   A true Coppy of this writing,
  Richard Cally/   or Gyft aboue written tran-
  Elyas Purrington/   scribed out of yᵉ originall &
                      yʳ with Compared this 18th day
                      of Novembʳ 1685 :
                      p Edw : Rishworth Re : Cor :

To all Christian people to whome these Presents shall come ; Know yee yᵗ I Robert Wadley of Lamprill River in the County of Norfocke, for an Consideration of my daughter Sarah young now the wife of John young, for her Marriage portion, hath given, granted, alienated, Enfeoffed, & Confirmed unto the aforesd John young of the same place & County aforesd, & by these Presents doth fully Clearely & absolutely giue, grant aliene, Enfeoff, & Confirme unto my sd son in Law, John Young his heyres, executors, Administrators & Assigⁿ for euer, one third part of my farme at Wells, which my father John Wadleigh deceased, gaue vnto mee by his last will & testament, which will is recorded in the County records, for yorke shire : Which third part is to bee on the South West side next unto the Town lott, both vpland, & Meddow & sault Marsh, begining at Webb hannet River, & so extends backeward into the Countrey, with all & singular its rights, priuiledges & appurtenances y^{r}unto belonging, also one third part of the falls, vpon that brooke which runneth down by my dwelling house which stands vpon the sd farme, for the bujlding of a Mill/

To haue, and to hould, the sd third part of Land, Meddow, or sault Marsh & priuiledg^s of ye brooke at the fall there of, with all & singular its rights, priuiledges, & appurtenances y^{r}unto belonging, unto the sayd John young & his heyres, & his & to y^r onely proper uss, & behoofe for euer: And I the sd Robert Wallcigh, for my selfe, my heyres, executors, & administrators, doth Couenant promiss, grant, & agree to & with the sd John young, his heyres, & Assignes, & euery of them by these Presents, shall & may by uertue & force here of from tyme to tyme, & at all tyms for euer here after, lawfully, & peaceably haue hould, uss, occupy possess & inioy all the Land, Meddow, & sault Marsh, & third part of ye falls afore mentioned, with out any lawfull lett, suite, trouble, deniall, interruption, Euiction, or disturbance, of the sd Robert Wadleigh his heyres, executors, administrators, or Assignes for euer: or of any other Person, or Persons, lawfully Clajmeing any iust right, title, or Interest unto the sd Premisses, or any part there of, from by or under mee/ in Confirmation hereof, I the sd Robert Wadleigh, haue here unto put my hand & seale, this first day of Septemb^r 1675:   Robert Wadleigh (his seale)

Signed sealed, & deliuered   This Deede was acknowledged
  in the Presence of us/   by Robert Wadleigh, to bee
        his   his volentary act & Deede,
  John ✝ Barber   this 11th of August 1676:
    marke   before mee
  John Wadleigh/   Samuell Daulton Comission^r

A true Coppy of this Instrument aboue written, transcribed out of the originall, & y^{r}with Compared this 18th day of Nouemb^r 1685:   p Edw: Rishworth Re: Cor:

Book IV, Fol. 47, 48.

This Indenture made this seuenth day of August, in the yeare 1685: Witnesseth, that I John young of Ecceter in the prouince of New Hampshyre, in Consideration of full satisfaction in hand receiued haue barganed sould alienated, Enfeofed & Confirmed vnto William Sawyer of Wells in the Prouince of Mayne, all my right title & interest in & unto one third part of that farme wch is given unto mee at Wells in the Prouince of Mayn aforesd by my father in Law Robert Wadleigh as doth fully appeare by his Deede of sayle, beareing date the first day of September in the yeare 1675: with all & singular its rights, priuiledges & appurtenances, y^{r}unto belonging, vnto the sd William Sawyer his heyres, & Assignes, & his & their proper vss, & behoofe for euer: To haue & to hould, all & singular, the aforesd barganed Premises [48] to him & his heyres for euer, free & Cleare, & freely & Clearely acquitted, & discharged from any former, or other bargane or sale, by mee or any other, from by or vnder mee, to any other Person or Persons whatsoeuer/ In confirmation hereof, I haue here unto set my hand & seale the day & yeare aboue written; Also I Saraih young, the wife of John young do fully Assigne, & make ouer all my title & Interest, vnto the aboue named William Sawyer, & his successors, which any ways in future tyme should or may belong unto mee/   John young (his seale)

Signed sealed & deliuered/   her
In the Presence of us/   Saraih ʃ young (her seale)
    his   marke
James 🜚 Daniell
   marke   John young & Saraih his wife, ac-
Henery h w Wadleigh   knowledged this Instrument to
   his marke   bee y^r act & Deede, this 7th of
                   August 1685: before mee
                      Robert Wadleigh Jus: pe

BOOK IV, FOL. 48.

Johh Wadleigh Eldest sonn of mee sd Robert Wadleigh doth Consent vnto, & allow off the alienation aboue written, as is further Attested this 11th of August 1685 : before me
Edw . Rishworth Jus : pe :
A true Coppy of this Instrum^t aboue written transcribed & Compared with originall this 23th of Novemb^r 1685 :
p Edw : Rishworth Re : Cor :

To all Christian people, to whome this Present Deede of Gyft shall Come/ Know yee that Wee Rowland young Senjo^r of yorke, in the prouince of Mayne, & Johaña young my beloued wife, for & in Consideration of the parentall loue, & naturall affection that wee beare vnto o^r Loueing sonn Samuell young, haue given & granted, & by these Prsents do giue grant & Confirme vnto our aforesd sonn Samuell young, one Tract of Land, to the valew or quantity of tenn acres, lijng & being, in part of a Tract of Land, granted vnto mee by the Town of yorke, at a publique Town Meeteing, held at yorke on the fineteenth day of Septeb^r 1667 : & layd out to mee & bounded, by the Select men of the Town of yorke, Aprill the ninth 1679 : Which will appeare by the sd Town grant vpon ReCords of the sd Town, & also by the returne of the aforesd Select men that layd out & bounded the aforesd Land wch sd granted land lijng behind my now dwelling house, & runns from thence vpon a North East lyne, or y^r abouts, till fourty Acres bee Measured, Which aboue sd Tenn Acres of Land, Wee do giue freely vnto the sd Samuell, Where he will haue it in the aforesd fourty Acres, as also which hee hath Chosen to bujld his house vpon, & hath fenced in a fejld, the sayd tenn acres of Land, with all ye priuiledges & appurtenances ; To haue & to hould to him the sd Samuell, his heyres executors & Assignes for euer ; And Wee do Ingage y^t Wee

haue full pouer, & authority in o'selues, the aboue sd Premisses to giue, & grant, & Wee the same will warrant, & Defend, & the sd Samuell, will saue & harmeless keepe, from any Person or Prson/ w'soeuer, laijng any right, title or Clayme legally y'unto, & Wee the sayd Rowland, & Joane young do promiss & ingage, for o' selues o' heyres executors, & Assignes vnto our beloued son Sam^ll young that wee will do & Prforme, all such act & Acts as the law requires, for the better Confirmation of ye Premisses as acknowledgment &c : & for the Present ratification of the aforesd Premisses Wee the aboue named Rowland, & Joanna young, haue here unto sett our hands & afixed our seales, this eighteenth of Aprill one thousand six hundred eighty & two/ Rowland young Senjo^r (his seale)
Signed sealed & deliuer'd   his Marke R
 In the Presence of/
Arther Bragdon/   Johanna young her (her seale)
Daniell Liueingstoone/   Marke C

Rowland young Senjo^r, & Johanna young his Wife, came before mee & owned this Instrum^t aboue written, to bee y^r act & Deed,   Edw : Rishworth, Jus : pe :

A true Coppy of this Instrum^t aboue written transcribed & with ye originall Compared this 23th of Novb^r 1685 :

p Edw : Rishworth ReCor :

To all Christian people to whome this Deed or Instrument shall come, Mary Booles of Portsmouth in New England sends Greeteing ; Now know yee y^t I the sd Mary Boolls relict of Joseph Bools deceased, of Wells, & Administratrix to the Estate of Morgan Howell of Cape Porpus deceased, vpon seuerall good Causes & Considerations mee y'unto moueing, & more especially for & in Consideration of the iust some of fiueteene pounds to mee in hand payd, & lawfully Assured to bee payd, by Samuell Snow of Boston, haue, for mee my heyres & successors by the Presents given, granted, barganed, & sould, Enfeoffed, & Confirmed, Do hereby give, grant, bargan, sell, Infeoff, & Confirme, freely fully & absolutely unto the aforesd Samll Snow, of Boston In the County of Suffocke in New England Cordwinder, his heyrs, & successors for euer, from mee my heyrs executors, Administrators & Assigns, my soole right Title & Interest of y^t Necke of Land ljing at Cape Porpus, which was formerly Morgan Howells, & in Prticular y^t place w^r Morgan Howells house formerly stood, contajneing by Estimatimation about fiuety Acres, bee It more or less, with all the profitts, priuiledg^s Comans, easements, Immunitys, with all & singular the appurtenances there vnto any wise appertajneing, freely & quietly, to haue & to hould with out any matter of Challenge Clajme or demand, of mee the sd Mary Bolls or any Person or Prsons from, by, or under mee, my heyres, executors, Administrators, & Assigns for euer : & further I the sd Mary Bolls, do hereby Couenant & promiss, in behalfe of my selfe, my heyres, executors, Administrators & Assigns to & with the sd Samll Snow his heyrs executors Administrators & Assigns that ye Land with all ye appurtenances, are free & cleare from all gyfts, grants, barganes, leases, dowrys, morgages, Judgm^{ts} or any other Incomberances w^{t}soeuer, do likewise promiss & Couenant, to warrant & defend the title, & Interest of the Premises, euery part & parcell y^{r}of, to him ye sd Samuell Snow, his heyres, executors, Administrators, & Assignes for euer ; from mee my heyres, executors, administrators, or from any Person or Persons ; under mee, or by mee, or my means, or any other by my procurement/ in testimony here unto, I haue afixed my hand & seale, this Twenteth day of June 1681 : In the Thirty secund yeare of ye Reign of our soueraigne Ld Charles secund, of England, Scotland,

BOOK IV, FOL. 48, 49.

France, & Ireland King, Defend{r} of the faith, one thousand six hundred eighty one/
[49] Signed, Sealed, & Deliuered/
 In Presence of vs/
 Samuell Austine/
 Jonathan Hamond/

Mary } Bools (her/seale)
 her marke

Mis Mary Booles did acknowledg this aboue Instrument to bee her act & Deede, this Twenty one day of June one thousand six hundred eighty one, before mee
   Samuell Wheelewright Jus : pe :
A true Coppy of this Instrument aboue written, transcribed out of the originall this 28{th} of Novemb{r} 1685 :
   p Edw : Rishworth Re : Cor :

Receiued by mee Nicholas Moorey, the Twenty fourth of Janvary one thousand six hundred eighty & foure tenn Neate Cattle Which is full satisfaction for the uss of Mr Jonathan Curwine of Salem & full ballance of all Accounts, from Joseph Storrer of Wells, Atturney to sd Currwine
Testes Benjamen Curtis/   p Nicholas Moorey/
Lewis Allene his marke

LA Benjamen Curtis, & Lewis Alline testifys vpon oath that they did see Nicholas Moorey Assigne this Instrum{t} as his Act & Deede, of which wee are witness too/ Dated this 4{th} of Septeb{r} 1685 : Sworne before mee Samull Wheelewright Jus : pe :
vera Copia of this receipt transcribed & with originall Compard this 4 : Deceb{r} 1685 : p Edw : Rishworth ReCor :

Know all men by these Presents, y{t} I Nicho{s} Mooey of Wells, Carpenter, in the Prouince of Mayn in New England being Atturney to & for Mr Jonathan Corwine of Salem M*r*chant, In the County of Essex in New England as aforesd, as by a letter of Atturney vnder the hand & seale of the sd Corwine dated the six*t* of August one thousand six hundred eighty foure, more at large doth & may appeare, for y*e* getting & recouering in of all debts due to him selfe, & to his now wife Elizabeth the Relict & Administratrix to Mr Robert Gibbs of Boston M*r*chant Deceased, haue by uertue of my sd pouer of Atturneyshipe haue receiued & accompted with Joseph Storer of Wells yeomā: In the prouince of Mayne, & haue made a full & a soole Issew of all Accounts between the sd Mr Jonathan Curwine, as hee is Interested by his sayd wife Elizabeth, & hath receiued full satisfaction of y*e* sd Joseph Storer/

Now know yee, that I the sayd Nicholas Moorey Atturney as abouesd, do acquitt & fully discharge the sd Joseph Storrer his heyrs, executors Administrators & Assignes, from all bills, bonds, obligatory, Booke debts, goods wares M*r*chandizes, Reckonings, accounts, sujte or sujtes of Law, Judgm*ts* executions, troubles Trialls, whatsoeuer, or howsoeuer, from the beginning of this world to this Present day, & shall warrant & Defend the sd Joseph Storer, his heyres, or Assignes, from the aboue named Mr Jonathan Curwine, or frō her as hee is related to the Estate of his sayd wife, thejre heyres, executors, administrators, & Assignes, for euer, by uertue here of; In witness whereof, I haue set too my hand & seale, the Twenty fourth day of Janvary one thousand six hundred Eighty & foure In the Thirty sixt yeare of the Reigne of our Soueraign Lord Charles the secund of England, Scotland, France, & Ireland King Defender of the faith &c: Nicholas Moorey (locus sigilli)

Signed, sealed, & Deliuerd/ Nicholas Moorey appeared before mee this 26*th* of Janva:
in Presence of/
Samuell Wheelewright/ 1684: & owned this Instrument to bee his Act & Deede
George Pearson/
Samuell Wheelewright Jus: pe:

Book IV, Fol. 49.

A true Coppy of this Instrument aboue written transcribed out of the originall & there with compared this 2: of Decemb^r 1685 :   p Edw : Rishworth Re : Cor :

Know all men by these Presents, that Jonathan Corwine of the Town of Salem, in In the County of Essex in New England M^rchant : Do by these Presents Constitute, & appoynt, my trusty and well beloued freind, Nicholas Morey of the Towne of Wells, In the Prouince of Mayne Carp'enter, to bee my true & lawfull Atturney, to Act for mee In all such Concernem^ts, of what kind or nature soeuer, as may mee Concerne, either to my owne P^rsonall Concerneme^t or w^t may mee Concerne, as my now wife Elizabeth was, & is the late relict, and administratrix to Mr Robert Gibbs, of Boston Merchant, deceased, In my name and steede, & to my uss, to aske, sue for, to leauy, require, and of all and euery Person or Persons whatsoeuer, all such somes of money, Lands, houses, Mills and kinds of debts dues & demands, of what kind & nature soeuer, as are due vnto mee from any Person or Persons w^tsoeuer, with in the aforesayd Prouince of Mayne, by these presents giueing and granting, vnto my sayd Atturney, my full and soole pouer, strength and authority, in & about the Premisses, to Act as hee shall see cause, impryson to cast out of pryson, to release & If hee see Cause, Compositions to make, to act and vss, all other Acts & thing & things, deuise or deuises in the Law, whatsoeuer needefull & necessary for the recouering, of all manner of dues, or demands, whatsoeuer is due to mee from any Person, or Persons whatsoeuer, by any ways, or meanes whatsoeuer, and hereby renoakeing & disanulling, all former letters of Atturney, by mee made to any Person whatsoeuer, concerneing the aboue mentioned Premises, by these Presents also giueing vnto my aboue mentioned Atturney, pouer If hee see Cause to appoynt one or more Atturneys vnder him as hee sees Cause to reuoake: p these Presents ratifijng, allowing & Confirmeing, and houlding firme, & stable, all and whatsoeuer my sayd Atturney, or any Athorized by him shall lawfully act, or do, or cause to bee acted, and done in my concernements, as aboue written to bee as valid to all Intents, Constructions, and purposes as I my selfe might or could do, If I were Prsonally Present, & had acted, and done the same; And In witness of the treuth hereof, I Jonathan Corwine haue here unto set my hand and seale, this sixt day of August In the yeare of our Lord 1684: one thousand six hundred eighty foure/ Annoq, Regni, regis, Carolj secundj Angliæ &c : 36 :

Signed, sealed, & Deliuered,   Jonathan Corwine (locus sigilli.)
In the Presence of us/   Mr Jonathan Corwine acknowl-
Samuell Beadle/   edged the aboue written In-
ffrancis Neale Senior/   strument to bee his Act &
                             Deede, Salem August the 7th
                             1684 : before mee/
                             John Hawthorne Assistant/

A true Coppy of this Instrument aboue written, transcribed out of the originall & yrwith Compared this 4th day of December 1685 :   p Edw . Rishworth Re :Cor :

[50] Bee It known vnto all men by these Presents, that I Samuell Snow of Boston Cordwinder, haue nominated, made ordayjned, & Constituted, & by these Presents do nominate, make, ordajne, Constitute, & in my stead & place haue putt, my trusty & beloued frejnd George Pearson of Boston Mrchant, my true & lawfull Atturney for mee, & in my name, & to my uss, to aske receiue, recouer & leauy all & singular debts, dues, & demands due by bills, bonds obligatory writeings, reckonings, accounts with all some, & somes of moneys owing or appertajneing unto mee Samll Snow by any Person or Persons In New England, with like lyberty

BOOK IV, FOL. 50.

to take into his possession, my houseings Lands, vplands, Meddows, to lett sell or dispose of, for my uss, & in my behalfe, all Lijng in the Townshipp of Cape Poipus, giueing & granting by these Presents unto my sd Atturney my full & lawfull pouer & authority for mee, & in my name & to my vss to sue arrest, Attatch declare, Implead, Imprison, Condemne, & release, the sd Debtors or any of them If neede require, & vpon thejr receipt of sd debts acquittance, or any lawfull discharge, for mee in my name, & as my act & deede to make & seale, & deliuer; One Atturney or more under him to ordajne make & at his pleasure agajne to reuoake, & generally to sue do execute, Prforme Conclude, & execute & finish w'soeuer matter or matters, thing or things, needfull & expedient in & about the Premisses, as Amply & æffectually as I my selfe might or Could do, If I were y^r Personally Present, allowing ratifijng Confirming & Establishing, w'soeuer my sd Atturney shall lawfully do or cause to bee done In & about the Premisses, to bee firme & uallid/ In witness where of, I haue here unto sett my hand seale, this Twenty secund day of June one thousand six hundred eighty fiue, 1685: In the first yeare of the Reign of o^r Soueraign Ld James, the secund, by the grace of god, King of England Scotland &c: Samuell Snow ($^{locus}_{sigilli}$)
Signed, sealed, & Deliuered/   his seale
    In the Presence of   Sam̄ll Snow Prsonally appeared
    Tymothy Dwight Junjo^r/   the 22th of June before mee
    Sam̄ll Nanny/   1685: acknowledged this
                                    aboue letter of Atturney to
                                    bee his Act & Deede/ Coram
                                    Elisha Cooke Assist^t
vera Copia of this Instrume^t aboue written, transcribed, & with the originall Compared, this 31: December: 1685:
                      p Edw: Rishworth Re: Cor:

Book IV, Fol. 50.

Boston 15th 1685:

Mr Pearson/ god sending you in safety to Wells, pray you to make yor application to walter Penewell of Cape Porpus, & make demand of the 1: Thirty pounds in moneys which is due to mee, & if hee pay you ye moneys, deliuer him vp the bill of sale for ye Land, but if hee refuse, then Demand the farme from him/

2ly If hee do not pay the moneys, pray make yor application to Nicholas Moorey of Wells, with whome I haue already treated, & uss your Endeauo^r to Compleate that bargane betweene us Concerneing the sd Farme, at Cape Porpus, vidz^t that of Mowntegues, & Mis Boolls is, & vpon your agreement with the sd Nicho^{ls} Moorey, or any other, If hee refuse, I will vpon yor order deliuer vp a bill of sale of ye sd Estate with all other writeings Concerneing the sd Land, & if you Comply with any, I would request you to speake with Mr Rishworth, that it may bee Entered vpon my Morgage that I haue receiued full satisfaction for y^t Land of Mountegues & Mis Bolls is, alias Morgan Howells Land at Cape Porpus, & w^t euer else you see cause to bee done in or about the Premisses, I will ratify & Confirme/ as witness my hand the day & yeare aboue mentioned/

your Loueing frejnd/
Tymothy Dwight/

A true Coppy of this letter transcribed, & with originall Compared this 31: day of Decemb^r 1685:

p Edw: Rishworth ReCor:

Bee It known to all men by these Presents, y^t Tymothy Dwight of Boston Gould Smith In New England In America, haue nominated, made, ordajned, Constituted, & appoynted in my steade & place, haue put my trusty & well beloued frejnd, George Pearson of Boston M^{r}chant as abouesd, to bee my true & lawfull Atturney, for mee & in my name, & for my uss, to aske, demand sue for arrest, recouer, & receiue all my debts, due by bill & booke, debts, dues, &

demands from any Prson, or Persons w'soeuer, or how soeuer, resciding in any part or place in New England, but espetially all these bills & Debts made ouer to mee by Sammuell Snow of Boston Cordwinder lijng at Cape Porpus, & else where, & if any Person, or Persons do refuse payment of those bills, or debts, I do Impoure my sd Atturney to sue arrest Implead, Imprison, & out of prison to cast and vpon receipt of any some or somes of Moneys, acquittance or any other discharges to giue for mee & in my name as my Act & Deede, & If neede to make demand & Constitute, one Atturney or more under him, & at his pleasure agajne to reuoake, & generally to do execute & Prforme all things needfull & expedient in and about the Premisses, and whatsoeuer my sayd Atturney or Atturneys shall lawfully do, or Cause to bee done In & about the premisses, I do here by ratify & Confirme by these Presents; In witness w'of I haue here unto set my hand & seale, this Twenty fourth of August one thousand six hundred eighty fiue, in the first yeare of the Reign of our Soueraigne Lord James secund of England Scotland King &c: Thymothy Dwight (his seale)

Signed sealed & deliuer̃d   Mr Tymothy Dwight acknow-
  In the Presence of us/   ledged this Instrument to bee
  Henery Messenger/   his Act & Deede, Boston
  Jabesh Newysh/   29th Septebr 1685: before
                  Samuell Nowell Assist't

A true Coppy of this Instrum't transcribed out of the originall, & y'rwith Compared this 1: Janva: 1685:

        p Edw: Rishworth Re: Cor:

Know all men by these Presents, that I Micom Mackcyntire, of yorke In ye the Prouince of Mayne, formerly of Newgewanacke, for & In Consideration of the sume of Twenty pounds to mee in hand payd & secured, to bee payd by Capt Charles ffrost, of Kittery, & Stephen Sewell

of Salem, haue exonerated released, remised quitt Claimed, & do by these Presents exonerate, release, remise & quitt Clajme, Mr Thom^s Broughton & Capt John Wincoll of Newgewanacke In the prouince of Mayne aforesd, of all manner of debts, bills bonds obligations acknowledgments or accounts dues or demands whatsoeuer, either for worke done about the Salmon falls Mills or Caused to bee done, by mee the sd Mackeyntire, or by any other way or means [51] whatsoeuer/ In witness to singular & euery one of the abouesd Premisses, I the sd Micum Mackeyntire, haue herunto afixed my hand and seale this tenth day of November 1685: The Marke
Signed sealed & Deliuered In the   of
  Presence of/ Stephen Sewell/   Micum Mackin- (locus sigilli)
  Samuell Bragdon/ Nicholas Gowen/ tyre/

Micum Mackeintyre, acknowledged the aboue written Instrume^t to bee his Act & Deede, this tenth of November 1685: before mee   Charles ffrost Jus: pe:

A true Coppy of this receipt or Instrument aboue written transcribed out of the Originall & y^{r}with Compared this 24th day of Janvary 1685: by   Edw: Rishworth ReCor:

Know all men by these Presents, that I Thomas Wills of Kittery In the Prouince of Mayne alias County of yorke In N: England, Mariner, do stand & am firmely bounden, & obleig'd vnto Capt Francis Champernown of Kittery aforesd Gentle: & Majo^r Nicho: Shapleigh of Kittery aforesd M^{r}chant & William Spencer of the same place Yeaman, ffeofees to Luce Chadborne Widdow, of Kittery aforesd, late the wife of Humphrey Chadborne whilst hee liued of Kittery aforesd, In ye full & whoole sume of Two hundred pounds, of Current pay of New England, due to bee payd vnto the sd Capt Francis Francis Champernown, Majo^r Nicho Shapleigh, & William Spencer, or to either of them, or to y^r lawfull Atturney, executors, Administrators, or Assignes, to yᵉ which payment Well & faithfully & truely to bee payd, I do bind mee my heyres, executors, & Administrators firmely by these Presents, sealed with my seale & Dated in Kittery aforesd, the Twenty fifth day of March, In the Twenty first yeare of the Reigne of oʳ most gratious soueraigne Lord Charles the secund, by the grace of God of England, Scottland, France & Ireland King, Defendʳ of the faith, one thousand six hundred sixty nine, Anno . Dom : 1669 :

The Condition of this Prsent obligation is such, yᵗ wʳas there is a Marriage agreed vpon & shortly (by gods Permission) to bee had & solemnized betweene the aboue bounden Thomas Wills, and the aboue named Luce Chadborne, and wheie as the sayd Luce Chadborne, In case it shall please god that shee decease before her Intended husband Thomas Wills, rescrueth unto her selfe a Lyberty to dispose of the full Moeity, or one halfe part of all the moueables that shee the sd Luce Chadborne is now possessed off, as by an Inventory here unto annexed, If yʳfore the sayd Thomas Wills shall for him selfe from tyme to tyme, & at all tyms hereafter the solemnizing thereof, Prmitt & suffer the sayd Luce Chadborne his wife to make her will, thereby giveing & bequeathing unto whom shee shall thinke meete all the Moueables aboue mentioned unto such Person, or Persons as shee shall please there in to nominate, & appoynt according to yᵉ true intent & meaneing of these Presents, & shall fullfill & Performe the same, without Couen, & fraude, or delay, yᵗ then this Present obligation to bee voyd, & of no æffect, or else to stand remajne, abide & bee in full pouer, force, strength & uertue/   Thomas Wills ($\genfrac{}{}{0pt}{}{his}{seale}$)

Signed sealed & deliuered/   Kittery 1ˢᵗ of Aprill 1669 .

  In yᵉ Presence of vs/   Thomas Wills acknowledged
  Edward Hilton/   this writeing or Instrumᵗ to
  John Shapleigh/   bee his free Act & Deede
  Richard Allexander/   before mee/
                           Elyas Stileman Comissioʳ/

Book IV, Fol. 51.

A true Coppy of this Instrument aboue written, transcribed out of the Originall & there with Compared, this 25th day of Febru : 1685 :   p Edw : Rishworth Re . Cor :

Know all men by these Presents that I Thomas Ryce of Kittery In the Prouince of Mayne In New England, seaman with the free Consent of Mary my wife, vpon good Considerations, mee y'unto mee moueing, & more espetially for & in Consideration of the iust sume of Twenty pounds, in money to mee In hand payd, by Capt Thom^s Doneil of Portsmouth In the Prouince of New Hampshire Esqr, the receipt w^{r}of, & euery part & Parcell y^{r}of, I do acknowledg & y^{r}with do own my selfe to bee fully satisfyd, contented & payd, & do for my selfe my heyrs executors Administrators & Assignes for euer acquitt & discharge sd Capt Thomas Doneil from the aforesd sume ; Haue by these Presents given, granted barganed sould, Enfeoffed, & Confirmed, & do here by giue, grant bargane, sell Enfeoff & & Confirme vnto the aboue Named Capt Thomas Daniel, his heyres, executors Administrators, & Assignes, my soole right Title & Interest, of the one halfe of a Certen Ysland, ljng & being in the Riuer of Pischataqua, between the now dwelling house of Mr Thom^s Withers, & Strawberry Banke, formerly granted by the sd Withers unto his too daughters, Mary, & Elizabeth æqually to bee divided, part w^{r}of sd Tho : Ryce & his wife liued vpon, in the tyme of ye Indean Warrs, Which Ysland was Confirmed by the sd Thos withers vnto his too Daughters, by his own act & Deede, acknowledged & ReCorded, as appeareth by that Deed beareing date July 24th 1671 :

To haue & to hould one halfe of ye sd Ysland, as granted & pos-essed by ye sd Thom^s Ryce, with all the priniledges profitts, & imunitys belonging y^{r}unto, from mee the sd Thomas Ryce my heyres, executors, Administrators, & Assignes for euer, unto sd Cap⁺ Daniell, his heyres, executors, administrators & Assignes for euer: acknowledging him selfe to bee true & lawfull owner thereof, haueing full pouer to dispose of the same, which Land at this Present is free from all appropriations Assignem⁺ˢ & Incomberances wᵗsoeuer, & do by these Presents stand bound to warrant & Defend the title yʳof, from all Prson or Persons whatsoeuer Pretending any Interest yʳunto, from by or vnder mee, or any by my procurement: In witness wʳof with the free Consent of Mary my wife I haue hereunto afixed my hand & seale in the Thirty third yeare of yᵉ Reigne of oʳ Soueraigne Ld Charles the secund, of England, Scotland, France, & Ireland King, Fidei Defensor: this 15ᵗʰ day of May, [**52**] one thousand six hundred eighty one/ 1681 :

Signed sealed & deliuered/   Thomas Ryce ($^{his}_{seale}$)
 In Presence of/
 Henery Dyer/   The Marke of
 Joshua ffryer/   Mary ⚡ Ryce ($^{her}_{seale}$)

A true Coppy of this Instrument, transcribed out of the Originall & yʳwith Compared this 25ᵗʰ day of ffebru: 1685 :
       p Edw:

 Articles, Couenants, agreements, had made, Convented, Concluded & agre'd vpon yᵉ tenth day of Novembʳ one thousand six hundred Eighty fiue, betweene Mis Alice Shapleigh of Kittery In the Prouince of Mayne, the Relict of Majoʳ Nichoˢ Shapleigh newly deceased, of the one party, & John Shapleigh of the same Town & Prouince of the other party are as followeth/

 1: It is agreed by & betweene the partys aboue named, & yᵉ sd Mis Shapleigh for the Considerations here after mentioned, hath granted, barganed sett, & to farme letten & by these Presents doth grant doth grant bargan sett & to farme lett, unto the sd John Shapleigh all her third part of Land

BOOK IV, FOL. 52.

Marsh & Meddow ground, with all Tymber wood trees standing, lijng, or belonging to her in Kittery as It was layd out by Court order, togeather with all her third part of the Corne, Mill & saw Mill, Dame & ponds there at Kittery aforesd, togeather with all vtensills belonging to ye sd Mills & Dame, as also her third part of the Barne Leantows or out houseing, togeather with foure steares of three years ould, & the three Cows & too Heffers of tow years ould & one Calfe, of this years, too Ewes, & two lambs with all her hay & fodder, already prouided reseruenig for my selfe the Milke of one Cow & the little garden at ye East End of the house, & ye too little yards at ye foreside of her dwelling Roome, with Lyberty of Cutting of Convenient fyre wood of the Land for her househould vss, with Lyberty to gather fruite in the garding or orchards for her own Prticular vss, in the house but for no other & liberty to gather greine peas or beanes for her selfe as aforesd, with lyberty & convenient way to & from her house, also convenient rowme to lay her fyre wood, neare ye house, also the Land her Negrow liues on, also reserued to his the sd Negros vss, being about three Acres; To haue & to hould all the third of Land Medow, Timber tree woods, Mills, dame pond all vtellensills y^rto belonging, the barne Leantow out housing, with all priuiledges & appurtenances belonging to all or any part or parts, with all the Cattle sheepe & lambs aboue mentioned unto the sd John Shapleigh, to his proper vss & benefitt, from the day of the Date here of, & to the end & tearme, & for & dureing the full tearme & tyme of seauen full whoole yeares, next Ensewing fully to bee Completed & Ended/

2ly It is agreed, & John Shapleigh doth hereby Couenant, promiss & grant too & with the sd Mis Alice Shapleigh by these Presents, y^t for & in Consideration of the houlding & Inioying of all the aboue barganed Premisses, for the tyme aboue mentioned doth hereby promiss to pay unto Mis Alice Shapley or her order, the full some of Twelue pounds in M{r}chtable pine boards in manner following, yearly & euery yeare dureing the whoole tearme & tyme abouesd to bee payd at Kittery, or Spruse Cricke, twise in euery yeare, six pounds at or before the last day of Euery Aprill dureing the whoole tyme in M{r}chtble pine boards, as they are Generally bought & sould for money, & y{e} other six pounds at or before the last day of euery October, in M{r}cħble boards as aforesd as they are bought & sould for money at the tyms of payment/

3ly It is further agreed that the Hay barne & Cattle, are to bee apprised by Indifferent men, & so returned to her agajne, & euery thing else at the end of seaven years, with this promiss that If it shall happen that warrs should arise with the heathen, & so by that means the Cattle hay or any thing else should bee destroy'd, or any ineuitable prouidence shall happen by fyre, or water, & not by John Shapleighs Neglect, hee shall not bee bound nor Compelled to make it good; otherwise to bee deliuered as aforesd, at y{e} end of seaven years, that is to say both Lands Mill & Dame, hay & stocke with out fraude or delay; It is further agreed y{t} John Shapleigh doth Ingage to deliuer unto Mis Alice Shapleigh abouesd, foure steres of three years ould & the vantage, three Cows, too Heffers of too years ould, & one Calfe of this years, too Ewes 2 lambs, with so much hay as is now prouided for her stocke to bee deliuered to her or her order, at the end of the tearme or tyme as aboue/ If any shall bee killed or lost with in the tyme aforesd, then the sd John Shapleigh stands ingag'd to make them good as now they are, that is to say any of the aboue mentioned Cattle/ In Confirmation, & for y{e} true Performance of all the Prticulars aboue mentioned, Wee the sd Alice Shapleigh, & John Shapleigh haue each to other haue set too y{r} hands & seales, to two Instruments both of one & y" same Tenure, the day yeare first aboue written/ Signed sealed & deliuered, In Presence of/ Joseph Hammond/ John Pickerine/

Alice Shapleigh (her seale) John Shapleigh (his seale)

Wee whose names are here vnderwritten, being desired to vew the Cattle aboue specifyd in the lease, & to valew the sd stocke what they are worth in good pay at Money price, haue accordingly apprised them as followeth to say the foure steres of three years ould & vantage at Twelue pounds, the three Cows at seaven pounds, the two Heffers at three pounds tenn shillings the Calfe at Tenn shillings, the whoole some is Twenty three pounds, & for the hay John Shapleigh is to Mow the same Marsh as Mis Shapleigh hath mowed & staked this yeare & so leaue it at the end of the tyme, to her the sd Alice Shapleigh in as good Condition as now It is, both English grass, & all other grass made into hay as now it is ualued by us vnder written the too sheepe & two lambs valewed at Twenty foure shillings/ Mis Alice Shapleigh is also to haue liberty to gather one Hodgsead of apples for her own vss, yearely/ this was agreed to by John Shapleigh, at y" tyme of o^r appriseing the stocke/   Joseph Hammond

A true Coppy of those articles of   Edw: Ayers/ agrement aboue written, & of Apprisall vnderwritten transcribed out of the originall & y^{r}with Compared this 25th of Febru: 1685:

p Edw: Rishworth Re: Cor:

[53] These may Certify to whome these. Prsents shall Come/ that w^{r}as Wee whose names are here vnderwritten, being mutually Chosen by Thos Donell & Samell Bragdon to runne the North East Lyne which is the diuission lyne of

thejr plantations, & according to Bragdons bill or Deede of sale & for the Ending of all Contriuercys from the begining of the world to ye Conclusion thereof, never to bee altered by the sd Bragdon, the Compass being sett by thejr Consents wee runne North East by the sayd Compass, & at the extent of the bounds was a stake sett in the fence of John Parker Senjo^r by the hands of sd Bragdon as a finall end of all contention, It being all done very Carefully (John Harmon being then as an eye witness by us) 6 : Janva : 168$\frac{2}{8}$ or sometyme in Janvary/ witness o^r hands/   John Penwill/
vera Copia of this writing or Instru-   Abra : Preble/
ment transcribed & with Originall Compared, this 2 : of March 168$\frac{2}{8}$

  p Edw : Rishworth Re : Cor :

These Presents may certify all whome It doth or may Concerne, that I Francis Hooke of Kittery of the Prouince of Mayne In New England, for sundrey good causes mee y^runto moueing, & more espetially for y^t Conjugall Loue, & affection which I beare vnto my well beloued wife Mary Hooke, & forasmuch as shee is the Proper heyre to an Estate, ljing in Barbadoes to the ualew of Two hundred pounds, which sd Estate, I the aforesd Francis Hooke am Interested in virtually, by the Marriage of my aforesd & dearly beloued wife Mary Hooke, for which causes I the abouesd Francis Hooke, do grant & giue Assigne make ouer, & deliuer unto my aforesd & Well beloued wife Mary Hooke, & by these Presents haue granted, given Assig^d made ouer, & deliuered unto my aforesd beloued wife Mary Hooke, these my too Negros male & female, named Thomas, & Hannah, they being part of ye produce of ye abouesd Estate, of Two hundred pounds the sayd two Negros ; To haue & to hould to her the sayd Mary as her owne proper & substantiall, & absolute Estate, for the benefitt of her own attendance & sceruice, granting unto my aforesd, & Well beloued Wife full pouer & lawfull authority, the aforesd too Negroes Thomas & Hannah to Nurture Traine vp Comand aliene, Assigne ouer & dispose of according as shee may see convenient or thinke meete, with out the least hinderance, or deniall of mee the sd ffrancis Hooke, or any other Person or Persons w'soeuer, disclaimeing my Interest or propriety in the abouesd too Negroe servants Thom⁹ & Hannah euer after this my deliuery & disposall to my aforesd & Well beloued wife/ In witness hereof I haue hereunto set my hand, & afixed my seale y⁹ ninth day of February one thousand six hundred eighty & fiue, 1685 : Annoq, Regni Regis Jacobus secund⁹/ ffrancis Hooke (Locus sigilli)

Signed sealed & deliuered/   Capᵗ Francis Hooke came before
   In the Presence of/   mee this 16ᵗʰ day of March
   John Harmon his   168⅘ & did acknowledg this
   Marke H   Instrumᵗ to bee his Act &
   Thymothy Yealls   Deede/
   Edw : Rishworth Jus : pe :

A true Coppy of yᵉ Instrument transcribed out of yᵉ originall & yʳwith Compared this 18ᵗʰ of March 168⅘
     Edw : Rishworth ReCor :

fforasmuch as the tyme Limited in the prouiso, on condition of the with in written Deede of Morgage for yᵉ redemption of the Estate therein barganed, & sould, is now fully past, & No part of the Money yʳin expressed, payd, I John Broughton the Granter do Confess the sayd Estate to bee truly forfited, & yʳfore for the auoyding of further trouble & charges, I haue in yᵉ Presence of the witnesses here vnder named, freely & fully surrendered & deliuered possession of all the with in granted Premisses, unto Capᵗ Charles Frost Atturney to yᵉ sayd Capᵗ Samll Seawell, one of the Administrators vnto the Estate of yᵉ late will of

BOOK IV, FOL. 53.

John Hull Esq[r] The with in named Grantee to haue & to hould the same unto him his heyres, & Assignes as his own proper & absolute estate for euer according to the Tenour of this Deede, this Eleventh day of Novemb[r] Anno Dom 1685 : John Broughton/

Signed & possession given,
    & receiued by y[e] respec-   The resignation of this Mor-
    tiue Prson aboue named/   gage, as surrendered into
    In Presence of us/   the possession of Cap[t]
    Stephen Sewell/   Charles ffrost Atturney to
    Thomas Abbett/   Mr Samell Sewell ; I John
    James Emery/   Broughton do by these
Presents, acknowledg to bee my Act & Deede, this 22th of ffebru : 1685 : Before mee Edw : Rishworth Jus : pe

vera Copia of this resignation transcribed out of y[e] originall & y[r] with Compared, this 18th March 168$\frac{5}{6}$

    p Edw : Rishworth Re : Cor :

To all Christian people to whome this Present Deed of Gyft shall Come/ Rowland young Senjo[r], with his well beloued wife, Joane young of yorke in y[e] Prouince of Mayne In New England sendeth Greeting ;

Now Know yee y[t] I the sd Rowland young, with the Consent & Concurrence of my well beloued wife Joane Young, for y[e] respect, & naturall affection y[t] wee beare vnto o[r] dutifull soun Rowland young of the Ysles of shoals the Northermost, haue given granted, & by these Presents, do giue aliene, & Confirme, as a full & free grant in an Inheritance of fee symple to him the sayd Rowland young our soun heyre Male, lawfully begotten of his body, & to him & thejrs for euer, One Certen tract, or parcell of Land, lijng & being on the North side of the River In yorke abouesd, part of which sd Tract of Land, was formerly y[e] homestall,

& in the possession of or Loueing father, Robert Knight deceased but now lawfully to us Convayed the Present Dowers: The other part a Certen Tract, or remaineing diuission of Land, adioyneing to the former aboue sayd & lijng to the North West of it, or yr abouts, & to carry as much breadth as our father Knights ould ffejld, till It meete with or sonn Roberts grant, & also Adioyneing to a Parcell of Land now in Tenure & possession of my Loueing sonn Robert young, which Wee the abouesd Doners, gaue also to the abouesd Robert Which sd Parcell of Land as abouesd bee It more or less, with all the priuiledges, appurtenances, proprietys, or benefitts, in euery & all respects, as to any part or Parcell there of, Wee freely & Consideratly, giue & grant to our dutifull sonn Rowland & to his as abouesd; And further Wee the sayd Rowland young & Joane my beloued wife, do thus order yt the sayd Rowland young shall haue a free & Coman out lett through our sonn Robert youngs Land which Wee gaue and granted to him, & lyes adioyneing to ye Present granted Tract, & that ye said [54] out lett shall give full & free passage, and repase, both for man & beast, both to the Mill, & also to ye Comans, in yorke, which passage or way in Common, to the sayd Rowland our sonn, for the Intents abouesd, shall remajne to Perpetuity, with all freedome of egress & Ingress, & regress, to through and from the sd way in euery respect to him the sd Rowland his heyres as abouesd, for euer: with out ye lett suite, deniall, or molestation, of the sd Robert young our son or any succeeding him, for euer; Always prouided yt If it should please almighty god, to take to the earth this our Loueing sonn Rowland by death & our loueing & Dutifull daughter his beloued & espowsed wife susanna should suruiue after him, wee thus order & determine in this our Deed of Gyft, that the sd Susanna, shall in that tyme of her Widdowhood or naturall life, remajneing a Widdow shall inioy the produce profitt, or benefitt, of the growth of ye sd Land, or any priuiledg, or any appurtenance yrto belonging, further

BOOK IV, FOL. 54.

declareing, yᵗ this sayd Tract of Land as abouesd in euery respect, as to any part or Parcell thereof, with all the priuiledges & appurtenances, is freely & Clearely quitt, & freely & Clearely quitted from all & former gyfts & grants, or from any Incumberance from by or under us the Doners in all respects, & that oʳ dutifull sonn Rowland & his successors, shall & may lawfully Inioy, hould, vsse & possess, the sd Tract of Land as his own proper inheritance in fee symple, to Perpetuity : And wee the sd Rowland young & Joane my beloued wife doners of the abouesd Premisses, will the same warrant & Defend to our beloued sonn abouesd, & the same both to him & his as abouesd, harmeless to keepe from all & Person, laijng any iust Claime, to all to all or any part of the afore mentioned Premises, from by or under us : And further yᵗ Wee Will do any Act, or Acts that may bee for the better Confirmation of the same, as acknowledgmᵗ & for true Prformance of each & euery Article aboue memtioned wee the sd Doners haue here unto sett our hands, & afixed our seales the 25ᵗʰ of August (1685) Annoq̃ Regni Regis Jacobus secundus, Anno Dom͞ : 1685 :

Signed sealed & Deliuer͞d   Rowland young
  In the Presence of/
  Samell Mathews   his R marke (ʰⁱˢ/ˢᵉᵃˡᵉ)

                                   Joane young her
  his ✗ marke/   marke A (ʰᵉʳ/ˢᵉᵃˡᵉ)
  Tymothy Yealles/

            Rowland young Senjoʳ & Joane young his
            wife, came before mee & acknowledged
            this Instrument to bee yʳ act & Deede/
            this 29ᵗʰ of August 1685
                      John Dauess Deputy President/

A true Coppy of this Instrument aboue written transcribed out of the originall & yʳwith Compared this 18ᵗʰ day of March 168⅘   p Edw : Rishworth Re : Cor :

Book IV, Fol. 54.

To all to whom these Presents shall Come/ I John Smith Senjoʳ of Cape Nuttacke in New England in the Prouince of Mayne, husbandman send Greeting &c: Know yee that I the sd John Smith for & in Consideration of the sume of Thirteene pounds, Current pay of New England, to mee in hand payd by Samell Bankes of Cape Nuttacke, in yᵉ Prouince of Mayn aforesayd Shipewright, before the Ensealing & deliuery hereof, the receipt wʳof I the sd John Smith do hereby acknowledg, & my selfe to bee fully satisfyed; haue for my selfe my heyrs executors, Administrators and Assignes, given, granted barganed, sould, deliuered, & Confirmed, And by these Presents do fully & freely & absolutely giue, grant, bargane, sell, & deliuer Confirme, unto the sayd Samll Bankes, his heyres, executors, Administrators, & Assignes from mee my heyres, executors, Administrators or Assignes, a Certen Tract of vpland Containeing about fourty eight Acres, lijng & being in the Riuer of Cape Nuttacke, on the North East side of the sd Riuer, being bounded in manner following, the West bounds begining at a Small Brooke neare yᵉ Mill, & so runnes North Nore West, to the extent of the bounds of the sd Smith: And on East begins at a Great Rocke, or Stumpe, at the vpper end of sd Bankes his Acre of Land, Wᶜʰnow his house stands, & from thence Nore north East vnto an Hemlocke tree Marked foure square, & from thence North Nore West to the extent of sayd Smith bounds, which Land as aboue bounded with all Tymber, trees, woods vnder woods, profitts priuiledges Comoditys & all other appurtenances wᵗsoeuer yʳunto belonging, to the sd Land as aboue expressed; To haue & to hould, the aboue named Tract of Land & Premisses hereby barganed & sould unto the sayd Samell Bankes his executors, administrators & Assignes, as his & yʳ own goods & proper Estate for euer: & to his & yʳ own proper vss & behoofe for euermore; And I the sd John Smith for my selfe, my executors, & Administrators, do Couenant, promiss & grant to & with the sayd Samell Bankes, his heyres, executors, Ad-

ministrators & Assignes, by these Presents y⁺ I the sd John Smith on the day of the Date here of, and at the tyme of the deliuery, and Ensealeing hereof, haue in my selfe full pouer, good right, and lawfull athority to giue, grant, bargane, sell deliuer & Confirme the sayd Land & Premises, hereby barganed & sould unto the sayd Samell Bankes, his executors, Administrators & assignes for euer more; In manner and forme aforesd, and also that hee the sayd Samell Bankes, his executors, Administrators & Assignes, shall and lawfully may from tyme to tyme, and at all tymes hereafter peaccably, & quictly haue, hould, vss, and Inioy yᵉ sayd Land and Premisses, hereby barganed, & sould, without any manner of Lett, Suite, trouble, euiction, Ejection, Molestation, disturbance, Challenge, Clajme, deniall, or demand what soeuer, of or by mee the sayd John Smith, my heyres, executors, Administrators, or Assignes or any of them, or of or by any other Person, or Persons whatsoeuer lawfully [55] Clajmeing, or to Claime, from by or vnder mee my Act & title; In witness whereof I haue here unto put my hand & seale this First day of March, one thousand six hundred eighty fiue & 86 :   John Smith ┼ (his seale)
Signed, sealed, & deliuered/   Senjoʳ ┼
   In the Presence of us/   Signum
   Timothy Yealles/   John Smith Senjoʳ came & acknowl-
   George Snell/   edged this Instrumᵗ to bee his Act
                     and Deede, vnto Samll Banks this
                     third day of March 168$\frac{3}{6}$
                     before mee ffrancis Hooke Jus : pe :
Mary Smith came before mee, this 14 : June 86 : & did acknowledge yᵉ Instrumᵗ aboue written to bee her Act & Deede/   Edw : Rishworth Jus : pe :
vera Copia of this Instrumᵗ aboue written transcribed out of the originall & there with Compared this 19ᵗʰ day of March 168$\frac{3}{6}$
          p Edw : Rishworth ReCor :

BOOK IV, FOL. 55.

To all Christian people to whome these Presents shall come/ Humphrey Spencer of Kittery In yᵉ County of Yorke shyre in the Massatusetts Jurisdiction in New England sends Greeteing: Now know yee that I Humphrey Spencer, for diuerse good causes & Considerations mee moueing here vnto, more espetially for & In Consideration of the some of nine pounds Steilg: in hand receiued of Beniamē: Barnard of Water Town in the County of Middlesex, and In the Coloney aforesayd, before yᵉ signeing & sealeing hereof, where with I acknowled my selfe to fully satistyd, Contented & payd, & of euery part & Parcell thereof, do acquitt, & for euer discharge the sd Benjā: Barnard by these Presents, Haue given & Granted, barganed, sould, aliend, Enfeoffed, & Confirmed, & do by these Presents absolutely giue, grant, bargane, sell, alliene, Enfeoff & Confirme vnto Benjamen Barnard, his heyres, executors, Administrators, & Assignes, a peece, or Parcell of Land being by measure Thirty Acres, being in the Town of Kittery, & lijng neare Whitts Marsh, being bounded as followeth, with the Land of George Gray on the West, & the Comans next the Riuer of Newgewanacke on the North, and with the Land of Nicholas Gillison on the East, & the land of the sayd Humphrey Spencer on the South:

To haue & to hould, the abouesayd peece and Parcell of Land with all appurtenances & priuiledges, yʳunto belonging, with the wood and Tymber vpon it to him the sayd Benj: Barnard, and his heyres for euer, & the sayd Humphrey Spencer do promiss, Couenant & grant, to and with the sayd Beniamen Barnard, that hee hath in him selfe good right full pouer lawfull authority the same to dispose of, & sell, and yᵗ the same is free & Cleare, and freely and Clearely acquitted exonerated, and discharged, of & from all manner of former Gyfts, grants, leases, Morgages, wills Entayles, executions, pouer of thirds, & all other of Incomberances of what nature and kind souer, had made, done, Committed or suffered to bee done, or Comitted, wʳby the sayd Benjamen

BOOK IV, FOL. 55.

Barnard his heyres or assignes, may bee any way Molested in, euicted, or Eiected out of any part or Parcell thereof, by any Person or Prsons whatsouer, haueing Claimeing or Pretending to haue or Claime any right, title or Interest of in, or to any of the aboue giuen granted Premisses/ and further the sayd Humphrey Spencer doth for him selfe, his heyres executors Administrators, & Assignes, Couenant promiss and grant to and with the sayd Benjamen Barnard, his heyres executors Administrators, & Assignes, the aboue mentioned peece or Parcell of Land with all the priuiledges & appurtenances there to belonging, for euer to defend by these Presents; In witness w{r}of the sayd Humphrey Spencer, hath here unto sett his hand & seale, this Twenteth day of December one thousand six hundred seaventy fiue, 1675: Signed sealed & Deliuered/   his maike
  In Presence of us/   Humphrey *HS* Spencer (his scale)
  George Broughton/
  John Broughton/   Humphrey Spencer appeared before mee & did acknowledg the aboue written Instrument to bee his Act & Deed, with his hand & seale to It, this twenteth day of December 1675: John Wincoll Assotiate/

A true Coppy of this Instrument aboue written, transcribed, & with the originall Compared this 5th day of Aprill 1686:   p Edw: Rishworth Re: Cor.

Thomas Abbett aged 43 yeares, & James Emery Junjo{r} aged 26 yeares testifyeth that about seaventeene years since, James Emery Senjo{r}, haueing sewed some of the Inhabitants for Cutting & Carrijng away of Creeke Thatch, from y{e} lower end of his house Lott, & recouered a Judgm{t} against them, the yeare after, John Roberts Senjo{r} of Douer, came & made Challenge of some March, In that which was

BOOK IV, FOL. 55, 56.

Called the fowling Marsh; These Deponents were Calld to go downe to sd Marsh, to see what Marsh sd Roberts Challinged, & hee Chalenged from the Poynt of Goodman Greenes Lott, & y^r sett down a Stake, & came from thence Southward, to a Poynt of Daniell Gooddines lott, & there set down seuerall stakes, to diuide between the sd Gooddins Land, & his, & then went further Southward so fare as hee thought good, no man opposing him, & then set down more stakes to diuide between James Emery Senjo^r, & him selfe, which the sd Emery agreed to, & the sd Emery hath Inioyed it peaceably euer since, till this yeare John Roberts Junio^r came & sett vp a fence vpon it/

Prouince of Mayne/ Taken vpon oath this 25th of March 1686: before mee   John Wincoll Jus: pe:

The aboue deponents owned these Depositions In Court 30th March: 86:   Edw: Rishworth ReCor:

vera Copia transcribed & Compared with ye Originall, this 6th Aprill 1686   p Edw: Rishworth ReCor:

Thomas Abbett aged about 43 years, & Benonie Hodgden aged 38 years testifyeth, y^t at the request of James Emery Senjo^r of Barwicke, & John Roberts Junjo^r of Douer, went to uew a Prcell of fence, at the lower end of James Emerys house Lott, whither sd fence stood vpon the Marsh Land or not, & haueing uewed the sayd fence as fare as the sd Robe·ts his bounds went: These Deponents found & declared it to ye sd Emery & Roberts, that ye sd fence stoode not [56] vpon any of the Marsh, & then the sd Roberts desired the sd Emery to lett the sayd fence stand seauen yeares, & hee would then remoue it/ & the sayd Emery answeared, hee would lett the sd fence stand foure yeares, If the sd Roberts would then remoue it, but the sd Roberts would not accept of It; And ye sd Emery then warned the sd Roberts not to set any

Prouince of Mayne

BOOK IV, FOL. 56.

fence below the bounds that was formerly sett by the sd Roberts his father, but ye sd Roberts answered hee would take no notice of It, & so they parted/ Taken vpon oath this 25th of March 1686 :
     before mee John Wincoll, Jus : pe :
The Deponents aboue written owned y^r depositions in Court March 30th 1686 : Edw : Rishworth Re : Cor :
vera Copia of these Depositions as ownd In Court, transcribed out of ye originall & y^{r}with Compared this 6th day of Apiill 1686 :   p Edw : Rishworth ReCor :

Daniell Stone aged about 43 years, testifyeth y^t sometyme in August last being desired by James Emery Senjo^r, to go & see what wrong was done to him by John Roberts Junjo^r of Douer In sd Emerys Marsh, at the lower end of his house lott in Barwicke; There lay too rafts of Connows, with thatch grass vpon them & sd Roberts comeing towards sd Connows, the sd Emery asked him who It was y^t had Cutt that Cricke thatch, there, & ye sd Roberts answeared, y^t It was hee & his Company had done It, & y^t hee would beare them out in It, & so the sd Roberts & his Company went to Cutting more of it forth with, in this Deponents sight, & It was vpon the same Land, that Ensigne Abbett testifys to bee ye sd Emerys Land, & sayd Emery warned the sd Roberts not to Cutt or carry away any of it, but sd Roberts answeared hee would Cutt & Carry it away In spight of his teeth

Taken vpon oath this 25th of March 1686 : this aboue Deponent owned this Deposition In Court, March 30th 1686 :
     Edw : Rishworth ReCor :

Daniell Goodine Junio^r aged 30 : years, testifyes to the treuth of ye aboue written testimony of Daniell Stoone,

BOOK IV, FOL. 56.

being Present with him at the same tyme/ Taken vpon oath this 25th of March 1686 : before mee John Wincoll Jus : pe :

A true Coppy of these too last depositions transcribed out of the original & y^{r}with Compared this 6th day of Aprill 1686 : p Edw : Rishworth ReCor :

Nathan Lawd Junjo^r aged 29 years

Testifyeth y^t about the latter end of summer 1684 : hee hyred a little peece of Cricke thatch, below the End of Goodmā : Emerys house Lott, in Barwicke of John Roberts Junjo^r of Douer, & ye sd Roberts owned the bounds betweene the sd Emerys Land & his, to bee a row of small slabbs, y^t stood vpon the hyer part of the Marsh land, & the lower part of sd Marsh hee owned to bee the sd Emerys/ taken vpon oath this 25th of March 1686 : before mee
John Wincoll Jus : pe :

vera Copia of this testimony aboue written transcribed & with originall Compared, this 6th day of Aprill . 1686 :
p Edw : Rishworth ReCor :

The testimonys of Abra : Conley & John Whitte/

Being examined made oath that Renald Jenkines bought a Parcell of vpland of John Newgroue, of about six Acres, lijng between Thomas Joanes & Dinnis Downeings Land, w^{r}on the sd Jenkines built a little house, & liued vpon it some Certen tyme/ & further sayth not/ Taken vpon oath this 13th of May : 1674 : before mee Edw : Rishworth Assoti^{ts} :

A true Coppy transcribed, & with originall Compared this 7th of Aprill : 86   p Edw · Rishworth Re : Cor :

BOOK IV, FOL. 56.

The Deposition of Renald Ginkens aged about 75 yeares/
This Deponent testifyeth y^t betweene fouity & fiuety yeares since, this Deponent bought six Acres of Land of John Newgroue, begining at the water side between the Lands of Thomas Joanes, & Joshua Downeing at Kittery, which land I the deponent built an house vpon, & liued in it some Certen tyme, & after that, I gaue or sould It for a small sume, to one Margery wife of William Euerett, sometyme liueing at Kittery or her Daughter Martha/ & further sayth not/

Taken vpon oath this 23th of June 1683 : before mee
        John Wincoll Jus : pe :
vera Copia transcribed & Compared with ye originall y^s 7th Aprill 1686 : p Edw : Rishworth Re : Cor :

The Deposition of Thom^s Turner aged about 73 : years/
This Deponent testifyeth y^t about fifteene or sixteen years since, Mr Dinnis Downeing of Kittery, agreed with this Deponent to set vp a Parcell of fence, on that side next Downings land, which is next to a Parcell of Land Comanly Called & known by ye name of Mr William Leightons six Acres, at Kittery, which I the Deponent did, & sd Downeing went & shewed mee where I should set it, & as I was at worke about It Majo^r Nicho : Shapleigh came by, & some dayes after, tould mee the Deponent I had done wrong/ I asked him in what/ sd Shapleigh replyed, I was come too fare out with the fence/ I tould him I did as my Imployer had directed mee/ Now this fence which I the Deponent had Sett vp by ye sd Downings order, was a great deale further out towards ye sd six Acres then any fence had beene before/ & further sayth not/

Taken vpon oath this 23th of June 1683 : before mee
        John Wincoll Jus : pe :
vera Copia transcribed, w^{t}h ye originall Compared this 7th day of Aprill 1686 : p Edw : Rishworth Re : Cor :

Book IV, Fol. 56, 57.

The Deposition of Thomas Hunscume aged about 60 years/
This Deponent testifyeth, that Joshua Downeings fence which is on y^t side his foild next the peece of Land (Comanly Called & known by the name of Mr Leightons six Acres) is further out next ye six acres considerably y^n the fence which was there in former tyme stood/ & further sayth not/
Taken vpon oath this 23th July 1683 : before mee
      John Wincoll Jus : pe :
vera Copia transcribed ye 8th day of Aprill 86.
      p Edw : Rishworth ReCor :

The Deposition of Martha Lawde ye wife of Nathan Lawd aged 42 years
This Deponent testifys w^n shee was little, her mother haueing tenn shillings of her, as the Deponent heard my mother say, which money the Deponents mother Margarett Euerett layd out for six Acres of Land wch shee bought of Renald Jenkins, which Land this Deponents husband would not accept of, vpon ye refusall w^{r}of the Deponents mother gaue him a steere in lew y^{r}of & her mother sould that six Acres of Land to Mr Will Leighton/ This six acres of Land lyeth between the Land of Thos Joanes & Joshua Downeing at Kittery, begining at the water side/ & further sayth not/
Taken vpon oath this 23 : of June 1682 : before mee
      John Wincoll Jus : pe .
A true Coppy transcribed & with originall Compared this 8th of Aprill 1686 : p Edw : Rishworth ReCor :

[57] To all people to whome these Presents shall come/ John Shapleigh of Kittery in the prouince of Mayne In New England sends Greeteing/ Now Know yee y^t I the aboue

BOOK IV, FOL. 57.

named John Shapleigh for diuerse good Causes mee y^{r}unto moueing, more especially for & in Consideration of Eighty pounds to mee in hand payd by James Johnsone of Hampton In ye Prouince of New Hampshyre Millwright, ye receipt w^{r}of, & euery part & Parcell y^{r}of I acknoledg & y^{r}with am fully satisfyd Contented & payd; Haue given granted barganed, sould, aliend Enfeoffed made ouer & Confirmed, & by these Presents for mee my heyres, executors, Administrators, & Assignes, do freely Clearely & absolutely giue, grant, bargane, sell, aliene, Enfeoffe, make ouer, & Confirme, vnto him the sd James Johnson his heyres, executors, administrators, & Assignes, for euer one quarter part of my saw Mill, & Corne Mill at spruse Cricke, in the Town of Kittery, in the Prouince of Mayne, with all the Implements & necessarys y^{r}unto belonging, as Crows, Doggs, saws & all other Iron Worke, y^{r}unto belonging togeather, with all the one quarter part of all the priuiledges of Tymber belonging to the sd saw Mill; To haue & to hould the aboue given & granted Premisses, with all ye priuiledges, & appurtenances y^{r}unto belonging or in any wise appertaineing, to him ye sd James Johnson his heyres executors, Administrators, or Assignes for euer, to vss occupy & Improue, to his or y^r own proper benefitt, & behoofe with out any Molestation, lett or hinderance, from any Prson or Persons, Clajmeing any title, right or Interest y^{r}unto, from by or vnder mee; And I the sd John Shapleigh doth Couenant & promiss to & with the sd Johnson, y^t at any tyme hereafter vpon the reasonable request of sd Johnson, his heyres, or assignes, to do & Prforme any act or thing, for ye better Confirmeing & sure makeing, of the Prmis^s aforesd/ In witness w^{r}of sayd Shapleigh hath here vnto sett his hand & seale, this

BOOK IV, FOL. 57.

fifth day of Aprill one thousand six hundred Eighty fiue/
Signed sealed & Deliuered/   John Shapleigh (his seale)
  In the Presence of/   Mr John Shapleigh came before
  John Purrington/   mee this 30th of March 1686. &
  Joseph Hamond/   owned this Instrument to bee
                his act & Deede/
                Edw : Rishworth Jus : pe :
A true Coppy of this grant transcribed out of ye originall
& there with Compared y^s 7th of Aprill 1686
                p Edw : Rishworth Re : Cor :

Know all men by these Presents that I Peter Wittum of
the Town of Kittery, & Prouince of Maine, Senjo^r, do by
these Presents Convey, Assigne & sett ouer, & Estate the
one halfe of the aboue specifyd Premisses, vnto William
Wittum my sonn, & his lawfull heyres after him for euer,
In as full & ample manner, to all intents & purposes as euer,
It was my own by all & euery Condition & Conveyance
w^{ts}oeuer, made to mee y^{r}of (one acre thereof excepted)
which I reserue for my own uss, dureing the tyme of my
owne, & my wifes naturall life, & to bee with in the fenced
ground of my sd sonn; & hee to keepe tenantable the out-
side fence for security thereof, which acre of Land shall bee
w^r I thinke most meete, & the first Choyce y^{r}of abide un-
changable: In Consideration of y^e Premisses my sonn is to
pay mee, dureing the tyme of my naturall life, foureteene
buslls to bee deliuered at my house of M^{r}ch$\bar{\mathrm{i}}$ble Indean
Corne, & dureing the life of my wife after mee seauen buslls

BOOK IV, FOL. 57.

ditto deliuered as aforesd, & in default of the payment as aforesd, the Land remaineth obliged/

Signed sealed & deliuered/   The signe ℘ of Peter (ʰⁱˢ ₛₑₐₗₑ)
  In the Presence of us/
  Siluanus Nocke/   Wittum Senoʳ
  William Gowen   March   The foureteene buslls of Corne
  alias Smith/   : 18 :   is to bee vnderstood to bee
                     : 1685 : payd Annually at the house
                               of Peter Wittum Senjoʳ &
                               seaven buslls of Corne to bee
                               payd yearely to Riddigon
                               Wittum dureing her his
                               wifes life, her husband dying
                               before her/

Wee Peter Wittum Senjoʳ & Riddigon his wife do acknowledg this Conuayance or Instrumeᵗ to bee our Act & Deede, this 5th of Aprill : 1686 : before mee

       Edw : Rishworth Jus : pe :

A true Coppy of this Instrumᵗ transcribed & with origall Compared yᵉ 9th of Aprill 1686 :

       p Edw : Rishworth ReCor :

Bee It known vnto all men by these Presents, yᵗ I william Wittum of yᵉ Town of Kittery In the Prouince of Mayne, for suerall good Causes & Considerations, mee here vnto moueing, but more espetially for & In Consideration of a Certen Tract of Land by mee in hand receiued of Peter Wittum Junjoʳ my brother, the which tract being the one halfe of a Certen Tract of Land purchased by my father of Joseph Hammond of the sd Kittery, ljng & being at a place Called Tompsons Poynt, between the Land of Thomas Roads on the one side, & the Land of William Furbush on yᵉ other side, & formerly known by the name of William Oliuers Land; the one halfe of which tract being given, granted, Confirmed, by Peter Wittum Senjo^r my father unto Peter Wittum Junjo^r my brother; Now Know yee y^t ffor & in Consideration of y^t halfe or Moeity so Assign'd, & Confirmed by my father to my brother; That I williā: Wittum by mutuall & free exchange with Peter Wittum my brother, do by these Presents, giue, grant, signe, & sett ouer to Peter Wittum my brother all my right & title to & in a Certen tract of Land, Contajneing about fifety acres more or less, part w^{r}of by mee Improued fronting on Sturgion Cricke, ljng & being between the now possession of Leonard Drowne on the one side, & William Sanders on ye other side, as also my right & title in Twenty acres of Land, granted to mee by the Town of Kittery, & beareing date 24th of June 1682: all which I do by these Presents Confirme & Conferr my whoole right y^{r}of & y^{r}in; to my brother Peter Wittum Junjo^r in as full & ample manner, as In any wise I can Estate the same, euen as fully & properly as euer It was my own, from mee my heyres executors, Administrators, or Assignes, to him & his for euer/ In witness w^{r}unto I haue here to affixed my hand & seale this sixt day of Aprill one thousand six hundred eighty six, In the first yeare of the Reigne of his Maiesty James the secund, of England, Scotland, France, & Ireland King, fidej Defeno^{rs} 1686:   William Wittum (his seale)

Signed, sealed, & Deliuered in Presence of/
Nicholas Smith/
John Howe/
his marke ЭН

William Wittum came before mee this 6th of Aprill 1686: & acknowledged this Instrum^t aboue written w^{r}unto hee hath afixed his hand & seale to bee his Act & Deede/
Edw: Rishworth Jus: pe:

A true Coppy of this Instrum^t transcribed, & with originall Compared, this 9th day of Aprill 1686:

p Edw: Rishworth Re: Cor:

BOOK IV, FOL. 58.

[58] Wee the select men of the Town of yorke, whose names are here subscribed haue layd out vnto John Twisden, a Tract of Land Contajneing one hundred & Twenty Acres, lijng & Adioyneing unto the brooke on the North East side of Phillip Addams his house lott of Land, & runneth in breadth from Richd Bankes his house lott of Land, North West, sixty poole or pearchs to the bounds of the Lands of Honory Sympsons which hee now liueth vpon, & runneth backewards from the Countrey highway into the woods North East 320 poole or pearch as Ric Bankes & Hene : Symsons lotts runnes & adioyīng to y{m} onely sd Twisden to leaue half an high way into y{e} Woods on the North West side of it out of the sd Land next to Henery Sympsons All which abouesd Tract of Land part w{r}of hee hath long possessed, Wee haue layd out & Confirmed, unto the aforesd John Twisden his heyres & Assignes for euer, with all the Interest the Town of yorke hath in the sayd Land/ Witness our hands this 12{th} day of June 1685 :   Job Allcocke/

y{s} grant mistaken in y{e} Entrey, & is Entered in the. 59   John Harmon/
pa This aboue written is Entered in y{e} Town booke of
yorke ReCords, this 16{th} of June 1686   John Sayword/
         p me Abraham Preble Town Clarke |

* A true Coppy transcribed, & with originall Compared this 28{th} of Aprill 1686 :   p Edw : Rishworth ReCor :

To all Christian people, to whome these Presents shall come ; Know yee y{t} I John Twisden in the Town of yorke in the Prouince of Mayne yemon, in New England send Greeting ; know yee that the sd John Twisden, for diuerse good Causes & Considerations, y{r}unto moueing, & more espetially for a ualewable some to mee In hand already payd, & secured, before y{e} Ensealeing & deliuery of these Presents, by Joseph Mowlton of yorke aforesd Yeamon, resciding in the sd Prouince, the receipt whereof I do acknowledg, & do for my selfe my heyres, executors, administrators, &

Assignes, acquitt & discharge the aboue named Jos: Mowlton, his heyres executors Administrators & Assignes from euery part & Parcell y'rof, haueing given, granted, & by these Presents do freely & absolutely giue, grant, bargane, sell aliene Enfeoff & Confirme, vnto Joseph Mowlton, his heyrs, executors, Administrators, & Assignes, one hundred & twenty acres of vpland, given & granted to mee by the Select men of the Town of yorke, in the aforesd prouince, lijng & Adioyning, unto the brooke on the North East side of Phillip Addams his house lott & Land, & runneth In breadth from Richd Bankes his house Lott, of Land North West sixty pooles, or pearch, to the bounds of the Land of Hene: Sympson which hee now liueth vpon, & runneth backeward from the Countrey high way North East three hundred & Twenty pooles, or pearches as Ric: Bankes his, & Hene: Sympsons Lotts runnes, & Adioyneing to them onely the sd Twisden is to leaue halfe an high way into the Woods, on the North West side of it out of the sd Land next to Hene: Symsons/ all wch abouesd Tract of Land part where of hee hath long possessed; Wee haue layd out & Confirmed unto the aforesd John Twisden, his heyres, & Assignes for euer with all the Interest the Town of yorke hath in the sd Land wch land as aboue bounded & is by these bounds & lymitts expressed with all my right title & Interest I now haue or out to haue at ye tyme & deliuery of these Presents in all ye Lands p. rch. as parsters fenced arrable Land, planted & unplanted, Commonages tymber Tymber trees woods, vnderwoods, profitts, priuiledges, & all manner of appurtenances, w'soeuer, there unto belonging, or in any wise app'rtaineing; To haue & to hould, all & singular the ye aboue granted, & barganed Premisses with all other rights & priuiledges, y'runto belonging unto mee the sd Twisden with euery part & parcell there of unto the sd Joseph Mowlton his heyres executors Administrators & Assignes, to his & y^r onely proper benefitt & behoofe for euer, & I the sd John Twisden do by these Presents, Couenant & promiss for my selfe, & in the behalfe of my heyres, executors, Administrators & Assigns that at & upon the Ensealeing of these Presents, I was the true & lawfull owner, of all & singular the aboue granted Premises, & I had & haue good right, & lawfull authority in my own name, to grant bargane sell aliene, Convay & Confirme as aforesd, the same aboue expressed; And y^t the sayd Joseph Mowlton his heyres, executors, & Administrators may & shall, by vertue of these Presents from tyme to tyme, & at all tymes for euer hereafter, lawfully & peaceably Inioy, haue, hould, vss, occupy & possess, all the aboue granted Premisses, with y^r appurtenances free & Cleare, & freely and Clearely acquitted & discharged, from all manner of gifts, grants, barganes, sales, Leases, Morgages, Joynters, Dowers, Judgm^{ts} executions, forfitures, troubles, & all other Incomberances w^{t}soeuer, had, made, done, or suffered to bee done, by mee John Tysden my heyres, executors, Administrators or Assignes, at any tyme or tymes before the Ensealeing & deliuery of these Presents, and that the sayd John Twisden In behalfe of him selfe, his heyres, executors, Administrators & Assignes, shall & will at all tymes & for euer hereafter warrant & Defend the right & Title of ye aboue granted, & mentioned Premisses, with the appurtenances, & euery part and Parcell there of unto the aforesd Joseph Mowlton, his heyres executors, or Administrators, against euery Person, & all Persons w^{t}soeuer laijng any Claime y^{r}to, or to any part there of from by or under mee, or any other by my procurement/ In testimony w^{t}of I haue here unto afixed my hand & scale, this tenth day of Aprill,

Book IV, Fol. 58, 59.

one thousand six hundred eighty fiue, Annoq, Regni, Regis Jacobi Secundi/   John Twisden (his seale)
Signed, Sealed, & Deliuered/   Always It is to bee under-
   In the Presence of/   stood y{t} Joseph Mowlton is
   Edw. Rishworth/   to pay y{e} proprietors rent
   Arther Bragdon y{e} sonn   When It is Demanded/
     of Thomas Bragdon/   Wee Susanna Twisden, & Samll
                           Twisden do giue o{r} free Consents
John Twisden Susanna   to this bill of Sale aboue writ-
   Twisden & Samll Twis-   ten, w{r}unto we haue afixed our
   den came before mee this   hands & seales
   10{th} of Aprill 1686: &   Susanna Twisden her (her seal)
   owned this Instrum{t} aboue
   written to bee y{r} act & Deede/   marke ST
     Edw: Rishworth Jus: pe: Samuell Twisden (his seal)
                             his marke ST

A true Coppy of this Instrume{t} aboue written, transcribed out of the originall & y{r}with Compared, this 28{th} of Aprill 1686:   p Edw: Rishworth Re: Cor:

[59] These Presents do bind mee Joseph Mowlton of the Town of yorke In the prouince of Mayne, my heyres, executors, Administrators & Assignes, In Consideration of a Parcell of Land, & swine which I bought of John Twisden, & of his Mother & brother Samell, who were also there in Concern'd, for y{e} sume of one hundred & eighty pounds, the sale w{r}of appeareth beareing date the 10{th} of Aprill 1685: do hereby stand obleiged to pay or Cause to bee payd the aforesd nine scoore pounds, according to tyme & Conditions following, from mee my heyres, executors, administrators, & Assignes, vnto the aforesd John Twisden, or in Case of his decease to his Mother Susanna Twisden, & after her decease to Samuell Twisden, or to whome y{e} longest suruiuer shall

appoynt, according to the seuerall tymes & Conditions thereof/

The first payment there of, is to bee pd In the yeare 1685 : being twelue pounds in goods at Current prises, & eight pounds in money/ And the other eight scoore pounds, is to bee payd unto John Twisden, & after him to the Longest suruiuer, namely tenn pounds Annually & euery yeare for the tyme & tearme of sixteene yeares, six pounds In goods, & foure pounds in money, vpon the Twenty ninth day of Aprill, & ye goods to bee at Current prises, the Issew of wch payments will end In Aprill Anno Dom : one thousand seauen hundred & too/

It is always to bee understoode, that It shall bee lawfull, If cause requir to take any Legall Course to recouer any of these Prticular payments, if Neglected/ In testimony w^rof I haue here unto afixed my hand seale this Tenth day of April one thousand six hundred Eighty & fiue 1685 :

Signed sealed & Deliuered/   Joseph Mowlton ($_{scale}^{his}$)
   In Presence of/   Joseph Mowlton came before
   Edw : Rishworth/   mee this tenth of Aprill one
   Arther Bragdon, the sonn   thousand six hundred eighty
   of Thom^a Bragdon/   six, & owned this Instrument
                                     within written to bee his Act
                                     & Deede/
                                     Edw : Rishworth Jus : pe :

vera Copia of this bill transcribed out of the originall & y^rwith Compared this 28th day of Aprill : 1686 :
                     p Edw : Rishworth Re : Cor :

Wee ye Select men of the Town of yorke, whose names are here subscribed, haue layd out unto John Twisden a Tract of Land Containeing one hundred & twenty Acres lijng & adioyneing unto a brooke, on the North East side of

Book IV, Fol. 59.

Phillip Addam house lot of Land, & runneth In breadth from Richd Bankes house lott of land North West, Sixty pooles or pearch to the bounds of the land of Hene : Sympsons, Which hee now liueth vpon, & runneth backeward from ye Countrey high way, North East, three hundred & Twenty pooles, or pearches, as Richd Bankes his lott, & Henery Sympsons lotts runnes, & adioyneing to them, onely the sd Twisden is to leaue halfe an high way into the woods, on the North West side of it, out of ye sd land next to Hene : Sympons, all which abouesd tract of Land, part w^{r}of hee hath long possess'd Wee haue laid out, & Confirmed, vnto ye aforesd John Twisden, his heyres & Assigns for euer, with all ye Interest ye Town of Yorke hath In ye sayd Land/ witness o^r hands this 12th day of June 1685.

This aboue written Entred in the Town   Job Allcocke/
   book of yorke ReCords, this 16th of   John Harmon/
   June 1685 :   John Sayword/
     p me Abra : Preble Town Clark :

A true Coppy of this Town grant, transcribed, & with originall Compared this 28th of Aprill 1686 :

         p Edw : Rishworth Re : Cor :

Receiued the 20th day of March 168$\frac{4}{5}$ of John Mills fourty shillings in moneys, and other pay which is in full payment for land my late father George Taylour sould to the sayd John Mills, & is in full payment of all bills, bonds, obligations, y^t euer my sayd father George Taylour euer had, or any other hath of sd John Mills in there hands/ I say receiued the sume abouesd/   p mee Andrew Taylour/
Signed sealed & deliuered/   Andrew Taylo^r acknowledged
   In the Presence of/   this receipt aboue to bee his
   George Pearson/   Act, & Deede, & signed &
                       deliuered by him March 20th
                       1685 : Before mee
                           John Richards Assist^t

Book IV, Fol. 59.

A true Coppy of this receipt aboue written, transcribed out of the Originall & there with Compared this 30ᵗʰ day of March 1686: p mee Edw: Rishworth Re: Cor:

George Taylours bill of sale/
Bee It known unto all men by these Presents, yᵗ I George Tayler & Margeret Taler my wife with one Consent Sell vnto John Mills our plantation of vpland, & possession of vpland, & a little Ysland, of Meddow belonging vnto it, vnto John Mills with all purtenances, & priuiledges yʳto belonging, unto John Mills, & John Mills is to pay, or cause to bee payd vnto Geo: Tayler, his heyres, executors, administrators & Assignes, the full & iust sume of thirteen pounds, in any pay yᵗ is payable from man to man, whereof the sayd Mills hath three years of payment, paijng fiue pounds a yeare, & the last yeare fourty shillings in Money, & the sayd George Tayler doth bind him selfe his heyres, executors, Administrators, or Assignes, in a bond of Thirty pounds to make good sale of the sd Land, & Meddow, aboue mentioned, & a small Necke of Meddow, belonging to the Ysland aboue mentioned/ In witness here of wee sett too our hands, & seale this 29ᵗʰ of Julie 1679:

Andrew Brown/ The Marke of George Tayler ⌐ (his seale)
William Burregh/ The marke ᘔᘈ of Margeret Tayler/

William Burregh Andrew Brown, did appeare before mee this 13ᵗʰ of Aprill 1686, & made oath that they did see George Tayler, & Margerett his wife sign seale & deliuer this Instrument unto John Mills, as thejr act & Deede, & Geo: Tayler gaue him possession by Turffe & Twigg, in part in lew of the whoole/

Taken vpon oath this 13ᵗʰ of Aprill 1686: before mee
Walter Gyndall Comissioʳ

BOOK IV, FOL. 59, 60.

vera Copia of this Deed aboue written transcribed out of
y⁰ originall & yʳwith Compared this first day of May 1686 :
p Edw : Rishworth ReCor :

To all Christian people to whome this Deede or Instrument shall Come/ Andrew Taler now of Boston Seaman,
In the County of Suffocke in New England In America,
sonn & heyre to George Tayler Yeamon formerly of Bla :
Poynt in yᵉ prouince of Mayne lately deceased, vpon seuerall good Causes, & Considerations mee yʳunto moueing, &
more espetially for & in Consideration of seauen pounds
eight shillings in moneys, to mee In hand payd by John
Mills of Bla : Poynt, in the Prouince of Mayne in New
England, the receipt wʳof I do acknowledg befoie the sealeing here of, & do acquitt the sd John Mills, his heyres, executors Administrators & Assignes, for euer, by these Presents : Giue, grant bargan, Sell, aliene & absolutely Confirme, unto yᵉ sd John Mills his heyres executors & Asignes,
[60] all yᵗ vpland &c : which my late father George Tayler,
formerly sould unto the sd John Mills, his heyres, executors
& Assignes for euer, & further I Andrew Taylor being now
at full age Twenty one years & vpwards, haue given granted,
barganed & sould unto the sd John Mills his heyres, executors, & administrators all that Meddow & Marsh ground
that lyeth on the North West side of yᵉ Pigsty Riuer, & all
other Meddow else where, lijng at Bla : Poynt, which formerly was in the possession of my late father Geo : Tayler,
& now in my owne right & pouer to sell & dispose of as
heyre unto my late father George Tayler, being about thirty
Acres of Meddow bee it More or less, & the vpland Con-
tajnes fiuety Acres bee It more or less, with all the profitts,
Comōnages easements Imunitys, & all & singular the priuiledges, & yᵉ appurtenances any wise appʳtajneing yʳunto,

quietly to haue & to hould, with out any matter of Challenge, Clajme or demand of mee the sayd Andrew Tayler, or any Person or Persons from by or under mee, my heyrs executors, Administrators or Assignes for euer & I do further Couenant & promiss that the Land & Meddows abouesayd, Which I Andrew Tayler now Sell & confirme unto John Mills his heyres & Assignes, I Andrew Tayler do Ingage, my selfe, my heyres, executors, Administrators, to & with the sd John Mills, his heyres, executors, Administrators and assignes, the vpland, & Meddows are free & Cleare from all Gifts, grants, barganes Sales, leases, Dowers, Morgages, Judgm^{ts} or any other Incomberances w^{t}soeuer, & do likewise warrant & defend the Title, & Interest of the premisses, & euery part & Parcell y^{r}of, to him y^e sd John Mills, his heyres, executors &c: for euer: from me my heyres, executors &c: or any other Person or Persons, from by or under mee, or by my procurement; In witness w^{r}of I haue here unto set my hand & seale, this 20th day of March one thousand six hundred eighty fiue six 168$\frac{5}{6}$ In the secund yeare of y^e Reigne of o^r Soueraigne Ld, James the secund, King of England, Scotland &c: Andrew Tayler ($^{his}_{seale}$)

Signed, sealed, & Deliuered,   Andrew Tayler appeared this
 In the presence of/   20th day of March 1685: &
 James Carre/   acknowledged this Instru-
 George Pearson/   m^t to bee his Act & Deede,
                                  before mee
                                  John Richards Assistant/

A true Coppy of this Instrum^t aboue written, transcribed out of ye originall & y^{r}with Compared, this first day of May 1686:   p Edw. Rishworth, Re: Cor.

Bee It known unto all men by these Presents, that I Andrew Tayler now of Boston seaman in the County of Suffocke, in New England in America being the rightfull sonn,

& heyre, of my late father George Taler of Blã: Poynt in the prouince of Mayne as abouesd, haue made, ordajned, Constituted, authorized & appoynted, & by these Presents, do make ordaine, & Constitute authorize, & appoynt, my trusty & well beloued frejnd John Mills of Bla: Poynt Yeoman, In the prouince of Mayne &c: my true & lawfull Atturney, to take & receiue peaceable & quiet possession, & seazine of, & in all y^t Messuage or tenement, that my late father George Tayler formerly sould him, & all other Meddows, or Marsh ground lijng on the North West side of pigsty Riuer or else w^r at Blã: Poynt, with all the rights, members, & app^rtenances sould by my late father George Taler & my selfe unto the sd John Mills, & the same possession so had, & taken, to detajne & keepe to his own vss & behoofe, his hejrs & Assignes, according to the Teno^r & true meaneing of ye Deede, w^rby the sd Premisses are Conuayed, unto the sayd John Mills, & If any refuse to giue quiett & peaceable possession, of the Premisses aboue méntioned, I do Impoure my sd Atturney, to sue arrest, Implead, Imprison, condemne & release, & to appeare before any Judges, Justises, y^r to answere reply, make answere, & psecute any y^t shall refuse deliuery, or giueing possession of sayd land, or Meddow, or do any other Act or thing that may bee for the secureing of the sd vpland & Meddows, ratifijng & Confirmeing all & w^tsoeuer my sd Atturney or his substitutes shall do or cause lawfully to bee done in & about the Premisses by these Presents/ In witness w^rof I haue here unto set my hand & seale, this Twenty & secund day of March one thousand six hundred eighty & fiue, six, In the secund yeare of ye Reigne of o^r soueraigne Ld James the secund King of England Scotland &c: 168 4/5   Andrew Taler (his seale)
Signed, sealed & deliuered/   Andrew Talo^r appeared & ac-
  In ye Presence of/   knowledged this letter of
  James Carr/   Atturney to bee his act &
  George Pearson/   Deede this 22th of March
    168 4/5 before mee
    John Richards Assistant

Book IV, Fol. 60.

vera Copia of this Instrument with written transcribed, & with the originall Compared, this 3d of May 1686:
     p Edw : Rishworth ReCor :

Know all men by these Presents, that I Renald Jenkines of Kittery in the County of Yorke In New England, for diuerse good causes & Considerations mee there unto moueing, haue given, & granted vnto my sonn Jabez Jenkines & by these Presents, do giue grant & Confirme vnto my sayd sonn Jabez, his heyres & Assignes for euer, my too lower most peeces or Parcells of sault Marsh, ljng on each side of Sturgeon Cricke, with all ye priniledges & benefitts there vnto belonging : To haue & to hould, the aboue mentioned Marshes, with out any Molestation, let or hinderance, from any laijng Claime there vnto, from by or vnder mee, In witness where of, I haue here unto sett my hand & seale, this tenth day of ffebr : one thousand six hundred seauenty and eight/   The marke of ν

Signed sealed & deliuered   Renold Jenkins (his seale)
 In the Presence of/   Renald Jenkins appeared before mee
 Jos : Hammond/   the 20th day of March one thousand
 Katherin Leighton/   six hundred seaventy and eight, &
         nine, seaventy, 167$\frac{8}{9}$ & did ac-
         knowledg the aboue written Deed
         of Gift, to bee his Act & Deede/
        John Wincoll Assotiate/

A true Coppy of this Deed of Gift aboue written, transcribed out of the Originall, & there with Compared this 13th day of May 1686 :   p me Edw : Rishworth Re : Cor :

Book IV, Fol. 60, 61.

To all before whome these Presents may come/ Bee It known y[t] I Thomas Mowlton Senj[or] of y[e] Towne of yorke In the prouince of Mayne, out of my naturall affection I beare vnto my too Sons, Jeremiah & Joseph Mowlton, & other Causes also mee y[r] vnto moueing, do freely giue, grant, & by these Presents fully Confirme vnto my too sons fore mentioned, & thejr heyres for euer, my whoole farme, vidz[t] All my land both arable, & pasture Land, all my Meddows fresh, & sault, also all my out lands app[r]tajneing in any wise unto mee, as well as that Which is Inclosed, togeather with my now dwelling house, & all out houses, with all my moueables, with in doores & with out, & to declare my right, & Title unto all the before granted Premisses, to bee iust & good, & from the Date here of do Invest, & possess: these my too sons with ye same for thejr own proper vsse & benefitt for euer, all which is to bee æqually diuided between my too sonns, & which is already done by them selues, [61] (the oarchard onely excepted) which haue before given to my sonn Joseph; All this to stand good, & abide firme for euer prouided there shall bee a Comfortable mantenance allowed to my selfe & beloued wife, dureing our naturall lifes; the Land and stocke before mentioned shall bee Carefully Improued, from tyme to tyme at ye soole & æquall Charge of these my too sonns, the Land shall bee tilled, all sorts of grajne, gathered in housed threshed out, & made fitt for vsse, & eight Cow kind with one Mare, shall bee at the Constant Comand of my selfe & wife so long as Wee shall liue, these Cattle shall bee prouided for both sumer & winter, with out any Cost of ours/ onely at the decease of my beloued wife, if shee out liue mee, shee may dispose of all her weareing Cloaths too platters, to whome shee pleaseth, & the bedd y[t] now wee ly vpon, shall bee my sonn Josephs; In witness w[r]of wee haue here unto set o[r]

hands & seales, this fifth day of June one thousand six hundred eighty foure/ 1684 :   Thomas Mowlton (his seale)
Signed sealed &   his ⁂ marke
  Deliuered in Presence   Martha Mowlton (her seale)
  of Shubeal Dumer/
  Charles Breissan/
  The aboue named Gyft from our father Thomas Mowlton Wee his too sonns Jeremiah & Joseph with the Conditions annexed do freely Accept, as witness our hands/
                    Jeremiah ✚ Mowlton
                    Joseph Mowlton
  All the Partys in this Instrument mentioned acknowledged the same to bee y^r Act & Deed, vidz^t Thomas Molton Senjo^r & his too sonns Jeremiah & Joseph Mowlton before mee September 26 : 1684 :   John Dauess Jus : pe :
  A true Coppy of this Deede with the acknowledgm^{ts} subscribed, transcribed out of the originall, & there with Compared this 14th day of May 1686 :
                       p Edw : Rishworth ReCor :

  Know all by these Presents y^t I Joshua Scottow of Bla͞ : Poynt, do bargane & sell vnto William Burrage of Scarbrough, for full & ualewable Considerations in hand receiued a Parcell of Marshland in sd Scarbrough begining with ye first Cricke, next vnto a fence or double ditch of Andrew Brownes & thence along ye sd Cricke vnto a fence of rails about Certen Small pounds, & from thence from it along to the head of another Cricke runing into the Riuer on the other side of the Necke, along y^t Cricke vnto a stake or poole set vp in the sd Cricke, from thence vpon a Streight lyne to the Southermost end of Robert Nicolls his Chymney, which was set vp before the last Indean Warr, & also hee is to haue from y^t poole all the Marsh belonging to the sd Scottow, & not Included in Andrew Browns Grant, which lyeth betweene sd Andrew Brown, & my ditch made before the sd Warr, all the aboue sayd Marsh as is expressd, To haue & to hould, with ye priuiledges y^runto belonging, free from all other barganes, & with out any Clajme of any other Persons, to bee vnto the sd William Burrage his heyres, or Assignes for euer, & y^t it shall bee warrantizd, & Confirmed by mee the sd Joshua Scottow mine heyres, executors, & Administrators vnto the sd William Burrage his heyres, or Assignes in witness of the Premisses I haue here unto set my hand & seale, made at Blacke Poynt this 19th day of October In the yeare of o^r Lord one thousand six hundred eighty fiue 1685 : In the secund yeare of o^r Soueraigne Ld James the secund, by the Grace of God, King of England &c · the Land aboue mentioned is bounded from the Cricke, aboue expressed vnto ye Lyne of Nichols his house, with the Riuer/   Joshua Scottow (his seale)

Witness/   Capt Scottow acknowledged this Instrume^t to bee his Act & Deed this 19th of Octob^r 1685 : before mee

                      Edw : Tyng Jus : pe :

A true Coppy of this Instrument aboue written transcribed out of the originall & there with Compared this 18th of May 1686 :   p Edw : Rishworth Re : Cor :

To the Marshall of the Province of Maine alias County of Yorke or his Deputy

In his Majestys name you are Required to leavy of the goods Cattle or Chattles, to the vallew of tenn pounds 7^s 5^d and 3^s 6^d for the Execution all as mony and for want thereof of the body of John Parker Senr form^rly his Maj^{ties} goale Keeper of this province to Sattisfie Henry Dering sometime

BOOK IV, FOL. 61.

of Piscattaqua now of Boston for a Judgm^t of Court, granted at a Court of Associates holden at Welds for this Province Aprill ye first 1673 & hereof faile not to make a true Returne under your hand dated the 9th Aprill 1686 :
                                        Edward Rishworth Recorder

 I served the within Execution upon the pasture land of John Parker Senr which was leagally prized by Richard Banks & Thomas Curtis and possession given unto Henry Dering according to law in full satisfaction of the within written Execution, being two acres & one fifth part of an acre, being butted and bounded as followeth ; West South west twenty foure poles by the high way from thence north nor west Sixteen pole by sd Jno Parkers tillage Land from thence East north East to the Runn of water & from thence by the Runn of water to the first departure being a loose great Stump at the Eastward Corner of the said pasture feild/ this thus done the 21th May 1686, the Land was measured by m^r John Penniwell in the Towne of Yorke westerly from the Meeting house by me
 Nathaniel Masterson Marshall of the Province of Maine
 vera Copia transcribed out of the originall & y^r with Compared this 22th of May : 1686 : p Edw : Rishworth Re : Cor :

 I whose name is vnderwritten, do acquitt the Loggers & Sawyers, James Oare, Hene Brown, & Nicholas Coole, for & in Consideration of the transactions ye yeare past, or before the date hereof, in & about the Mill at Mowsome/ In witness w^{r}unto I haue set my hand, this fiueteenth of August one thousand six hundred eighty foure/
 William Frost   Nicholas Morey/
 Robert Hillton/ Nicho^s Morey came before mee & ac-
       knowledged this receipt to bee his
       Act & Deede, this 26th of May
       1686 : Edw : Rishworth Jus : pe :

Book IV, Fol. 61.

A true Coppy of this receipt transcribed & with originall Compared this 31 : of May 1686 :   p Edw : Rishworth ReCor

These may Certify any whome It may Concerne, y^t y^r was proclamation sett vp at Sacoe, y^t the Cr^s that had any thing due from the Estate of Jo^n Batson deceased, should bring in y^r Accots, to the Court of pleas at Wells, the 25th day of May 1686 : & likewise at Wells, & Cape Porpus/
Witness/ Jonathan Hammond
　　　　　Francis Backehouse
A true Coppy of this publi-　John Miller his ✝ marke
cation transcribed out of
ye originall & y^r with Compared this 31 : May, 1686 :
　　　　　p Edw : Rishworth ReCor :

To all Christian people to whome this Present Deed shall come/ Samell Snow of Boston Cordwinder in New England, & Executor to Margerett Mountegue the relict of Griffine Mountegue, formerly of Cape Porpus in New England In the prouince of Mayne, lately deceased, & Saraih his wife sends Greeteing ; Know yee y^t the sd Samll Snow executor as abouesd & Sarah my wife, for & in Consideration of the sume of sixty pounds, in moneys & other Current pay of New England to them at or before the sealeing & deliuery here of by Nicholas Morey, of Wells Carpenter, Well & truely payd, the receipt w^{r}of I the sd Samuell Snow, & Saraih my wife, do hereby acknowledg, & y^{r}with to bee fully satisfyd, & Contented, & y^{r}from & from euery part, & Parcell y^{r}of, for them selues, thejr heyres, executors, & Administrators, doth exonerate acquitt & fully discharge, him the sayd Morey his heyres, executors, & Administrators, &

Assigns for euer by these Presents: Hath given, granted, barganed & sould, alliend, [62] Enfeoffed, & Convayed & Confirmed, vnto the sd Nicholas Morey his heyres & Assignes, & do hereby fully & freely, clearely & absolutely give grant bargane sell aliene Enfeoff, Convay & Confirme, vnto him one hundred Acres of vpland & Meddows bee It more or less, lijng at Cape Porpus, adioyneing to Morgan Howells Land vpon & neare the Necke, all which vp land & Meddows was given mee by Margerett Mowntogue, as executor to her last will more largely will appeare, which Lands were her late husbands, Griffine Mountegues, & all my right title & Interest of that Necke of Land lijng at Cape Porpus, Which was formerly Morgan Howells Land, where he formerly dwelt adioyneing to the Griffine Mountegues Land · Being fiuety Acres more or less, which I lately bought of Mis Mary Booles of Wells as by Instrument under her hand & seale, more largely doth & may appeare, with all houseing & out houseing arrable Land with fence or otherwise/ To haue, & to hould, the sd vpland & Meddows, togeather with all the houseings, Woods, vnderwoods, Mines, Mineralls, priuiledges appurtenances to ye sd vplands & Meddows, and other priuiledges thereto belonging, or in any wise app^{r}tajneing, And all the Estate right Title, Interest vss & propriety possession Claime & Demand whatsoeuer, of mee the sd Samuell Snow, & Saraih my wife of in or to the sayd vpland, Meddows, houseings, To haue & to hould the sd vpland, & Meddows, houseing &c: vnto the sd Nichol^s Mory his heyres & Assignes for euer; To his & thejr own proper vss, & behoofe for euer; And the sayd Samell Snow & Saraih his wife, for them selues & y^r respectiue heyres, executors Administrators do Couenant promiss & grant, And with Nicholas Morey his heyres & Assignes by these Presents, & vntill the deliuery here of, vnto the sd Nichol^s Morey, to the vss of him selfe, his heyrs & Assignes for euer, were the true & rightfull owners unto the aboue barganed Premisses, & that they in thejr own right, full pouer and lawfull authority, the Premisses to grant barganc, & Sell, & Confirme as aforesd, & that the same is free & Cleare, & freely discharged & acquitted, or otherwise at all tyms by the sd Samell Snow & Saraih his wife, thejr heyres executors saued harmeless of & from all & singular the former & other grants Barganes, sales, Morgages, leases gyfts, Estates, Titles, Charges troubles & Incomberances whatsoeuer, had, made, done, or suffered to bee done by the sayd Samuell Snow, or Saraih his wife or any other Clameing lawfully by or from them, & that the sayd Nicholas Morie, his heyres & Assigns shall & may henceforth, for euer, lawfully & peaceably & quietly haue hould vss Occupie, possess & Inioy the sd barganed Vpland, Meddows houses, with all other Arrable Land & with the priuiledges & appurtenances y^{r}unto belonging, with out ye let suite, trouble Molestation, deniall, Euiction Eiection or disturbance of the sayd Samll Snow, & Saraih his wife or any other Person or Persons w^{t}soeuer Claimeing or to Clajmc any Estate right title Interest Claime demand, w^{t}soeuer in & to the barganed Premisses, or any part or Parcell there of, from by or vnder them ; In witness w^{r}of I the sd Samuell Snow & Saraih his wife, haue here unto set y^r hands & seales this secund day of February one thousand six hundred eighty fiue, & in the first yeare of the Reigne of o^r Soueraigne Ld James ye secund of England Scotland &c : King : the estate aboue mentioned doth all ly In the prouince of Mayne In New England/

Signed sealed & deliuered/   Samell Snow (his scale)
  in the Presence of/   Saraih Snow her
  Solomon Raynsford/   marke ʃ (her scale)
  Joseph Cowell/

Samuell Snow acknowledged this writing to bee his Act & Deed, this 9th day of March 1685 : before mee

                    Robert Pike Assistant/

BOOK IV, FOL. 62.

Mr Solomon Raynsford appeared before mee, & made oath that hee did see Samell Snow, & Sarah his wife signe seale & deliuer this writeing, & yᵗ him selfe & Joseph Cowell did sett yʳ hands to it as witnesses/

Sworne March the 9th 1685 : before mee

Robert Pike Assista ͞:

vera Copia of this Instrument with in written, transcribed out of yᵉ originall & yʳ with Compared this first day of June 1686 p Edw : Rishworth Re : Cor :

Know all men by these Presents yᵗ I William Burrage of Scarbrough In the Prouince of Mayne In England for & in Consideration of the sume of six pounds, tenn shillings to mee in hand payd well & truely payd before yᵉ scaleing & deliuery here of, by Siluanus Dauis of Falmouth in Cascoe bay, in the prouince of Mayn in New England, the receipt wʳof as a ualewable sume of Money I do hereby acknowledg, & yʳof, & of euery part, & Prcell yʳof, do exonerate acquitt & discharge, the sd Siluanus Dauis his heyres, executors & Assignes, for euer, for euer by these Presents, haue granted barganed, sould, & Confirmed & by these Presents, do fully & absolutely grant, bargan, sell Enfeoffe & Confirme, unto the sd Siluanus Dauis all yᵗ my peece or Parcell of Meddow, six Acres & a halfe or yʳabouts, as It is measured lijng scituate in the Townshipe of sd Scarbrough, at a place yʳ Comanly Called Nonesuch Marshes butted & bounded, with the vpland on the Noreward side Nonsuch Riuerlett, on the South side Joⁿ Skillings & Geo : Ingersolls Junjoʳ thejr Marsh on yᵉ East side, & Marsh belonging to Siluanus Dauis on the Westward side, bee yᵉ quantity of Acres, Meddow & swampe more or less, as It is butted & bounded, or reputed to bee bounded ; To haue & to hould all & singular all the aforesd Parcell of Meddow swamp & vpland within the aforesd bounds, with all yᵉ rights priuiledges & appurtenances yʳvnto belonging, with priuiledge to fence vpon the vpland, neare Adioyneing to the sd Meddow, unto the sd Siluanus Dauis his heyres, & Assigns, & to thejr proper vss, & behoofe for euer; And I the sd William Burrage do hereby auouch my selfe at yᵉ tyme of the Ensealeing, & vntill the deliuery of these Presents, to bee true & lawfull owner of all the aboue barganed Premises, freely & clearely acquitted & discharged, from all former & other barganes, sales, titles, & Incomberances, & do bind my selfe my heyres, executors Administrators to warrant, & defend all the sd granted Premises & appurtinances vnto yᵉ sd Siluanus Dauis his heyrs, & Assigns for euer, against all Persons [63] whomsoeuer lawfully Claimeing the same or any part there of, as witness my hand here unto Set with my seale this eight day of May sixteen hundred eighty & six, in the secund yeare of the Reigne of our Lord King James the secund, by the grace of god King of England, Scotland, France, & Ireland Defendʳ of the faith &c:

Signed, sealed, & deliuered/   William Burrage (his seale)
   in Presence of vs/   Saraih Burrage her
   George Ingersall Senjoʳ/   marke ⁊ (her seale)
   Elizabeth Tyng

     William Burrage acknowledged the aboue
     Instrument to bee his Act & Deede,
     for yᵉ vss of Capᵗ Siluanus Dauiss this
     8ᵗʰ of May 1686: before mee
         Edw: Tyng Jus: pe:

Saraih Burrage acknowledged her Consent, to the aboue Deede to which shee hath set her hand & scale this 18ᵗʰ of May 1686:   before mee Edw: Tyng Jus: pe:

George Ingersall Senjoʳ did appeare this eight day of May 1686: & testify yᵗ he did lay out the aboue six acres & an halfe of Meddow as aboue expressed, & by the sd Burrage order helpe measure it, & also hee did see the abouesd Wil-

Book IV, Fol. 63.

liam Burrage, deliuer yᵉ same into yᵉ possession of Siluanus Dauis, by Turffe & Twidg/ Taken vpon oath this 8th day of May (1686) before mee   Edw : Tyng Jus : pe :
 vera Copia of this Instrument transcribed out of yᵉ Originall Compared this 2cund day of June 1686 :
              p Edw : Rishworth Re : Cor :

Bee It known vnto all men by these Presents, that John Wadleigh of Ecceter In prouince of new Hampshire, In New England, send Greeteing/ Know yee, yᵗ I the sd John Wadleigh for a valewable Consideration to mee In hand payd, or sufficient security yʳfore by Peter Follssam of Ecceter aforesd, do yʳwith acknowledg my selfe fully satisfyd, Contented & payd, & yʳof, & of eueɪy part & Parcell yʳof, do acquit, exonerate & discharge, the sd Peter Fallsan his heyres, executors, Administrators & Assignes for euer; by these Presents, Haue given granted bargained, & sould, aliend, Enfeoffed, & Confirmed, & by these Presents do giue, grant, bargane, & sell, aliene Enfeofe & Confirme vnto yᵉ sayd Peter Foullsam his heyres, executors, & Administrators for euer, a Certen Parcell of vpland & Meddow, or Marsh (excepting the one halfe of fiue acres & an halfe heretofore alienated of Marsh being thus excepted) the third part of the farme & liueing of my Grandfather John Wadleigh deceased, & now mine by yᵉ disposure & gift of my Loueing father Robert Wadleigh, as by his fathers Gift may appeare, lijng & being in the Town of Wells In the prouince of Mayne aforesd, In New England, & bounded on the one side with yᵉ Land of my Ouncle Thomas Mills, & on the other side with the Land of the sd Peter Follsam, which hee lately bought of my father Robert Wadleigh; To haue & to hould (excepting as aforesd) the sd third part of the vpland, & Meddow or Marsh, lijng being & bounded as

aforesd with a third of ye Falls in the brooke, runneing between ye demised Land, the Land of my aforesd Ouncle Thomas Mills, with all & singular the Wood, trees Tymber & all other the appurtenances in any wise belonging, or appertajneing to ye sd Peter Follsam his heyres, executors, administrators & Assignes for euer, Also I the sd John Wadleigh do couenant promiss & Ingage, to & with the sd Peter Follsam that I the sd John Wadleigh am ye true proper & undoubted owner of the sd barganed Premisses, and that the sayd premisses were free & Cleare, & freely & Clearely exonerated, acquitted, & discharged of from all, & all manner of former barganes, sales, gifts, grants, titles, Morgages suits Dowrys, & all other Incomberances w^{t}soeuer, from the begining of the world to ye date hereof, & further I the sayd John Wadleigh do Couenant promiss & Ingage to & with the sd Peter Follsam his heyres, executors, & Administrators, all & singular the app^{r}tenances, with the Premisses there unto belonging to warrant acquit, & defend, for euer, against all Persons w^{t}soeuer, from by or vnder mee, Clajmeing any right title or Interest of & into the same, or any part or parcell there of, & in testimony hereof I the sd John Wadleigh, with Abigayle my now wife, haue herunto set our hands, & seales, this Twelth day of August, Anno Dom̅: 1685: Annoq̅ Regni Jacobj Regis Secundj, p^{r}o: John Wadleigh (seal)
Signed Sealed & deliuered/ Abigayl Wadleigh (seal)
in the Presence of/ John Wadleigh & his wife Abigayl
Edw Smith/ owned the Instrument aboue written, to bee y^r Act & Deed ye Day
John Foullsam/
& yeare aboue written, before mee/

Robert Wadleigh Jus: pe:
A true Coppy of this Instrument aboue written transcribed & Compared with the originall this 3d day of June 1686: p Edw: Rishworth Jus: pe

Bee It known vnto all men by these Presents, that I Robert Wadleigh Senjo^r of Ecceter, In the prouince of New Hampshire, in New England Gentle: send greeteing; Know yee that the sd Robert Wadleigh, for a ualewable Consideration to mee In hand payd, or sufficient security y^rfore, by Peter Foullsam of Ecceter Planter, do there with acknowledg my selfe fully satisfyd Contented & payd, & y^rof & of euery part & Parcell y^rof, do exonerate, acquitt & discharge the sayd Peter Foullsum his heyres, executors, administrators, & assignes for euer, by these Presents; Haue given granted, barganed sould, alien'd Enfeoffed & Confirmed, & by these Presents do giue, grant, bargane, Sell, aliene Enfeof & Confirme, vnto the sd Peter Foullsam, his heyres, executors, & Administrators for euer, a Certen Parcell of Meddow, & vpland (excepting the forth part of fiue Acres & an halfe, heretofore alienated of the sd Meddow) the rest being accounted the sixt part of the farme, or Estate of my father, John Wadleigh deceased: Lijng & being in the Town of Wells, in the prouince of Mayne, [64] in New England aforesd, & the same Meddow & vpland, being bounded on ye one side, with the Land of my sonn Wadleigh, & on the other side with land which I the sd Wadley, lately sould unto William Sawyer; To haue & to hould, ye sd accounted sixt part of the Meddow, & vpland, with all & singular the Wood, trees, Tymber, houses, barnes, out houses, & all other appurtenances, y^rvnto in any wise appertajneing, or belonging, vnto the sd Peter Foullsum his heyres, executors, administrators, & Assignes for euer/ Also I the sd Robert Wadleigh, do promiss, Couenant, & Ingage to & with the sayd Peter ffoullsam, that I the sayd Robert Wadleigh am ye true proper & undoubted owner of the suyd barganed Premisses, and y^t the sayd barganed were free, & freely, & Clearely exonerated, acquitted & discharged of & from all, & all manner of former barganes, sales, grants, Gifts, titles, Morgages, suites, Dowrys, & all other Incomberances w^tso-

euer, from ye begining of the world vntill the date hereof, and further I the sayd Robert Wadleigh, do also Couenant promiss and Ingage, to & with the sd Peter Foullsam, his heyres, executors, and administrators, & either of them, all & singular the appurtenances with the Premisses, ther unto belonging to warrant & acquitt and Defend for euer against all Persons whatsoeuer, (from by or under mee) Clajmeing any right title or Interest of, or into the same, or any part or Parcell thereof; And In testimony hereof I the sayd Robert Wadley, with the Consent of Saraih Wadleigh, my now wife, and John Wadleigh my Elldest sonn, haue here unto set o^r hands & seals, this Twelth day of August one thousand six hundred eighty fiue, Annoq, Regni Regis Jacobi secundj, pr^o   Robert Wadleigh (his seal)
Signed sealed, & Deluered/   Saraih Wadleigh (her scale)
  In the Presence of/   John Wadleigh (his seal)
  Edw: Smith/   Robert Wadeigh & Saraih his wife & John
  John Foullsam/ Wadleigh his Elldest sonn, did all appeare before mee this tenth day of May, 1686: and acknowledged this aboue Instrume^t to bee y^r Act & Deede/   Henery Greene Jus: pe:

A true Coppy of this Instrument aboue written transcribed out of ye Originall this 4th of June 1686:

         p Edw: Rishworth Re: Cor:

To all Christian people, to whom these Presents shall come; Know yee that I John Wadleigh of Wells In the County of yorke, haue given, & granted, & by these Presents do giue & grant, Assigne & make ouer unto my Daughter Mary Mills, & her children & thejr heyres, & successors for euer, all my right title & Interest, in & to that Lott of Land, which they now dwell vpon at this Town of Wells, &

Book IV, Fol. 64.

all the Marsh, before the sd lott downe vnto Webhannett River, as it is bounded, & layd out already, and the vpland is to begin on the South West side at the foote bridg which is neare vnto my ould garden, & so to runne up North East vnto Samuell Austines Lott, & so to runne vp into the Countrey, vpon the same Lyne, as my now dwelling lott doth, and too Acres of Marsh lijng neare Webhannet Riuer, by the Town Lott, & all the Marsh which is in thejr possession, at the Necke of Land, all which Land & Marsh aforesd, I do firmely giue, & grant unto my daughter Mary Mills, & her children for euer, only reseruing to my selfe, my heyrs & successors for euer, free priuiledg for ye placeing of a Mill, & to make a Dame vpon the sd Brooke where It is most Conueniett/ In Confirmation hereof I have here unto subscribed my hand & seale, this 18th day of July 1664:

Sealed, signed, & deliuer'd
  In the Presence of us/
William Symonds/
John Barrett
his marke ⊂⊃

The signe ⟨M⟩ of John
Wadleigh (his seal)
A true Coppy of this Instrument transcribed out of the originall & y^r with Compared this 4th day of June 1686
    p Edw: Rishworth ReCor:

I Robert Wadleigh of Ecceter in the prouince of New Hampshire, being proper heyre, & Ecceecutor to the last will & testament of my father John Wadleigh of Wells In the prouince of Maine deceased, Do by these Presents fully freely & absolutely ratify & Confirme this Deede of sale on the other side, to haue & to hould the aforesd Land & Premisses, to them & y^r heyres, executors, Administrators & Assigns for euer, according to y^e true Intent, & meaning

BOOK IV, FOL. 64.

thereof, from mee & my heyres, executors, & Administrators/ Witness my hand & seale, this 16th day of Aprill 1683 :
Signed sealed, & Confirmed/   Robert Wadleigh ($_{seale}^{his}$)
In the Presence of us/   Robert Wadleigh came before
John Gillman Senjo^r/   mee this 18th day of Aprill,
John Wadleigh/   1683 : & owned this Instrument or Writeing to bee his act & Deede/
                               Ralph Hall Jus : pe :
A true Coppie of this Confirmation of that bill of sale Enterd on the other side giuen by John Wadleigh to Mary Mills & her children, transcribed & with y^e originall Compared this 4th of June 1686 :   p Edw : Rishworth Re : Cor

Know all men by these Presents, that I ffrancis Wanewright In the County of Essex, for & in Consideration of the some of Twenty & seauen quint^{lls} & $\frac{1}{2}$ of good dry M$^{rch^t}$ble Cod fish to mee either payd in hand, or to mee secured by bill, with a Parcell of fish formerly receiued, haue sould vnto Roger Kelly of Smuttinose Ysland of the Ysles of Shoales, in the prouince of Mayne, in New England, & do by these Presents, fully, clearely & absolutely grant, bargan, sell & Confirme vnto the sd Roger Kelly, the house with too leantows, with land Adioyning, pileing places, & traine fatt all adioyneing to ye sd house, I formerly bought of Richd Endle, with all my right title, of sayd house & Land, y^{r}unto belonging (onely too long flakes excepted) wch flakes runnes neare the doore of Hugh Allard, unto neare the parsonidg house of Mr Samell Belcher Minister of the Ysles of shoales, w^r hee now liueth, to him ye sd Roger Kelly all y^t house & leantows, & Land (excepting the too long flakes afore mentioned to him, to haue & to hould for euer, his heyres, executors, Administrators, &

Assigns, & do warrantize yᵉ sale of sd house & Land, with yᵉ priuiledges & appʳtenances appʳtajncing, to him the sd Roger Kelly for euer, & do Confirme to yᵉ sd Roger Kelly, that yᵉ sale of the abouesd Premisses to bee firme & good [65] & freely discharged from all former gifts, grants barganes, sales, Morgages Dowrys, Judgmᵗˢ, executions, or any other Intanglements or Incomberances wᵗsoeuer, & that It shall & may bee lawfull for yᵉ sd Roger Kelly & his heyres, & Assignes from hence forth & for euer, To haue vss, possess & Inioy, all the sd house & Land to his own proper vss, & behowfe & benefitt, to him the sd Roger Kelly & his heyres for euer: with out any lett hinderance, deniall, interruption or Molestation from mee the sd Francis Wanewright my heyres, executors, Administrators, from by or vnder mee, any Person wᵗsoeuer for euer, makeing any Claime to the abouesd house & Land; In witness wʳof I haue here vnto put my hand & seale/ Dated In Ipswich this first day June in the yeare of oʳ Ld one thousand six hundred eighty six, 1686:   ffrancis Wanewright (ʰⁱˢ seale)
Signed, sealed, & Deliuered/   vpon the 5ᵗʰ day of June
In the Presence of us/   1686: Mr Francis Wane-
John Fabes/   wright acknowledged this
John Wanewright/   Instrumenᵗ to bee his act
    & Deede, before mee/
    John Fabes Jus: pe:
vera Copia of this Instrumᵗ transcribed & with originall Compared this 8ᵗʰ day of June 1686:
          p Edw: Rishworth ReCor:

Bee It known unto all men by these Presents, that I John Ryall of North Yarmouth In Cascoe bay, haue with yᵉ Consent of my brother William Ryall, in the Prouince of Mayne in New England, for in Consideration of a valewable sume to mee in hand payd before ye signeing sealeing & deliuery of these Presents, by mee John Ryall, for which I acknowledg my selfe, fully satisfyd, payd, & Contented, haue barganed & sould, given granted Enfeoffed, aliened, & Confirmed, & by these Presents I John Ryall do fully Clearely & absolutly bargane, sell, Enfeoffe, & Confirme vnto Amos Stephens of Boston, Marriner, a parcell of Land about fiueteene acres bee It more or less, Which is a Small Necke lijng next adioyneing to the sd John Ryall, onely a Cricke parting, & at the vpper end of the sd Cricke, It lyeth bounded by marked trees, South East & by East & North west, & by west, & on the north west side by the Wood land, down to ye Riuer, to a marked Oake tree, & so to the Riuer at low water marke South & by West, with priuiledg^s of Com̅anidg, with a large Cart way out of the sd Land, all wch land I haue sould, given & granted, Enfeoff & Confirme, vnto the sayd Amos Stephens, his heyrs, executors, administrators or Assignes for euer: all the right Title, & interest I haue & might, & out to haue vnto ye sd Land, with all the trees, woods, vnderwoods, with all the priuiledges, benefitts & profetts, of w^tsoeuer y^runto is belonging, or any ways app^rtajneing; I the sd John Ryall with ye Consent of my brother William, & Elizabeth my wife, do by these Presents, absolutely bargane, sell, & Enfeoff & Confirme to him the sd Amos Stephens his heyres & Assignes for euer; To haue & to hould, the hereby barganed Premisses, to the onely use, & behoofe of him the sayd Amos Stephens his heyres, & Assigns for euer; And I the sayd John Ryall do Couenant & agree to & with the sayd Amos Stephens his heyres, & Assigns y^t at ye signeing & deliuery of these Presents, the hereby barganed Premisses, is my true right & Interest, & is free, & Cleare, of & from all other bargans, sales, Morgages, Gifts incomberances, & intalements of what nature soeuer, made by mee, my Cause, knowledg, or procurement, & I John Ryall do hereby empty my selfe heyres, executors

& Administrators of, & from all Claime title, & Interest to the aboue mentioned barganed Premisses, or any part y^{r}of, to ye onely vsse of sd Amos Stephens, his heyres & Assigns: Mee John Ryall, my brother William & Elizabeth my wife, my heyres, executors or Assignes, or any other Persons, claimeing from by or under mee, them or any of them shall & will warrant & defend; And In witness of the treuth hereof I John Ryall haue set too my hand & seale this eight day of Nouember, one thousand one thousand six hundred Eighty & too, 1682: also It is agreed vpon that, before the signeing & sealeing, & deliuery hereof, y^t If sd Amos Stephens shall see cause not to hue on the sd Land, y^t w^{t}soeuer the sd Stephens shall lay out either in building or otherwise, the sayd John Ryall shall haue ye refuse of it/

Signed sealed & deliuered/   The Marke of
In the Presence of us/   John Ryall R (his seal)
The marke of Richd Pows-

land T   John Ryall came before mee,
    & did acknowledg this to bee
Henery Harwood/   act & Deede, unto Amos
Mathew Paulling/   Stephens of Boston this 9th
Nicholas Tredby/   of Novemb^r 1682 : befor mee
    Anthony Brackett Commissioner

John Ryall appeared before mee this 16th of March 168$\frac{4}{5}$ & acknowledged the aboue Instrument to bee his act & Deed betore mee   Edw: Ting Jus: pe:

Richd Powsland, & Mathew Paulling made oath that they did see John Ryall signe, seale, & deliuer this Instrume^t unto Amos Stephens/ Taken vpon oath this first of October 1685/ before mee   Edw: Tyng Jus: pe:

A true Coppy of this Instrument aboue written with all ye appendences under written, transcribed out of ye originall, & y^r with Compared this 7th of June 1686:

    p Edw: Rishworth Re: Cor:

Book IV, Fol. 65, 66.

To all Christian people, to whome this writeing shall come/ Know yee that I Joseph Barnard of the parish of Barwicke, in the Town of Kittery, in the prouince of Mayne, in New England for & in Consideration of the full & iust some of fourty one pounds, & fiue shillings, in Current Money of New England, payd to mee in hand by my brother Benjam͞: Barnard, of Douer in the prouince of New Hampshire, in New England aforesd, w^{r}of & of euery part & Parcell thereof, I do hereby acquitt, exonerate, & discharge ye sayd Benjam͞: Barnard, his heyres, executors, & Administrators, for euer, & am there with fully Content, & satisfyd, & do by these Presents, in Consideration there of giue, grant, bargane, sell, Enfeoffe, & Confirme, unto Beniam͞ Barnard, a Certen tract, or Parcell of Land, scituate, & lijng in the parish of Barwicke, & Town of Kittery ye prouince of majne aforesd, Contajneing fiuety Acres, with all the Tymber thereon either growing, or lijng, on the sd land with all buidings & fences y^{r}on, with all priuiledges & appurtenances, in any wise there to belonging, as It is bounded by the Land of Ric: Tozier on ye South, the River y^t diuid^s Douer, & Kittery on the West, & the Land of Capt Price, on the North, & ye Com͞ons on the East, as It was bought of Benonj Hodgsden, & by the Deede of sale beareing date June 30th 1681 : more amply appeareth, & now by mee, sd Joseph Barnard, sould unto aforesd Beniam͞: Barnard, aforesd; To haue & to hould all the aboue barganed Premisses, with all & [66] singular the appurtenances & priuiledges in any wise there unto belonging, or appertajneing, to him the sd Beniamen Barnard, his heyres, executors, Administrators & Assignes for euer, & to his & thejr only proper vss, & behoofe for euer/ and the sayd Joseph Barnard do for my selfe, my heyres, executors, and Administrators, Couenant & promiss to & with the sd Beniamen Barnard his heyres, executors, Administrators, & Assigns, that I ye sayd Joseph Barnard haue in my selfe haue good right, full pouer, & lawfull authority, the abouesayd granted Premisses to sell, & dispose of, & that the same & euery part & Parcell thereof are free, & cleare, & freely & Clearely acquitted & discharged, of & from all manner of former Gyfts, grants, leases, morgages, wills Intailes, Judgm^{ts}, executions, thirds, & pouer of thirds, and all other Incomberances whatsoeuer, had made done or suffered to bee done, w^{ch}by the sayd Beniamen Barnard, his heyres, executors, Administrators, or Assignes, shall or may any ways bee molested, or eiected out of the aboue granted Premisses, or any part y^{r}of by any Person whatsoeuer, haueing, claimeing, or Pretending to haue any legall right, to any of the aboue granted Premisses, defending the same against all Persons whatsoeuer, makeing any lawfull Claime thereto (the Lord proprietor onely excepted) In Confirmation of the treuth hereof, I the abouesd Joseph Barnard, haue here unto set my hand, & seale, this first day of Janvary, in the yeare of o^{r} Ld god, one thousand six hundred eighty & fiue, & six, 168$\frac{5}{6}$ & in the first yeare of the Reign of o^{r} soueraign Ld James the secund, by the grace of god King of England, Scotland, France, & Ireland Defend^{r} of y^{e} faith &c : Joseph Barnard/ ($^{locus}_{sigilli}$)

Signed, sealed, & deliuer'd Prouince of Mayne/
  in the Presence of us/ Joseph Barnard acknowledgd
  Icabod Playstead/ this aboue written Deede of
  Edw Taylour sale to bee his free Act &
  his ℰ marke/ Deede, this 12th day of January 168$\frac{5}{6}$ before mee
    John Wincoll, Jus: pe:

A true Coppy of this Instrument, or bill of sale transcribed out of the originall, & y^{r} with Compared this 14th June 1686: p Edw: Rishworth Re: Cor

Book IV, Fol. 66.

yorke Prouince of Mayne, March first/
1684/5

Where as there was a Certen Instrument drawn out beareing date, the 19th of Nouember 1684, as a testimoniall of the mind & will (as wee vnderstand) of Mathew Austine Senjo:r a little before his death, which not so Clearely & Methodically done to y:e understanding & satisfaction either of authority, & some others of sd Mathew Austines relations, who were most espetially Concern'd therein, uidz:t Mary Austine his wife, & Mathew Austine his onely sonn; The p:misses Considered, do mutually Consent & agree, according to y:t Aduise given us by o:r frejnds, Arther Bragdon, & John Sayword, whom wee haue made Choyce of, to rectify & put into good order, w:tsoeuer they shall find a miss in poy:mt of Method, & to settle It in substance as neare as may bee Consonant to the former Instrument, Which is as followeth/

1: I Mathew Austine Senjo:r do giue unto my beloued wife Mary Austine, after my decease, the soole vss, Aduantage, & benefitt, of one halfe of all my Lands, Arable, & Pasture lands which are now under my Improuem:t, with y:e vss & benefitt of too thirds of my Oarchard with all the profitts belonging y:rto, dureing the full Tearme of her naturall life/

2ly I the sd Mathew Austine do further giue & bequeath unto the sd Mary wife, all my moueables, both of quicke stocke, & househould stuffe, with in doores, & with out, for her own proper vss, to bee at her soole disposall, for her own & childrens more Comfortable mantenance dureing her naturall life. & at her death shall haue pouer by these Presents to dispose of w:t moueable goods are then remajneing, to whome shee shall Judge most Conuenient/

2: I do giue & bequeath unto my sonn Mathew Austine all those lands which hee hath already built vpon, being one halfe of my arable & pasture Lands, w:ch I formerly possessed, & one third part of the orchard, dureing the

BOOK IV, FOL. 66.

naturall life of my sayd wife Mary Austine, & at my wifes decease, I do giue & bequeath all my lands barne houseing, Pasturs, Oarchards, gardens, grass plotts, with all priuiledges y^rto app^rtajneing, to my sonn Mathew Austine to his heyres & Assignes for euer, as his & y^r owne proper Interest, & Inheritance; always prouided, as I euer intended, It is to bee so understood, that the sd Mathew Austine my sonn is to pay unto his three sisters, Mary, Saraih, & Sebellah Austine, each of them fiue pounds a peece in good, M^rchable sufficient pay, with in one Twelph Moenth after hee Enters into the Premisses, if demanded/

I do further giue & beqneath unto my sonn Mathew Austine, my own Loume which I my selfe vsed to work in, with all the wollen, & halfe ye Cotton Tackelling/

I do desire y^t my seruant Abra: Place, being newly Entred into the Trade of a weauer, may bee further Instructed, & brought vp in art of Weaueing/

4. I do giue & bequeath that fourty Acres of vpland, y^t lyes aboue ye fall Mills, granted to my father Dauis, by the Town of yorke, which lands sd Dauis gaue to mee & bequeath unto my too Elldest daughters, Mary, & Saraih, to bee æqually diuided between them/

5 I do giue and bequeath, a Certen Parcell of Land, lijng aboue yorke bridg Contajneing about   Acres of vpland, which was given mee by the Town of yorke unto my daughter Sebellah hir heyres & Assigns for euer/

These Gyfts, legacys, & seuerall bequessts as aboue express'd, were signed & sealed by the aboue sd Mathew Austine Senjo^r, as his last will & testament, which are freely allowed & Consented too/ Confirmed, & acknowledged by us as o^r free Act & Deede/ as witness o^r hands & seals this first day of March 168¾

Signed, sealed & Deliuer'd   Mary Austine (her seale)
 in the Presence of/   Mathew Austine (his seale)
  Arther Bragdon Senjo^r/   Before the signeing & sealeing
  John Sayword/   here of, It is mutually agreed

by us Mary Austine, & Mathew Austine wife & sonn to Mathew Austine deceased notwithstanding w'soeuer is mentioned in the first & secund articles of this Instrum^t aboue written, referring to the sd Mathew Austine Junjo^r, his haueing the uss of all those arable & pasture lands, which Mathew Austine his father formerly Improued (that the sd Clawse of Mathew A : Junjo^n, haueing the one halfe of the Arable & pasture Lands, is reuersed) & that ye aforesd Mary Austine wife to Mathew Austine deceased, shall possess & improue w'soeuer Lands & pastures sd Austine made uss of before his decease, dureing her naturall life, & what Lands Mathew Austine Junjo^r made uss of before his fathers death, hee is likewise to Inioy & Improue, as witness o^r hands at the day & yeare aboue written   Mary Austine/
Witness   Mathew Austine/
   Arther Bragdon Senjo^r Mary Austine & Mathew Austine
   John Sayword/   came before mee this first day of March 168$\frac{5}{6}$ & owned this Instrument aboue written, & the postscript underneath to bee y^r free Act & Deede/
                      Edw : Rishworth Jus : pe :

Wee Jonathan Sayword, & Saraih Austine do own this Instrument aboue written, w^{r}vnto [67] our Mother Mary Austine, & o^r brother Mathew Austine haue subscribed, to bee our free Act & Deede, & freely do Consent y^{r}unto, owned before mee by Jonathan Sayword, & Sary Austine this 6th day of June 1686 : Edw : Rishworth Jus : pe :

A true Coppy of this Instrume^t with in written, & of y^r agreement & acknowledgm^{ts} y^{r}unto transcribed out of the originall, & y^{r}with Compar'd this 15th June 1686 :
                p Edw : Rishworth Re : Cor :

BOOK IV, FOL. 67.

Humphrey Chadborne aged 25 yeares, & William Playstead aged 26 yeares, testifyeth y^t being desired by Nicholas Frost, to new the bounds of the late Abraham Conleys Lands, on the West side of his house at Sturgeon Cricke, they found onely one brooke about sixty or seauenty poole westward of the sd house, & the place ye sd Frost shewed them, w^r hee sayd y^t Majo^r Shapleigh, Richd Nason, James Emery, & Christoph^r Banefejld, had lately layd out the sd Conleys Land, vidz^t at a place called Greenhams Gutt, there was no appearance of any brooke there, nor runne of water/ & further sayth not/ Taken vpon oath this 18th day of June 1678 : before mee John Wincoll Assōte

vera Copia of the euidences transcribd & with originall Compar'd this 24th day of June 1686 :

p Edw : Rishworth Re : Cor :

The Depositions of Stephen Jenkins aged about 28 yeares, & Jabez Jenkins aged 27 yeares or there abouts, testifyeth, that w^{as} there is a difference between Nathan Lawde Senjo^r, & Nicholas Frost, about a brooke of water, which difference hath Occasioned much trouble between ye sd partys, now wee do hereby testify, y^t at the water side of the Ceaders, so called, is an apparent brooke of water, which brooke runneth betweene a peece of sault Marsh now in the possession of Capt Charles Frost, & that peece of ground comanly known by the name of the Ceaders, & neare ye mouth of the sayd brooke, where it runnes into Sturgeon Cricke, neare the East Corner of Capt Frosts Marsh, there lyes an ould Whitte oake tree blown up by ye rootes, y^t hath one ould Cutt on the side of it, like an ould bound marke, & a little vp ye the sd brooke y^r grows a pine tree with Antient Markes vpon the sids of it, like an ould bound tree/ And y^t

Book IV, Fol. 67.

place called Greenhams Gut, is no brooke of water, neither doth any runne y^r but by thawes, or greate Raynes/

Taken vpon oath this 29th of May 1682, before mee

       Charles Frost Jus: pea:

A true Coppy of these euidences transcribed, & with ye originall Compared this 24th d: of June 1686.

      p Edw: Rishworth ReCor:

Portsmouth Anno Dom: 1680:

Mr Nathan Bedford is Dr/				Nathan Bedford p Contra is Cr/			
Aprill To 40 yards of Onistone at 2^s 7^d				June p Cash payd Mr Nicolls	lb	s	d
14 p yard.	5	03	4	2 | mate	.00	02	00
It 6 gross of Gympe buttons at 2^s 6^d				20th by 28 Quintlls ½ of Refuge			
	00.	15	00	fish at 9^s p Q^ll	.12	16	06
It one peece of scarge 60 skeyns of				lb	12	18	6
silke at	03	05.	00	Dr. . .18 06 09			
13 yd^s ½ of colourd Keyrsey at 4^s 6^d				Cr. 12 18 06			
p yd . . .	.03	00	09	£05 08 03			
It 33 yd^s ½ of blew lining at 12^d	01	18	06	Due to ballance fish as money,			
It one Castor hatt at 14^s . .	00	14	00	Advance ¼ to bring it into			
Agreed for ye aboue Goods to bee £14 16 07				fish price Current 01 07 3 | 0 15 3¾			
payd In fish at Money price |							
15 To 7 yd^s of worsted Camlet at 2^s	lb	s	d	Nathan Bedford Dr			
p yard	00	14	00	To Cash payd Mr John Nicolls	lb	s	d
It one bagg of silke buttonones at 18^s	00.	18	00	his mate . .	00:	07·	0
It 14 skines of silke at 14d . . .	00	01	02	Septr 11 one gross of buttones			
26 It To ⅜ of silke Tabby 3s 6d .	00	03	06	at 3s 6d, Cash 5s .	00	08	6
29 To one yd & a quarter of Tabby by				Aprill: 5. To a felt hatt at. . .	00	09	0
yor ord^r to James Harbert .	00	04	09		01.	04	6
30 To a new bead for an Hodsead pd							
James Robinson . . .	.00.	01	03				
June lb				14 16 7			
28 It to 12 of Oakum payd wild in Cash 00 03 00				03 10 2			
		02 05 8		18 06 09			

Book IV, Fol. 67.

Mr Nathan Bedford is Dr			P Contra is Cr		
To sundreys at price Current in fish to six June			P fish in Company with Mr El-liott	lb s d 36 01 10	
5 dozen of Cod lynes at 30s	....	10 16 00	It 76 Qintlls of Mount fish at 14s		
It Two Hodgs of Molosses . .		06 00 00	p Q .	53 04 00	
It 31 yds of broad Cloath at 7s 6 p yd		11 12 06		89·05 10	
It 24 Hodgeds of sault at 12s 6d p H		15 00 00	P balla receiued, of Mr Robert		
It Too peeces of Canting at	.	02 02 00	Elliett	25 03 8¼	
28 ft 7 yds ½ Canvice at		03 10 06		114 09 06¼	
Septebr					
9th It 38 yds of the best Nowells at 2s p yard & Twine .		03 18 06			
It 26 yds ½ fine locerum at 2s 2d p yd		2.19.05			
It to Nehemiah Partridge 13 lb			13 00 00			
It 15 busils of peas at 50 p busll		03 15 00			
It 81¼ lb of porke at 3d ½ p lb	..	...12.11.4			
March					
10 It to Too barrells of Macharell at 03 10 0			New Hampshire Septembr 26 1683		
It Tenn Hodgeds of sault at	.	07.00 00	The with written Accont was Sworne to		
11 It to 66 yds of Hall Cloath at		06 12 00	bee a true Accont from the booke by		
It one peece of Seaige at	. ..	. 03 07 00	John Hinkes with in named before ye		
	107 14 3	107 14. 03	Judg & Assistants in this Court			
	006 15 3		R. Chamberlne Protheni·		
	114 09 6				

Aprill 7th 1683 : The ballance of this with in Account was Omitted to bee allowed, wn the Comittee sat for want of the Account appeareing, Now It is come to hand wee do allow it, the some being allowed by us of the Committee, 25 : 03 : 8d¼   John Dauess/

vera Copia transcribed out of ye   Samll Wheelewright/
originall & yr with Compared   Jonathan Hamonds/
this 16 : of July 1686 : Er-
rours excepted
     p Tho Scottow Recordr

To all Christian people to whome this Present writeing shall Come/

Articles of agreement made & Concluded, betweene vs the Select men of the Town of yorke, in behalfe of sd Town, wrunto our hands are subscribed, on ye one Party, & John Saywoid an Inhabitant & rescident In the sd Town, on the other Partie, These Presents withesseth y̑ Wee the Select men afoꞅesd, according to pouer given vs by the Town, & in there behalfe, do give & grant vnto the sd John Sayword Certen Tracts, & Parcells of Land swamps & Tymber, fitt for sawing, with all the priuiledges there unto belonging, the land excepted, reserued for the Town, as more Prticularly are hereafter mentioned, to the sd Sayword his heyres or Assigns for euer, Vpon his Prformance of such Conditions, as are in this agreement vnder written, Wee grant & give to him a Certen Parcell of Swampe, & Marsh, commanly & known & Called by the name of the bell Marsh, lijng & being aboue the head of John Twisdens Marsh Contajneing about the quantity of Twenty Acres, bee It more or less/

2 : Secundly wee do give unto him Twenty Acres of Land, neare & Adioyneing to yᵉ brooke, Called by yᵉ name of folly brooke, with soolᵉ propriety of the sd Brooke, so fare as the Towns pouer extends, togeather with yᵉ fall Mill Brooke, that place where the Fall Mill stood, onely excepted, with free lyberty & propriety giuen unto him the sd John Sayword for building & Erecting any Mill or Mills vpon the sd Brooke, or brookes, except any grant granted before by the Town which is layd out, with some sutable quantity of Land adioyneing there unto necessary for bujlding yʳof, wʳby hee may haue free Egress & Regress for his Accomodations in that Worke, & wee do furthei grant unto him for his accomodation of Tymber for sawing, at the sd Mill or Mills, the soole propriety of all pine & Oake Tymber, lijng between Bass Coue Brooke, & the fall Mill brooke with yᵉ same priuiledges of the Comans as other Inhabitants haue/

3 : Thirdly wee do further giue & grant unto the sd John Sayword, all y̑ Parcell of swampe, & Marsh [68] neare & below Cape Nuttacke Pond, with Twenty acres of vpland, Adioyneing yʳunto, with wᵗ other Conveniencys of Tymber yʳ may bee had, If it may bee had vpon the Comans, suta-

ble for sawing or being sawne, which accomodations of Lands, Meddow, Tymber trees, brookes &c : as aboue mentioned, with all the priuiledges, profitts, & appurtenances there to belonging ; Wee the Select men aforesd do grant & Confirme unto the sd John Sayword, his heyres, executors, administrators & Assignes for euer/ vpon these following Considerations/

1 First that ye sd Sayword shall build or cause to bee built at ye meeteing house at yorke, three sufficient Gallerys, with three Conuenient seats in each Gallery & one beanch besid^e in ye hyest Rowme, in euery gallery If the sd Conueniency of Rowme will beare it, the fronture seate hee is to make with barresters, & too peyre of stayres to go vp into the Gallerys, one for ye men & another for the wimine/

2 : The sd John Sayword stands Ingag'd, to seate the sd Meeteing house below with Conuenient Seates, too seats to barrestred below, one for men, & ye other for wimine/ & repayreing of ye defects y^t are in the ould seates, & by makeing & Adding so many new Seats more, as shall bee necessary for ye full & decent seateing of the whoole house/ Which worke in makeing of Gallerys, & seateing the lower part of the sayd house, is by John Sayword to bee done & finished at his own proper Charge (nayles onely excepted) which the Town is Ingag'd to prouide uery speedily at or before the last of Octob^r next Insewing, Anno : Dom : 1681 : as witness o^r hands the 10th of December 1680 :

Signed sealed & deliuered/   John Dauess/
   in Presence of us/   Richd Bankes/
John Penwill   John Twisden/
Mathew Austine/   A true Coppy of this grant transcribed, & with ye originall Compared August 2th 1686 :

       p Tho : Scottow Record^r

BOOK IV, FOL. 68.

Know all men by these Presents that I Richard Cutt of Kittery, in the prouince of Mayne In New England, for & in consideration of fiueteene pounds of Current money of New England, to mee in hand payd by William Scriuine of the sd place, the receipt w^rof I do hereby acknowledg, & my selfe y^rwith fully satisfyd & pd & from which sume, & euery part y^rof, I do y^rfore exonerate, acquitt & discharge, the sd william Scriuen his heyres, executors, & Admmistrators for euer; Haue giuen, granted, sould, barganed alien'd, Enfeoffed, & Confirmed, & by these Presents do for my selfe my heyres, executors, administrators, & Assignes, giue, grant, bargane, sell, aliene Enfeoffe & Confirme, vnto the sd William Scriuen, a Certen peece or Parcell of Land, scituate & being In ye Town of Kittery aforesd & lijng against spruse Cricke, contajneing by measure Twenty Acres bee It more or less, being bounded on the East by Michell Endles Land, the lyne begining at the Cricke by the bridg ouer against a Hemlocke tree, marked W : S : & R : C : from thence North East to a Hemlocke tree marked W : S : 1 : on the North East by the Land of John Mogaridg, by a North West, & by West Course, to a branch of Spruse Cricke then West, by the Cricke to a Certen poynt, then by the Cricke West & South West to the head of the sd Cricke, from thence along the Gully by Mary Cutt her Land to a Maple tree M : C : W : S : from thence forth South West & by West, to a bla͠ Ash marked W : S : & from thence forth South East, by Certen marked trees to a Hemlocke, by the bridg ouer the Cricke marked W : S : R : C : w^r the Land first begane : To haue & to hould, all the aboue barganed Premisses, togeather with all & singular the priuiledges, y^runto belonging, or any ways app^rtajneing, unto him the sd william Scriuine, his heyres, executors, Administrators, & Assignes for euer, cleaie & Clearely discharged, & acquitted of & from all & all manner of former & other gifts, grants, barganes, leases, Morgages, Joyneturs, deuises, Judgm^{ts}, executions, wills, Entayles forfitures, & of & from all other titles, troubles, Charges, & Incomberances, w'soeuer, had made, Committed, done, or suffered to bee done by my selfe, or my Assignes, before the Ensealeing, & deliuery here of; And I the sd Richd Cutt, the aboue demised Premisses & app'rtenances, & euery part y'of, as is aboue expressd, for my selfe my heyrs executors, Administrators & Assignes unto the sd William Scriuen his heyres executors Administrators & Assigns shall & will warrant & for euer Defend against all Pisons Clajmeing, or too Clajme any right or title y'in, or to any part y'of/

In witness, & for Confirmation w'of, the sd Richd Cutt to this Instrument in writeing hath set his hand & seale with out frayd this Twenty secund day of July in the yeare of our Ld one thousand six hundred eighty & six, & in ye secund yeare of the Reigin of Soueraigne Lord James secund of England, Scotland, France & Ireland King, Defend^r of the faith &c :   Richd Cutt (his seal)

Signed sealed & deliuered/
   In the Presence of us/   Richard Cutt came before mee
   Joseph Rayn/   the 22th of July 1686 : &
   Nicholas Heskines/   owned this aboue written
                           Instrum^t to bee his Act &
                           Deede/ John Hinkes
                                 of the Councill/

A true Coppy of this Instrument transcribed out of the originall, & y^r with Compared this 26th of July 1686 :
                  p Thomas : Scottow Record^r

To all people to whome this Present Instrument In writeing shall come/ Richard Cutt of the Townshipe of Kittery In the Prouince of Mayne In New England yeoman sends greeteing; Know yee y^t I the sd Richard Cutt as well for &

in consideration of the naturall affection & brotherly loue, & good will which I haue & beare unto my well beloued sister Mary Cutt of the sd place as also for diuerse other good Causes & Considerations mee here unto espetially moueing, have giuen granted & Confirmed, & by these Presents, fully Clearely & absolutly giue, grant & Confirme, unto my sayd sister Mary Cutt, one Certen Tract or Parcell of Land Contajneing about Twenty Acres bee It more or less, scituate lijng & being in spruse Cricke, In the sd Prouince of Mayne, In the sayd Townshipp of Kittery, bounded on the West side of William Scriuens Land, On broad Coue, & being a Poynt or Necke of Land, between a little Cricke on the sd westerne side of William Scriuens Land, on sayd broad Coue head, And from broad Coue the lyne begining at a little Beach tree, marked with a letters M: C: & from thence running ouer by a South & by East Course unto a Maple tree Marked M: C: meeteing or butting vpon the sayd William Scriuens Land. To haue & to hould the sd Tract of Land, bee It twenty Acres more or less, togeather with all the woods, & vnderwoods, priuiledges, water Courses, easements, Emoluments, & Conueniences, y^{r}unto belonging, unto her ye sayd Mary Cutt, & to her heyres for euer; But If she the sayd Mary Cutt dyes & hath no heyre, then the sd Tract or Necke of Land is to returne unto ye sayd Richard Cutt agajne, hee paijng & allowing unto his sd sisters Assignes, all & w^{t}soeuer In her life tyme shee payd & disbursed in bulding on, or fenceing on the sd Land, or any part thereof, & after sd reimbursement & payment made: The sd Land to bee reinioyd & possessed [**69**] by sd Richard Cutt, as formerly: And if the sd Mary Cutt haue heyres, then the sayd Richd Cutt for him selfe his heyres, executors, & administrators, all & singular the aboue demised Premisses, unto the sayd Mary Cutt & her heyrs shall & will warrant & for euer defend against all other Prsons Claimeing, or to Claime any right, title, or property in the sd Land, or

BOOK IV, FOL. 69.

any part thereof: In witness & Confirmation hereof, I the sd Richard Cutt haue here unto with out fraud, sett his hand & seale, this Twenty secund day of July In the yeare of o{r} Lord one thousand six hundred Eighty & six, & in the secund yeare of y{e} Reign of o{r} Soneraign Lord King James the secund/ Richard Cutt (locus sigilli)
Signed sealed & deliuered/

In Presence of vs/   Richd Cutt came before mee
Joseph Rayn/   this 22th day of July 1686:
Nicholas Heskins/   & acknowledged the aboue written Instrument to bee his act & Deede/

John Hinkes of y{e} Councill/

A true Coppy of this Instrument aboue written, transcribed out of the Originall & y{r}with Compared this 27th of July 1686: p Tho: Scottow: Record

This bill bindeth mee Nathan Bedford, my heyres, executors & Administra{rs} to pay or cause to bee payd, unto Margerett Joclein the wife of Hene: Jocelyn the some of Twenty one pounds tenn shillings in Current pay in money in New England, at or before the Twenty ninth day of Septemb{r} next, being y{e} feast of Sa{t} Michell/ witness my hand this 24{th} of August 1679: this bill not to sta.. in force vntill the fineteenth day of July next, after y{e} signeing hereof/

Witness/   Nathan Bedford/
William Start/   This bill allowed by
The marke of   the Comittee this
Thomas Lott   25{th} day of Sep-   Samll Wheelewright
   teb{r} 1683: as wit-   John Dauess/
   ness our hands/   Jonathan Hamonds/

Book IV, Fol. 69.

Receiued in part of this too buslls of Indean Corne, & foure Gallons of Molosses/ witness my hand this 25th of August 1679 :   Margerett Jocelyn/
Witnesses   The aboue bill as witnesseth
  Wia^m Start   Wil^m Start & Thom^s Lott
  The marke of   vpon oath before mee was
  Thos Lott ⨍   signed & deliuer̃d by the
                          sayd Nathan Bedford unto
Hene : Jocelyn Jus : in quor̃ : Mis Margerett Jocelyn the
                          24th day of August 1679 :
                          Taken vpon oath before
                          mee at Pemaquid this 22th
                          of May 1680 :
                              Thom^s Sharpe Com̃and^r/

These are to signify y^t I & my wife Margerett do Assigne this bill unto my frejnd Mr John Hinkes of Pischataqua, M^rchant his heyres & Assignes, given under o^r hands this Twelth of May on . thousand six hundred & eighty/
Witnesses here unto/ Witnessed by us/ Hene : Jocelyn
  Francis Smale/ Andrew Sampson/ Margerett Jocelyn
  Portsmouth In ye Prouince of New Hampshyre the 5th of November 1680, Francis Smale came & made oath y^t hee saw Mr Hene : Jocelyn, & Margerett Jocelyn sign & deliuer the aboue written, vnto wch him selfe & Andrew Sampson were witnesses, before mee Elyas Stileman of the Councill/

A true Coppy of this bill aboue written, with ye Assigment y^rof, transcribed out of ye originall & y^rwith Compared this : 27th : of July : 1686/   p Thomas : Scottow . Record^r

Scarbrough May 17th 1682/ We the Select men whose names are here under written Do giue and grant unto Robert Tidey a parcel or parcels of upland Lying on the South

BOOK IV, FOL. 69.

East Side of the highway that goeth to Richd Huniwells from Black point, being bounded as followeth, on the upside of the high way toward the Meeting house, with a pine tree about a pole from the way and So along by ye high way till about two poles from Goodman ffickets field with an other pine tree and So leaving a highway between the said ffickets field it goes up to Goodman Huniwells corner of his field and So across over the field toward the Swamp on the East side of the field the Said parcel or pcells of upland being Six Acres more or less as it is now bounded, with all ye priuiledges thereof formerly granted to the said Tidey.

The Select men { Robt Eliot / William Burredge / John Jackson / John Simson }   Recorded in the Records of ye town book by John Simson the Town Clerk of Scarbrough the 27 of May 1682.

This is a true Copie taken out of the Records.

A true Copie of ye originall Copie Transcribed and Compared Septemb^r 15th 1702   p Jos: Hamond Regist^r

May 17th 1682/ We the Select men of Scarbrough whose names are here under written Do give and grant unto Robert Tidy a parcel of Swamp called called the Beaver Dam to the quantity of Six Acres with all ye priviledges thereof

The Select men { Robert Ellet / William Burredge / John Simson. / John Jackson. }   A true Copie of the originall Transcribed and compared Septemb^r: 15: 1702.

p Jos: Hamond Regist^r

[Folio 70 is blank. The first page of folio 71 is blank.]

BOOK IV, FOL. 71.

[71] To all to whome this presents shall come I Francis Champernoone of Kittery, in New England Gent[ll] In the Province of Main, Owner of the Land, called Champernoon Island in Kittery aforesaid lying and being bounded, with M[r] Nathan[ll] Fryer on the West & Broad boat Harbour on the East, send Greeting &c, Know yee that I the sd Francis Champernoone for diverse good causes, and considerations, there unto me moving, & more especially for and in consideration of the tender Love, and indeared affection that I bear unto my well beloved wife Mary Champernoon, Have for my self my Heires, Executors, Administrators, & Assignes, given, granted, delivered & confirmed, and by these presents, doe fully, freely, and absolutely, give, grant, deliver, and confirm, unto my said wife Mary Champernoone, her Heires, Executors, Administ[r] or Assigns all the Housing that is on my sd Island, with the half part of the sd Island, the whole Island in two equall Parts being divided together with the one halfe to be devided, of all & singular, Timber, Timber Trees, Woods, Under woods, Marsh and appurtenances whatsoever, to the s[d] Island now belonging, or in any wise appertayning To haue & to hold all the s[d] Houseing & half part of the s[d] Island and premises, hereby freely given, unto my well beloved wife Mary Champernowne, her Heires, Executors, Administrators, and Assigns, as her, and their own proper Goodes & Estate forevermore, and to her and their own proper use, and behoof forevermore, after my decease/ And now full possession of the whole, for our advantage, on the ensealing & delivery hereof — And I the sd Francis Champernowne, do covenant promise, and Grant, to and with my s[d] wife Mary Champernowne, her Executors, Administrators, and Assignes, by these presents, that I the s[d] Francis Champernowne on the day of the date hereof, and at the time of the ensealing, and deliuery hereof, haue in my selfe, full power, good Right, and lawfull Authority, to give, grant, deliver and confirm the whole Houses afores[d]

with the half part of the s^d Island, and premises, hereby freely given unto my well beloved wife, Mary Champernowne, her Heires, Executors, Administrators, and Assignes foreuermore, in manner and form afores^d. And allso that my s^d well beloved wife Mary Champernowne, her Heirs, Executors, Administrators, and assignes, or any of them, shall and lawfully may, from time, to time, and all times hereafter, peaceably and quietly, haue hold use, and Injoy, the whole Houses, and half part of the said Island, and premises, hereby freely given, without any manner of Lett, suit, trouble, eviction, ejaction, Molestation, disturbance Challenge, claime, deniall, or demand, whatsoever, of or by me the s^d Francis Champernowne, my Heirs, Executors, Administrators or Assignes, or any of them, or of or by any other person or persons [72] whatsoever, lawfully clayming, or to clayme, from by, or under me, my Act or Title. In wittness whereof, I have hereunto put my hand & seale this 19th day of May, Anno Domini 1684

Sealed signed and delivered,   Francis Champernowne (seal)
  in the presence of us,   Capt Francis Champernowne came
  John Penwill/   before me the 19th May as above,
  Sarah S P Penwill   and owned the aboues^d Instru-
  marke.   ment to be his free Act & Deed/
        John Davis Dep^t Presid^t

A true Copy of the Originall Instrument transcribed & compared this 8th Septemb^r 1686 as Attests,
        Tho : Scottow Dep^t Regist^r

Know all men, by these presents, that I George Ingersoll Junr of Fallmoth, in Casco Bay, do for himself, his Heires Eec^r Adm^r give, grant bargain, & sell, for, and to properly belong to the Partners, in their Saw mill, & for the use of that Saw Mill, the one half of all his fresh Meadow, being part of a Meadow, commonly known & called by the Name of Nonsuch meadow, lying in the Towneship of Scarborough/ the s^d Meadow, is to belong forever to the proper use of the Saw mill, that now is in Partnership, betwixt George Ingersoll Juu^r, John Ingersoll, Cap^tne John Phillips, Syllvanus Davis, John Endicott, James Inglish, as witnesse his hand, this 13th March 168¾ & to Remain to they their Heires & either of them, their Heirs, Exec^r Adm^r or Assignes forever, as wittnesse his hand the day & year abovewritten

<small>Geo. Ingersoll, to Syllvanus Davis</small>

Signed & delivered in presence,   George Ingersoll.
of us,
Valentine Potter,
Sarah Baker,

George Ingersoll Junr owneth the above Instrument to be his Act & deed, this 13th March 168¾ before,

                      Edw: Tynge, Jus^t P^r

Katharine Ingersoll the wife of George Ingersoll Junr owneth her free consent to the aboue Instrument this 13th March 168¾ before   Edw: Tynge Just Peace

A true Copy of the originall Instrument, transcribed, and compared this 8th September, 1686
                   Tho: Scottow: Dep^t Regis^tr

Know all men by these presents, that I Richard Kirle of Kittery in the County of Yorke, as well for my naturall affection & parentall Love wch I bear to my well beloved Son in law, Samuell Knight of s^d Towne & County, as allso for diverse others good Causes & Considerations, me at present especially moving, have freely given & granted, & by these Presents do give & grant to sd Samuell Knight, Six Acres of Land being part of a Towne Grant of fifteen Acres of Land, lying & beeng in Kittery, s^d Knight Part

Book IV, Fol. 72.

Rich Kirle to Sam¹¹ Knight

shall begin at the Great Cove, & so run sixty eight Pole next to the Land, which is now Remmicks Land, and such breadth, as makes up the forementioned Summ of Acres — To have & to hold, all & singular the s⁴ six Acres of Land to s⁴ Knight, his Heires, Executors, Administrators, & Assignes forever to their own proper Use & Behoof, freely and Quietly without any matter of Challenge or claim, or demand, of me the s⁴ Kirle, or of any other person or persons w'soeuer for me, in my name, by my cause, meanes, or procurement, and without any money or other thing to be yeilded or paid, unto me sd Kirle, my Heires, Executors or Assignes/ And I said Kirle all the sd Land to the sd Knight his Heires, Executors, Administrators, & Assignes, to the use aforesaid against all People doth Warrant & defend by these presents/ And further Know that the s⁴ Kirle, hath put s⁴ Knight in peaceable and Quiet Possession of the sd Land, at the delivering & Sealing of the presents, as witnesse my hand Seale this twenty seventh day of July one thousand, six hund, & seventy six   Richard Kirle/ (seal) Locum segilli

Signed Sealed & delivered
in the presence of us/
marke

John ⌁ Green/

Thomas Spinney/

Mʳ Thomas Spinney & John Green came & made Oath, that this Instrument is the Act & Deed of Richard Kirle, unto Samuell Knight & that they saw the sd Kirle, sign, seale, & deliver it to the said Knight/ taken upon Oath, this 24ᵗʰ, May 168¾ before me
Francis Hooke Jusť Pec

Richard Kirle owned that he put his hand to this Instrument, but saith allso that he was not himself, but was, d headed/ owned this 2ᵈ August 1684

Before me Francis Hooke Jusť Pe

BOOK IV, FOL. 72, 73.

A true Copy of the Originall Instrument, transcribed & compared this 9th Septemb'r 1686, As Attests,
Tho : Scottow, Dep, Regist/

[73] To all Cristian People, unto whom this present Deed of Guift shall come, John Parker of Kennebeck, within the Province of Main, in New England Fisherman sendeth Greeting/ Know yee that I sd John Parker, with the free & full consent of Margarett my wife, for diverse good causes & considerations me there unto moving, more especially for & in consideration of that naturall Love & affection, which I have & bear unto my Daughter Sarah, now the wife of William Baker of s^d Kennebeck, House Carpenter, and for the dowry & Mariage Portion of the Sarah, Have given granted, assigned, enfeofed and confirmed and by these presents, Do fully freely & absolutely, give, grant, bargain, sell, alien, assigne, enfeofe, convey, & confirme unto the s^d William Baker, and Sarah his wife my Daughter, in there own present possession, and by me all ready layd out to them all that my tract, or parcell of Land, scituate, lying, and being in Kennebeck aboves^d beginning at a Point of Land lying to the Northward, of Cap^{ne} Syllvanus Davis his house, on the North side of the Brooke, and up along the Westerly side of the Salt Marsh Creeck, that runneth up towards Laitons, so far as to the Rock, commonly called Stovers Rock, and from thence running along the Cart way

<small>Jo^s Parker to William Baker</small> over to Winnegense Marshes, and round the North east head of s^d Marshes, to a Point of Upland running in to s^d Marshes, and from s^d Point of Upland upō a strtaight line over a Cove of Marsh to the Top of a great Rock a little Rock lying in the saddle of s^d great Rock, and from sd Rock along the Marsh side Westernly, to the westward end of s^d Marshes,

all the Upland, Swamps, Meadows, and Marshes contained, and lying within & betwixt, the afore mentioned, lines & boundes Northeruly, and the Boundes of Cap^{ne} Syllvanus Davis Southernly, in the full dimensions of Length and breadth, be quantity thereof, for number of Acres more or lese, according as it is now set out, & bound trees marked, Together with all the trees, timber, woods, vnderwoodes, stones fences poundes, Springs waters, herbage & feedings, growing lying or being upon the s^d Landes, and of every part & parcell thereof, with all edifeces & buildings & improvements, made by s^d William Baker thereupon, having been in his Possesion (for the space of sixteen years last past, or more) and all rights, libertyes & Comonages, profitts previledges, members, herediments & appurtenances there unto belonging. Allso all the estate, right Title, Interest, use, property possession claim, & demand, whatsoever of me the s^d John Parker, of in & to the same, To have and to hold, the s^d tract or parcell of Land, both upland, swamp meadows and marches, as above described, and bounded, be the contents, or quantity thereof more or lesse, with all other the premises, libertyes, priviledges and appurtenances thereof unto him the s^d William Baker and Sarah his present wife, and to the Heires of the Body of the s^d Sarah lawfully begotten, and to be begotten, to the only proper use, benefitt and behoofe of them, their Heires and Assignes forever, next and immediately after the decease of the s^d William Parker and Sarah his present wife, and the longer liver of them, freely peaceably, and quietly, to have hold, use, occupy possesse, and injoy all the above given and granted premises, without any payment to be made, or any account reckning, or answer therefore to be rendred or given unto me or mine at any time to come, So that neither I the sd John Parker, my heires Exec^{rs} adm^{rs} or assignes, shall or may at any time or times forever hereafter, have, aske, claim challenge or demand, any estate, Right Interest, claim or demand of in or to the above granted premises, or any part or parcell thereof. But from all action of right, title or claime thereunto, wee and every of us to be utterly excluded, and forever debared by vertue of thesse presents, And farther, I the said John Parker, for me my heires, Execrs and admrs do covenant and promise, to warrant maintain and defend, all the sd premise with their appurtenances, unto the sd William Baker & Sarah his present wife. and to the Heires of their body lawfully begotten, and to be begotten and their Heires and Assignes for ever against the lawfull claimes, or demands of any person, or person whatsoever. In Wittnesse, whereof I the above named John Parker, & Margarett my wife (in token of her consent & and full Relinquishment of all right of Dowre or power of thirds to be had, or claimed in the premises) have hereunto put or handes, & affixed our seales, this thirty day of January Anno Domᵉ one thousand six hundred eighty and four, Annoqᵉ RRˢ Caroli secundi Angliæ &c tricessimo sexto

Signed sealed and delivered   marke
  in the presence of us/
  Tho: Parker   Syll/ Davis   John *J P* Parker (seal)
  John P Paine   Jeams Inglish : Margarett Parker (seal)
  mke

John Parker and Margerett his wife did owne this Instrument, to be their Act and Deed to William Baker, & his wife Sarah, as is within specifyed, this 25th of February 168⅔ at Harwich in the province of Main before me,

                              Syllvanus Davis Commisr

A true Copy of the Originall Instrument transcribed, and compared this 8th Septembr 1686, as attests:

                    Tho : Scottow : Dept Regist

BOOK IV, FOL. 74.

[74] To all Cristian People to whom these presents shall come—Know yee that I Dennis Morrough of Fallmoth, in the Province of Main Yeoman in the County of Yorke there in America sendeth Greeting/ Know yee, that the s^d Dennis Morrough for divers good causes & considerations me thereunto moving but especially for the sum of eight Poundes, to mee in hand paid, by Philip Breton, the receipt where of I do acknowledge my selfe fully satisfyed & paid, & for my self my Heires, Exec^r Adm^r & Assignes, from every part & parcell thereof, have given granted, & by these presents, do fully, freely, & absolutely, give grant, Bargain, sell, alien, assigne, & sett over unto Philip Breton his Heires, Exec^r Adm^r or Assignes, thirty Acres of Land, with all the Marsh lying within the Boundes of s^d Land. Which Land lyeth on the South side of Casco River, & is bounded as followeth, to begin on the Western side, of Jeames Frees land, and so along by the water side, whom to Mr Clarke land, which is the full breadth of s^d Land by the Water side, and so to run the sam breadth, into the Woodes between Clarks & Frees Land, till thirty acres be accomplished & compleated, with

<small>Dennis Morrough to Philip Breton:</small> all my right Title & Interest, that I now haue, or ought to haue, at the time of the sealing of these presents, with all the Woods, underwoodes mines, mineralls, commonges profitts, priveledges & appurtenances there unto belonging, as was given me by the select men of this Town of Fallmoth, as the Town records will plainly make appear/ To haue and to hould, all & singular the above granted & bargained premises to euery part & parcell with all & singular other priveledges, & to every part & parcell unto me belonging with all my right Title & Interest thereof unto the s^d Philip his Heires, Exec^r Adm^r & Assignes, to their own proper use benefit & behoof for ever, of o^r from me the s^d Dennis Morrough, my Heires, Exec^r Adm^r & Assignes forever, And for the tru performance I

Book IV, Fol. 74.

have hereunto set my hand & Seale, this 2ᵈ of September, one thousand six hundred & eighty six

Signed sealed & delivered, &, Possession given, in presence, of us/
Tho. Scottow:
Ben Rolfe.

Dennis ✗ Morrough/ (seale)
      marke

Jane } Morrough (seal)
    marke

 Fallmoth the 3ᵈ September 1686, Dennis Morrough & Jane Morrough appeared before me one of his Majestyes Council, & acknowledged this Instrument to be their free act, & deed/ Edwᵈ Tynge.

A true Copy of the originall Instrument transcribed and compared this 9ᵗʰ September 1686
     Tho: Scottow: Repᵗ Regisᵗ

 Know all men, by these presents, that I Samuell Webber of casco Bay, in the Province of Main, in New England, Millright for and in consideration of the Summ of thirty two Poundes to me in hand before the ensealeing and delivery hereof well & truely paid by Syllvanus Davis of aforesᵈ Casco Bay, the Receipt where of, as a valuable summ of money, I doe hereby Acknowledge & thereof & of every part & parcell thereof, exonerate, acquitt & discharge, the sᵈ Syllvanus Davis, his Heires, Execʳ Admʳ & Assignes forever by these presents, Have granted, bargained sould & confirmed, & by these presents do fully & absolutely grant bargain, sell, enfeoffe & confirm, unto the sᵈ Davis, one full moiety of all that my Saw Mill, & the River on the which it stands, commonly known and called by the name of Long Cricke, scituate & at Fallmoth in Casco Bay aforesᵈ within the Province of Main, granted unto me by the select men of the aforesaid Towne of Fallmoth, as doth appear by the Towne Records, with the full moiety of one hundred Acres of Land granted by the afores⁴ select men, for the accomodation of the s⁴ Saw Mill, with the Previledge of the Falls, and timber with one halfe of the Land on both sides of the Falls sufficient for accomodation to the s⁴ Mill, the other half of s⁴ Mill & the half of the one hundred Acres of Land, I have sould unto John skilling before the ensealing hereof. the Boundes of the sd Hundred Acres of Land is divided betwixt s⁴ Davis and Skilling, to say the deviding line to run from corner to corner athwart s⁴ Land, beginning at a black Stump, upon the Southeast side of fores⁴ Long Crick, & to run to the West Northward Corner marked Tree S⁴ Davis to haue his half of the hundred Acres upon the North ward side of s⁴ line, or boundes, and John Skilling to have his half of s⁴ hund Acres upon the South westwardly side of the fores⁴ thwart line or Boundes, allso Davis is to have all the meadow & swamp that is capable to make Meadow within John Skillings Part of s⁴ hund Acres, with the Priveledge of the moiety of all Woodes, trees, timber standing & lying or growing upon any part of s⁴ hundred Acres of Land, and free liberty for Cart wayes for yᵉ use & benefitt of s⁴ Mills with the moeity of all Priveledges granted unto me by the select men of fores⁴ Fallmoth, be it in one Kinde or other, for the use of s⁴ Mill, allso I do grant unto s⁴ Davis my dwelling house & feild now standing and lying on the Northward side of s⁴ Mill, and allso ten Acres of swamp or meadow granted unto me by s⁴ select men, more then the fores⁴ hundred Acres of Land, which s⁴ swamp or meadow lyes up a branch of the fores⁴ Mill River, having been in my Possession & improvement, euer since I built the fores⁴ Mill/ To have & to hould the said granted premises with all waters, Damms, utensills, libertyes, priveledges, accommodations and appurtenances thereunto belonging, or any wayes appertayning unto him

Sam Webber to Syll. Davis

[75] the s^d syllvanns Davis, his heires and assignes and to their proper use & only behoof forever, and I the afores^d Samuell Webber, do hereby avouch my self at the time of ensealing & untill the delivery of these presents to be the true & lawfull Owner of all the above bargained premises, freely and clear acquitted and discharged from all former and other bargains, sales & Incumbrances, morgages, dowryes, or titles of dowrys, whatsoever, In wittnesse whereof I the abovenamed Samuell Webber & Deborah my wife in token of her consent, and full relinquishment of all right of dowry, or power of thirds to be had or claymed in the premises, have hereunto put o^r hands and fixed o^r seales, this 23th day of Novembr 1685, in the first year of the Reign of o^r Soveraign Lord King James the second, by the Grace of God Defend^r of the faith, &c

The word third day Interlined before the signing hereof Sealed Signed and delivered with quiet & peaceable possession given in presence of us,

John I S Skilling, his signe,
Joseph Webber:

Samuell Webber : (seale)
Deborah ✝ Webber (seal)
her signe

Samuell Webber appeared before me this 23^d of Novembr 1685 & acknowledged this Instrument to be his Act & deed/ Deborah Webber ownes her consent to the aboves^d Deed of Sale, the day & year aboue written as attests
    Edw : Tynge Just peace

A true copy of the originall Instrument transcribed and compared this 8th of Septembr 1686 as attests,
    Tho : Scottow : Dep^t Regis^t

Book IV, Fol. 75.

To all Christian People, to whom this present Deed of Sale, shall come, Bartholomew Gidney of Salem, in the County of Essex, in the Colony of the Masachusetts in New England Esqr and Hannah his wife, send greeting, Know yee, that the s^d Bartholomew Gidney, and Hannah his wife, for and in consideration of the Summ of one hundred & fifty Pounds of Currant money of New England, to them in hand at or before the ensealing, and delivery of these presents by Walter Gendall of Casco in the Province of Main, in New England afores^d Yeoman well and truly paid, the receipt whereof they do hereby Acknowledge, and themselves therewith fully satisfyed and Contented, and thereof, and of every part and parcell thereof, do Acquitt, Exonerate, and Discharg the s^d Walter Gendall, his Heires, Execut^{rs} Administrators and Assignes, and every of them by these presents, Have given, granted, bargaind, sould, aliend, enfeofed, and confirmed, And by these presents Doe fully, freely, clearly and absolutely, giue, grant, bargain, sell, Alien, Enfeof and confirm, unto the s^d Walter Gendall, his heires, and Assignes forever, All that their tract or parcell of Land scituate, lying, and being in Casco afores^d on the North side of the Bay there, the front whereof next the Sea lyeth within the Township of North yarmoth in New England aforesaid as the same Land was formerly granted by severall Indian Sagamores unto Thomas Stevens of Kennebeck Yeoman, as by Deed of Sale under the hands and Seales of the said Indian Sachems bearing date, the 19th day of January 1673 reference whereunto being had more fully, and at large doth and may appear, And one Moiety whereof was granted by the s^d Stevens unto the s^d Gidney, as by Deed of Sale beareing date the 12th day of October 1674, more fully may appear, And the other Moiety thereof was granted by the s^d Stevens, unto Henry Seaward, & by him Morgaged unto the s^d Bartholomew Gidney, and afterwards the same became forfeited into the hands of the s^d Gidney,

Together with all and singular the Houses out houses, Edifices Buildings, Yards, Gardens, Orchards Lands, Meadows, Marshes, Swamps, Woods, underwoods, Trees Rivers, Ponds, Damms, Headwares, fishings, fowlings, [76] wayes Easements, waters watercourses, profitts, priveledges, rights, Libertyes, commodityes, herediments and appurtenances whatsoever to the s^d Tract or parcell of Land belonging or in any wise appertayning/ And also all Deeds writings whatsoever touching or concerning the Premises, only or only any part or parcell thereof, To have and to hold the said tract or parcell of Land scituate, lying and being as afores^d with all other above granted premises, with their appurtenances, and every part and parcell thereof unto the s^d Walter Gendall his Heirs, and Assignes, and to the only proper use, benefitt, and behoofe of the said Walter Gendall, his heires and Assignes forever, And the s^d Bartholomew Gidney and Hannah his wife for themselves, their Heires, Exec^r and Administrators, do hereby covenant and promise and grant to and with the s^d Walter Gendall his heires and assignes, in manner and form following (that is to Say) that the s^d Walter Gendall his heires and Assignes, shall and may by force and vertue of these presents, from time to time, and at all times, forever hereafter, lawfully peaceably & quietly, have, hold, use, occupy possesse & Injoy the above granted premises, with their appurtenances and euery part and parcell thereof, as a good perfect and absolute Estate of Inheritance in ffee simple, without any manner of condition, reversion or limitation whatsoever, Soe as to alter, change, defeat or make void the same, free and Clear & clearly acquitted and discharged off or from all former and other gifts Grants, bargaines, sale Leases, Morgages Joynters Dowers, Judgements, Executions Intailes, forfeitures, and of and from all other, titles, troubles, charges, and Incumberances whatsoever, had, made, committed done or suffered to be done by them the s^d Bartholomew Gidney, and Hannah his wife or either of them, their or either of their, heires or assignes, at any time or times before the ensealing hereof, And further that the s^d Bartholomew Gidney, and Hannah his wife their heires, Executores, Administrators and Assignes shall and will from time, to time, and at all times for ever hereafter warrant and defend the above granted tract, or parcell of Land, with all other the above-granted premises, with their appurtenances, and every part thereof, unto the said Walter Gendall his heires and Assignes against all and every person and persons whatsoever, any way lawfully clayming or demanding the same or any part thereof by from or under the s^d Bartholomew Gidney, and Hannah his wife, their or either of their Heires or Assignes/ In witnesse whereof the s^d Bartholomew Gidney, and Hannah his wife have hereunto set their hands and seales, the twelvth day of July, Anno Domini one thousand six hundred, eighty and one, Annoq, Regni R^s Caroli secundi xxxiii/

Signed Sealed and delivered in the   Bartholomew Gidney
presence of us by the within   (seal)
named Bartholomew Gidney   (seal)
John Hayward,
Eliezer Moody Servt

This Instrument acknowledged by the within named Bartholomew Gidney as his Act and Deed in Boston this 12th of July 1681 before me   Thomas Danforth Presid^t

A true Coppy of the originall Instrument, transcribed and therewith compared this 9th Novemb^r 1686 as attests
           Tho · Scottow Dep^t Reg^t

Know all men by these presents that I Walter Gendall of Casco in the Province of Main, have released & forever quitt claimed and by these presents, remise, release, & for me my heires and Assignes for euer quitt claime unto Bartholomew Gidney of Salem In the Colony of the Massachusetts, all my right Title & Interest, that I have or ever had, in or unto the Land to me Sould according to the within written Instrument of Conveyance to the s^d Gidney, to have and to hold the same to him, his heires, Executors, administrators & assignes forever, and I the s^d Gendall do hereby Ingage my self, my heirs and Executors, Administrators & assignes [77] to warrant, acquitt and defend, the Quiett and peaceable Possession, to maintaine unto the said Gidney his heires and Assignes against all persons laying claim thereunto by from, or under me, or my Heires or Assignes — having allready forfeited on a Morgage for non payment & In Wittnesse hereof have sett my hand and Seale this 17th day of July 1684

See Book 3 page 96 for ye Orig^l Deed

Signed Sealed and delivered   Walter Gendall, (seal)
  in the presence, of
  William Gidney,
  Benjamin Hiliard

Walter Gendall of Casco acknowledged this above written Instrument to be his Act and Deed Salem July the 7th 1684
                 before me John Hathorne Assis^t

A true Coppy of the originall Instrument transcribed and compared this 10th of Novemb^r 1686 as attests
            Tho : Scottow Dep^t Reg^tr

To all Chrystian People to whom this present Deed of Morgage shall come, Know yee that we Henry Harwood and Elizabeth his wife, now in Boston, in New England for & in consideration of fivety Poundes in Hand Received currant money of New England before the ensealing of these presents by Bozoun Allin of Boston Tanner well and truly paid, the Receipt whereof to full content and satisfaction they do hereby Acknowledge and thereof and every part thereof & parcell, do exonerate Acquitt and discharge the s^d Bozoun Allin, his heires Executores, Administrators forever by these presents, have granted Bargained sold aliened enfeofed conveyed and confirmed, and by these presents, do fully, freely, and absolutely, grant bargain sell, alien assigne enfeofe convey, and confirm, and by these presents unto s^d Bozoun Allin, his heires, and assignes forever, all that their messuage, Tenement or dwelling house, with the ground thereto belonging, scituate lying and being in the Towneship of ffallmoth, in Casco Bay in the Eastern Parts of New England, the which we exchanged with the reverend Mr George Burroughs for, and was purchased by the s^d Burroughs of John Skilling of Casco bay afores^d together with all the Gardens Orchards houses outhouses, Barns, Stables, Edifices, Buildings and other Rights, priviledges profitts, commoditves & appurtenances whatsoever to the Premises belonging, or in any wise appertaining, and all the estate title and right, propriety possession clayme or demand, that we or either of us have or at any time might have had, in or unto the Premises or to any part thereof, To have and to hold, the above granted dwelling house and Land, with all the Libertyes priviledges and appurtenances thereof unto the s^d Bozoun Allen of Boston Tanner his heires and assignes, to his and their only Proper use, benefitt and behoof from hence forth and forever, And the s^d Henry Harwood Cordwind^r and Elizabeth his wife for themselves and their respective heires Executores Administrators, do covenant promise and grant to & with the s^d Bozoun Allen, his heires, Execut^{rs} Administrators and Assignes, that they are the true Right and proper owners of the above bargained premises, and have in themselves full power, and good Right the same to bargain sell & Confirm unto the s^d Bozoun Allin, his heires, Exec^{rs} & Assignes in manner as aforesaid, and that the bargained premises are at the Sealing and delivery hereof free and

BOOK IV, FOL. 77, 78.

clear, acquitted and discharged off and from all former and other gifts, grants, bargains, sales, Leases, morgages, titles, troubles, acts, alienations and Incumbrances whatsoever, and that we will warrant and make good the sale of the above bargained premises and all the libertyes, priviledges and appurtenances thereunto belonging to the s^d Bozoun Allen his heires, Exec^{rs} Adm^{rs} and Assignes, against all persons lawfull clayming any Right to, or Interest therein from henceforth and foreuer, and that the s^d Elizabeth Harwood, the wife of Henry Harwood Cordwinder doth allso hereby, Renounse relinquish and discharge all her Right, Title and Interest of in or unto the premises forever by these presents. Provided allwayes that it is the true Intent of these presents, that if the s^d Henry Harwood Cordwinder or Elizabeth his s^d wife, they or either of them their heires Exec^{rs}, Adm^{rs}, or assignes, doe shall or well and truly pay or cause to be pd unto the abovenamed Bozoun Allen his heires, Exec^{rs}, Administ^{rs} or assignes, the abovesaid Summ [78] of fivety Poundes Currant money of New England at the now dwelling house of aboves^d Allen, on or before the first day of July 1686 then this Deed of Morgage to be void or of none effect, or else to stand and remain and abide, in full force power and vertue, In wittnesse whereof the s^d Henry Harwood and Elizabeth Harwood have hereunto sett their handes and Seales, the first day of August Anno Dom^i 1685

Signed Sealed & delivered in pres- Henry Harwood
 ence of, the word house in the   (sea.)
 12th line, and words interlined in Elizabeth Harwood
 the fourteenth line is, & they are   (a^l)
 interlined before signing, & Sealing

 The mark ┼ ∫ of Mary Wright
 The mark | a of Priscilla Woodberry,

Boston the August 5th 1685, then and there personally ap peared Henry Harwood and Elizabeth his wife and acknowledged this Instrument to be their volvntary Act & Deed before Elisha Hutchison Assist

A true Coppy of the originall Instrument transcribed & compared this 10th of Novembr 1686

p Tho: Scottow Dept Registr

February the 3d 168$\frac{4}{5}$

Articles of Agreement made between John Smith of Yorke in the Province of Main of the one Party and Mary Smith of the Same Town of the other Party, I the Said John Smith do give grant Enfeofe and Confirm unto the Said Mary Smith the wife of my late deceased Father John Smith, a Certain parcel of Land being bounded by a White Oak Tree on the North West Side of a Runn of Water being at the head of a Crick on the Northeast Side of Samuell Bankes his house and the other Side being bounded by Samuell Bankes his Land, and so far to Runn to a Certain Hemlock Tree NorthWest from the River which Hemlock Tree Samuell Bankes Pretends to be his Corner Boundes, and yrfor to Run on a North west line on both Sides, as far as my father Land doth Goe, which parcell of Land I the Sd John Smith do give grant Infeofe and Confirm unto the Said Mary Smith, her heires Execrs, and Admrs and Assignes forever, with all Priviledges, appurtenances thereunto belonging from by or under me, my heires Execrs Admrs and Assignes, which for and in Consideration hereof I the Said Mary Smith my heires Execrs, Admrs and Assignes deliver all ye Right and Title of any Land which was formerly my husband Smiths, and will not henceforth and forever lay any Claim or challenge to any thirds or part or parcell thereof, but do from henceforth Acquitt and Clear the Said Smith and owne my Self to be Contented and fully Satisfyed, which being fully Agreed and possession given on both Sides we bind our Selves in a Bond of One hundred Pound each to the Other for to Stand to what is here written/ Sealed Signed and Delivered in the Presence of us

 Samuell Webber   John ✗ Smith his m^{ke} (seal)
 John Webber/
        Mary 𝓜 Smith
         her marke   (Sigill)

John Smith and Mary Smith Acknowledged this above Instrument to be their Act and Deed this 29th February 168$\frac{7}{8}$
    Before me Sam^{ll} Wheelright Jus^t Peace

A true Copy of the Originall Instrument transcribed and Compared this 1th March 168$\frac{7}{8}$

       p me Tho: Scottow Dep^t Regis^{tr}

[79] To all Christian people before whom these presents shall come/ John Shapleigh of Kittery in y^e Prouince of Mayn in New England Send greeting, Now Know y^e that I John Shapleigh of Kittery in y^e Prouince of Mayn afores^d/ for diuers good causes me thereunto mouing, More Especially for and in Consideration of Ninety pounds to me in hand payd by Edward Ayers of Kittery in the Prouince afores^d Blacksmith, The receipt whereof and of euery part & parcell thereof I acknowledge & therewith fully Satisfied contented and payd, haue giuen granted bargained Sold Aliened Enfeofed made ouer and confirmed, And by these presents for me my heires Execut^{rs} Administrat^{rs} and Assigns doe freely cleerly & absolutely giue grant bargain Sell Alien Enfeoffe make ouer, and confirm unto him the s^d Edward Ayers his heires Execut^{rs} Administrat^{rs} and Assigns foreuer all that house & land orchard Barn or other buildings formerly in ye possession of William Elingham late of Kittery Deceased, Scituate lying and being in Kittery afores^d on y^e

Book IV, Fol. 79.

Riuer of Piscataqua, being about Sixteen Acres be it more or less, Together with thirty Acres of land and Marsh purchased of Antipas Mauerick late of s^d Kittery Deceased, by Maj^r Nicholas Shapleigh of s^d Kittery Deceased, as more amply appeares by his Deed bearing Date the Sixteenth day of June one thousand Six hundred Seuenty and Eight lying and being next adjoyning unto ye land formerly possessed by ye aforesaid Elingham bounded by a creek on ye North west side comonly known by ye name of Daniells creek And by ye land formerly s^d Mauericks on ye South East Side and Soe ranging back upon an East North East line, and by ye Side of s^d creek upon a parralell line into the Woods till ye s^d Thirty Acres be compleated To haue & to hold the aboue giuen and granted premises with all ye priuiledg^s & appurtenances thereunto belonging or in any way appurtaining, To him ye s^d Edward Ayers his heires Execut^{rs} Administrat^{rs} and Assigns for euer And ye s^d John Shapleigh for himselfe his heires and Assigns doth couenant & promise to and wth ye s^d Edward Ayers his heires Execut^{rs} Administrat^{rs} and Assigns for euer to warrant & Defend ye aboue giuen & granted premises against all psons what soeuer Claiming any Right Title or Interest thereunto from by or und^r him ye s^d John Shapleigh his heires or Assigns/ In Witness wherof the Said Shapleigh hath Set his hand & Seal this Eight & twentieth day of December, one thousand Six hundred Eighty & fiue, 1685. John Shapleigh (Seal)
Signed Sealed & deliuered Alice Shapleigh (Seal)
   in the presents of us Sarah Shapleigh (Seal)
   John Pickerin Mr John Shapleigh & his wife came this
   Jos Hamond 24° of ffebruary one thousand Six
   hundred Ninety fiue and owned this
   bill of Sale to be their act and Deed-
         Job Alcock Justis of pe/

Book IV, Fol. 79.

A true Copie of ye origenall Instrument Transcribed & compared This 25º ffebruary 169⅔

p me/ Jos : Hamond Reg^r

Know all men by these presents that I Thomas Trafton of York in the Prouince of Maine Yeoman, many good causes me hereto mouing, Especially in consideration that I haue had and haue a Real loue and fatherly affection to and towards my welbeloued Daughter Elizabeth, And in like manner to and towards her husband John Rackliff haue of my own free will & upon good and Real consideration freely giuen granted made ouer Released and deliuered unto my Said Son in law John Rackliff, a parcell or Tract of land with a house & orchard thereupon, lying and being nere that part of ye Town of York abouesaid comonly called Rogeres Coue, containing twenty Acres, ten of which formerly belonged to Mr Edward Godfry With all ye benefits profits conueniences priuiledges and appertenances therein thereon or in any manner thereunto belonging or appertaining, to him ye Said John Rackliff during his Naturall life and afterwards to ye Eldest lawfull begotten Son of the s^d John Rackliff upon ye body of ye afores^d Elizabeth and for want of Such Son then Suruiuing, to ye next in kindred, Either Son or Daughter, To whom and their heires for Euer I ye aforesaid Thomas Trafton doe freely giue and bequeath the aforesaid twenty Acres of land in manner aforesaid/ Onely prouided that ye said land may be shall and s . . . . continue to ye right and true Intent of this my Deed of free gift, to wit, that ye said John Rackliff during his life Shall Inherit possesse and enjoy the s^d twenty Acres of land, in manner afores^d then to be and continue to ye lawfull heires of ye s^d John Rackliff begotten upon ye body of ye afores^d Elizabeth and Soe from heire to

Traftons Deed of gift to his daughter

heir for euer/ and for want of Such heires to return without trouble or Molestation to me or my heires In witness of y̅e̅ truth and for true meaning and Real performance of all and euery aboue written, I the abouesaid Thomas Trafton haue hereunto put my hand and affixed my Seal the fifth day of Nouemb̅r̅ in y̅e̅ year of our Lord God one thousand Six hundred Ninety & one and Seal

    Being present   Thomas T Trafton (Seal)
    Matthew Nelson
        mark   his mark
William W Rackliff   Thomas Trafton owned this aboue
         his   Instrum̅t̅ to be his act and Deed
Joseph Alexander   before me
                       Abraham Preble Justis peace

This Deed here Entred on Record Jan: 24° 169$\frac{2}{1}$ and with y̅e̅ origenall compared

                      p Jos Ham̅ond Reg̅r̅

[80] To all People to whom this present Deed of Sale Shall come I Sarah Whinnick Relict & Administratrix unto Joseph Whinnick late of Black point Alias Scarbrough ffisherman Dec̅d̅ Send Greeting/ Know yee that for and in consideration of y̅e̅ Sum of twenty and three pounds in currant money of New England to me and to my Dec̅d̅ husband in hand well and truly payd at and before y̅e̅ ensealing & deliuery of these presents by Richard Hun̅well of Scarbrough in y̅e̅ Prouince of Maine aforesaid, Yeoman, the receit whereof I doe hereby acknowledge and my Selfe therew̅t̅h̅ to be fully Satisfied and contented and payd and thereof & of and from euery part and pcell thereof for me the Said Sarah Whinnick my heires Executers Administrat̅r̅s̅ and Assigns doe Exonerate acqut and fully discharge him the s̅d̅ Rich̅d̅ Hunniwell his heires Execut̅r̅s̅ Administrat̅r̅s̅ and Assigns

by these presents for euer/ I the s^d Sarah Whinnick Haue
giuen granted bargained Sold Aliened enfeoffed and confirmed And by these presents doe for me my
heires Execut^rs Admiuistrat^rs and
Assigns fully freely and absolutely,
giue grant bargain Sell Alien En-
feoffe conuey & confirm unto him ye s^d Richard
Hunniwell his heires and Assigns all that my place or
parcell of land and Meadow lying and being Scituate at
Black point which was formerly Sold to the said Hunniwell
by my Dec^d Husband by a verball agreem^t and has been possessed by ye said Richd Hunniwell about fifteen years past
and is bounded on ye Southerly Side by Black point Riuer
on ye North by a Riuer commonly known by ye name of the
black riuer by the N. West part thereof by Bass creek And
is Surrounded with water at Spring Tides, containing forty
Acres more or less however else bounded or reputed to be
bounded Together wth all the profits priuiledges and Appertenances to ye s^d land Marsh & Meadow belonging or in any
wise Appertaining To haue and to hold ye s^d peece or pcell
of land Marsh and Meadow with ye Appertenances thereto
belonging with all right title Interest claim & demand which
I ye said Sarah Whinnick now haue or in time past haue had
or wch I my heires Execut^rs Administraters or Assigns in
time to come may might Should or in any wise ought to
haue of in or to ye aboue granted premises or any part
thereof to him the s^d Richd Hunniwell his heires or Assigns
for euer And to ye Sole & proper use benefit and behoof of
him ye said Richd Hunniwell his heir Execut^rs &c for euer
more/ And I ye said Sarah Whinnick for me my heires Exe-
cut^rs Administrat^rs and Assigns doe couenant promise and
grant to and with him the s^d Richd Hunniwell his heires and
Assigns That at and before ye ensealing and deliuery thereof

Sarah Whinnicks Deed to Richd Hunniwell

Whinnicks Deed to Hun- well

I am yᵉ true Right and proper Owner of yᵉ aboue pʳmises and the Appertenances And that I haue in my Selfe full power good Right and lawfull Authority the Same to grant and confirm unto him yᵉ said Richᵈ Hunniwell his heires and Assigns as afoʳesᵈ, And that yᵉ Same & euery part thereof is free & cleare acquitted and discharged of and from all former and other gifts grants bargains Sales leases Mortgages titles troubles Acts Alienations and Incomberances whatsoeuer And that it Shall and may be lawfull to and for yᵉ said Richᵈ Hunniwell his heires & Assignes the afoʳesᵈ pʳmises and euery part thereof from time to time and at all times for euer here after To haue hold use improue occupie possess and enjoy lawfully peaceably and quietly without any lawfull lett deniall hinderance Molestation or disturbance of or by me or any other pson or psons from by or under me or by my procuremᵗ, And that yᵉ Sale thereof and of euery part thereof against my Selfe my heires Executʳˢ Administratʳˢ and Assigns and against all other psons whatsoeuer lawfully claiming yᵉ Same or any part thereof I will for euer Saue harmless warrant and Defend by these presets And that I my heires Executʳˢ and Administratʳˢ Shall and will make pform and Execute Such other further lawfull and reasonable act or acts thing or things as in law or Equity can be deuised or required for yᵉ better confirming and more Sure making of the pʳmises unto yᵉ said Richᵈ Hunniwell his heires Executʳˢ Administratʳˢ and Assigns According to the laws of this Prouince. In witnesse whereof I the said Sarah Whinnick haue hereunto Set my hand and Seal the thirtieth day of Nouembʳ in yᵉ Sixth year of the Reign of their Majesties William & Mary

Sarah Whinnicks Deed to Richard Hunniwell

Book IV, Fol. 80.

King and Queen ouer England & ct Anno Domini One thousand Six hundred and Ninety four: 1694.

Signed Sealed & Deliuered   Sarah whinnick ($\genfrac{}{}{0pt}{}{her}{Seal}$)

In the p^rsents of us —

          his   her **2** mark

Henry H Lewes   Boston psonally appeared before me
      mark   y^e Subscrib^r one of their Majesties
Sarah Knight   Justices of peace Sarah Whinnick
                             & acknowledged this Instrum^t to
                             be her Act & deed this 30° of
                             Nouemb^r 1694/

                                         Timothy Prout

This Deed here Entred on Record, and with ye origenall compared January 24° 169⅘   p Jos Hamond Regist^r

---

Mrs Jordan & Rob Jordans Deed of Sale to Hunnwell

Know all men by these presents that we Sarah Jordan Widow and Robert Jordan of Spurwinck Relict & Son of ye late Robert Jordan of ye sd Spurwinck Clark, haue Bargained Sold Enfeoffed and confirmed and by these p^rsents Doe bargaine Sell Enfeoffe and confirm to Richd Hunniwell for and in consideration of two Cows and two oxen to ye s^d Robert Jordan deliuered to him before ye Signing and Sealing hereof, ten Acres of fresh & Salt Marsh-land be it more or less Scituate and lying in ye said Town of Scarbrough and bounded as followeth viz with a Brook called Mooty brook westerly with black point Riuer Southerly with ye body of Marsh belonging to and in ye possession of ye said Robert Jordan Easterly and with a little creek according to a bound Stake Set up between ye said pcell of land Sold to ye said Richard Hunniwell and ye rest of ye land Northerly — To haue and to hold ye said ten Acres of land whether it be more or less according to ye limmits and bounds aboue Expressed, together with all y^e

priuiledges profits and appertenances thereunto belonging, to the Sole and proper use & behoof of ye said Richd Hunniwell his heires or Assignes for euer and the s^d Mary and Robert Jordan Joyntly and Seuerally for themselues their heires Execut^rs and Administrat^rs doe hereby couenant and grant to & with the said Richard Hunniwell his heires and Assigns that they ye s^d Sarah Jordan and Robert her Son are and Stand lawfully possessed [81] To their own use and behoofe of the said bargained p^rmises and appertenances in a good perfect and absolute Estate of Inheritance in ffee Simple and haue in them Selues full power Right and Absolute Authority to grant bargain Sell convey and asure ye Same in manner and form aboue said And that he ye said Richd Hunniwell his heires or Assignes and each or euery of them Shall and may for euer hereafter peaceably and quietly haue and hold ye Said bargained p^rmises with all the Appurtenances free from all Dowers incumbrances intanglements or Molestations whatsoeuer either from them ye said Sarah or Robert Jordan or either of them or from their or either of their heires Execut^rs or Administrat^rs or from any pson or psons by or from under them or any of y^m or of any other pson or psons whatsoeuer claiming any right or title thereunto/ In witness of ye truth of what is aboue And confirmation thereof, the said Sarah Jordan and Robert Jordan haue hereunto Set their hands and Seales made at Black point in ye said Town of Scarbrough the twentieth day of January in ye year of our Lord 1684. And in the xxxvi year of ye Reign of our Soueraign Lord Charles ii^d by the grace of God King of England Scotland ffrance and Ireland &^ct

Read Signed Sealed and Deliuered In p^rsents of —
Jeremiah Jordan
mark
Susaña ∫ fford

mark
Sarah ⌠ Jordan ⟩ (her seale)
Robert Jordan ⟨ (his seale)
2 : 8 : 1685 : This Deed was acknowledged & done in presents of
Josh : Scottow Justice p—

BOOK IV, FOL. 81.

A true Copie of yᵉ origenall Instrumᵗ Transcribed and Compared This 24º of January 169¾ p Jos Hamond Registʳ

Know all by these presents that I James Tobey Senʳ of the Town of Kittery in yᵉ County of York yeoman, for diuers good causes and considerations me hereunto mouing, but Especially for yᵉ loue I bear unto my two Sons John and William Tobey Haue giuen granted Alienated and confirmed, And doe by these presents ffreely giue grant Alienate Enfeoff and confirm all my housing and lands lying in yᵉ Township of Kittery, that is to Say my house & house lot and all my other lands Excepting yᵉ four Acres of land which I haue giuen unto my Sonne Stephen Tobey whereon his house now Standeth Alsoe I giue unto my two Sons John & William Tobey all the Timbʳ wood & woods and undʳ wood trees strees standing lying or growing on yᵉ aboue mentioned pʳmises as alsoe all priuiledges appertinances high wayes Easmᵗˢ of what kind Soeuer unto yᵉ sᵈ John Tobey & William Tobey and their heires & Assigns for euer Alsoe I doe freely giue unto my two Sons John Tobey & William my Stock of cattle to them and their heires for euer/ To say two oxen three steeres four cows three heifers one Bull twelue Sheep three Sows and one Mare/ To haue and to Hold all yᵉ aboue house & housing lands Appertinances priuiledges Stock of cattle, aboue mentioned to The onely use benefit and behoofe of them the sᵈ John Tobey and William Tobey then heires and Assigns for euer/ Equally to be Deuided between them the said John and William Tobey abouesᵈ Yeelding and paying yearly and euery year unto me yᵉ sᵈ James Tobey Senʳ, during my Naturall life the one halfe part of all yᵉ Increase of yᵉ aboue Specified Stock of cattle & one halfe part of yᵉ produce of yᵉ fruites of yᵉ Earth

James Tobyes Deed of gift to his Sons

Book IV, Fol. 81.

as corn apples Cyder butter cheese and all whatsoeuer ye s^d plantation produceth And also convenient Roome in my now dwelling house I do reserue for my own use during my naturall life Alsoe I doe freely giue unto my two Sons John Tobey & William Tobey all my houshould goods to them and their heires for euer excepting my bed and furniture which I giue unto my daughter Mary Tobey, vizt all my woollen & Linnen and Pewter & brass & Iron & vessels of wood I doe freely giue unto my s^d Sons/ Always provided and to be understood that my said Sons John & William Tobey doe well and truly pay render or cause to be payd unto me ye s^d James Tobey Senr ye halfe Increase aboue mentioned during my Naturall life And at my Decease to pay fiue Shillings in money to my Son Stephen Tobey & one heifer to my Son James Tobey And to my two Sons Rich^d and Isaac Tobey fiue pounds Each And to my Daughter Mary my younger daughter ten pounds one halfe in money and the other halfe in currant pay And furthermore I ye said James Tobey doe couenant with ye s^d John and William Tobey that ye p^{r}mises are free from all manner of incombrance whatsoeuer and ye peaceable possession thereof to maintain against all manner of psons whatsoeuer/ Witness my hand & Seal this Second day of Septemb^r One thousand Six hundred Ninety & fiue —

In presents of us   The Signe of
    Richard Rogers   James . ◯ . Tobey (his Seal)
    Mercy Gowen
    Richard Carter   James Toby psonally appearing before me this 16° day of Septemb^r 1695/ did acknowledge this aboue written Instrum^t to be his free Act & Deed:
                        Charles ffrost Justice : peace

A true Copie of y^e Origenall Instrum^t transcribed & compared this : 24° day of January 169$\frac{5}{6}$ p Jos Hamond Regist^r

[82] Know all men by these presents that I Henry Sayword of York in y[e] County of York Millwright for diuers good Considerations there unto me Mouing, doe giue grant Alien & Confirm unto M[r] Nathan[ll] ffryer of y[e] great Ysland in y[e] Riu[r] of Piscataqua March[t] & hereby haue giuen granted Aliened and confirmed from me my heires Execut[rs] Administrat[rs] and Assignes, unto the Said Nathan[ll] ffryer his heires Execut[rs] Administrat[rs] and Assignes for euer for his own proper use and behoofe, A certain tract or parcell of upland containing three hundred & Seuenty Acres in y[e] whole being 350 Acres of upland and about twenty Acres of grassy Swamp lying and being on y[e] South West Side of York Riuer Adjoyning to that tract of land w[ch] formerly was Thomas Beesons on y[e] Southermost Side thereof and now y[e] said land is in the Possession of Edward Rishworth, according to a grant made to the said Henry Sayword by the Town of York, bearing date y[e] Second day of March One thousand Six hundred Sixty & fiue To haue and to hold y[e] afoies[d] Tract of land according to y[e] conditions by Henry Sayword made with y[e] sd Town, with all y[e] profits priuiledges Imunities & Appurtenances whatsoeuer belonging or in any wise Appertaining thereunto from me my heires Execut[rs] Administrat[rs] and Assignes to

Henry Saywords Deed to M[r] ffryer for land at York Assigned

y[e] said Nathan[ll] ffryer his heires Execut[rs] Administrators and Assignes for euer/ And doe further couenant and promise, that y[e] Said land is free clere from all troubles titles claims & incombrances whatsoeuer And to Defend y[e] Right and Title thereof from all psons whatsoeuer by from or under me unto y[e] Said Nathan[ll] ffryer his heires and Assigns for Euer/ The condition of this Deed of Sale grant or Morgage is Such that if y[e] said Henry Sayword Shall pay or cause to be payd Deliuer or cause to be deliuered twenty eight thousand foot of good Merchantable pine boards at Some conuenient landing place at Newgewanacke at or before y[e] twentieth day of June Next Ensuing, Then this

Book IV, Fol. 82.

Deed of Sale grant or Morgage is to be of noe Effect nor stand of any Vallue/ If not pformed then to be and remaine and Stand in full force Efficacie and power as all other Deeds doe unto all intents and purposes whatsoeuer/ As Witness my hand and Seal this 17º day of Aprell : 1674 :
Signed Sealed and deliuered   Henry Sayword (his Seal)
   in the presents of   Henry Sayword doth acknowledge
   Edw : Rishworth   this Instrum^t to be his act & Deed
   Susaña Rishworth   this 17º of March 1674 Before me
                            Edw : Rishworth Asso^{te}
A true Copie of the Origenall Instrument Transcribed and Cōpared : January 24º 169¾   p Jos Hamond Regist^r

Know all men by these presents That I Nathaniel Fryer Senr of the Great Island Merchant my heires Execut^{rs} and Administrat^{rs} Mentioned and Named in the wthin Deed, Doe by these presents ffreely fully and absolutely Giue Grant and Assign ouer unto my welbeloued Son Joshua Fryer his heires Execut^{rs} administrat^{rs} and Assigns for euer, all my Right &

Cap^{tn} Fryers Deed of gift to his Son Joshua   Title to, and Interest in the within Deed as his and their own proper Estate To haue and to hold for euer from me my heires Execut^{rs} and Administrat^{rs} for Euer unto him the s^d Joshuah Fryer his heires Execut^{rs} Administrat^{rs} and Assigns And to his and their own use benefit and behoofe for Euer In Testimony whereunto I haue put my hand and Seal this 28th day of February 169¾
   Witness : William Redford   Nathaniel Fryer (his Seal)
   Charles Frost Junr
   Cap^{tn} Nathaniel Fryar acknowledged the aboue written Instrument to be his Act & Deed this 28th March 1694
                         Charles ffrost Just^e peace
A true Copie of the origenall Instrument Transcribed and therewith compared Jan : 24th 169¾
                     p Jos Hamond Regist^r

Book IV, Fol. 83.

[83] Be it known unto all men by these presents that I James Toby of Kittery in y⁵ County of York doe for and in consideration of Diuers good causes me mouing thereunto, but more Especially y⁵ fatherly affections and tender care and loue that I bear unto my beloued Son Stephen Toby, doe by these presents freely grant and giue unto him my beloued Son aforesaid And to his lawfull heires for euer a certain tract and parcell of land Scituate & lying in the aforesaid County of York in y⁵ Town of Kittery Joyning to the aforesaid Stephen Toby his house at y⁵ North Side of John Greens his land and Joyning thereto, bounded on y⁵

<small>James Tobyes Deed of gift to his Son Stephen</small>

South Side with said Greens land And on y⁵ North Side with the Mast way a great Rock being y⁵ head bounds, And runing from thence towards y⁵ Riuer of Piscataqua till it contains four Acres thus butted and bounded And containing four Acres as aforesaid, To haue and to hold y⁵ aboue said land with all y⁵ Priuiledges and appurtenances thereunto belonging to him and his heires for euer as aboue said without any let hinderance or Molestation by me or any under me, Unto which daly gift I doe hereby ffreely and Volluntarily giue and grant as aboue said unto my Son Stephen aforesaid for euer unto which Deed of gift I doe hereunto freely Set my hand and Seal, This Seuenth day of May And in y⁵ year one thousand Six hundred Ninety & fiue

Signed Sealed and Deliuered in the presents of
Jacob Remick

James ⟩ Toby (his Seal)
mark

Thomas Hunscom James Toby psonally appearing before me on y⁵ 16° day of Sep⁵ 1695 did Acknowledge this aboue written Instrum⁵ to be his ffree Act & deed

Charles ffrost Jus⁵ peace

A true copie of the origenall Instrum⁵ Transcribed & compared this 29° of January 169⅝/

p Jos Hamond Regist⁵

Book IV, Fol. 83.

To all christian people to whome these pres^ts shall come/ Barnabas Wixon of North Ham in ye County of Barnstable in ye Prouince of ye Massachusets Bay Sends Greeting/ Now know ye that I ye aboue Mentioned Barnabas Wixon Administrat^r to ye Estate of John Green late of Kittery Marrin^r Deccased, for Diuers good causes me thereunto mouing More Especially for and in consideration of ten pounds of lawfull money of New England to me in hand payd by Stephen Tobey of Kittery in ye County of York Shipwright, the receipt whereof I acknowledge And therewith fully Satisfied contented & payd and of all and euery part & pcell thereof haue freely and clearely acquitted Exonerated and discharged him ye said Tobey his heires & Assigns for euer, haue 'giuen granted bargained Sold Enfeoffed and confirmed, And by these presents doe for me my heires Execut^rs Administrat^rs and Assigns freely clerely & absolutely give grant bargain Sell Enfeoffe and confirm unto him ye said Stephen Tobey his heires Execut^rs Administrat^rs and Assigns for Euer, all that piece or parcell of land which

Wixons Deed to Stephen Tobey

was given to my Predesess^r John Green afors^d by his father Richd Green of Kittery afores^d as more fully appears by an Instrument under ye said Richd Grens hand bearing date June ye Nineteenth 1697 — being by Estimation ffifteen Acres more or less, Scituate lying and being in Kittery nere ye Riuer of Piscataqua, Joyning to ye land of James Tobey on ye North Side And on that Side begining at ye couc on ye uper Side of ffranks ffort and butting to ye home lot of ye afores^d Richd Green And from James Tobeys land running on a square to a Hemlock tree and on ye Same line till it comes to ye Middle of ye afores^d lot of land of ye s^d Richd Greens And then to run up through ye Middle of ye lot to ye head of ye said Richd Greens land/ To haue and to Hold the afores^d premises with all ye Priuiledges, and appurtenances thereunto belonging or in any wayes Appurtaining, To him ye said Stephen Tobey his heires Execut^rs Administrat^rs and Assigns

BOOK IV, FOL. 83, 84.

for euer And that y̅e̅ s̅d̅ Stephen Tobey Shall and may from time to time and at all times hereafter occupie improue and make use of y̅e̅ aboue giuen and granted p̅mises w̅th̅out any Molestation let deniall or hinderance from me y̅e̅ said Barnabas Wixon or any other p̅son or p̅son claiming any Right Title or Interest thereunto from by or under me/ In witness whereof I haue hereunto Set my hand and Seal this thirteenth day of January Anno Domini one thousand Six hundred Ninety & fiue Ninety Six. 169⅝

        The mark ᴎ of Barnabas Wixon (his Seal)

Signed Sealed and Deliuered   Barnabas Wixon came before
  in the presents of   me this fourteenth day of
  Christian Remick   January 169⅝ and owned
  Jos Ham̅ond   this Instrum̅t̅ to be his Act
                              and Deed before me
                              Job Alcock Justes of peace

A true Copie of y̅e̅ origenall Instrum̅t̅ Transcribed & compared this 29° day of January : 169⅝—

                           p Jos Ham̅ond Regist̅r̅

[84] Let all men know by these presents that we Thomas Spencer of the Parish of Unitie in y̅e̅ County of York planter and Patience my now wife being now or of late possest of one lot of land containing by Estimation two hundred Acres be it more or less giuen and granted unto mee y̅e̅ said Thomas Spencer and to my heires and Assigns for euer by the Town grant of Kittery, Which land lyeth and is within y̅e̅ foresaid Parrish of Unitie/ Now these presents witness that I the said Thomas Spencer and Patience my now wife for and in consideration that Thomas Etherington hath Married with Mary our daughter And for y̅e̅ loue and Naturall affection that we y̅e̅ said Thomas and Patience Spencer doe beare unto the foresaid Thomas Etherington and Mary his

Book IV, Fol. 84.

Thomas
Spencers
Deed to
Tho: Etherington

wife And for their better liuelyhood hereafter haue and by these presents giue and grant unto yᵉ Said Thomas Etherington and Mary his wife, All that tract of land being by Estimation twelue Acres or thereabouts be it more or less as it is now marked and laid out It being bounded with yᵉ lands of Richᵈ Nason on yᵉ or nere yᵉ South an West, And on yᵉ North and West with yᵉ Residue of Thomas Spencers land now in his Possession And with Daniel Goodings land on yᵉ North and East, lying Directly by a line by Daniel Goodings land Soe farr as it lyeth adjoyning to it from yᵉ begining to yᵉ end of it as it lyeth adjoyning And on the East Adjoyning to a lot of land that yᵉ said Thomas Etherington lately purchased of John Gattinsby And there is yᵉ dwelling house of the said Thomas Etherington that he built now Standing on yᵉ foresaid lot Soe bounded & was part and parcell of the foresaid lot of two hundred Acres and is now in yᵉ Possession of yᵉ said Thomas Etherington To haue and to hold the foresaid twelue Acres of land with the appurtenances unto them yᵉ sᵈ Thomas Etherington and Mary his Now wife their heires Executrˢ Administratrˢ and Assigns for euer, in as ample manner to all constructions as I the said Thomas and Patience Spencer can or may Estate yᵉ Same or grant or giue the Same/ And we yᵉ said Thomas Spencer and Patience my now wife for us our heires Executrˢ & Administratrˢ Warrant yᵉ said Thomas Etherington and Mary his now wife, their heires Executrˢ & Administratrˢ against all pson or psons that Shall lawfully Claim under us or either of us, or under our Estate or Title/ In witness whereof we haue here-

Book IV, Fol. 84.

unto Set our hands and Seales Euen y° twentieth day of June in y° year of our Lord God 1662.
Signed Sealed and Deliuered   The mark of
In the presents of us   Thomas ⌒ Spencer (his seal)
Andrew Searle   Patience Spencer (her seal)
Humphrey H S Spencer
John ⌒ Gattensby   Thomas Spencer & his wife acknowledge this writing to be their act and Deed, this 26. Novemb^r 1669.
Richd Waldern Comission^r
A True Copie of the origenall Deed Transcribed & compared this 25° of March: 1696 p Jos Hamond Regist^r

Let all men by these presents that we Thomas Spencer of the Parish of Vnitie in the County of York planter, and Patience my now wife, being possest of one lot of land containing by Estimation too hundred Acres be it more or less, giuen and granted unto the said Thomas Spencer and to his heires and Assignes for euer by the Town grant of Kittery, which land lyeth and is within the foresaid Parish of Vnitie/ Now these presents Witness that I the said Thomas Spencer and Patience my now wife for and in consideration that John Gattinsby hath Marryed with our daughter Susaña, the now wife of the said John Gattinsby, As alsoe the loue and Naturall affection that we the said Thomas and Patience Spencer doe bear unto the fores^{d}John Gattinsby and Susanna his now Wife, And for their better liuelyhood haue giuen & granted unto the said John Gattinsby and Susanna his wife, All that Tract of land it being by Estimation twelue Acres or thereabouts be it more or less as it is now marked and laid out/

BOOK IV, FOL. 84.

Thomas
Spencers
Deed of
Gift to
Jn⁰ Gattinsby

It being bounded with yᵉ lands of one Richard Nason on or near the South Side, and with yᵉ lands of Daniel Gooding, & a Marsh called Parkers Marsh on the North and East/ And yᵉ lands of Thomas Etherington on yᵉ West according as it hath formerly been laid out by the sᵈ Thomas Spencer, And is part and pcle of that foresᵈ lot of tw hundred Acres as aforesᵈ granted, And is lying and being within yᵉ Parish of Vnitie aforesᵈ & Town of Kittery and County of York/ To haue and To hold the foresᵈ twelue Acres of land with yᵉ said appurtenances unto them yᵉ said John Gattinsby Susanna his wife and their Assignes for euer in as large and Ample mañer to all constructions as we the said Thomas Spencer and Patience his wife can or may Estate or grant the Same/ Warranting yᵉ said John Gattinsby against my heires Execut`s` and Administrat`s` And against all pson or psons lawfully Claiming from by or under me yᵉ sᵈ Thomas Spencer or under my Estate or title/ In witness hereof we haue hereunto Set our hands & Seals Euen yᵉ fiue & twentieth day of June in yᵉ year of our Lord God, one thousand Six hundred Sixty and two. 1662 : The marke of

This is a true Copie of the origenall Deed of Gift Signed & Sealed by the aboue said Thomas Spencer and Patience his wife
Andrew Seare
William Spencer
Humphrey 𝓗𝓢 Spencer

Thomas C Spencer (his Seal)
Patience Spencer (her Seal)

William Spencer appeared before me this 24⁰ of Octobʳ 1694, and made oath that he Saw yᵉ abouesᵈ Thomas and Patience Spencer, Signe and Seal ye abouesᵈ Instrument and that he did Set to his hand as a Witness, and that yᵉ other two witnesses Set to their hands at yᵉ Same time Sworn before me— Charles ffrost Justice peace

A true Copie of yᵉ origenall Deed Transcribed and Compared this 25⁰ of March 1696   p Jos Hamond Registʳ

[85] Know all men by these presents that we John Gattinsby of Wells in ye County of York planter, And Susanna my now Wife for and in consideration of ye Sum of fourteen pounds in hand payed before ye insealing and deliuery hereof by the hands of Thomas Etherington of ye Parish of Vnitie and County of York Marrin^r The receit whereof I ye said John Gattensby doe hereby acknowledge and thereof doe acquit ye said Thomas Etherington his heires Execut^rs and Administrat^rs for euer, haue granted bargained and Sold unto ye said Thomas Etherington, all that tract of land it being by Estimation twelue Acres or thereabouts be it more or less And is part of a greater lot of two hundred Acres granted unto Thomas Spencer And is that Tract of land that ye said Thomas Spencer for a good Consideration granted unto ye said John Gattensby as by his Deed bearing Date ye fiue & Twentieth day of June Anno Domi one thousand Six hundred Sixty & two it more plainly doth and may appear and is lying and being within ye Parish of Vnitie and County of York afores^d/ To haue and to hold ye said Tract of land with thappurtenances unto him ye said Thomas Etherington his heires and Assigns for euer in as large and Ample manner as I ye said John Gattensby can or may grant or Estate ye Same, Warranting him ye Said Thomas Etherington his heirs Execut^rs Administrat^rs and Assignes against all manner of pson or psons whatsoeuer Claiming from by or under me ye said John Gattinsby or my wife Susanna or under either of us, or under our or either of our Estate or title/ In Witness whereof we ye said John Gattinsby and Susanna my now Wife haue hereunto

Gattinsbys Deed to Etherington

Set our hands and Seales, Euen the Twentieth day of October Anno Dom : 1664
Sealed & Deliuered
In ye presents of us/
Andrew Searle
William Spencer
Humphrey H S Spencer

The mark of
John ⌒ . Gattinsby (his seal)
The mark of
Susanna ◯ Gattinsby (her seal)

John Gattinsby appeared before me and acknowledged this Deed to be his Act this 26° Nouemb^r 1669 :
Richd Waldron Comiso^r

A true Copie of ye origenall Deed Transcribed and Compared March 25th 1696.   p Jos Hamond Regist^r

[86] This Indenture made the Nine and twentieth day of ffebruary in ye twenty Eight year of the Reign of our Soueraign Lord Charles the Second, by the grace of God of England, Scotland ffrance and Ireland, King Defend^r of the ffaith &c/ between John Wincoll of the Town of Kittery in the County of York Shiere and in the Collony of the Massachusets in New England of the one partie And William Spencer of the Same Town and County of the other partie Witnesseth/ That the said John Wincoll both and as well for and in consideration of a Marriage by Gods permission in a conuenient time to be had made Solemnized and compleated, between the said John Wincoll and one Marie Etherington Daughter of Thomas Etherington late of Kittery Deceased as also for and in consideration of a certain Estate of house and Seuerall Tracts of land giuen granted and confirmed unto the said John Wincoll before ye Sealing hereof by the Said William Spencer, Trustee and Guardian for the Said Mary Etherington, during her Minoritie for her Mar-

riage Portion as also for her better and more comfortable liuelyhood if She Shall happen to Suruiue and out liue the Said John Wincoll her intended husband, haue giuen granted Infeoffed and confirmed And doth by these presents for himself his heires Execut^{rs} and Administrat^{rs} giue grant Infeoffe and confirm unto ye Said William Spencer all those Seuerall Tracts of land viz: one hundred and twenty Acres of land Scituate and lying in the Town of Kittery, being the land on which the Dwelling house of the said Wincoll lately Stood, part of which land ye Said Wincoll bought of George Veazie Deceas^d and ye rest was granted by ye Town of Kittery and together is bounded with the land of Clement Short on the North west, and on ye South west with ye Riuer that runneth to the Selmon ffalls And on the South east with ye land on Benoni Hodsden And on the North east with comon land, As also Seuerall Tracts or pcells of land made ouer by Deed of Sale from Thomas Spencer and William Spencer to the said Wincoll viz: all that dwelling house and lot of land on which ye dwelling house Standeth being by Estimation twenty and four Acres, and bounded with ye land of Richard Nason on ye South & West And on ye North & west with part of Thomas Spencers land And on ye East and North with Daniel Goodwins land And on ye East in part with Humphrey Spencers land and with part of Thomas Spencers land on ye South/ As alsoe Sixty and fiue Acres of land more bounded on ye South with the high way by Wilcocks pond And on ye East with ye land of ye foresaid Thomas Spencer And on ye North with ye land of ye fores^d William Spencer, and on ye South with the land layd out for ye use of the Ministry To Haue and to hould all ye said house and parcells or tracts of land with their and euery of their apurtenances unto him the Said William Spencer and Mary Etherington ye Intended wife of ye said John Wincoll for euer for and to ye onely

Indent^s between Cap^{ta} Jno Wincoll and Wm Spencer

Book IV, Fol. 86.

use benefit & behoofe of her the Said Mary and her heires and Assigns and for and to no other use Intent or purpose whatsoeuer, And the Said William Spencer doth hereby for himself his heirs Execut[rs] Administrat[rs] and Assigns and for euery of them couenant promise and agree to and with y[e] said John Wincoll and Mary his Intended wife their heires Execut[rs] and Administrat[rs] And to and with euery of them that he the said William Spencer his heires Execut[rs] or Administrat[rs] upon request made to him them or either of them by the Said Mary her heires Execut[rs] Administrat[rs] or Assignes or any or either of them at any time after the Death of him the said John Wincoll Shall Surrend[r] and deliuer up this present writing to her them or either of them Soe requesting y[e] Same, And alsoe put her or them in quiet and peaceable possession of all the aboue said house land and other the Premises and Hereditaments with their and euery of their Appurtenances with an account of the profits if any Shall be in his or their hands at that time of request made as afores[d] without any lett Sute Charge trouble deniall or delay, And the Said John Wincoll doth hereby for himselfe his heires Execut[rs] and Assigns and for euery of them couenant & promise to and with the Said William Spencer his heirs Execut[rs] Administrat[rs] and to and with euery of them, And it is the true intent and meaning & Mutuall Agreement of the parties to these presents that if the Said Mary, the Intended wife of the Said John Wincoll doe happen to die without Issue And the Said John Wincoll partie to these presents liuing, Then he y[e] Said John Wincoll shall and may from time to time and at all times during his Naturall life quietly and peaceably haue hold possess and enjoy, all that house and Seuerall Tracts of land with euery part and parcell thereof with their and euery of their Appurtenances that was the proper Estate of the said Mary Etherington before Marriage And after y[e] Death and Decease of y[e] Said John Wincoll, to return unto Patience Etherington Sister to

the said Mary Etherington and to her heires for euer/ In witness hereof both parties to this Indenture haue Set to their hands and Seales the day aboue written In the year of our Lord one thousand Six hundred Seuenty fiue.
Sealed Signed and Deliuered   John Wincoll (his Seale)
  In the presents of us—   Cap^{tn} John Wincoll came be-
  Andrew Searle ⎱ Witnesses   fore me this Second day of
  Daniell Stone ⎰   Aprill 1686 and did ac-
                                          knowledge this Instrum^t
                                          aboue written to be his
                                          Act & Deed
                                          Edw : Rishworth Jus : pe
A true Copie of this Indenture Transcribed & compared This 25° of March 1696   p Jos Hamond Regist^r

Know all men by this presents that I Jane Wethers with ye consent of my Daugter Elizabeth wethers of Kittery in the County of York in New England for the consideration of ye Sum of three pounds and three Shillings in manner as followeth—twenty Shillings in Siluer, to be payd at ye Sealing of it/ and forty thre shillings to be payd in Searge & Indian Corn at ye acknowledging of it before a Magestrate—we doe alsoe own to haue bargained and Sold Aliened Assigned and Set and Set ouer unto the aforesaid Peter Lewis his heires Execut^{rs} Administrat^{rs} or Assigns for euer a

<small>Jane & Elizabeth Wethers Deed to Peter Lewis</small>

parcell of land behind his lot of land that he know liues on, twenty Rod in depth be it more or less and Sixty Nine Rod in breadth which conteneth ye hole breadth of ye s^d Lewis his land/ And for ye true Performance we hous names are aboue Ritten doe bind our heires Execut^{rs} Administrat^{rs} and Assignes for euer, to keep him harmless from any pson or psons that Shall lay any claim thereto, as witness our hands and Seales, this twenty fifth day of Nouember in the year of our Lord one thousand Six hundred Jeghty and fiue—

Sealed Signed and Deliuered The mark of
In the presents of us— Jane ⊥ Wethers (her/seal)
Witness Elizabeth Wethers (her/seal)
John Deament Elizabeth Berry came and before me
The mark ₵ of this 2 day of July 1695. And ac-
Sarah Brukin. knowledged this Instrument to be
  her act & Deed/
  Samuel Donnell Justis peace

A true Copie of the origenall Deed Transcribed and Compared March: 21th 169⅔ p Jos Hamond Regist^r

Receiued of Peter Lewis in full Satisfaction of this Instant Deed twenty Shillings in Siluer and Six bushells and three peck & a halfe peck of Indian corn, and fiue yards & a halfe of Serge Nouemb^r the twenty 9—I say Receiued by me
Elizabeth Wethers

A true Copie p Jos Hamond Regist^r

[87] This Indenture made this Eighteen day of Decemb^r in the year of our Lord one thousand Six hundred Ninety fiue and in the Seuenth year of the Reign of our Soueraign Lord William of England Scotland ffrance and Ireland King Defender of the ffaith—Between Robert Jordan formerly of Cape Elizabeth and now Inhabitant on the great Island in New Castle in ye Prouince of New Hampshiere Yeoman, And Robert Elliot of the Same place Merch^t Witnesseth that ye said Robert Jordan formerly of the Prouince of Maine in New England for and in Consideration of the Sum of two hundred and thirty pounds Nineteen Shillings and eight p^s of Lawfull mony of New England in hand payd to

him the said Robert Jordan by the said Robert Elliot, at & before the ensealing & deliuery of these presents, the Receipt whereof the said Robert Jordan doth hereby acknowledge and thereof and of euery part thereof doth hereby alsoe fully acquit & clearly discharge the said Robert Elliot his heires and Assigns, And for diuers good causes and Considerations him the said Robert Jordan thereunto mouing hath demised granted bargained and to ffarm Letten, & by these presents doth Demise grant and to ffarm Let unto the said Robert Elliot his heires Execut^{rs} Administrat^{rs} and Assigns, All that Interest Title Claim Propriety and Demand, which I the said Robert Jordan haue of unto or in a Cape or Tract of Land called the Cape Elizabeth aforesaid, Scituate and lying in the Prouince of Maine and now in ye Township of ffalmouth in New England aforesaid, together with all the out houses Stages fflakes & fflakerooms, Meadows, Marshes, Swamps woods and underwoods, ponds watercourses or Riuers Emolluments and conueniences therein, thereon, or thereunto belonging, The Land containing in all fiue or Six hundred Acres be it more or less And alsoe I ye said Robert Jordan for and in consideration of full Satisfaction to me in hand payd by said Robert Elliot at or before ye ensealing and deliuery of these presents doe hereby Demise grant Bargain Sell & Surrender unto ye Said Robert Elliot, All that Interest Title property Claim or Demand which I now haue or hereafter may haue of in unto or into all or any part of the Marsh and Marsh Land and Thatch banks Scituate lying and being on Spurwink Riuer in the Prouince of Mayn in New England aforesaid To Haue and to Hold the said Demised premises together with euery part and parcell thereof with their appurtenances unto him the Said Robert Elliot his heires Execut^{rs} Administrat^{rs} and Assigns for euer, hereby alsoe Renoking making voyd & disannulling all and all manner of writings promises contracts bargains or entan-

Mr Rob
Elliots
Deed
from
Robert
Jordan

BOOK IV, FOL. 87.

glements formerly made or done by me the said Robert Jordan to any other pson or psons whatsoeuer In, of, or about the aboue Demised Premises, And further I the Said Robert Jordan my heires Execut^{rs} Administrat^{rs} and Assigns The Sale and Alienation of all the aboue Recited Articles, unto the Said Robert Elliot his heirs Execut^{rs} Administrat^{rs} and Assigns Shall and will Warrant and for euer defend the Same against all manner of Persons whatsoeuer Witness my hand and Seal the day and year aboue written

Signed Sealed and deliuered   Robert Jordan (his Seal)
  In presents of us
       mark of
Richard R Oliuer

Robert Jordan appeared this Eighteen day of March in the year of our Lord 169⅝, Eighth year of Majesties Reign & acknowledged this aboue Instrument to be his Act & Deed before me,   Henry Dow Justice of peace in New Hampshier

A True Copie of this origenall Instrument Transcribed and Compared this 25° of March: 1696
                           p Jos: Hamond: Reg^r

Know all men by these presents that I Gowen Willson for diuers good Considerations but more Especially in regard of ye relation between Andrew Haley of Spruce Creek who Married my Daughter, Deborah, And for and in consideration of my Daughters Portion, doe giue freely and grant unto ye Said Andrew Haly his heires Execut^{rs} Administrat^{rs} and Assigns a Small Tract of land contayning Eleauen acres or there abouts, be it more or less, which land lyeth in Spruce Creek on the Eastern Side of Robert Mendums his land, And is part of ye forty fiue Acres of land granted to me by the

Wilsons Deed of gift to Haly

BOOK IV, FOL. 87, 88.

Select men of Kittery, twenty three or twenty four years past, which land is to run from Robert Mendums bounds, Eleauen pole in breadth within fence, And Soe to run from y" water Side North east up into y" woods Eight Score pole/ I doe further alsoe freely giue unto the Said Haly a Small orchard which was formerly a Cow yard & Inclosed and moreouer besides this I doe promise to allow the s^d Haly unto ye land before Mentioned a Sufficient lane to goe up into ye woods/ To haue and to hold the Said land aboues^d to him and his heires for euer more/ Unto which Deed of Gift I doe hereunto Volluntary and freely Set my hand this Second day of June : 1684/ It is to be understood [88] That the heires aboue mentioned must be Such as is born of my Daughters body, and Soe to remaine in that generation/ As Attests my hand and Seal.   Gowen Wilson (his Seal)
Signed Sealed & Deliuered
   in the presents of us   Gowen Wilson came & owned
   Mary Hooke   this Deed of Gift to be his Act
   the mark of   and Deed, to Andrew Haly
   Johana H Crocker   This 2. June. 1684 before me
                     ffrancis Hook Justice pea
A true Copie of ye origenall Deed Transcribed & compared this : 28° of May 1696   p Jos : Hamond Regist^r

Know all men by this presents that I James Emery of Kittery in ye Prouince of Mayn in New England
Emerys Deed to R Dauis   haue giuen and granted unto Richard Dauis of the Same Town ten Acres of land out of that fiftie Acres that ye Town gaue unto me James Emery about four years agoe/ And it is layd out by Captain John Wincoll Surveigh^r of ye Town of Kittery—I James Emery doe acknowledge to haue giuen and granted for euer unto Richard Dauis his heires or Assigns all that Right I had of ye Town by vertue of a grant unto me, whereunto I haue Set

BOOK IV, FOL. 88.

my hand 19 of Desember in ye year of our Lord 1687 and in ye third year of ye Reign of Souerain King James the Second of England Scotland Ireland and ffrance

 Witness   James Emerey my
 Zechariah Emerey   hand & Seal   (his seal)
 Noah Emerey.

A true Copie of ye origenall Deed Transcribed & compared : June : 1st 1696 p Jos Hamond Regist^r

County York

Know all men by these presents that I Samuel King now Resident in Kittery in the County of York Planter, for diuers good causes & considerations me hereunto mouing, but more Especially for the considerations me hereunto mouing, but more Especially for the consideration of fifty fiue pounds in Money to me in hand payd by Isaac Goodrich of the Same place Yeoman, haue giuen granted bargained and Sold Enfeofed and confirmed/ And doe by these pres^ts bargain Sell Alenate Enfeoffe & confirm, All that tract of land lying in the Township of Kittery known by the name of Kings place Joyning to a Coue fformerly called Mast Coue, and was lately in ye Ocupation of Mistress Margeret Adams, and is that tract of land wherein my ffather Wm King formerly dwelt, and is by computation thirty four Acres or thereabouts as doth more at large appear by my Grandfather Palmers Deed of Gift to my ffather Wm King and is on Record and alsoe by Kittery Town Grant to my ffather bearing Date May the twenty Eighth one thousand Six hundred Seuenty & four, and layd out by Cap^tn Wincoll Surv^r and is bounded at ye Southwest end with Piscataqua Riuer and at ye other end and both Sides by ye lands of Mistress Mar-

Book IV, Fol. 88, 89.

Sam^{ll} Kings Deed to Isaac Goodrich

garet Adams, together with all ye wood & under wood appurtenances and priuiledges thereunto belonging, water courses coues flats and all whatsoeuer belonging thereto as is aboue Specified Euery part & parcell thereof unto ye s^d Isaac Goodrich his heires Execut^{rs} Administrat^{rs} or Assigns for eu^r To haue and to hold, the Same and euery part & parcell thereof, unto ye onely use benefit and behoof of him the Said Isaac Goodrich his heires Execut^{rs} Administrat^{rs} or Assigns for euer moreouer I ye s^d Samuel King doe couenant with ye said Isaac Goodrich his heires and Assignes for my Selfe my heires Execut^{rs} and Administrat^{rs} that I am the true and proper owner thereof and of euery part and parcell thereof, and that I am lawfully Siezed thereof at the time of the Sale hereof and furthermore I ye said Samuel King doe couenant with ye said Isaac Goodrich and his heires that the premises are from all Incombrances whatsoeuer as seruices heriots Joyntures Dowers Rents gifts Sales Mortgages Legacies, and that it Shall and may be lawfull for ye said Isaac Goodrich to take use and ocupie and improue ye premises and any and euery part thereof without the least hinderance Molestation lett or trouble of me the s Samuel King my heires or Assignes the quiet and peaceable possession thereof to Warrant and maintain against all manner of psons laying lawfull claime thereunto, unto the s^d Isaac Goodrich his heires or Assignes for euer/ Witness my hand and Seale this Sixteenth day of June in the year of our Lord one thousand Six hundred Ninety & Six   Samuel King (his Seal)
Signed Sealed & Deliuered

in presents of us
Mary Addams
Wm Godsoe
John Newmarch

The 18° of June 1696 : Samuel King came and acknowledged this Instrument to [89] be his Act and Deed before me
           Wm Peprell Js pes

BOOK IV, FOL. 89.

King to Goodrich

Memorandum that Quiet and peaceable possession was giuen by Samuel King to Isaac Goodrich in presents of us
 Mary Addams A true Copie of the origenall Deed Tran-
 Wm Godsoe scribed and compared June 26° 1696 —
       p Jos Hamond Regist^r

Know all men by these presents that I Sarah King Daughter of Wm King late of Kittery in the County of York Spinster haue for Diuers good causes and considerations me thereunto mouing but Especially for a valluable consideration to me in hand payd before ye Sealing and Signing hereof, and doe acknowledge my self therewith content and payd, haue giuen granted Alenated and Sold And doe by these presents bargan Sell Enfeoffe and confirm unto my beloued brother Samuel King all my Right title and Interest in my late ffather Wm Kings lands and Estate whatsoeuer lying in the Township of Kittery, both what he had of my Grandfather William Palmer as by Deed appears and his Town grant Joyning together, To haue and to hold all ye aforesaid lands or all my Right title and Interest in and to the Same to ye onely use benefit & behoof of him ye Said Samuel King his heires or Assignes for euer from me ye said Sarah King my heires Execut^rs or Administraters or any from by or under me, the peaceable and Quiet possession thereof to maintain against all psons whatsoeuer/ Witness my hand and Seale this Seuenteenth day of June one thousand Six hundred Ninety and Six

Signed Sealed and Deliuered Sarah King aboues^d came and
 in presents of us   acknowledged this Instrum^t
 John Hancock   to be her act & Deed this
 John Wheelwright Seuenteenth of June 1696
        Before me Samuel Wheelwright
           Justice peace

BOOK IV, FOL. 89.

A true Copie of y® origenall transcribed and compared
June 26° 1696   p Jos Hamond Regist^r

Know all men by these presents that I Christian Remich
of the Town of Kittery in the County of York Yeoman, for
diuers good causes & considerations me hereunto Mouing,
Especially for the loue I bear unto my beloued Son Isaac
Remich, haue giuen and granted and doe by these presents
giue grant Alineat Enfeoffe and confirm unto my beloued
Son Isaac Remich All that Tract of land Lying and Scituate
in y® Township of Kittery afores^d and on the North Side of
my Addition and Joyning to y® Same that was granted unto
me by the Town of Kittery to my old lott, lying on the East
Side of the great coue where my Son Isaac Remich now
dwells Containing ten Acres being part of three Grants layd
out to me in May the twentieth : one thousand
Six hundred Seuenty and four, together with all
the Timber wood or under Woods appurtenances and priuiledges thereunto belonging. To
haue and to hold all the aboue giuen and granted
premises unto the said Isaac Remich to him and

Christian Remichs Deed of Gift to his Son Isaac

to his heires Lawfully begotten of his body to him & to them
for euer to their only proper use and behoofe for euermore/
And furthermore I the s^d Christian Remich Doe Warrant
and ingage the aboue giuen and granted premises to be free
from all former gifts and grants or Sales or Mortgages or
Incombrances by me made and the peaceable possession
thereof to maintain against all persons laying Claim thereto
from or under me, Our Soueraign Lord and Lady the King
& Queens Majesty Excepted/ Witness my hand and Seal
this thirtieth March one thousand Six hundred Ninety and

four/ Memorandum that one word is enlined the twelfe line yᵉ word Coue.   Christian Remich (ʰⁱˢ/Seal)
Signed Sealed and Deliuered in presents of us

   Joshua Remich   Christian Remich came and Ac-
   the Sign of   knowledged this Instrument to
   Lidia ℒ Remich   be his act and Deed to his Son
        Isaac Remich, this thirtieth of
   Wᵐ Godsoe   Septembʳ 1694, before me ffran-
        cis Hook of yᵉ Council and
        Justice peace

A true Copie of the origenall Instrument Transcribed & compared this 19º of Septembʳ 1696   p Jos Hamond Regʳ

Know all men by these presents that I Christian Remich of Kittery in the County of York for and in Consideration of a valluable Sum of money to me in hand payd by Isaac Remich of the Town of Kittery in the County aforesaid at and before the Sealing hereof, haue bargained and Sold and by these presents doe bargain & Sell fully Clearely and absolutely unto the Said Isaac Remich, a Certain parcell and tract of land Containing twenty Acres Situate and lying in the Town of Kittery, butting and bounded as followeth Vizᵗ [90] on the North Side with Isaac Remich his own Land, and on yᵉ South Side Samuel Spinney and Christian Remich their land, prouided that the said Isaac Remich leaue a way of twenty four foot broad on that Side next to Samuel Spinney his land/ which way Shall run up to yᵉ head of Said Spinneys land, the East end is bounded with John Shapleigh his land And on yᵉ West end wᵗʰ the Riuer/ To haue and to hold the Same land with all the pruiledges and apurtenances thereunto belonging, to yᵉ said Isaac Remich his heires Executʳˢ Administratʳˢ and Assigns to his and their proper use and uses for euer/ And I yᵉ said Christian Remich my

heires Execut^{rs} Administrat^{rs} and Assigns and euery of us the said land unto ye said Isaac Remich his heires Execut^{rs} Administrat^{rs} and Assigns against all psons from by or under me Shall and will for euer acquit and Defend by these presents prouided always that ye Said Isaac Remich Shall giue way to Christian Remich or any ordered by him for to cut and Carrow away from of the said land herein Sold one hundred and ffifty Cord of wood within ye Term of twenty yeares thence next following the day of the Date hereof/ In witness whereof I haue hereunto Set my hand and Seal this twentieth day of June in y^e year one thousand Six hundred Ninety and four.   Christian Remich (Seal)
Signed Sealed & Deliuered in presents of

    Jacob Remich   Christian Remich came and acknowl-
    Joshua Remich   edged this Instrument to be his act
    Peter $\mathcal{P}$ Staple and Deed unto his Son Isaac Remich this thirtieth Septemb^r 1694
    his mark   Before me
                  ffrancis Hook of Council and Just : peace
A true Copie of the Origenall Instrument Transcribed & compared this 19º day of Septemb^r 1696
                        p Jos. Hamond Regist^r

I under written doe ffreely and Volluntarily giue up all my right and Title which I Euer had or might haue to ye land Sold by my ffather Christian Remich on ye other Side mentioned/ In witness whereof I haue Set my hand this 20º day of June 1694   Abraham Remich
Signed and deliuered in presents of us/

    Jacob Remich   A true Copie of ye origenall as it was
    Joshua Remich   upon the back Side of ye aboue written Instrument Transcribed & compared this 19º of Septemb^r 1696   p Jos Hamond Regist^r

Book IV, Fol. 90.

To all christian people before whome these pres^{ts} shall come — Samuel Miller of Kittery in the County of York in the Prouince of the Massachusets Bay in New England Sends greeting/ Now know ye that I the aboue mentioned Samuel Miller for Diuers good causes me thereunto mouing, More Especially for and in consideration of forty & four pounds to me in hand payd before ye Signing and Deliuery hereof by Joseph Hill, of Dover in ye Prouince New Hampshire, the receipt whereof and of euery part & parcell thereof I acknowledge and therewith fully Satisfied contented & payd haue giuen granted bargained Sold Aliened Enfeoffed made ouer and confirmed, And by these presents doe for me my heires Execut^{rs} Administrat^{rs} and Assigns freely clearly and absolutely Giue grant bargain Sell Alien Enfeoff make ouer and confirm unto him ye s^d Joseph Hill his heires Execut^{rs} Administrat^{rs} and Asssigns for euer, All that my house and land in Kittery which was formerly my father Richard Millers late of s^d Kittery Dec^d, Scituate lijng and being on ye South east Side of Peter Staples land, and Joyning to it and alsoe Joyning to ye Northwest Side of a parcell of land of Waymonth Lidstons and part of ye Ministry land, begining at ye head of ye land which was formerly John Simons his land running back upon a Northeast and by East line a hundred and twenty poles and is in breadth forty poles, containing Thirty Acres which land was granted to my father Richard Miller by ye Town of Kittery and Measured and layd out by the Surueigher of said Town, as doth more Amply Appear on Record in Kittery Town Book, together with fiue and twenty Acres of land lying back in the Woods Joyning to ye Bay land in part which land was Measured and layd out to me ye S^d Samuel Miller June ye 14° 1694, as appears on Record in ye s^d Town Book — To haue and to hold the afores^d house and lands with all ye priuiledges and Appertenances thereunto belonging, with Right Title Interest Claim

Sam^{ll} Millers Deed to Jos: Hill

and Demand which I ye s^d Samuel Miller now haue or in time past haue had; or which I my heirs Execut^rs Administrat^rs or Assigns in time to come, may might Should or in any wise ought to haue, off in or to ye aboue granted premises or any part thereof, To him ye s^d Joseph Hill his heires Execut^rs Administrat^rs or Assigns for euermore/ And I the said Samuel Miller for me my heires &^c doe couenant promise & grant to and with him the s^d Joseph Hill his heires Execut^rs &^c that at & before the Ensealing and Deliuery thereof. I am ye true right and proper owner of the aboue premises and the Appertenances And that I haue in my Selfe good Right full power and lawfull Authority the aboue giuen & granted premises to Sell and dispose off, And that ye Same and euery part thereof is free and clear and freely and clearly Acquitted Exonerated & discharged off and from all and all manner of Wills entailes Judgments Executions power of thirds and all other Incombrances whatsoeuer, And that it Shall & may be lawfull to and for ye said Joseph Hill his heires Execut^rs Administrat^rs or Assigns the aboues^d premises and euery part thereof to haue hold use improue ocupie possess and enjoy lawfully peaceably and quietly without any lawfull let deniall hinderance Molestation or disturbance of or by me or any other pson or psons from by or under me or by my procurement And that ye Sale thereof and of euery part thereof against my Selfe my heires Execut^rs Administrat^rs and Assigns and against all other psons whatsoeuer lawfully Claiming the same or [91] any part thereof I will for euer Saue harmless warrant & defend by these presents And that I my heires Execut^rs &^c Shall and will make perform and Execute Such other further lawfull Act or Acts thing or things as in law & Equitie can be deuised or required for the better confirming and more Sure making of the premises unto the s^d Joseph Hill his heirs Execut^rs or Assigns According to ye laws of this Prouince In Witness whereof I the s^d Samuel Miller haue here-

BOOK IV, FOL. 91.

unto Set my hand and Seal This Nineteenth day of October in y^e Eighth year of the Reign of our Soueraign Lord William the third, by the grace of God, King of England &^{c}. Anno Domini one thousand Six hundred Ninety and Six : 1696
Signed Sealed & deliuered/   Samuel Miller ($^{his}_{Seal}$)
In the presents of us/   mark of
Richard Cater/   Mary 〜 Miller
Jos Hamond/   Kittery ffeb^y 15. 169$\frac{5}{6}$ Christop^r Banfield
                & Grace his wife came before me y^e
                Subscrib^r, and freely gaue up her Right
                of thirds to y^e Lands aboue mentioned
                y^e s^d Grace being Mother to y^e abones^d
                Miller   Charles ffrost Justice of peace
A true Copie p Jos : Hamond Register : ffeb^y 16 · 169$\frac{5}{6}$
Possession of the aboue premises was deliuered unto Joseph Hill by Samuel Miller this 21° of October 1696 In the presents of
Richard Rogers
Jos : Hamond   Prouince of New Hampshiere Octob^r
                22^d 1696 Samuel Miller and Mary his
                wife Acknowledged the aboue Instru-
                ment to be their free Act and Deed/
                before me Geo : Jaffrey Jus^t of peace
A true Copie of the origenall Deed Transcribed & compared this 29° day of Octob^r 1696 p Jos Hamond Regest^r

To all People to whome this presents come Greeting, Know yea that I Samuel Miller of Kittery in the Prouince of the Massathusets Bay in New England planter, And Administrat^r to the Estate of my late honour^d father Richard Miller Deceased, for Diuers good causes and consideration me hereto mouing, haue giuen granted Aliened and Set ouer and doe by these presents for euer from me my heirs giue grant Alien and Set ouer unto my Honor^d Mother

Book IV, Fol. 91.

Grace Banfield (wife to Christopher Banfield of Kittery afores^d Carpenter) one parcell of land lying in ye Town of Kittery afores^d and abutting on ye water Side in the Long Reach in ye Riuer of Piscataqua on ye Southwest and by west and on the High way Northeast and by east and bounded betwixt the land of Richard Rogers and Peter Staples, with all houses barnes leantoes Gardens orchurds trees, with all wayes Easments conueniences and priuiledges thereto belonging or in any wise Appertaining To haue and to hold the said land houses barns leantoes gardens orchurds trees with all Easmements conueniences and priuiledges thereto belonging, to her ye Said Grace Banfield her heires and Assigns for euer and to their proper use benefit and behoof and noe other, prouided always that whereas I the said Samuel Miller haue two Sisters named Mary Miller and Martha Miller to whom there is remaining due Some part or portion of my late Honor^d father Richd Millers Estate, to be payd to them when they are of age or Marryage day, Now if my s^d honor^d Mother doe pay or cause to payd to my said two Sisters Mary Miller & Martha Miller their portions/ Then the land to remain to the s^d Grace Banfield, and her heires and Assigns for euer but if not, then the s^d land after ye Decease of my s^d Mother is to be Equally Deuided betwixt my two Sisters Mary and Martha afores^d, And that to be in full for their portions. In witness whereof I ye s^d Samuel Miller haue hereunto Set my hand and Seal, and Mary Miller doe hereby relinquish all my Right and Claim of Dowre thereto and haue hereto Set my hand and Seal, this twenty Second day of Octob^r In ye Eighth year of ye Reign of our Soueraign Lord William the third King of England &^{c} and in ye year of our Lord 1696. Dated in New Castle in New Hampshiere in New England.

Signed Sealed & deliuered   Samuel Miller (his Seal)
  In the presents of us   her
  Joseph Hill
  Phesant Eastwicke.   Mary X Miller
                                mark   (her Seal)

Book IV, Fol. 91, 92.

A true Copie of the origenall Deed Transcribed and compared this 29º day of Octob^r 1696 p Jos Hamond Regest^r

[92] Know all men by these presents that I Joseph Hill of Douer in the Prouince of New Hampshiere, doe own and acknowledge my Selfe to owe and be Indebted unto Christopher Banfield of Barwick in the County of York the full and Just Sum of Eight pounds fifteen Shillings of lawfull money of New England to be payd to him the Said Banfield his heires Execut^{rs} Administrat^{rs} or Assigns at his or their Demamand.

The Condition of this Obligation is Such that if the aboue bounden Joseph Hill doe well and truly pay or cause to be payd unto Mary Miller, daughter of Richd Miller late of Kittery Dec^d the full and Just Sum of Eight pounds fifteen Shillings in Merchantable Goods at money price to her Acceptance when She Shall Ariue to ye Age of Eighteen yeares, or in case of her remouall by death or otherwise to be payd to her heirs Execut^{rs} Administrat^{rs} or Assignes, Then this present Obligation to be voyd and of none Effect, otherwise to Stand & remain in full Strength and vertue/ In witness whereof I haue hereunto Set my hand and Seal this twentieth day of Octob^r Anno Domini 1696. And in ye Eighth year of the Reign of our Soueraign Lord William the third King ouer England &c.   Joseph Hill (his Seal)
Signed Sealed and deliuered

   In the presents of—   A true Copie of ye origenall Tran-
   Jos Hamond   scribed and compared this 2^d of
   Joseph Hamond Junr Nouemb^r 1696.
                                p Jos Hamond Regist^r

Book IV, Fol. 92.

Know all men by these presents that I Joseph Hill of Douer in ye Prouince of New Hampshiere doe Acknowledge my Selfe to Owe and be Indebted unto Christopher Banfield of Barwick in ye County of York in ye Prouince of the Massachusets Bay, the full and Just Sum of Eight pounds fifteen Shillings of lawfull money of New England, to be payd to him the s^d Christopher Banfield his heires Execut^{rs} Administrat^{rs} or Assignes at his or their Demand/ The condition of this obligation is Such that if the aboue bounden Joseph Hill doe well and truly pay or cause to be payd unto Martha Miller, daughter of Richd Miller late of Kittery Deceased, her heirs Execut^{rs} Administrat^{rs} or Assigns the full and Just Sum of Eight pounds fifteen Shillings Merchantable pay to her or their Acceptance when She the s^d Martha Shall ariue to ye age of Eighteen years. Then this present Obligation to be voyd and of none Effect, otherwise to stand abide & remain in full force Strength and Vertue. In witness whereof I haue hereunto Set my hand and Seal this twentieth day of Octob^r Anno Domini 1696. And in ye Eight year of ye Reign of our Soueraign Lord William the third King of England &c.
Signed Sealed & deliuered   Joseph Hill (his Seal)
  In the presents of
  Jos Hamond
  Joseph Hamond Junr
  A true Copie of ye origenall Transcribed & compared This 2^d of Nouemb^r 1696.   p Jos: Hamond Regist^r

To all Christian people to whome these presente wrighting Shall come and appear/ I Charles Adams of ye Township of Douer in the Prouince of New Hampshiere in Piscataqua in New England Sendeth greeting/ Know ye that ye s^d Charles Adams for good Causes, and considerations me mouing thereunto, And more Especially for and in consideration of ye Sum of foity fiue pounds in money or goods Aqueafelent to money in hand payd or Secured to be payd before ye Ensealing and Deliuering of these presents by ye hands of John Moriell off the Toun of Kittery in ye Prouince of Main the receipt whereof he doth Acknowledge himselfe Satisfied and payd of euery pences theeareoff doth for euer Acquett & dischardge the S^d John Morrell his hires Executores Admenestratores by these presents hath absolutely giuen granted bargained Sold Infeofed and confirmed and by these presents doth giue grand bargain & Sold unto John Morrell a peaces off Land or peaces of land which was my father Phelepe Benmores dessesed and now mine by Maring Tempiances the Dafter of s^d Benmore Lying and being one Kittre Sid near Sturgeon Crecke and one ye other upon John tomson all which said peacs or peses of land that my father Benmore bought of Jeames Emore upon Kittery Sid as afores^d with all preueledges and appurtinances thereto belonging and appurtaining unto ye Said Charles Adams with all my hole right belonging to it shall be for the Sole uess benefet and behoufe of ye s^d John Morrell his hires Executores Admenestratores and Assignes for euer To haue and to hold the premeses afores^d And ye s^d Charles Adams doth for himselfe his hires Executores Admenestratores Couenant & promise to and with ye s^d John Morrell him his heires Execut^r Administrat^r warrant to maintain and make good the Same aboue granted peaces of land to ye uttermost of my right and power without any Molestation from me my hires Executores Admenestratores or any person or persons by or through mine or there menes consent permet or procurement In witness hereof the s^d Charles Adams hath heareunto Seat his hand and Seale this twentie Sixth day of March one thousand Six hundred Nintti two and in ye fourth year of ye Raines of our Souerenes King William and quea Mary defender off the ffaith before ye Seling and Deliuery of thes

Book IV, Fol. 92, 93.

presents the words in ye twelth line Chrast out was a mistake it is Jeames Emori   Charles Adams (_{Seal}^{his})
Sealed Singed and Deleuered   his Assines
In the presents of us
Henery Nock.   Edward Allen/ March 30th 1696

Temporances Adeams Relict and Administratrix unto the Estate of her late husband Charles Adams Deseased came & acknowledged ye aboue Instrument to be her free act and deed before me, before me Job Alcock Justis of pe

A true Copie of ye origenall Transcribed & compared this 17 of Nouemb^r 1696   p Jos Hamond Reg^r

[93] Know all men by these presents that I Temprance Addams a Relict of and Administratrix to ye Estate of Charles Addams late of ye Town of Douer in the Prouince of New Hampshiere planter Deceased haue Demised released and for euer Acquitted Claime And by these p^rsents doe Demise release and for euer quit Claim to John Morrell of the Town of Kittery in the Prouince of Maine Brick-layer his heires Execut^{rs} and Administrat^{rs} of all and all manner Action or Actions Sutes bills bonds writings obligations debts duties Accompts Sum and Sums of Money leases Mortgages Judgments by confession or otherwise obtained Executions extents quarrels Controuersies Trespasses Damages and demands whatsoeuer which in law or Equitie or otherwise howsoeuer I ye s^d Temprance Addams against ye s^d John Morrell had and which I my heires Execut^{rs} or Administrat^{rs} shall or may haue claim challenge or demand for or by reasons means or Couler of any matter cause or thing whatsoeuer from the beginning of ye World to ye day of ye date of these presents. In witness whereof I haue hereunto Set my hand and Seale this thirteen day of Nouemb^r in ye Eighth year of ye Reign of our Soueraign Lord William the

third King of England &c. And of mans Redemption one thousand Six hundred Ninety Six.

Signed Sealed & deliuered   Temprance Addams (her/Seal)
  In ye presents of us   her ✘ mark
  Siluanus Nock   A true Copie of the origenall original
  Nicholas Morrell   instrument transcribed & compared
                       this. 1st day of Decemb^r 1696
                           p Jos Hamond Regist^r

County York/ Kittery Nouemb^r ye 17° 1696 Then layd out unto John Morrell Senr forty Acres of Land toward ye head of Stirgeon Creek, it being ye Remaining part of his Deuident part of Land granted unto Anthony Emery and Nicholas ffrost. March : 3^d 1651 at Stirgeon creeks mouth And was in part layd out by ye Select men of Kittery in ye year 1672 as by ye Records more at large doth appear And was purchased by s^d John Morrell of Charles Addams who Deriued his Title from one Benmore And said Benmore of s^d Anthony Emery afores^d/ The s^d tract of land takes its beginning at a black Ash marked on four Sides in a Swamp, with Benmores name on it, where ye Select men afores^d left of from s^d black Ash, Eighty poles East to a little birch and an old hemlock—and from thence North Eighty pole to a Maple tree Marked on four Sides and . M . And from thence West ye Same breadth, And South ye Same it being Square, bounding on Stirgeon Creek, with allowance for ye s^d Creeks turning & winding and alsoe for a high way if Seen Needfull of four poles for ye use of the Town of Kittery out of the Same—by me Wm Godsoe Suru^r

  A true Copie of ye origenall Transcribed and Compared this : 1st day of Decemb^r 1696 : p Jos Hamond Regist^r

BOOK IV, FOL. 93, 94.

County
York

At a meeting of the Select men of York and Kittery Decembʳ yᵉ 30 by Appointment of both Townes for yᵉ orderly running out of the bounds between both Townships And marking the Deuiding line but more Especially in obedience to a beneuolent Act made by his Excellency the Gouernʳ and Generall Assembly intituled an Act for Regulating of Townships and Choyce of Town officers And Setting forth their power In which Act it is required that all towns Should run out their bounds and new Mark them once in three years and in psuance and obedience to yᵉ said Act we the Select men aforesᵈ whose Names are under written for York and Kittery Decembʳ yᵉ 30° and 31° and January 13ᵗʰ and 14° run out yᵉ old Stated bounds,

Bounds
between
York &
Kittery

begining at a white Oak near the Bridge at Braueboat Harbʳ and from thence on a N. W. B. N. Course a little Westerly by old marks, to a pine tree Standing on a little Neck at yᵉ head of yᵉ Western branch of York Marshes, Marked with a Y. and a K. And from thence on a due North line to a pine tree Marked. Y and K Standing on yᵉ South Side and Eastern end of a great pond called York pond And from thence on a N E B N course to Bakers Spring where stands a red oak tree Marked on three Sides. To the truth of yᵉ aboue written we haue hereunto Set our hands this 14° of January: 1695·

Select men { Samuel Donnel
for York   { Thomas Trafton

Select men { John Shapleigh
for Kittery { Wᵐ ffernald
            { Benᵒ Hodsden

A true Copie of yᵉ origenall Transcribed, and compard this. 1ˢᵗ of March: 169⅔ — p Jos Hamond Registʳ

[94] To all Christian People to whom this present writing Shall come Know yee that whereas ffrancis Morgan and Sarah his wife of yᵉ Town of Kittery in New England did

BOOK IV, FOL. 94.

Sell unto Captain Brian Pendleton of Portsm^o Merchant, and John ffabes of ye Island of Shoales one hundred Acres of Land Scituate and being in Spruce Creek in the Said Township of Kittery as by Deed of Sale may and doth at Large appear, the said Deed bearing Date the first day of Apr^{ll} in the year of Our Lord One thousand Six hundred Sixtie and fiue, ffrancis Champernowne and Mary his wife, for a valluable consideration and Satisfaction made rendered and payd by the said Pendleton & ffebins In times past, Haue remised released and for euer quit Claimed and by these presents for our Selues our heires Execut^{rs} and Administrat^{rs} doe fully clearly and absolutely Remise Release and for euer quitt Claime unto ye Said Brian Pendleton and John ffebes in their Joynt and Seuerall full & peaceable possession and Seizin and to Joint and Seuerall their heires Execut^{rs} Administrat^{rs} and Assignes for euer All Such Right title Interest Estate and propriety and Demand whatsoeuer As they the said ffrancis Champernown or Mary his wife had or ought to Haue of in or to all the aboue Mentioned one hundred Acres of Land or to any part thereof by any wayes or means whatsoeuer/ To Haue and to hold all the said Land unto ye Said Brian Pendleton and to ye said John ffebins their Heires & Assigns Joyntly and Seuerally for euer, Soe that neither the s^d ffrancis Champ^{r}noun nor Mary his wife nor his nor their Heires nor any other pson or psons for them or in their names Rights or Steads of any of them Shall or will by any way or means hereafter Haue claim Challenge or demand any Estate Right Title or Interest of in or unto ye Premises or any part or parcell thereof But from all and euery Action Right Estate Title or Interest or Demand of in & unto the Premises or any part or parcell thereof they and euery of them Shall be utterly Excluded and Barred for euer by these presents And alsoe the s^d ffrancis Champernown and Mary his wife his and their heires Execut^{rs} Administrat^{rs} and Assignes the said one hundred Acres of Land with y⁸ Appurtenances priuiledges & properties thereof unto y⁸ sᵈ Brian Pendleton and John ffebes theirs and hers heires Executʳˢ Administratʳˢ and Assignes to their proper use and uses in manner and form afore Specified against all psons Shall & will Warrand and for euer defend by these presents In witness whereof the sd ffrancis Champernown and Mary his wife haue hereunto Set their hands and Seales this fifteen day of March In the year of Our Lord one thousand Six hundred Eighty and Six. Annoq̃ Regni Regis Jacobi Secundi Secundo Angliæ Scotiæ ffranc̃ et Hiberniæ Rex.

Signed Sealed and
  Delivered in prestˢ of us   the mark of
  Robert Elliot   ffrancis F Champernown (his seal)
  Nicolas Tucker   (Seale)
  the mark of Richᵈ R A Abbot/

A true Copie of y⁸ origenall Deed Transcribed & compared this 21ˢᵗ of Decembʳ 1696
                    p Jos: Hamond Register

To all Christian people to whome these presents Shall Come Greeting Know ye that I Dominicus Jordan Administratʳ to Ralph Trustrum Late of Winter Harbour Deceased, for and in Consideration of fforty fiue pounds of Currant Money of New England in hand receiued, the receipt whereof sᵈ Dominicus Jordan Acknowledgeth and himselfe to be fully Contented Satisfied and payd And thereof doth Acquit Exonerate and Discharge Captain Edward Sergeant of Newberry Vintnʳ his heires Executʳˢ Administratʳˢ and Assigns for euer As also for Diuers other good causes and Considerations thereunto Especially Mouing haue giuen granted bargained and Sold, And by these presents doe giue grant bargain Sell Alien Enfeoffe release deliuer and Confirm to s^d Edward Sergean a parcell of Land Sometime in the hand of Ralph Trustrum aboues^d and in the possession of me s^d Dominicus Jordan this time Lying and being in Saco alias Winter Harbour, Containing about one hundred Acres more or less, bounded on the Land of John Sergeant s^d Edward Sergeants father Northerly, Easterly on ye fflats Joyning to Winter Harbour Southerly upon the Land of Mr Walter Penuel Deceased & Soe runing backward till all the formentioned Land be Compleated As alsoe a parcel of Meadow Containing about fifteen Acres Adjoyning to ye Meadow of s^d John Sergeant Northerly bounding upon ye Northwest upon ye Land that was formerly Symon Booths together with ten Acres of Meadow in two parcels Lying in or on Little River, All in the Township of Saco Alias Winter Harbour All which Land was formerly aboues^d Ralph Trustrums and Lawfully Descended to me Dominicus Jordan, together with all benefits priuiledges & and Appertenances in and upon S^d boundiary any wayes belonging and Appertaining/ To have and to hold the s^d giuen granted & bargained premises to s^d Edward Sergeant his heirs Execut^rs Administrat^rs and Assigns for euer And s^d Dominicus Jordan for himselfe his heires Execut^rs Administrat^rs doth Couenant promise and grant with ye Consent of Hannah his wife, to and with s^d Edward Sergeant his heires Execut^rs Administrat^rs and Assigns and to and with euery of them by these presents that all and Singular the s^d premises before giuen granted bargained and Sold at ye time of the Ensealing and Deliuery of these, are and be and at all times hereafter Shall be continue and remaine Clearly Acquitted Exonerated discharged and Kept harmless of & from all and all manner of former and other bargains Sales Gifts Grants Leases Charges Dowers titles troubles and encombrances whatsoeuer had made Committed Suffered or done or to be had made Comitted Suffered or done by the s^d Dominicus Jordan his heires

Book IV, Fol. 94, 95.

Execut^{rs} Administrat^{rs} or Assigns or any other person whatsoeuer or persons whatsoeuer laying any Leagall Claim to ye aboue s^d premises, As Witness my hand & Seal this first of July one thousand Six hundred and Ninety fiue.

Signed Sealed & deliuered   Dominicus Jordan (his Seal)
In presets of us—   Hannah Jordan (her Seal)
Sam^{ll} Penhallow
Jos Hamond   July ye 6° deay 1695, Dominicus Jordan
John Pickerin   came and Acknowledged ye aboue
                 written Dead of Sale to be his fiee
                 Acte and Deade And Hannah his wife
                 Acknowledged to Surrend^r up onto
                 ye s^d Sargeant his Ares & all her Right
                 & Dowrey to and in the aboues^d Deate
                 of Salle bee for mee
                       William Peprell Justes pes
A true Copie of ye origenall Transcribed and Compared,
ffeb^{ry} 16 : 169 9/8   p Jos Hamond Regist^r

[95] To All Christian people to whom these presents Shall Come Greeting Know yea that I John Woodman of Kittery in ye County of York yeoman haue for ye Consideration of ten pound in money to me in hand paid by Samuel Spinney of ye Same place yeoman before ye Signing and Sealing hereof and doe acknowledge my Selfe Satisfied and Contented for Euery part and parcel thereof doe by these p̅sents bargaine Sell Enfeof and Confirm unto Sam^{ll} Spinney afores^d all my Right title and interest that I haue or might haue in a Certaine grant or tract of land Containing twenty acres Granted unto me by ye town of Kittery in ye year of our lord one thousand Six hundred ninty and four may ye Sixteenth as by ye town grant may more at large appeare with all ye priuilidges and Appurtainences there

unto belonging or that might Accrew unto me yͤ sᵈ John Woodman by vertue of yͤ sᵈ Grant: To haue and To hold the sd grant and Euery Pᵗ and psell thereof to yͤ only use bennefit and beehoofe of him yͤ sᵈ Samuel Spinney his heires or Assigns for Euer and yͤ sᵈ John Woodman doth Couenant to and with the sᵈ Samuel Spinney that ꝑmisses are free from all maner of Incumberances by me made or done or Suffered to be done and that it Shall and may be lawfull for yͤ sᵈ Samuel Spinney to take use occupy all and Euery pᵗ and psell thereof to his own use and his heirs for Euer, and yͤ peaceable possession thereof to Warrant and maintaine against all psons laying Claim thereto Witness my hand: Seale this fifth day of Decembʳ one thousand Six hundred ninty and Six. And in yͤ Eighth year of his Maᵗⁱᵉˢ Reign King William yͤ third.

In ꝑsents of us,   John Woodman (sele)
  James Emerson
  William Godsoe

A true Copie of the origenall Transcribed and Compared this 21° of Decembʳ 1696   p Jos Hamond Registʳ

John Woodman Appeared before me the Subscriber and owned this Instrumᵗ to be his free Act and Deed this 25° day of Decembʳ 1696/

         Samˡˡ Wheelwright Just: pece

A true Copie of this Acknowledgment: transcribed out of the Origenall   p Jos Hamond Registʳ

Be it known unto all men by these presents that James Denmarke of the Town of Wells in the County of York in New England with the free Consent of Elizabeth my wife, Diuers good Causes and Considerations me thereunto mouing, And Especially for and in consideration of twelue pounds to me in hand payd by Joseph Storer of the aboue said Toun and County wherewith I doe acknowledge my Selfe to be fully Satisfied and Contented, haue giuen granted Enfeoffed and confirmed. And by these presents doe giue grant Enfeoff and confirme freely fully and abso-

Denmarks Deed to Storer

lutely unto the aboue Named Joseph Storer from me my heirs Execut^{rs} and Assigns, a certain tract or point of Salt Marsh Scituate and being in the Toun of Wells and bounded as followeth it being the Lower end of that parcle of Marsh which was formerly John Barrets Marsh Adjoyning to the aboue^d Joseph Storers And on ye other Side to a pacell of Marsh now belonging to Nicholas Cole, the bounds of said Marsh to begin at ye Riuer Comonly known by the Name of Webhannt or ye Great Riuer from thence to run the whole breadth of ye s^d Marsh which Contains about thirty Rods be it more or less untill it comes up to a Small pond lying on the Northeast Side of the aboue s^d Joseph Storers home Lot which is about fiftie Rods from the lower end of the bounds at ye Great Riuer, the bounds are to run up to the Northern part of s^d pond and from thence upon a Square the whole breadth as aforesaid, with all the Appertenances and priuiledges thereunto belonging quetly and peaceably to haue and to hold for euer, without any matter of Challenge Claim or demand of me the Said James Denmark or any pson or psons either from by or und^r me my heirs or Success^{rs} for euer and he the s^d Joseph Storer his heires Execut^{rs} Administrat^{rs} and Assigns I doe hereby declare to be truly and Rightly possessed of euery part and parcell of the premises aboue Mentioned And that he ye Said Joseph Storer his heirs and Success^{rs} Shall peaceably and quietly haue hold and Enjoy the aboue mentioned premises for euer, And I doe hereby Couenant and promise to and with ye Said Joseph Storer, that I am ye true lawfull and Right owner before ye Ensealeing hereof, of the aboue Said Marsh And that I haue full pouer of my Selfe to make lawfull Sale of the Same and I doe further promise that the parcel of Marsh wch I haue here Sold is free and Cleare from all former gifts grants bargains Leaces Dowries Legasies Joyntures Morgages Judgments and all other Incombrances whatsoeuer And doe promise to Warrant maintain and Defend ye Title & Interest of s^d Marsh to him ye said Joseph Storer and his heires for euer from me my heirs Execut^rs and Assigns or any other pson or psons whatsoeuer laying any Just Claim thereunto. In Testimony whereunto I haue Set my hand and Seal this Sixteenth day of June, and in ye Eighth year of this Reign of our Soueraign Lord William 3^d of England King &^c. 1696

Signed Sealed & deliuered   James Denmarke (his seal)
  In presence of   Elizabeth Denmarke
  Nicholas Cole   James Denmark and Elizabeth Denmark
  Jonath Hamond   his wife came before me this 20° day
          of June 1696, and did acknowledge
          this Instrument to be their Act & Deed
          p Samuel Wheelwright Jus peace

A true Copie of y^e origenall Deed Transcribed and compared this : 18° day of January : 169$\frac{9}{10}$

         p Jos : Hamond Regist^r

[96] Know all men by these presents that I Miles Thompson Senr Carpenter of y^e town of Barwick of the Prouince of the Massachusets for diuers good causes and and considerations me hereunto moueing, but Especially for the Loue that I beare unto my Naturall Son Bartholomew Thompson, haue given granted Alienated and Confirmed unto the said Bartholomew his heires Execut^rs Administrat^rs and Assigns All that Tract of Land both upland & Meadow lieing and being in the Towne and Prouince abouesaid Con-

Book IV, Fol. 96.

Miles Thompsons Deed of gift to his Son Bartholomew

taining forty Acres more or less which I bought of Abraham Tilton as may Appear by a bill of Sale from s^d Tilton bearing Date March ye Eighth 167½ which said bill is entred into the Records of the County of York page 141. Nouemb^r 17th 73. The said tract of Land with all its Appurtenances belonging to it or that may hereafter belong Shall be to my Son Bartholomew free from all Molestation for from by or under me or any other pson or psons whatsoeuer laying any Leagall Claime thereunto as a quiet and peaceable Possession, to haue and to hold ye Same in ffee Simple for euer I doe alsoe hereby Engage that my wife Ann Thompson Shall render up her thirds in the aboues^d tract of Land. To the true prformance of the aboue written I haue Set my hand and Seal This Decemb^r y^e fourth one thousand Six hundred Ninety and four.   Miles Thompson

Signed Sealed & deliuered
  In the presents of us—   his $\mathcal{M}$ marke (his Seale)
Edward Tompson
Benony Hodsden   Ann ⌒ Thompson (her Seale)
James Neaull. i. e. Neal   her mark

Miles Thompson and Ann Thompson Acknowledged y^e aboue written Instrument to be their Act & Deed this 28° of Decemb^r 1694 before me Charles ffrost : Just : peac

A true Copie of the origenall Deed Transcribed and Compared this 20th of Jan^ry 169_7   p Jos Hamond Regist^r

To all Christian people to whom this present Deed of Sale shall Come, I James Emery Senr of Barwick in the County of Yorke, in the Prouince of the Massachusets Bay in New England Send Greeting/ Now know y^e that I the aforementioned James Emery for diuers good Causes me thereunto Mouing, more Especially for and in Consideration of one

BOOK IV, FOL. 96.

hundred and twenty pounds of lawfull money of New England to me in hand well and truly paid at and before the Ensealing and Deliuery of these presents by Phillip Hubbord of s^d Barwick Joyn^r the receipt whereof I acknowledge and therewith fully Satisfied Contented and payd and thereof and of Euery part and parcell thereof for me the s^d James Emery my heires Execut^rs Administrat^rs and Assigns by these pres^ts for euer, Haue giuen granted bargained Sold Aliened Enfeoffed and Confirmed, and by these presents doe for me my heires Execut^rs Administrat^rs and Assigns fully freely and absolutely Giue Grant bargain Sell alien Enfeoffe and Confirm unto him the s^d Phillip Hubbord his heires and Assignes, All that my Land and building Scituate lying and being in Barwick afores^d, Containing forty Acres be it more or less butted and bounded as followeth vidz^t begining at a Red oak tree Standing in the fence between my s^d Land and the Land of Daniel Goodwin Junr runing South till it Comes to a fence between the s^d Land and Mr John Playsteds or birchen point Lot Soe called, And Soe to the Main Riuer Side, and up the s^d Riuer Northward to a Small brook and valley which is a parting bounds between s^d Land and Daniel Stones Land, And from thence runing as the fence now Stands to a tall white oak stump Standing within Daniel Stones Garison/ And from s^d Stump upon a Streight Course to ye first mentioned red oak tree where it began together with all my Right title and Interest of and to the Marsh Comonly Called the fouling Marsh Joyning to s^d Land, with all the profits priuiledges and appertenances to the said Land and Marsh belonging or in any wise Appertaining, Excepting and reseruing always out of said Land a burying place of four Rods Square Joyning to ye highway And alsoe halfe an Acre of land which I formerly gaue to my Son James Emery where his house now Stands and Joyning to the high way. To haue and to hold ye s^d Land and Marsh with all ye wood Stand-

James Emereys Deed to Ph: Hubord

ing and Lying, ffruit trees with all other the appeitenances thereto belonging with all Right title Interest Claim and Demand, which I y̆ᵉ s̆ᵈ James Emery now haue or in time past haue had or which I my heires Execut̆ʳˢmi Adnistıat̆ʳ or Assignes in time to come may might Should or in any wise ought to haue of in or to the aboue Granted premises or any pait thereof, To him y̆ᵉ said Phillip Hubbard his heires or Assignes for euer And to the Sole and proper use benefit and behoofe of him the Said Phillip Hubbord his heirs &ᶜ, for euermore/ And I y̆ᵉ s̆ᵈ James Emery for me my heires Execut̆ʳˢ Administrat̆ʳˢ and Assignes doe Couenant promise and grant to and with the s̆ᵈ Phillip Hubbord his heires &ᶜ. that at and before y̆ᵉ Ensealing and Deliuery thereof I am the true Right and proper owner of the aboue premises and the appertainances, And that I haue in my Selfe good Right full power and lawfull Authoritie the Same to Sell and dispose off And that y̆ᵉ Same and euery part thereof is free and Clear, and freely and Clearly Acquitted Exonerated and Discharged of and from all and all manner of former Gifts grants bargains Sales Leaces Mortgages Alienations and Incombrances whatsoeuer/ And that it Shall and may be lawfull to and for the S̆ᵈ Hubbord his heires and Assigns the aforesᵈ premises and euery part thereof Except before Excepted from time to time and at all times hereafter to haue hold use improue ocupie possess and enjoy Lawfully peaceably and quietly without any lawfull let hinderance Molestation or disturbance of or by me or any other pson or psons from by or under me or by my procurement And that the Sale thereof against my Selfe my heirs or Assigns And against all other psons whatsoeuer Lawfully Claiming the Same or any part thereof except before excepted I will for euer Saue harmless warrant and Defend by these presents.

In witness whereof I the s̆ᵈ James Emery haue hereunto Set my hand & Seal the fiue and twentieth day of January In the Eighth year of the Reign [**97**] of our Soueraign Lord

William the third by the grace of God of England Scotland ffrance and Ireland, King Defender of the ffaith, Anno Domini one thousand Six hundred Ninety and Six, Seuen/ 169⁶/₇.   James Emery   (his Seal)
Signed Sealed and deliuered   her
   In the presents of us —   Elizabeth X Emery (her Seal)
   Tests Jos : Hamond   marke
   Joseph Hamond Junr James Emery Senr and Elizabeth
                            his wife appeared before me
                            this twenty Seuenth of January
                            169⁶/₇ and Acknowledged this
                            Instrument to be their act and
                            Deed, And the s^d Elizabeth gaue
                            up her Right of thirds to the
                            Same/ Charles ffrost Just peace
   A true Copie of the origenall Deed of Sale Transcribed and Compared this 4 : of ffebruary : 169⁶/₇ —
                                     Jos Hamond Regist^r

Deliuery of Ingosells land   The within mentined tract of Land was De-
              liuered by turfe and twig to the within mention
before us
Richard Cutt   A true Copie p Jos Hamond Regist^r
Richard Endell
the mark of
Joseph ⨯ Wilson

Know all Christian people by these presents that I Elihue Gunnison of Kittery in the County of York in New England Shipwright for and in Consideration of a certain & valluable Sum of Money being twenty pounds Currant money of New England to me in hand payd by John Engorsel of the

Same Town and County afores^d, with which Said Sum doe acknowledg my Selfe fully Satisfied, hereby Acquitting the Said John Engorsell from all and euery part thereof for euer, haue giuen granted bargained and Sold and doe by these presents giue grant bargain Sell Aliene Infeoffe confirm and make ouer unto ye said John Engorsell his heires Execut^{rs} Administrat^{rs} and Assigns a certain Tract of land Setuate lying and being In Spruce Creek in Kittery in the County afores^d which is to Say twenty pole ffronting by the high way from Richd Endles fence and Soe to run Northeast Aight Score pole back and then twenty pole Norwest back to Richard Endles bounds and Soe Sowest back upon Richard Endles afores^d line to our first Station togather with all Appertenances & priuiledges thereunto belonging, To haue and to hold to him ye said John Engorsell his heires Execut^{rs} Administrat^{rs} and Assigns for euer with all manner of priuiledge thereunto belonging And I the Said Elihue Gunnison doe hereby engage and oblige my Selfe my heirs Execut^{rs} Administrat^{rs} and Assigns for euer to warant and defend the aboue said tract of Land together with all ye appertenances thereunto belonging unto the s^d John Engorsell his heires Execut^{rs} Administrat^{rs} & Assigns from any manner of pson or psons whatsoeuer that Shall proue any Lawfull Claim Right title or Interest to any part or parcel thereof from by or under me/ In Testimonie of all and Singular the premises aboue ritten I haue hereunto Set my hand and Seal this Sixteenth day of Nouemb^r In ye year of our Lord 1696.

Gunnisons Deed to Ingersoll

Signed Sealed & deliuered Elihue Gunnison (his Seal)
  In the presents of us The 28° Desember 1696
  Richard Cutt Elihew Gunnison Cam and Ac-
  Richard Endell knowledged enstrerement to
  the mark of bee his ffree ackt and Dead
  Joseph A Wilson Bee Bee for mee
                              Wm Peprell Js pes

Book IV, Fol. 97, 98.

A true Copie of the origenall Deed of Sale Transcribed and Compared this : 18° day of ffeb^ry 1694̸

p Jos : Hamond Register

To all Christian People to whome this present deed of Sale Shall come greeting Know yee that wee Allexand^r fforgisson and Daniel Emery with ye Concent of our mother in Law Ellizabeth Gowen and our wiues Ellizabeth fforgison and Maigrat Emory, of ye town of Kittery in Yorke Sheire in ye Prouince of ye Mattachets bay in New England for and Consideration of the Sume of forty and three pounds Curant money of New : England to them in hand paid att & before ye Enseahng and deliuery of these presents well and truely paid by Jabaz Jenkins of ye town of Kittery aboues^d haue giuen granted bargained Sold and by these presents doe fully and absolutly giue grant bargaine Sell release Enfeoffe and Confirm unto ye s^d Jabez Jenkins for ye aboue s^d Sume of money the which they heareby acknowledge to haue Receiued two Sartaine parsels of Land bounded as [98] ffoweth viz one parsel being about Eleuen accres bounded on ye north with the land formerly Adrian fryes and Stirgion Creeke on ye west with maine Riuer on ye South with John Morrels and on the East with John Morrel the other parsel being about forty nine accres bounded by Stirgion Creek on ye South near bare Coue and on ye west and East with John Morrel and William Tomsons Land, and on ye South as it may appeare on Reccord all ye aboue mentioned Sixty accres of Land butted and bounded as aboue or howeuer otherwise all ye Estate Right title Interest use propriety possession Claime and demand whatsoeuer of them or Either of them of in and unto the s^d land and Euery part or peace thereof, To haue and To hold ye afore granted primises with ye liberties, priuilges Commodityes benifits and appurtenances thereunto belonging in as large and ample maner and Sort unto yᵉ sᵈ Jabaz Jenkins his heirs and Assigns for Euer to be unto yᵉ only proper use benifit and behoofe of yᵉ sᵈ Jabaz Jenkins his heirs and Assigns for Euer/ and yᵉ sᵈ Allexander fforgisson Daniel Emery for them Selues their heirs and Assigns doe Couenant and promiss to and with yᵉ sᵈ Jabaz Jenkins his heirs and Assigns Shall and may at all times for Euer hereafter Lawfully peaceably and quietly haue hold use occupie possesse and Injoy all yᵉ sᵈ peces of land with yᵉ priuiliges and abartenances thereof without yᵉ lest let hinderence or Claiing any Right or Euiction by or from them or Either of them or by or from all and Euery other person or persons hauing or Claiming any Right title or Interest therein by from or under yᵉ sᵈ Allexander fforgisson and Daniel Emory In Wittness whareof they haue hereunto Set their hands and Seales yᵉ Sixth day of ffebʳʸ in yᵉ yeare of our Lord one thousand Six hundred Ninty and Six Seuen and in yᵉ Eighth year of yᵉ Raine of our Soueren Lord William yᵉ third King of England &ᶜ.   Daniel Emory   (his Seal.)

Signed Sealed and Deliu-   Allexandʳ fforgisson   (his Seal.)
ered In Presents of us.   Ellizabeth ℰ Gowen
John Belcher   her mark
Charles ffrost Junʳ   allias Smith   (her Seale.)

                        her
Ellizabeth ⟨mark⟩ ffergisson   (her Seale.)

Margrit Emery   (her Seale.)

This Instrument was acknowledged by the fiue persons Subscribing to be their volentary act and Deed
Kittery ffebʳʸ yᵉ 6º 169⁶⁄₇   before me Charles ffrost
                                   Justice of Peace

A true Copie of yᵉ origenall Deed Transcribed and Compared this 25º of ffebʳʸ 169⁶⁄₇   p Jos. Hamond Registʳ

BOOK IV, FOL. 98.

To all Christian people to whome this presents Shall Come I Israel Hodsden Now resident in Portsmouth in New Hampshiere in New England Greeting, Know ye that I ye aboues^d Israel Hodsden for Diuers good Causes and consideration me hereunto mouing more Especially for and in Consideration of Eleauen pounds in hand payd before ye Ensealing and deliuery of these presents hereof by Daniel Emery of Kittery in York Shiere in ye Prouince of the Massachusets in New England, wherewith I acknowledge my Selfe fully Satisfied contented and payd and hereof and of euery part and parcell hereof doe acquit and for euer discharge the said Daniel Emery his heires and Assigns & by these presents haue absolutely giuen granted bargained and Sold Alienated and Confirmed and Enfeoffed unto ye aboue Said Daniel Emery a piece or parcell of Land Containing twelue Acres of Land Situate and Lying in Kittery bounded as followeth bounded on the North with Etheringtons land on ye East with william Gowen, on the South with Trustrum Harris Land and William Gowens land, on ye West with the Land formerly layd out to Jeremiah Hodsden, be it more or less, together with fiftie Acres of land lying in Kittery afores^d near the third Hill bounded on ye East with Edward Waymouths Land, on the South with William Gowens and John Breadies land on ye West wth Comons on ye North with Stephen Jenkins Land be it more or less To haue and to hold the aboue mentioned pieces or parcells of land with all ye woods Timb^r and all the Appertenances and priuiledges thereunto belonging or anwise appertaining to him ye s^d Daniel Emery his heires or Assignes for euer and to his own proper use and behoofe and benefit for euer And the s^d Isral Hodsden for himselfe his heires and Assigns doth Couenant & promise to and with the said Daniel Emery his heires and Assigns that ye s^d Isral Hodsden hath in himselfe good Right full power and Lawfull Authority the aboue giuen and granted premises to Sell and Dispose of and that freely and Clearly Acquitted Exonerated and discharged of and from

Book IV, Fol. 98, 99.

all manner of gifts grants Leases Morgages Wills Entailments Judgments Executions power of thirds and all Incombrances whatsoeuer and the s[d] Israel Hodsden doth for himself his heires Execut[rs] Administrat[rs] and Assigns Couenant and promise to and with y[e] Said Daniel Emery his heires and Assigns the aboue granted premises and to warrant and Defend him by these presents In witness whereof y[e] aboue s[d] Israel Hodsden hath hereunto Set his this Seuenth day of ffebruary in the year of our Lord Christ one thousand Six hundred Ninety and Six & Seuen In y[r] Eighth year of y[e] Reign of our Soueren Lord William King of England &[c].

Signed Seled and deliuerd
in presents of us
Job Alcock
Edward Ayers

his
Israel ─┼─ Hodsden (Seal)
mark (=)
Ann Hodsden

Israel Hodsden and Ann his wife Acknowledged this Instrement to be their Act and Deed before me ffebruary y[e] Ninteenth one thousand Six hundred Ninety Six Seuen. Job Alcock Just ps

A true Copie of y[e] origenall Deed Transcribed and Compared March: y[e] 8 : 169$\frac{6}{7}$ — Jos Hamond Regis[tr]

[99] Know all men by these presents that I Richard Selly of Winter Harbour in New England Marrin[r] doe Confess my Selfe to owe and to be Justly Indebted unto Henry Kemble of Boston in New : England afores[d] Black Smith in y[e] Just quantety of ten thousand foot of Merchantable pine boards to be deliuered unto y[e] said Henry Kemble or to his Certain Atturney heires Execut[rs] Administrat[rs] or Assignes in Boston aforesaid upon Demand/ for performance whereof I bind me my heires Execut[rs] and Administrat[rs] to him y[e] Said Henry Kemble his heires Execut[rs] Ad-

Richard
Sellyes bill
for 10000
of boards
to Henry
Kemble

Book IV, Fol. 99.

ministrat{rs} or Assignes in Double the vallue of y{e} aboues{d} quantetie of boards. In witness whereof I the said Richard Selly haue hereunto Set my hand & Seale this Ninth day of May in the Yeare of our Lord One thousand Six hundred & Seuenty : 1670
Signed Sealed & Deliuered   Richard R⩔ Selly
In the presence of us   his Mark (his Seal)
  John Rule
  Thomas Kemble
A true Copie of y{e} origenall Transcribed and Compared, March y{e} 4 : 1696   p Jos Hamond Regist{r}

Know all men by these presents that I Richard Selly of Saco in New England doe confess my Selfe to owe and to be Justly Indebted unto Henry Kemble of Boston in New England Ancor Smith in y{e} full and Just Sum of twenty and Six pounds of Lawfull money of New England, to be payd to the said Henry Kemble or to his Certain Atturney his heires Execut{rs} Administrat{rs} and Assignes at or before y{e} last of May next Ensuing after y{e} Date hereof, for y{e} well and true performance whereof I bind me my heires Execut{rs} Administrat{rs} and Assigns firmly by these presents/ And for y{e} further and better Securitie of him the Said Henry Kemble for y{e} paym{t} of the aboue said Sum I bind ouer and Assigne unto him the said Henry Kemble his heires and Assignes All that my housing and Land whether upland or Meadow and all my Interest therein, Scituate in Saco or winter harbour in New-England, And all the profits and priuiledges thereunto belonging firmly by these presents In witness whereof I haue hereunto Set my hand and Seal this Seuenth day of Decemb{r} in

[margin: Rich{d} Sellyes bill of 26 14 to Hen Kemble]

[margin: The Assignm{t} is on y{e} other side]

BOOK IV, FOL. 99.

the yeare of oʳ Lord One thousand Six hundred and Seuenty. Annoq Regni Re Caroli Secundi Anglia &ᵗ xx y⁰ 1670

The Condition of the aboue written obligation is Such that if the aboue bounden Richard Selly his heires Executʳˢ Administratʳˢ or Assigns Doe and Shall well and truly pay or Cause to be payd unto y⁰ aboue named Henry Kemble or to his Certain Atturney, his heires Executʳˢ Administratʳˢ of Assignes or any or either of them the full and whole Sum of fourteen pounds in Currant money of New England at one Intire payment at or before the last of May next Ensuing the Date here of without ffraud or further Delay/ Then this present Obligation to be voyd and of None Effect or Else to remain in full force Strength and vertue

Signed Sealed and Deliu-
ered In the presents of   Richard   Selly (his Seal)
us and the words Scitu-   his marke
ate in Saco or Winter
Harbʳ in New England
interlined before Sealing
and deliuery of these presents
Witness as abouesᵈ Thomas Kemble Senʳ
                Thomas Kemble Junʳ

A true Copie of y⁰ origenall Transcribed & compared March : 4. 1696.   p Jos Hamond Registʳ

Receiued by me under written of Richard Selly in part of pay of this bill wᵗʰin written as followeth, to Say two thousand foot of boards at Seuerall payments & by a bond of fourteen pounds bearing Date y⁰ Seuenteenth day of Decembʳ in the year of our Lord 1670 Soe there remaineth one thousand foot of boards yet due, which boards I doe Assign ouer to Mʳ Robert Brimsdon or to his Assigns the which thousand foot of boards being payd is in full of y⁰

payment of this within written bill as witness my hand this 19th 10 : 70.   p me Henry Kemble (his/seal)
Signed Sealed and Deliuered

in presents of us   Know all men that I Robert Brims-
Thomas Eldredg   don of Boston Merchant doe As-
Daniel Richards   sign ouer this (as it is written on
                    both Sides) to Cap^{tn} John Hill of
                    Wells to him his heires and As-
                    signes as witness my hand Octob^r
Witness   31st 1693.

Thomas Johnston   Robert Brimsdon (Seal)
Jam^s Conuers

A true Copic Transcribed out origenall and therewith Compared This. 4 day of March : 1696 —

p Jos Hamond Regist^r

I Henry Kemble of Boston Ancor Smith doe Assigne all my Right Title and Interest of this within men-
Hen. Kembles Assignm^t of ye obligation on ye other Side tioned wrightins, ouer unto Robert Brimsdon Merchant of Boston or to his heires and Assigns as Witness my hand this Nineteenth day of
Decemb^r 1670   Henry Kemble (Seal)

Signed Sealed and deliu-   Daniel Richards made oath the
ered in the presents of us 13° of the 9th mo. 1671, that he
Thomas Eldredg   was present and did see this
Daniel Richards   Assignment Signed & Sealed
                           and did Set his hand thereto as
                           a witness before
                           Anthony Stoddard Comissi^r

A true Copie of ye origenall : Transcribed and Compared this 4th day of March : 1696 —   p Jos Hamond Regist^r

Book IV, Fol. 99, 100.

Know all men that I Robert Brimsdon of Boston in y̆ᵉ County of Southfolk in the Prouince of the Massachusets Bay in New England Merchᵗ doe Assigne make ouer and Confirm unto Capᵐ John Hill of Wells in the County of Yorke in the Prouince of yᵉ Massachusets Bay in New England aforesᵈ Yeoman All my Right Title and Interest in and unto this within Written bond or Obligation to him his heires Executʳˢ and Assigns for euer As Witness my hand and Seale this 31ˢᵗ of Octobʳ 1693, and in the Sixth year of their Majestics Reign. Robert Bronsdon (his Seal)
Sealed and deliuered in presents of
   Thomas Johnston   Then Appeared before me yᵉ Sub-
   Jamˢ Conuers.   scribʳ one of their Majesties Justices of the peace for yᵉ County of Suffolk, Robert Brimsdon and Acknowledged this Instrumᵗ to be his Act & Deed this first day of Nouembʳ 1693.   Tımothy Prout Justice

A true Copie of the origenall Transcribed and Compared March : 4 : 1696.   p Jos Hamond Registʳ

[100] Know all men by these presents that I Richard Zelly of or resident neare unto Winter Harbour neare the Riuer of Saco in New-England Marrinʳ am bound and firmly obliged unto Robert Brimsdon of Boston in the Massachusets Collony in New-England aforesᵈ Merchant, in the Sum Sixty pounds of lawfull Money of and in New-England, to the which payment well and truly to be made and done, I bind my Selfe my heirs Executʳˢ Administratʳˢ and Assignes firmly by these pʳsents unto the Said Robert Brimsdon or to his heires Executʳˢ Admınistratʳˢ or Assignes firmly by these presents/ Witness my hand this Sixth day of Decembʳ Anno Domini, 1670 Annoq̨ Regnı Regis Charole Secundi uigessimo Secundo.

Book IV, Fol. 100.

Rich⁴ Zellyes obligation of 60ᵥ to Rob: Brimsdon

The Condition of this obligation is Such that if the aboue bound Richard Zelly or his heires Execut⁽ʳˢ⁾ Administrat⁽ʳˢ⁾ or Assignes doe pay or Cause to be payd unto yᵉ aboue Named Robert Brimsdon or to his heires Execut⁽ʳˢ⁾ Administrat⁽ʳˢ⁾ or Assignes the full and Just Summe of thirty pounds ffifteen Shillings and two pence of Lawfull money of and in New-England afores⁽ᵈ⁾, at or before the last day of May next Ensuing the Date here of, which will be in yᵉ year of our Lord One thousand Six hundred Seuenty and one, at yᵉ dwelling house of yᵉ s⁽ᵈ⁾ Robert Brimsdon or in any other place of his appointment and order, That then this Obligation aboues⁽ᵈ⁾ and yᵉ Surrender hereunto anexed in writing Shall be voyd and of None Effect, otherwise to remain in full power force and vertue giuen under my hand without ffraud the day and Year aboue written

Signed Sealed & deliuered
  In presents of us
    Thomas
    Beauis
    Daniel Richards
    Nicholas Heskins

mark of
Richard /₹₂/ Zelly (Seal)

Nicholas Heskins made oath yᵉ 12ᵗʰ of 10ᵗʰ mo. 1670 that he was present and did See this Instrum⁽ᵗ⁾ Signed & Sealed and Set his hand thereto as a Witness—before me
        Anthony Stoddard Comiss⁽ʳ⁾
Daniel Richards made oath likewise the 13ᵗʰ of 9ᵗʰ mo: 1671. before me
        Anthony Stoddard Comiss⁽ʳ⁾

A true Copie of yᵉ origenall Transcribed and Compared this 4° day of March: 1696:   p Jos Hamond Regist⁽ʳ⁾

Know all men by these presents that I Robert Brimsdon of Boston in the County Southfolke in the prouince of the Massachusets Bay in New-England Merchant, for and in Consideration of a valuable Sum of money to me well and truly payd in hand p Cap⁽ᵗⁿ⁾ John Hill of Wells in the

Book IV, Fol. 100, 101.

Rob. Brimsdons Assigmt to Capn Hill of ye obligation on ye other Side

County-Yorke in the Prouince afores⁴ Yeoman haue Assigned and made ouer, and doe by these presents fully freely and absolutely Assign and make ouer unto yᵉ afore Said John Hill all my Right title and Interest in and unto this within written bond or Obligation to him his heires Execut^rs Administrat^rs and Assignes for euer/ as Witness my hand and Seale this 31ˢᵗ of Octobʳ 1693/ Annoq̃ Reg. Rs & Regine Guilielmi & Marie Angliæ &ᶜ quinto.

Signed Sealed and Deliuered   Robert Bronsdon (his Seal)

In presents of—
Thomas Johnston
Jamˢ Conuers

Then Appeared before me yᵉ Subscribʳ one of their Majesties Justices of the peace for yᵉ County of Southfolk Robert Brimsdon did Acknowledge this Instrument to be his Act and Deed this first day of Nouembʳ 1693

Timothy Prout Justice

A true Copie of yᵉ originall Transcribed and Compared March yᵉ 4ᵗʰ 1696. p Jos Hamond Regʳ

[101] To all Christian people to whom this present Writing Shall come I Richard Zelly of the Harbour Called Winter Harbour neare yᵉ Riuer of Saco in New-England Send Greeting/ Know yee that I the Said Richard Zelly for and in Consideration of a Penall bond giuen and acknowl-⁻ edged unto Robert Brimsdon of Boston in the Massachusets Collony in New England afores⁴ Merchant for the Just Sum of thirty pounds fifteen Shillings and two pence to be payd at or before the last day of May Next Ensuing the Date hereof in Good and Currant Money of New England haue in

Zellyes Mortgage or Obligation to Robt Brimsdn of his housing and Lands

Case of Default and payment not made of the Said Sum at the time mentioned in the Said bond Granted and by these presents doe Grant Aliene and Surrender unto the Said Robert Brimsdon his heires Executrs Administratrs or Assignes all my Estate Right Title and Term of Yeares yet to Come and unexpired use possession Rent Reuersion propertie Claime and Demand whatsoeuer of in and unto all those Lands Mesuages tenements or Hereditaments Goods Chattells or Worldly Estate with which I ye said Richard Zelly am possessed of by vertue of any Deed writing Inheritance or any other way whatsoeuer Leagall giuing and by these presents Granting unto my Said Creditr Robert Brimsdon for my Selfe my heires Executrs Administratrs or Assignes full power and Authority in and about ye aboue recited premises, untill ye said penall bond be fully Satisfied/ Giuen under my hand and Seale this 7th day of Decembr 1670, Annoq Regni Regis Charoli Secundi xxii.

Sealed and Deliuered
In presents of us/
Thomas Beauis
Nicholas Heskins

mark of
Richard R Z Zelly (his Seal)

Nicholas Heskins made oath, 12th 10th mo 1670 that he was present and did See this writing Signed and Sealed And Set his hand thereto as a Witness, before

Anthony Stoddard Comissir

A true Copie of the originall Transcribed and compared May the 4th 1696 — p Jos : Hamond Registr

Know all men by these presents that I Robert Brimsdon of Boston in the County of Southfolk in the Prouince of the Massachusets Bay in New-England Merchant for and in Consideration of valluable Sum of Money to well and truly payd in hand by Captn John Hill of Wells in the County of York in the Prouince afores^d yeom haue Assiagned made ouer and fully Confirmed unto the Said John Hill this within written bond Mortgage or Obligation To haue and to hold ocupie possess and enjoy ye Same to him his heires and Assignes for euer In as full and Ample manner as I my Selfe did or might haue done, to all intents and Purposes in the Law/ As witness my hand and Seale this 31st of Octob^r 1693 Annoq, Ri Rs & Reginæ Guihelmi & Mariæ Nunce Angliæ &^c Quinto.   Robert Bronsdon (his Seal)

Sealed and Deliuered   Then Appeared before me the Sub-
  In presents of   scrib^r one of their Majesties Jus-
  Thomas Johnston   tices of ye peace for ye County of
  Jam^s Conuers   Southfolke Robert Brimsdon And
                        Acknowledged this Instrum^t to be
                        his Act and Deed this first day of
                        Nouemb^r 1693 —
                            Timothy Prout Justice

A true Copie of the origenall Transcribed and Compared this 4° day of March 1696, p Jos Hamond Regist^r

[102] Whereas I John Hill of Saco in the County of Yorke in the Prouince of the Massachusets Bay in New England haue Seuerall obligations Assigned and made ouer to me by Robert Brimsdon of Boston in ye Prouince afores^d Merchant Namely one bill of ten thousand foot of boards by Richard Zelly, payable to Henry Kemble of Boston Black Smith, bearing Date the Ninth day of May one thousand Six hundred and Seuenty, And by the Said Kemble Assigned and made ouer unto Robert Brimsdon of Boston afores^d/ Said Assignm^t bearing Date ye 19th 10 . 70, and by the Said Brimsdon Assigned to me Octob^r ye 31st 1693, as more at large appears p s^d bill and Assignm^ts And one obligation from s^d Richard Zelly unto s^d Henry Kemble of twentie Six

pounds of Lawfull money of New England, for Securitie of ye which, the s^d Zelly makes ouer all his houses Lands and Meadows at Saco, with ye Appertenances as at large Appears by s^d obligation under his hand and Seal bearing Date Decemb^r the Seauenth day of Decemb^r 1670 And by said Kemble Assigned to Robert Brimsdon as appears under his hand and Seal bearing Date Decemb^r ye Nineteenth 1670, And by s^d Brimsdon Assigned to me Octob^r ye 31st 1693, as appears under his hand and Seal And alsoe an Obligation of Sixtie pounds of Lawfull money of New England for the paym^t of thirty pounds fifteen Shillings and two pence of like money by Richard Zelly afores^d unto ye afores^d Robert Brimsdon bearing Decemb^r ye Sixth 1670, and by s^d Brimsd~ Assigned unto me octob^r ye 31st 1693, as appears by ye Assignm^t on ye back Side of the obligation, As alsoe a writing or Morgage giuen by ye said Richard Zelly unto s^d Robert Brimsdon of all his Lands Messuages, Tenem^ts Hereditaments Goods Chattells or worldly Estate which he ye said Richard Zelly was possessed off, for ye payment of thirty pounds fifteen Shillings and two pence good and Currant money of New England bearing Date Decemb^r the 7° 1670, and Assigned unto me by s^d Brimsdon octob^r 31st 1693

John Hill to Jos Hill

Now Know all men by these presents that I the aboue mentioned John Hill for Diuers good Causes and Considerations me thereunto Mouing haue Assigned made ouer and Confirmed unto my Dear & Louing Brother Joseph Hill of Saco all my Right Title and Interest of in and unto the aboue Recited premises and all and euery of them and euery part thereof, to Improue and use as his own prop^r Right Title and Interest, to him his heirs and Assigns for euer. In witness whereof I haue hereunto set my hand and Seal this Sixth day of March one thousand Six hundred Ninety and Six or Seuen: 169⁶⁄₇ And in the Eighth year of y^e Reigne of our Soueraign Lord William y^e third by y^e grace of God of

BOOK IV, FOL. 102.

England Scotland ffrance and Ireland, King Defender of y^e Faith.	John Hill (his Seal)
Signed Sealed & Deliuered	Kittery this Sixth day of March
In the presents of us	169$\frac{4}{}$ Cap^{tn} John Hill came
John Belcher	before me and Acknowledged
Charles ffrost Juñ^r	the aboue written Instrument
	to be his act & Deed
	Charles ffrost Just peace
A true Copie of y^e origenall Transcribed and compared :	
March : y^e 8 : 169$\frac{4}{}$	p Jos Hamond Regist^r

To all Christian people to whom this p^rsent Deed of Sale Shall come Greeting Know yee that I Richard Joce of Portsmouth in the Prouince of New Hampshere in New England M^rch^t and Hannah my wife for and in Consideration of the Sum of twentie pounds Cur^t money of New England to us in hand payd and Secured to be payd by Samuel ffernald of ye town of Kittery in the Prouince of Mayn in New England afores^d Shipwright the receipt whereof I doe Acknowledge my Selfe to be therewith fully Satisfied and payd and thereof Exonerate Acquit and discharge the Said Samuel ffernald his heires Execut^{rs} Administrat^{rs} for euer, haue by these presents giuen granted bargained Sold Alienated Enfeoft Conueied released assured and Confirmed and by these presents doe fully freely Absolutely Sell Alien and Enfeoff assure and Confirm unto ye said Samuel ffurnill his heires and Assignes for euer, To Say the one halfe part of twenty Acres of upland more or less granted by the Select men of the Town of Kittery in the Prouince of Mayn afores^d unto Joseph Alcocke his heires or Assigns for euer, as by Record of the Said Town of ye 14° June one thousand Six hundred fiftie and Nine may more fully appear, which said Land lieth within the Great Coue aboue William Palmers and goeth

BOOK IV, FOL. 102.

back into the woods by an East lyne and goeth by the water side North East as appears by Seuerall marked trees which bounded the Said Lott/ And all the priuiledges to y̆ said Land belonging and appertaining/ To haue and to hold the said Land Appertenances and priuiledges thereunto belonging to him y̆ said Samuel ffurnill his heires Execut[rs] Administrat[rs] or Assigns for euer from me the s[d] Richard Joce and Hannah my wife our heires Execut[rs] Administrat[rs] and Assigns for euermore And for noe other Intent use or purpose, And we the said Richard Joce and Hannah my wife to hereby Auouch y̆ Sale hereof by us made and that we haue good Right and Lawfull Authoritie in our Selues to Sell and Dispose of the Same and that y̆ Land and premises is absolutely ffree and Cleare from all manner of titles or Claims troubles Mortgages Leases rents Dowries Rights of Dowries thirds and Widows thirds or any other other Incombrance whatsoeuer And further we bind our selues our heires and Execut[rs] and Administrat[rs] to warrant and for euer defend the said Samuel ffernald his heires Execut[rs] Administrat[rs] or Assigns against all persons whatsoeuer lawfully Claiming or pretending any Right or title or Interest in the Said Land or premises or to any part thereof from by or under us our heirs Execut[rs] Administrat[rs] or Assigns In Testimony whereof we the s[d] Richard Joce and hannah his wife haue hereunto put our hands and Seales this thirty day of Nouemb[r] in the year of our Lord : 1696

Sealed Signed and deliuered   Richard Jose (his Seal)
  In presents of   Hannah Jose (her Seal)
  John Partridge   M[r] Richard Jose psonally Appeared this
  Hen : Penny   14th of Jan[ry] 169$\frac{6}{7}$ and Acknowledged
                    the aboue Instrum[t] to be his volluntary
                    & free Act and Deed before me
                              Tho : Packer Jus[t] peace
  A true Copie of y̆ origenall Deed Transcribed and Compared, March : 8° 169$\frac{6}{7}$ p Jos Hamond Regist[r]

BOOK IV, FOL. 103.

[103] To all Christian people to whome this presents Shall come/ I Israel Hodsden now Resident in Portsmouth in New Hampshiere in New England Greeting, know y^e that I y^e aboues^d Israel Hodsden for diuers good Causes and Considerations me hereunto mouing, More Especially for and in Consideration of Eleuen pounds in hand payd before the Ensealing & deliuery of this presents hereof by Daniel Emery of Kittery in york Shiere in the Prouince of the Massachusets in New England, wherewith I Acknowledge my Selfe fully Satisfied Contented and paid And hereof and of euery part and parcell hereof doe Acquit and for euer dischaige ye s^d Daniel Emery his heires and Assigns and by these presents haue absolutely giuen granted bargained and Sold Alienated and Confirmed and Enfeofed unto the aboue-s^d Daniel Emery a piece or parcell of Land containing twelue Acres of Land Situate and Lying in Kittery bounded as followeth — is bounded on the North with Etheringtons land on ye East with William Gowen on the South with Trustrum Hareses land and William Gowens land, on ye West with the land formerly laid out to Jeremie Hodsden, be it more or less together wth ffifty Acres of land lying in Kittery afores^d neare the third Hill bounded on ye East with Edward Waimouths land on ye South with William Gowens and John Bredys land on ye West with Comons on the North with Steuen Jenkins land be it more or less To haue and to hold ye aboue mentioned pieces or parcells of Land with all ye woods timber and all the Appertenances and priuiledges thereunto belonging or any wise appertaining to him the s^d Daniel Emery his heires or Assigns for euer and to his onely proper use and behoofe and benefit for euer And ye s^d Israel Hodsden for himselfe his heires and Assigns doth Couenant and promise to and with the S^d Daniel Emery his heires and Assigns that he ye said Israel Hodsden hath in himselfe good Right full power and lawfull Authoritie to ye aboue giuen and granted premises to sell

Book IV, Fol. 103.

and dispose of, and freely and Clerely acquited Exonerated and discharged of and from all maner of gifts grants leases Morgages wills Entailments Judgments Executions power of thirds and all Encombrances whatsoeuer And the s^d Israel Hodsden doth for himselfe his heires Execut^rs Administrat^rs and Assigns Couenant and promise to and with the s^d Daniel Emery his heirs and Assigns the aboue granted premises and to warrant and Defend him as by these presents In witness whereof the aboues^d Israel Hodsden hath hereunto Set his hand and Seale this Seuenteenth day of ffeb^ry in ye year of our Lord Christ one thousand Six hundred Ninety and Six & Seuen in ye Eight year of the Reign of our Soueren Lord william King of England &^c.

Signend Sealed and deliuered   Israel ✗ Hodsden (his/Seal)
  In the presents of us   mark
  Job Alcock   Ann Hodsden
  Edward Ayers

Israel Hodsden and Ann his wife Acknowledged this Instrument to be their Act & Deed before me ffeb^ry the Nineteenth one thousand Six hundred Ninety Six Seuen

                              Job Alcock Jusis ps
A true Copie of the origenall Deed Transcribed & Compared this: 23. day of March. 169⅚   p Jos Hamond Regist^r

To all Christian People to whome these presents Shall come Know ye that we Humphrey Spencer and Grace Spencer my wife Now Inhabitants on the Great Island in the Prouince of New Hampshier in the Town of Portsmouth In New England for Diners good Causes and valluable Considerations us thereunto mouing Haue remised released and for euer quit Claimed and by these presents for our selues our heires Execut^rs and Administrat^rs Doe fully Clearly and absolutely Remise Release and for euer quit Claim unto Robert Elliot Merchant on ye said Great Island and of the Town of Portsm^o in New Hampshiere in New England afores^d in his full and peaceable possession & Seizin and to his heires and Assigns for euer All Such Right Estate Interes & Demand whatsoeuer as we the said Humphrey Spencer and Grace Spencer my wife haue had in times past or ought to haue of in or to a Certaine Tract of land Situate lying and being in Newchowaninck Situate lying and being on one Side or part by the Land of Daniel Gooden Senr and Cap^{tn} Wincoll by Marked trees and at the end by the land of Moses Spencer and Eliakim Hutchinson Containing in all be it more or less Thirty Acres, To haue and to hould all the s^d Tract of land unto the s^d Robert Elliot his heirs and Assigns for euer Soe that neither he the Said Humphrey Spencer nor Grace Spencer nor his nor her heires Nor any other pson or psons for him her or them or in his or their Names, or in the Name Right and Stead of any of them Shall or will by any way or meanes hereafter haue Claim Challenge or Demand any Estate Title or Interest of in or to the premises aboue Named or any part or parcell thereof, but from all and euery Action Right Estate, Title Interest and Demand of in or unto the premises or any part thereof they and euery them the said Humphrey & Grace Spencer and their heires Execut^{rs} Administrat^{rs} and euery of them Shall utterly Excluded and Barred for euer by these presents, And the said Humphrey and Grace Spencer and his or her heires the premises and Appurtenances Specified unto him ye said Robert Elliot his heirs and Assigns to his and their proper use in manner and form aforesaid Shall Warrant and for euer Defend by these presents In witness whereof we haue hereunto Set our hands and Seales

Marke of

Signed Sealed and Deliu- Humphrey *HS* Spencer (Seal)
ered in presents of us —
Nicho. Heskins Grace *RL* Spencer (Seal)
William Broad

Book IV, Fol. 103, 104.

A true Copie of y^e origenall Deed or relese Transcribed and Compared, this 24th day of March 169$\frac{9}{8}$
                                p Jos Hamond Regist^r

These presents Declare and Witness that I Robert Elliot mentioned in this Instrument in writing doe hereby make ouer Surrender and Deliuer unto Allen ffuz of Nechowannick in the Prouince of Maine in New England this said Instrument in writing together with all the particulars herein Mentioned And all my Interest and Concerns I haue herein from me s^d Robert Elliot and mine to him ye s^d Allen ffuz and his/ Witness my hand this thirteenth day of July in ye Yeer of our Lord one thousand Six hundred Eighty and Nine
Witness Nicho: Heskins   Robert Elliot (Seal)

I Allen ffuz aboue mentioned for my Selfe my heires Execut^{rs} [**104**] and Administrat^{rs} doe hereby Surrender and make ouer this Deed or Instrument in writing, together with all the particulars therein Contained unto Humphrey Spencer of Newchowannick his heires Execut^{rs} and Administrat^{rs}/ Witness my hand and Seal, this Eleuenth day of June one Thousand Six hundred Ninety fiue: 1695
Signed Sealed and deliuered   mark of
  In presents of us—   Allen **A** ffuz (his Seal)
  William Spencer   New Castle June y^e Eleuenth 1695
  Nicho Heskins   Allen ffuz came before me and Acknowledged the aboue written to be his Act & Deed
                        Shadrach Walton Jus pes
A true Copie of the origenall Surrender or Assignments Transcribed and Compared, this 24 of March 169$\frac{9}{8}$
                                p Jos Hamond Regist^r

Book IV, Fol. 104.

Know all men by these presents that I the within Named Ephraim Joy doe by these present Assign and Confirm this within written Deed of Sale unto James Stackpole Senr of Barwick in the County of Yorke in New England to him his heires Execut^rs Administrat^rs and Assignes, for and in Consideration of ffifteen pounds in Currant Money of New England, which money is already Deliuered and Receiued as Witness my hand this the Second day of Nouember and in the year of our Lord God One thousand Six hundred Ninetie and Six.

         Ephraim E Joy (his Seale)
Signed Sealed & deliuered
in the presents of us   his mark
Witness:

James Warren Junr Ephrem Joy Senr Acknowled this
Thomas Abbott Senr aboue written Instrument to be
James Emery Junr   his Act and Deed this 30° of
          Decemb^r 1696
       Before me Charles ffrost Jus^t peace

A true Copie of the origenall Assignment Transcribed and Compared this 27° of March 1697 (The within written Deed mentioned in this Assignm^t whereunto this refers is Entred in the Eleuenth Page of this Booke by Mr Edward Rishworth)   p Jos Hamond Regist^r

---

     Berwick ffebruary the 27th 169$\frac{4}{5}$

These presents testifie a Deuision between Nicholas and John Gowen, according to an agreement made January 22° 169$\frac{4}{5}$.

Impr. That Deuiding line aboue the County Rode is as followeth from y^e Rode to the now dwelling house and Soe to the Barn and all y^e Yard Round the Barn to the Rode to ly for the benefit of both parts, full breadth between both orchurds then from the North Corner of s^d Yard aboues^d to goe to the Rockie hill, upon an East Northeast a quarter Easterly line, on which line a Rod on each Side to be left for a way for our Conueniency It is to be understood that where the way cannot goe direct on the line it is to goe to ye Conuenents Side thereof, The deuiding line below ye Rode begins twenty Six pole and a halfe from ye aboues^d yard Norerly as the Rode lies and from thence Southwest by West half Westerly to ye Brooke runing out of Mr Broughtons Swamp, which lines is the deuiding lines of all the Land which I the s^d Nicholas was bound to Deuide between us the aboues^d Alsoe a way on s^d line two pole Wide one on each Side thereof to ye foot bound at Mr Broughtons Swamp/ for ye Difference of the aboues^d two parts I reserue that part of the orchard from ye Well to ye house backward for Seuen years Space, to be for ye benefit of him that Shall haue the Nothermost part, after which time to return to him that Shall haue the Southermost part/ Alsoe a way is allowed to ye Well for both parts/ Alsoe he that has the Nothermost part Shall haue both Barns and Trustrums house And he that has ye Southermost part Shall haue the house that was our fathers and Shall haue ffortie Shillings from ye other part towards building of a Barn upon s^d part or any other Improuement upon s^d Land &^{c}.

Now John is to Chuse which part he best fancies to be his and after his Choyce my Selfe to haue y^e other part/ As Witness my hand   Nicholas Gowen.
Witness Daniel Emery
  Alaxander fforguson

     March the 4° 169$\frac{3}{4}$ I John Gowen Alias Smith haue made Choyce of the Southermost part of the land aboue written to be mine As Witness my hand.
Witness Alexander fforguson   John Gowen, Alias Smith
  Daniel Emery

  Nicholas Gowen and John Gowen Alias Smith acknowledged this Instrument to be their Act & Deed this 4° of March 169$\frac{3}{4}$ Before me Charles ffrost: Just peace

BOOK IV, FOL. 104, 105.

A true Copie of The aboue agreement of a Deuision of Lands between Nicholas and John Gowen Alias Smith Transcribed and Compared this 27º day of March 1697
p Jos Hamond Regist^r

[105] To all Christian People to home this present Shall Come, I James Emery Senr of Kittery in the County of Yorke now in the Prouince of the Massachusets in New England Greeting, Now know ye that I ye aboue s^d James Emery for Diuers good Causes & considerations me hereunto mouing More Especially for and in Consideration of thirty and fiue pounds in hand payd before the Signing and Sealing hereof by James Emery Junr and Daniel Emery and Job Emery, my three Sons of Kittery aboues^d, wherewith I Acknowledge my Selfe fully Satisfied Contented and payd And hereof and of euery part and parcel hereof doe Acquit and for euer discharge the aboues^d James Emery Junr Daniel Emery and Job Emery their heires and Assigns by these presents, Haue giuen granted bargained and Sold alienated Enfeoffed and Confirmed, And by these presents doe absolutely giue grant bargain Sell alien Enfeoff and Confirm unto the aboue Named James Emery Junr Daniel Emery and Job Emery in Equall Shares, a piece or parcell of Land Containing Sixty Acres, with all ye Wood timber that is either Standing or lying upon ye aboues^d land with all ye Appurtenances and priuiledges thereunto belonging or in any wayes Appertaining of what nature or kind soeuer, the s^d Land lying in Kittery aboues^d bounded as followeth vizt with ye land of Daniel Gooden on ye North on ye East upon ye Rocey hill, on ye South with Siluanus Nock, and John Plaisted, on ye West with ye Stoney Brook/ To haue and to hold the aboue mentioned piece or parcell of land with all the Appurtenances aboues^d to them the s^d James Emery Daniel Emery and Job Emery their heires and Assigns for

euer, and to their only proper use and behoofe, only it is to be understood that I haue reserued one Acre of this land for two years and the timber upon that Acre to my disposing, Alsoe I James Emery Senr doe reserue the use of the aboues^d land my life time if I demand it with Seuen years, and if not to be free for euer, And I ye s^d James Emery Senr for my Selfe my heires and Assignes doe Couenant and promise to and with the aboue s^d James Emery Junr Daniel Emery and Job Emery their heires and Assigns that he the s^d James Emery Senr hath in himselfe good Right full power and lawfull authority to the aboues^d land to Sell and dispose of and that ye Same and euery part & parcell thereof as free and clear and freely and Clerely acquitted Exonerated and Discharged of and from all manner of Gifts grants leases Morgages Wills Entailm^{ts} Judgments Executions power of thirds and all Incombrances whatsoeuer and ye s^d James Emery Senr doth for himselfe his heires Execut^{rs} Administrat^{rs} and Assignes doe Couenant and promise to and with the aboues^d James Emery Junr Daniel Emery and Job Emery their heires Execut^{rs} Administrat^{rs} and Assignes as by these pres^{ts} In witness whereof I haue Set to my hand and Seal this first day of March in ye yeare of our Lord Christ one thousand Six hundred Ninety Six and Seuen in the eight year of the Reign of our Lord William King of England &^{c}. It is to be understood that whereas my two Sons Daniel Emery and Job Emery has payd me for ye aboues^d land that if my Son James Emery doe not pay pay to them the third part of the price aboue mentioned then to haue noe part of y^e aboues^d Land this done before y^e ackowledgm^t of this Instrum^t.

Signed Sealed and deliuered   James Emerey (his Seal)

in presents of us—

Alexander fforguson   James Emery Senr kame before
      his   me this 17 of March : 169$\frac{6}{7}$
James 2 Treworgie   and owned this Instrum^t to be
   mark   his Act and Deed before me
Samuel Winch   Job Alcock Justis pes

Book IV, Fol. 105.

A true Copie of y^e origenall Deed Transcribed and Compared March. 27° 1697. p Jos Hamond Regist^r

Know all men by these presents that I Thomas Hunscom of Kittery in the County of Yorke Shipwright haue for the Consideration of Eight pounds in Money to me in hand payd by Samuel Spinney of ye Same place, And doe Acknowledge my Self therewith fully Satisfied Contented and payd for ye aboues^d ConSideration haue bargained and Sold and doe by these presents bargain Sell Enfeoff Alenat and Confirm unto the Said Samuel Spinney a Certain tract of Land Containing twenty Acres Granted unto me by the Town of Kittery, May the Sixteenth one thousand Six hundred Ninety and four as by the Records of said Town Doth more at Large appear; together with all my Right title and Interest in the Same or that may any ways Accrue unto me the Said Thomas Hunscum by Vertue of s^d Grant aboues^d To haue and to hould the Said twenty Acres of Land unto the only use benefit and behoofe of him the s^d Samuel Spinney his heires Execut^{rs} Administrat^{rs} or Assigns for euermore and that it Shall and may be Lawfull for the said Samuel Spinney or his order to take use Ocupie and possess the Same without any manner of lett or Molestation from me the Said Thomas Hunscum or any under me, the peaceable and quiet possession thereof to Warrant and Maintain against all persons from by or under me/ Witness my hand and Seal this Sixteenth day of March on thousand Six hundred Ninety Six Seuen : 169⅚ Thomas Hunscom (his Seal)

In presents of us
John Woodman
W^m : Godsoe

A true Copie of the origenall Deed Transcribed and Compared April 3^d 1697. p Jos Hamond Regist^r

Book IV, Fol. 106.

[106] Know all men by these presents that I Timothy Dorman of Boxford in the County of Essex in his Majesties Prouince of the Massachusets Bay in New England husbandman for and in Consideration of a valluable Sum of money in hand payd to my full Satisfaction receiued of Ephraim Dorman, Sen[r], of Topsfield in the County aboues[d] haue giuen granted bargained and Sold, alienated Enfeoffed and confirmed & by these presents doe giue grant bargain Sell Alienate infeoff and confirm unto the Said Ephraim Dorman Sen[r] his heires Execut[rs] Administrat[rs] & Assigns foreuer a certain parcel or quantetie of Land Situate lying and being beyond Wells in the Prouince of Maine in New England at a place called Coxhall Now called Swansfield Containing by Estimation fiue hundred Acres be it more or less which is part of that Tract of land of Six Miles square which M[r] Halakenden Symonds formerly purchased of Lieu[t] Sanders Sen[r] and John Bush and Peter Turbut, who purchased y[e] s[d] land of the Indian Sogamore Called Sosowon and was Confirmed as by writing will appear by s[d] Sagamores onely Son Called ffluellin and by the testimonies of Seuerall Indians as well as English, which Land by this writing is bounded as followeth to wit bounded by Lieu[t] Thomas Bakers land towards y[e] South and bounded by Caporpus Riuer Alias Mousum Riuer towards y[e] West and the east end bounded towards Sawco Riuer/ And from y[e] Southerly Side to y[e] Northerly Side forty fiue Rods in breadth all along from end to end lying Six Miles in Length, All which fiue hundred Acres afores[d] I the Said Timothy Dorman bought of M[r] Harlakenden Symonds as will appear by Record under his hand/ All the aboues[d] fiue hundred Acres as it is bounded I the said Timothy Dorman doe Acknowledge I haue bargained for and Sold and made ouer to y[e] s[d] Dorman with all y[e] trees Rocks mines Swamps upland and Meadow ponds and water Courses and whateuer doth properly belong to the Said land with all y[e] priuiledges and Appertenances

belonging thereunto Contained in ye length and breadth aboue mentioned: To haue and to hold and peaceably to injoy without any let hinderance Molestation deniall or disturbance And I the aboues^d Timothy Dorman Doe ingage to Defend it from any lawfully laying Claim to all or any part of the aboues^d premises from by or under me or any other pson whatsoeuer/ And to ye true peformance hereof I doe bind my Selfe my heires Execut^{rs} Administrat^{rs} & Assigns to y^e s^d Ephraim Dorman his heires Executers Administrat^{rs} & Assigns for euer In witness whereof I haue hereunto Set my hand and Seal this fifth of January one thousand Six hundred and Ninety Six or Seuen

Signed Sealed and deliuered Timothy Dorman ($_{seal}^{his}$)
in the presents of us . Essex ss Timothy Dorman psonally appeared this 15° January 169$\frac{6}{7}$ before me the Subscrib^r being one of his Majesties Justices for s^d County, & Acknowledged this aboue written Instrument to be his Act and Deed.   Jonathan Corwin

Witnesses
Thomas Baker
Ephraim Dorman Senr
Mary Dorman Junr

A true Copie of the origenall Deed transcribed and Compared this 12° of April : 1697 p Jos Hamond Regist^r

To all Xten people to whom this present writing Shall Come, know yee that whereas Mr John Cutt of Portsm^o Sometime President in ye Prouince of New Hampsh^r Deceased, did in his lifetime purchase of ffrancis Morgan and Sarah his wife one hundred and ten Acres of Land lying and being Spruce Creek adjoyning to Goose Coue and thence down to Marsh Coue as may at large appear by Deed of Sale under s^d Morgan and his s^d wifes hand bearing Date ye twenty Second of April one thousand Six hundred Sixty

Book IV, Fol. 106.

and fiue As alsoe fourteen Acres more purchased of s^d Morgan and Sarah his wife by said Cutt Neare Adjoyning to ye afores^d Land as will alsoe at large appear by Deed of Sale under their hands bearing Date the twentith of June one thousand Six hundred Sixty & eight As alsoe thirty Acres of land adjoyning to ye Same tract purchased by ye s^d Cutt of one Ephraim Lyn as will appear by Deed of Sale under s^d Lyns hand bearing Date the thirtieth day of March one thousand Six hundred Sixty and Eight/ Now Know all persons Concerned that I Samuel Cutt Suruiuing heir to the aboues^d John Cutt Deceased for the Consideration of fliftie pounds as money in hand payd and Secured to be payd unto me ye s^d Samuel Cutt, the receipt whereof I doe hereby Acknowledge and my Selfe to be fully Satisfyd contented and payd and of euery part and penny thereof doe by this presents Exonerate Acquit and Discharge Elihue Gunnison of Kittery in the Prouince of Main and his heires for euer haue bargained and Sold & by this presents doe bargain Sell Alienate and make ouer unto the said Elihue Gunnison his heires and Assigns for euer, to Say all & euery of the before mentioned tracts of Land together with all ye priuiledges and appurtenances whatsoeuer thereto belonging or in any ways appertaining with all timber trees woods and underwoods &^c in as full large and ample manner as my s^d father had them by Vertue of s^d Deed aforementioned. To haue and to hould all ye before mentioned lands & euery part thereof with all ye benefits and priuiledges thereunto belonging or in any ways appertaining unto him ye s^d Gunnison his heirs Execut^rs Administrat^rs and Assigns for euer without the least let hinderance Interuption of me ye s^d Samuel Cutt my heires Execut^rs or Administrat^rs &^c or any from by or under me them or any of them or any other pson or psons whatsoeuer Claming any Right title or Interest to all or any part of the aboue bargained and Sould Lands &^c either from my Selfe my heires Execut^rs and administrat[rs] and from all manner of psons Claiming any Right or Interest from by or by vertue of Right from my Deceased father John Cutt afores[d] by any manner of ways whatsoeuer/ And alsoe I doe hereby for euer Acquit and Discharge the s[d] Elihue Gunnison his heires Execut[rs] Administrat[rs] and that for euer from all Debts dues and Demands whatsoeuer due, owing or belonging to the Estate of my s[d] Deceased father from y[e] begining of y[e] world to y[e] Date hereof/ for y[e] true performance of all and euery part and pticular in this writing contained I haue hereto Set my hand and Seal, this fifteenth day of June 1695   Sam[ll] Cutt (his Seal)

Signed Seled & deliuered   Portsm[o] New Hampshiere. June
   in presents of   19th 1695 M[r] Sam[ll] Cutt came
   John Pickerin   and Acknowledged the aboue
   Sam[ll] Penhallow   Instrum[t] to be his free Act and
                            Deed before me
                            Geo. Jaffray Jus[t] of peace

A true Copie of the originall Deed of Sale Transcribed & compared this 12. day of Aprill : 1697.

                          p Jos Hamond Regist[r]

[107] This Indenture made the. 11. day of June in the year of our Lord one thousand Six hundred Eightie and three, between Elihue Gunnison of the Town of Kittery in the Prouince of Maine & John Pickerin of the Town of Portsm[o] in the Prouince of New Hampshier on the other party witnesseth that y[e] Said Elihue Gunnison for and in consideration of y[e] full and Just Sum of one hundred pounds in money and other goods in hand payd by the s[d] John Pickerin, the receit whereof the s[d] Gunnison doth hereby acknowledg and himselfe to be fully Satisfied content and payd and of euery part parcell and penny thereof doth cleerly acquit and discharge y[e] s[d] John Pickerin his heires

and Assigns and for Diuers other good causes and considerations him yᵉ sᵈ Elihue Gunnison thereunto mouing hath giuen granted bargained and Sold and by this presents doth giue grant bargain and confirm unto the sᵈ John Pickerin his heirs Execut⁽ʳˢ⁾ Administrat⁽ʳˢ⁾ and Assigns all that dwelling house and barn with all yᵉ Neck of land thereunto belonging where the sᵈ Gunnison liueth, in the Town of Kittery in yᵉ Prouince of Maine aboue said which house and barn & land Standeth and Lyeth at yᵉ entring in of Spruce Creek Soe called and known by that name, and lyeth on yᵉ West or Norwest Side of yᵉ entring of sᵈ Creek/ together with four Acres of land up the Creek next Adjoyning to a parcel of land of Ephraim Crockets, which four Acres I bought of William Adams/ Excepting out of all yᵉ land onely ten Acres or thereabout Adjoyning to yᵉ house where Mʳ Cowel now liueth And Adjoyning to ffrancis Trickies Land/ to haue and to hold yᵉ before hereby granted and bargained premises with all the priuiledges and appertens thereunto belonging or any ways appertaining, with all the trees woods underwoods Corn Standing growing and lying excepting onely yᵉ ten Acres or thereabout aboue excepted unto yᵉ sᵈ John Pickerin his heires and Assigns Executers or Administrat⁽ʳˢ⁾, to haue hold and injoy from yᵉ day of yᵉ Date hereof and thence forward: untill yᵉ full end and Term of Ninety nine years be computed completed and ended to be to yᵉ soll use benefit and behofe of yᵉ sᵈ John Pickerin his heirs Execut⁽ʳˢ⁾ Administra⁽ʳˢ⁾ or Assigns during yᵉ holl time or term of Ninety nine years as aboues⁽ᵈ⁾ without yᵉ lawfull let Sute or Interuption of him yᵉ sᵈ Elihue Gunnison his heires Execut⁽ʳˢ⁾ Administra⁽ʳˢ⁾ or Assigns free and Cleare from all and all manner of Gifts grants bargains Morgages Sales or any other incombrance whatsoeuer Suffered or done by them or either of them/ Prouided alwayes and it is Neuertheless agreed and Concluded by and between saied parties to this presence and it is the true intent and meaning thereof, that if the said Gunnison his heirs Execut[rs] Administrat[rs] or Assigns or either of them Shall well and truly pay or cause to be payd unto the s[d] Pickerin his heires Execut[rs] Administrat[rs] or Assigns or any of them at y[e] now dwelling house of y[e] s[d] John Pickerin in Portsmouth aboues[d] the full and intier Sum of one hundred pounds in good Sound fish and other goods at y[e] price as can by for fish at price Currant, at or before y[e] last day of July which will be in y[e] year of our Lord one thousand Six hundred Eighty and Eight, that then this present Indenture bargain and grant and euery Claus and article therein contained Shall Seace Determine and be utterly voyd and of none effect to all intents and purposes whatsoeuer, Any thing in this presents Contained to y[e] contrary notwithstanding/ otherwise to be in full power and force/ In confirmation of all y[e] aboue written I y[e] s[d] Elihue Gunnison haue put to my hand and Seal the day and year first aboue written.

Signed Sealed and deliuered Elihue Gunnison (his Seal)
 In the presents of us Elihue Gunnison came and Ac-
 Mary Stanyan knowledged this Instrum[t] to be
 the marke of his Act and Deed this. 12 day
 Sarah ◯ Reed of June 1683 before me
      ffrancis Hooke Just : pea

A true Copie of the origenall Instrument Transcribed and Compared this 20 of Aprill. 1697. p Jos Hammond Regist[r]

This presents Wittnesseth that I John Pickerin Sen[r], of Portsm[o] in the Prouince of New Hampshiere doe hereby Acknowledge to haue Receiued of M[r] Elihue Gunnison of Kittery in the Prouince of Maine, full Satisfaction for all the housing & Lands mentioned in y[e] Indenture or Morgage Contained on y[e] other Side this paper and haue and doe by this presents for euer, both for my Selfe my heires Execut[rs] and Administrat[rs], Quitt all and all manner of Claim and Claims and Demands to the whole Estate within mentioned

BOOK IV, FOL. 107.

Pickerin to
Gunnison

And that it is and Shall remain Clerely holly & absolutely the said Gunnisons as it was before the making the within Deed to my Selfe and furthermore I doe by these presents Acquit and discharge the s⁴ Gunnison his heirs and Execut⁽ʳˢ⁾ &ᶜ of and from all and all manner of Debts Dews and Demands whether by bill book or Accounts or any other way or means whatsoeuer due to me from the beginning of the world to yᵉ Date hereof, he yᵉ s⁴ Gunnison Discharging me alsoe ffor Confirmation hereof I haue hereto Set my hand and Seale this. 2ᵈ day of Apr¹¹ one thousand Six hundred Ninety & Seuen.

Signed Sealed & deliuered   John Pickerin (his seale)
   In presents of us   Prouince New Hampshiere/ John
          his   Pickerin Senʳ Came and Ac-
Christifer C K Keniston knowledged the aboue Dis-
      marke   charge and Acquittance to be
   John Pickerin Junⁱʳ   his ffree Act and Deed, this
                           Second day of April : 1697 :
                           before me John Hinckes
                                    President.

A true Copie of the origenall Discharge or Acquittance Transcribed and Compared this 20ᵒ of Apr¹¹ 1697.

                         p Jos Ham̄ond Registʳ

To all Christian People to whome this present Deed of Sale Shall Come, I Joseph Banks of Yorke in the County of Yorke in the Prouince of the Massachusets Bay in New-England Send Greeting/ Know yee that for and in Consideration of yᵉ Sum of twelue pounds Currant money of New England to me in hand well and truly payd all and before the Ensealing and deliuery of these presents by Peter Nowel

BOOK IV, FOL. 107, 108.

Joseph Banks
to
Peter Nowell

of Salem in ye County of Essex in ye Prouince afores^d Blacksmith, the receipt whereof I doe by these presents Acknowledge, and my Selfe therewith to be fully Satisfied contented and pay'd and thereof and of and from euery part and parcell thereof, for me the s^d Joseph Banks my heires Execut^rs Administrat^rs and Assigns doe Exonerate Acquit and fully discharge him the s^d Peter Nowell his heires Execut^rs Administrat^rs and Assigns by these presents for euer I the s^d Joseph Banks haue giuen granted bargained sold Aliened Enfeoffed and Confirmed and by these presents doe for me, my heires Execut^rs Administrat^rs and Assignes, fully freely and absolutely giue, grant, bargain Sell Alien Enfeoff Conney and Confirm unto him the Said Peter Nowell his heires Executors Administrat^rs and Assigns, all that my piece or parcell of Land Lying & being Scituate in the Township of York aboues^d in the Prouince aboues^d by Estimation ten Acres more or less Butted and bounded by York Riuer on ye Southwest, by ye Land Daniel Dill on ye Northwest, by the highway on ye Northeast, And by the land of Henry Lampril on ye Southeast, or however otherwise bounded or reputed to be bounded, together with all ye profits priuiledges and Appurtenances to ye s^d land belonging or in any wise appurtaining/ To haue & to hold the s^d piece or parcel of land With all the Right, title Interest Claim and demand which I the s^d Joseph Banks now haue or in time past haue had, or which I my heires Execut^rs Administrat^rs or Assigns in time to Come may might Should or in any wise ought to haue off in or to [108] the aboue granted premises or any part thereof, to him the s^d Peter Nowell his heires and Assignes, And to ye Sole and proper use benefit & behoofe of him his heires and Assignes for euer more/ And I ye s^d Joseph Banks for me my heires Execut^rs Administrat^rs and Assignes doe Couenant promise and grant to and with him the s^d Peter Nowell his heires Execut^rs and Assignes, that at and before yᵉ Ensealing and Deliuery hereof I am yᵉ true Right and proper owner of yᵉ aboue granted premises & their Appurtenances And that I haue in my Selfe full power good Right and Lawfull Authoritie the same to grant and Confirm unto him yᵉ sᵈ Peter Nowell his heires & Assignes as aforesᵈ/ And that yᵉ Same and euery part thereof is free & clear Acquitted and discharged of and from all former and other gifts grants bargains Sales leases Mortgages titles troubles Acts Alienations and Incumbrances whatsoeuer/ And that it shall and may be lawfull to and for yᵉ sᵈ Peter Nowell his heires and Assignes yᵉ aforesᵈ premises and euery part thereof, from time to time and at all times foreuer hereafter, to haue hould use improue ocupie possess and Enjoy, Lawfully peaceably and Quietly without any lawfull lett deniall hinderance Molestation and Disturbance of or by me or any other pson or psons from by or under me or my procurement And that yᵉ Sale hereof and euery part thereof against my Selfe my heires Execut^rs Administrat^rs and Assignes and against all other psons whatsoeuer lawfully claiming and Demanding yᵉ Same or any part thereof, I will for euer Saue harmless warrant and Defend by these presents And that I my heires Execut^rs Administrat^rs and Assignes Shall and will make perform and Execute Such other further lawfull and Reasonable Act or Acts thing or things as in law or Equity can be deuised or required for the better confirming and more Sure making of yᵉ premises, unto yᵉ sᵈ Peter Nowell his heires Execut^rs Administrat^rs or Assigns according tó yᵉ laws of this Prouince In witness whereof I yᵉ sᵈ Joseph Banks haue hereunto put my hand and Seal this Eighteenth day of ffebruary in the year of our Lord one

Banks to Nowell

Book IV, Fol. 108.

thousand Six hundred Ninety and four fiue Annoq, Regni Rx
Ræ Guilielmi Mariæ Angliæ Scotiæ &^{c} Se^{mo}
Signed Sealed and deliuered　　　Joseph Banks ($^{his}_{Seal}$)
　In presents of us—　Joseph Banks came and Acknowl-
　John Hancock　　　　edged this Instrum^t to be his
　Lewes Bane　　　　　Act and Deed this 14 Octob^r
　Abrā Preble　　　　　1695 Before me
　　　　　　　　Samuel Donnell Justis of y^e peace
A true Copie of y^e origenall Deed of Sale Transcribed
and Compared this. 20th of April. 1697
　　　　　　　　　　　p Jos Hamond Regist^r

To all christian People to whome this present Deed of
Sale Shall come/ I Richard Coman of Salem in the County
of Essex in the Prouince of the Massachusets Bay in New
England Tayler Send Greeting/ Know yee, that for and in
ye consideration of ye full and Just Sum of twenty pounds
Currant Money of New England to me in hand well and
truly payd by Peter Nowell of York in the County of York
in ye Prouince afores^d Blacksmith at and before ye Ensealing
and deliuery of these presents, whereof and from euery part
whereof I the s^d Richard Coman haue discharged and Acquitted ye s^d Peter Nowell himselfe his heires Exec^{rs} Admin^{rs}
& Assigns, as Acknowledging my Selfe herewith to be fully
Satisfied contented and payd, I Richard Coman aboues^d haue
giuen granted bargained Sold Aliened Enfeoffed and Confirmed, And by these presents doe for me my Selfe my heires
Exec^{rs} Admin^{rs} and Assignes giue grant bargain Sell Alien
Enfeoff conuey and confirm unto ye s^d Peter Nowell his
heires Exec^{rs} Admin^{rs} and Assignes A certain piece or par-
cell of Land lying and being Scituate in the Township of
York formerly the Prouince of Maine now in ye County of
York in the Prouince of the Massachusets Bay, which par-

Book IV, Fol. 108.

cel of land being by Estimation ten Acres more or less is butted and bounded on the Southwest Side by York Riuer,
Coman
to
Nowell
on ye Southeast by the land of Mary ffrethee Alias Blacklidge, Just aboue Bass Coue, on ye Northeast by the high way going up to Scotland, on ye Northwest by the land of Peter Nowell, or howeuer otherwise bounded or reputed to be bounded/ Together with all house timber Stones, and all ye Rights Titles Priuiledges and appurtenances thereunto belonging or in any wise appurtaining, To him ye s^d Peter Nowell his heires and Assigns, And to his and their Sole and proper use benefit and behoof for euermore, and that I ye s^d Richard Coman at and before the Ensealing of these presents am ye Sole and lawfull owner and proprietour of ye aboue granted and Demised premises, And that I haue in my Selfe good Right full power and lawfull Authority to Alien and dispose these premises as aboue, and doe Couenant and Engage that it shall and may be lawfull for ye s^d Peter Nowell his heires Exec^{rs} Admin^{rs} and Assignes from henseforth and for euer hereafter the aboues^d premises To haue and to hold use Improue ocupie possess and enjoy lawfully peaceably Quietly, without any let hinderance Molestation or disturbance from me my heires Exec^{rs} Admin^{rs} or Assignes or from any other pson or psons by from or under me or my procurement and that I will Defend and maintaine ye premises from all psons whatsoeuer lawfully Demanding or Claiming any right or title thereunto and that I will further confirm ye premises to ye s^d Peter Nowell his heires Exec^{rs} & Assignes by all Such further lawfull and Reasonable Act or Acts thing or things as in Law or Equity can be Deuised or required for the more Sure making ouer ye aboue granted premises according to ye Laws of this Prouince/ In Witness whereof I ye s^d Richd Coman haue hereunto put my hand and Seale this fourteenth day of October In ye year of our Lord one thousand Six hundred Ninety and fiue. Annoq,

Regni Regis Guilielmi Tertii Angliæ Scotiæ ffranciæ & Hiberniæ Septimo
Signed Sealed and deliuered
In presents of us —
John Hancock
Matthew Austin
Joseph Banks

Richard R Coman (his Seal)
his mark

Richard Coman aboues^d came and Acknowledged this Instrum^t to be his Act Deed this 14 Octob^r 1695 before me Samuel Donnell
Justis of ye peace

A true Copie of ye origenall Deed of Sale Transcribed and Compared Apr^{ll} 22 : 1697 p Jos Hamond Regist^r

[109] To all Christian People to whom this present Deed of Sale Shall come/ Siluanus Nock of Douer in the prouince New Hampshiere, Sends Greeting/ Now Know yee that I ye aforementioned Siluanus Nock for Diuers good Causes me thereunto mouing more Especially for and in Consideration of the Sum of fiue & twenty pounds of lawfull money of New England to me in hand payd by Nathan Lord of Barwick in ye County of York in ye Prouince of ye Massachusets Bay in New England the receipt whereof I acknowledge and of euery part and pcell thereof and therewith fully Satisfied Contented and payd, haue giuen granted Bargained Sold Aliened Enfeoffed and Confirmed And doe by these presents for me my heires Execut^{rs} Admin^{rs} and Assignes freely clearly and absolutely giue Grant bargain Sell Alien Enfeoff and Confirm unto him ye s^d Nathan Lord his heires and Assignes for euer, a certain piece or parcell of Land which was giuen to me by my father in law James Emery as at large aypears by a Deed of Gift und^r his hand and Seal bearing date ye Second day of March one thousand Six hundred Ninety and four fiue, lying and being in ye Town & County afores^d being butted and bounded as followeth,

Book IV, Fol. 109.

Vidz^t bounded Southerly on ye land of s^d Nathan Lord, Westerly on ye land of John Plaisted and on ye land of Zechariah Emery till you Come to a Small white oak Northerly, which s^d white oak is marked with. **I. E.** on the North Side of ye tree and **S. N.** on the South Side and Soe to run on ye North Side by Seuerall marked trees of ye Same mark to an Ash tree And then to run Southeast by Seuerall marked trees till you come to ye Rockie hill to a white oak marked And then to run from that s^d white oak on a South

Siluenus Nocks Deed to Nath Lord

west line twenty Rods and Soe to run to a Marked tree which is s^d Nathan Lords bound marke, Containing Eighteen Acres more or less To haue and to hold the s^d piece or parcell of land with all ye priuiledges & appertenances thereto belonging or in any wise Appertaining to him ye Said Nathan Lord his heires Execut^{rs} Administrat^{rs} and Assignes for euer And to his and their own proper use benefit and behoofe/ And I the s^d Siluanus Nock doe Couenant and promise and Grand to and with ye said Nathan Lord his heires Execut^{rs} Admin^{rs} and Assignes that at and before ye Ensealing and Deliuery thereof I am ye true Right and proper owner of ye aboue premises and ye appertenances And that I haue in my Selfe good Right full power and lawfull authority ye Same to Sell and dispose off And that ye Same and euery part thereof is free and cleare acquitted Exonerated and Discharged of and from all and all manner of former Gifts Grants Mortgages Alienations power of thirds and all other Incombrances whatsoeuer/ And that it Shall and may be lawfull for him ye s^d Lord his heires &^c the aboue premises and euery part thereof to haue hold use improue ocupie possess & enjoy fully peaceably and quietly without any Molestation deniall let hinderance or disturbance of or by me or any other pson or psons from by or under me or by my procurement: And that ye Sale thereof against my Selfe my heires and Assigns and against all other psons

Book IV, Fol. 109.

whatsoeuer lawfully claiming ye Same or any part thereof I will for euer Saue harmless Warrant and Defend by these presents/ In witness wherof I haue hereunto Set my hand and Seal this twentieth day of Aprill in ye year of our Lord one thousand Six hundred Ninety and Seuen And in ye Ninth year of ye Reign of our Soueraign Lord William ye third of England Scotland ffrance and Ireland, King Defend^r of ye ffaith :   Siluanus Nock (his Seal)
Signed Sealed and Deliuered

    In ye presents of us—   Siluanus Nock Acknowledged
    Jos Hamond   this Instrum^t aboue written
    Jos. Hamond Junr   this. 6. day of May 1697. to
                                 be his Act and Deed, before
                                 me Charles ffrost Just : peace

Elizabeth Nock ye wife of Siluanus Nock personally appearing this Sixth day of May. 1697. deliuered up her Right of Dowery to ye aboue granted premises before me.
                             Charles ffrost Just : peace

A true Copie of ye origenall Deed of Sale : Transcribed & compared : May : ye 8° 1697   p Jos Hamond Regist^r

To all Christian People to whome this Publique Instrument of bill of Sale Shall come or may concern/ Captⁿ Ezekiel Rogers Gent : of Ipswich in the County of Essex In ye Prouince of ye Massachusets Bay in New England In America Sendeth Greeting in our Lord God Euerlasting Know yee that ye said Ezekiel Rogers for and in consideration of the Sum of one hundred and thirtie pounds to him ye s^d Rogers in hand payd and Secured to be payd in good Currant Money of New England by Jeremiah Moulton of York in the Prouince of Mayn within their Majesties Teritory and Dominion of New England Yeoman, payd to ye Satisfaction of s^d Rogers, wherewith and of euery part thereof he

BOOK IV, FOL. 109.

doth Acknowledge himselfe fully Satisfied contented and payd, doe by these presents Giue Grant, Bargain, Sell Aliene Assign Set ouer and confirm unto y⁰ said Mʳ Jeremiah Moulton, his heires Execut⁽ʳˢ⁾ Administrat⁽ʳˢ⁾ and Assigns for euer haue Giuen Granted bargained Sold Enfeoffed and Confirmed from him y⁰ Said Rogers his heires Execut⁽ʳˢ⁾ Administrat⁽ʳˢ⁾ and Assigns for euer, To haue and to hold, a certain dwelling house Scituate & being in the Town of York in y⁰ Prouince of Maine, with a pcell of Land adjoyn-

Capᵗⁿ Rogʳˢ Deed of Sale to Jeremiah Moulton

ing thereunto ffronting to Yorke Riuer, together with all out houses Barnes Stables Orchards Arable Land & Pasturage Comonages Priuiledges Church Priuiledges Imunities high wayes Waterwayes Wood under Wood and all other the Appurtenances thereunto belonging or any wayes Appertaining, bounded by sᵈ Riuer South, and by y⁰ Land of Mʳ Eliakim Hutchesons West: and John Brauns Northerly, which Land or house Lot Contains ten Acres be it more or less, within y⁰ sᵈ bounds And likewise a Pasture of ten Acres more or less being a Town Grant and three Ares of Marsh with the Creek thatch and Appertenances, together with Eight Acres of upland Joyning to y⁰ sᵈ Pasture, that being onely the Town Grant, part of which Land herein Mentioned. is Expressed in two Deeds made by Mʳ Edward Rishworth, one bearing Date y⁰ 27 day of March. 1675. the other the. 24. day of ffebruary. 1680—with all other priuiledges & Appurtenances to aboue mentioned houseing land and Priuiledges belonging, As well not Mentioned as Mentioned, To haue and to hold, the aboue Land and premˢ to him y⁰ sᵈ Jeremiah Moulton his heires Execut⁽ʳˢ⁾ Administrat⁽ʳˢ⁾ and Assigns for euer, And to his and their Execut⁽ʳˢ⁾ Administrat⁽ʳˢ⁾ and Assigns for euer, and to his and their own proper use benefit and behoofe to haue hold use ocupie Possess and Quietly to enjoy y⁰ Same and euery part thereof without let hinderance or Molestation of him sᵈ Ezekiel Rogers or his

heires Execut[rs] Administrat[rs] or Assigns or any other pson or psons whatsoeuer Laying Lawfull Claim thereunto or any part thereof, or at any time hereafter, and that at Ensealing hereof hath in himself full power and absolute Right to y[e] Land and Premises in this Deed Mentioned and that it is free and Cleare from all former Gifts grants Bargains Sales Mortgages Dowries Joyntures and from all or any Incombrances whatsoeuer or howsoeuer And ffurther Confirmation Shall and will at any time or times giue and make under hand and Seal Instrument or Instruments to Establish and Confirm y[e] within Mentioned Demised premises Excepting and Reseruing thirtie foot broad and ffortie foot Long out of y[e] aboue Demised Premises formerly Sold unto M[r] Joseph Pennuwell of York Lying on y[e] backside of y[e] s[d] Homesteed by the highway/ In Testimong whereof [110] he hath hereunto Set his hand and Seal/ Dated in York in the Prouince of Maine in New England this twenty third of July Anno Domini One thousand Six hundred Ninetie and four, Annoq, Regni Regis & Reginæ Guilielmi & Mariæ Angliæ &[c] Sexto
Signed Sealed and Deliuered   Ezekiel Rogers (his Seale)
  In presents of us—   This Instrument Cap[tn] Ezekiel Rog-
  James Plaisteed   ers acknowledged to be his Act
  John Hancock   and Deed before me Samuel Don-
                            nel Esq[r] one of his Majesties
                            Iustices of the Peace in y[e] County
                            of York This 16th August 1694—
                                   Samuel Donnel
  A true Copie of the origenall Deed of Sale Transcribed and Compared, here Entered upon Record this. 29° Iune. 1697   p Jos Hamond Regist[r]

Know all men by these presents that I Walter Allen of Barwick in y[e] County of York in New England, doe for my

Book IV, Fol. 110.

<small>Walter
Allins
Receipt</small>
Selfe Ayres Execut^rs Administrat^rs Acquit Exonerate & Discharge the Administrat^rs and Relict of ye Estate of late Deceased Thomas Holmes of ye Same Town and County of all Legasies Dues Debts and Demands from ye Said Estate, In Consideration of hauing and Receiuing of and from s^d Estate three young Cattell of two years old and a pcell of Bills Due to s^d Holmes Deceased the which I y^e Said Walter Allen doe Acknowledge to Receiue as a full Portion for my wife Mary y^e Daughter of Said Holmes Deceased In witness whereof I haue Set to my hand and Seal this twentie & ffifth day of ffebruary. 169$\frac{6}{7}$ and In y^e Seuenth year of William the Second ouer England & Cet. King/   Walter Allin. (his Seal)
Signed Sealed & Deliuered
  in presents of us —
John Plaisted
Job Burnum
  A true Copie of the origenal Receipt or Acquittance Transcribed and Compared. this. 29° June 1697
                     p Jos Hamond Regist^r

  Know all men by these presents, that I John Seward of Portsmouth in the Prouince of New-Hampshiere Shipwright with ye free consent of Ann my wife, haue for and in Consideration of thirty pounds of Lawfull money of New England to me in hand paid by James ffernald of Kittery in ye County of York Husbandman, the receipt thereof I doe acknowledge and my Selfe therewith Satisfied contented and paid and euery Parcell thereof, and doe Acquit the s^d James ffernald for ye Same and euery Part thereof, And haue Giuen granted bargained and Sold Aliened Enfeoffed and confirmed and by these presence doth Bargain and Sell Alien Enfeoffe and confirm unto the s^d James ffernald, all that Tract of Land

Situate lying and being in ye Town of Kittery in ye County of York at a place called ye Great Cone below ye boyling Rock And is bounded with ye Great Cone Eastward forty pole in breadth North and South And by ye Land of John ffernald on ye South and with ye Lands of ye late Stephen Paul on ye North, in length Eighty pole into ye woods on an East line Containing Twenty Acres and is that Tract of Land which was Granted John Simmons by the Town of Kittery in ye year 1661. July ye 17 : as by the Records doth more at large appear and alsoe all wayes paths passages trees woods and under woods Easments Comoditie and the Appttenances whatsoeuer in any wise appertaining thereunto, To have and to Hold the s^d Tract of Land and euery Part and Parcell thereof unto ye s^d James ffernald his heires and Assigns for euer, the s^d John Seward doth for himselfe his heires Execut^rs Administrat^rs Couenant with ye s^d James ffernald his heires Execut^rs Administrat^rs or Assigns that he ye s^d John Seward is the true and proper owner of ye aboue mentioned land at ye time of Signing and Sealing of these presents And that ye Same is ffree from all manner of Encombrances as Gifts Ioyntures Sales Mortgages or Dowries and that it Shall and may be Lawfull for ye s^d James ffernald or any other under him to take possess use & Ocupie ye Same and euery Part thereof to ye onely use benefit and behoofe of him ye s^d Iames ffernald his heires and Assigns for euer, As alsoe ye Peaceable and quiet Possession thereof to Warrant and Maintain against all manner of psons whatsoeuer Lawfully laying Claim thereunto ye Kings Matie the King of England and his Lawfull Successors only Excepted/ Witness my hand and Seal this Senenteenth day of September

Jno Sewards Deed to Ja ffernald

Book IV, Fol. 110, 111.

one thousand Six hundred Ninety and Seuen and in y⁰ Ninth
year of his Majesty Reign William the third.
Signed Sealed and deliuered   John Sewar ($_{Seal}^{his}$)
   In the presents of us — John Seward appeared before me
   John Spinney   and Acknowledged this In-
   Thomas Spinney   strum^t to be his Act and Deed
   James Spinney   witness my hand y^e 18th of Sep-
                             temb^r 1697.
                     Job Alcock Jus^t pes
                      The mark of

               Agnes   Sewer ($_{Seal}^{her}$)

Ann Seward appeared before me and
   ffreely gaue up her Right of Dowry
   in y^e aboue tract of Land/ Witness
   my hand This 18th of Septemb^r 1697
          Job Alcock Jus : pes

   [111]   Memorandum that Peaceable and Quiet Possession
            was giuen by Mr John Seward of Portsmouth
Possession
giuen   unto ye within Mentioned James ffernald of Kit-
            tery of ye Lands within Mentioned this 17° day
of Septemb^r 1697 in presents of us whose Names are under
written
   John Spinney
   Thomas Spinney
     the Sign of
   John   I F   ffernald

Receiued of Nathaniel Kane thirty one Kintolls & halfe of
Marchata : fish and one piece of Kenten and twelfe thousand
& three hundred foot of March^t boards & Six pounds Seuen
Shillings & Six pence all which I own to haue receiued in
part of Satisfaction for a serten tract of land I haue Sold

BOOK IV, FOL. 111.

him in Spruce Creek at y" head of the Western Creek containing one hundred Acres I say receiu^d p me John Shapleigh which land he is in possession of

<table>
<tr><td>Kittery y° 23 of July 1691</td><td>Mr John Shapleigh owned</td></tr>
<tr><td>Test   her</td><td>this Instrument to be his</td></tr>
<tr><td>Patience P Downing</td><td>Act & Deed to Mr Nathan-</td></tr>
<tr><td>   mark</td><td>iel Kane the 22^d of July:</td></tr>
<tr><td>Sarah Shapleigh</td><td>1693 Before me—</td></tr>
<tr><td></td><td>ffrancis Hooke Jus^t peace</td></tr>
</table>

A true Copie of the origenall Transcribed & compared this third day of Jan^{ry} 169$\frac{7}{8}$—   p Jos Hamond Regist^r

Portsm° May 12th 1691

Mr Shapleigh/ Sr Whereas Nathaniel Keen Stands engaged to y^r Selfe for a Certain tract of land Some time Since purchased; these are to Signifie that I will pay on Demand to you or y^r orders Six pounds Sil[l] and thirtie Shillings as money, prouided you will outset Seuen thousand and half of boards of that Compliment which he yet Stands engaged to you for which you lately promised to comply with/ Noe more at present—I remain y^r ffriend to Serue y^u

                                      Ursula Cutt

1691: June 13 day. Rec^d in part of this Note Six pounds Seuen Shillings and Six pence/ I say Rec^d p me

                                      John Shapleigh

Rec^d In full Satisfaction of the within written Note of Mrs Ursula Cutt upon ye acco^t of Nathaniel Kane Seuen pounds ten Shillings in Money I say receiued p me

                                      John Shapleigh

Kittery 9th of Nouemb^r 1692.

Mr John Shapleigh owned this Instrum^t to be his Act to Mr Kane this 22 of July 1693 Before me

                               ffrancis Hooke Just: Peace.

A true Copie of the origenall: Transcribed and compared this: 3^d of Jan^{ru} 169$\frac{7}{8}$ p Jos Hamond Regist^r

BOOK IV, FOL. 111.

To all Christian people to whome this p'sent Deed of Sale Shall come I Katharine Nanney, Alias Nayler of Boston in the County of Suffolk in the Prouince of the Massachusets Bay in New England Widdow Send Greeting/ Know yee that I ye sd Katharine Nanney als Naylr for and in Consideracon of the Summe of fiue pounds Currant money of New England to be annually payd unto me ye sd Katharine Nanney als Nayler and Secured to be paid by Samuel Wheelwright of Wells in the County of York in the Prouince aforesd Gent, as by a writing or Couenant Obligatory under the hand and Seal of the sd Samuel Wheelwright, reference thereunto being had doth and may more fully appear and for diuers other good consideracons me thereunto moving Have giuen granted bargained Sold Aliened Assigned Set over released and confirmed And by these presents Doe giue grant bargain Sell Alien Assign Set ouer releas and confirme unto ye sd Samuel Wheelwright his heires and Assignes for euer All that Tract of land or ground which my husband Robert Nanney late of Boston deceased bought of Mr Coole containing by Estimacon five hundred Acres (be it more or less) of Upland Meadow and Marsh ground with the Appurtenances lying and being together in Wells aforesd, and is bounded by a Creek which runneth between the sd tract of Land and the land that was giuen by my father John Wheelwright with me in Marriage unto my sd husband Robert Nanney on the one Side and a Spring or Small brook Deviding between ye sd tract of land and the land formerly of Stephen Batson of Wells aforesd of the other Side And likewise Thirty Acres of Marsh ground with the Appurtenances lying and being in Wells aforesd Excepted always out of the land bought of Mr Coole one tract of land being twenty fiue pole in breadth beginning at the Northeast Side of Samuel Austins Land which sd tract of Land was formerly giuen in Exchange to William Hammond/ Alsoe one hundred and fifteen Acres of

Katherine Nanney to Samll Wheelwright

Upland and ten Acres of Marsh with fiftie Acres of Upland more & fiue Acres of Marsh more bought of William Hamond which in all amounts to one hundred Sixty fiue acres of Upland and fifteen Acrs of Marsh lying and being within the precincts of ye Town of Wells afores^d And also two hundred and thirty acres of Upland and twenty Acres of Upland bought by the said Robert Nanney of William Symonds, which s^d land Lyeth in Wells afores^d And likewise all that Land that was in the Possession lately of John Wakefield lying in Wells afores^d between the Land of John Sanders and Mr Coole, together with all and Singul^r the houses buildings Lands Arable and Meadow pasture woods und^r woods and Comon and all other Priuiledges and Appurtenances to them or any of them belonging or in any wise Appurtaining—And also all my Right Title Interest use revertion possession claim and demand to the Same or any part or pcell thereof. To haue and to hold the s^d Land and ground and all other ye premises with their Appurtenances to ye said Samuel Wheelewright his heirs & Assignes for euer to the onely Use and behoofe of the s^d Samuel Wheelwright and of his heirs and Assigns for euer/ And [112] I the said Katharine Nanney a̅ls Nayler for my Selfe my heirs Exec^rs Adm^rs doe Covenant grant and Agree to and with the said Samuel Wheelwright his heirs and Assignes That at all times hereafter upon the reasonable request & Cost and Charges in ye Law of the said Samuel Wheelwright or his Assignes I shall will doe make knowledge and Suffer or cause to be made knowledge done and Suffered all and euery Such reasonable Act and Acts thing and things as the s^d Samuel Wheelwright or his Learned Councel in the Law Shall be reasonably devised or required for ye more & better conveyance and Sure making of the premises aforegranted and their Appurtenances to ye s^d Samuel Wheelwright his heirs and Assigns for euer/ In witnes whereof I y^e said Katharine Nanney a̅ls Nayler haue to this p^{r}sent Deed of

Book IV, Fol. 112.

bargain & Sale Set my hand and Seal this Sixth day of July Anno Domini 1694. and in the Sixth year of the Reign of King William and Queen Mary of England Scotland &c.

Sealed & Deliuered   Katharine ($_{Seal}^{her}$) Nanney.
 In the pres^{ts} of   Boston 6th July. 1694.
 Elizabeth Pearson   Mrs Katharine Nanney with in
 Wm Milborne   Named appeared before me the
           Subsriber and Acknowledged
           this Instrument within written
           to be her Act & Deed/
             Jer: Dumer J. P.

A true Copie of the origenall Deed of Sale Transcribed and Compared this. 20th day of Novemb^r 1697

         p Jos Hamond Regist^r

Richd Cutt to John Morgrage

To all christian people/ Know yee that I Richard Cutt of the town of Kittery in the County of York Gent^l haue giuen granted bargained and Sold Enfeoffed and confirmed, And doe by these presents giue grant bargain and Sell unto my well beloued friend John Mugridg of the Same place Yeoman for the consideration of a Valluable Sum of money to me in hand payd before the Sealing of these presents — all that Tract of Land lying and being Cituate in the township of Kittery known by the name of spruce Creek And is that tract of Land whereon the s^d Mugridg doth now dwell and is bounded with Spruce Creek it Selfe and broad Coue and the Mill Creek And the lands of Mr William Scriuen as alsoe the Lands of the late Michael Endle, now in the possession of the s^d John Mugridg To have and to hold all the aboue said tract of land unto the s^d John Mugridg to him and his heires and Assigns for euer And furthermore I the s^d Richard Cutt my heirs Executors and Administrat^{rs} doe couenant with y^e

s^d John Mugridg his heirs Execut^rs or Administrat^rs that the aboue s^d land is cleare and ffree from all incumbrances by me the s^d Cutt made or Suffered to be done in any respect And that I am the true and proper owner thereof and that I am Lawfully Seized of the Same and of euery part and parcell thereof And further I the s^d Richard Cutt aboues^d doe couenant with ye s^d John Mugridg his heirs or Assignes the Peaceable and quiet Possession thereof to maintain against all psons laying lawfull Claim thereunto the Kings Majestie the King of England his heirs Excepted And that it Shall and may be lawfull for the said John Mugridg to take use ocupie and Possess all and euery part and parcell of the aboue giuen and granted premises to his own proper use and his heirs for euer/ Witness my hand and Seal this twenty eighth day of June one thousand Six hundred Ninety and fiue And in the Seuenth year of his Majesties Reign William the third King of England Scotland ffrance and Ireland Defend^r of the ffaith &^c   Richard Cutt (his Seal)

Signed Sealed and deliuered   The 24th January 169¾ — then
  in the presents of us —   Mr Richard Cutt came and
  William Screuen   acknowledged this Instru-
  ffrancis Nicolle   ment to be his Act and
  Wm Godsoe   Deed before me.
                      Wm Pepprell Is pece

A true Copie of the origenall Deed Transcribed and Compared this 6th day of Decemb^r 1697.   p Jos Hamond Regest^r

---

To all christian People to whom these presents Shall come Greeting Know yee that I Thomas Spinney of the Town of Kittery and County of York Yeoman on ye one part, and John Spinney Son of the s^d Thomas Spinney afores^d on the other part Witnesseth that ye s^d Thomas Spinney hath Let and to ffarm

Tho Spinney to his Son John

Book IV, Fol. 112, 113.

Letten and Set ouer unto my Son John Spinney During the Naturall liues of us the s^d Thomas Spinney & Margery my wife, all this my house and land and Stock of Cattle To Say all my land Joyning to my house with the barns outhouses and leantos orchurds Gardens and tooles for husbandry with four Cows two heifers one bull and two oxen and eight Sheep/ the s^d Stock of Cattle to be taken off the place by me ye Said Thomas Spinney at the end of ffiue years, but the Increase to remain [113] on the place for euer Yeelding and paying yearly and euery year for euer during the Naturall liues of the aboues^d Thomas Spinney and his wife aboues^d the one halfe of the whole Produce of the house & land & Stock of Cattle To Say the one halfe of the Corn English and Indian And to plant three Peck of Corn Annually and to pay the one halfe of the butter and cheese that is Produced of the cows and halfe the Increase of the aboues^d cows with halfe the Lambs and Wool of the Sheep and milk for our own use with halfe the Cyder and halfe the ffruit that remains, the one halfe of the Garden Stuff and halfe the Swine that are raised on the plantation and halfe Increase of any horse kind keep on the place, the English grain to be paid in when threshed out And as further consideration of the Premises it is Mutually agreed between both parties that ye s^d Thomas Spinney doth engage to bear the one halfe of the charges of fencing the said lands and to pay the one halfe of the Rates and ye one halfe part of repairing the houseing And to allow ye said John Spinney the benefit of wood for fireing at my land ouer the great Coue Ioyning to my Son Sam^ll Spinneys house lott And that Dureing my Naturall life and my wiues afores^d.

Tho Spinney to his Son John

And in consideration of a conveiance of the aboues^d house and housing and land bearing Date this Instant moneth of March : 1694 made by me the afores^d Thomas Spinney to his Son John Spinney the s^d John Spinney doth Engage to continue with his father

and mother dureing their Naturall liues to be Ayding and Assisting them as Necessity Shall require: And as these Articles aboue doth express/ but if the said John Spinney Shall Se cause to Decline or not perform the Premises herein Mentioned Then it is concluded and agreed by both parties that the s^d Conveyance bearing Date March the 23^{third} 1694 Shall be Null Voyd and of noe Effect/ but if he ye s^d Thomas Spinney doe faile or not Maintaine or withdraw or not perform what he hath promised and Set ouer on his part, to pay or forfit ye Sum of one hundred pounds to the said John Spinney his Son afores^d It is likewise concluded and agreed that if it Should please God that the s^d John Spinney Should Decease that Mary his now wife Shall haue the benefit and Aduantage of the Premises performing that Obligation her husband hath made with her father aboues^d as long as She remains a Widdow/ In confermation hereof both parties haue Set to their hands and Seales this twentieth and third day of March one thousand Six hundred Ninety and four. Thomas Spinney (his Seal)
Signed Sealed and deliuered John Spinney (hhs Seale)
in presents of us. The 9th of July 1698/ Then Thomas
James Spinney Spinney & John Spinney both ap-
Wm Godsoe peared before me & Acknowledged
 this Instrument to be their Act &
 Deed one to ye other/ before me
  Wm Pepperrell. Justis pease
A true Copie of ye origenall Transcribed & Compared. this. 10th July. 1698 – p Jos Hamond Regist^r

Know all men by these presents that I Peter Staple Senr of ye town of Kittery and in the County of York in New England Yeoman haue giuen granted Alienated Enfeofed and Set ouer unto my beloued Son Peter Staple and doe by

Book IV, Fol. 113.

these presents Giue grant alienate and Set ouer unto my beloued Son Peter Staple all my house and land lying in the townShip of Kittery in the County afores^d, being bounded by the Main Riuer and Richard Hilton and Samuel Millerd on the Southeast And on the Northwest with the Lands of Richard Rogers or that called Millard Lott and Soe back into the woods as far as my land goeth to the Northward And Joyning to my house Lott — containing Eighty Acres of Land more or less with all my out housing & barns and Appertenances thereto belonging, Excepting and reseruing unto my Selfe during the Naturall life of me the s^d Peter Staple and my Now wife Elizabeth, the one halfe of my dwelling house And Excepting foreuer out of the Premises two Acres of land ffronting the Main Riuer Next to Richard Rogers/ Alsoe I doe freely giue unto my Said Son the whole Stock of Cattle of all Sorts that I am now Possessed with/ To haue and to hold all the aforesaid housing and lands unto

Peter Staple to his Son Peter

the said Peter Staple to him and to his heirs Lawfully begotten to him and to them and that foreuer Except the afores^d Excepted and reserued out of the Premises/ Always Provided and to be understood that the s^d Peter Staple Junr Shall husband & Manage and Manure the aboues^d giuen and granted Premises at his own Proper cost and charge/ and yeeld and pay or cause to be payd During the Naturall liues of me the s^d Peter Staple and Elizabeth my now wife the one halfe of the Prouce of said house and land, and Stock of Cattle, but in Case that either I the s^d Peter Staple Senr or Elizabeth my wife Shall Decease, then ye s^d Peter Staple to pay but ye one third of the Produce as afores^d/ And at ye Decease of the longest liuer of the two to pay Six head of Neat Cattell at ye age of three or four years old as they Shall appoint or Eighteen pounds in Siluer/ And further I ye Said Peter Staple Senr doe Couenant to and with the s^d Peter Staple Junr that the Premises are ffree of all Incombrances or gifts bargains or Mortgages whatsoeuer by me made And that I am the Proper owner thereof and in Actuall Possession of all the Premises And the Quiet and peaceable Possession thereof to Maintain against all persons Laying Claim thereunto, our Soueraign Lord & Lady Excepted/ Signed Sealed and Deliuered this twentieth day of August one thousand Six hundred Ninety and four And in the Sixth year of their Maj[ties] Reign King William & Queen Mary —

Signed Sealed & Deliuered in the presents of —
Samuel Nellson
the Sign of
Mary Nelson
Ebenezar Wentworth
W[m] Godsoe.

The Sign of Peter P Staple (his Seal)
Peter Staple Sen[r] came and acknowledged this Iustrum[t] to be his Act and Deed unto his Son Peter Staple Jun[r] this. thirteenth day of Sept: 1694 — Before ffrancis Hook of y[e] Councill & Iust: Peace

A true Copie of the origenall Deed of Gift Transcribed and Compared this. 29th of Decemb[r] 1697

p Jos Hamond Regist[r]

[¹↳] Nathan Lord aged 25 yeares and Abraham Lord aged about 23 years. Testifie that about the latter end of June or y[e] beginning of July. 1680. being in Thomas Abbets house, where there was John Green Sen[r] & these Deponants were going out of the s[d] house to their work, the s[d] John Green called them back again and desired them to bear Witness that he gaue his out Lott and y[e] Meadow Joyning to it to his two Grand Children Moses Abbet and John Gillison/ & ffurther these Deponents Say not

Taken upon oath this. 7th day of ffebruary. 1681, before me
John Wincoll Just[ce] of peace

A true Copie of y[e] origenall Transcribed & compared this. 8th day of ffebruary: 169[7] — p Jos Hamond Regist[r]

Book IV, Fol. 114.

To all Christian People to whome this present Deed of Sale Shall come/ I Matthew Austine of York in the County of York in ye Prouince of the Massachusets Bay in New England Send Greeting/ Know yee that for and in consideration of foure and ffourty pounds good and Lawfull money of New England to me in hand well and truly payd at and before ye Ensealing and Deliuery of these pres^{ts} by Daniel Black of York in ye County afores^d, and in ye Prouince afores^d Weauer the receipt whereof I doe hereby Acknowledge and my Selfe therewith to be fully Satisfied contented and payd and thereof and of and from euery part & pcell thereof for me the s^d Mathew Austine my heires Execut^{rs} Administrat^{rs} and Assignes, doe Exonerate Acquit and Discharge him ye s^d Daniel Black his heires Executors Administrat^{rs} and Assignes for euer, I the s^d Mathew Austin haue Giuen Granted Bargained Sold Aliened Enfeoffeed & conveied & confirmed, and by these presents doe for me my heires Execut^{rs} Adminis^{rs} and Assignes fully ffreely and Absolutely Giue, Grant, Bargain, Sell, Aliene, Enfeoffe, conuey & confirm unto him ye said Daniel Black his heires Execut^{rs} Administrat^{rs} and Assignes a Certain piece or parcell of Land lying and being Scituate in ye Township of York in the Prouince afores^d by Estimation three Acres more or less being and lying wthin ffence on the South Side of the high way going down to ye house that was formerly Maj^r John Dauisses of York and is the whole lott within the said ffence, Excepting half an acre belonging to the hovse of Mr John Penwill late of York, And is bounded on the Northwest by the Land of Rowland Young Deceased, Southerly by the Creek comonly called ye Meeting house Creek Esterly with a Small creek or run passing into ye Meeting house Creek and on the Northeast by the highway aboues^d, or howeuer otherwise bounded, together wth the Dwelling house now upon it with all the Stones trees and all other the Priuiledges and

Mathew Austin to Dan · Black

Appurtenances thereunto belonging or in any wise Appertaining — To haue & to hold the s^d house and Land together with all and Singular the Rights, Titles, Priuiledges, Interests, Claims & Demands, which I ye s^d Mathew Austin my heires Execut^{rs} or Assignes, now haue or in time past haue had or in time to come may, Should, or in any wise ought to haue in and to ye aboue granted Premises or any part thereof And alsoe in like manner a certain Lott of woodland lying Connenient for s^d house of Six Acres to be Annexed & layd out unto ye Premises, To him ye s^d Daniel Black his heires and Assignes for euer And to his and their Sole and proper use benefit and behoof, Moreouer I the s^d Mathew Austin doe couenant promise and Grant that at & before the Ensealing and deliuery of these presents I am the true Right and proper owner of the aboue granted premises and their Appurtenances And that I haue in my Selfe good Right, full power, and lawfull Authority the Same to grant and confirm unto ye s^d Daniel Black as aboues^d/ And that ye Same and euery part thereof is free and cleare Acquitted & Discharged of and from all former and other gifts grants bargains Sales leases Morgages Dowers Titles troubles and Incumbrances whatsoeuer And that it Shall and may be Lawfull to & for the s^d Daniel Black his heires Execut^{rs} Adminis^{rs} & Assignes the aboue granted premises and euery part there of from time to time and at all times for euer hereafter to haue & to hold use improue ocupie possess and enjoy Lawfully peaceably Quietly without any lawfull lett hinderance Molestation or disturbance Euiction or Ejection of or by me or any other psons by from or und^r me or my procurment And that ye Sale thereof and euery part thereof I will Maintain against me my heires Execut^{rs} Administrat^{rs} and Assignes and against all other psons whatsoeuer Lawfully Claiming or Demanding the Same or any part thereof And will furthermore make perform and Execute Such other Lawfull and reasonable Act or Acts thing or things as in law or Equitie can be Deused or required for yᵉ better confirming and more sure making ouer of these presents unto yᵉ sᵈ Daniel Black his heires Executʳˢ Administratʳˢ and Assignes According to the Lawes of this Prouince/ In witness whereof I yᵉ sᵈ Mathew Austin with Mary my wife haue hereunto put our hands and Seales this Sixth day of ffebruary in yᵉ year of our Lord one thousand Six hundred Ninety & fiue Six. Annoq Regni Regis Guilielmi Tertii Angliæ Scotiæ ffrantiæ & Hiberniæ, Septimo

Signed Sealed & deliuered   Mathew Austin (ʰⁱˢ Seal)
   In presents of   Mary Austin
   Joseph Ware   her ∕∕∕∕∕ mark (ʰᵉʳ Seal)
   Phillip ⚹ Welch   Mathew Austin abouesᵈ came &
     his mark   Acknowledged this Instrument
   John Hancock   to be his Act and Deed this
                        Sixth of ffebruary 169 before
                        me Samuel Donnell Justis
                        peace and alsoe Mary his wife—

A true Copie of the origenall Deed of Sale Transcribed & compared this 8ᵗʰ of ffebruary : 169⅞
                p Jos Hamond Registʳ

[115] Know all men by these presents that I John Honewell of Middletown in the Collony of Conecticot Brickmaker for yᵉ Sum of ffifteen Shillings in money receiued by me of John Stainford of Ipswich, in the Massachusets Prouince Cordwainer unto full Satisfaction, and for diuers other good causes and considerations me hereunto Especially moning, haue and doe by these presents giue grant bargain Sell Infeoff and confirm, unto yᵉ sᵈ John Stainford his heires Executʳˢ Administratʳˢ and Assignes for euer, a pcell of Land Upland and Meadow Lying and being Scituate at Winter Harbour in the Prouince of Mayn, commonly called by yᵉ

name of Honewells Neck formerly in the Ten^r of Roger Honewell Deceased, containing forty Acres more or less, bounded on ye Southeast by Parkers Neck, on ye Northwest by ye Land of William Chillson, Deceased, called Windmill hill, on ye North-East by ye Sea And on ye Southwest by the flats, together with all & Singul^r the priuiledges and Appurtenances, trees, underwood, ways & comodities thereunto belonging or in any wise Appurtaining whatsoeuer/ To haue and to Hold, to him ye s^d Stainford his heires Execut^{rs} Administrat^{rs} and Assignes for euer, without any let Moles-

tation or disturbance of him the said Honewell

<small>J^{ne} Honewell to John Stainford</small> his heirs Execut^{rs} Admimstrat^{rs} or Assignes for euer/ Moreouer the s^d Honewell hereby Coue-

nanteth that at ye Insealing hereof to the Said Stainford he is Legally Possessed of all ye s^d granted Premises & that he hath Right and Lawfull Authority in his own name to Sell ye Same and that it Shall & may be Lawfull for ye s^d Stainford to use ocupie Possess & enjoy by himself his heirs Execut^{rs} or Assigns, ffree & freely discharged of and from all other and former Gifts grants bargains Sales Morgages Dowries or Incombrances whatsoeuer as his and their good & perfect Estate of Inheritance in ffee Simple without any contradiction Soe as to alter ye Same, by me ye s^d Honewell my heires Execut^{rs} Administrat^{rs} &c^t And ye s^d Honewill his heirs Execut^{rs} Admin^{rs} & Assigns by these pres^{ts} shall saue & keep harmless the s^d Stainford his heirs Execut^{rs} &c from all & euery person or psons whatsoeuer, Claiming any Right Title or Interest unto ye s^d bargained p̱mises or any part or pcell thereof, from by or under him them or any of them for euer/ In witness hereof I ye s^d John Hone-

BOOK IV, FOL. 115.

will haue hereunto Set my hand and Seale, the: 18th of Decemb`r` 1692   the mark of
Signed Sealed & deliuered
  In the presents of us   John 𝐈 Honewell (his Seal)
Dillingem Caldwell   John Honewell personally appear-
Caleb Steuens.   ing before me y`e` Subscrib`r` one
of their Ma`tus` Councill for y`e`
Prouince of the Massachusets
Bay in New England And ac-
knowledged y`e` aboue written
Instrument to be his Act &
Deed this. 20th day of December
1692 — Barth`l` Gedney

A true Copie of y`e` origenall Deed Transcribed & compared this 8th day of ffebruary : 169$\frac{2}{3}$ Jos Hamond Regist`r`

    To all Christian Peope to whome this present Deed of Sale Shall come/ I Benjamin Gouge of York in the County of York in y`e` Prouince of y`e` Massachusets Bay in New England Taylor Send Greeting/ Know yee, that ffor and in consideration of the Sum of three pounds Six Shillings good and Lawfull Money of New England to me in hand well and truly payd at and before y`e` Ensealing and Deliuery of these presents, by Daniel Black of York in y`e` County and Prouince afores`d` Weauer, the receipt whereof I doe hereby Acknowledge And my Self therewith to be fully Satisfied contented and payd And thereof and of and from euery part and parcell thereof from y`e` s`d` Benjamin Gouge my heires Execut`rs` Adminis`rs` and Assigns doe Exonerate Acquit and Discharge him y`e` s`d` Daniel Black his heires Execut`rs` Adminis`rs` and Assignes for euer, I y`e` s`d` Benjamin Gouge haue giuen, granted, bargained, Sold, Aliened, Enfeoffeed & confirmed and by these presents doe for me, my

BOOK IV, FOL. 115.

Self my heires Execut[rs] Adminis[rs] and Assignes fully freely & absolutely giue, grant, bargaine, Sell, Aliene, Enfeoffe, conuey and confirm unto y[e] s[d] Daniel Black his heires and Assignes, a certain piece or parcell of Land, Upland & Swamp lying & being Scituate in the Township of York aboues[d] by Estimation ten Acres more or less And is butted & bounded on y[e] Southeast being twenty pole in breadth the ffront by the Neck of Land that was formerly Henry Donnells, And in length backward fourscore pole, being bounded on y[e] Northeast by Peter Wares Land, on the North west by the Land of M[r] Suball Dummer And on y[e] Southwest by a Lott of land granted

Ben Gooch
to Daniel
Black

by the Town of York to y[e] aboues[d] Henry Donnell, together with all y[e] Stones timber brush wood & under wood, herbage Messuage and all other the priuiledges and Appurtenances thereunto belonging or in any wise appurtaining — To haue and to hold the Same with all y[e] Right Title Interest Claim and Demands, which I y[e] s[d] Benjamin Gouge my heires or Assignes now haue or in time past haue had or in time to come may Should or in any wise ought to haue in and to y[e] aboue granted Premises or their appurtenances, to him y[e] S[d] Daniel Black his heirs and Assignes and to his and their Sole and proper use benefit for euermore, Moreouer I the s[d] Benjamin Gouge doe couenant promise and Engage that at and before y[e] Ensealing and Deliuery of these presents, I am the true Sole Right and proper owner of y[e] aboue granted premises & their appurtenances and that I haue in my Selfe good Right full power and Lawfull Authority the Same to grant and confirm unto y[e] S[d] Daniel Black as aboues[d] and that the Same and euery part thereof is free and clear Acquitted & Discharged of and from all former and other gifts grants bargains Sales Leases Mortgages Titles troubles and Incombrances whatsoeuer and that it Shall and may be Lawfull to and for y[e] s[d] Daniel Black his heirs Execut[rs] Adminis[rs] and Assignes the aboue granted

Premises and euery part thereof from time to time and at all times for euer hereafter To haue & to hold use Improue ocupie enjoy Lawfully peaceably Quietly without any lawfull let hinderance Molestation or Disturbance Euiction or Ejection of or by me or any other person by from or under me or my procurement And that the Sale thereof and of euery part thereof I will maintain against my Selfe my heirs Execut^{rs} Adminis^{rs} and Assigns and against all other persons whatsoeuer Lawfully Claiming or Demanding the Same or any part thereof, And will ffurthermore make performe and Execute Such other Lawfull and reasonable Act or Acts thing or things as in Law or Equity can be Deuised or required for ye better confirming and more Sure making ouer ye Premises unto ye s^d Daniel Black his heirs or Assigns According to ye Laws of this Prouince In witness whereof I ye s^d Benjamin Gouge haue hereunto put my hand and Seal this tenth day of ffebruary in ye year of our Lord one thousand Six hundred Ninety & fiue Six, and [116] In the Seuenth year of his Majesties Reign ouer England &^{c}.

Signed Sealed & Deliuered   Benjamin Gooch (his Seal)

  In presents of —   Benjamin Gooch came & Acknowl-
  Matthew Austin   edged this Instrument to be his
  Joseph Ware   Act and Deed this tenth day of
  John Hancock   ffebruary 169⅚ before me
                          Samuel Donnell Justis peace

A true Copie of the origenall Deed of Sale Transcribed & compared this 8th day of ffebruary : 169⅚

                        p Jos Hamond Regist^r

Know all men by these presents that I John Harris Senr of Ipswich in the County of Essex in New England for and in consideration of the Sum of twenty pounds to me in hand payd before ye Ensealing hereof, by James Smith of Marble-

Book IV, Fol. 116.

Head in ye County afores^d in ye Prouince of the Massachusets Bay, whereof I the s^d Harris doe Acknowledge ye receipt, And my Self therewith fully Satisfied contented & paid, and doth hereby fully freely Clearly and absolutely Acquit Exonerate & Discharge ye s^d Smith his heires Execut^{rs} Admin^{rs} and Assignes for euer by these presents, hath with ye consent of Hester his Now wife, who with ye aboue s^d payment Acknowledgeth her Self fully contented and paid in refference to her Right of Dowry or thirds, bargained Sold giuen granted Infeoffed confirmed and deliuered and Doth by these presents Giue grant bargain Sell Infeoff confirm and Deliuer unto ye s^d Smith his heirs Execut^{rs} Admi^{rs} and Assignes for euer, A certain pcell of Land and Meadow Lying and being Scituate at Coxhall in ye County of York shiere in the Prouince of Mayne, Contaning four hundred Acres, being a part of that Land that I ye s^d Harris with Seuerall others bought of Harlackindine Symonds, as may appear by a Generall bill of Sale of ye thirtieth of June. 1688 as refference thereunto being had may more fully at Large appear, together with all & Singular ye Appurtenances and Priuiledges thereunto belonging or in any wise Appertaining To have and to hold ye s^d four hundred Acres of Land to be layd out in ye first Deuision with ye s^d Purchasers, together with all and Singular the Appurtenances & Priuiledges & comodities ways Easments profits, Emoliments, Mines, Mineralls, Swamps, Springs, water, water-Courses in any wise Appertaining or that Shall at any time to come Accrue or belong thereunto or any part thereof, for or by reason of any Deusion amongst ye s^d Propriet^{rs}, together with all the trees wood underwood Standing Lying or being thereon & euery part thereof unto him ye s^d Smith his heirs Execut^{rs} Administrat^{rs} and Assignes quietly and peaceably without any let hinderance disturbance Molestation Interuption or deniall of me ye s^d Harris or Hester my wife, my heirs Execut^{rs} Administrat^{rs}

[margin: John Harris his Deed to James Smith]

BOOK IV, FOL. 116.

or Assignes for euer/ And further I y{e} s{d} Harris doe hereby Couenant promise and grant, to and with y{e} s{d} Smith that that before at y{e} Ensealing hereof I haue Leagall Right full power and Lawfull Authority in my own name to Sell and Conuey y{e} Same as aboue/ and will therefore Warrantize and Defend y{e} s{d} bargained Premises from all manner of Persons whatsoeuer laying any Claime thereunto or any part thereof from by or under me my heirs Execut{rs} Administrat{rs} or Assignes for euer/ And that it shall and may be Lawfull to and for y{e} s{d} Smith his heirs Execut{rs} Administrat{rs} & Assigns for euer, to haue hold use ocupie possess Enjoy & Improue to his and their use and uses, all y{e} Demised premises free and Clear as a good perfect & absolute Inheritance in ffee Simple without any condition or reseruation whatsoeuer, Soe as to alter change or make voyd the Same/ In witness and Confirmation whereof I y{e} s{d} Harris haue hereunto Set my hand and Seal this. 27{th} of Decemb{r} Ann : Do : one thousand Six hundred Ninety fiue and in y{e} Seuenth of his Majesties Reign William by y{e} grace of God King of England &{ct} John Harris (his Seal)
Signed Sealed & deliuered

In presents of— M{r} John Harris aboue named psonally
Tho : Wade appeared and Acknowledged the
Thomas Newmarch aboue written Instrument to be his
James Taylor. Act & Deed/ Alsoe his wife Esther
Harris freely Yielded up her Right
of Dowry in y{e} aboue Premises Decemb{r} 28{th} 1695 Before me
Tho : Wade Justice of Peace

A true Copie of the origenall Deed Transcribed & compared this 23{d} day of ffeb{ry} 169$\frac{4}{5}$ p Jos Hamond Regest{r}

Book IV, Fol. 117.

[117] To all christian People to whome these presents shall come, Greeting Know yee that I Samuel Willis of Hartford in the Collony of Conecticot in New England Gen^t for Diuers good causes & considerations me thereunto Mouing and for and in consideration of the Loue & respects which I bear unto my late wiues brother John Taylor of Hampton in ye Massathusets Prouince in New England and in consideration of the Sum of thirty pounds of currant Money of New England to me in hand payd by him ye s^d John Taylor, the receipt of which & of euery part of which I doe hereby Acknowledge, In consideration whereof I haue and by these presents doe giue grant bargain Alienate, Enfeoff and confirm unto him ye s^d John Taylor his heirs and Assignes for euer, All those my housing and Lands Scittuate Lying and being at ye Salmon falls in ye Township of Kittery upon ye Riu^r of Piscataqua Containing two hundred Acres be it more or less, together with all trees timber woods under woods Meadows pastures Areable Lands comons brooks ponds ways and all other priuiledges Immunities and Appurtenances whatsoeuer thereunto belonging or in any ways Appurtaining being butted and bounded as followeth Viz^t Upon Piscataqua Riuer West, On undeuided Lands East, on Lands belonging to James Smith North, and on Lands belonging to Mr Plaisted South/ hereby Granting and confirming al my Right Title & Interest whatsoeuer of me ye s^d Samuel Williss and my heirs in and unto all and Singular the aboue Demised premises, unto ye s^d John Taylor and his heirs and Assignes foreuer, hereby hensforth Granting that at all times hereafter it Shall and may be Lawfull to and for the Said John Taylor his heires Execut^rs Administrat^rs or Assignes to enter into haue hold use ocupie Possess and Injoy all and Singular the aboue Demised Premises to him his heirs or Assignes for euer, without any Let Suite trouble Deniall Euiction Ejection, Disturbance or Interuption of by

Sam^ll Willis to Jno Taylor

or from me the s^d Samuel Williss his heirs Execut^rs Administrat^rs or Assignes, or from or by any other person or persons in by or under them, together with twenty thousand of Brick, & Iron Ware or Implements of Husbandry which ye S^d Williss hath at Piscataqua hereby Ratifying and confirming all ye aboues^d Lands & Demised Premises with all priuiledges and Appurtenances whatsoeuer thereunto belonging, And for a full confirmation and Establishment of all and Singular ye Premises, I haue hereunto Set my hand & Affixed my Seal this tenth of March in ye year of our Lord One thousand Six hundred Ninety and fiue Six and in ye Eighth year of y^e Reign of o^r Soueraign Lord William by the grace of God King of England Scott^d &^ct

Signed Sealed and Deliuered   Samuel Willis (his Seal)
  In the presents of   Samuel Willis Esqr Gen^t psonally
  Caleb Stanly Junr   appeared in Hartford this 10th day
  Sarah Stanly   of March Anno Dom: 169$\frac{5}{6}$ and
                          Acknowledged y^e aboue written
                          Instrument to be his free & Voluntary Act & Deed, before me
                          Caleb Stanly, one of y^e Council
                          of his Majesties Collony of Conecticott in New Engl^d

A true Copie of y^e origenall Deed Transcribed & compared ffeb^ry 25° 169$\frac{5}{6}$ p Jos Hamond Register.

To all People To whom this present writing Shall come, John Taylor of Hampton in the Prouince of New Hampshier in New England yeom̄ Sendeth Greeting/ Know yee that the s^d John Taylor for and in consideration of y^e Sum of Eighty pounds of Currant Money of New-England to him in hand paid before ye Ensealing & Deliuery hereof by Edward Sargent of Newbury in y^e

BOOK IV, FOL. 117.

County of Essex in yᵉ Prouince of the Massachusets Bay in New England Vintner, the receipt whereof he doth Acknowledge and himself therewith fully Satisfied and contented, Haue Giuen granted bargained Sold Alienated Enfeoffeed and confirmed, And doth by these presents fully clearly and absolutely Giue grant bargain Sell Alienate and confirm unto the sᵈ Edward Sargent, to him his heirs Executʳˢ Administratʳˢ or Assignes a piece parcell or tract of Land Lying being & cituated at yᵉ Salmon-falls in the Township of Kittery on the Eastern Side of Piscataqua Riuʳ in New England, containing two hundred Acres of Land be it more or less, And is bounded and abutted as ffolloweth,

John Taylor to Edw. Sergᵗ

Upon Piscataqua Riuer aforesᵈ West, on undeuided Land East, on Lands belonging formerly to James Smith North, and on Lands belonging to Mʳ Plaisted South with all the housing timber wood orchard, Gardens trees & fence upon yᵉ Same/ which Land and premises was formerly in the Possession and ocupation of William Loue late of Kittery Deceased. And alsoe all and euery Town Grants right of comōns Deuisions and Sub deuisions of uplands or Meadows alredy granted or to be granted unto the sᵈ William Loue Deceased or his heirs or Assignes in the Township of Kittery aforesᵈ and are either layd out or still to be layd out unto the Said Loue Deceased his heirs or Assignes as aforesᵈ, And Especially three Grants Vizᵗ one at a Town Meeting held at Kittery July 5ᵗʰ 1667 for thirty Acres of Swamp ground or Land that may be fit to make Marsh of/ the other grant March 20ᵗʰ 167$\frac{2}{3}$, for three Acres of Swamp land and alsoe and other Grant August 21ᵗʰ 1685 for Sixty Acres of Land as may more fully appear by sᵈ Grants reference thereunto being had To haue and to hold the abouesᵈ two hundred Acres of Land be it more or less bounded and abutted as aforesᵈ And alsoe all yᵉ housing timber orchards Gardens trees and fence upon yᵉ Same and all Deuision Subdeuisions Rights of commons and Land and all y̆ˢ aboueˢᵈ Grants wᵗʰ all and euery other the Premises with their Appurtenances, and euery part and parcell thereof unto yᵉ sᵈ Edward Sargent his heires Executors Administratʳˢ or Assignes, with all yᵉ Rights priuiledges & Appurtenances thereunto belonging or in any ways Appurtaining as a ffree Estate in ffee Simple for euer/ And the sᵈ John Taylor for himselfe his heirs Executʳˢ and Admʳˢ doth couenant and promise to and with the sᵈ Edward Sargent his heirs Executʳˢ Admʳˢ and Assignes that at yᵉ time of yᵉ Ensealing and Deliuery hereof he is the true Lawfull and propʳ owner of all yᵉ aboue Granted and bargained premises and that and that [118] he hath full good Right and Lawfull Authority to Sell and dispose of yᵉ Same as aboue said/ And that yᵉ Same and euery part and parcell thereof is free and cleare and ffreely and clearely Acquitted and Discharged of & from all other and former Gifts grants Sales bargains Alienations Enfeoffments confirmations Rights Dowryes Right of thirds Morgages Extents Executions Judgments Titles claimes charges Troubles and Incumbrances wᵗˢoeuer and that he will warrant and foreuer Defend the Same and euery part and parcell thereof unto yᵉ sᵈ Edward Sargent his heirs Execᵗʳˢ Admʳˢ & Assignes against all persons whatsoeuer Laying hauing or pretending to haue any Legall Claims Title or Interest thereunto/

And he will doe or cause to be done any other or further Act or Acts thing or things that Shall be needfull for a more Sure conueiance of yᵉ Same as abouesᵈ, when he Shall Legally thereunto be called In witness whereof yᵉ sᵈ John Taylor hath hereunto Set his hand and Seale the twenty Second day of Aprill in yᵉ year of our, one thousand Six hundred Ninety Seauen, and in yᵉ Eighth year of yᵉ Reign of our

Book IV, Fol. 118.

Soueraign Ld William the third of England Scotland ffrance & Ireland, King Defend^r of y^e ffaith &^c.

Signed Sealed and deliuered   John Taylor ($^{his}_{Seale}$)
 In presents of —   New Hampshier
 John Rudsby   John Taylor personly apeared this
 Joseph Lobdell   eight day of Decemb^r 1697 and Ac-
 Nicholas Dauison   knowledged this Instrument to be
          his free & volluntary Act and Deed,
          Before me
           Nath^ll Weare Iustice of peace

A true Copie of ye origenall Deed of Sale, Transcribed and Compared this 23^d day of ffebruary : 169¾.

         p Jos Hamond Reg^r

Know all men by these presents that we Jonathan Wade & Thomas Wade of Ipswich in the County of Essex in the Prouince of the Massachusets Bay in New England Execut^rs to ye last Will and Testament of Mr Thomas Wade late Deceased, who was Administrator to ye Estate of Mr Jonathan Wade of s^d Ipswich Deceased, Haue Assigned ordained and made and in our Stead & place by these presents put and constituted our trustie and well beloued brother Mr John Wade of Barwick Minist^r to be our true and Lawfull Atturney. for himself and in his own name & to his use to ask, Sue for, Leuie, require, recouer and receiue of Mr John Woodman of Kittery, Administrator to ye Estate of John Diemond of Kittery Deceased, All & euery Such Debts and Sums of Money which are now due unto us by any manner of ways or meanes whatsoeuer, Giuing and granting unto our s^d Atturney our whole power Strength and Authority in and about ye premises/ And upon ye receipt of any Such Debts or Sums of money afores^d Acquittances to make or other discharges in our names to make and deliuer and all &

BOOK IV, FOL. 118, 119.

euery Such Act & Acts whatsoeuer in ye Law for the recouery of all or any Such Debts or Sums of money as afores^d and in our names to doe Execute and perform as fully largely and Amply in euery respect to all Intents and purposes as we our Selues might or could doe if we were in our own persons present/ Ratifying allowing and holding firm and Stable all & whatsoeuer our s^d Atturney Shall Lawfully doe or cause to be done in or about the Execution of the premises by vertue of these presents In witness whereof and for the confirmation of all that is aboues^d We the s^d Jonathan Wade & Thomas Wade haue hereunto Set our hands & Seales this. 12th day of May. 1697

Signed Sealed & deliuered   Jonathan Wade (his Seal)
in the presents of us   Thomas Wade (his seal)
Elizabeth Appleton.

Mr Jonathan and Thomas Wade personally appeared before me the Subscriber one of his Majesties Iustices of the peace within ye County of Essex in N. England Acknowledged the aboue written Instrument to be their Act & Deed/

Ipsw^ch May. 14. day. 1697   John Appleton

A true Copie of the origenall Instrum^t Transcribed & compared this 6th of Aprill : 1698 p Jos Hammond Regist^r

[119] To all Christian People to whom this Present Deed of Sale Shall Come : I Isaac Remich Late of Kittery in the County of York in the Prouince of the Massachusets Bay in New : England Send Greeting Know ye that I Isaac Remich afores^d for diuerse good Causes me there unto mouing more Especially for and in consideration of one hundred pounds Lawfull Money of New : England to me in hand well and truly paid at and before the Ensealing and Deliuery of these presents by John Denit of Portsm° in the Prouince New : Hampsheir Carpenter the Receipt whereof I acknowledge

Book IV, Fol. 119, 120.

thereof from time to time and at all times hereafter to haue hold use Improoue occupie possess and enjoy Lawfully peaceably and quietly without any lawfull Let Deniall hindrance Molestation or Disturbance of or by me or any other pson or psons from by or und^r me or by my Procurem^t and that ye Sale hereof and euery part thereof against my Selfe my heirs Execut^{rs} Administrators and assigns or any other pson or psons Lawfully Claiming ye Same or any part thereof I will for euer Saue harmless warrant and Defend by these psents and that I my heirs Execut^{rs} and Administrat^{rs} Shall and will make pform and Execute Such other further Lawfull and Reasonable act or acts thing or things as in Law or Equity can by the s^d John Dennet or his Learned Councill in ye Law be Diuised or Required for the better Confirming & more Sure making of the Primises unto ye s^d John Dennet his heirs Execut^{rs} Administrat^{rs} and assigns according to ye Laws of this Prouince/ In Witness whereof I ye s^d Isaac Remich haue hereunto Set my hand and Seal ye Second day of May in the tenth year of ye Reign of our Soueraign Lord William ye third of England Scotland ffrance and Ireland King Defend^r of the ffaith &^{c} and in the year of our Lord God Anno Domini one thousand Six hundred Ninty and Eight/ 1698   Isaac Remich (his Seal)

[120] Signed Sealed and Deliuered

In the presents of us— Isaac Remich Came 2^d day of
Thomas Phipps   May: 1698 before me the
Jno Snell   Subscrib^r and acknowledged
    her   this aboue Instrument to be
Doritha ✗ Alcock   his free act and Deed/
    mark   Job Alcock Just: Peace

A true Coppie of ye originall Deed is here Entred on Record and therewith Compared this 19 day of may 1698/
p Jos Hamond Reg^r

Know all men by these presents that Whereas I Christian Remich haue giuen and granted unto my Son Isaac Remich

Book IV, Fol. 120.

two peils of land in ye township of Kittery, the one peill containing twenty acres bareing Date Octob^r ye 16 : 1686 and the other containing ten acres bareing March ye 30 : 1694 and Whereas there is Somthing Inserted therein which may Seem to appear and Look Something Like an Entailm^t I doe by these presents Declare that I neuer Intended any thing therein to Debarr or hind^r my s^d Son from Disposeing thereof for his best aduantage, and I doe freely consent and allow of the aboue Deed of Sale Which he has made of it to John Dennet In Witness Whereof I haue hereunto Set my hand and Seal this 2^d day of May 1698

Signed Sealed and Deliuered   Christian Remich/ (Seal)
  In ye Presents of—   In° Snell Doritta Alcock and Thomas
  Thomas Phipps   Phipps came the 2^d day of May
  Jn° Snell   1698 before me the Subscrib^r and
    her mark   gaue oath that that they See Isaac
  Doritha **A** Alcock   Remich Sign Seal & Deliuer this
                       aboue Deed of Sale to be his act
                       and Deed   Job Alcock
                                      Just : Peace

Xtian Remich came ye 2^d day of may 1698 before me ye Subscrib^r & acknowledged this aboue Instrum^t to be his free act and Deed   Job Alcock Just Peace

A true Coppie of the originall Instrum^t is here Entred on Record and therewith Compared this 19 day of May 1698
                 p Jos Hamond Regest^r

Know all men by these Presents that I Isaac Remich Late of Kittery in the County of York in the Prouince of the Massachusets bay in New England/ Now of South Carolinea doe owe and am Indebted unto John Dennet Senr of Portsm° in ye Prouince New : Hampshier Carpinter the full and Iust Sum of fiue hundred pounds Cur^t Money of New : England

Isaac Remick
to Jn° Denet

to be paid to him y̌ᵉ sᵈ Dennet his heirs Execut͏ʳˢ Administrat͏ʳˢ or Assigns at his or their Demand for which paymᵗ well and truly to be made I bind me my heires Execut͏ʳˢ Administrat͏ʳˢ and Assigns ffirmly by these presents In Witness wherof I haue hereunto Set my hand and Seal this Seccond day of May Anno: Domini: 1698

The Condition of this obligation is Such that if y̌ᵉ aboue bounden Isaac Remich his heirs or Assigns doe for euer Saue harmless Warrant and Defend the sᵈ John Dennet his heirs &ᶜ in Reference to a Certaine house and Land with y̌ᵉ appurtenances as p a deed of Sale undᵣ said Remichs hand and Seal bareing Date with these Presents being Scituate in Kittery in y̌ᵉ County of york against themselues their heirs and assigns that then this present obligation to be void and of none Effect otherwise to Stand Remaine and abide in full force Strength and uertue.   Isaac Remich (Seal)
Signed Sealed and Deliuered

In the presents of—   Isaac Remich Came the 2ᵈ Day of
Thomas Phipps   May 1698/ before me the Sub-
Jn° Snell   scriber and acknowledged this
                            aboue Instrumᵗ to be his free
                            act and Deed.
                                  Job Alcock Just͏ᵉ Peace
A true Coppie of the Originall Bond is here Entred on Reccord and therewith Compared this 19 day of May: 1698
                            p Jos Hamond Regestʳ

[121] To all Christian People to whom this present Deed Shall Come and Consern/ Know yee that I Robert Elliot Some time of Black point Allias Scarbrough in the Prouince of Maine in New: England Sendeth Greeting in our Lord God euer Lasting for Diuerse good Couses and

Considerations me thereunto moouing and more in Speciall for that John Pickerin Jun[r] of Portsm[o] in y[e] Prouince of New : Hampshier with whom I now liue hath Promissed and Ingaged the taking Care and Maintaining me with meat drink washing & Lodging : Suitable and Conuenient Duering my naturall life as becometh a Christian the which I doe Except of and my Selfe fully Satisfied therewith and for his Satisfaction in that behalfe haue Giuen Granted bargained and confirmed and by these presents doe fully freely and absolutely giue grant, Allienate and Confir: unto y[e] s[d] John Pickerin his heirs & Execut[rs] Administrat[rs] and Assigns for euer to Say a Certaine peill of upland & Meadow Lying and being in Black point Allias Scarbrough on y[e] North Side of nonsuch Riuer as allso another peill of Marsh : on y[e] other Side togather with a Little point of Marsh on the East Side of Jameco path y[e] Bounds of all which s[d] lands and meadows will more at Large appear by the s[d] town Reccords as Granted to me by y[m] : To Hauue & to Hold all y[e] here before mentioned Lands and Meadows with all y[e] trees timber woods and underwoods with all y[e] Priuiledges and appurtenances thereunto belonging or in any Appertaining with all oth[r] Rights and Priuiledges that doth or may belong to me in and from the s[d] town as I haue been an Inhabitant unto y[e] s[d] John Pickerin and his heirs Execut[rs] Administrat[rs] and Assigns for euer without y[e] Least truble or Molestation from me my heirs Execut[rs] Administrat[rs] or Assigns or any one of y[m] or any other pson whatsoeuer Claiming any Right Title or Interest to all or any part of y[e] before Mentioned pmisses but that the Same shall foreuer Remaine y[e] s[d] Pickerins Right in fee Simple for Confirmation whereof

BOOK IV, FOL. 121.

I haue hereunto Set my hand and Seal, This 22ᵈ day of ffebʳʸ 169⅜ the mark & Seal
Signed Sealed & Deluered of Robert R Elleot (ʰⁱˢ Seal)
In ᵽsents of us
John Pickerin Robert Eliot appeared this twenty Sec-
Wᵐ Colton cond day of ffebʳʸ 169⅜ & acknowl-
John Lincoott edged yᵉ aboue Instrumᵗ to be his act
and Deed Before me
Thoˢ Packer Justˢ Peˢ
A True Coppie of this Instrunᵗ is here Entred on Rec-
cord and with yᵉ originall Compared this 20ᵗʰ of May 1698
ᵽ Jos Hamond Registʳ

This Indenture made the twenty Eighth day of ffebʳʸ in the year of our Lord According to Computation, one thousand Six hundred and Eighty nine: Between Benjamin Woodbridge of the town of Kittery in the Prouince of Maine Ministʳ on the one parte and Joseph Crocker of the Said town and Prouince and Dennis Hicks of the town and Prouince aforesᵈ on the other party/ Witnesseth, that the sᵈ Benjamin Woodbridge For and in Considʳation

Benjamĩ Woodbridg To Crocket & Hicks

of the Summe of Thirty Six pounds to him in hand paid or Secured to be paid by the sᵈ Joseph Crocket & Dennis Hicks att and before the Ensealing and Deliuery of these pʳsents the Receipt whereof he the sᵈ Benjamin Woodbridge doth hereby acknowledge and thereof doth acquitt and Discharge yᵐ the sᵈ Joseph Crocket and Dennis Hicks their heirs Executʳˢ and administratʳˢ foreuer by these presents and alsoe for Diuerse good Causes and considʳations him the sᵈ Benjamin Woodbridge thereunto mouing Hath granted Bargained Sold allienned Enfeoffed and Confirmed and by these pʳsents doth Grant Bargaine Sell allien Enfeoffe and Confirm unto the s^d Joseph Crocket & Dennis Hicks their heirs and Assigns foreuer/ All that tract or p^{r}cill of Land Lying in the s^d town of Kittery Containing By Estcemation Thirty Six Acres be it more or Lesse and begining att Crockets Crick on the Southward Side thereof and thence Running up into the woods unto a Brook of water Colled Ashing Swamp Brook on the Northward part on a North and by East course Bounded By land of Rog^r Dearings on the Eastward part and Land late of Thomas Crockets on the Westward part thereof: they the s^d Crocket & Hicks leueing a Suffitient High way Togather with all ways waters water courses woods commons Proffits and Commodities Priuilidges and Aduantages whatsoeuer to the Same belonging or in any wayes appertaining and the Reuertion and Reuertions Remaind^r and Remaind^{rs} thereof and Euery part thereof and all the Estate Right Title and Interest of him the s^d Benjamin Woodbridge or his heirs of in or to the Same and True Coppies if Required of all Such deeds Euidences and wrightings which Concern the Same or any p^t thereof To Haue and To Hold: the s^d p^{r}cill of Land and [122] Euery part thereof with the appurtenances unto the s^d Joseph Crocket and Dennis Hicks their heirs and Assigns foreuer to and for the onely and proper use and Behooffe of y^m the s^d Joseph Crocket and Dennis Hicks their heirs and Assigns for Euer And the s^d Benjamin Woodbridge doth for himselfe and his heirs Couenant Promiss and grant to and with the s^d Joseph Crocket and Dennis Hicks their heirs and Assigns in manner and form ffollowing That is To Say That he the sd Benjamin Woodbridge now at the Sealing and Deliuery of these p^{r}sents Doth Stand Lawfully Seized of and in the aboues^d p^{r}cill of Land with the appurtenances of a good

Ben$\text{J}$ Woodbridge To Crocket & Hicks

p^{r}fect absolute and Indeseazible Estate of inhertance in fee Simple and that he hath full pow^r and good Right to grant and conuey the s^d Land to the s^d Joseph Crocket and Dennis Hicks. their heirs and Assigns foreuer and alsoe that they the s^d Joseph Crocket and Dennis Hicks their heirs and Assignes Shall and Lawfully may from time to time and att all times hereafter peasably & and quietly haue hold use occupie Possess and Enjoy the Said p^rcill of Land with the appurtences without the Lawfull Let Suite truble Deniall Ejection Euiction or Disturbance of him the s^d Benjamin Woodbridge or his heirs or of any oth^r p^rson or p^rsons whatsoeuer haueing or Lawfully Claiming to haue any Estate Right Title or Interest of in or to the Same or any p^rt thereof his Majesty now King of England his heirs and Success^rs onely Excepted And alsoe that the Said hereby Sole p^rmisses with the appurtenances now are and be and Soe from time to time and att all times hereaft^r Shall be Remaine and continue vnto the s^d Joseph Crocket and Dennis Hicks and their heirs free and Clear and freely and Clearly acquited Exon^rated and Discharged of and from all form and other gifts grants Bargains Sales Leases Joyntures Dowryes Judgm^ts Executions Extents and of and from all Titles trubles Charges & Incumbrances Whatseuer had made Commited done or Suffered by him the s^d Benjamin Woodbridge or by any other p^rson or p^rsons Whatsoeuer Except before Excepted and alsoe that he the s^d Benjamin Woodbridge and his heirs or Eith^r of y^m Shall and will att any time or times for and During the Space or terme of Seuen years next Ensuing the Date hereof at the Reasonable Request and att the proper Costs and Charges in ye Law of y^m the s^d Joseph Crocket and Denis Hicks make p^rform and Execute or Cause to be made p^rformed and Executed all and Euery Such furth^r & other Lawfull and Reasonable act and acts Conney-

Benjamin Woodbridge To Crocket & Hicks

ances and Assurances in the Law whatsoeuer for the better assurance and Conueying of ye s^d Land unto the s^d Joseph Crocket and Dennis Hicks and their heirs as by y^m or Eith^r of y^m Shall be reasonably required Be it by fiue ffeofm^t Acknowledgment recouery release or confirmation Deed or

Deeds Recorded the Recording of these p'sents or by any oth' act way or means Whatsoener all which s'd acts as afores'd Soe hereafter to be done made acknowledged or Executed Shall be and enure and Shall be construed Deemed adjudged and taken to be and enure to and for the onely and proper use and behoofe of y'm the s'd Joseph Crocket and Dennis Hicks and their heirs and Assignes for euer and to & for none other use intent or purpose whatsoeuer In Witness whereof the s'd Benjamin Woodbridge hath hereunt Set his hand and Seal the day and year first aboue written

                         Benjamin (Seal) Woodbridge.

Memorand'm that the s'd Benjamin Woodbridge doth not by uertue of y'e within deed of Sale any way infrindge himselfe of liberty of Seting a mill below y'e s'd land if he See occation any thing in this Deed to the Contrary notwithstanding/ Dated y'e day and year first within written

Sealed and Deliuer'ed and Liuery and Seizin giuen and Deliuered of y'e w'th'in p'r'misses in y'e p'r'sence of us y'e words/ they the s'd Crocket & Hicks leuing a Suffitient high way being first interlined in y'e Sight of us und'r'writen between y'e twelueth and thirteenth Lines
        Roger Dearing
        Will'm Hooke.

I Dennis Hicks doe assign and make ou'r all y'e Right Title and Interest that I haue of this deed unto Mary Ball and her heirs and assigns for Euer as attests my hand this 30° of octob'r 1696/
                Denis Hicks
Test: Joseph Couch   his   mark
    Joseph Couch
[123] Prouince
       of   } ss
      Maine

BOOK IV, FOL. 123.

Memorand{m} that this day being the 20{th} of ffeb{ry} 1689 : M{r} Benjamin Woodbridge appeared before me and acknowledged the within Instrum{t} to be his Act and Deed —
ffrancis Hooke Just : Pea
A True Coppie of this Instrum{t} is here Entred on Reccord and with the originall Compared this 20{th} of May 1698°
p Jos Hamond Regist{r}

To all CHristian People before whom these presents Shall Come Richard Estis of Salem in the County of Medlesex in New : England Sends greeting — Now Know Yee : That I the aboue mentioned Richard Estis for Diuerse good causes me thereunto moouing more Especially for and in consid{r}ation of one hundred pounds to me in hand paid at and before y{e} Sealing and Deliuery of these p{r}sents by Nicholas Morrell of Kitt{r}y in y{c} Prouince of Maine in New : England afores{d} the Receipt whereof I acknowledge and therewith fully Satisfied contented and paid and thereof and of Euery part and

Richard Estis to Nicholas Morrel

p{r}cill thereof I doe Clearly acquit Exon{r}ate and Discharge y{e} s{d} Nicholas Morrell his heirs Execut{rs} administrat{rs} and Assigns for Euer by these p{r}sents haue giuen granted bargained Sold Alliened Enfeoffed made ouer and confirmed, and by these p{r}sents for me my heirs Executers Administrat{rs} and Assigns for euer doe fully clearly and absolutely Giue Grant bargaine Sell Allien Enfeoffe make ouer and confirm unto him y{e} s{d} Nicholas Morrell his heirs Execut{rs} administrat{rs} and Assigns foreuer all that piece or p{r}cill of Land which I bought of William Racklift Scituate lying and being in y{e} town of Kittery afores{d} butting upon y{e} Riũ of Piscataqua on y{e} Sout west : and on y{e} Northeast Joyning to y{e} Land of Allexand{r} Dennet and in Bredth to goe half way from s{d} Dennets to M{r} Shapleighs Northwest line and Soe to run back from yᵉ sᵈ Riuer upon a Northeast and by East line till forty Acres be Compleated and ended as appears by sᵈ Racklifts Deed of Sale bareing Date the Sixth day of Januaʳ 1686 To Have and To Hold, the above giuen and granted pʳmisses with all yᵉ buildings Edifises houses Barns Erected being and Standing upon sᵈ land togathʳ with all yᵉ Priuilidges benifits commodities wood Timbʳ trees gardens orchards fences Pastures with all and Singular yᵉ appurtenances thereunto belonging or in any ways appertaining unto him yᵉ sᵈ Nicholas Morrell his heires Executʳˢ Administratʳˢ and assigns for euer and to his & their own propper use benifit and behoofe to occupie Improoue and make use off: without any Molestation let Deniall or hinderance and further I yᵉ sᵈ Richᵈ Estis doe Declare that I haue at yᵉ Sealing and Deliuery hereof Just Right full Power and Lawfull authority the aboue Giuen and Granted pʳmisses to Sell and Dispose of and yᵗ all and Euery part and pʳcill thereof is free and clear and freely and clearly acquitted Exonʳated and Discharged of and from all and all mañer of Wills entayles Judgments Executions Powʳ of thirds and all other Incombrances of what kind or nature Soeuer and that I yᵉ sᵈ Estis doe Ingage and Promiss the aboue giuen and granted pʳmisses by these pʳsents foreuer to warrant and Defend against any pson or psons whatsoeuer Claiming any Right Title or Interest thereunt from by or undʳ me yᵉ sᵈ Richard Estis. In Witness whereof I haue hereunto Set my hand and Seal this Eith day of ffebruary in yᵉ year of our Lord Anno Domini one thousand Six hundred Ninty and two Ninty three/ 169$\frac{2}{3}$ and in yᵉ fourth year of yᵉ Reign of our Soueraign Lord and Lady William and Mary by yᵉ grace of

Richᵈ Estis
To
Nichᵒ Morrᵉˡˡ

god of England Scotland ffrance and Ireland King and Queen : Defend^r of the ffaith &^{c}

Signed Sealed and Deluered   Richard Estis ($^{his}_{Seal}$)
   in the Presence of us —   Elizabeth Estis —
   John Shapleigh.   Richard Estis Personally appeared
   Jos . Hamond.   Before me the Subscrib^r Salem May y^e 19th 1698, and acknowledged y^e aboue writen Instrum^t to be his act and Deed and Elizabeth Estis his wife alsoe acknowledged y^e Same and freely Resined up her Right and Title of Dowre therein —
         John Hathourn Just^s Peace

[124] A true Coppie of this Instrument is here Entred on Record and with ye originall Compared this 23 day of may 1698   p Jos Hamond Regist^r

To all People To whom this Present wrighting Shall Come Edward Sergent of Newbury in the County of Essex in the Prouince of the Massachusets Bay in New : England Vintner Sends Greeting Know Yee that the s^d Edward Serge^t for and in consid^{r}ation of ye Sume of twenty two pounds Ten : Shillings of Curant Money of New : England to him in hand paid before the Ensealing and Deliuery hereof by William Peperell of Kittery in ye Prouince of Maine in New England ye Receipt whereof he doth Acknowledge and himselfe therewith fully Satisfied and contented Haue giuen : granted Bargained Sould Allienated Enfeoffed and confirmed and Doth by these p^{r}sents fully Clearly and absolutly Giue Grant Bargaine Sell Allien Enfeoffe and confir : unto ye s^d Wm Peprell his heirs Execut^rs Administrators and Assigns ye full one halfe or Moiety of a p^{r}cill of land Lying and being in

Sacoe Allias Wint[r] Harbour containing Eighty
acres of upland be it more or Less and is
bounded Northerly by the Land of y[e] s[d] Edward
Sergent Easterly by a small Brook running on
y[e] Southern Side of an orchard of y[e] s[d] Sergents and the
flatts Joyning to Wint[r] Harb[r] Southerly by y[e] Land of
M[r] Walter Penuel deceased and Soe running backward
till all y[e] fore Mentioned Land be Compleated y[e] s[d] Peprill to haue his halfe or Moiety of s[d] p[r]cill of Land upon
y[e] Souther Side thereof next Adjoyning to y[e] Land of
M[r] Walter Penuell Deceased and to be as good in quantity
and quallity as the other halfe or Moiety as alsoe a p[r]cill of
Meadow containing fifteen acres y[e] one halfe or Moiety
thereof which Meadow adjoyns to y[e] Meadow of John Sergent Northerly Bounding vpon y[e] Northwest upon the land
was formerly Simon Booths togather with y[e] one halfe or
Moiety of ten Acres of Meadow in two p[r]cills lying in or
on Little Riuer all in y[e] Township of Sacoe allias Wint[r]
Harb[r] with all y[e] timb[r] treese woods underwoods waters and
watercourses Priuilidges and Appurtenances thereunto belonging which Land and Meadow was fformerly Dominicus
Jordans administrat[r] to Ralph Trustrum Late of Winter
Harb[r] Deceased. To Have and to Hold: the one halfe or
Moiety of all the aboue granted and Bargained
p[r]misses to him y[e] s[d] William Peprell his heirs
Execut[rs] Admin[rs] and Assigns w[th] all y[e] Rights
Priuiledges and appurtenances thereunto belonging or any wayes appertaining as a ffree Estate in fee Simple
for euer And y[e] s[d] Edward Sergent for himselfe his Heirs
Execut[rs] and Administrat[rs] doth couenant and Promiss to
and With y[e] s[d] William Peprell his heirs Execut[rs] Administrat[rs] and Assigns and to and with Euery of y[m] by these
presents that all and Singular the s[d] p[r]misses before Giuen
Granted Bargained and Sold at y[e] time of y[e] ensealing and
Deliu[ry] of these are and be and at all times hereafter Shall

*Edw[d] Sergent
To
W[m] Peprill*

*Edw Sergent
To
W[m] Peprell*

BOOK IV, FOL. 124, 125.

be Continue and Remaine Clearly Acquited Exonerated Discharged and kept harmless of & from all and all Manner of form^r and other Bargains Sales Gifts grants Leases Charges Dowryes Titles Trubles and Incumbrances whatsoeuer had made Comitted Suffered done or to be had made Committed or Suffered to be done by the s^d Edward Sergent his heirs Execut^{rs} Administrat^{rs} or Assigns or any from by or under him In Wittness whereof ye s^d Edward Sergent with Elizabeth his wife haue hereunto Set their hands : and Seals this fourth day of Aprell Annoq, Domin: one Thousand Six hund^rd ninty Eight in ye Tenth year of ye Reign of our Soueraign Lord William the third of England : Scotland ffrance and Ireland King Defend^r of ye faith &^c :

Signed Sealed & Deliuered   Edward Sergent (his Seal)
  In Presents of   th : 4 apr^{ll} 1698° Then Edward
  Samuel   Sergent of newbury came and
  Bridgiot Night   acknowledged this Instrum^t to
                               be his act & deed before me y^e
                               Subscrib^r
                               Job Alcock Jus^{te} peace

[125] The Interlining und^r ye Twentieth line of woods trees timb^r and water Courses was writen before the ensealing and Deliuery of these p^rsents.

A True Coppie of this Instrum^t is here Entred on Reccord and with ye Originall Compared this 23^d day of May 1698°   p Jos Hamond Regist^r

To all People unto whome this present Deed of Sale Shall come/ James Gooch of Boston in the County of Suffolk within the Prouince of ye Massachusets Bay in New England Marrin^r, Eldest Son & heir of his father James Gooch late of Wells in ye County of York within ye afores^d Prouince yeoman Deceased Intestate and Elizabeth his s^d wife

BOOK IV, FOL. 125.

Send greeting/ Know y⁰ that I y⁰ sᵈ James Gooch and Elizabeth his sᵈ wife for and in consideration of y⁰ Sum of Seuenty pounds Current money of New England to them in hand well and truly paid before the ensealing & deliuery of these presents by John Wheelwright of Wells in the County of York aforesᵈ yeoman the receipt whereof to full content and Satisfaction they doe hereby Acknowledge, and thereof and of euery part and parcell thereof doe acquit Exonerate and discharge the sᵈ John Wheelwright his heirs Executʳˢ Administratʳˢ and Assignes and euery of them for euer by these presents, Haue giuen granted bargined Sold Aliened Enfeoffed Conueied and confirmed, And by these presents for them Selues and their heires doe fully freely Clerely and absolutely giue grant bargain Sell Alien enfeoff conuey & confirm unto the sᵈ John Wheelwright his heirs and Assignes for euer, The Seuerall parcels of upland and Salt Marsh hereundʳ mentioned and expressed Scituate lying and being in Wells aforesᵈ Appertaining to the Estate of the sᵈ James Gooch Deceased, and whereof he died Seized, bounded and described as followeth, Vizᵗ one parcell thereof being part Upland & part Salt Marsh, containing Twenty fiue poles in breadth begining at Sam: Austines land on y⁰ Northeast Side, which is in controuersie, And from thence to run twenty fiue poles to a certain pine tree marked with N. & W. and Soe to run down to y⁰ Riuer, along by an Elbow in y⁰ Main Creeke, with all the point yᵗ runs out to y⁰ Creek, and Soe to y⁰ Mussell Ridge Soe called, and from thence to run up into y⁰ Countrey as high as other Lots goes/ And one other parcel thereof being upland lies on y⁰ Southwest Side of a certain Island comonly called and known by the name of Drakes Island Next y⁰ aforesᵈ Mussell Ridge and Soe to y⁰ Seawall And Soe Joying to y⁰ Marsh hereinafter bargained and Sold/ And y⁰ remaining parcel thereof being Salt Marsh, containing by Estimation twelue Acres be the Same more or less lying on the Southwest Side of yᵉ last mentioned upland is butted and bounded Southeast and Southwest by the afore mentioned Sea wall Nothwest by a creek called Nannyes Crek, and Northeast by yᵉ last aforementioned upland or howeñ otherwise yᵉ premises are bounded or reputed to be bounded Together with all and Singular the timbʳ trees woods and underwoods Standing & growing thereon, ways easments waters watercourses profits priuiledges rights comodities hereditaments Emoluments and appurtenances whatsoeuer to the said granted and bargained premises belonging or in any wise Appurtaining or therewith now, or heretofore used ocupied or enjoyed, and yᵉ reuertion And reuerc̃ons remder and remainders rents Issues and profits thereof And alsoe all the Estate Right Title Interest Inheritance use possession Dower thirds propeity claim and demand whatsoeuer of yᵉ sᵈ James Gooch and Elizabeth his sᵈ wife and of either of them of in and to the Same and euery part thereof, with all Deeds writings and euidences onely relating thereto. To have and to hold all yᵉ aboue and before mentioned granted and bargained premises with th'appurtenances and euery part and parcel thereof unto yᵉ sᵈ John Wheelwright his heirs and Assignes for euer to his and their own Sole and proper use benefit and behoofe from henceforth and foreuermore, Absolutely without any manʳ of condition redemption or reuocation in any wise/ And the sᵈ James Gooch for himself his heirs Execut and Adminʳˢ doth hereby Couenant promise grant & agree to and with yᵉ sᵈ John Wheelwright his heirs and Assignes in manner and form following, that is to Say, That at yᵉ time of this present grant bargain Sale and untill yᵉ ensealing and deliuery of these presents the sᵈ James Gooch and Elizabeth his sᵈ wife are true Sole and Lawfull ownʳ of all th' aforebargained premises and Stand Lawfully Seized thereof in their or one of their own proper right of a good Sure and Indefeazable Estate of Inheritance in ffee

Simple, Hauing in themselues full power good Right and Lawfull Authority to grant Sell conuey and assure ye Same in manner & form afores^d ffree and cleare and cleerly acquitted Exonerated and discharged of & from all and all manner of former and other gifts grants bargains Sales Leases releases Mortgages Joyntures Dowers Judgments Executions Entailes fines fforfitures and of and from all other titles troubles charges and Incombrances whatsoeuer/ And ye s^d James Gooch for himself his heirs doth hereby couenant and grant that he and they the before hereby granted and bargained premises with the appur^{ses} unto ye s^d John Wheelwright his heirs & Assignes against ye s^d James Gooch and Elizabeth his wife and his heirs & assiges and against all other and euery person & persons whatsoeuer Claiming by from or under him them or any of them or under or in Right of ye s^d James Gooch his Dec^d ffather, Shall and will warrant acquit and for euer Defend by these presents/ In witness whereof ye s^d James Gooch and Elizabeth his s^d wife haue hereunto Set their hands & Seales the ninth day of June Anno Dom : 1698 Annoq, R R^s Guiliclmi Tertij Anglia &^{c} Decimo   James   Gooch
            Elizabeth (Seal) (Seal) Gooch
            Signed Sealed and deliuered
            in presents of us—
            Abigail Littlefield
            Eliezar Moody

[126] Rec^d the day and year first within written of the within named John Wheelwright the Sum of Seuenty pounds Current money in full paym^t Satisfaction and discharge of the purchase Consideration within Expressed/

p James Gooch.

Boston June 9th 1698/ The within named James Gooch and Elizabeth his wife psonally appearing before me the Subscrib^r one of ye members of the Council of his Ma^{tis} Prouince of the Massachusets Bay in New-England and Justice of peace in ye Same Acknowledged this Instrumt to be their free & Volluntary Act & Deed — Samll Wheelwright

A true Copie of ye origenall Deed of Sale Transcribed & Compared, this 25th June : 1698   p Jos Hamond Registr

This Indenture made the Seuenteenth day of June Anno Domi one thousand Six hundred Ninty and fiue in ye Seuenth year of ye Reign of our Soucraign Lord William ye ye third of England &c Between Samuel Wheelwright of Wells in ye County of York within his Majtys Prouince of ye Massachusetts Bay in New-England Gent and Esther his wife of the one part and John Wheelwright of Wells aforesd yeoman Son of ye sd Samuel Wheelwright on ye other pt Witnesseth that whereas Katherine Naneny allias Nayler of Boston in ye County of Suffulk and Prouince aforesd Widdow by deed of Burgaine and Sale under her hand and Seal Bareing Date the Sixth day of July anno Domini 1694 for and in consideration of ye Summe of ffiue pounds Curant money of New-England therein mentioned to be Annually paid unto ye sd Katherine Nanney Als Nayler and Secured to be paid By ye sd Samuel Wheelwright as By a wrighting or Couenat obligatory under ye hand and Seal of ye sd Samuel Wheelwright referance thereunto being had doth and may more ffully appear did giue grant Bargaine Sel aliene assign Set ouer Release and confirm unto him ye sd Samuel Wheelwright his heirs and assigns for euer all that Tract of Land or ground which her husband Robt Nanney Late of Boston Deceased bought of Mr Cooly containing By estimation fiue hundred Accres be it more or Less of upland Meaddow and Marsh ground with ye appurtenances Lying and being together in wells aforesd and is Bounded by a Creek which Runneth between ye said Tract of Land and the

[margin: Samll Wheelwright Esqr to Mr John Whelwrigh]

Book IV, Fol. 126.

Land that was giuen by her father John Wheelwright with her in mariage unto her husband Robt Nanney on ye one Side and a Spring or Small Brook diuiding between ye said tract of land and ye land form^{r}ly of Stephen Batson of Wells aforesaid of ye other Side and Likwise thirty accres of Marsh ground with ye appurtenances: lying and being in Wells afores^d Exepted always out: of the land Bought of Mr Coole one Tract of Land being twenty fiue pole in Bredth Beginning att ye Northeast Side of Samuel Austines Land which said Tract of Land was formerly giuen in Exchange to William Hammonds allso one hundred and fifteen Accres of upland and tenn accres of Marsh with fifty accres of upland more and fiue Accres of Marsh more Bought of William Hammonds which in all amounts to one hundred Sixty fiue accres of upland and ffifteen accres of Marsh/ lying and being within ye precincts of ye Town of Wells aforesaid and also two hundred and thirty acres of upland and twenty accres of Meddow Bought by ye s^d Robert Nanney of William Simonds which s^d land lyeth in Wells afores^d and Likewise all that land that was in ye Possession latly of John Wakfield lying in Wells afores^d Between ye Land of John Sanders and Mr Coole with all and Singular ye houses Buildings Lands Arable and Meaddow Pastures Woods under woods common and all other priuiledges and appurtenances to y^m or any of y^m belonging or in any Wise appertaining as by ye s^d Deed Reference whereto Being had more ffully may appear. Now This Indenture Further Witnesseth/ that ye Said Samuel Wheelwright and Esther his s^d wife for and in consideration of ye naturall loue good will and affection which they haue and doe bare unto their Louing Son ye s^d John Wheelwright as also for and in consideration of ye s^d John Wheelwright or his heirs paying ye one Moity of ye Summe of fiue pounds Cura^t Money of New England annually unto ye said Katherine Nanney Allias Nayler ac-

[margin: Sam^ll Wheelwright Esqr To Mr John Wheelwright]

cording to yᵉ Tennour of yᵉ sᵈ Recited Wrighting and for diuerse other good couses and considerations yᵐ thereunto moouing/ They yᵉ sᵈ Samuel Wheelwright and Esther his Wife haue giuen granted aliened Enffeoffed Released Assigned and confirmed, and by these pʳsents doe ffully [127] ffreely Clearly and absolutely giue grant alliene Enfeoffe assign Release and confirm unto yᵉ sᵈ John Wheelwright his heirs and assigns for euer The one ffull Moiety or halfe part of all and Singular yᵉ Before mentioned Seueral granted and Bargained Tracts and Pʳcill of upland Meaddow and marsh ground lying Scituate bounded and Described as aforesᵈ with one full Moiety of all and Singular yᵉ houses Buildings Woods under Woods Commons and all other profits Buildings Rights com̄odities hereditamᵗˢ Emollumᵗˢ and appurtenances to yᵉ Same Belonging or in any kind appertaining and also all yᵉ Estate Riᵗ Title Interest use possession Dower thirds claim reuertion Remaindʳ property Claim and demand whatsoeuer of yᵉ sᵈ Samuel Wheelwright and Esther his Wife of in and to yᵉ Same and Euery part thereof To haue & To Hold, all yᵉ afore mentionᵈ granted Enfeoffed and confirmed pʳmisses with yᵗ appurᶜᵉˢ unto yᵉ sᵈ John Wheelwright his heirs and Assigns for euer to his & their own sole and propper use Benifit and Behoofe from

Samˡˡ Wheelwright Esqʳ
To Mʳ
John Wheelwright

hence forth and for euer more ffreely Peaceably and quietly without any maner of Reclaime challeng or contradiction of yᵉ sᵈ Samuel Wheelwright and Esther his said Wife or either of yᵐ their or either of their heirs Executors Adminʳˢ or assigns or of any other pʳson or pʳsons whatsoeuer By their or either of their means Title or procuremᵗ in any manʳ or wise and without any accompt Recconing or Answer therefore to yᵐ or any in their names to be giuen rendred or done in time to come So that Neither yᵉ sᵈ Samuel Wheelwright nor Esther his said Wife their Heirs Executors Adminʳˢ or Assigns or any other pʳson or pʳsons whatsoeuer by

BOOK IV, FOL. 127.

y^m for y^m or in their names or in ye Name of any of y^m at any time or times hereafter may aske claim Challenge or demand in or to ye p^rmisses or any part thereof any Right title Interest use Possession Dower/ But from all and euery action of right Title Claim Interest use possession and Demand thereof: they and euery of y^m to be utterly Excluded and for euer Debared by these p^rsents In Witness Whereof ye s^d Samuel Wheelwright and Esther his Wife haue hereunto Set their hands and scales ye Day and year first aboue writen.

 Sam^ll (his seal) Wheelwright Esther (her seal) Wheelwright
Signed Sealed and Deliuered by the within named Samuel Wheelwright in p^rsents of us/

        Elizur Holyoke Junr
        Eliazer Moody/ Ser :
Signed Sealed and Deliuered By y^e within named Esther Wheelwright on y^e 24 day of June 1696, In p^rsents of us.
       Nathaniel Clark
          his
     Benjamin X Maires
         mark

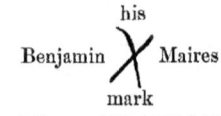

Sam^ll Wheelwright Esqr To Mr John Wheelwright

 Boston New : England June : 17th 1695/ The within named Samuel Wheelwright psonally appeared Before me y^e Subscrib^r one of y^e memb^rs of his Maj^tys Councill for y^e Prouince of ye Massachusets Bay in New England—and a Justice of Peace in ye Same Ackuowledged ye within written Instrum^t to be his act and Deed Elisha Hutchinson

Wells New : England June 24 1696 ye within named Esther Wheelwright psonally appearing Before me ye Subscriber one of ye memb^rs of his Majest^s Councill for ye Prouince of ye Massachusets Bay in New-England and a Justice of Peace in ye Same Acknowledged ye within written Instrum^t to be her act and Deed/ Sam^ll Wheelwright.

Book IV, Fol. 127, 128.

A true Coppie of y⁸ Originall Deed Transcribed and Compared: 2ᵈ day of July 1698/ p Jos Hamond Registr

Know all men by these presents that I Robt Nanny of Boston Merct, haue Sold unto Will Hamonds of Wells in the County of York, all my right and title of part of that tract of Upland and Marsh which I the sᵈ Nanny bought of Mr Cole Deceased, to him & his heires and Assignes foreuer, which Land is twenty fiue pole in breadth, begining at Sam: Austins land on yᵉ Northeast side which is in controuersie and Soe 25 poles to a certain pine tree marked with N. & W. And Soe to run down to yᵉ riuer along by an Elbow in the Main Creek, with all yᵉ point that runs out to the Creek and Soe to yᵉ Mussell ridge, and to run up into the Country as high as other lots goes [128] And in consideration thereof the aforesᵈ Hamonds is to giue me one hundred Sixty fiue Acres of upland and fifteen Acres of Marsh that lyes aboue the great plain aboue the towns lots as it is layd out by the lot layers of Wells and I the aforesᵈ Nanny doe bind me my heirs Executⁿ and Assignes firmly by these presents, that yᵉ sᵈ Hamonds Shall not be Molested by me or any under me of from yᵉ heirs Executⁿ or Assignes of Mr Cole Decesed/ And for further Confirmation I haue hereunto Set my hand and Seal the 10 of Nob in yᵉ year of our Lord one thousand Six hundred Sixty one/   Robert Nanney (his Seal)
Sealed Signed & deliuered

  in the presents of us —   This bill of Sale was Acknowl-
  Ezekiel Knights   edged before us yᵉ 11 of Nob.
  Jos Bolls.   61.   Ezekiel Knights
                                  Comissionr

A true Copie of yᵉ origenall Deed Transcribed & compared this 6ᵗʰ July. 1698 — p Jos Hamond Registr

Book IV, Fol. 128.

Know all men by these presents that I William Hamond of Wells in the Prouince of Main Alias County of York in New England for my Self my heirs Execut^rs Administrat^rs and Assignes, haue Assigned Sold and made ouer, And by these presents doe Assigne and make ouer unto James Gooch and his heirs all the Land and Marsh as is Expressed in this bill of Sale from Mr Robert Nanney to my Selfe, together with my now dwelling house and out housing with all ye priuiledges & Appurtenances thereunto belonging/ I Say to him ye s^d James Gooch his heirs and Assigns To have and to hold and peaceably enjoy for euer/ Whereunto I haue Set my hand & Seal this third day of ffeb^ry in ye year of our Lord one thousand Six hundred & Sixty Seuen

Signed Sealed & deliuered   I Benedictus Hamond wife of
  in presents of us —   William Hamond, And Jona-
  Robert   Junr   than Hamond Son of William
  Will. Symonds.   Hamond doe consent to this
                        writing

                      Will Hamond. (his Seal)
                      Jona^n Hamond

William Hamond and Jonathan Hamond Acknowledged this Instrum^t to be their Act and Deed : this 4th of July 1698
          before me Sam^ll Wheelwright. Ius : peace

A true Copie of ye origenall Deed or Assignment/ transcribed and compared. this 6th of July. 1698 —
                p Jos Hamond Regist^r

Know all men by these presents that I Abraham Remich of Eastham in the County of Barnstable, for and in consideration of a Vallable Sum of money to me in hand paid by Peter Staple of Kittery in the County of York, at and before the Sealing hereof haue bargained and Sold and by these presents doe bargain and Sell fully clearly and absolutely unto the s^d Peter Staple a Certain parcell and tract of Land containing thirty Acres Scituate and lying in the afores^d Town of Kittery, butting & bound as appears by the return, and is bounded on the Northwest by Christian Remichs land, on the Northeast with James Spinneys land and William Tetherly/ And on the Southeast with Samuel Spinney Wil-

<small>Abraham Remich to Peter Staple</small>
liam Rocklys land thus butted and bounded with all ye Priuiledges and Appurtenances thereunto belonging. To haue and to hold the Same land to ye s^d Peter Staple his heires Execut^{rs} Adm^{rs} and Assignes, to his and their own proper use and uses for euer/ And I the s^d Abraham Remich my Self my heires Execut^{rs} Adm^{rs} and Assignes and euery of us, the s^d land unto the S^d Peter Staple his heires Execut^{rs} Adm^{rs} and Assignes against all persons from by or under me Shall and will defend and Acquit for euer by these presents In witness whereof I haue hereunto Set my hand and Seal this Nineteenth day of June, in ye year, one thousand Six hundred Ninety and four/   Abraham Remich (his Seal)

Signed Sealed & deliuered   her
  In presents of us —   Elizabeth ϑ Remich
  Christian Remich   mark
  Jacob Remich.   Christian Remich Jacob Remich and
  Isaac Remich   Isaac Remich came and made oath
  Joshua Remich   that they Saw Abraham Remich
  Peter Staple   Signe Seale and deliuer this In-
  Nathaniel Atkins   strument to Peter Staple of Kittery Senr this thirteenth day of Septemb^r 1694 as his Act and Deed/ before me
        ffrancis Hooke Just peac

A true Copie of the origenall Deed of Sale Transcribed & compared this 9th day of June 1698 p Jos Hamond Regist^r

BOOK IV, FOL. 128, 129.

Anno Regni Regis Georgij Quinto —
At a Court of General Sessions of ye peace holden for & within ye County of York at York April ye 7th 1719/ Joshua Remich & Peter Staple made Oath that they Saw ye within Named Abraham Remich Sign Seal & Deliver ye within Instrum^t as his Act & deed and that they Set their hands as witnesses thereunto at ye Same time
       Attest Jos Hamond Cler
Recorded according to ye Original April 7th 1719
       p Jos Hamond Reg^r

[129] Know all men by these presents that I John Neale of the Town of Kittery in the County of York or Province of Mayn doe bargaine Sell and by these presents doe confirm unto Nathan Lord Senr of the Town afores^d in the aforesaid County or Province of Mayn his heires or Assignes/ All my Right and Title of a parcell of land and house containing About twenty fiue Acres more or less Lying and being upon the Northeast Side of Piscataquach Riuer being the one half of a tract of land which I ye s^d John Neal bought of Alexander Maxell of the Town of York, the said fiue and twenty Acres of land being upon ye North Side of the

John Neal
To
Noth Lord

s^d tract of land, with fiue Acres of Marsh ground lying and being neare a place comonly called by the name of Whites Marsh, for and in consideration of Eighty pounds Starling to me to be in hand payd by the s^d Nathan Lord his heires or Assigns and furthermore I the s^d John Neal doe hereby bind my Self my heires and assignes for euer, to bare the s^d Nathan Lord his heires and Assignes for euer harmless from any cause or causes arising for from or by me my heires or Assignes for euer/ And for the performance of the contents of this bill

Book IV, Fol. 129.

of Sale I haue hereunto Set my hand this 7th 9mo in the year of our Lord 1662
Sealed & Deliuered
  in the presents of us   John   Neale
  James Heard
  Peter ⟨⟩ Grant   his mark
    his mark   (his Seal)

        John Neal Acknowledged the aboue written Instrument to be his Act and Deed this 22th of May 1683 — before me
            Charles ffrost Jus. of peace

A true Copie of the origenall Deed of Sale Transcribed & compared this 14th of June. 1698/
            p Jos Hamond Registr

    Know all men by these presents that I Mary Twisden Widow and Relict of unto Peter Twisden lately of the Isles of Sholes ffisherman, for and in consideration of the Sum of twelue pounds money to me in hand alredy paid by Samll Small of Kittery, with which sd Sum doe acknowledge my Self fully Satisfied, and hereby Acquit ye sd Samll Small his heires Executrs and Administratrs from all and euery part thereof for Euer — haue giuen granted bargained and Sold and doe by these presents giue grant bargain sell Alien Enfeoffe confirm and make ouer unto ye sd Samuel Small, one certain lot or parcell of Marsh Consisting of three Acres whether it be more or less, which was formerly bought by my said husband Peter Twisden of Robert Edge of York, which sd lott lies in ye Westermost branch of sd York riuer, and bounded as ffolloweth : Vidzt, on ye Southeast by a piece of Marsh that was formerly Mr John Alcocks And on the Northwest by that which was formerly Philip Adamms, one end bounded by the upland, and the other by the Riur/ To

haue and to hold to him yᵉ sᵈ Samˡˡ Small his heires Executʳˢ Admʳˢ and Assigns, all the aboueˢᵈ lott of Marsh of three Acres let it be more or less as purchased by my sᵈ husband of said Edge together with all the priuiledges and Appurtenances thereunto belonging or in any ways Appurtaining for euer/ And I the said Mary Twisden doe oblige my Self my heires Execʳˢ and Admʳˢ to warrant and defend yᵉ sᵈ Marsh as Specified together with all yᵉ Pruiledges unto him yᵉ sᵈ Samˡˡ Small his heires Executʳˢ Admˡⁿ & Assigns for Ever from all manner of person or persons whatsoeuer pretending or laying any manner of Lawfull Claim from by or under me or any of mine. In Testimony to all and Singular the Premises I haue hereunto Set my hand and Affixed my Seal, July. 20ᵗʰ 1696   the mark of
Signed Sealed & deliuered   Mary M Ŧ Twisden
 in the presents of us   Massachuset June, 30ᵗʰ 1697 (her Seal)
  Job Alcock   Mary Twisden appeared befor me,
  Alexander Dennett   one of his Maᵗⁱᵉˢ Justices for
         this Prouince, and Acknowl-
         edged this Instrument to be her
         Act and Deed   Sam Sewall

A true Copie of yᵉ origenall Deed of Sale Transcribed & compared this. 16ᵗʰ June 1698—   p Jos Hamond Registʳ

To all People to whome these presents Shall come Peter Wittum of Kittery in the County of York in yᵉ Prouince of the Massachusets Bay in New England Sends Greeting/ Now know yee that I the aboue mentioned Peter Wittum for Diuers good causes me thereunto mouing, More Especially for and in consideration of yᵉ Summ of Sixty pounds to me in hand paid by Samuel Small of Kittery aforesaid, of Lawfull money of New England, the receipt whereof I acknowledge and of euery part and parcell thereof And therewith fully Satisfied

Peter Wittum to Samˡˡ Small

contented & and payd, haue freely and clearly Acquitted Exonerated and discharged him the Said Small his heires Execut[rs] Admin[rs] and Assignes for euer, haue giuen granted bargained Sold Aliened Enfeoffed made ouer and confirmed, And by these presents doe for me my heires Execut[rs] Admin[rs] and Assignes for euer, fully clerely and absolutely giue grant bargain Sell Alien Enfeoffe make ouer and confirm unto him y[e] s[d] Sam[ll] Small his heires Execut[rs] Admin[rs] and Assigns for Euer, All that Messuage or Tenement which I formerly liued on and possessed, with about Sixteen Acres of land thereunto belonging Scituate lying & being at Stirgeon Creek in y[e] town of Kittery afores[d] on y[e] Southwest Side of s[d] Creek and Joyning to it together with an orchard thereto belonging, with all y[e] profits priuiledges Appurtenances and benefits thereunto belonging or in any wise appertaining [130] To haue and to hold the s[d] Messuage or Tenement with y[e] land and orchard and Appurtenances thereunto belonging, with all Right Title Interest claim and demand which I y[e] s[d] Wittum now haue or in time past haue had or which my heires Execut[rs] Admin[rs] or Assigig in time to come may might Should or in any wise ought to haue, of in or to y[e] aboue giuen and granted Premises or any part thereof to him y[e] s[d] Sam[ll] Small his heires or Assignes for euer, and to the Sole and proper use benefit and behoofe of him y[e] s[d] Samuel Small his heires Execut[rs] Admin[rs] and Assignes for efimore And I y[e] s[d] Wittum for me my heires Execut[rs] Admin[rs] or Assigns doe couen[t] promise & grant to and with him y[e] s[d] Sam[ll] Small his heirs & Assignes y[t] at and before y[e] ensealing and deliuery thereof I am y[e] true right & proper owner of y[e] aboue premises and y[e] Appurtenances, And that I haue in my Self good right full power and Lawfull Authority the aboue giuen & granted premises to Sell and dispose off, and that y[e] same & euery part y[r]of is free and cleare & freely & clerely Acquitted Exonerated and Discharged of and from all and all manner of former & other gifts grants bargains Sales leases Mortgages troubles

Book IV, Fol. 130.

& incumbrances whatsoeuer And that it Shall and may be lawfull to and for y[e] s[d] Sam[ll] Small his heires and Assigns the aboues[d] Premises and euery part thereof from time to time and at all times hereafter to haue hold use improue ocupie and possess lawfully peaceably and quietly, without any Lawfull deniall hinderance Molestation or disturbance of or by me or any other pson or psons from by or under me or by my porcurement and that y[e] Sale thereof and of euery part thereof, against my Self my heires Execut[rs] and assigns & against all other psons whatsoeuer Lawfully claiming the Same or any part y[r]of I will for euer Saue harmless Warrant and Defend by these presents — and that I my heires &[ct] Shall and will make perform & execute, Such other further Lawfull and reasonable Act or Acts thing or things as in law or Equitie can be deuised or required for y[e] better confirming and more Sure making of the premises unto s[d] Sam[ll] Small his heires &[ct] According the Laws of this Prouince/ In witness whereof I y[e] said Peter Wittum haue hereunto Set my hand and Seal this twelfth day of Decemb[r] in y[e] year of our Lord one thousand Six hundred Ninety Six and in y[e] Eighth year of the Reign of our Soueraign Lord William the third, King ouer England &[ct]

Signed Sealed and deliuered   Peter P Wittum (his Seale)
    in pres[ts] of   his mark
    John Shapleigh
    John Heard   Peter Wittum Sen[r] and Redigon his wife appeared before me and Acknowledged this Instrum[t] to be their Act and Deed And y[e] s[d] Redigon did freely & Voluntaryly giue up all her Right title and Interest thereunto this ffifteenth of January. 169$\frac{6}{7}$ Before me
                           Charles ffrost Just : Peace

A true Copie of y[e] origenall Deed of Sale Transcribed & compared this. 16. of June 1698 — p Jos Hamond Regist[r]

Book IV, Fol. 130.

This Indenture made the Eighteen day of July one thousand Six hundred Ninety Eight In the tenth year of y̅e̅ Reign of our Soueraign Lord King William the third, of England Scotland ffrance and Ireland, &c between John Brawn of Piscataqua in y̅e̅ County of York w̅th̅in their Majesties Prouince of the Massachutus Bay in New England husbandman, and Anna his wife on the one part and William Pepperell of Piscataqua in y̅e̅ County afores̅d̅ Mercht on y̅e̅ other pt Witnesseth that the s̅d̅ John Brawn and Anna his wife for and in consideration of y̅e̅ Sum of thirteen pounds Currant money of New England to them in hand att and before y̅e̅ Ensealing and Deliuery of these pres-

John Brawn to Wm Pepperell

ents well and truly payd and Secured in y̅e̅ law to be paid by y̅e̅ s̅d̅ William Pepperrell the Receit whereof to full content and Satisfaction they doe hereby Acknowledge and thereof doe Acquit the s̅d̅ William Pepperrell his heirs Execut̅rs̅ Admin̅rs̅ & Assigns & euery of them for euer by these presents haue giuen granted bargained Sold conueied & confirmed, by these presents doe freely fully and absolutely giue grant bargain Sell conuey and confirm unto y̅e̅ s̅d̅ William Pepperrell his heires and Assignes for euer, All that their piece or parcell of Upland at Piscataqua. Lying and being in Kittery, containing by Estimation one halfe Acre or thereabouts And is butted and bounded by the Sea on y̅e̅ South Side and William Pepperrell on y̅e̅ North and East & West Side, together w̅th̅ all and Singular the house now upon it with orchit trees and all Appurtenances thereunto belonging or in any wayes thereunto Appurtaining To haue and to hold the s̅d̅ piece or parcell of upland house and orchit with all y̅e̅ aforementioned to be granted and bargained premises unto y̅e̅ s̅d̅ William Pepperrell his heires Execut̅rs̅ & Assignes to his and their onely proper use benefitt and behofe for euer, and y̅e̅ s̅d̅ John Brawn & Anna his wife for them Selues their heires Execut̅rs̅ Admin̅rs̅ or Assigns doe couenant promise grant and agree, to and with y̆ᵉ s̆ᵈ William Pepperrell his heires Execut̆ʳˢ Admin̆ʳˢ and Assigns by these presents in manner following that is to Say that at yᵉ time of this bargain and Sale and untill yᵉ ensealing & deliuery of these presents, they the sᵈ John Brawn and Anna his wife are the true owners of yᵉ aforesᵈ bargained premises, and haue in themselues full power good right & lawfull Authority to grant bargan for, Sell convey the Same in manner as abouesᵈ being free and clear of and from all former gifts grants titles troubles Charges and incumbrances whatsoeuer And will warrant and Defend the Same unto yᵉ sᵈ William Pepperrell his heirs and Assigns for euer, Against the lawfull Claims and demands of all & euery pson or psons whomsoeuer [131] And lastly will doe or cause to be done any other Act or Acts for yᵉ furthʳ confirmation and more Sure making of yᵉ aboue bargained premises as by his or their Councill learned in yᵉ law Shall be reasonable Aduised Deuised or required/ In witness whereof John Brawn & Anna his wife haue hereunto Set their hands & Seals this day & year first aboue written/

Signed Sealed Deliuered   John ⤴ Brawn (Seal)
in yᵉ presents of us —   Anna Bran (Seal)
William ffernald
John Shapleigh   John Brawn and Anna Brawn his wife
Abraham Preble   came before me yᵉ 18ᵗʰ July 1698
      and Acknowledged this to be their
      ffree Act and Deed/ Before me
      Samuel Donnell Just : peace

A true Copie of the origenall Deed of Sale. Transcribed and compared this 18. of July. 1698/
     p Jos Hamond Registʳ

To all Christian People to whom this present Deed of Gift Shall come I ffrancis Nicholls of Kittery in the

BOOK IV, FOL. 131.

Province of the Massachusets Bay in New-England wth the consent of Iane my Wife : Send Greeting Know ye that for diuerse good causes and considerations me thereunto mouing haue giuen granted alliened Enfeoffed conueyed and confirmed unto Mr Richard Cutt of Kittery in ye County of york in ye Prouince of ye Massachusets : Bay yeoman in New-England and

Nicholls
To
Richd Cutt

doe by these p^rs^ts for my Selfe my heirs Executors Admin^rs and assigns ffully ffreely and absolutely giue grant allien enfeoffe conuey and confirm unto him ye s^d Richard Cutt his heirs and assigns Certain Tracts or p^rcills of Land Togather with all ye appurtenances and Priuiliges Belonging or in any wayes thereunto appertaining all of y^m Scituate Lying and Being in the Township of ffalmouth in cascoe Bay The contents and Bounds whereof are as ffolloweth vizt Two accres granted By ye Inhabitants and freehold^rs of ffalm^o at my first Settlem^t there as their Town Records may make appear allso Six Accres more att another place Butting upon ye Land of Capt Ting allso Sixty accres more Bounded By the Land commonly called corbans Lott all which tracts of Land were granted to me By ye Town of ffallmoth as their Town Reccords will manifist : also three accres more which was giuen By ye Township of falmo^th to Jonathan Orriss Bounded By ye Six accres here mentioned also Richard Smiths house Lot Lying and Being near fort loyall which I purchased of him with all ye Profits and Priuiledges unto s^d house Lot Belonging or appertaining/ To Haue and To Hold ye s^d Tracts of Land with all ye appurtenances thereunto Belonging with all ye Right Title Interest claim and Demand

Nichols
To
Richd Cutt

which I ye s^d ffrancis Nicholls and Iane my Wife now haue or in time past haue had or which I my heirs Execut^rs Admin^rs or Assigns may might should or in any wise ought to haue in time to come of in or to ye aboue granted p^rmisses or any p^t Thereof To him ye s^d Richard Cutt his heirs and assigns

BOOK IV, FOL. 131, 132.

for euer and to yᵉ sole and proper use Benifit and Behoofe of him yᵉ sᵈ Richard Cutt his heirs executorˢ Administrators and Assigns for euer more and I the sᵈ frances Nichols with Iane my Wife for me my heirs Execrˢ Adminrˢ and assigns doe couenanᵗ promiss and grant to and wᵗʰ yᵉ sᵈ Richard Cutt his heirs and assigns that at and Before yᵉ ensealing and deliuery hereof the aboue mentioned and euery pᵗ thereof is free and clear acquitted and Discharged of and from all former and other gifts grants Bargains Sales leases mortgages dowries titles Trubles acts Allienations and Incumbrances whatsoeuer and that it Shall and may be Lawfull to and for yᵉ sᵈ Richard Cutt his heirs and assigns yᵉ abouesᵈ pʳmisses and euery part thereof from time to time and at all times forever hereafter to haue hold use occupie Improue possess and enjoy Lawfully Peacably and quietly without any Lawfull Deniall hindrance Mollestation or Disturbance of or by me or any pʳson or pʳsons from By or under me or By my Procuremᵗ In Witness whereof I the sᵈ ffrances Nichols and Iane my Wife haue hereunto Set our hands and Seals the Nineteenth day of Octobʳ Anno Domini one Thousand Six hundred ninty and Six/ Añoq̃ Regni Regis Gulielmi Angliæ &ᶜ octauo/ The words Thereunto in yᵉ eighth line [132] was Inserted Before Signing and Sealing and Deliuery   Frances Nichols (his Seal)

Signed Sealed & Deliuered   her
  In the Presence of us   Iane Nichols / o (her Seal)
  John Newmarch Junʳ
  John Lary   mark
  Samuel Scriuen

The 20 : of octobʳ 1696 : Then ffrances Nichols Came and Acknowledged This aboue Instrument to Be his ffree Act and Deed Before me, Wᵐ Pepperel Js Pes

A true Coppie of the origenall Deed of Gift Transcribed and compared this 6ᵗʰ day of Augost 1698 —

                pʳ Jos Hamond Registʳ

BOOK IV, FOL. 132.

Know all men By these p'sents that I Richard Cutt of Kittery in the County of York in the Prouince of ye Massachusets Bay in New-England for and in consideration of one hundred pounds money of New-England to me in hand Paid By my Brother Robert Cut of ye s^d Place ye receipt whereof I doe hereby acknowledge and my Selfe therewith fully Satisfied & Paid and ffrom which Summ and euery part thereof I doe therefore Exon'ate acquit and Discharge ye s^d Robert Cut

Richd Cutt
To
Robt Cutt

his heirs Executors Admin^{rs} and assigns for euer haue giuen granted Sold Alliened and confirmed and p these p'sents doe for my Selfe Executo^{rs} administrators and assigns guue grant Bargaine Sell and Confirm unto ye s^d Robt Cutt the one halfe of my land on which I now Dwell in ye Town as aboue s^d which halfe is Laid out to s^d Robt Cutt next to Mr Meridies and is Bounded as ffollows upon ye S : E : with Meredes on ye East and N : E with Willm Scriuen and Mary Churchwoods on ye North with my own Land and from thence South to a White Ash tree and to ye water/ To Haue and To Hold the aboue Bargained p'misses togather with all and Singular Priuiliges thereunto Belonging or any wise appertaining Exepting William Scriuens Land on Barnses point giuen him p me Before this which is allwayes Excepted to him ye s^d Robert Cutt his heirs Executors Admin^{rs} and Assigns for euer Clear and Clearly acquited and discharged of and from all other and former gifts grants Bargains leases Mortgages Joyntures Judgm^{ts} Executions Wills Entailes forfitures and from all other trubles and Incumbrances whatsoeuer done or to be done p my Selfe or assigns Before the Sealing and Deliuery hereof and I ye s^d Richard Cutt ye aboue s^d p'mises doe promiss to warrant and Defend against all maner of psons whatsoeuer claiming any part or p'cill thereof by from or und^r me my heirs Executors Administrators or assigns In Witness whereof I the s^d Richard Cutt haue Set my hand

Richd Cutt
To
Robt Cutt

BOOK IV, FOL. 132, 133.

and Seal June 28: 1694 and in ye Sixth year of their Maj^ties Reign.   Richard Cutt (his Seal)
Signed Sealed & Deliuered
  in Presence of us   Mr Richard Cutt Acknowledged this
  William Scriuen   Instrum^t to Be his act and Deed
  Frances Nicholls   to Mr Robt Cutt this 23^d of June
                        1694:   Frances Hook Just pea
    A true Coppie of the origenall Deed Transcribed & compared this 6th day of Augost 1698   p Jos Hamond Reg^r

[133] To all People to whom this Present Deed of Mortgage shall come ffrances Hooke of Kittery Point in the Prouince of Mayne in New-england and Mary his wife send greeting Know Ye that the said ffrances Hooke and Mary his Wife doe Acknowledge to be indebted and Iustly to owe the full and Iust Sume of one hundred and fifty Pounds curant Money of New-England unto Henry Dearing of Boston in the County of suffulk in Newengland afores^d Being for sundry goods wch they ye s^d ffran^s Hooke and Mary his wife haue at Diuerse Times heretofore Bought and Rec^d of the s^d Henry Dearing In Consideration of wch Summe of one hundred and fifty Pounds By them formerly Receiu^d as afores^d of the said Henry Dearing the Rec^t whereof they doe hereby Acknowledge and themselues therewith to be fully Satisfied and Paid and absolutely acquit and Discharge him the s^d Henry Dearing his heirs and Assigns for euer They the s^d ffrances Hooke and Mary his Wife haue giuen granted Bargained Sold Allienned enfeoffed and confirmed and by these p^rsents for themselues their heirs Executors admin^rs and assigns doe fully freely and absolutely giue grant Bargaine sell allien Enfeoffe and confirm unto him ye s^d Henry Dearing his heirs and assigns all that their peice or p^rcill of

Maj^r Hook
   To
Mr Henry
Dearing

Book IV, Fol. 133.

Land Bought formerly of the Late Nic° Shapleigh and his Wife with the Dwelling houses and Barn on the same Scituate and Being within the said Town of Kittery Being Butted and Bounded with a creeck on the North east and Piscataqua Riuer on the South west the Late Nic° Shapleighs land on the north west and Easterly on the Land of said Nich° Shapleigh or howeuer Butted and Bounded Togather will all woods Trees houses Buildings waters water courses fences Pastures feedings Profitts Rights Memb^{rs} and Appertenances to the same Belonging or in any Wise Appertaining as Also my Tenn cows and Negroe Boy called Tom and my Two fishing shallops the one named Arabella and the other Penellapy with all Sails Roads anchors and all other things whatsoeuer Belonging to them with all the fish of their next Winter voyage To Haue and To Hold: The said Peice or p^{r}cill of Land wch containeth three acres more or Less Butted and Bounded as afores^d with the s^d houses Barn and all other Profits Priuiliges and appurtenances — and my tenn cows and Negroe Boy Tom and my two fishing shallops and all things Belonging to them With all the fish of their next Winter voyage unto him the said Henry Dearing, his heirs Executors Administrators and assigns for euer more And the said ffrances Hook and Mary his Wife for themselues their heirs Executors Administrators and assigns Doe couenant Promiss and grant to and with him the said Henry Dearing his heirs Executors Admin^{rs} and assigns that at and Before the Sealing & Deliuery hereof they are the True and lawfull owners and Possessers of the p^{r}misses and that the same and euery part thereof is free and clear and freely and clearly acquited Exonerated and Discharged of and from all and all maner of former and other gifts grants Bargains Sales Leases Mortgages Indentures Dowries Extents Seizures entails forfitures Judgm^{ts} Executions and of and from all other

Book IV, Fol. 133, 134.

Major Hooke
To
Mr Dearing

titles trubles and Incumbrances whatsoeuer and that it shall and may Be Lawfull and free to and for the s^d Henry Dearing his heirs and assigns from time to time and at all times foreuer hereaft^r the Primisses with their appurtenances to enter Possess haue hold use occupy and enjoy as an Estate of Inheritance in fee Simple without any condition limitation or Reuertion whatsoeuer so as to alter and make voyd the same and that the same and euery part thereof unto the said Henry Dearing his heirs and assigns against themselues and against all other p^rsons whatsoeuer from By or under them Lawfullly claiming the Same or any part thereof they shall and will from time to time and at all times foreuer hereafter well and suffitiently saue harmless warant and Defend and that they shall and will doe and p^rform all and such further and other Lawfull and Reasonable acts and things for the Better confirmation and sure making of ye same as afores^d as in Law and equity can Be Diuised or Required Prouided allwayes and it is hereby Declared to Be ye true intent and meaning hereof as ffolloweth that if ye s^d ffrances Hooke and his Wife shall well and Truly pay or cause to Be payd unto the said Henry Dearing his heirs or Assigns the full and just summe of one hundred and fifty pounds curant money of new England at [134] The Dwelling house of the said Henry Dearing in Boston afores^d on or Before the first day of octob^r next Ensuing the Date hereof without fraud or further Delay that then and from thence forth this Present Deed and grant and euery article therein contained Shall be voyd and of none Effect and to all Intents and Purposes shall utterly cease and Determine any thing contained herein to the contrary hereof in any wise notwithstanding and it is Mutually couenanted and agreed By and Betwen the s^d Frances Hooke and his Wife and the said Henry Dearing that if uppon the non paym^t of the aboues^d Summe of one hundred and fifty Pounds at ye day and Place afores^d the s^d Henry His heirs and assigns shall from thence forth haue full and free Power and authority By uertue hereof to sell grant allien and confirm ye Primisses for so much money as he cann in order to satisfie the fores^d sume and ye s^d Henry Dearing shall Return and pay the ouerplus aboue the s^d Summe of one hund: and fifty Pounds Togather with all costs and Damages of the p^{r}misses shall be sold for any/thing aboue the s^d summe & Damages unto the s^d ffrances Hook his heirs and assigns upon demand after he hath Rec^d it/ and the s^d ffrancis Hook doth firmly Bind and oblige himselfe his heirs Executors and Administ^rs unto Henry Dearing his heirs and assigns in ye summe of two hundred Pounds Money of New-England on cōdition that he shall well and Truly Pay or cause to Be Payd and Satisfied unto Henry Dearing his heirs or assigns all such summe and summs of money which shall be wanting or fall short of the said summe of one hundred and fifty Pounds upon the sale and allienation of the p^{r}misses By the s^d Dearing his heirs or assigns so that ye s^d summe of one hundred and fifty Pounds with all manner of Damages shall Be fully satisfied to ye s^d Henry Dearing according to ye true Intent and meaning hereof/ In Witness whereof the s^d ffrancis Hooke and his Wife haue hereunto Set their hands and Seals this thirty day of Decemb^r in the year of our Lord one thousand Six hundred Eighty fiue.

Major Hook To Mr Dering

Sealed and Deliuered in P^{r}sence   ffrances Hooke (his Seal)
  of us: Arthur ffarmer
Nicholas Tucker

Major Hook To Mr Dearing
        Capt Frances Hooke came Before me this 16: March 168$\frac{3}{4}$ and did acknowledge this Instrum^t abouc written to Be his Act and deed—
                       Edw Rishworth Jus: Peace

Seuerall Summs of money payd since this Instrum^t was made and I rec^d allso goods seuerall times my Booke will clear it.

BOOK IV, FOL. 134, 135.

Kittery the 8th of Aprill 1686 Capt Frances Hooke gaue Henry Dearing Possession and Deliuery of the within mentioned p'misses the Land By Turfe and Twigg and the cattle By the horne one in Lew of the whole and ye houses in Possession and one Negroe Boy named Thomas or Tom Before and in Presence of us as Witnesses as Witnesseth/

     John Bray
     Stephen   *O*   Presby
     his mark

A True Coppy of the origenall Instrumt Transcribed & compared this 6th day of August 1698

     p Jos : Hamond Registr

This Indenture made the fifth day of Iune Anno Domi one Thousand Six hundrd Ninty and one anncq R Rs et Regena Guliclmi et Mariæ Nunc &c Terto : Between Samuel Phillipps of Boston in the County of Suffulk in their Majests Collony of the Massachusets Bay in New-England victuallr Son of Major William Phillipps Late of Boston aforesd formerly of Saco in the Prouince of Mayn in New-England aforesd Gent Decd and Sarah his Wife on the one part and George Turfrey of Boston aforesd Mercht on ye other part Witnesseth Whereas the sd William Phillipps in and By his Last Will and Testament made in the month of ffebruary Anno: Domini 1682 and Executed the twenty ninth Day of Septembr 1683 amongst Diuerse other Legacyes did therein giue and Bequeath unto his Wife Bridget Phillipps his Eldest Son Samuel Phillipps and youngest Son William Phillipps and to their heirs and assigns for euer in Equall [135] Proportions three Quarter parts of a certain p'cil of Land and three Quarter parts of the Sawmill Built thereon which Land lieth on Saco Riuer in the Prouince of Mayne

(margin: Samll Phillipps To Geo Turfrey)

in New England aforesd Beginning at a Brook called Dauids Broock and from thence runns four miles up the Riuer of Saco and from the s^d Riuer of Saco runns four miles into the Country wth all the priuilidges & appur^{ces} thereunto Belonging Exept onely about twenty or thirty accres of s^d Land wch s^d William Phillipps Sold to William ffrost and timb^r sold to his Son in Law John Alden as By Deed is Exprest the other fourth part which makes up the whole he fformerly Sold to Mr Willia^m Taylor for Mr Haenan fformerly of ffyall also in and By s^d Will did giue and Bequeath unto them an Island Called cow Island Lying and Being in Saco Riuer afores^d Together with one halfe part of another Island called Bonitons Island Lying on Saco riuer afores^d Purchased By s^d William Phillipps Dec^d of John Boniton Senr Now THis Indenture Further Witnesseth that ye s^d Samuel Phillipps and Sarah his wife for and in Consideration of the Summe of Eighty Pounds Curant money of New-England to them in hand well and Truly paid Before the ensealing and Deliuery of these Presents By the said George Turfrey the Receipt whereof to full content and satisfaction they doe hereby acknowledge and thereof and of Euery Part thereof doe acquit Exonerate and Discharge the said George Turfrey his heirs Executors and administrators and Euery of them for euer By these p^{r}sents haue giuen granted Bargained Sold Alliened Enfeoffed Conueyed and confirmed and By These p^{r}sents doe fully freely clearly and absolutely giue grant Bargaine Sell Allien Enfeoffe conuey and confirm unto the s^d George Turfrey his heirs and Assigns for euer all the Estate Right Title Interest Inheritance Property Possession reuerc͠on Claim and Demand Whatsoeuer that the s^d Samuel Phillipps and Sarah his wife or either of them euer had now haue or which they or either of them their or either of their heirs may might should or ought to haue and claim of in and to all and Singular the Lands Islands and Mills Before

*Saml Phillipps
To
Geo Turfrey*

menc̃oned and expressed with the Tenem^{ts} thereon Being one quarter Part of the Same Scituate Lying and Being on Saco River in the Prouince of Mayn afores^d Together with all and Singular the Pastures Trees woods und^rwoods Swamps Marshes meddows Arable Lands Ways waters wat^rcourses milldamms mill Ponds head Wares And going Mill gears ffishings ffowlings huntings easements commons common of Pasture Passages Stones Breaches fflatts Wharfes Profits Priuilidges rights Libertys Im̃unitys commodities and appurten^ces whatsoeuer to s^d Quarter Part Belonging or in any kind appertaining or therewith all now or heretofore used occupied or Enjoyed or Reputed Taken or known as Part p^rcell or memb^r thereof By fforce and uertue of s^d Will and Testam^t or howsoeuer otherwise without any Prejudice to the Right and Interest of their mother Mrs Bridgett Phillipps and Brother William Phillipps or either of them

Sam^ll Phillips
To
Geõ Turfrey

therein To Haue & To Hold all and Singular ye aboue granted and Bargained Primisses with their and euery of their Rights Memb^rs and Appurtenan^ces and euery Part and p^rcell thereof unto the s^d George Turfry his heirs and assigns for euer to his and their only Sole and Proper use Benifit and Behhoofe from hence forth and foreuer more and the said Samuel Phillipps and Sarah his Wife for themselues their heirs Executors and Adm^rs do covenant Promiss grant and agree to and wth the said George Turfrey his heirs Executors Adm^rs and assigns By these p^rsents in manner and fform ffollowing that is to say that the s^d Samuel Phillipps and Sarah his Wife or one of them for and not withstanding any act matter or thing committed or suffered By them or either of them att the time of the ensealing and Deliuery of these p^rsents are the true Sole and Lawfull owner and stand Lawfully Seized of and in all the aforebargained p^rmisses wth their and euery of their appurtenances of good Perfect and Indefeazable Estate of Inheritance in fee Simple and for and notwithstanding any

BOOK IV, FOL. 135, 136.

such act Matter or thing as afores[d] haue good right full Power and absolute authority to grant Bargaine Sell conuey and assure the same in manner and form as afores[d] and that it shall and may Be Lawfull to and for the s[d] George Turfrey his heirs and assigns and and euery of them Lawfully Peaceably and Quietly to enter into and upon haue hold use occupy Possess and enjoy the aboue granted p̃imisses with their and euery of their appur[ces] and to haue receiue and take y[e] rents Issues and Profits theirof w[t]hout y[e] Lawfull and equitable Let Sute truble Deniall Disturbance expulc̃on euiction ejection interuption hindrance [136] Or Mollestation Whatsoeuer of them the s[d] Samuel Phillipps and Sarah his Wife or either of them their or either of their heirs or assigns or of any other By them or any of their means act consent Defalt Priuity or Procurement and that the grantors nor either of them haue not done or Suffered to Be done any matter act or thing whereby the aboue granted p[r]imisses or any Part thereof may Be any ways charged or Incumbred in Estate title or charge or other Incumbrance

Sam[ll] Phillipps
To
Geo Turfrey

Whatsoeuer and Lastly that the said Samuel Phillipps and Sarah his Wife their heirs Executors and Adm[rs] shall and will from hence forth and foreuer hereafter Warra[t] and Defend the aboue granted p[r]imisses w[th] their Appurtenances and euery part thereof unto the s[d] George Turfrey his his heirs and assigns foreuer against the Lawfull Claims and Demands of all and euery p[r]son and p[r]sons whatsoeuer from By or und[r] them or any or either of y[m] In Witness whereof the s[d] Samuel Phillipps and Sarah his Wife haue hereunto set their hands and Seals the day and year first aboue written.

Samuel (his Seal) Phillipps.   Sarah (her seal) Phillipps.

Signed Sealed and Deliuered By the within named Samuel Phillipps in p[r]sence of us —
John Hill
Eliezer Moodey Ser:

BOOK IV, FOL. 136.

Memorand that on the first Day of Iuly Anno Dom 1697º the within Named Samuell Phillipps and Sarah his Wife came p'sonally Before me the Subscrib' one of his Majest' Councill of the Prouince of the Massachusets Bay and Justice of Peace within the Same and acknowledged the within written Instrum^t to Be Their Act and Deed and also the s^d Samuel Phillipps acknowledged to haue Rec^d from the within named George Turfrey at the day of the date of these p'sents the Summe of thirty Pounds money Part of the Sum within mentioned and now at this day ye said Phillipps Rec^d from the s^d George Turfrey the Sum of fifty pounds money in full Paym^t in P'sence of—
        Nathaniel Thomas

A True coppie of the origenall Instrum^t Transcribed and Compared this 10th day of Aug^st 1698.
       p Jos Hamond Regist^r

This Indenture made the day of July. Anno Dom^i one thousand Six hundred ninety and fiue in the Seuenth year of ye Reign of our Soueraine Lord King William the third of England &^c Between John Morton of Boston in the County of Suffolk and Prouince of the Massachusets Bay in New England yeoman and Martha his Wife on the one part and Enoch Greenleafe of the same Boston sadler on the other

Morton   part Witnesseth that the s^d John Morton and
To   Martha his s^d Wife for and in Consideracon of
Greenleafe   the Summe of Twenty pounds Currant Mony of
       New England to them in hand well and truly paid Before thensealing and Deliuery of these p'sents By the said Enoch Greenleafe the Receipt whereof to full content and satisfaction they doe hereby acknowledge and thereof and of euery Part thereof Doe acquit Exon^rate and Discharge the s^d Enoch Greenleafe his heirs Execcutors and Adm^rs and

euery of them for euer By these p'sents as also for diuerse good causes and consid'acons them hereunto moueing they the s^d John Morton and Martha his s^d Wife haue giuen granted Bargained and sold alliened Enfeoffed conueyed released and confirmed and By these p'sents doe for themselues and their heirs fully freely and absolutely giue grant Bargain sell allien Enfeoffe release conuey and confirm unto the s^d Enoch Greenleafe his heirs and assigns for euer all that their Certaī [137] Tract or pcill of upland cntaining By Estimation one hundred accres Be the same more or Less with all the Meadow adjoyning and thereunto Belonging which he the s^d Morton formerly Purchased of John howell of Black point dec^d Scituate Lying and Being at a Certaine Place or village commonly called or known By the name of Dunston within the Township of Scarborrough in the County of York within the Prouince of the Massachusets Bay afores^d Being Butted and Bounded on ye Northeasterly Side By common or Wild^rness Lands and on all other sid^s wholly Surrounded By the Riuer There Together with all and Singular the houses Ediffices and Buildings standing thereon orchards Profits Priuilidges Rights comons comon of Pasture Trees woods und^rwoods comodities Immunityes heredam^ts Imollum^ts and appurtenances whatsoeuer to the s^d Granted Primisses and to euery part and parcill thereof Belonging or in any wise appertaining or therewith now or heretofore used occupied enjoyed accepted reputed taken or known as part p^rcell or memb^r thereof and the Reuercon and Reuercons remaind^r and remaind^rs Rents issues and Seruices thereof and also all the Estate Right title Interest Inheritance use Possession Dower Power of thirds claim and Demand whatsoeuer of the s^d John Morton and Martha his s^d Wife and of either of y^m of in and to the same and euery part thereof with all Deeds wiitings and Euidences Relating thereunto To Haue and To Hold all the Beforemencōned

Morton
To
Greenleaf

granted and Bargained Primisses with their appur^{cs} and euery part and pcell thereof unto the s^d Enoch Greenleafe his heirs and assigns foreuer to the onely sole and propper use Benifit and Behoofe of him the said Enoch Greenleafe and of his heirs and assigns foreuer absolutly without any maner of condition Redemption or Reuocation in any wise and the said John Morton for himselfe his heirs Execcutors and Adm^{rs} Doth hereby couenant Promiss grant and agree to and wth the said Euoch Greenleafe his heirs and assigns in maner and form following That is To Say that at the Time of this p^rsent grant Bargaine and Sale and untill thensealing and Deliuery of these p^rsents he the said John Morton is the true Sole and Lawfull owner and stands Lawfully Seized of all the aboue granted and Bargained Primisses in his own Propper Right of a good Sure and Indefeasible Estate of Inheritance in fee Simple without any maner of condition Reuercon or Limitation of use or uses whatsoeu^r so as to alter change Defeate or make uoyd the same hauing in himselfe full Power good Right and Lawfull Authority to grant Sell conuey and assure the Same unto the s^d Enoch Greenleafe his heirs and assigns foreuer in maner and form as afores^d free and clear and clearly acquited Exoncrated and

<small>Morton
To
Greenleafe</small> Discharged of and from all and all maner of former and other gifts grants Bargains Sales Leases Releases Mortgages Joyntures Dowries Judgm^{ts} Executio^s Entailes fines forfitures Seizurs amerciam^{ts} and of and from all other titles Trubles charges and Incumbrances whatsoeu^r and Further Doth hereby couenant Promiss Bind & oblige himselfe his heirs Executors and Adm^{rs} from henceforth and foreuer hereafter to Warra^t and Defend all the aboue granted and Bargained Primisses wth the appurtenances and euery part thereof unto the said Enoch Greeleafe his heirs and assigns foreuer in his and their Peaceable Possession and Seizen against the Lawfull claims and Demands of all and euery p^rson and ps^rons what-

BOOK IV, FOL. 137, 138.

soeuer In Witness whereof the said John Morton his s^d Wife haue hereunto set their hands and Seals the Day and year first aboue written.

The ℬ mark of   The ⊘ Marke of
John (his Seal) Morton   Martha (her Seal) Morton

Signed Sealed and Deliuered in Presence of us —
Elizabeth Trusedalle
Daniel Clark
Eliezer Moody Ser:

[138] Suffolk, ss/ Boston New England July 16th 1695/

The within Named John Morton and Martha his Wife p'sonally appearing Before me the Subscrib^r one of his Majesties Justices of Peace within the County of Suffolk afores^d acknowledged the within written deed to Be their act and Deed —   Is^a Addington.

A true Coppie of the origenall Deed Transcribed and compared this tenth day of Augst   p Jos Hamond Reg^r
1698

To all CHRIStian People to whome this p'sent Deed of Sale Shall come greeting whereas George Litten Late of Kittery in the County of york Marin^r Dec^d was while he liued and att the time of his Death Possessed of a Certaine house and Land at Crooked Lane on Piscataqua Riu^r and after the Decease of the s^d Litten and his wife administracõn was granted unto Richard King and John Lary on s^d Littens Estate they being the husbands of s^d Littens two Daughters Mary and Sarah By Name Now Know yee that wee Richard King Mary King his Wife and Sarah Lary Relict Widdow of Jno Lary afores^d Dec^d all of Kittery in the County of york in the Prouince of the Massachusets Bay in New England, for

Richd King &^o To Rog^r Kelly Esqr

BOOK IV, FOL. 138.

Diuerse good causes us thereunto mouing more Especally for and in consideraĉon of the Summe of Sixty two pounds Cura^t money of New-England to us in hand well and truly payd at and Before the ensealing and Deliuery of these p^{r}sents By Rog^r Kelly of the Isles of Shoals in s^d Prouince Esqr the Receipt whereof we doe hereby acknowledge and our selues therewth to be fully Satisfied contented and paid and thereof And of and from Euery part and percil thereof for us the said Richard King Mary King and Sarah Lary our heirs Execcutors Adm^{rs} and assigns doe Exonerate acquit and fully Discharge him the s^d Roger Kelly his heirs Execcutors Adm^{rs} and assigns By these p^{r}sents foreuer haue giuen granted Bargained Sold Alliened Enfeoffed and confirmed and By these p^{r}sents for us our heirs Execcutors Adm^{rs} and assigns doe fully freely and absolutely giue grant Bargaine Sell Alien Enfeoffe conuey and confirm vnto him the said Roger Kelly his heirs and Assigns all that house and Land formerly our father George Littens Lying and Being Scituate at Crooked lane on the Riu^r of Piscataqua in the Township of Kittery afores^d Being ten acres it Being the one half or

Richd King &^{c}
To Roger
Kelley Esqr

Moiety of twenty acres of Land Purchased By our s^d father George Litten of John White as By Deed of Sale und^r said Whites hand and Seal Bearing Date May the Ninth 1670 — Referance whereunto Being had will more at Large appeare it Being halfe the Bredth of that Twenty acres that is mentioned in that Deed of Sale from s^d White to our s^d father George Litten Being Bounded on the northwest By the Land of John Amerideth on the Southeast By the Land of Edward Litten and so to Run Back into the woods By the same Bredth upon a Northeast Line till ten acres Be compleated as p the Town grant to the s^d John White Bearing Date June 19° 1654 as more at Large appears on Kittery town Records Refarance thereunto Being had or howeuer Elce Bounded or Reputed to be Bounded together with all the

Book IV, Fol. 138, 139.

out houses Ediffices Buildings orchards with all and Singular the profits Priuiledges and appur^{ces} to the said house and Land Belonging or in any wise appertaining To Haue and to Hold the said house and Land with the appurtenances thereunto Belonging with all Right Title Interest claime and Demand which wee the s^d Richard King mary King and Sarah Lary now haue or in time past haue had or wch wee our heirs Execut^{rs} Adm^{rs} and Assigns in time to come may might should or in any wise ought to haue of in or to the aboue [139] Granted Primisses or any part thereof to him the said Rog^r Kelley his heirs or assigns foreuer and to the Sole and prop^r use Benifit and Behoofe of him the s^d Roger Kelley his heirs Execcutors &^c: foreuermore and wee the said Richard King Mary King and Sarah Lary for us our heirs Execcutors Adm^{rs} and Assigns Doe couena^t Promiss and grant to and with ye s^d Roger Kelley his heirs and assigns that at and Before the ensealing and Deliuery thereof Wee are ye true Right and Propper owners of ye aboue p̄imisses and ye appur^{ces} and that wee haue in our Selues good Right full Power and Lawfull authority ye Same to grant and confirm unto him the s^d Roger Kelley his heirs and assigns as afores^d and that the same and Euery part thereof is free and Clear acquited and Discharged of and

<small>Richd King &c To Roger Kelley Esq</small> from all former and other gifts grants Bargains Sales Wills Entails Power of thirds Mortgages Leaces Allienations and Incumbrances whatsoeuer and that it Shall and may Be Lawfull to & for ye s^d Roger Kelley his heirs and Assigns the afores^d p^rmisses and euery part thereof from time to time and at all times hereafter to haue hold use Improue occupy Possess and Enjoy Lawfully Peaceably and Quietly without any Lawfull Let Deniall hind^rance mollestation or disturbance of or By us or any other p^rson or p^rsons from By or und^r us or By our Procurm^t and that the Sale thereof and of euery part thereof against our Selues our heirs Execcutors Adm^{rs}

Book IV, Fol. 139.

and Assigns and against all other psons Lawfully Claiming the same or any part thereof wee will foreuer saue harmless warant and Defend By these ℘sents and that wee our heirs Exeecutors and Adm^{rs} shall & will make perform and exicute such other further Lawfull and reasonable act or acts thing or things as in Law and Equity can By him the his heirs or assigns his or their Learned Councill in ye Law Be deuised or required for the Better confirming and more Sure making of the Primisses Vnto him the s^d Roger Kelley his heirs Exeecutors Admin^{rs} and assigns according to the Laws of this Prouince In Witness whereof wee the said

Richd King &^{c} To Roger Kelley Esqr

Richard King Mary King and Sarah Lary haue hereunto Set our hands and Seals the three and Twentieth Day of July in the Tenth year of the Reign of our Soueraigne Lord Wilham ye third By the grace of god King of England Scotland ffrance and Ireland Defend^r of the ffaith &^{c} and in ye year of our Lord one thousand Six hundred Ninty and Eight 1698

Signed Sealed & Deliuered
  in the presence of us —
  John Coopper
  Jacob Smith
  Jos: Hamond Ser/

                his
Richard R King (his Seal)
       mark
Mary   King (her Seal)
  her
Sarah ʃ Lary (her Seal)
  marke

The 28th of Apr^{ll} 1699: then these Subscrib^{rs} Richd King & Mary his wife & Sarah Lary all appeared before me & Acknowledged this aboue Instrum^t to be their Act & Deed as witness my hand—   Wm Pepperrell Js pes

A true Copie of ye origenall Deed transcribed & compared this 28th July 1699/   p Jos Hamond Regist^r

To all Christian People to whome this Deed of Mortgage shall come, Nathaniel ffryer of Piscataway Riuer in New England Merch[t] Sendeth Greeting, Know y[e] that y[e] s[d]

ffryer to Bronsdon

Nathaniel ffryer for & in consideration of the Sum of four hundred pounds And Eighty pounds in Currant Money of New England to him in hand well and truly payd by Robert Bronsdon of Boston in New England afores[d] Merch[t] the receit whereof he doth hereby acknowledge and himselfe therewith to be fully Satisfied and contented And there of and of and from euery part & pacell thereof for himselfe his heires Execut[rs] and Administrat[rs] doth Exonerate Acquit and discharge the s[d] Robert Bronsdon his heires, Execut[rs] Administrators and Assignes firmly and for euer by these presents hath giuen granted bargained Sold Aliened Enfeoffed and confirmed, And by these presents doth fully freely clearly and absolutely giue grant bargain Sell Alien Enfeoffe conuey and confirme unto the s[d] Robert Bronsdon his heires Execut[rs] and Assignes all that his Island, Scituate lying and being on the Eastern Side and at the mouth of the said Riuer commonly called and known by the name of Champeroons Island, which he the s[d] ffryer bought of Captain ffrancis Champeroon of Piscataway Riuer afores[d] Gen[t] containing one thousand Acres of Land be it more or less, Excepting Eighty Acres of Land lying upon the s[d] Iland which he y[e] s[d] ffryer hath giuen to his Son in Law M[r] John Hincks together with all housing and buildings upon the s[d] Iland and all y[e] Land as well upland as Marsh or Meadow Salt and fresh to s[d] Iland belonging, And all y[e] wood underwood timber and timber trees Mines Mineralls Liberties [140] Priuiledges Imunities and Appurtenances whatsoeuer to y[e] s[d] Iland belonging or in any wise Appurtaining And alsoe all the stock of Cattle both great & small being upon y[e] s[d] Iland, to say twenty Cowes three breeding Mares four oxen four and twenty Sheep four hoggs and all other Cattle now being upon y[e] s[d] Iland of what kind

soeuer/ All which Iland Excepting as before Excepted and
all other the afore bargained premises and Appurtnnces he
y[e] said Robert Bronsdon is to haue and to hould and peaceably to possess & enjoy to him his heires Execut[rs] Administrat[rs] and Assigns for euer, and to his and their Sole and
proper use benefit and behoofe from hence forth for euer—
And the said Nathaniel ffryer for himselfe his heires Execut[rs] and Admin[rs] doth couenant promise and grant to and
with the s[d] Robert Bronsdon his heirs Execut[rs] Admin[rs] and
Assignes that he y[e] s[d] Natnaniel ffryer is the true Right Sole
and proper owner of the afores[d] Iland and of all and Singular other y[e] bargained Premises and Appurtnnces, and hath
in himselfe full power good Right and Lawfull Authority
the Same to giue grant bargain Sell Alien and confirm unto
the said Robert Bronsdon his heires Execut[rs] and Assignes in
manner as afores[d] And that y[e] said Iland and all other y[e]
bargained Premises and Appurtenances Excepting as before
Excepted, Are at the Sealing and deliuery of these presents
free and clear and clearly Acquitted and discharged of and
from all former and other Gifts, grants, bargains, Sales,
Leases, Mortgages, Joyntures, Dowries, Wills Entayles
Judgments Executions, titles, troubles Acts Alienations and
Incumbrances whatsoeuer And that the said Robert Bronsdon his heires Execut[rs] and Administrat[rs] Shall and may from
henceforth for euer hereafter peaceably & quietly haue hold
use Improue possess and enjoy the afores[d] Iland and other
the aboue bargain Premises and Appurtenances without y[e]
lett trouble hinderance Molestation or Disturbance of him
the said Nathaniel ffryer his heires Execut[rs] Admin[rs] or
Assignes or of any other person Lawfully Claiming any
Right thereto or Interest therein from by or under them or any
or either of them And that he the said Nathaniel ffryer shall
and will warrant the said Iland and other the bargained
Premises to him the said Robert Bronsdon his heires Execut[rs] and Assignes for euer by these presents—Prouided

alwayes and it is the true intent of these presents That if the said Nathaniel ffryer his heires Execut^rs Admin^rs doe or shall well and truly pay or cause to be paid unto the aboue named Robert Bronsdon or to his Atturney his heires Execut^rs Admin^rs or Assignes, the full and whole Summe of four hundred Eighty fiue pounds in currant Money of New England at or before the fiue and twentieth day of October which will be in the year of our Lord one thousand Six hundred and Ninety one, with the Interest that Shall be due thereupon All to be payd in Boston afores^d And ye Interest after ye Rate of Six p cent at the end of euery twelue moneths during the said Term, Then this Deed of Mortgage is to be utterly void and of none Effect to all Intents and purposes, but in default thereof to stand remaine and abide in full force strength power and vertue/ In witness w^rof The said Nathaniel ffryer hath hereunto Set his hand and Seal the Six & twentieth day of October, Anno Domini 1688 Annoq, Regni Regis Jacobi Secondi Angliæ &^c Quarto/

Signed Sealed and deliuered
In the presents of us—
Jonathan Euans
Joseph Bronsdon
Thomas Kemble
Acknowledged ye 26th of Octob^r 1688 before me the Instrum^t aboue written—

Memorand that whereas there is mentioned aboue, all other Cattle of what kind soeuer, it is to be understood that the said ffryer makes ouer only twenty Cowes three breeding Mares four oxen four & twenty Sheep and four hoggs—

Edw Randolph   Nathanell ffryer (his Seal)

Jonathan Euans appeared before me the 9th of August 1690 and made oath y^t he Saw Mr Nathaniel ffryer Senr signe this aboue Instrument as his Act and Deed And likewise saw Joseph Bronsdon and Thomas Kemble Signe with my Selfe/ toake upon oath 9th day aboue written

John Dauis Depty Presid^t

Book IV, Fol. 140, 141.

A true Copie of the origenall Deed of Mortgage Transcribed and Compared this 19th day of Septembr 1698
p Jos Hamond Registr

Know all men by these presents that I Robert Bronsdon of Boston in New England Mercht Doe by vertue of these presents Assigne make and Set ouer the within Instrument or bargained Premises that is to Say the within mentioned Island and all the Appurtenances thereunto belonging together with all the Cattle and Creatures as p the other Side is more particularly Exprest & Incerted, to haue and to hold to him the sd Robert Elliot his heires and Assigns for euer In witness whereof I haue hereunto Set my hand and Seal this twentieth day of August Anno Dom: 1698 Annoq R Rs Gulielmi Tertii Angliæ & Decimo

Bronsdon to Elliot

Sealed & Deliuered Robert Bronsdon (Seal)
In pi esents of— p John Watson p Letter of
Nathaniel Elliot Atturney Recorded in York 19th
Nicho Heskins. Augst 1698

A true Copie of ye origenall Assignment Transcribed & compared this 19th Septembr 1698/ p Jos Hamond Regr

[141] Know all men by these presents that I Robert Bronsdon of Boston in the County of Suffolk in the Prouince of the Massachusets Mrchant for and in consideration of ye Sum of Six hundred and twenty pounds in Currant Money of New England to me in hand well and truely payd by Robert Elliot of New Castle in ye Prouince of New Hampshiere Mrchant doe for me my heires Executrs Adminrs and Assignes Remitt Release and for euer Acquit and discharge Nathaniel ffryer of New Castle aforesaid Mrchant him his heires Executrs and Adminrs of and from all & euery Act or Action cause and causes of Action Bill Bond Couents contracts Leases Mort-

Bronsdon to ffryer

Book IV, Fol. 141.

gages Debt Dues Duties and Demands whatsoeuer which I euer had May or might haue had, for or by reason of any Act thing heretofore done whatsoeuer In witness whereof I haue hereunto Set my hand & Seal this twenty fourth day of August Annoq, R R^s Gulielmi Tetii Angliæ &^{c} Decimo/ Anno Dom̄: 1698   Robert Bronsdon ($^{his}_{Seal}$)
Sealled and deliuered   p Letter of Atturney Re-
   In presents of—   corded in York 19th August :
Nathaniel Elliot   98 to John Watson
Nichō Heskins

John Watson Atturney to Robert Bronsdon, psonally appeared Acknowledged the aboue Instrument to be his Act and Deed, this 25th August 1698   p John Hinck Presid^t

A true Copie of the origenall Acquittance Transcribed and Compared this. 19th Septemb^r 1698
                         p Jos Humond Reg^r

To all Christian People to whome this Instrument in Writing or Deed of Sale shall come, I Robert Iordan Iun^r Son of Robert Jordan Senr Decased and in time past liuing at Richmond Island in the Eastern parts of New England Send Greeting in our Lord God Everlasting/ Know ye that I the s^d Robert Jordan Junr for and in consideration of the Sum of Eightie pounds to me in hand paid and Secured to be paid by Mr Nathaniel ffryer of ye Township of Portsmouth in New England afores^d Merchant, with which I doe hereby Acknowledge my Selfe Satisfied and fully contented, Have giuen and granted And by these presents doe giue grant & confirm fully freely and Absolutely unto the s^d Nathan^{ll} ffryer Senr his heires Executors Administrators and Assignes The one halfe and Deale or half part of one Certain Tract or

Jordan   parcell of Land comōnly called or known by the
to ffryer   name of Cape Elizabeth in the Eastern parts of
              New England afores^d, bounded with a Small gut

or Stream of water running into the Sea out of a Small Marsh lying behind the long Sands to y² westward and Soe to run up into y² Main Land in a Straight line to y² pond comonly called y² great Pond/ Prouided & it is hereby Intended and Appointed that y² s² Nathan¹¹ ffryer his heires Executors Administrators or Assignes Shall at noe time or times hereafter Interfere take away Molest or Diminish any part or parcell of the said Marsh or upland that lyeth between the s² Marsh & y² s² Great Pond to the said Streight line to pass as afores² Northwards And soe to run down upon the said Pond to the Sea taking unto y² s² Premises Mentioned one little Island Scituate on the East Side of y² s² Pond together with y² Marshes on both Sides of a Creek runing out of the said Pond into the Sea at Alewife Coue and alsoe not to Intrench upon y² Main upland or plains thereunto Adjacent aboue the Extent of twenty Measured poles Always reseruing granting giuing & allowing unto my brother John Jordan of Richmonds Island aforesaid or unto his Assignes or persons concerned with him, convenient Ingress regress and egress fully and freely at all times & Seasons to y² s² Alewifes coue and there and thence to procure fetch & carry away Bait for his or their ffishing uses at terms and times Seasonable To haue and to hold the s² one half part of y² s² Tract of Land together with the priuiledges Accomodations profits Appurtenances & conveniences thereof unto the said Nathaniel ffryer his heires [142] Executors Administrat²² or Assignes foreuer, freely and quietly without any hinderance or Interruption as it was granted and giuen to me by my father Robert Jordan & my Mother Sarah Jordan as by a Deed of Gift bearing Date y² twenty Ninth day of ffebruary in y² year of our Lord one thousand Six hundred Seuenty and fiue may and doth at large Appear And moreouer whereas my father Robert Jordan did by his last Will and Testament giue and graunt unto me Robert Jordon and the rest of my brothers One Certain parcell of Marsh &

BOOK IV, FOL. 142.

Land Scituate and being in Spurwink Riuer in ye eastern parts of New England afores^d to be Diuided in Equall parts among us as by s^d Will may Euidently Appear, I Robert Jordan aboues^d Haue giuen and granted and by these presents fully and freely doe giue grant and confirm unto ye s^d Nathaniell ffryer in manner and altogether as the first granted Premises aboue Mentioned are, The one half or half & Deale part of the s^d Marsh and Land in whatsoeuer place thereof my Lot shall be, after it is Diuided And it is hereby Intended granted & Mutually agreed on by me the Vendor with ye Vendee that in ye halfing or Diuiding any or all of the aboue recited premises, there shall be a Just complyance each with other that in Quantity quallity convenience as much as may be our proportions may be alike/ And I the s^d Robert Jordan for my Self my heires Executors and Administrat^{rs} Doe hereby Couenant and engage to Warrant and for euer Defend unto ye s^d Nathaniel ffryer all ye premises Mentioned in this writing together with the priuiledges thereof and unto the s^d ffryer his heires Execut^{rs} and Administrat^{rs} and Assignes peaceably quietly & without Interruption to enjoy the Same/ Witness my hand and Seal this fourteenth day of July in the year of our Lord One thousand Six hundred Seuenty and Nine.   Robert Jordan (his Seal)

Jordan to ffryer

Signed Sealed and Deliuered
   in presents of us.   July ye 16th 1679. Mr Robert Jordan
   Tho : Cobbett   came and Acknowledged this In-
   Nicho : Heskins   strument to be his ffree Act and
                      Deed before me.
                              Elias Stileman Comis^r

A true Copie of ye origenall Instrum^t Transcribed and Compared this 1st day of Septemb^r 1698.
                              Jos Hamond Regist^r

BOOK IV, FOL. 142, 143.

To all Christian People whome it may or doth concern I Nathaniel ffryer my heires Execut^{rs} Administrat^{rs} and Assignes Doe and by these presents haue Surrendered made ouer, Surrend^r and Deliuer this within present Deed of Sale or Instrument in writing together with all & euery particular therein Mentioned and all my Interest and Concern wch I formerly had or haue therein, Unto Robert Elliot Esqr Merchant on the Great Island in New Castle in New England, to him ye Said Robert Elliot Esqr his heires Execut^{rs} Administrat^{rs} & Assigns for euer Excepting what was Sold by me Nathaniell ffryer Senr to John Holicomb Tho: Sparks Edward Vittery and John Parret or what Shall appear by Deed of Sale giuen under the hand and Seale of Nathaniel ffryer Esqr/ Which ouerture and Assignment is for and in consideration of the Sum of Six hundred and twenty pounds in Money to me the s^d Nathaniel ffryer Senr to be payd by the said Robert Elliot/ As witness my hand and Seale this 23th day of August In the tenth year of of our Souereign Lord William King of England Scotland ffrance and Ireland &^{c}

ffryer to Elliot

Signed Sealed and deliuered   Nath ffryer (his Seal)
In the presents of us —
John Neail
Richard Parsons

A true Copie of ye originall Transcribed and compared, this 1st Septemb^r 1698   p Jos Hamond Reg^r

[143] To all Christian People to whome these presents shall come, Know ye that I Edward Gilman of Exet^r in the Province of New Hampshiere for Divers good causes me thereunto Moveing more Especially for and in consideration of twelue pounds to me in hand payd by Alexander Dennet of Kittery in the Province of Maine the receipt where of

and of euery part thereof I acknowledge and therewith fully
Satisfied contented & paid Have giuen granted bargained
Sold Aliened made ouer & confirmed & by these presents
doe for me my heires Execut^{rs} Administrators and Assigns
giue grant bargain Sell Alien make ouer and confirm unto
him the Said Dennit his heires Execut^{rs} Administrat^{rs} and
Assignes for euer a certain piece or parcell of Land containing twenty Acres, Scituate Lying and being in the Town of
Kittery being bounded as followeth vizt to begin at the head
of Edward Ayers his Land and Soe to run back upon a
North-East and by east line between Samuel Hills Land and
s^d Dennets Land to ye head of s^d Dennets Land Joyning to
both Lands and what that wants of twenty Acres to be
made up at the head of ye Land afore mentioned & the head
of s^d Dennets Land/ To have and to hold ye afores^d piece
or parcell of Land, with all the priviledges and Appertenances thereunto belonging or in any wayes appertaining, to
him the s^d Dennet his heirs Execut^{rs} Administrat^{rs} and Assignes for euer, And his and their proper use benefit and
behoofe without any Molestation let or hinderance from or
by me ye s^d Gilman my heires or Assignes and from all
other persons laying any Just claime thereunto for euer to
warrant and Defend by these pres^{ts} In witness whereof I
haue Set my hand and Seal this Seuen and twentieth day of
Aprill one thousand Six hundred Eighty & Six — 1686.
Signed Sealed and Delivered   Edward Gillman (his Seal)
  In presents of —   Edward Gilman came and Acknowl-
  Christian Remich   edged the aboue written bill of
  Jos Hamond   Sale this 27th of Aprill 1686 before
    me   Charles ffrost Justis of peace
Stephen Paul and Katharine his wife freely consents to
the above written Instrument and gaue up all their Right
title and Interest therein this 27th of Aprill 1686 before me
    Charles ffrost Justis peace
    Stephen Paul (his Seale)
    Katharine Paul her mark : K : (her Seal)

Book IV, Fol. 143.

A true Copie of the origenall Deed Transcribed & compared this 2ᵈ octobʳ 1698   p Jos Haṁoud Registʳ

To all Christian People before whome this present writing Shall come Know yee that I Iohn Redden of Ipswich in the County of Essex in New England ffisherman & Iane Redden his wife for Diuers good and Valuable causes and Consideration me thereunto moving but Especially for and in Cosideration of Eight pounds of good and Lawfull Money of New England unto me in hand payd & received before the Signing and Sealing hereof, and for which I doe Acknowledge my Selfe to be fully Satisfied contented & payd, hath giuen granted bargained Sold Enfeoffed made ouer Alienated & confirmed unto William Baker Glover of the Same Town & County abovesᵈ, a certain parcle of Land containing one hundred Acres as it was at first laid out be it more or Less, the sᵈ Land being in the Township of Wells in the Province of Maine in the Massachusets Collony in his Majesties Territory and Dominion of New England in America and is bounded in manner and order as followeth Viz: on the Southwest Side by Samuel Hatch it tis bounded, And tis bounded on the east and be North Side by Jonathan Littlefield and the Clay brook, and on the South East end by Norgunkiet River it tis bounded, and on the Norwest end bounded by the Common, which land according to the bounds abovesᵈ, I the abovesᵈ John Redden bought of yᵉ said Samuel Hatch, Doe make over with all and euery of the Priviledges and Appurtenances thereunto belonging To have and to hold & peaceably and quietly to Possess and Enjoy unto the abouesᵈ William Baker his heires Executʳˢ Adminʳˢ and Assignes for euer, as his own proper Right and Inheritance, the aforesᵈ Lands together with all and Singular the Priviledges Profits accom-

Reding to Baker

ondations and Appurtenances thereupon or thereunto belonging, without any let hinderance Molestation or Interuption from me & from my wife Jane Redden or any of our heires Execut^{rs} Administrat^{rs} or Assignes or any of them for euer, or any other person or persons whatsoeuer, making or Claiming any Right or Title to or unto any part or parcell thereof for euer/ ffurther I the aboues^d John Redden and Jane Redden haue Real Right and Lawfull Authority to make Sale of ye aboue said land and therefore warrantize the Sale thereof to be good and free from all former Gifts grants Sales Deeds Rights Titles thirds Dowries Judgments Executions Morgages Entailments or any other Incombrance whatsoeuer/ And it Shall be Lawfull to and for ye s^d William Baker his heires and Success^{rs} from time to time and at all times hereafter, to Haue hold use ocupie Possess and Enjoy all and euery part of the Premises hereby Demised.

[144] In witness whereof, I the aboues^d John and Jane Redden haue hereunto Set our hands and Scales/ Dated the twenty Seuenth day of January in the year of our Lord one thousand Six hundred Ninety Seuen Ninety Eight.

Signed Sealed and deliuered
in piesence of us
Witnesses
Joseph ffuller
Judth Wood

his
John ℐ Ridden (Seal)
mark and Seal
her
Jane ℛℯ Ridden (Seal)
mark and Seal

Ipswich January twenty Seuenth day 169⅞ John Reddene & Jane Reddene personally appeared before me and owned this Instrum^t to be their Act and Deed/

John Appleton J^{ta} peace

A true Copie of the origenall Deed of Sale Transcribed and Compared this 23^d day of Novemb^r 1698

p Jos Hamond Regist^r

BOOK IV, FOL. 144.

Witnesseth these presents that I Alyce Shapleigh of the Town of Kittery in the Province of Maine, Widdow Relict and Administratrix to y[e] Estate of my Deceased husband Major Nicholas Shapleigh for Diuers good causes and considerations thereunto me moueing, and by order of Court & their Approbation and in payment of my husbands Debts and more Especially for and in consideration of the full and Just Sum of twenty fiue pounds in currant money of New England to me in hand already payd at y[e] Sealing and deliuery of these presents, the receipt whereof I doe acknowledge my Selfe to be fully Satisfied contented and payd, and thereof and euery part and pcell thereof I the said

Alice Shapleigh to Jo Downing

Alyce Shapleigh doe acquit and discharge Joshua Downing of Kittery in the said Province afores[d] his heirs Execut[rs] Administrat[rs] or Assignes for euer by these presents and haue hereby granted bargained Enfeoffed conueyed assured deliuered and confirmed and by these presents doe fully giue grant bargain Sell Enfeoff convey Assure deliuer and confirm unto the afores[d] Joshua Downing his heires Execut[rs] Administrat[rs] and Assignes, a certain tract or parcell of Land containing the quantety of twenty Acres or there abouts, the bounds whereof being as followeth, four Acres of the s[d] land lying on the South Side the highway bounded with Thomas Jones on y[e] West to a Small white oak tree upon y[e] s[d] Downings own Land on y[e] East & the high way on the North/ And Sixteen Acres more on the North Side y[e] high way bounded with M[r] Shapleighs Land on th West & North, and the Land called y[e] Bay land on the East and y[e] high way on y[e] South and it runs from a rock in his new Pasture upon y[e] hill Eighty fiue pole to a Crochett white oak tree North East & by North and from thence the head line runs South east & by South finety four pooles to y[e] afor[sd] Bay Land which land as aboue bounded with all Timber trees wood und[r]woods Profits Priviledges comodaties and all other Appurtenances whatsoever, with all y[e] Right Title Interest use

Book IV, Fol. 144.

Possession or whatsoeuer doth belong thereunto with all and Singular before mentioned Premises/ To haue and to hold the aboue named tract of Land as above bounded with all y⁵ Appurtenances thereto appertaining, from me my heires Execut[rs] Adm[rs] and Assignes or und[r] my beloved husband Maj[r] Nicholas Shapleigh his heires Execut[rs] Administrat[rs] and Assignes or any of them, unto y⁵ said Joshua Downing his heires Execut[rs] Administrat[rs] and Assigns for euer And doe further Couenant and Promise to and with y⁵ s[d] Joshua Downing his heires and Assignes &c that y⁵ s[d] Land is free and Clere from all former gifts grants Morgages bargains Sayles leases Dowres or thirds of Dowres Titles Judgments Executions and all other Troubles and Incombrances w[t]soeuer had made Comitted or done or to be made comitted or Suffered to be done by s[d] Alyce Shapleigh her heires Execut[rs] Administrat[rs] or Assignes or of or by her Deceased husband Maj[r] Nicholas Shapleigh his heires Execut[rs]

Alice Shaply
to
Jos. Downing

Adm[rs] or Assigns and by her and them to be Sufficiently Saued and kept harmless from all manner of persons w[t]soeuer from by or under them or her or any other by their Procurem[t] whereby said Downing shall peaceably Injoy quietly possess the aboue bargained Premises to him Selue his heires Exeq[rs] Adminis[rs] and Assignes for euer — In Witness whereof I haue hereunto affixed my hand and Sayle this Second day of June one thousand Six hundred Eighty three, In the thirty fifth year of y⁵ Rayn of our Soveraign Lord Charles of great Brittain ffrance & Ireland King: Anno: Domini. 1683/ Defend[r] of the ffaith/ the word Second interlined in the thirty Second line before y⁵ Sealing and deliuery hereof. (her seal)

Signed Scaled & deliuered   Alice Shapleigh
   In the presents of us   M[rs] Alice Shapleigh came before
   ffrancis Johnson   me the Second day of June
   John Penwill   1683, and owned y⁵ aboues[d]
                           Instrum[t] to be her Act &
                           Deed.   John Dauis
                                      Dep[ty] President

Book IV, Fol. 144, 145.

ffrancis Johnson and John Penwill came before me did Acknowledge that y° did See M^s Alice Shapleigh Sign Seal & deliuer y° aboue written Instrument whereunto y° haue giuen y^r oath the 3th of June 1685.

John Dauis Dep^{ty} presid^t

A true Copie of the origenall Deed of Sale Transcribed & compared this 22^d of Decemb^r 1698/

Jos. Hamond Regist^r

[145] This Indenture made the Eleuenth day of June, in the first year of ye Reigne of our Souraign Lord and Ladie William & Mary by the grace of God King & Queen of England Scotland ffrance and Ireland Defend^r of ye ffaith/ And in ye year of o^r Lord according to ye computation of ye Church of England one thousand Six hundred Eighty & nine, by and betwixt John Amerideth and Ioan his wife of the Town of Kittery in ye Province of Maine in New England on ye one partie And Roger Dearing and Joseph Couch of the Town of Kittery afores^d and in ye Province afores^d Shipwrights on ye other partie Witnesseth, That ye said John Amerideth and Joan his wife for and in the consideration of the Sume of ffiftie pounds of good & Lawfull money of New England to them at and before ye ensealeing & deliuery of these presents in hand well and truly paid by ye s^d Roger Dearing and Joseph Couch, the receipt whereof the s^d John Amerideth and Joan his wife doe hereby acknowledge and themselues therewith fully Satisfied & paid and thereof and of euery part thereof doe clearly acquit and discharge the said Roger Dearing and Joseph Couch forever, by these presents hath giuen granted bargained Sold enfoffed and confirmed, and by these presents doe giue grant, bargaine,

Book IV, Fol. 145.

<small>John Ame rideth to Rog⁰ Dering & Couch</small>

Sell, Alien, Enfeoffe and confirm unto y⁰ s⁴ Roger Dearing and Joseph Couch, their heires and Assignes for euer, ffiftie Acres of Land lying and being in the Town of Kittery afores⁴ and Province afores⁴, being butted and bounded as followeth Viz⁴ beginning at the Stepping Stones and bounded by Diggary Jeofryes and Clement Dearings land by a North and by east line untill it make up Six Acres, And then from an old Hemlock tree by John Brays fence east and by South Sixty eight pole in breadth, and then runneth North and by east to a beech tree Marked. R. D. by the Same breadth to make up the ffiftie acres, with all and Singular its Rights members Jurisdictions easments Meadows ffeedings pastures wood under wood wayes profits Comodities common of Pastures heredittaments and Appurtenances whatsoever to the said Land or any part or parcell thereof any ways belonging or appertaining To have and to hold the said Land and other y⁰ Premises before by these presents Mentioned unto the said Roger Dearing and Joseph Couch their heires and Assignes and to their onely proper use behoofe and benefit for ever/ And the said John Amerideth and Joan his wife for and notwithstanding any Act done by him or her y⁰ s⁴ John and Joan Amerideth to the contrary at or before the ensealeing and deliuery of these presents are and stand lawfully Seized in all y⁰ Land and Premises afores⁴ as a ffee Simple in their own Right and to their own use without any condition, Limitation, other use or trust to alter change or determine the said Land before mentioned to be hereby Aliened bargained granted and Sold, and of euery part and parcell thereof And that y⁰ s⁴ Joseph Couch and Roger Dearing according to y⁰ true Intent and meaning of these presents shall have full power Just right and Lawfull Authority to use ocupie possess and enjoy grant bargaine or sell the Same and euery part and parcell thereof with all the Appurtenances and coveniences thereto belonging, And that the s^d Land with all woods and under woods and other conveniences Shall from henceforth and for euer remaine and continue unto ye s^d Roger Dearing & Joseph Couch and to their heires and Assignes Acquitted Discharged and Exonerated of and from all and all manner of former bargains Sales gifts grants rent Charges arreages of rent Annuities Uses Entails Judments Dowers Joyntures leases forfitures executions intrusions and incumbrances whatsoeuer and of and from all & all manner of other charges titles troubles and incumbrances whatsoeuer had made or comitted or done by us John Amerideth and Jone his wife or any other Person whatsoever, the rents and Services to grow Due to ye Chiefe Lord or Lords of the fee or fees of ye Premises for and in respect of their Seignory onely excepted and foreprised And further that the Said John Amerideth & Jone his wife their heires Execut^rs or Administrat^rs shall and will at all times hereafter upon ye rsasonable request and at cost and charges of ye s^d Roger Dearing and Joseph Couch their heires or Assignes make Suffer doe Acknowledge and execute or cause to be made done Suffered Acknowledged and executed all Such further Act or Acts thing or things device or devices, conueiance or conveyances and assurances for ye better Assuring and Sure making of ye premisses hereby bargained and Sold to ye s^d Roger Dearing and Joseph Couch, their heires and Assignes for euer And the s^d Joan Amerideth her heires Execut^rs and Administrat^rs Shall and will Defend at all times, ye title of ye s^d land to noe other intent and purpose whatsoeuer against any manner of Claimes made by any pson whatsoeuer for all or part of the said Land. In witness whereof the said John Amerideth and Joan his wife haue to this present Indenture

Book IV, Fol. 145, 146.

Set to their hands and Seales the day and year above Written.

     The mark of Joan ⟊ Amerideth ($^{her}_{Seal}$)

Signed Sealed & deliuered   The 26. of July. 1695.
 In the presents of us   Mrs Joan Amerideth came & Ac-
 William Stacie   knowledged this above Instru-
 James ffoy   ment to be her Act & Deed to
         Mr Roger Dearing and Joseph
         Couch, betore me—
         William Pepperrell
           Justes peace

A true Copie of the origenall Deed of Sale Transcribed and compared this. 22^d of Decemb^r 1698.
       p Jos Hamond Regist^r

[146] To all Christian People to whome this present Deed of Sale Shall come/ I Joseph Weare of York in the County of York in the Province of the Massachusets Bay in New England Sayler, Send greeting—Know yee that for and in consideration of the Sum of forty pounds currant Money of New England to me in hand paid at & before ye Ensealeing and deliuery of these presents by Matthew Austin of Yorke afores^d weaver, the Receipt whereof I doe hereby Acknowledge and my Selfe therewth to be fully Satisfied contented and paid and thereof and of and from euery part and parcell thereof for me the s^d Joseph Weare my heires Execut^{rs} Administrat^{rs} & Assignes doe Exonerate Acquit and fully Discharge him the s^d Matthew Austin his heires Execut^{rs} Administrat^{rs} & Assignes by these presents for ever, I the s^d Joseph Weare Have giuen granted bargained Sold Aliened Enfeoffed and Confirmed and by these presents doe for me my heires Exec^{rs} Admin^{rs} & Assignes fully freely and Absolutely giue, grant, bargaine, Sell Alien, Enfeoffe and

confirme unto him the s^d Matthew Austin his heires Exec^rs Admin^rs & Assignes my certaine dwelling house and land about it, lying and being Scituate in the Town of York afores^d in ye Province afores^d by Estimation three Acres more or less being and lying within fence Excepted halfe an Acre of Land belonging unto ye dwelling house of Mr John Penwill late of York and is bounded on the Northwest by the land of Rowland Young, on ye South by the Meeting house creek, on ye east by a small creek coming out, of the Meeting house creek, on ye Northeast by the high way, or however otherwise bounded or reputed to be bounded, together wth all the Priviledges thereunto belonging or in any wise appurtaining — To have & to hold the s^d house & land with all the Appurtenances with all ye Rights Titles Interest claime & demand which I ye s^d Joseph Weare my heires Exec^rs Admin^rs or Assignes have now, or in time past haue had or in time to come may Should or any wise ought to haue in or to ye above granted Premises or any part thereof And alsoe in like manner a lot of Woodland lying covenient for the house and land of Six Acres to be Annexed unto the Premises, To him the said Matthew Austin his heires and Assignes for euer and to their Sole and proper use benefit and behoofe And I ye s^d Joseph Wear for me my heires Exec^rs Admin^rs and Assignes doe covenant Promise and grant to and wth him the said Matthew Austin his heires & Assignes that at and before the Ensealing and delivery hereof I am the true, Right, and proper owner of the above granted Premises and their Appurtenances And that I have in my Selfe full power good Right and Lawfull Authority the Same to grant and confirm unto the s^d Matthew Austin his heirs Assignes &^c as afores^d, And that the Same and euery part thereof is free and clere Acquitted and discharged of and from all former and other gifts grants bargains Sales leases Mortgages Titles troubles and Incumbrances whatsoeuer And that it shall and may be

Jo: Weare to Math Austin

Lawfull to and for the s⁴ Matthew Austin his heires and Assignes, the afores⁴ Premises and euery part thereof from time to time, and at all times foreuer hereafter to haue hold use improue ocupie possess and Enjoy lawfully peaceably and quietly without any Lawfull let deniall, hinderance, Molestation and disturbance for of or by me or any person or persons from by or under me or by my procurem⁺ and that the Sale thereof and every part thereof against my Selfe my heires Exec⁺ʳˢ Administrat⁺ˢ and Assignes and against all other persons whatsoeuer Lawfully Claiming and demanding the Same or any part thereof I will forever Save harmless warrant and defend by these presents And that I my heires Exec⁺ʳˢ and Assignes Shall and will make peform and Execute Such other Lawfull and Reasonable Act or Acts thing or things as in Law or Equity can be devised or required for yᵉ better confirming and more sure making of the Premises unto yᵉ s⁴ Matthew Austin his heires & Assignes according to yᵉ Laws of this Province In witness whereof I the s⁴ Joseph Weare have hereunto Set my hand and Seale this Eighteenth day of January in yᵉ year of our Lord, one thousand Six hundred Ninety and four five Annoq̱ Regni R Rˢ : Rᵐ / Guilielmi & Mariæ Sexto/

Signed Sealed and delivered   Joseph Weare (his Seale)
   In the presents of us —   her
   John Hancock   Hañah ℒ Weare (her Seal)
   Edward Beale   marke

          Joseph Weare and Hañah his wife appeared and made Acknowledgcm⁺ of this Instrum⁺, to be their Act & Deed before me this. 18ᵗʰ Jan : 94/5/

          Samuel Donnell Justis pea
A true Copie of the origenall Deed of Sale Transcribed & compared this. 5ᵗʰ day of Jan⁷ 169⅘ —

          p Jos Hamond Regist⁺

To all Christian people to whome these presents shall come/ Knoy ye that I Matthew Austine of the Town of York in ye County of York in the Province of the Massachusets Bay in New England, for Diuers good Causes me thereunto Moveing, More Especially for and in consideration of the Summe of Sixty five pounds to me in hand well & truly paid at and before ye Ensealing and diliuery of these presents, by William Pepperrell of Kittery in ye County & Province afores^d Merchant, the Receipt whereof I acknowledge and therewith fully Satisfied contented and paid and thereof and of and from every part and parcell thereof have freely and clerely acquitted Exonerated and discharged him the s^d William Pepperrell his heires & Assignes for ever, Have given, granted, bargained, Sold, Aliened, Enfeoffeed, made over and confirmed, & by these presents doe freely clerely and absolutely give, grant, bargain, Sell, Alien, Enfeoffe make over and confirm unto him the s^d William Pepperrell his heires Execut^{rs} Administrat^{rs} and Assignes, All that my house and Land which was formerly my father Matthew Austins, Scituate lying and being in the Township of York afores^d and on the Western Side of the new Mill Creek Joyning to the Bridge that is ouer [147] the s^d Ciick running upon a Northwest line one hundred & Sixty poles in length, and fourty pole in breadth Southwest & Northeast, together with all other ye houses Barnes out houses Edifices and buildings Gardens, orchards pastures, trees & fences thereon To have and to hold the above given and granted Premises, with all and Singular the Priviledges Appurtenances and comodities thereunto belonging or in any wise Appurtaining with all ye woods under wood timb^r trees waters water courses to him ye s^d William Pepperrell his heires or Assignes for ever and to their own proper use benefit and behoofe, peaceably and quietly to enjoy ye Same without any Molestation let deniall or hinderance from me

Matthew Austin to Wm Peprrll

BOOK IV, FOL. 147.

the s^d Matthew Austine my heires Exec^{rs} Admin^{rs} or Assignes or any or either of us, further that I the said Matthew Austine at and before ye Ensealing and deliuery of these presents am ye true Right owner of the aboue giuen and granted Premises and of all & euery part thereof And that all and every part thereof is free and clere Acquitted Exonerated and discharged of and from all and all manner of former and other gifts grants bargains Sales Mortgages Wills Entails Judgments Executions power of thirds and all other Incumbrances of what kind or Nature soev^r and that I have in my Selfe good Right, full power, and Lawfull authority the Same to Sell and dispose of And I the s^d Matthew Austine my heires and Assignes shall and will from time to time and at all times hereafter for ever warrant and defend the title thereof against my Selfe my heires Executors Admin^{rs} and assignes and against all other persons whatsoeuer Claiming any Right title or Interest thereunto from by or under me my heires or Assignes And that the s^d William Pepperell his heires or Assignes shall and will from time to time and at all times hereafter, use improve ocupie possess and enjoy the aboue giuen and granted Premises with ye Appurtenances as their own proper Right by vertue of these presents. Alwayes provided and it is to be understood that if the s^d Matthew Austine his heires Exec^{rs} Admin^{rs} or Assignes Shall well and truly pay or cause to be paid unto him the said William Pepperrell his heires or Assignes the full and Just Sum of Sixty fiue pounds Currant money of New England, at or before the thirtieth day of Decemb^r wch will be in ye year of o^r Lord one thousand Seven hundred and two 1702/ at ye now dwelling house of the s^d William Pepperrell at Kittery, that then this present obligation Shall be voyd and of nône Effect, or otherwise to abide and remaine in full force and vertue. In witness whereof I the s^d Matthew Austine have hereunto Set my hand and Seale this fifth day of Jan^{ry} in y^e year of o^r Lord

one thousand Six hundred Ninety Eight nine and in y^e tenth year of y^e Reign of our Soveraign Ld William y^e third by the grace of God of England Scotland ffrance and Ireland, King Defend^r of y^e ffaith &^{c}/   Matthew Austine ($^{his}_{seal}$)
Signed Seled & deliuered   her
   in p$^{rs^{ts}}$ of us   Mary 𝒱 Austine ($^{her}_{seal}$)
   Jos Hammond   mark
   Joseph Ware   Matthew Austine & Mary his wife appeared before me y^e Subscrib^r on of the memb^{rs} of his Maties Council of y^e Prouince of y^e Massachusets Bay, and Justice of peace within y^e Same, and acknowledged this aboue Instrument to be their Act and Deed Jan^{ry} 5th 169$\frac{8}{9}$ Sam^{ll} Wheelwright

A true Copie of y^e origenall Transcribed & compared this 5th Jan^{ry} 169$\frac{8}{9}$ —   p Jos Hammond Regist^r

County York — Kittery. June the Seventeeth 1696/ Know all men by these presents that I Isaac Goodrich of the township of Kittery in the County of York Yeoman, for the consideration of fiftie pounds in money to me in hand paid by my Aunt Mistres Margret Adams before the Signing and Sealeing hereof have bargained Sold and doe by these presents bargaine Sell Alienate Enfeoffe and confirm unto my s^d Aunt Margret Adams all that Tract of Land I ye s^d Isaac Goodrich bought of Samuel King as appears by an Instrument bearing Date the Sixteenth of this Instant moneth one thousand Six hundred Ninety & Six, And is that tract of Land that was formerly Wm Kings late of Kittery Deceased. To have and to hold all the s^d tract of Land be it more or less unto the onely use Benefit and behoofe of her ye s^d Margret Adams her heires or Assigns for ever from me the s^d Isaac Goodrich and my heires for ever, And furthermore I ye s^d Isaac Goodrich doe covenant with ye s^d Margret Adams and her heires, the peaceable and Quiet Possession thereof to Defend & Maintain against all manner of Persons Laying Claime thereunto And alsoe that the Same is ffree from all Encumbrances whatsoever by me made or done Always provided that if the s^d Isaac Goodrich Shall well and truely pay the full and Just Sum of fiftie pounds in money at or before ye Eighteenth of June which will be in the year of our Lord one thousand Six hundred Ninety and Seven to the s^d Margret Adams her heires or Assignes without any maner of ffraud or Deceit, then this Instrument to be voyd and of none Effect otherwise to remaine and abide in full force power and vertue and Pleadable in any of his Maj^ties Courts of Judicature/ Witness my hand & Seale the Seventh day of June one thousand Six hundred Ninety and Six.

Goodridge to Adams

Witness   Isaac Goodridge (his Seal)
  Mary Addams   June. 18th 1696. Isaac Goodridge psonally appearing Acknowledged this within written Instrument to be his Act and Deed/ before me.
  Wm Godsoe

                          Wm Pepperrell Js pes
A true Copie of the origenall Instrument Transcribed and compared. this 18th Jan^ry 169⅚.   p Jos Hamond Regist^r

[148] To all Christian People to whome this present Deed of Sale Shall come, We William Hilton Senr and Arthur Beal of York in ye County of York in the Province of the Massachusets Bay in New England husbandman Send greeting/ Know ye that for and in consideration of ye Sum of Nine pounds good and Lawfull money of New England to us well and truely paid at and before ye ensealeing and

deliuering of these presents by Daniel Black of York in yͤ town & County & Province afores^d Weaver, the receipt whereof We doe hereby Acknowledge and our selues therewith to be fully Satisfied contented and paid and thereof and of & from every part and parcell thereof for us the s^d William Hilton and Arthur Beal our heirs Execut^rs Admin^rs and Assignes doe Exonerate acquit Discharge him ye s^d Daniel Black his heires Execut^rs Admin^rs and Assignes for ever, We ye s^d William Hilton and Arthur Beal have giuen granted Bargained Sold Aliened Enfeoffed and confirmed unto and by these presents doe for us our Selues our heires Execut^rs Admin^rs and Assignes fully freely & Absolutely give grant bargain Sell Alien Enfeoff convey and confirm unto s^d Daniel Black his heires and Assignes a certain piece or parcell of Salt Marsh Lying & being Scituate in ye township of York afores^d, by Estimation three Acres more or less & is butted and bounded on ye Southwest Side of York Riuer a little below ye partings and leis bounded between ye Marsh formerly called Mr Edward Rishford and the Marsh

Hilton
to
Black

formerly called Henry Simpson, being bounded by s^d Rishfords Marsh with a Ditch from ye Riuer to ye upland and by s^d Simpsons Marsh it is bounded by Small brook or gutter that runs from ye upland into ye Riuer, together with ye Crick and all other the priviledges and Appurtenances thereunto belonging or in any wise Appurtaining To haue and to hold ye Same with all ye Right and title Interest clames and Demands which we ye s^d William Hilton and Arthur Beal our heires or Assignes now haue or in time past haue had or in time to come may Should or in any wise ought to haue in and to the aboue granted Premises or their Appurtenances, to him ye said Daniel Black his heires and Assignes and to his and their Sole and proper use benefit for evermore/ More over we ye s^d Hilton & Beal doe covent^t promise and engage that at & before ye ensealing and deliuery of these presents we are the true Sole right & proper owners of ye above granted

Book IV, Fol. 148.

Premises & their appurtenances And that we have in ourselves good right & full power and Lawfull Authority the Same to grant and confirme unto ye s^d Daniel Black as aboues^d and the same and every part thereof is free & cleare acquitted & discharged of and from all former and other gifts grants Bargains Sales Leases Morgages titles troubles and incumbrances w'soever and that it shall and may be Lawfull to and for ye s^d Dan^ll Black his heires Execut^rs Admin^rs and Assignes the above granted Premises and every part thereof from time to time and at all times for ever hereafter to have and to hold use improve Ocupie Possess enjoy Lawfully peaceably quietly without any let hindrances Molestation or disturbance Eviction or Ejection of or by us or any other Person by from or under us or our procurement And that ye Sale hereof and of every part thereof we will Maintain against our Selves or our heires Execut^rs Admin^rs & Assigns and against all other psons Lawfully Claiming or Demanding the Same or any part thereof/ And will furthermore make pform & execute Such other Lawfull and reasonable Act or Acts thing or things as in Law or Equity can be devised or required for ye better confirming & more Sure making ouer ye Premises unto ye s^d Daniel Black his heires or Assignes according to ye Laws of this Prvince/ In witness whereof We ye s^d William Hilton and Arthur Beal have hereunto put our hands and Seales this Sixteenth day of January in y^e of our Lord one thousand Six hundred Ninety and Eight. or. Nine and in y^e tenth year of his Majesties Reign.

Signed Sealed and deliuered

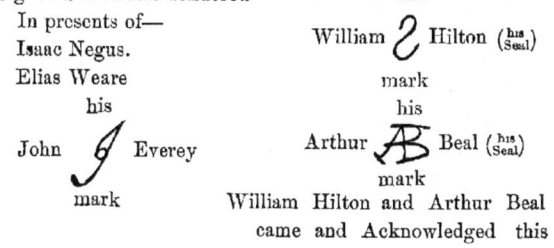

In presents of—
Isaac Negus.
Elias Weare

John (his mark) Everey

William (his mark) Hilton (his Seal)

Arthur (his mark) Beal (his Seal)

William Hilton and Arthur Beal came and Acknowledged this

Book IV, Fol. 148, 149.

Instrum⁺ to be their Act & Deed this Seventeenth day of January : 169⅔. before me
Samuel Donnell Justis pea
A true Copie of yᵉ origenall Transcribed & compared this.
24ᵗʰ of Jan⁽ʳʸ⁾ 169⅔.   p Jos Hammond Regist⁽ʳ⁾

[149] To all Christian People to whome these presents may come to be Seen Read or heard/ Know ye that I Humphrey Spencer of yᵉ Great Island in the Townshᵢp of Portsmouth in New Hampshiere in New England Carpenter for and in consideration of yᵉ Sum of ten pounds to me in hand payd by Mʳ Robeɪt Elliot Merchant. The receipt whereof I doe hereby Acknowledge and my Selfe therewith fully Satisfied contented and paid at & before yᵉ Ensealing and Deliuery of these presents Have bargained and Sold and by these presents doe fully clerely and absolutely bargaine and Sell unto yᵉ sᵈ Robert Elliot Merchant and Inhabitant in yᵉ Town of Portsmouth in New Hampshʳ in New England aforesᵈ, one Certain tract of Land conteyning fiftie Acres being a town Graunt and ten Acres of Swamp bounded with yᵉ land of George Gray on yᵉ West, Nicholas Gillison on yᵉ East : and Thomas Spencer and Richard Nasons Marsh, and bounded on yᵉ South with yᵉ brook that runs out of Wilcocks Pond and his own Addition and bounded on yᵉ North with the Comons next yᵉ River All which Demised Premises are Scituate lying and being in Nichewanick in yᵉ Province of Maine in New England aforesᵈ To have and to hold yᵉ sᵈ ffifty Acres of Land and ten Acres of Swamp

Spencer
to
Elliot

bounded as above and Laid out and Measured by John Wincoll & Roger Plaisted Surv⁽ʳˢ⁾/ And as the said Premises are recorded Or however unto yᵉ Said Robert Elliot his heires Execut⁽ʳˢ⁾

Admin[rs] and Assignes to his and their proper uses and behoofs for ever And I y[e] s[d] Humphrey Spencer my heires Execut[rs] Admin[rs] and every of us the s[d] fiftie Acres of Land and ten Acres of Swamp above Specified Unto y[e] s[d] Robert his heires Execut[rs] Admin[rs] and Assignes Shall and will Warrant and forever Defend/ hereby Revoking making voyd and Disannulling all & all manner of Premises contracts writeings or Agreements formerly made or done to any other pson or psons in New England in of or concerning the Premises Demised as abovesaid or any part thereof And y[e] s[d] Humphrey Spencer doth and by y[e] vertue of these Premises hath Aliene Sell Enfeof and graunt unto y[e] aboves[d] Robert Elliot his heires Execut[rs] Admin[rs] and Assignes two fifth parts of the Marsh commonly called y[e] further Marsh And lying & Adjoyning to Richard Nasons and y[e] land aboves[d] and which Marsh was formerly belonging to Thomas Spencer Deceased the father of said Humphrey Spencer And I y[e] s[d] Humphrey Spencer all y[e] first and last Demised land Swamp and Marsh for my Selfe my heires Execut[rs] and Admin[rs] together with all the priviledges Accomodations thereof Shall and will Warrant & for ever Defend by these presents/ Witness my hand and Seal without ffraud this Second day of Aprill in y[e] year of our Lord One thousand Six hundred Eighty and Six. 1686

Signed Sealed & Deliuered in the presents of us

· Nicho: Heskins
William Broad

mark of
Humphrey H S Spencer (Seal)
Grace B L Spencer (Seal)

Nicholas Heskins came before me Nathan[ll] ffryer & made Oath that Humphrey Spencer and Grace Spencer in his Sight did Signe Seal & delifi this Deed in his Sight and that he Saw William Broad write his name & was witness wth him Selfe to y[e] Same/ Sep[t] 12. 1694

Nathanll ffryer Jes peis

Book IV, Fol. 149.

A true Copie of y[e] origenall Deed Transcribed & compared this. 7th ffer : 169⅝ —   p Jos Hamond Regist[r]

I Robert Elliot doe hereby for my Selfe my heires Execut[rs] and Administrat[rs] Make over and Surrend this Deed together with all y[e] concernm[ts] therein Mentioned Unto Allen ffuz of Nichewanick Planter or to his heires Execut[rs] Admin[rs] or Assignes/ Witness my hand/ Dated in New-Castle, this Eleventh day of Iune in y[e] year of our Lord one thousand Six hundred Ninetie five : 1695   Robert Elliot

<small>Elliot to ffuz</small>

Signed Sealed & deliuered
in presents of —   New Castle June y[e] Eleu-
William Spencer   enth : 1695 Robert Elliot
Humphrey Spencer   Esq[r] came and Acknowl-
                      edged this above written
                      to be his Act & Deed
                      Before me
                      Shadrach Walton
                              Jus : pes

A true Copie of y[e] origenall Deed of Sale on y[e] other Side together with y[e] aboue Assignment Transcribed and Compared this 7[th] day of ffebr : 169⅝ — p Jos Hamond Regist[r]

To all People to whome this p[r]sent Deed of Sale shall come, I Martha Lord Relict-widdow and Administratrix unto Nathan Lord late of Kittery In the County of York in y[e] Province of the Massachusets Bay in New-England Deceased Send Greeting Know ye that for and in consideration of y[e] Sum of Eight and twenty pounds in Currant money of New England to me in hand paid at and before y[e] Ensealing & Delvery of these p[r]sents by Joseph Hamond (Sen[r]) of Kittery in y[e] County and Province afores[d], the receipt whereof I doe hereby Acknowledge and my Self therewith to be fully

<small>Martha Lord to Jos: Hamond</small>

Book IV, Fol. 149, 150.

Satisfied contented and paid & thereof, and of and from every part and parcell thereof for me ye s^d Martha Lord my heires Execut^rs Administrators and assignes Doe Exonerate Acquit and fully Discharge him ye s^d Joseph Hamond his heires Execut^rs Adm^rs and assigns by these presents for ever I the s^d Martha Lord (by vertue of power granted to me at a Superiour Court held at Boston for s^d County on the twenty fifth of October. Anno: 1698 — Have given granted bargained Sold Aliened Enfeoffed and confirmed And by these presents doe for me my heires Execut^rs Adm^rs and assignes fully freely and absolutely Give grant bargain Sell Alien Enfeoffe convey and confirm unto him ye s^d Joseph Hamond his heires & assignes all that piece or parcell of Meadow Lying and being Scittuate at Sturgeon Creek in the township of Kittery aforesaid being butted and bounded as followeth — vizt Southeastward by John Heards Meadow which he had of Nathan [150] Lord And on ye Southwestward by the upland, and on ye Northwest by Mr Shapleighs Meadow or Ditch, And on the Northeast by s^d Sturgeon Creek or however Els butted or bounded or reputed to be butted and bounded being about five or Six Acres more or less, together with all profits priviledges and Appurtenances thereunto belonging or in any ways appertaining — To have and to hold the s^d piece or parcell of Meadow with all ye appur^ces thereto belonging, with all Right title Interest Claime and Demand wch I the s^d Martha Lord now Have or in time past have had or which I my heires Execut^rs Adm^rs or assignes in time to come may might Should or in any wise ought to have of in or to the above granted premisses or any part thereof to him the s^d Joseph Hamond his heires or assignes for euer And to his and their own proper use benefit and behoofe And I ye said Martha Lord doe Covenant promise and grant to and with the s^d Joseph Hamond his heires and assignes that at and before the ensealing and delivery hereof I am ye true right and proper owner of the above p^rmisses and the appurtenances And that I have in my Self full power good Right and Lawfull Authority ye Same to grant and confirm

Book IV, Fol. 150.

unto him ye s^d Joseph Hamond his heires and assignes as aforesaid and that ye Same and every part thereof is free and Clear acquitted and discharged of and from all former and other gifts grants bargains Sales Leases Mortgages titles troubles and Incumbrances whatsoever and that it shall and may be Lawfull to and for ye s^d Joseph Hamond his heires and assignes the afores^d p^rmisses and every part thereof from time to time and at all times for ever hereafter to have hold use Improve ocupie possess and enjoy ye Same Lawfully peaceably & quietly without any Lawfull Let deniall hinderance Molestation or Disturbance of or by me or any other person or persons from by or under me or by my procurement And that the Sale thereof against my Self heires Execut^{rs} Am^{rs} and assignes and against all other persons whatsoever Lawfully Claiming ye Same or any part thereof I will for ever Save harmless warrant and Defend by these p^rsents— In witness whereof I have hereunto Set my hand and Seale this Eighth day of ffebruary in y^e tenth year of the Reign of our Soveraign Lord William y^e third by the grace of God of England Scotland ffrance and Ireland King Defend^r of y^e faith &^c Annoq_e Domini one thousand Six hundred Ninety & eight, nine : 169$\frac{8}{9}$ Martha Lord (her Seal)
Signed Sealed and delivered in p^rsence of us

Witnesses
- Daniel [his mark] Gooden
- John [his mark] Key
- Samuel Smalle

York ss. August. 25th 1702.
The within named Martha Lord personally appearing before me y^e Subscriber one of her Ma^{tys} Justices of y^e Peace for s^d County Acknowledged this Instrument to be her Act & deed
            Ichabod Plaisted

Book IV, Fol. 150.

A true Copie of the originall Transcribed August 25ᵗʰ 1702— p Jos Hamond Registʳ

This Indenture made the Second day of Ianuary one thousand Six hundred Ninety Eight. 9. In yᵉ tenth year of the Reign of our Soveraign Lord King William the third, of England Scotland ffrance & Ireland between Ioseph Crocket of Kittery in yᵉ County of York Planter within his Majesties Province of yᵉ Massachusets Bay in New England and Hannah his wife on yᵉ one partie & William Pepperrill of Kittery in yᵉ County of York aforesᵈ Merchant of the other partie Witnesseth That the sᵈ Joseph Crocket and Hannah his sᵈ wife for and in consideration of yᵉ Sum of Six pounds Currant money of New England to them in hand at and before the Ensealing and Deliuery of these Presents well & truly paid and Secured in yᵉ Law to be paid by yᵉ sᵈ William Pepperrell The receipt whereof to full content & Satisfaction they doe hereby Acknowledge and thereof doe Acquit yᵉ sᵈ William Pepperrell his heires Executʳˢ Administratʳˢ and Assignes and every of them for ever by these presents have given granted bargained Sold Conveied & confirmed by these presents doe freely fully and Absolutely giue grant bargain Sell convey & confirm unto yᵉ sᵈ William Pepperrell his heires Executʳˢ Administratʳˢ & Assigns for euer All that their piece or parcell of upLand & Swamp or Meadow att Kittery Lying and being in Piscataqua Riuer on yᵉ North Side of Diggery Jeofreys land, containing by Estimation fortie five Acres or thereabout more or less And is butted and bounded by Marked trees containing a hundred and Sixty Pole in Length North & by East & forty five pole in breadth East and by South, westerly with John Dearings land And on yᵉ North & on yᵉ East and on yᵉ South with present Comons, which Land was giuen to sᵈ Crocket in two Severall Town

Jos Crocket to William Pepperrell

grants, Together with all & Singular the Woods under Woods Water Water Courses Stones trees Timber and all other y⁶ Profits Priviledges Unto y⁶ Same belonging or in any wayes thereunto Appurtaining. To have and to hold y⁶ s^d piece or parcell of Upland Swamp or Meadow with all y⁶ afore Mentioned to be granted & bargained Premises Unto y⁰ s^d William Pepperrell his heires and Assignes to his and their onely proper use benefit & behoofe for euer And the s^d Joseph Crocket and Hannah his wife for themselves their heires Execut^rs & Admin^rs & Assignes doe covenant Promise grant and agree to and with y⁶ s^d William Pepperrell his heires Execut^rs Admin^rs and Assignes by these presents in Manner following that is to Say that at y⁶ time of this bargain and Sale and untill y⁶ Ensealing and deliuery of these presents they y⁶ s^d Ioseph Crocket & Hannah his wife are the true owners of y⁶ afores^d bargained Premises And haue in them Selues full power good Right & Lawfull Authority to grant bargain ffor Sell convey the Same in manner as aboues^d being free and clere of and from all former gifts grants titles troubles Charges & Incumbrances whatsoeuer, Will Warrant and Defend y⁶ Same unto y⁶ s^d William Pepperrell his heires [151] Execut^rs Admin^rs and Assignes for ever against y⁶ Lawfull Claimes & Demands of all and euery person or persons whome soeuer by and under me & lastly will doe or cause to be done any other Act or Acts for the further confirmation and more Sure making of the aboue bargained Premises as by his or their Councill Learned in y⁶ Law Shall be reasonably devised or required In witness whereof y⁶ s^d Joseph Crocked and Hannah his s^d wife have hereunto Set their hands and Seales the day and year first aboue Written.

Signed Sealed & Deliuered
  in presents of us—
  Andrew Pepperrell.
  Thomas Corbet.
  Sam^ll Pecher.

Joseph ✝ Crocket (Seal)
  y⁶ mark of
Hannah h. Crocket (Seal)

A true Copie of ye origenall Deed of Sale Transcribed and Compared this 28th ffebr : 169⅞

                        p Jos Hamond Regist^r

York ss/ Kittery Iune 17th 1700—

The aboue named Ioseph Crocket psonally appearing, Acknowledged ye above Instrument to be his Act & Deed.

                  Before me Jos Hamond Jus^{ts} Peace

A true Copie of this Acknowledgm^t Entred here Iune 17 : 1700/   p Jos Hamond Reg^r

The Deposition of Christian Remich aged 67 years or thereabout Testifieth & Saith that he well knew Dennis Downing now Deceased Liued on the ffarm or plantation which his Son Joshua Downing now Possesseth and that ye s^d Dennis Downing Possessed it in ye year fifty one & that he Possessed it Quietly Seuerall years And this Deponent never knew or heard that any body Molested Said Downing on ye s^d place all his life time he being a near Neighbour to s^d Downing/ this Deponent further Saith that he knew s^d Downing pay Rates for the said Land as an Inhabitant of ye Town and never knew s^d Downing to pay Rent or Acknowledgm^t to any body for ye s^d ffarm.

<small>Remich & Rogers oaths</small>

Sworn in Court this 4th Jan^{ry} 169⅘

                      p Jos Hamond Cler

Richard Rogers appeared at ye same time and made oath to ye truth of what Christian Remich had Sworn to, as to Dennis Downings Possession &^c.

                Sworn in Court, p Jos Hamond Cler

A true Copie of ye origenall oaths. Transcribed and Compared this 30th Jan^{ry} 169⅘—   p Jos Hamond Regist^r

BOOK IV, FOL. 151.

This Indenture made the Sixteenth day of December: one thousand Six hundred Eighty Seven Anno, R. R. Iacobi Anglia &c Secudi Tirtio, between Robert Tufton Mason Esq' Grandson and heir of Cap^tn John Mason late of London Esq' Deceased, on ye one part And Eliakim Hutchinson of Boston within his Majesties Territory & Dominion of New England Merchant of ye other part Witnesseth—

Whereas our Soveraign Lord King Iames ye first by his letters pattents under ye great Seal of England Dated at Westminster the third day of Novemb^r In ye Eighteenth year of his Maties Reigne for ye considerations in ye Same etters Patteuts Expressed, did absolutely Giue Grant & confirm unto ye Council Established at Plimouth in the County of Devon ffor ye Planting Ruleing ordering and Governing of New England in America And to their Successr^s and Assignes for ever, All ye land of New England afores^d Lying and being in breadth from forty Degrees to forty

<small>Robert Tufton Mason to Eliak Hutchinson</small> Eight Degrees Northerly Latitude Inclusiuely, Together with all firm Lands Soyles grounds Havens Ports Riv^rs waters fishing hunting haukinging fowling and all Mines Mineralls &c as in and

by the s^d letters Pattents amongst divers other things therein contained More at large it doth and may appear And whereas ye s^d Councill by their Indenture under their comon Seal bearing date the two and twentieth day of Aprill Anno one thousand Six hundred thirtie fiue made between ye s^d Councill by ye name Councill Established at Plimouth in ye County of Devon for ye Planting Ruleing ordering and Governing of New England in America of the one part, and S^r ffardinando Gorges of London Knight of ye other part for ye considerations in ye s^d Indenture Expressed Did giue grant bargain Sell Enfeoffe and confirm unto ye s^d S^r ffardinando Gorges his heires and Assignes for ever All that Part Purport or Portion of the Main Land of New England afores^d begining at ye entrance of Piscataqua horbour. Soe to Pass up ye Same Unto the Riuer of Nichewannick through yᵉ Same unto yᵉ farthest head thereof And from thence Northwestward untill Sixty Miles be finished And from Piscataqua Harbour aforesᵈ Northeastwards along yᵉ Sea Coast unto Sagadehock & up the Riuer thereof to yᵉ Riuer of Kenebeck and throughout yᵉ Same unto yᵉ head thereof and Soe up into yᵉ Land Northwestward untill Sixty Miles be finished from yᵉ Mouth or entrance of Sagadehock from which Period to cross over yᵉ land to the Sixty Miles end formerly accounted up into yᵉ land from Piscataqua harbour through Nichewanick River/ which amongst other Lands are granted unto yᵉ sᵈ Sʳ ffardinando Gorges/ together with all Mines Mineralls precious Stones woods Marshes Riuers waters fishins hunting fowlings &ᶜ [152] with all and Singular their Appurtenances &ᶜ/ As by the sᵈ Indenture doth at large doth appear, And whereas the sᵈ Sʳ ffardinando Gorges for diuers good causes and considerations him thereunto Moveing in and by a certain Indenture under his hand and Seal bearing Date yᵉ Seventeenth day of Septembʳ Anno One thousand Six hundred thirty fiue did giue grant bargain Sell Enfeoff & confirm unto Captⁿ Iohn Mason of London Esqʳ his heires and Assignes for ever all that part or portion of land begining at yᵉ entrance of Nichewanick Riuer and Soe upward along the sᵈ Riuer and to yᵉ farthest head thereof And to contain in breadth throughout all yᵉ length aforesᵈ three Miles within yᵉ Land from euery part of sᵈ Riuer and halfe way over yᵉ sᵈ Riuer, together with all & Singular harbours Cricks Marshes woods Riuers waters Lakes Mines Minerall precious Stones fishings hawking hunting & fowling &ᶜ comodities & Heredittaments whatsoeuer, with all and Singular their and every of their Appurtenances to be holden of his Majestie his heirs and Successʳˢ as of his manner of East Greenwich in yᵉ County of Kent in free and common Soccage and not in Capite or by Knights Service. Yeelding and paying unto his Majestie his heires & Successʳˢ the fifth part of yᵉ ore of Gold and Silver that from time to time and at all times thereafter Shall be there

BOOK IV, FOL. 152.

gotten had and & obtained for all Services duties & demands as in and by the s⁴ Letters Pattents are reserued and by the s⁴ Recited Indenture it doth more at Large appear/ Now this Indenture further Witnesseth that yᵉ aboue named Robert Tufton Mason Esqʳ Grandson & heire of yᵉ s⁴ Capᵗⁿ John Mason Esqʳ for and in consideration of yᵉ Sum of Sixty pounds in currant Money of New England to him in hand at & before the Ensealing and deliuery of these presents well and truly paid by the aforenamed Eliakim Hutchinson in full payment & Satisfaction for all past Rents and Demands whatsoeuer, the receipt whereof yᵉ s⁴ Robert Tufton Mason doth acknowledge and thereof doth Exonerate Acquit and Discharge the s⁴ Eliakim Hutchinson his heires Execuᵗʳˢ Administratʳˢ and Assignes for euer by these presents Alsoe in farther consideration of yᵉ yearly Rent & payments, hereafter in these presents Expressed and reserved on yᵉ part of the s⁴ Robert Tufton Mason to be paid by yᵉ s⁴ Eliakim Hutchinson his heires Execuᵗʳˢ Administratʳˢ or Assignes, hath giuen granted released Enfeoffed and confirmed And by these presents doth freely fully and Absolutely Giue grant Alien release Enfeoff & confirm unto yᵉ s⁴ Eliakim Hutchinson his heires and Assignes for ever, The full quatetie of fiue hundred Acres of Land Lying Scituate on both Sides the little Riuer of Newgewanick Alias Newichewanick within the Township of Kittery in the Province of Maine in New England aforesᵈ, four hundred & fourteen Acres whereof was formerly Surveighed and Measured by Capᵗⁿ Iohn Wincoll as appears by a Draught or Plat thereof by him made & Signed the fiue and twentieth day of May: 1682, being now in yᵉ actuall possession of yᵉ s⁴ Hutchinson, and yᵉ remainᵈʳ to compleat yᵉ s⁴ fiue hundred Acres to be made up out of yᵉ Adjacent lands backwards and Severall other parcells and spots of Land Marsh or Meadow Lying upon yᵉ aforesᵈ Riuer which were formerly granted by the Town of Kittery unto Richard or George Leader or to yᵉ s⁴ Hutchinson And all Rights and grants of Timbʳ made by-

the s^d Town of Kittery unto the said Richard or George
Leader or s^d Hutchinson and other timb^r convenient to be
brought unto ye s^d Hutchinsons Mill Standing or Lying
within the s^d Masons Right not heretofore Granted Excepting pine trees of four and twenty Inches Deamiter fitting to
make Masts for ye Kings Ships, & the Sole Propriety in the
ffalls on which s^d Hutchinsons Mill now Stands, with y^e
Stream water water courses Damms Bank priviledges and Appurtenances thereto belonging reserving ye priuiledge of y^e
Riuer and Stream for ye Transportation of timb^r Loggs &
boards &^c as is usuall and hath been formerly Accustomed,
together with all woods underwoods timb^r and trees (Except
as afores^d) Stones Mines and Mineralls whatsoever upon y^e
afore mentioned to be granted lands or any part or parcell
thereof Springs waters water courses fishing fowling hawking hunting Rights libertis priuiledges comodities profits and
Appurtenances thereto belonging reseruing unto his Matie his
heirs and Success^rs one fifth part of ye ore of gold and Silver
that from time to time and at all times hereafter shall be
there gotten had and obtained/ To have and to hold the s^d
quantety or tract of Land of fiue hundred Acres and other
ye Seuerall parcells or spots of land Marsh or Meadow aboue
Mentioned with ye woods trees timb^r & grants of timb^r Sole
Propriety in ye ffalls and all other ye afore granted Premises
with ye Rights memb^rs Priviledges and Appurtenances thereof Excepting and reseruing as is above Excepted and reserved, Also all ye Estate Right Title Interest use property
possession claim Challenge & Demand whatsoever of him y^e
s^d Robert Tufton Mason or his heires of in & to ye Same and
to euery part and parcell thereof unto ye s^d Eliakim Hutchinson his heires and Assignes to his and their onely proper
use benefit and behoofe for ever/ And the s^d Robert Tufton
Mason for himself his heires Execut^rs and Administrat^rs doth
covenant promise grant & agree to and with ye s^d Eliakim
Hutchinson his heires & Assignes by these [153] presents
in manner following, that is to Say that he s^d Eliakim Hutch-

inson for his heires or Assignes shall and may from time to time and at all times forever hereafter by fo·ce and vertue of these presents Lawfully peaceably and quietly have hold use ocupie possess and enjoy to his and their proper use benefit and behoofe all and euery of the aboue granted premises with the Rights memb^{rs} profits priviledges and Appurtenances thereof free & clear and clerely acquitted Exonerated and Discharged of & from all former and other gifts grant bargains Sales Mortgages titles troubles charges incumbrances claimes and Demands whatsoever and doth further couenant promise bind and oblige himselfe his heires Execut^{rs} and Administrat^{rs} from time to time and at all times for euer hereafter to warrant maintaine and defend all and every of ye s^d granted Premises unto ye Eliakim Hutchinson his heires and Assignes against all and every pson & persons whatsoever And at ye Cost and Charges in ye Law of the s^d Eliakim Hutchinson his heires or Assignes upon request or demand thereof to doe make Seal and Execute Acknowledge and Suffer Such other & farther deeds Instruments writing Act or Acts Device or Devices in ye Law for the more Sure making and Confirmation of ye s^d bargained Premises with ye memb^{rs} and Appurtenances thereof unto ye Said Eliakim Hutchinson his heires and Assignes for ever as his or their Councill learned in ye Law Shall Devise Aduise or require And the s^d Eliakim Hutchinson doth by these presents Covenant promise grant and agree for himselfe his heires Execut^{rs} Administrat^{rs} and Assignes well and truly to pay or cause to be payd unto ye s^d Robert Tufton Mason his heires Execut^{rs} Administrat^{rs} or Assignes the full and Just Sum or quit Rent of forty Shillings in Currant money of New England p Annum for ye s^d fiue hundred Acres of Land to be paid upon ye fiue & twentieth day of Decemb^r Yearly And in euery year Successiuely from the fiue and twentieth of Decemb^r Anno one thousand Six hundred Eighty and Eight Thenceforth for euer if Demanded And in like proportion for Soe many Acres as ye s^d other parcells or Spots of Land

Book IV, Fol. 153.

Marsh or Meadow Shall Appear to contain upon a Survey and Measure thereof to be made and for ye grants and Priuiledges for the use of ye S^d Saw Mill the full and Just quantity of three thousand foot of Boards for every hundred thousand foot which from time to time and at all times for ever hereafter Shall be there Sawn, Soe always that the afores^d paiments be in full of all rents acknowledgement duties Services and payments for ye aboue granted Premises And euery of them whatsoeuer and to whomesoeuer except the fifth part of the ore of gold and Siluer afore reserved to be paid to his Majestie his heirs or Success^{rs} In witness whereof the s^d parties to these presents haue Interchangeably Set their hands and Seales the day and Year first aboue Written Alsoe there is further granted to y^e s^d Eliakim Hutchinson his heires &^{c} a Strip of Land of about one Acre more or less Lying upon y^e Side of the Riuer comonly called Pipe staff point formerly bought of Richard Nason.

Signed Sealed & Deliuered Robert Tufton Mason ($_{Seale}^{his}$)
in presents of us — after enterlining y^e words
Grandson & heire of Cap^{tn} John Mason Esqr

Nich^o Page   Robert Tufton Mason Acknowledged
William Ardell   the within written to be his Act &
Isaac Addington   Deed the Seuenteenth day of Decemb^r 1687. before me. John Usher

The within written Instrument hauing been pused by us underwritten was Sealed and Executed by our ffather Robert Tufton Mason Esqr in our presents and is freely and fully consented unto and approved by us and each of us & Soe far as we or either of us Are are may or hereafter might haue been any wayes or Interested in ye Premises or any of them therein Mentioned to be granted we and each of us respetiuely for our Selues and for our Severall and respectiue heires Execut^{rs} and Administrat^{rs} doe grant release Ratifie confirm and for euer quit Claim unto ye s^d Hutchinson his heires and Assigns for euer All and euery of our Estate Right Title Interest reversion and Reversions Claim Challenge and demand to and in and all and euery the within granted Premises with their appurtenances—

Signed in presents us   John Tufton
   Thomas Grafford   Maj^r John Tufton psonally Appearing Acknowledged y^e Subscription aboue & the Instrument to which it is under written to be his Act and Deed.
   Sam^{ll} Penhallow

                         Before J. Dudley
               March y^e 12th 1687

A true Copie of the origenall Indenture Transcribed & compared this 18th of ffebruary : 169$\frac{8}{9}$—

                 p Jos Hamond. Regist^r

[154] To all People to whome these presents shall come Greeting. Know y^e that I John Davis of Portsm^o in the Province of New Hampshiere New England Smith, ffor and in consideration of a valluable Sum to me in hand already paid by James Plaisted of York in ye County of York in New England, the receipt whereof I doe by these presents Acknowledge and full Satisfaction therewith and thereof & of every part thereof doe fully clerely and absolutely Acquitt Exonerate and Discharge ye s^d James Plaisted his heires Execut^{rs} and Administrat^{rs} for ever by these presents have granted bargained and Sold Aliened enfeoffed & confirmed to him ye s^d James Plaisted his heires and Assignes for ever all ye Right title or Interest I have, euer had, or ought to have either by Town grant, Purchase Possession by priviledge of Landing place Hay Yard or by any other ways or meanes whatever, To a certain tract of land lying in York afores^d in the place called ye New Mill creek between ye Land of Thomas Moulton & the land of Mr Edward Rishworth be it more or less as by any means may be made to Appear/ To have & to hold ye above granted and

BOOK IV, FOL. 154.

bargained Premises with all ye Priviledges and Appurtenances to ye Same Appertaining or in any wise belonging, to him ye s^d James Plaisted his heires & Assignes forever to his & their onely proper use and behoofe Soe that neither I ye s^d John Davis my heires Execut^rs Administrat^rs nor Assigns nor any other pson or psons by us for us or in our names or in ye name or names of us or of any of us at any time or times hereafter may Ask claime Challenge or Demand in or to ye Premisses or to any part thereof any Interest right title use or possession by from all Claime Shall be excluded and for ever Debarred And he ye s^d James Plaisted his heires & Assigns Shall and may at all times and from time to time forever quietly & peaceably have hold ocupie Possess and enjoy ye Premises in and by these presents granted bargained and Sold and every part thereof without the Lawfull let hinderance contradiction or deniall of me the above named John Davis or of my heires Execut^rs Administrat^rs or Assigns or of any of them or of any other pson or psons whatsoever Claiming or having any Right title or Interest therein or to any part or peell thereof by from or under me/ In witness whereof I have hereunto Set my hand and Seal this thirty first day of March in the tenth year of his Majesties Reign, and in ye year of our Lord God Everlasting: 1699.   John Davis (his Seale)

Signed Sealed & Deliuered   Docter John Davis came before
 in presents of us—   me this: 1st day of Aprill:
 Roger Swaine   1699 And did then Acknowl-
 Thomas Phips   edge the above Instrument
                             to be his free Act & Deed—
                             Nathaniel ffryer Jus: peace

A true Copie of ye origenall Instrument or Deed of Sale.
Transcribed and Compared: this 4th day of Aprill: 1699—
                    p Jos: Hamond Regist^r

BOOK IV, FOL. 154.

Know all men by these presents that I Ann Ieofrey Relict and Administratrix to ye Estate of Thomas Crocket late of Kittery in the County of York have for the consideration of ye Motherly love and dear affection I bear unto my beloved Son Epraim Crocket, but more Especially for ye consideration of ffifteen pounds & eleven Shillings paid for my Deceased husband Thomas Crocket as alsoe for twelve pounds in Money paid to my daughter Mary Barton for her Legacie, as alsoe twenty pounds in Money paid to my Son Joshua Crocket by my aboves^d Son Ephraim Crocket, for the consideration aboves^d have giuen granted bargained and sold, and doe by these presents bargain Sell Enfeoffe make over Alien^ts and confirm unto my Son Ephraim Crocket and his heires for ever all that tract of Land on lying Crockets Neck being bounded in part by Spruce Creek and the lands of my Son Hugh Crocket and ye lands of William Roberts and John Parrot containing all that tract of land within the s^d bounds as it was formerly laid out and bounded by Cap^tn Wincoll To have and to hold all ye s^d tract of Land unto ye s^d Ephraim Crocket and his heires Lawfully begotten of his body to him & to them and their heires for ever and that it shall and may be Lawfull for ye s^d Epraim Crocket and his heirs to take use ocupie and improue ye s^d tract of land and every part & parcell thereof to ye onely proper use benefit and behoofe of them ye s^d Epraim Crocket and his heires for ever from me ye s^d Ann Jeofrey or my heires Executors Admin^rs or Assignes or any other pson under me and further I ye s^d Ann Jeofrey doe covenant with ye s^d Ephraim Crocket and his heires that ye s^d lands are free from all Incumbrances whatsoever by me made or Suffered to be done or any by my direction or order/ And further more I ye s^d Ann Jeofrey doe engage and Covenant for my Self and my heires the Peaceable & quiet possession thereof to Warrant and Maintain against all persons Laying Lawfull Claim thereunto, the kings Majestie & his Lawfull Success^rs Ex-

Book IV, Fol. 154, 155.

cepted/ Witness my hand and Seale May ye twentieth one thousand Six hundred Eighty and Eight/

Signed Sealed and Deliuered
  in presents of us whose
  names are Subscribed—
Henry Barter
Wm Godsoe

The Signe of
Ann ⟨⟩ Jefory (her Seal)

The. 7th of July. 1697 then came Ann Jefery and Acknowledged this Instrum^t to be her free Act and Deed before me Wm Pepperrell Js pes

A true Copie of ye origenall Instrument Transcribed & Compared this 25. day of March : 1699—

p Jos Hamond Reg^r

[155] Know all men by these presents that I Ann Ieofrey Relict & Administratrix of the Estate of Thomas Crocket late of Kittery in ye County of York for Diuers good Causes and considerations me hereunto Moving but more Especially for and in consideration of a Sum of Money paid unto my Deceased husband Thomas Crocket by my Deceased Son Ephreaim Crocket, which s^d Sum was for a bargain and Sale and did bargain & Sell a certain tract of Land and Marsh Lying in Braveboat Harbour, containing Eighty Acres as it was bounded be it more or Less/ the s^d bargain & Sale was made and compleated in the Year of our Lord one thousand Six hundred Seventy and three Iune ye third the & whole money then paid and every part thereof unto my Deceased Husband Thomas Crocket & Acquittances giuen for ye Same but ye Deed of Sale or conveiance was Neglected and delayed which Should have then ben giuen Therefore I ye aboues^d Ann Jeofrey Administratrix doe by these presents Ratifie bargain and Sell Set ouer and Alienate and confirm And doe by these presents bargain and Sell Enfeoffe and confirm all that tract of Land and Marsh for ye consideration aboue said unto my beloued Daughter in Law

Book IV, Fol. 155.

Ann Crocket Relict of my said Son Epraim Crocket and his heires heires for ever All that tract of land and Marsh Lying in Braueboat Harbour that was in ye tenure and occupation of ye late Richard White that was my late husbands Thomas Crockets the s^d Land and Salt Marsh is now held in ye Right of s^d Richard White or his Assignes and lies on ye Western Side of Braueboat Harbour the Marsh begins at ye head of s^d harbour and soe down along ye Westerly Side of ye Creek to a Marked tree Standing on the Westerly Side of a Cove of Salt Marsh which runs up to the next run Westerly from ye Bridge and Soe bacward into the Woods untill Eightie Acres be compleated with all ye priuledges and Appurtenances unto ye Sole benefit and behoofe of her ye s^d Ann Crockett and my Son Ephraime Crockets heires and that for ever. To haue and to hold all ye s^d tract of Land and Salt Marsh to ye only use and behoofe of her ye s^d Ann Crocket and ye heires or Assignes of my Deceased Son Ephraim Crockett and that for ever more wthout any Claim let hinderance Molestation or Deniall of ye s^d Thomas Crockets heires or me the s^d Ann Jeofrey or any und^r either of us And further I ye s^d Ann Jeofrey aboves^d my heires and Assignes doe covenant to and with ye s^d Ann Crocket and ye heires and Assignes of Ephraim Crocket aboues^d to warrant and defend the Premises and ye Peaceable Possession thereof to Maintaine against all persons laying Lawfull Claime thereunto.

Witness my hand and Seal this   day of July one thousand Six hundred Ninety and fiue. And in y^e Seventh year of his Majestys Reign William y^e third.

Signed Sealed & Deliuered in   the mark
y^e pres^{ts} of us
Sam^{ll} Winkley   of   Ann Jeofrey ($^{her}_{Seal}$)
Sam^{ll} Palmer

July y^e 9th day 1695/ Ann Jeofrey came & Acknowledged this Deed of Sale to be her ffree Act & deed, before me—
Wm Pepperrell Justes pes

Book IV, Fol. 155.

A true Copie of y^e origenall Deed Transcribed & compared this 25th day of March 1699— p Jos Hamond Regist^r

To all Christian People to whome these presents shall come greeting — Know ye that I Iames Gibbons of Sacoe in ye Province of Mayn in New England planter for and in consideration of ye Sum of ten pounds at and before ye ensealing and Delivery of these presents to me in hand paid by Richard Rogers of Sacoe in ye Prouince of Mayn afores^d Cooper, have giuen granted Aliened bargained Sold Enfeofeed & confirmed and by these presents doe fully clerely & absolutely giue grant Alien bargaine Sell Enfeoffe and confirm unto ye s^d Richard Rogers his heires and Assignes for ever All that two hundred Acres of Land bounded as followeth Viz^t To begin at his now dwelling house and from thence along ye Sea Shore Northeasterly to ye next Current of fresh water Issuing out of ye woods to ye Sands or Salt Sea, and from thence to ye S^d house againe Westerly and from thence to ye Riuer of Goose faire on ye Same line to a knot of pines near ye s^d Riuer and soe to ye Riuer with all the thatch grass comonly Soe called in or on ye Northeast Side of that Riuer And Soe from both bounds to run upon a Streight line with an Equall bredth Northwesterly up into ye Maine land untill two hundred Acres be compleat & ended with all ye Meadow within ye s^d bounds being part of ye s^d two hundred Acres with all ye Sandy Ridge of land along ye Sea from both bounds to high water Mark thereunto granted but not to be within ye Compass or Mensuracon of ye s^d two hundred Acres before expressed but over & aboue ye Same as alsoe all ye woods underwoods and all other priviledges & Rights whatsoever thereunto belonging or in any wise Appertaining And alsoe all ye Estate Right Title Interest use possession property Claime & Demand whatsoever of me ye s^d Iames Gibbons my heires or Assignes of in and

BOOK IV, FOL. 155, 156.

to y° Same/ To have and to hold y° s^d two hundred Acres of Land And all and Singular other y° Premises hereby granted bargained & Sold with every of their Right member & Appurtenances whatsoeuer unto y° s^d Richard Rogers his heirs and Assignes to y° onely proper use and behoofe of y° s^d Richard Rogers his heires and Assignes for ever. And y° s^d Iames Gibbons for himselfe and his heires Execut^rs & Admin^rs the s^d two hundred Acres of land and all and Singular other y° Premises before granted bargained and Sold with y° Appurtenances unto y° s^d Richard Rogers and his heires to y° only proper use and behoofe of y° s^d Richard Rogers his heires and Assignes for ever against him y° s^d Iames Gibbons his heires and Assignes for ever and against y° heires and Assignes of Robert Haywood of y° Island of Barbadoes Dec^d and all and euery other psons whatsoever Lawfully Claiming by from or under him them or any of them Shall and will Warrant and for ever Defend by these presents In witness whereof I y° s^d James Gibbons haue hereunto put my hand & Seale this twenty fifth day of May in y° third year of our Soveraign Lord James the Second, of England Scotland ffrance & Ireland King &° Annoq Domini : 1687 Signed Sealed and Deliuered in   the mark of

  presents of us   James   Gibbons ($^{his}_{Seal}$)
  [156] Phillip ffoxwell
  Elizabeth Sharp   Boston Iuly y° 7. 1692/ Iames Gib-
  Wm Milborn   bons psonally appeared before me
                        and Acknowledged this Instrum^t
                        to be his Act and Deed before me
                                        Jer : Dumer

A true Copie of y° origenall Deed Transcribed & compared this 22^d March 169⅔   p Jos Hamond Regist^r

To all People to whome this present Deed of Sale Shall come, I ffrancis Avant of Kittery in y° Prouince of y° Masachusets Bay in New England Yeoman Send greeting Know yᵉ that for and in consideration of yᵉ Sum of Six pounds in Currant Money of New England to me in hand well and truly paid at and before yᵉ Ensealing and Deliuery of these presents by Mʳ Richard Cutt of yᵉ Same Town County and Prouince aforesᵈ Yeoman, the receipt whereof I doe hereby Acknowledge and my Selfe therewith to be fully Satisfied and paid and from euery pait and pcell thereof for me yᵉ sᵈ ffrancis Avant my heires Execut[rs] Admin[rs] and Assignes doe Acquit and fully Discharge him the sᵈ Richard Cutt his heires &ᶜ by these presents for ever, I the sᵈ ffrancis Avant haue giuen granted bargained Sold and by these presents doe for me my heires Execut[rs] Admin[rs] and Assignes fully freely and absolutely giue grant bargain Sell convey and confirm unto him yᵉ sᵈ Richard Cutt his heirs and Assignes A certain tract of Land Scituate and lying in yᵉ township of Kittery Comonly called by yᵉ Name of Crockets plaine Containing ten Acres be it more or less as it is butted and bounded on yᵉ East end by yᵉ land of William Godsoe with a Northwest & by North line twenty pole And from thence Southwest & by west Eighty pole to a black birch & an hemlock growing together and from thence Southeast & by South twenty pole to two Marked trees And from thence Northeast & by east to our first Station being a great Hemlock Marked on four sides by yᵉ high way, together with all yᵉ Right title and Interest which I ffrancis Avant have to a parcell of Land granted by the town of Kittery to Joshua Crocket in yᵉ year of our Lord one thousand Six hundred Seventy and Nine on yᵉ twenty Eighth of July. And Measured out on yᵉ Second of Octobʳ in yᵉ Same year abouesᵈ containing twenty Acres which Tract of land I ffrancis Avant haue bargained with yᵉ sᵈ Crocket for and haue paid him forty Shillings towards it which bargain I doe by these presents make ouer to Richard Cutt his heires Execut[rs] Admin[rs] &ᶜ To haue and to hold the abouesᵈ tracts of land with all yᵉ profits priviledges & Appurtenances there unto belonging, or in any wise appertaining with all y" Right Title Interest Claim and Demand which I ffrancis Avant now haue or in time past haue had or which I my heires &c may might Shold or in any wise ought to haue in time to come of in or to y" aboue granted Premises or any part thereof to him y" s^d Richard Cutt his heirs and Assignes for ever and to y" Sole and proper use benefit and behoofe of him y" s^d Richd Cutt his heires &c foreuermore and I the s^d ffrancis Avant for my Selfe my heires Execut^{rs} Admin^{rs} & Assignes doe Covenant promise and grant to and with him y" said Richd Cutt, his heires and Assignes that at and before y" Ensealing & Deliuery here of the aboue Mentioned Premises and euery part thereof is free and Cleare Acquitted and Discharged of and from all former and other gifts grants bargains Sales Mortgages Dowries titles troubles Acts Alienations and incumbrances whatsoever And that it shall & may be lawfull to and for y" s^d Richard Cutt his heires and Assigns the afores^d Premises and every part thereof from time to time and at all times for ever here after to haue hold use ocupie Improve possess and enjoy Lawfully peaceably and quietly without any lawfull lett deniall hinderance Molestation or disturbance of or by me or any pson or psons from by or under me or by my procurement & that y" Sale thereof and euery part thereof against my Selfe my heires Execut^{rs} Admin^{rs} and Assignes and against all other psons whatsoever, Claiming and lawfully Demanding y" Same or any part thereof, I will for ever Saue harmless warrant & Defend by these presents/ In Witness whereof I ye s^d ffrancis Avant haue hereunto Set my hand and Seal after ye incertion of ye words Six hundred in y^e Eighteenth line This Nineteenth day of Octob^r Anno Dom: one thousand Six hundred Ninety

BOOK IV, FOL. 156, 157.

and Six, Annoq, Regni Regis Anglia Scotia &c Guilielmi octavo.

Signed Sealed & Deliuered
in the presents of us —
John Newmarch Junr
Samuel Scriven
John Larry

ffrancis A Auant ($^{his}_{Seal}$)
his mark

The 20th of octob^r 1696 ffrancis Auant came before me & Acknowledged this aboue Instrument to be his ffree Act and Deed.

before me Wm Pepperrell Js pes

A true Copie of y^e origenall Deed Transcribed & compared this 22^d day of March : 169$\frac{8}{9}$.

p Jos Hamond Regist^r

[157] Know all men by these presents that I Ioshua Crocket of Dover in y^e Province of New Hampshiere Shipwright have for y^e consideration of fourteen pounds in Money to me in hand paid by Richard Cutt Gentleman, in the Town of Kittery in y^e County of York and doe Acknowledge my Selfe fully Satisfied contented and paid and of every part and parcell thereof haue giuen granted bargained and Sold Enfeofft and confirmed And do by these presents bargain sell Enfeoffe convey and Set ouer and confirm unto the aboues^d Richard Cutt Gentleman and his heires for ever a Certain tract of Land containing twenty Acres ly and Scituate in ye town of Kittery afores^d at a place comonly called and known by the name of Crockets plaine and is that tract of Land that was granted unto me by ye Town of Kittery Iuly 28th 1679 — and laid out unto me the s^d Ioshua Crocket by Cap^{tn} John Wincoll october ye 2nd 1679 — being Eighty pole in Length and forty pole in breadth and lies between ye lands of ye s^d Richd Cutt he lately purchased of

Book IV, Fol. 157.

ffrancis Auent and ye land of my brother Epraim Deceased, wth all ye Appurtenances and Priuiledges thereunto belonging or any wise appertaining, as Timb^r wood woods or underwood Standing or ly thereon to ye only use benefit and behoof of him ye s^d Richard Cutt his heires or Assignes for ever/ To have and to hold all ye aboves^d twenty Acres of land as it is bounded and Described untoth Sole and only Use benefit and behoofe of him ye s^d Richd Cutt his heires and Assignes for ever more and furthermore the said Joshua Crocket doth Covenant for himselfe and his heires and Assignes with ye s^d Richd Cut his heires Execut^{rs} or Admin^{rs} or Assignes that ye above tract of land is free from all encumbrances whatsoever as Dowers Joyntures Sales gifts Mortgages Services or ye like And that I am at ye Sealing and Signeing hereof Lawfully Seized of every part and pcell thereof and that it Shall and may be lawfull for ye s^d Richd Cutt his heires or Assigns to take use ocupie improve & possess all and every part of ye Premises with all ye Appurtenances and Priviledges above Mentioned and ye peaceable and quiet possession thereof to warrant and Maintaine against all persons laying Claim thereunto. Witness my hand & Seale this Eighteenth day of Jan^{ry} one thousand Six hundred Ninety & Six. Seven : 169⅚ The Signe of

Signed Sealed & Deliuered   Joshua   C   Crocket (his Seal)
  in piesents of us —
Richard Bryar   The 26th of Septemb^r 1698
Thomas Harford   Then Joshua Crocket came & Ac-
Wm Godsoe   knowledged this above Instrum^t to
                    be his free Act and Deed to M^r
                    Richd Cutt before me
                              Wm Pepperrell Js pes

A true Copie of ye origenall Deed Transcribed and Compared this. 22^d day of March : 169⅚—p Jos Hamond Regist^r

BOOK IV, FOL. 157.

To all People to whom this present Deed of Sale shall come I Richard Cutt of Kittery in y" County of York in y" Province of y" Massachusets Bay in New England Yeoman Send Greeting/ Know ye that for and in consideration of y" Sum of twenty two pounds of Currant Money of New England to me in hand Well and truly paid at and before y" Ensealing and Deliuery of these presents by Richard Rogers Jun[r] of y" Same Town County and Province afores[d] Coop[r] the receipt whereof I doe hereby Acknowledge and my Selfe therewith to be fully Satisfied and paid and from every part and parcell thereof for me y" s[d] Richd Cutt my heires Execut[rs] Admin[rs] and Assignes doe Acquit and fully discharge him the s[d] Richard Rogers his heires &[c] by these presents for ever, I the s[d] Richard Cutt haue giuen granted bargained Sold Aliened Enfeoffed conveyed and confirmed and by these presents doe for my Selfe my heires &[c] ffully freely and absolutely giue grant bargain Sell Alien Enfeoffe convey and confirm unto him y" s[d] Rich[d] Rogers his heires and Assignes a Certaine tract of Land Scituate Lying and being in y" Township of Kittery Commonly called by y" name of Crockets plaine Containing thirty Acres butted & bounded as followeth, on y" East end by y" Land of William Godsoe with a Northwest and by North line, Sixty poles, and from thence Southwest and by West Eighty poles, and from thence Southeast & by South, Sixty poles, and from thence Northeast and by east to our first Station being a great Hemlock Marked on four Sides by y" highway together with all y" profits priviledges and Appurtenances to the Said land belonging or in any wise appertaining To have and to hold the aboves[d] tract of land with all y" Appurtenances thereunto belonging with all y" Right title Interest Claim and Demand which I Richard Cutt now haue or in time past haue had or w[ch] I my heires &[c] may might Should or in any wise ought to haue in time to come of in or to y" aboue granted Premises or any part thereof to him y" s[d] Richard

Rogers his heires and Assignes for euer and to yᵉ Sole and proper use benefit and behoofe of him yᵉ sᵈ Richᵈ Rogrˢ his heires &ᶜ for evermore. And I the sᵈ Richard Cutt for me my heires Executʳˢ Adminʳˢ & Assignes doe Covenant promise and grant to and with him yᵉ sᵈ Richard Rogers his heires or Assignes that at & before yᵉ Ensealing and Deluery hereof the above Mentioned Premises and every part thereof is free & clere Acquitted and Discharged of and from all other and former Gifts grants bargains, Sales Mortgages, Dowers, titles, troubles Acts Alienations and encumbrances whatsoever/ And that it shall and may be lawfull to and for the said Richard Rogers his heires and Assignes the aforesaid Premises and every part thereof from time to time and at all times for ever hereafter to haue hold use Ocupie improve possess and enjoy as his own proper Right of Inheritance, in ffee Simple, lawfully peaceably [158] And quietly without any lawfull lett deniall hinderance Molestation or Disturbance of or by me or any pson or psons from by or under me or by my procurement, And that yᵉ Sale thereof and euery part thereof against my Selfe my heires Executʳˢ Adminʳˢ and Assignes I will for ever Saue harmless Warrant and Defend by these presents. In witness whereof I the sᵈ Richard Cutt and Joanna my wife have hereunto Set our hands & Seales. this. twenty fourth day of Decembʳ anno Domini one thousand Six hundred Ninety and Seven, Annoq Regni Regis Gulielmæ Anglia Scotia &ᶜ nono.

Signed Sealed & Deliuered   Richard Cutt (ʰⁱˢ Seal)
   in yᵉ presents of us   Joanna Cutt (ʰᵉʳ Seal)
   Robert Cutt   The 26ᵗʰ of Septembʳ 1698
   John Newmarch   then Richᵈ Cutt came and Acknowl-
   Sarah More.   edged this Instrument to be his free
                    Act and Deed. before me
                            Wᵐ Pepperrell Js pes

A true Copie of yᵉ origenall Deed of Sale Transcribed & compared this 22ᵈ day of March 169⅞

BOOK IV, FOL. 158.

Be it known unto all men by these presents that I William Hilton Inhabitant in York being Justly Indebted unto Mr Robert Elliot of Portsmouth Merchant in New England the Sum of thirty pounds Currant Money of New England, I doe hereby make over Surrend^r and deliuer unto ye s^d Robt Elliot or to his ord^r and Assignes three Cows two Yearlings and one heifer two Mares & two Colts, and alsoe my now dwelling house and land in ye township of York on the Western Side of ye Riuer Lying between Thomas Trafton & Timothy Yeales his plantation, hereby Annulling making voyd & of noe Effect all manner of former Mortgages promises or contracts of or concerning any or all y^e aboue mentioned Premises or any part thereof, Witness my hand & Seale this Eighteenth day of ffebruary in y^e year of our Lord one thousand six hundred Eighty & Eight. Annoq Regni Regis Jacobi Secundi Quarto :   Marke of
Signed Sealed & deliuered
  in presents of —   William ⌠ Hilton ($^{his}_{Seale}$)
  John Davis
  Nich^o Heskins New Castle in New England this Ninth day of March. 169$\frac{8}{9}$. William Hilton came before me and owned y^e aboue writing to be his Act & Deed
                    Nathaniel ffryer Justis peace
A true Copie of y^e aboue Mortgage or obligation Transcribed & compared this : 8 day of Aprill : 1699—
                p Jos Hamond Regist^r

Know all men by these presents that I Richard King of Kittery in the Province of Maine Shipwright for Divers good causes me thereunto Moving more Especially for and in Consideration of a valluable Sum of Money to me in hand paid by Richard Gowell of ye Town and Province afores^d, the receipt whereof and of every part and parcell thereof I Acknowledge & therewith fully Satisfied and contented and paid haue giuen granted bargained Sold Aliened made ouer and confirmed And by these presents doe for me my heires Execut^{rs} Administrat^{rs} and Assignes for euer ffreely clearly and absolutely giue grant bargain Sell Alien make ouer and confirm unto him ye s^d Richard Gowell his heires Execut^{rs} Admin^{rs} and Assignes for ever three Acres of Land be it more or less Scituate lying and being upon ye great coue below Thomas Spinneys bounded with John Slopers land on ye South Side and ye great Coue on ye west Side and a Brook of water on ye North Side and Richard Gowells former Lott on ye East Side/ To have and to hold to him ye s^d Richard Gowell his heires Execut^{rs} Admin^{rs} or Assignes the aboue giuen and granted Premisses and that the s^d Gowell Shall and may from time to time and at all times hereafter Ocupie improve and make use of ye Same without any Molestation lett deniall or hinderance from or by me ye s^d King or any other person or persons whatsoeuer Claiming any Right title or Interest thereunto from by or under me/ In witness whereof I haue hereunto Set my hand and Seal this thirtieth day of Decemb^r in ye year of our Lord Anno Domini One thousand Six hundred Eighty & Six. 1686.

Signed Sealed & deliuered
  In ye presents of
    Tests.

Gabriel his mark Tetherly

Jacob Remich.

The mark of Richard King (his Seal)

her
Mary King (her Seal)
mark

A true Copie of ye origenall Deed Transcribed & compared. this. tenth day of Aprill: 1699—

                           p Jos Hamond Regist^r

York ss/ Decr 25th 1718

Book IV, Fol. 158, 159.

Richard King psonally appeared & Acknowledged this above written Instrum^t to be his Act & Deed before me
    Jos : Hamond J : peace
Recorded as above p Jos Hamond Reg^r/

[159] Know all men by these presents that I Ann Hunscom of Kittery in the County of Yord Administrat^r to ye Estate of her Son John Hunscom Dec^d haue bargained and Sold. And by these presents doe bargain and Sell fully clearly and Absolutely unto Richard Gowell of Kittery in ye County of York afores^d a grant of twenty Acres of Land granted unto ye s^d John Hunscom bearing Date May ye Sixteenth. one thousand Six hundred Ninety and four, for and in Consideration of a valluable Sum of Money alredy to me in hand paid by ye S^d Richd Gowell before ye Sealing hereof/ To haue and to hold ye Same grant of land to the S^d Richard Gowell his heires Execut^{rs} Admin^{rs}, against all persons to Defend and acquit the s^d grant, I bind my Selfe my heires Execut^{rs} Admin^{rs} and Assignes unto ye s^d Richd Gowell his heires Execut^{rs} Admin^{rs} for ever.

In witness whereof I ye s^d Ann Hanscom have Set my hand & Seal this twenty Second day of Novemb^r in ye year one thousand Six hundred Ninety and Seven.

Signed Sealed & deliuered
  in ye presents of us
  Wm Godsoe
  Jacob : Remich
  John Tomson

Ann (her mark) Hanscom (her Seale)

A true Copie of ye origenall Deed. Transcribed and compared this 10th day of April. 1699. p Jos Hamond Regist^r

BOOK IV, FOL. 159.

These presents doe witness that I Rowland Young of York ffisherman with the free consent of my wife Joane doe in Consideration of ye Sum of Nine pounds to me in hand paid by Cap^{tn} John Davis and other considerations thereunto me Moveing; doe giue grant Sell and confirm unto Daniel Dill of the Saide town his heirs Executors Admin^{rs} for ever a Certain tract or pcell of Land containing ye full quantety of ten Acres more or less, lying and being between Bass Cove and John Chirmihills land, bounded with John Alcocks Lott on ye Northwest Side and Richard Banks his his Lot on ye Southeast Side to run twenty pole by ye Riuer Side and Soe backward till ye ten Acres be Extended According to town giant whereby ye s^d land was giuen me bearing July the 3^d 1653 — which ten Acres of land, with all ye Appurtenances and Priviledges thereto appertaining, I the s^d Rowland Young on ye former consideration of that Nine pounds paid me by Daniel Dills order from Cap^{tn} Davis doe hereby in ye behalfe of my Selfe heires and Assignes. Ratifie and confirm unto aforesaid Daniel Dill his heires and Assignes for ever, the s^d Dill paying what yearly Acknowledgm^t Shall Appear to be Due if Demanded. As witness my hand and Seal this 4th Day of Decemb^r 1666 in y^e Eighteenth year of our Soveraigne Lord y^e King Charles y^e Second.   Rowland Young ($^{his}_{Seal}$)

Signed Sealed & Deliuered   his R mark
  in y^e presents of
  Edw Rishworth   Rowland Young & Joan Young his
  John Twisden   wife doe Acknowledge this In-
  Daniel Liuingstoun   strum^t above written to be their
                                      Act & Deed. this 4th of Decemb^r
                                      1666 Before me
                                           Edw : Rishworth Jus^t pea

A true Copie of the origenall Instrum^t Transcribed and Compared this 16th May. 1696 — p Jos Hamond Regist^r

BOOK IV, FOL. 159, 160.

Witness these presents that I Iohn Daves of York have Sold to James Warren, forty Acres of Upland lying betwixt ye s^d Daues Marsh & the bridge, And ye s^d Warren is to have halfe ye breadth of ye fourscore Acres which ye town of York gaue to the Said Daves & William More & John Harker, that is to Say halfe ye breadth by the water Side, with all ye Right that ye s^d Daues has in that forty Acres as Records Shall make Appear, which land ye s^d Daues has Sold with ye consent of Mary Daves his wife And all ye Right that they have in it/ Witness our hands the. 6. of 8. Month 1662. & Sayle/   John Daves (Seale)

                              the mark
Witness to ye Sealing hereof   of Mary M̶D Daues (Seale)
   Attests   ffrancis Johnson
   Timothy Yeales   John Penwill
   Benjamin Whitney.

These may Certifie that I Iohn Daves doe Acknowledge to have Received of James Warren full Satisfaction for ye with Mentioned land/ I say Rec^d by me/ Witness my hand/ York ye 16th of Aprill 1686.   John Daves

A true Copie of ye origenall Instrum^t together wth y^r Receipt on ye back Side Transcribed & Compared this. 23^d May 1699.   p Jos Ham̃ond Regist^r

[160] Know all men by this Present Bill of Sale that I Robert Ellet formerly of Scarbrough on None Such Riuer in the Prouince of Maine Now Inhabitant in Portsmouth in New hampsh^r NewEngl and for Diuers good Causes and Considerations me thereunto mouing But more Especially for and in Consideracõn of a valluable Summ of money to me in hand Paid by John Batson of Cape Porpus Carpenter the Receipt whereof I doe hereby acknowledge and my Self to be therwth fully Satisfied Contented and Payd : Have giuen granted Bargained and Sould and By these Presents doe

BOOK IV, FOL. 160.

giue grant Bargaine Sell allieane assigne Enffeoffe allienate and Confirme unto the said John Batson his Heirs Executors Administrators and Assigns to Have And to Hold a Certain p^rcell of vpland and Medow Cittuate lying and Being at Cape Porpus in ye Prouince of Maine in New-England Containing By Esteemačon Seuenty Acrees be it more or less Adjoyning unto ye said John Batson on ye South West and By the Cape riuer on ye North West. To Have & To Hold to him the said John Batson his heirs Execut^{rs} Adm^{rs} and Assignes foreuer and ye s^d Robert Ellet Doth hereby and hereafter shall Warant and Defend the Sale hereof unto the said John Batson his heirs Execut^{rs} &c^a from by and und^r him ye said Robert Ellet or from and By or und^r his heirs Execut^{rs} or administrat^{rs} But the same Quietly to Possess and Peaceably to Enjoy wthout any Disturbence or Mollestation — Together with ye Priuiledges Profits Highwayes water wayes woods und^r woods and all other Emolluments Whatsoeuer which Land aboue mentioned did of Right Belong unto me the said Robert Ellet as Coming to me by Mariage of my wife whose Maiden Name was Margery Batson &c^a to all and euery the aboue mentioned Premised Couenanted Bargained Premises To Confirm haue to this my Bill of Sale Set to my hand and Affixed my Seale in Presence of the Witnesses this twenty Seuenth day of Iune Anno Domini one thousand Six hundred Ninty and Two.

Signed Sealed & Deliuered   his
  In Presence of us
  John Partridge   Robert *RE* Ellet (_{Seale}^{his})
  Henry Crown Sc̃r
                            mark

                      the North riuer interlined between
                       ye nineth and tenth line done by
                       consent of Robert Ellet Before me
                           Geō: Jaffrey Just of Peac
Portsmouth in New Hampsheir Septemb^r 9th 1695.

BOOK IV, FOL. 160, 161.

Robert Ellet aboue mentioned Came before me one of his Maties Justices of Peace for this Prouince and acknowledged ye aboue Deed of Sale to Be his free act and Deed
        Geō : Jaffry Just of Peace
A true Coppie of the origenall Deed of Sale Transcribed and Compared this 10th day of July 1699
       p Jos Hamond Regist^r

[161] Articles of agreement made between ffrancis Backhouse on the one Party and John Hill on the other Party both of ye town of Sacoe in the Province of Mayne, referring to ye building of a Saw Mill in s^d Fran : Backhouse his Crick as followeth —

1 : The s^d ffrancis Backhouse doth hereby giue and grant free liberty to his kinsman John Hill afores^d to Joyn with him in Equall Partnership, & Charges to be Eqully disbursed between them for the building of a good Sufficient Saw Mill in Said Backhouse his Crick which runeth down by his house.

2ly Its further agreed that ye s^d Backhouse & Hill having built & compleated ye s^d Saw Mill with all Nessessaries & Implem^ts appetaining to her upon an Equall proportionable Charge, or halfe Moety, that it Mutually was agreed & Concluded that upon those considerations the s^d ffrancis Backhouse doth by these presents, giue grant & confirm unto John Hill heires & Assignes for ever, all ye priviledges of timber with all ye propriety for ye s^d Saw Mill, with all Nessessary conveniencies belonging thereunto, to him & his heires for ever — provided always & it is hereby Intended & concluded that s^d John Hill shall after he hath had a convenient Oppertunity of being Instructed by a workman how to Kilter ye saws and keep them in Due order, he s^d Hill is hereby Ingaged to whet & keep them in good order he is to doe that work at his proper Charge from which care and

BOOK IV, FOL. 161.

trouble s^d ffran: Backhouse shall Totally be ffreed/ And further it is agreed between ye psons afores^d, that if either of them shall find cause to dispose of their Interests of s^d Mill & Accomodations then each pty Selling shall in ye first place Preferr to each other by tendering ye Sale thereof before any other pson whatsoeuer, and provided he will giue for it as much any other will giue he shall have ye first refusall of ye Premises.

In witness whereunto we have hereunto Set our hands. this 28th day of Iune. 1686
ffrancis Backhouse
John Hill.

ffrancis Backhouse & John Hill came both before me this 28th day of June 1686—and did own and Acknowledge these Articles of Agreement aboue written to be their ffree Act and Deed at this present Date

June ye 28th 1686.   Edw: Rishworth Jus: Pea:

A true Copie of ye origenall Agreem^t transcribed & compared this. 25th day of July. 1699. p Jos Hamond Regist^r

Memorandum. That I Ambrose Berry, of Boston, Marrin^r doe by these presents for me my heires Execut^rs & Admin^rs giue liberty unto John Hill of Sacoe and his Assignes to Set up, Maintaine and uphold, two Damms for ye Stoppage of water for ye use of a Mill or Mills belonging to ye s^d John Hill or his Assignes, upon my land now adjoyning to Bulleys Creek in Sacoe afores^d for ever/ In witness w^r of I have hereunto Set my hand this Eighteenth day of Septemb^r 1686   Ambrose Berry

Signed in the presents of
  Pendleton ffletcher
  Edward Sergeant
  Samuel Webber

Book IV, Fol. 161.

A true Copie of the origenall, transcribed and compared this 25th day of July : 1699   p Jos Hamond Registr

All men shall know by these presents that I Robert Eliot Esqr of the great Island in ye town of New Castle in ye Province of New Hampshier in New England Merchant am holden and firmly bounden unto Nathaniel ffryer Esqr of ye great Island in ye town aforesd in ye Sum of twelue hundred pounds of good and Lawful money of New England to be paid to the sd Nathaniel ffryer his certain Atturney heirs or Executrs, to ye which paiment well and truly to be made I the sd Robert Eliot bind my Selfe my heires Executrs and Administratrs firmly by these prests Sealed with my Seal in ye town of New Castle aforesd this twenty fourth day of August in ye tenth year of the Reign of our Soveraign William the third King of great Brittain &c and in ye year of our Lord. 1698.

The condition of this obligation is Such that whereas the aboue bounden Robert hath paid for the aforesd Nathaniel ffryer the Sum of Six hundred & twenty pounds in Currant money of New England and ye sd Nathaniel ffryer hath made ouer and Mortgaged to ye sd Robert Eliot his houses Lands & all his Estate as well Moveables as other for the Security of ye Same that ye sd Sum of Six hundred and twenty pounds Shall be paid by the sd Nathaniel ffryer or his heirs to ye sd Robert Eliot or his heirs at or before ye twenty fourth day of August in the year of our Lord Seuenteen hundred and one as by the Indenture bearing date with these presents may more fully Appear/ Now if ye sd Robert Eliot Should depart this life before ye sd Nathaniel ffryer, the heirs or Executrs of ye sd Robert Eliot may let ye sd Sum Still remain upon ye same Security after ye Expiration of ye said time during ye Naturall life of ye Said Nathaniel ffryer without any Interest or consideration or otherwise to receive

BOOK IV, FOL. 161, 162.

Annually but the Interest of Six pounds for one hundred pounds proportionably And upon yᵉ payment of yᵉ sᵈ Sum the sᵈ Robᵗ Eliot his heires or Assigns Shall deliuer up to yᵉ sᵈ Nathaniel [162] ffryer the said Indenture with a discharge for the Same, Then this Obligation to be voyd and of none Effect or else to Stand in full force power and vertue.

Signed Sealed and delivered   Robᵗ Elliot (his Seal)
   in yᵉ presents of us —   30ᵗʰ Apr : 1700/
   (the word Annually, inter-   Sarah Eastwick appearing
   lined before Sealing —   before me Acknowledged
   Sarah Eastwick   that She Signed her name
   Phesant Eastwick   to the above Instrumᵗ as a
     witness And that Phesant
     Eastwick did then Sign it
     as a Witness, before
     Theo Atkinson I : Pea :

A true Copie of yᵉ origenall Transcribed and Compared,
Aprˡˡ 30ᵗʰ 1700   p Jos Hamond Registʳ

The End of this Book —

INDEX.

INDEX OF

Date.	Grantor.	Grantee.	Instrument.
1686, Mar. 25	ABBETT, Thomas and James Emery, jr.	James Emery, sr.	Deposition
1686, Mar. 25	ABBETT, Thomas and Benoni Hodgden	James Emery, sr.	Deposition
1692, Mar. 26	ADAMS, Charles	John Morrell	Deed
1696, Mar. 30	ADAMS, Temperance	John Morrell	Deed
1696, Nov. 13	ADAMS, Charles, estate of, by Temperance Adams, administratrix	John Morrell	Release
169$\frac{2}{3}$, Feb. 25	ALLIN, Walter	Thomas Holmes's estate	Release
1689, June 11	AMERIDETH, Joan	Roger Dearing Joseph Couch	Deed
168$\frac{8}{9}$, Mar. 1	AUSTINE, Mary and Matthew Austine Sarah Austine Jonathan Sayword	One another	Agreement
169$\frac{5}{6}$, Feb. 6	AUSTINE, Matthew et ux.	Daniel Black	Deed
169$\frac{8}{9}$, Jan. 5	AUSTINE, Matthew et ux.	Wm. Pepperrell	Mortgage
	AUSTINE, Matthew, see Mary Austine		

GRANTORS.

Folio.	Description.
55	Concerning Emery's possession of part of the "Fowling Marsh," in *Berwick*, and counter claim by John Roberts, jr.
55	As to location of fence between Emery's and John Roberts's land in *Berwick*.
92	Land in *Kittery* near Sturgeon creek, received as marriage portion of his wife, Temperance, from Philip Benmore and by him bought of James Emery.
92	Quitclaim of all her rights to property described above.
93	General discharge.
110	General discharge, and receipt for marriage portion of his wife Mary.
145	6 acres between Diggory Jeofery and Clement Dearing at the Stepping Stones; also 44 acres adjoining John Bray; all in *Kittery*. This purports also to be John Ameredith's deed, but he does not sign it.
66	Ratifying the provisions of an imperfect will of Matthew Austine, sen., devising land and bequeathing personal estate in *York*.
114	3 acres more or less, between Meeting-house creek, a small creek and the highway (except half an acre of John Penwill's) in *York*.
146	All his lands, formerly his father's, Matthew Austine, sen.'s, west of the new mill creek, adjoining the bridge in *York*.

Index of Grantors.

Date.	Grantor.	Grantee.	Instrument.
	AUSTINE, Sarah, see Mary Austine		
1696, Oct. 19	AVANT, Francis	Richard Cutt	Deed
1686, June 28	BACKHOUSE, Francis and John Hill	One another	Contract
	BACKHOUSE, Francis, see Jonathan Hammond		
169$\frac{6}{7}$, Feb. 15	BANFIELD, Grace et ux	Joseph Hill	Deed
169$\frac{5}{6}$, Feb. 18	BANKS, Joseph	Peter Nowell	Deed
1669, July 31	BAREFOOTE, Walter	George Pearson	Assignment
168$\frac{5}{6}$, Jan. 1	BARNARD, Joseph	Benj. Barnard	Deed
167$\frac{8}{9}$, Feb. 18	BASTON, Thomas	Thomas Wells	Deed
167$\frac{3}{4}$, Feb. 8	BATSON, Stephen	John Batson	Deed
1688, Apr. 6	BEALE, Arthur	William Craffts	Deed
	BEALE, Arthur, see William Hilton		
1679, Aug. 24	BEDFORD, Nathan	Margaret Jocelyn	Prom.
1683, Apr. 7	BEDFORD, Nathan, estate of	Robert Elliett	Commis'r's report
1686, Sept. 18	BERRY, Ambrose	John Hill	Deed
1684, Sept. 18	BERW'CK, parish of	Eliakim Hutchinson	Bond
	BICKHAM, Richard, see Robert Vickers		

Index of Grantors.

Folio.	Description.
156	10 acres called Crocket's plain; also assigning right to conveyance of 20 acres town grant to Joshua Crocket; all in *Kittery*.
161	Of co-partnership, to build and conduct a saw-mill on Backhouse's creek in *Saco*.
91	Quitclaim of dower in land in *Kittery*, sold to Hill by Samuel Miller et ux. *q. v.*
107	10 acres northeast of the river, between it and the highway, and lands of Daniel Dill and Henry Lamprill, in *York*.
30	Of a bond of Francis Champernowne's to pay £40.
65	50 acres in *Berwick* bought of Benoni Hodgsden, between the river and the commons and lands of Tozier and Price.
4	100 acres upland and 10 acres meadow at Merryland in *Wells*, bought of Francis Littlefield and Peter Cloyce.
1	18 acres upland and 25 acres marsh, between the main river, Little river, Middle creek, and the creek from Beaver pond, in *Cape Porpoise*.
29	21 acres at Brave-boat harbor, near the bridge, south of William Moore's land, as per town grant of and in *York*.
69	To pay £21 : 10.
67	Allowing claim of £25 : 3 : 8¼.
161	License to build and maintain two mill dams upon grantor's land, across Bulley's creek in *Saco*.
23	To maintain Rev. John Emerson, or some other settled minister, or in default thereof to reconvey 10 acres land donated by Hutchinson.

INDEX OF GRANTORS.

Date.	Grantor.	Grantee.	Instrument.
1683, Jan. 10	BLANY, Elizabeth	Richard Wharton	Deed
1682, Nov. 7	BODG, Henry	Joseph Curtis	Deed
1674, July 9	BOLLES, Joseph et ux.	John Batson	Deed
1683, Dec. 12	BONIGHTON, John	Benj. Blackeman	Deed
1668, Oct. 13	BRACKETT, Thomas	George Munjoy	Deed
1670, July 21	BRACKETT, Mary	George Munjoy	Deed
1671, June 2	BRACKETT, Thomas	Elizabeth Harvy	Bond
	BRAGDON, Samuel, see Thomas Donell		
1698, July 18	BRAWN, John et ux.	Wm. Pepperrell	Deed
1685, Aug. 15	BRAY, Richard	John Attwell	Deed
	BRIDGHAM, Elizabeth et ux., see Elizabeth Pouning		
1693, Oct. 31	BRONSDON, [Brimsdon], Robert	John Hill	Assignment
1693, Oct. 31	BRONSDON, [Brimsdon], Robert	John Hill	Assignment
1693, Oct. 31	BRONSDON, [Brimsdon], Robert	John Hill	Assignment
1698, Aug. 20	BRONSDON, Robert, by John Watson, attorney	Robert Elliot	Assignment
1698, Aug. 24	BRONSDON, Robert, by John Watson, attorney	Nathaniel Fryer	Release

INDEX OF GRANTORS. 7

Folio.	Description.
17	Quitclaim to the Way and Purchase patent in *Pejepscot*.
25	5 acres bounded north by Eastern creek, east by a highway, and Wilson's and Hammon's land; also 5 acres at the Pudding-hole, all in *Kittery*.
3	50 acres in *Cape Porpoise* granted by Thomas Gorges to Morgan Howell.
22	Tract two miles wide east of Saco river, part of Lewis and Bonighton's patent, south of James Gibbons's division, in *Saco*.
34	50 acres in *Falmouth* adjoining Ware creek.
35	Quitclaim to the above.
12	For support and maintenance.
130	Half an acre bounded by the sea and land of grantee in *Kittery*.
44	60 acres adjoining Thomas Maynes, on West side of Ryall's river [in *North Yarmouth*.]
99	Of Richard Selly's mortgage of lands in *Saco* to Henry Kemble to secure £14.
99, 100	Of Richard Selly's bond to Brimsdon to pay £30:15:2.
101	Of Richard Selly's mortgage of all his estate to Brimsdon, to secure the above bond.
140	Of Nathaniel Fryer's mortgage of Champernowne's island and chattels in *Kittery* to Bronsdon to secure £485.
141	General discharge.

Index of Grantors.

Date.	Grantor.	Grantee.	Instrument.
1685, Nov. 11	BROUGHTON, John	John Hull's estate	Deed
1639, Mar. 18	BURDETT, George	Ann Messant	Mortgage
1685, July 25	BURRAGE, William	John Mills	Deposition
1686, May 8	BURRAGE, William et ux.	Sylvanus Davis	Deed
1684, June 9	CARTER, Richard	John Mayne	Deposition
	CARTER, Richard, see Henry Donell		
1678, June 18	CHADBORNE, Humphrey and William Playstead	Abraham Conley's estate.	Deposition
1669, July 30	CHAMPERNOWNE, Francis	Walter Barefoote	Bond
1684, May 19	CHAMPERNOWNE, Francis	Mary Champernowne	Deed
1684, July 8	CHAMPERNOWNE, Francis	Mary Champernowne Elizabeth Cutts	Deed
1684, July 8	CHAMPERNOWNE, Francis	Nat'l Raynes Francis Raynes	Deed
1685, Apr. 15	CHAMPERNOWNE, Francis	William Moore	Deed
1686, Mar. 15	CHAMPERNOWNE, Francis	Brian Pendleton John Fabes	Deed
[1684, Jun.28]	CHAMPERNOWNE, Francis and Francis Raynes	Each other	Agreement
1684, Mar. 19	COFFIN, Peter	John Shapleigh	Deposition
1695, Oct. 14	COMAN, Richard	Peter Nowell	Deed
167$\frac{3}{8}$, Mar. 14	CONLEY, Abraham	Peter Wittum	Deed

INDEX OF GRANTORS.

Folio.	Description.
53	Quitclaim to the eighth part of the two saw mills, &c., in *Berwick*, mortgaged Book III. 47.
20	Farm and stock [in *York*] to secure £112.
43	As to Mills's possession of marsh [in *Scarborough*] and warning trespassers.
62	6½ acres marsh at Nonesuch marshes in *Scarborough*.
11	As to Mayne's possession of marsh in Sysquissett creek [in *North Yarmouth*].
67	As to the bounds of Conley's lands at Sturgeon creek in *Kittery*.
30	To pay £40.
71	Half of Champernowne's island in *Kittery*.
12	The other half of Champernowne's island in *Kittery* to Mary for life, remainder of said half to Elizabeth, reserving life estate to himself.
21	Quitclaim to farm [at Braveboat harbor in *Kittery*], conveyed grantees by Capt. Francis Raynes.
36	Quitclaim to two acres marsh bought by Moore of Ann Godfrey, northeast of Braveboat harbor [in *York*].
94	Quitclaim to 100 acres at Sturgeon creek in *Kittery*, sold grantees by Francis Morgan et ux.
12	Vesting in Raynes and his heirs, disputed land at Braveboat harbor [in *Kittery*].
41	That Nicholas Shapleigh stated John Shapleigh was his brother's son whom he had brought from his mother in England, and that John should be his heir.
108	10 acres northeast of York river above Bass cove, adjoining Freethee and Nowell in *York*.
3	3½ acres 16 poles land between Conley's marsh and the highway in *Kittery*.

Index of Grantors.

Date.	Grantor.	Grantee.	Instrument.
1674, May 13	Conley, Abraham and John Whitte	[Wm. Leighton]	Deposition
1669, June 25	Coole, Nicholas	Thomas Wells	Deed
168⅔, Mar. 23	Cossones, John	John Attwell	Deposition
1684, May 15	Cossons, John	John Mayne	Deposition
1683, June 13	Crockett, Elihu	Aaron Ferris	Deed
1683, Aug. 4	Crockett, Ephraim	Aaron Ferris	Acknowledgment
169⅔, Jan. 2	Crocket, Joseph et ux.	Wm. Pepperrell	Deed
169⅘, Jan. 18	Crocket, Joshua	Richard Cutt	Deed
1688, May 20	Crocket, Thomas, estate of, by Ann Jefory, administratrix	Ephraim Crocket	Deed
1695, July —	Crocket, Thomas, estate of, by Ann Jeofrey, administratrix	Ephraim Crocket's estate	Deed
1683, Apr. 2	Cross, Joseph et ux.	Fr. Littlefield, sr.	Deed
1684, May 29	Cross, Joseph et ux.	Samuel Austine	Deed
1684, Feb. 11	Curtis, Benjamin	William Young	Deed
168¾, Mar. 18	Curtis, Thomas	Henry Lamprill	Deed
1683, May 25 1683, June 20 1683, Nov. 13	Cutt, John, estate of, by Reuben Hull, agent of John Cutt, executor	Edw. Rishworth	Receipts(3)

Index of Grantors.

Folio.	Description.
56	As to Renald Jenkins's purchase and occupation of six acres in *Kittery* [afterwards by mesne conveyances Leighton's].
12	Upland bought of Francis Littlefield, sen., and interest in grant of marsh in *Wells*, reserving family burying ground.
37	As to Atwell's purchase of Richard Bray of 60 acres in Casco Bay [*North Yarmouth*].
11	As to Mayne's possession of marsh on Sysquissett creek [in *North Yarmouth*].
1	20 acres between Spruce creek and another creek, adjoining Joseph Crockett's, reserving a highway, in *Kittery*.
1	Quitclaim to above property.
150	45 acres upland and meadow adjoining Jeofferys, Dearing, the commons, as by town grants, in *Kittery*.
157	20 acres at Crocket's plain in *Kittery*, between grantee's and Ephraim Crocket's land.
154	All lands lying on Crocket's neck, bounded in part by Spruce creek in *Kittery*.
155	80 acres at the head of Braveboat harbor in *Kittery* near the bridge.
88	Five parcels aggregating 176½ acres in *Wells*, most bordering Ogunquit river.
10	One half of Drake's island; also one half of his father Cross's marsh north of the island in *Wells*.
31	20 acres and house on southwest side of northwest branch of York river above the bridge, in *York*.
7	10 acres fronting York river adjoining Bass cove and the road to Scotland in *York*.
30	Upon account.

Date.	Grantor.	Grantee.	Instrument.
1686, July 22	CUTT, Richard	William Scrivine	Deed
1686, July 22	CUTT, Richard	Mary Cutt	Deed
1694, June 28	CUTT, Richard	Robert Cutt	Deed
1695, June 28	CUTT, Richard	John Mugridg	Deed
1697, Dec. 24	CUTT, Richard et ux.	Richard Rogers, jun.	Deed
1695, June 15	CUTT, Samuel	Elihu Gunnison	Deed
1691, May 12	CUTT, Ursula	[John] Shapleigh	Letter
	DARUMKINE, see Warumbee		
1662, Oct. 6	DAVES, John et ux.	James Warren	Deed
1684, Dec. 8	DAVESS, John	James Freathy	Deed
1684, July 7	DAVIE, Humphrey by William Goodhew, sen. and John Wilde, agents	Roger Kelly James Blagdon	Receipts(2)
1699, Mar. 31	DAVIS, John	James Plaisted	Deed
1696, June 16	DENMARKE, James et ux.	Joseph Storer	Deed
1666, Jan. 9	DIXON, James	John Brawn	Conditional deed
168⅔, Mar. 24	DONELL, Henry and Richard Carter	John Attwell	Deposition
168⅝, Jan. 6	DONELL, Thomas and Samuel Bragdon	Each other	Reference and award
169⅘, Jan. 5	DORMAN, Timothy	Ephraim Dorman, sen.	Deed

Index of Grantors.

13

Folio.	Description.
68	20 acres at Spruce creek, near the bridge in *Kittery*.
68	20 acres at Broad cove in Spruce creek in *Kittery*.
132	Half of the land on which he dwelt in *Kittery*.
112	Land between Spruce creek, Broad cove, mill creek and Scriven's land in *Kittery*.
157	30 acres called Crocket's plain in *Kittery*.
106	Three parcels aggregating 154 acres, at Goose cove in Spruce creek in *Kittery*.
111	Agreeing to accept orders for £7:10, on account of Nathaniel Keen.
159	40 acres between grantor's marsh and the bridge in *York*.
30	12½ acres at Bass cove on the north east of the path to the marshes adjoining William Dixon in *York*.
13	For an anchor and cable.
154	Land at new mill creek between Thomas Moulton and Edward Rishworth [in *York*].
95	Marsh on Webhannet river adjoining grantee's in *Wells*.
47	Of all interests under his father William Dixon's will, subject to a gift to Dorothy Moore [in *York*.]
37	As to Atwell's purchase of Richard Bray of 60 acres in Casco Bay [*North Yarmouth*].
53	Determining dividing line between their plantations [in *York*].
106	500 acres in *Coxhall* on Mousam river, part of the Symonds purchase.

Index of Grantors.

Date.	Grantor.	Grantee.	Instrument.
1684, July 16	Downs, Richard, sen.	Fr. Wainwright	Mortgage
1664, Aug. 24	Drake, Thomas	Richard Bray	Deed
1685, —— 15	Dwight, Timothy	[George] Pearson	Letter
1685, Aug. 24	Dwight, Timothy	George Pearson	Power of attorney
1692, June 27	Ellet, Robert	John Batson	Deed
169⅔, Feb. 22	Elleot, Robert	John Pickerin, jr.	Deed
1689, July 13	Elliot Robert	Allen Fuz	Deed
1695, June 11	Elliot, Robert	Allen Fuz	Deed
1698, Aug. 24	Elliot, Robert	Nathaniel Fryer	Bond
1683, Jan. 10	Ellkine, Jane et ux.	Richard Wharton	Deed
	Emery, Daniel et ux., see Alex. Forgisson et ux.		
1687, Dec. 19	Emery, James	Richard Davis	Deed
169⅔, Jan. 25	Emery, James, sen., et ux.	Philip Hubbord	Deed
169⅔, Mar. 1	Emery, James, sen.	James Emery, jr. Daniel Emery Job Emery	Deed
	Emery, James, jun., see Thomas Abbett		

INDEX OF GRANTORS. 15

Folio.	Description.
13	Tenement and outhouses, flakes and room, stage, shallop and appurtenances at Hog island, *Isles of Shoals.*
32	Plantation between Goodman Carter's and John Mayne's [in *North Yarmouth*].
50	About negotiations for purchase of land formerly Morgan Howell's at *Cape Porpoise.*
50	To collect debts, especially of Samuel Snow at *Cape Porpoise.*
160	70 acres at *Cape Porpoise* adjoining grantee's, which was portion of grantor's wife, Margery.
121	Three parcels at Black point, *Scarborough*, on Nonesuch river.
103	30 acres at Newichewannock in *Berwick*, conveyed to grantor by Humphrey Spencer et ux. *q. v.*
149	50 acres near Wilcock's pond; also two-fifths in common of the "further marsh," all in *Berwick*, conveyed to grantor by Humphrey Spencer et ux. *q. v.*
161	Conditioned to extend the time for the payment of a mortgage by Fryer, in case of obligor's prior death. See *ante* fol. 142.
17	Quitclaim to the Way and Purchase patent in *Pejepscot.*
88	10 acres out of a town grant of 1683, in *Kittery.*
96	40 acres on the main river in *Berwick*, between Dan'l Goodwin, jun., and John Plaisted, or Birchen point, reserving four rods square for a burying ground; also all right in the "Fowling marsh."
105	60 acres in *Kittery* [*Berwick*] between Rocky hill, Stony brook, and lands of Gooden, Nock and Plaisted, equally to each, but if Job default in payment, in halves to James and Daniel, reserving for seven years right to demand estate for life to grantor.

INDEX OF GRANTORS.

Date.	Grantor.	Grantee.	Instrument.
169¾, Feb. 8	ESTIS, Richard et ux.	Nicholas Morrell	Deed
1671, Mar. 25	EVERITT, William	Wm. Leighton's assigns	Acknowledgment
1674, Nov. 23	EVERITT, William, estate of by Martha Lawd, administratrix	Wm. Leighton's assigns	Acknowledgment
1684, May 26	FLETCHER, Pendleton	Edward Sargeant	Deed
169⅚, Feb. 6	FORGISSON, Alexander et ux. and Daniel Emery et ux. Elizabeth Gowen *alias* Smith	Jabez Jenkins	Deed
	FORGISSON, Mary, see William Furbush		
1683, Dec. 4	FREATHY, William et ux.	Samuel Freathy John Freathy	Deed
1688, Oct. 26	FRYER, Nathaniel	Robert Bronsdon	Mortgage
169¾, Feb. 28	FRYER, Nathaniel	Joshua Fryer	Assignment
[1698]Aug.23	FRYER, Nathaniel	Robert Elliot	Deed
1681, Jan. 18	FURBUSH, William and Thomas Rodes	Joseph Rayne	Prom. note
1680, Apr. 12	FURBUSH, William and Mary Forgisson	Each other	Reference and award
1695, June 11	FUZ, Allen	Humphrey Spencer	Deed
1664, Oct. 20	GATTINSBY, John et ux.	Thomas Etherington	Deed
1684, July 17	GENDALL, Walter	Bartho. Gidney	Deed

INDEX OF GRANTORS.   17

Folio.	Description.
123	40 acres on Piscataqua river in *Kittery*, adjoining Alex. Dennet, as by deed from William Racklift.
5	Quitclaiming land in *Kittery* conveyed by Isaac Nash et ux. [Book I. i. 75].
5	Quitclaiming the above property.
45	Land at Winter Harbor, *Saco*, formerly Simon Booth's.
97	11 acres adjoining the main river and Sturgeon creek; also 49 acres on Sturgeon creek near Bear cove in *Kittery*.
5	Parts of his farm [in *York*] in severalty, part in common to be divided, reserving life estate to themselves.
139	Champernowne's island in *Kittery*, except 80 acres conveyed to John Hincks.
82	Of Henry Sayword's mortgage of 370 acres on southwest side of York river in *York*.
142	All his lands [half of *Cape Elizabeth*, see Book III. 69] except small parcels conveyed. See Elliot's bond to reconvey, *post* fol. 161.
6	Joint and several to pay £16:1:7.
35	Fixing division line between their home lots [in *Kittery*].
103	30 acres at Newichewannock in *Berwick*, conveyed by grantee to Robert Elliot and by him to grantor, *q. v.*
85	12 acres in Unity parish [*Kittery*] conveyed grantor by Thomas Spencer.
76	Quitclaim to lands [in *North Yarmouth* conveyed grantor by grantee, Book III. 96].

Index of Grantors.

Date.	Grantor.	Grantee.	Instrument.
1683, Dec. 12	GIBBONS, James et ux.	Benj. Blackeman	Deed
1687, May 25	GIBBONS, James	Richard Rogers	Deed
1684, Aug. 6	GIBBS, Robert, estate of, by Elizabeth Corwine, administratrix, by Jona. Corwine, agent	Nicholas Moorey	Power of attorney
1684, Jan. 24	GIBBS, Robert, estate of, by Nicholas Moorey, attorney	Joseph Storer	Receipt
1684, Jan. 24	GIBBS, Robert, estate of, by Nicholas Moorey, attorney	Joseph Storer	Release
1681, July 12	GIDNEY, Bartholomew	Walter Gendall	Deed
1685, May 19	GIFFARD, John	John Sargeant	Deed
1686, Apr. 27	GILLMAN, Edward and Stephen Paul et ux.	Alexander Dennet	Deed
1683, June 23	GINKENS [Jenkins], Renald	Wm. Leighton's assigns	Deposition
1684, Mar. 9	GLANFEILD, Peter et ux.	Christopher Addams	Deed
169⅔, Feb. 10	Gooch, Benjamin	Daniel Black	Deed
1698, June 9	GOOCH, James et ux.	John Wheelwright	Deed
1683, Dec. 3	GOODHUE, William, sen.	Jos. Hammond	Power of attorney
1696, June 7	GOODRIDGE, Isaac	Margaret Adams	Mortgage

Folio.	Description.
22	Tract 3½ miles along Saco river by 2 miles back, being the second division to grantors in Lewis and Bonighton's patent in *Saco*.
155	200 acres along the sea shore next Goosefair river in *Saco*.
49	General power, with substitution.
49	In full of all accounts.
49	General discharge.
75	The tract in *North Yarmouth* bought by Thomas Stephens of the Indians.
42	60 acres in two parcels and 6 acres meadow at Winter Harbor in *Saco*.
143	20 acres in *Kittery*, adjoining grantee's, Ayer's and Hill's lands.
56	As to his purchase, occupation and sale of land in *Kittery*, afterward by mesne conveyances William Leighton's.
31	26 acres, more or less, in two parcels, in *Kittery*, bought of William Palmer and Samuel Knight.
115	10 acres between lands of Donnell, W[e]are and Dummer at *York*.
125	Land adjoining the river; land adjoining Drake's island; also 12 acres marsh, all in *Wells*, formerly his father James Gooch's.
3	To take possession of and sell the land in *Kittery* mortgaged by William Oliver. See Book II. 149.
147	Land in *Kittery* formerly William King's bought of Samuel King.

Index of Grantors.

Date.	Grantor.	Grantee.	Instrument.
1683, July 14	GODDINE [Goodwin], Daniel, sen.	Thos. Goddin James Godine	Deed
1686, Mar. 25	GOODINE [Goodwin], Daniel, jun.	James Emery, sr.	Deposition
1643, July 18	GORGES, Sir Ferdinando, by Thomas Gorges, deputy governor	Town of Gorgeana	Deed
169$\frac{8}{9}$, Feb. 27	GOWEN, Nicholas and John Gowen *alias* Smith	Each other	Partition
169$\frac{5}{6}$, Jan. 13	GREEN, John, estate of, by Barnabas Wixon, administrator	Stephen Tobey	Deed
1683, June 11	GUNNISON, Elihu	John Pickerin	Mortgage
1683, June 11	GUNNISON, Elihu	John Pickerin	Mortgage
1696, Nov. 16	GUNNISON, Elihu	John Engorsel [Ingersoll]	Deed
	HAMMOND. Jonathan, see Wm. Hammond et ux.		
1686, May 25	HAMMOND, Jonathan and Francis Backehouse John Miller	John Batson's estate	Certificate
1667, Feb. 3	HAMMOND, Wm. et ux. and Jonathan Hammond	James Gooch	Deed
1695, Dec. 27	HARRIS, John, sen. et ux.	James Smith	Deed
1667, May 8	HARVY, Elizabeth	Thomas Brackett	Deed
1680, July 8 1683, Sept. 5	HARVY, Elizabeth	Thaddeus Clarke	Assignment
1685, Aug. 1	HARWOOD, Henry et ux.	Bozoun Allen	Mortgage

INDEX OF GRANTORS.

Folio.	Description.
21	30 acres in *Berwick* bought of James Grant, with reservations.
56	As to controversy between Emery and John Roberts, jun., over marsh in *Berwick*.
46	Neck of land at the harbor's mouth, except Rev. Mr. Burdett's 20 acres; marsh at Braveboat harbor; all marsh and islands south of Gorgeana river; reserving the timber and right to set the fishermen by the shore.
104	Of land in *Berwick* above the county road, near Rocky hill adjoining the brook from Broughton's swamp.
83	15 acres near Piscataqua river, in *Kittery*, at the cove above Frank's fort.
6	House and land at Spruce creek, *Kittery*, and 4 acres more bought of William Adams.
107	Re-record of the above, made when the indorsed discharge was left for record.
97	20 acres adjoining Richard Endle at Spruce creek in *Kittery*.
61	That the creditors of said estate had been notified to bring in claims.
128	Land and marsh in *Wells* conveyed by Robert Nanny, and by him bought of Mr. Cole.
116	400 acres at *Coxhall* bought by grantor and others of Harlakenden Symonds.
34	50 acres at Ware creek [in *Falmouth*], as part of his wife Mary's dowry.
12	Of Thomas Brackett's bond, *q. v.*
77	Land in *Falmouth*, exchanged with Rev. George Burroughs, and by him bought of John Skilling.

Index of Grantors.

Date.	Grantor.	Grantee.	Instrument.
	HAYNES, Joyce, see Thomas Haynes		
1678, Aug. 2	HAYNES, Thomas et ux.	Edward Cricke	Deed
1684, July 21	HAYNES, Thomas and Joyce Haynes Sampson Penley	[Richard Wharton]	Deposition
1696, Oct. 30	HICKS, Dennis	Mary Ball	Deed
169$\frac{4}{5}$, Mar. 6	HILL, John	Joseph Hill	Assignment
	HILL, John, see Francis Backehouse		
1696, Oct. 20	HILL, Joseph	Christo. Banfield	Bond
1696, Oct. 20	HILL, Joseph	Christo. Banfield	Bond
1682, May 18	HILTON, William, sen.	Timothy Yeales	Deed
1688, Feb. 18	HILTON, William	Robert Elliot	Deed
1698, Jan. 16	HILTON, William, sen. and Arthur Beale	Daniel Black	Deed
	HODGDEN, Benoni, see Thomas Abbett		
169$\frac{4}{5}$, Feb. 7	HODSDEN, Israel et ux.	Daniel Emery	Deed
169$\frac{4}{5}$, Feb. 17	HODSDEN, Israel et ux.	Daniel Emery	Deed
1692, Dec. 18	HONEWELL, John	John Stainford	Deed
1685, Dec. 30	HOOKE, Francis	Henry Dearing	Mortgage

INDEX OF GRANTORS. 23

Folio.	Description.
19	200 acres upland and 5 acres marsh called Barberry marsh at Maquoit [in *Casco Bay*].
19	That Francis Smale bought Sebascodegan island of the Indians for Major Nicholas Shapleigh.
122	Quitclaim of his interest in common of 36 acres between Crocket's creek and Ashen Swamp brook, in *Kittery*.
102	Of the bonds and mortgages by Richard Zelly [Selly] assigned to assignor by Robert Brimsdon [Bronsdon], *q. v.*
92	Conditioned to pay £8:15, portion to Mary Miller, stepdaughter of obligee.
92	Conditioned to pay £8:15, portion to Martha Miller, stepdaughter of obligee.
43	One-half in common of Ingleby lot on west side of York river containing 100 acres: also half of Ingleby's meadow containing 3 acres, all in *York*.
158	Quitclaiming house and land on west side York river between Yeales and Trafton; also farm stock, in *York*.
148	3 acres of marsh near the partings of York river, in *York*.
98	12 acres bounded by Etherington, Gowen, Harris and Hodsden; also 50 acres near the Third hill, all in *Kittery*.
103	Re-record of the above.
115	Honewell's neck at Winter Harbor in *Saco*.
133	House and land on Piscataqua river, adjoining land formerly Nicholas Shapleigh's, and of him bought, in *Kittery*, also chattels.

Index of Grantors.

Date.	Grantor.	Grantee.	Instrument.
1685 Feb. 9	HOOKE, Francis	Mary Hooke	Bill of sale
1684, Nov. 12	HOOLE, John et ux.	Joseph Curtis	Deed
1681, July 18	HOWELL, John	John Mills	Deposition
1681, June 20	HOWELL, Morgan, estate of, by Mary Booles, administratrix	Samuel Snow	Deed
1685, April 3	HOWLEMAN, John	John Attwell	Deposition
	HUNNEWELL, see Honewell		
1697, Nov. 22	HUNSCOM, John, estate of, by Ann Hanscom, administratrix	Richard Gowell	Deed
1683, July 23	HUNSCUM, Thomas	Wm. Leighton	Deposition
169$\frac{6}{7}$, Mar. 16	HUNSCUM, Thomas	Samuel Spinney	Deed
1685, June 24	INGERSALL, George	Robert Corben's heirs	Deposition
168$\frac{3}{4}$, Mar. 13	INGERSOLL, George et ux.	Geo. Ingersoll, jr. John Ingersoll John Phillips Sylvanus Davis John Endicott James Inglish	Deed
1683, Aug. 4	JEFFERY, Ann	Aaron Ferris	Acknowledgment
1684, Apr. 28	JEFFRAY, George	John Macgowen	Power of attorney
	JENKINS, see Ginkens		
	JENKINS, Jabez, see Stephen Jenkins		
1678, Feb. 10	JENKINS, Renold	Jabez Jenkins	Deed

Folio.	Description.
53	Of negroes, Thomas and Hannah.
38	135 acres near Spruce creek in *Kittery*, part bought of Thomas Withers, and part by town grant.
43	As to Mills's occupancy of marsh by the river and path to Nonesuch [in *Scarborough*].
48	50 acres upon that neck at *Cape Porpoise* formerly Howell's, and where his house stood.
37	As to John York's fencing in and refusing to surrender land bought by Attwell of Richard Bray [in *North Yarmouth*].
159	20 acres by town grant of and in *Kittery*.
57	As to location of fence between lands of Joshua Downing and Leighton in *Kittery*.
105	20 acres by town grant of and in *Kittery*.
43	As to Corben's occupation and possession of meadow [in *Falmouth*].
72	One-half in common of grantor's part of Nonesuch meadow in *Scarborough*.
1	Quitclaim to land in *Kittery* conveyed to grantee by Elihu Crocket, *q. v.*
9	General power.
60	Two pieces of salt marsh on each side Sturgeon creek [in *Kittery*].

Date.	Grantor.	Grantee.	Instrument.
1682, May 29	JENKINS, Stephen and Jabez Jenkins	Nicholas Frost's estate Charles Frost	Deposition
1679, Aug. 25	JOCELYN, Margaret	Nathan Bedford	Receipt
1680, May 12	JOCELYN, Margaret et ux.	John Hinks	Assignment
1684, Oct. 17	JORDAN, Dominicus et ux. and David Trustrum	Edward Sargeant	Deed
1679, July 14	JORDAN, Robert, jun.	Nathaniel Fryer	Deed
1695, Dec. 18	JORDAN, Robert	Robert Elliot	Deed
	JORDAN, Robert, see Sarah Jordan		
1684, Jan. 20	JORDAN, Sarah and Robert Jordan	Ric. Hunniwell	Deed
1696, Nov. 30	JOSE, Richard et ux.	Samuel Fernald	Deed
1696, Nov. 2	JOY, Ephraim	James Stackpole, sen.	Deed
1670, Dec. 19	KEMBLE, Henry	Robert Brimsdon [Bronsdon]	Assignment
1670, Dec. 19	KEMBLE, Henry	Robert Brimsdon [Bronsdon]	Assignment
1684, Oct. 2	KEMBLE, Thomas	John Shapleigh	Deposition
	KING, Mary et ux., see George Litten's estate		
1686, Dec. 30	KING, Richard et ux.	Richard Gowell	Deed
1696, June 16	KING, Samuel	Isaac Goodrich	Deed
1696, June 17	KING, Sarah	Samuel King	Deed

Index of Grantors.

Folio.	Description.
67	As to bound marks of a parcel of land near the Cedars at Sturgeon creek, in *Kittery*.
69	Endorsed upon Bedford's promissory note.
69	Of Nathan Bedford's promissory note, *q. v.*
44	House and lot adjoining John Sargeant and 5 acres marsh near Little river, in *Saco*.
141	One half in common of tract of land between the Long Sands and Great pond, at Cape Elizabeth [in *Falmouth*], also his rights to marsh on Spurwink river.
87	Of all his remaining rights being 500 or 600 acres at Cape Elizabeth in *Falmouth*, also rights in common to marsh on Spurwink river.
80	10 acres of marsh on Black Point river in *Scarborough*.
102	One half in common of town grant of 20 acres to Joseph Alcock in *Kittery*.
104	3¼ acres on the way to Hutchinson's saw mill in *Berwick*. See folio 11.
99	Of Richard Selly's bond, *q. v.*
99	Of Richard Selly's mortgage, *q. v.*
41	As to Nicholas Shapleigh's intended disposition of his estate.
158	3 acres upon Great cove, below Thomas Spinney's in *Kittery*.
88	34 acres at Mast cove on Piscataqua river, formerly his father William King's, by gift from his grandfather, William Palmer, and also by town grant, in *Kittery*.
89	All title to her father William King's land in *Kittery* by gift from William Palmer, and by town grant.

Index of Grantors.

Date.	Grantor.	Grantee.	Instrument.
1676, July 27	KIRLE, Richard	Samuel Knight	Deed
1683, Sept. 1	KITTERY, town of	William Sanders	Survey
1695, Jan. 14	KITTERY, town of	Town of York	Survey
1696, Nov. 17	KITTERY, town of	John Morrell, sr.	Survey
	LARY, Sarah, see George Litten's estate		
	LAWD, see Lord		
1685, May 16	LEATHERBY, William	John Attwell	Deposition
1698, July 23	LITTEN, George, estate of, by Richard King, surviving executor, and Mary King et ux. Sarah Lary	Roger Kelly	Deed
1683, Apr. 2	LITTLEFIELD, Francis, sr.	John Elldridg	Deed
1685, July 9	LIVEINGSTOONE, Daniel and Joanna Liveingstone and children not named	Each other	Agreement
	LIVEINGSTONE, Joanna, see Daniel Liveingstoone		
	LORD, Abraham, see Nathan Lord		
1682, June 23	LORD, Martha	Wm. Leighton	Deposition
Recorded 1684, Mar. 14	LORD, Martha et ux.	Wm. Leighton	Acknowledgment
169$\frac{8}{9}$, Feb. 8	LORD, Nathan, estate of by Martha Lord, adm'x	Jos. Hammond, sr.	Deed

Folio.	Description.
72	6 acres, part of a town grant at Great cove in *Kittery*. In a postcript grantor attempts to revoke this conveyance.
24	30 acres adjoining the commons, land of Francis Blachford and Captain Frost.
93	Of the dividing line between the towns.
93	40 acres near the head of Sturgeon creek.
37	That the land John York lives on in *North Yarmouth* was formerly possessed by Attwell who bought of Richard Bray.
138	10 acres and house at Crooked Lane in *Kittery*.
39	156 acres at Ogunquit river falls and 11½ acres marsh, in *Wells*.
45	To unite in improving 40 acres land in *York;* after death of Joanna to be divided in halves between Daniel and three children not named.
56	As to her mother Margaret Everett's buying 6 acres in *Kittery*, of Renald Jenkins, and selling same to Leighton.
5	Quitclaiming the above property.
149	6 acres more or less of meadow, at Sturgeon creek in *Kittery*.

Index of Grantors.

Date.	Grantor.	Grantee.	Instrument.
1686, Mar. 25	LORD, Nathan, jun.	James Emery	Deposition
1681, Feb. 7	LORD, Nathan and Abraham Lord	Moses Abbet John Gillison	Deposition
1685, Nov. 10	MACKINTYRE, Micum [Malcolm]	Thos. Broughton John Wincoll	Release
1687, Dec. 16	MASON, Robert Tufton	Eliakim Hutchininson	Deed
1684, June 28	MASSACHUSETTS, by Thos. Danforth, pres.	John Mayne	Executive order
[No date.]	MASSACHUSETTS, by Thos. Danforth, pres.	John Mayne	Executive order
1685, June 26	MASSACHUSETTS, by Thos. Danforth, pres.	Edmund Whitte	Executive order
1683, Nov. 7 1684, July 25	MASSACHUSETTS, General Court of	Richard Wharton	Order and survey
	MAYNE, Elizabeth, see John Mayne		
1684, Jan. 3 1684, Feb. 16	MAYNE, John and Elizabeth Mayne	George Pearson	Deposition
	MIHIKERMETT, see Warumbee		
1685, June 25	MILLER, John	Francis Champernown	Receipt
1685, June 26	MILLER, John	Francis Champernown	Deposition
	MILLER, John, see Jonathan Hammond		

Folio.	Description.
56	As to John Roberts, jun.'s, acknowledgment of the bounds between him and Emery.
114	As to John Green, sen.'s intended disposition of his estate.
50	General and especial receipts for labor done at Salmon Falls mills at *Berwick*.
151	500 acres on both sides Little Newichewannock river in *Kittery*, and parcels of marsh formerly granted by town of Kittery to Hutchinson, or George or Richard Leader, rererving an annual quit-rent.
28	Confirming to John Mayne, land possessed and improved by him at Casco, [in *North Yarmouth*.]
29	Re-record of the above.
46	Confirmation of title to Chebeague island in Casco bay, formerly granted by George Cleeve to Walter Merry.
23	Confirming Wharton's former grant of 1000 acres, and report of surveyors appointed, that they had laid out 650 acres being the westerly half of Chebeague island, and 350 acres on the main land west of Maquoit, in *Casco Bay*.
31	That 60 acres of land sold by Richard Bray to Pearson, adjoining deponent at Mayne's point [in *North Yarmouth*], had been occupied 35 years or more.
42	For £36 in full satisfaction of a note of Champernown's, by mesne transfers now property of deponent.
42	As to the transfers of the above note, which, becoming property of deponent, had been satisfied by Champernown; the paper now lost or in the hands of George Pearson.

Index of Grantors.

Date.	Grantor.	Grantee.	Instrument.
1696, Oct. 22	MILLER, Richard, estate of, by Samuel Miller, administrator	Grace Banfield	Conditional deed
1696, Oct. 19	MILLER, Samuel et ux.	Joseph Hill	Deed
1684, Aug. 15	MOREY, Nicholas	James Oare Henry Brown Nicholas Coole	Discharge
1686, Sept. 2	MORROUGH, Dennis et ux.	Philip Breton	Deed
1695, July —	MORTON, John et ux.	Enoch Greenleafe	Deed
1682, Sept. 8	MOUNTEGUE, Margaret, estate of, by Samuel Snow, executor	Timothy Dwight	Mortgage
1685, Feb. 2	MOUNTEGUE, Margaret, estate of, by Samuel Snow, executor	Nicholas Morey	Deed
1684, June 5	MOWLTON, Jeremiah	Thomas Mowlton et ux.	Agreement
1684, June 5	MOWLTON, Joseph	Thomas Mowlton et ux.	Agreement
1685, Apr. 10	MOWLTON, Joseph	John Twisden Susanna Twisden Samuel Twisden	Bond
1684, June 5	MOWLTON, Thomas et ux.	Jere. Mowlton Joseph Mowlton	Conditional deed
168⅔, Jan. 26	MUNJOY, George, est. of, by Mary Lawrence, adm	Dennis Maraugh [Morrough]	Deed
1694, July 6	NANNEY, Katherine, *alias* Nayler	Samuel Wheelwright	Deed

INDEX OF GRANTORS. 33

Folio.	Description.
91	Land at the Long Reach in Piscataqua river, in *Kittery*, conditioned that Grace pay portions to Richard Miller's daughters, Mary and Martha; but in default to be to Grace for life, remainder over equally to Mary and Martha.
90	30 acres and house formerly granted by and in *Kittery* to his father, Richard Miller.
61	Of claims growing out of the transactions at the mill at Mousam [in *Wells*].
74	30 acres on the south side of Casco river, as by town grant of and in *Falmouth*.
136	100 acres and meadow appurtenant, at Dunstan in *Scarborough*, bought of John Howell.
10	100 acres adjoining Morgan Howell's, also 100 acres on Kennebunk river, and the commons; also 100 acres more at the Desert marshes, all in *Cape Porpoise*.
61	100 acres formerly Griffin Montague's; also 50 acres, the Neck, formerly Morgan Howell's, in *Cape Porpoise*.
61	Accepting conditions of Thomas Mowlton's deed, *q. v.*
61	Accepting conditions of Thomas Mowlton's deed, *q. v.*
59	To secure payment of £180.
60	All his estate real and personal in *York*, with reservations for support of self and wife.
35	50 acres at Ware creek in *Falmouth* conveyed by Elizabeth Harvey to Thomas Brackett.
111	500 acres, except tract sold to William Hammond; also 30 acres marsh bought by her husband, Robert Nanney of Mr. Coole; also 165 acres and 15 acres marsh, bought by Robert of William Hammond; also 230 acres, bought by Robert of William Symonds, all in *Wells*.

INDEX OF GRANTORS.

Date.	Grantor.	Grantee.	Instrument.
1661, Nov. 10	NANNEY, Robert	Wm. Hammonds	Deed
1685, July 25	NANNEY, Robert, est. of, by Katherine Nanney, *alias* Nayler, executrix, by Ed. Rishworth, att'y	Jere. Mowlton and others	Caution
1662, Nov. 7	NEALE, John	Nathan Lord, sr.	Deed
	NEHONONGASSETT, see Warumbee		
1696, Oct. 19	NICHOLS, Francis et ux.	Richard Cutt	Deed
1697, Apr. 20	NOCK, Sylvanus et ux.	Nathan Lord	Deed
	NUMBANUET, see Warumbee		
1679, Aug. 29	PARKER, Isaac	John Wentworth	Mortgage
1661, June 1	PARKER, John	Sylvanus Davis	Deed
1684, Nov. 30	PARKER, John	Sylvanus Davis	Deed
1684, Jan. 30	PARKER, John et ux.	William Baker et ux.	Deed
1686, May 21	PARKER, John, sen.	Henry Dering	Levy on execution
1684, Oct. 29	PARRETT, John	Nath'l Fryer, sen.	Mortgage
	PAUL, Stephen et ux., see Edward Gillman		
	PENLEY, Sampson, see Thomas Haynes		
1691, June 5	PHILLIPS, Samuel et ux.	George Turfrey	Deed

Folio.	Description.
127	Tract 25 poles wide, between Main creek and Mussel ridge, in *Wells*.
43	Claiming title to Mr. Gorge's neck in *York*.
129	25 acres and house and 5 acres marsh, near White's marsh in *Kittery*.
131	2 acres, 6 acres and 60 acres by town grant; also 3 acres by town grant to Jonathan Orris; also Richard Smith's house lot near Fort Loyal, all in *Falmouth*.
109	18 acres near Rocky hill in *Berwick* adjoining lands of grantee, John Plaisted and Zachariah Emery, by gift from James Emery, Nock's father-in-law.
21	Land and house bought of mortgagee [in *York*].
33	Land on Kennebec river between two rivulets three-quarters of a mile apart, thence across to Casco bay.
34	In confirmation of the above, on west side of Kennebec river.
73	Land north of Davis on Kennebec river, to Stover's rock and Winnegance marshes.
61	2¼ acres by the highway westerly from the meeting-house in *York*.
26	House, land, boats and appurtenances at Cape Elizabeth
134	One-fourth in common of saw-mill and tract of 16 square miles on Saco river, except 20 acres and timber sold out; also one quarter of Cow island, and one eighth Boniton's island, all in *Saco*.

INDEX OF GRANTORS.

Date.	Grantor.	Grantee.	Instrument
1684, Aug. 11	PHILLIPS, William, est. of, by Bridget Phillips, ex'x	Walter Barefoote and others	Caution
1697, Apr. 2	PICKERIN, John	Elihu Gunnison	Discharge
1679, Aug. 4	PLAYSTEAD, Roger, estate of, by William Playstead for self and attorney for joint adm'rs	Thomas Clarke	Deed
	PLAYSTEAD, William, see Humphrey Chadborne		
	POUNING [Pounding], Daniel, see Henry Pouning's estate		
1684, Oct. 13	POUNING [Pounding], Henry, estate of, by Elizabeth Pouning, administratrix, Elizabeth Bridgham et ux. Sarah Pouning Daniel Pouning	Jabez Jenkins	Deed
1684, Oct. 13	POUNING, Henry, est. of, by Elizabeth Pouning, administratrix, Elizabeth Bridgham et ux. Mary Pouning Sarah Pouning Daniel Pouning	Jabez Junkins	Deed
	POUNING, Mary, see Henry Pouning's estate		
	POUNING, Sarah, see Henry Pouning's estate		
1674, Nov. 14	PRITCHETT, John	Jane Pritchett, their son and daughter Richard Pritchett John Burrell	Conditional deed
1683, Jan. 10	PURCHASE, Elizabeth	Richard Wharton	Deed

INDEX OF GRANTORS.

Folio.	Description.
20	Claiming title to saw-mills at Saco river falls in *Saco*.
107	Of the mortgage recorded at folio 107.
9	Quitclaiming premises mortgaged to Playsted, and John Hull by John Wincoll, recorded at folio 8.
27	6 acres as by town grant of and in *Kittery* between lands of John Whitte and Anthony Emery. Mary Pouning is named as a grantor, but does not sign.
28	By same description, evidently to cure defect of Mary's not signing the above.
36	Lands and chattels at *Sagadahoc* to wife and to son and daughter in equal shares, except a neck of land to brother Richard, conditioned upon their joining him, or coming to look after the premises, otherwise all the premises to Burrell.
17	Quitclaim to the Way and Purchase patent at *Pejepscot*.

Index of Grantors.

Date.	Grantor.	Grantee.	Instrument.
1683, Oct. 25	PURCHASE, Thomas, estate of, by Elizabeth Blany, administratrix	Richard Wharton	Deed
1684, July 8	RAYNES, Francis et ux.	Nathaniel Raynes Francis Raynes	Deed
1684, July 10	RAYNES, Francis and Nathaniel Raynes	Alice Shapleigh	Mortgage
	RAYNES, Francis, see Francis Champernown		
	RAYNES, Nathaniel, see Francis Raynes		
169⅔, Jan. 27	RIDDEN, John et ux.	William Baker	Deed
1694, June 19	REMICH, Abraham et ux.	Peter Staple	Deed
1694, June 20	REMICH, Abraham	Isaac Remich	Deed
1694, Mar. 30	REMICH, Christian	Isaac Remich	Deed
1694, June 20	REMICH, Christian	Isaac Remich	Deed
1698, May 2	REMICH, Christian	Isaac Remich John Dennet	Deed
169⅔, Jan. 4	REMICH, Christian	Joshua Downing	Deposition
1698, May 2	REMICH, Isaac	John Dennet	Deed
1698, May 2	REMICH, Isaac	John Dennet	Bond
1684, Nov. 4	RENALDS, John	Peter Rendle	Deed
	RODES, Thomas, see William Furbush		

Index of Grantors.

Folio.	Description.
16	One half in common of the Way and Purchase patent of lands at Pejepscot and adjacent, reserving seven lots.
21	The farm they live on [in *York*], life estate to Nathaniel, remainder to Francis, reserving life estate to themselves
24	Farm and buildings in *York*, where Ann Godfrey formerly dwelt, conveyed by Alice Shapleigh, folio 20.
143	100 acres on Ogunquit river and Clay brook, adjoining lands of Hatch and Littlefield and the commons in *Wells*.
128	30 acres in *Kittery*, adjoining Christian Remich, Spinney's, Tetherly's and Rackley's lands.
90	Quitclaim to 20 acres in *Kittery* conveyed by Christian Remich to grantee, folio 89, *q. v.*
89	10 acres on the east side of Great cove in *Kittery*, being part of three town grants.
89	20 acres on the river in *Kittery* adjoining grantor, Spinney and Shapleigh.
120	Quitclaim of the above two tracts releasing the entail.
151	That Dennis Downing lived on and possessed the farm now possessed by Joshua [in *Kittery*].
119	House with 77 acres in *Kittery*, as by deeds from his father Christian Remich, and by town grants.
120	Conditioned to warrant the titles to above conveyance.
29	100 acres, the former plantation of his father, William Renalds, 127 rods up the river from Peter Turbett's former plantation in *Cape Porpoise*.

Index of Grantors.

Date.	Grantor.	Grantee.	Instrument.
1694, July 23	ROGERS, Ezekiel	Jere. Moulton	Deed
169⁸⁄₉, Jan. 4	ROGERS, Richard	Joshua Downing	Deposition
1682, Nov. 8	RYALL, John	Amos Stephens	Deed
1681, May 15	RYCE, Thomas et ux.	Thomas Daniel	Deed
1674, Apr. 17	SAYWORD, Henry	Nathaniel Fryer	Mortgage
	SAYWORD, Jonathan, see Mary Austine		
1682, May 17	SCARBOROUGH, town of	Robert Tidy	Grant
1682, May 17	SCARBOROUGH, town of	Robert Tidy	Grant
1669, Aug. 24	SCOTTOW, Joshua	Peter Hinxen [Hinkeson]	Deed
1668, Aug. 1	SCOTTOW, Joshua	Peter Hinkeson	Deed
1680, Jan. 1	SCOTTOW, Joshua	Benj. Blackeman et ux.	Deed
1681, Jan. 18	SCOTTOW, Joshua	Benj. Blackeman et ux.	Deed
1685, Oct. 19	SCOTTOW, Joshua	William Burrage	Deed
1678, Nov. 15	SEELY, William, estate of, by Elizabeth Seely, administratrix	William Screven	Deed
1670, May 9	SELLY, Richard	Henry Kemble	Bond
1670, Dec. 7	SELLY, Richard	Henry Kemble	Mortgage
1670, Dec. 6	SELLY [Zelly], Richard	Robert Brimsdon [Bronsdon]	Bond

Index of Grantors.

Folio.	Description.
109	House and 31 acres in four parcels on York river, adjoining Eliakim Hutchinson and John Braun in *York*.
151	That Dennis Downing lived on and possessed the farm now possessed by Joshua [in *Kittery*].
65	15 acres adjoining grantor and the river [in *North Yarmouth*].
51	One half in common of an island in Piscataqua river, between Strawberry Bank and Thomas Withers's house, and by him conveyed to his two daughters.
82	350 acres upland and 20 acres swamp, on south west side of York river, as by town grant of and in *York*.
69	6 acres by the highway from Black Point to Hunnewell's.
69	6 acres of swamp called the Beaver dam.
40	10 acres marsh near Pine tree creek in *Scarborough*.
40	23 acres upland at Black Point in *Scarborough*, with certain restrictions and quit rent reserved. Executed Aug. 9, 1676.
22	10 acres near the ferry place at Black Point; also marsh called Crooked lane marsh on the river to Dunstan in *Scarborough*.
23	10 acres at Black Point in *Scarborough*.
61	Marsh in *Scarborough* between the ditches of grantor and Andrew Brown.
41	10 acres called Carle's point on the west side of Spruce creek in *Kittery*.
99	To pay 10,000 feet of merchantable pine boards.
99	In form of a bond to secure £14, of house and land at Winter Harbor in *Saco*.
100	To pay £30 : 15.

Index of Grantors.

Date.	Grantor.	Grantee.	Instrument.
1670, Dec. 7	SELLY [Zelly], Richard	Robert Brimsdon [Bronsdon]	Mortgage
1698, Apr. 4	SERGENT, Edward	Wm. Pepperrell	Deed
1697, Sept. 17	SEWARD, John et ux.	James Fernald	Deed
1683, Feb. 5	SHAPLEIGH, Alice	John Shapleigh	Lease
1683, Feb. 6	SHAPLEIGH, Alice	Nicholas Shapleigh and other children of John Shapleigh	Bill of sale
1684, July 8	SHAPLEIGH, Alice	Francis Raynes Nath'l Raynes	Deed
1683, Aug. 20	SHAPLEIGH, Alice and John Shapleigh	Each other	Arbitration and award
1685, Nov. 10	SHAPLEIGH, Alice and John Shapleigh	Each other	Agreement & appraisal
1685, Dec. 28	SHAPLEIGH, Alice	Edward Ayers	Deed
1685, April 5	SHAPLEIGH, John	James Johnson	Deed
1685, Dec. 28	SHAPLEIGH, John et ux. and Alice Shapleigh	Edward Ayers	Deed
1691, June 13 1691, July 23 1692, Nov. 9	SHAPLEIGH, John	Nathaniel Kane	Receipts(3)
	SHAPLEIGH, John, see Alice Shapleigh		
1688, June 2	SHAPLEIGH, Nicholas, estate of, by Alice Shapleigh, administratrix	Joshua Downing	Deed

Index of Grantors.

Folio.	Description.
101	Of all his estate, real and personal, wherever situate, to secure above bond.
124	One half in common of 80 acres on the sea, of 15 acres of meadow, of 10 acres of meadow in two parcels, all at Winter Harbor and Little river in *Saco*.
110	20 acres in the Great cove below the Boiling rock in *Kittery*.
2	Of her third of the revenue of the saw mills at Spruce creek in *Kittery*.
2	Of household stuff set out to her from the estate of Nicholas, her late husband.
20	Farm formerly Ann Godfrey's in *York*.
2	Choosing arbitrators to set out Mrs. Shapleigh's thirds in Major Nicholas Shapleigh's estate, with an inventory of the same.
52	Dividing parts of Major Nicholas Shapleigh's estate, &c., and an appraisal thereof.
79	Quitclaiming land conveyed by John Shapleigh et ux., folio 79, *q. v.*
57	One fourth in common of his saw mill and corn mill and appurtenances in *Kittery*.
79	16 acres formerly William Ellingham's, on Piscataqua river; also 30 acres formerly Antipas Maverick's, all in *Kittery*.
111	Together in full for land sold at Spruce creek [in *Kittery*].
144	20 acres in *Kittery*, 4 acres south of the highway, adjoining Thomas Jones, 16 acres north of highway, adjoining grantor and the Bay land.

INDEX OF GRANTORS.

Date.	Grantor.	Grantee.	Instrument.
1684, July 23	SHAPLEIGH, Nicholas, estate of	Sam'l Shrympton Eliakim Hutchinson John Purrington John Penwill Nathaniel Fryer Edw. Rishworth	Commis'r's report
1684, Sept. 6	SHAPLEIGH, Nicholas, estate of	Alice Shapleigh	Commis'r's report
1684, Sept. 6	SHAPLEIGH, Nicholas, estate of	Alice Shapleigh	Commis'r's report
1684, Feb. 11	SHRIMPTON, Samuel et ux	Richard Cutt	Deed
	SKINNER, Edward, see Elias White		
1685, Apr. 3	SMALE, Francis, sen.	John Shapleigh	Deposition
1682, Nov. 3	SMYTH, John, sen., et ux.	William Sawyer	Deed
1684, Aug. 1	SMITH, John, sen.	John Smyth	Conditional deed
1684, Dec. 3	SMITH, John, sen.	John Sayword	Deed
1685, Apr. 21	SMITH, John, sen.	John Smyth, jun.	Receipt
1685, June 23	SMYTH, John, sen.	Robert Jordan's heirs or assigns	Deposition
1686, Mar. 1	SMITH, John, sen. et ux.	Samuel Bankes	Deed
168¾, Feb. 3	SMITH, John and Mary Smith	Each other	Partition
	SMITH, Mary, see John Smith		
1685, June 22	SNOW, Samuel	George Pearson	Power of attorney

Folio.	Description.
26	Allowing several claims against the estate.
24	Assigning her as dower 253 acres adjoining the dwelling house; also 9 acres marsh at Sturgeon creek; also one third of two mills and chattels, all in *Kittery*.
26	Re-record of the preceding.
32	800 acres between Spruce creek and Crooked lane in *Kittery* levied from the estate of Robert Cutt.
41	That he heard Major Nicholas Shapleigh say that he had brought John from his mother in England, and promised he should be heir to his whole estate, failing children, &c.
4	80 acres and 8 acres meadow in *Wells* at Little river, which came to his wife Mary from her father George Farrow.
19	Confirming former deed of land [in *York*] upon conditions and reservations.
36	All interest in saw mill and 4 acres of land at Cape Neddick [in *York*].
32	For £30: full consideration for land sold him.
41	That being marshal of the province, he levied execution in favor of Jordan upon a neck of land in *Saco*, as property of Richard Vines.
54	48 acres on Cape Neddick river [in *York*].
78	Of John Smyth, senior's real estate, setting off to Mary a parcel near Samuel Banks in *York*, she releasing to John all the other real estate.
50	General and especially to manage property at *Cape Porpoise*.

Index of Grantors.

Date.	Grantor.	Grantee.	Instrument.
1675, Dec. 20	Spencer, Humphrey	Benj. Barnard	Deed
1686, Apr. 2	Spencer, Humphrey et ux.	Robert Elliot	Deed
Recorded 169$\frac{4}{5}$, Mar. 24	Spencer, Humphrey et ux.	Robert Elliot	Deed
1682, June 30	Spencer, Patience	Moses Spencer	Deed
1662, June 20	Spencer, Thomas et ux.	Thomas Etherington et ux.	Deed
1662, June 25	Spencer, Thomas et ux.	John Gattinsby et ux.	Deed
1684, May 23	Spencer, William	Susanna Joy et ux.	Deed
	Spinney, John, see Thomas Spinney		
1694, Mar. 23	Spinney, Thomas and John Spinney	Each other	Lease and bond
1694, Aug. 20	Staple, Peter	Peter Staple	Conditional deed
1684, Sept. 22 1684, Oct. 12	Stephens, Edward	John Cossons's assigns	Depositions
1686, Mar. 30	Stone, Daniel	James Emery, sr.	Deposition
1685, May 22	Swett, Clement	Thomas Sparke	Deed
168$\frac{2}{3}$, Mar. 20	Tayler [Taylour], Andrew	John Mills	Release

INDEX OF GRANTORS. 47

Folio.	Description.
55	30 acres near Whitte's marsh and the commons next Newgewannock river [in *Kittery*].
149	Town grant of 50 acres and 10 acres of swamp on Wilcox's pond brook; also two fifths in common of the Further marsh [in *Berwick*].
103	30 acres at Newichewannock [in *Kittery*] bounded by lands of Daniel Goodwin, Capt. Wincoll, Moses Spencer and Eliakim Hutchinson.
7	What remained undivided of a 200 acre town grant, at Slut's corner; also 30 acres and half the meadow; also her third of Tom Tinker's and Great swamps [in *Berwick*].
84	12 acres, part of town grant of 200 acres in Unity parish, [*Kittery*].
84	12 acres, part of town grant of 200 acres in Unity parish, [*Kittery*].
11	3½ acres by the highway to Hutchinson's mill in *Berwick*.
112	Of all grantor's estate in *Kittery*, conditioned upon John's managing upon halves during lives of Thomas and wife.
113	80 acres, house and farm in *Kittery*, reserving 2 acres and all stock, conditioned upon grantee maintaining grantor and wife.
24	As to deed of Sir Ferdinando Gorges to Cossons, and his occupation of two islands called by his name in *Casco Bay*.
56	As to controversy between Emery and John Roberts, jun., about right to cut hay on marsh claimed by Emery [in *Berwick*].
38	House and 20 acres adjoining John Parrott's at Cape Elizabeth [in *Falmouth.*]
59	General discharge as heir to his father, George Tayler, and receipt of consideration for land sold.

Index of Grantors.

Date.	Grantor.	Grantee.	Instrument.
168⅔, Mar. 20	TAYLER, Andrew	John Mills	Deed
168⅔, Mar. 22	TAYLER, Andrew	John Mills	Power of attorney
1679, July 29	TAYLER, George et ux.	John Mills	Deed
1681, July 25	TAYLER, George	John Mills	Deposition
1697, Apr. 22	TAYLOR, John	Edward Sargent	Deed
1695, May 7	TOBEY, James	Stephen Tobey	Deed
1695, Sept. 2	TOBEY, James, sen.	John Tobey William Tobey	Conditional deed
1694, Dec. 4	THOMPSON, Miles et ux.	Bartholomew Thompson	Deed
1684, July 20	TOMPSON, John	John Wincoll James Emery	Bond
1691, Nov. 5	TRAFTON, Thomas	John Rackliff et ux.	Deed
	TRUSTRUM, David, see Dominicus Jordan		
1695, July 1	TRUSTRUM, Ralph, estate of, by Dominicus Jordan, administrator	Edward Sergeant	Deed
1672, July 9	TUCKER, Francis	John Batson	Receipt
Acknowledged 1687, Mar. 12	TUFTON, John	Eliakim Hutchinson	Release
1683, June 23	TURNER, Thomas	William Leighton	Deposition

Index of Grantors.

Folio.	Description.
59	Confirmation of land sold by his father George Tayler, *q. v.*; also 30 acres of meadow on Pigsty river, and elsewhere in Black Point [*Scarborough*].
60	To take possession of land sold by his father Geo. Tayler, *q v*
59	Plantation and island of marsh [in *Scarborough*].
43	As to Mills's warning Anthony Libby not to cut hay on his marsh [in *Scarborough*].
117	200 acres at Salmon falls; also three town grants aggregating 60 acres and 33 acres of swamp, formerly William Love's [in *Berwick*]
83	4 acres on the mast way, adjoining grantee's house in *Kittery*.
81	All his lands, except 4 acres to Stephen Tobey, and chattels in *Kittery* with exceptions, and conditioned for support, &c.
96	40 acres in *Berwick*, bought of Abraham Tilton.
35	To save them harmless as administrators of estate of his father, William Tompson, and to protect town of Kittery from charges on account of his brother, James Tompson.
79	20 acres at Rogers cove in *York*.
94	100 acres and 25 acres meadow in two parcels at Winter Harbor in *Saco*.
31	For 24½ quintals of fish.
153	Of all rights in land conveyed by his father Robert Tufton Mason, *q. v.*
56	As to Dennis Downing's possession of 6 acres, afterwards Leighton's in *Kittery*.

INDEX OF GRANTORS.

Date.	Grantor.	Grantee.	Instrument.
1685, April 10	TWISDEN, John and Samuel Twisden Susanna Twisden	Jos. Mowlton	Deed
	TWISDEN, John, see Peter Weare		
1696, July 20	TWISDEN, Mary	Samuel Small	Deed
	TWISDEN, Samuel, see John Twisden		
	TWISDEN, Susanna, see John Twisden		
1674, Mar. 4	VICKRIS, Robert and Richard Bickham William Williams	Francis Tucker	Power of attorney
1697, May 12	WADE, Jonathan, est. of, by Jonathan Wade and Thomas Wade exec'rs	John Wade	Power of attorney
1664, July 18	WADLEIGH, John	Mary Mills and her children not named	Deed
1683, Apr. 16	WADLEIGH, John, estate of, by Rob't Wadleigh, executor	Mary Mills and her children not named	Deed
1685, Aug. 11	WADLEIGH, John	William Sawyer	Release
1685, Aug. 12	WADLEIGH, John et ux.	Peter Follsam	Deed
	WADLEIGH, John, see Robert Wadleigh		
1675, Sept. 1	WADLEIGH, Robert	John Young et ux.	Deed
1685, Aug. 12	WADLEIGH, Robert, sen. et ux. and John Wadleigh	William Sawyer	Deed
1685, Aug. 12	WADLEIGH, Rob't, sen. et ux. and John Wadleigh	Peter Foullsam	Deed

Folio.	Description.
58	120 acres, as by town grant, on the country highway and the brook near Philip Adams's house lot, in *York*.
129	3 acres marsh on the west branch of York river, bought by Peter Twisden of Robert Edge, in *York*.
13	To collect debts of William Bickeham and others in New England.
118	To collect debts due from estate of John Diamond of *Kittery*.
64	House lot and marsh on Webhannet river in *Wells*.
64	Confirmation of the above deed.
48	Quitclaim to one third part of farm in *Wells*, conveyed by John Young et ux.
63	One third part of a farm in *Wells* formerly his grandfather's John Wadleigh's, as by gift from his father Robert Wadleigh.
47	One third part of the farm in *Wells* formerly his father's, John Wadleigh's.
45	One sixth part of the farm of John Wadleigh in *Wells*.
63	One sixth part of the farm of John Wadleigh in *Wells*.

Index of Grantors.

Date.	Grantor.	Grantee.	Instrument.
1686, June 1	WANEWRIGHT, Francis	Roger Kelly	Deed
1684, July 7	WARUMBEE, and Darumkine Mihikermett Weeden Domhegon Numbanuett Nehonongassett Indian sagamores	Richard Wharton	Deed
1675, June 29	WATTS, Henry	John Mills	Deposition
1683, Oct. 10	WAY, Eleazer	Richard Wharton	Deed
169$\frac{3}{4}$, Jan. 18	WEARE, Joseph et ux.	Matthew Austine	Deed
1685, June 13	WEARE, Peter and John Twisden	Joseph Preble	Deposition
[No date]	WEBBER, John	[John Cloyce]	Deposition
1685, Nov. 23	WEBBER, Samuel et ux.	Sylvanus Davis	Deed
	WEEDEN DOMHEGON, see Warumbee		
1684, July 15	WHARTON, Richard	John Parker	Deed
1695, June 17	WHEELWRIGHT, Samuel et ux.	John Wheelwright	Deed
1694, Nov. 3	WHINNICK, Joseph, estate of, by Sarah Whinnick, adm'x	Richard Hunniwell	Deed
1684, July 18	WHITE, Elias and Edward Skinner	William Wharton	Deposition

Index of Grantors.   53

Folio.	Description.
64	House, land and appurtenances on Smuttynose island *Isles of Shoals*.
15	Tract from Androscoggin falls 4 miles west, and so down to Maquoit, and by the Pejepscot river, and from the other side of Androscoggin falls, all the lands from the falls to Pejepscot and Merrymeeting bay to Kennebec and toward the Wilderness bounded by a southwest and northeast line to extend from Androscoggin uppermost falls to Kennebec river, and all the land from Maquoit to Pejepscot to Atkins bay in Kennebec river, also Mericoneag neck and Small Point harbor, and Sebascodegan island in Casco bay, and all islands in Kennebec and Pejepscot rivers and Merrymeeting bay.
13	As to Mills's possession and occupation of marsh on Nonesuch river [in *Scarborough*].
18	One half in common of the Way and Purchase patent of lands at *Pejepscot* and adjacent.
146	House and 3 acre lot, except half acre of John Peniwell's, on Meeting House creek, also 6 acre woodlot, in *York*.
46	That 15 acres in *York*, originally William Johnson's, are now Joseph Preble's by mesne conveyances.
24	That he voyaged to Boston with Cloyce.
74	One half in common of a saw mill and 100 acres on Long creek in *Falmouth*
17	Tract 6 miles in length between Casco bay and Kennebec adjoining Winnegance creek.
126	One half in common of the tracts conveyed by Katherine Nanney, *q. v*, in *Wells*.
80	46 acres on Black Point river and Bass creek in *Scarborough*.
19	That Richard Wharton delivered possession of Sebascodegan island in Casco bay to John Parker to the use of William Wharton.

Date.	Grantor.	Grantee.	Instrument.
	WHITTE, John, see Abraham Conley		
168¾, Mar. 24	WHITNEY, Benjamin et ux.	Jona. Sayword	Deed
	WILLIAMS, William, see Robert Vickris		
169⅜, Mar. 10	WILLIS, Samuel	John Taylor	Deed
1669, Mar. 25	WILLS, Thomas	Francis Champernown Nic. Shapleigh William Spencer trustees of Lucy Chadborne	Bond
1684, June 2	WILSON, Gowen	Andrew Haley et ux.	Deed
1671, April 6	WINCOLL, John	John Hull Roger Playstead	Mortgage
1675, Feb. 29	WINCOLL, John	William Spencer trustee of Mary Etherington Patience Etherington	Deed
	WITHERS, Elizabeth, see Jane Withers		
1685, April 22	WITHERS, Jane	Elizabeth Withers	Deed
1685, Nov. 25	WITHERS, Jane and Elizabeth Winters	Peter Lewis	Deed
1679, Nov. 25	WITHERS, Thomas	Rowland Williams	Deed
1682, June 12	WITHERS, Thomas	Joseph Curtis	Deed
1683, Jan. 9	WITHERS, Thomas	Joseph Berry	Deed
1684, Dec. 22	WITHERS, Thomas et ux.	Elizabeth Withers	Bill of sale

Folio.	Description.
37	House and 20 acres as by two town grants of and in *York*.
117	200 acres and house at Salmon falls, on the river [in *Berwick*].
51	In the nature of a marriage settlement, between the obligor and Lucy Chadborne.
87	11 acres at Spruce creek, part of town grant of and in *Kittery*.
8	2 saw mills and appurtenances at Salmon falls in *Kittery*, with timber rights, &c.
86	By way of marriage settlement, with remainder over to Patience, several tracts in *Kittery* aggregating 209 acres.
36	20 acres about the late Thomas Withers's dwelling house in *Kittery*, reserving life estate therein.
86	Lot 69 by 20 rods adjoining grantee's lot in *Kittery*.
5	Lot 75 poles long between lot of John Phillips, Nicholas Weeks and Enoch Houchings and Spruce creek in *Kittery*.
25	80 acres east of and near the head of Spruce creek in *Kittery*.
11	Half acre, 10 rods along the river, adjoining Withers's house lot in *Kittery*.
35	Of cattle.

Index of Grantors.

Date.	Grantor.	Grantee.	Instrument.
1685, Mar. 18	WITTUM, Peter et ux.	William Wittum	Deed
1696, Dec. 12	WITTUM, Peter et ux.	Samuel Small	Deed
1686, Apr. 6	WITTUM, William	Peter Wittum, jr.	Deed
1689, Feb. 28	WOODBRIDGE, Benjamin	Joseph Crocket Dennis Hicks	Deed
1696, Dec. 5	WOODMAN, John	Samuel Spinney	Deed
1681, Sept. 23	WORMESTALL, Arthur	John Abbett	Deed
1684, Nov. 16	WORMESTALL, Arthur	William Daggett et ux.	Deed
1685, Aug. 7	YOUNG, John, et ux.	William Sawyer	Deed
1666, Dec. 4	YOUNG, Rowland et ux.	Daniel Dill	Deed
1683, Oct. 16	YOUNG, Rowland et ux.	Edward Martine	Deed
1682, Apr. 18	YOUNG, Rowland, senior et ux.	Samuel Young	Deed
1685, Aug. 25	YOUNG, Rowland, senior et ux.	Rowland Young et ux.	Deed
1680, Dec. 10	YORK, town of	John Sayword	Conditional grant
1683, Dec. 21	YORK, town of	Edw. Rishworth	Survey
1685, June 12	YORK, town of	John Twisden	Survey
1685, June 12	YORK, town of	John Twisden	Survey
1695, Jan. 14	YORK, town of	Town of Kittery	Survey
	ZELLY, see Selly		

Index of Grantors.

Folio.	Description.
57	One half in common of land at Tompson point in *Kittery*, purchased of Joseph Hammond.
129	Messuage and 16 acres on south west side of Sturgeon creek in *Kittery*.
57	50 acres on Sturgeon creek, also 20 acres by town grant of and in *Kittery*.
121	36 acres between Crocket's creek and Ashen brook swamp in *Kittery*.
95	20 acres, town grant of and in *Kittery*.
43	40 acres upland and 6 acres salt marsh near water side at Winter harbor in *Saco*.
27	7 acres upland, 4 acres salt meadow, also half undivided of land bought of Thomas Williams, all in *Saco*.
47	One third in common of a farm in *Wells*, conveyed by Robert Wadleigh, *q. v.*
159	10 acres at Bass cove in *York*.
13	Dwelling house and appurtenances on Smuttynose island, *Isles of Shoals*.
48	10 acres, part of town grant of and in *York*.
53	The former homestead of Robert Knight north of York river; also tract adjoining the above and Rob't Young, in *York*.
67	20 acres called the Bell marsh, 20 acres on Folly brook, and mill privilege, 20 acres and swamp below Cape Neddick pond, with timber rights, conditioned upon Sayword's building galleries and seats in the meeting house.
28	74 acres as by town grant of April 22, 1661.
58	120 acres adjoining the brook, north east of Philip Adams's house lot.
59	Re-record of the above.
93	Of the dividing line between the towns.

INDEX OF

Date.	Grantee.	Grantor.	Instrument.
1681, Sept. 23	ABBET, John	Arthur Wormestall	Deed
1681, Feb. 7	ABBET, Moses and John Gillison	Nathan Lord Abraham Lord	Deposition
1684, Mar. 9	ADAMS, Christopher	Peter Glanefeild et ux.	Deed
1696, June 7	ADAMS, Margaret	Isaac Goodridge	Mortgage
1685, Aug. 1	ALLEN, Bozoun	Henry Harwood et ux.	Mortgage
168$\frac{2}{3}$, Mar. 23	ATTWELL, John	John Cossones	Deposition
168$\frac{2}{3}$, Mar. 24	ATTWELL, John	Henry Donell Richard Carter	Deposition
1685, Apr. 3	ATTWELL, John	John Howleman	Deposition
1685, May 16	ATTWELL, John	William Leatherby	Deposition
1685, Aug. 15	ATTWELL, John	Richard Bray	Deed
168$\frac{2}{3}$, Mar. 1	AUSTINE, Mary and Matthew Austine Sarah Austine Jona. Sayword	One another	Agreement
169$\frac{3}{4}$, Jan. 18	AUSTINE, Matthew	Joseph Weare et ux.	Deed
	AUSTINE, Matthew, see Mary Austine		

GRANTEES.

Folio.	Description.
43	40 acres upland and 6 acres salt marsh near water side at Winter harbor in *Saco*.
114	As to John Green, senior's intended disposition of his estate.
31	26 acres, more or less, in two parcels, in *Kittery*, bought of William Palmer and Samuel Knight.
147	Land in *Kittery* formerly William King's bought of Samuel King.
77	Land in *Falmouth*, exchanged with Rev. George Burroughs, and by him bought of John Skilling.
37	As to Atwell's purchase of Richard Bray of 60 acres in Casco Bay [*North Yarmouth*].
37	As to Atwell's purchase of Richard Bray of 60 acres in Casco Bay [*North Yarmouth*].
37	As to John York's fencing in and refusing to surrender land bought by Attwell of Richard Bray [in *North Yarmouth*].
37	That the land John York lives on in *North Yarmouth* was formerly possessed by Attwell who bought of Richard Bray.
44	60 acres adjoining Thomas Maynes, on West side of Ryall's river [in *North Yarmouth*.]
66	Ratifying the provisions of an imperfect will of Matthew Austine, sen., devising land and bequeathing personal estate in *York*.
146	House and 3 acre lot, except half acre of John Peniwell's, on Meeting House creek, also 6 acre woodlot, in *York*.

INDEX OF GRANTEES.

Date.	Grantee.	Grantor.	Instrument.
1684, May 29	AUSTINE, Samuel	Joseph Cross et ux.	Deed
	AUSTINE, Sarah, see Mary Austine		
1685, Dec. 28	AYERS, Edward	Alice Shapleigh	Deed
1685, Dec. 28	AYERS, Edward	John Shapleigh et ux. Alice Shapleigh	Deed
1686, June 28	BACKEHOUSE, Francis and John Hill	One another	Contract
1684, Jan. 30	BAKER, William et ux.	John Parker et ux.	Deed
169¾, Jan. 27	BAKER, William	John Ridden et ux.	Deed
1696, Oct. 30	BALL, Mary	Dennis Hicks	Deed
1696, Oct. 20	BANFIELD, Christopher	Joseph Hill	Bond
1696, Oct. 20	BANFIELD, Christopher	Joseph Hill	Bond
1696, Oct. 22	BANFIELD, Grace	Richard Miller's estate, Samuel Miller, adm'r	Conditional deed
1686, Mar. 1	BANKES, Samuel	John Smith, sen. et ux.	Deed
1684, Aug. 11	BAREFOOTE, Walter and others	William Phillips' estate, Bridget Phillips, exc'x	Caution
1669, July 30	BAREFOOTE, Walter	Francis Champernowne	Bond
1675, Dec. 20	BARNARD, Benjamin	Humphrey Spencer	Deed

Index of Grantees.

Folio.	Description.
10	One half of Drake's island; also one half of his father Cross's marsh north of the island, in *Wells*.
79	Quitclaiming land conveyed by John Shapleigh et ux., folio 79, *q. v.*
79	16 acres formerly William Ellingham's, on Piscataqua river; also 30 acres formerly Antipas Maverick's, all in *Kittery*.
161	Of co-partnership, to build and conduct a saw-mill on Backhouse's creek in *Saco*.
73	Land north of Davis on Kennebec river, to Stover's rock and Winnegance marshes.
143	100 acres on Ogunquit river and Clay brook, adjoining lands of Hatch and Littlefield and the commons in *Wells*.
122	Quitclaim of his interest in common of 36 acres between Crocket's creek and Ashen Swamp brook, in *Kittery*.
92	Conditioned to pay £8:15, portion to Mary Miller, stepdaughter of obligee.
92	Conditioned to pay £8:15, portion to Martha Miller, stepdaughter of obligee.
91	Land at the Long Reach in Piscataqua river, in *Kittery*, conditioned that Grace pay portions to Richard Miller's daughters, Mary and Martha; but in default to be to Grace for life, remainder over equally to Mary and Martha.
54	48 acres on Cape Neddick river [in *York*].
20	Claiming title to saw-mills at Saco river falls in *Saco*.
30	To pay £40.
55	30 acres near Whitte's marsh and the commons next Newgewannock river [in *Kittery*].

Index of Grantees.

Date.	Grantee.	Grantor.	Instrument.
168$\frac{5}{6}$, Jan. 1	BARNARD, Benjamin	Joseph Barnard	Deed
1672, July 9	BATSON, John	Francis Tucker	Receipt
167$\frac{2}{3}$, Feb. 8	BATSON, John	Stephen Batson	Deed
1674, July 9	BATSON, John	Joseph Bolles et ux.	Deed
1686, May 25	BATSON, John, estate of	Jona. Hammond Fr. Backehouse John Miller	Certificate
1692, June 27	BATSON, John	Robert Ellet	Deed
1679, Aug. 25	BEDFORD, Nathan	Margaret Jocelyn	Receipt
1683, Jan. 9	BERRY, Joseph	Thomas Withers	Deed
169$\frac{3}{8}$, Feb. 6	BLACK, Daniel	Matthew Austine et ux.	Deed
169$\frac{5}{6}$, Feb. 10	BLACK, Daniel	Benjamin Gooch	Deed
1698, Jan. 16	BLACK, Daniel	Wm. Hilton, sen. Arthur Beale	Deed
1680, Jan. 1	BLACKEMAN, Benjamin et ux.	Joshua Scottow	Deed
1681, Jan. 18	BLACKEMAN, Benjamin et ux.	Joshua Scottow	Deed
1683, Dec. 12	BLACKEMAN, Benjamin	John Bonighton	Deed
1683, Dec. 12	BLACKEMAN, Benjamin	James Gibbons et ux.	Deed

INDEX OF GRANTEES. 63

Folio.	Description.
65	50 acres in *Berwick* bought of Benoni Hodgsden, between the river and the commons and lands of Tozier and Price.
81	For 24½ quintals of fish.
1	18 acres upland and 25 acres marsh, between the main river, Little river, Middle creek, and the creek from Beaver pond, in *Cape Porpoise*.
3	50 acres in *Cape Porpoise* granted by Thomas Gorges to Morgan Howell.
61	That the creditors of said estate had been notified to bring in claims.
160	70 acres at *Cape Porpoise* adjoining grantee's, which was portion of grantor's wife, Margery.
69	Endorsed upon Bedford's promissory note.
11	Half acre, 10 rods along the river, adjoining Withers's house lot in *Kittery*.
114	3 acres more or less, between Meeting-house creek, a small creek and the highway (except half an acre of John Penwill's) in *York*.
115	10 acres between lands of Donnell, W[e]are and Dummer at *York*.
148	3 acres of marsh near the partings of York river, in *York*.
22	10 acres near the ferry place at Black Point; also marsh called Crooked lane marsh on the river to Dunstan in *Scarborough*.
23	10 acres at Black Point in *Scarborough*.
22	Tract two miles wide east of Saco river, part of Lewis and Bonighton's patent, south of James Gibbons's division, in *Saco*.
22	Tract 3½ miles along Saco river by 2 miles back, being the second division to grantors in Lewis and Bonighton's patent in *Saco*.

Index of Grantees.

Date.	Grantee.	Grantor.	Instrument.
	BLAGDON, James, see Roger Kelly		
1667, May 8	BRACKETT, Thomas	Elizabeth Harvy	Deed
	BRAGDON, Samuel, see Thomas Donell		
1666, Jan. 9	BRAWN, John	James Dixon	Conditional deed
	BROWN, Henry, see James Oare		
1664, Aug. 24	BRAY, Richard	Thomas Drake	Deed
1686, Sept. 2	BRETON, Philip	Dennis Morrough et ux.	Deed
1670, Dec. 6	BRIMSDON, Robert	Richard Selly [Zelly]	Bond
1670, Dec. 7	BRIMSDON, Robert	Richard Selly [Zelly]	Mortgage
1670, Dec. 19	BRIMSDON, Robert	Henry Kemble	Assignment
1670, Dec. 19	BRIMSDON, Robert	Henry Kemble	Assignment
	BRIMSDON, Robert, see Robert Bronsdon		
1688, Oct. 26	BRONSDON, Robert	Nathaniel Fryer	Mortgage
	BRONSDON, Robert, see Robert Brimsdon		
1685, Nov. 10	BROUGHTON, Thomas and John Wincoll	Micum[Malcolm] Mackintyre	Release
1685, Oct. 19	BURRAGE, William	Joshua Scottow	Deed
	BURRELL, John, see Jane Pritchett		

Folio.	Description.
84	50 acres at Ware creek [in *Falmouth*], as part of his wife Mary's dowry.
47	Of all interests under his father William Dixon's will, subject to a gift to Dorothy Moore [in *York.*]
32	Plantation between Goodman Carter's and John Mayne's [in *North Yarmouth*].
74	30 acres on the south side of Casco river, as by town grant of and in *Falmouth*.
100	To pay £30 : 15.
101	Of all his estate, real and personal, wherever situate, to secure above bond.
99	Of Richard Selly's bond, *q. v.*
99	Of Richard Selly's mortgage, *q. v.*
139	Champernowne's island in *Kittery*, except 80 acres conveyed to John Hincks.
50	General and especial receipts for labor done at Salmon Falls mills at *Berwick*.
61	Marsh in *Scarborough* between the ditches of grantor and Andrew Brown.

INDEX OF GRANTEES.

Date.	Grantee.	Grantor.	Instrument.
1669, Mar. 25	CHADBORNE, Lucy and Francis Champernown Nicholas Shapleigh William Spencer Trustees	Thomas Wills	Bond
[1684, Jun. 28]	CHAMPERNOWN, Francis and Francis Raynes	Each other	Agreement
1685, June 25	CHAMPERNOWN, Francis	John Miller	Receipt
1685, June 26	CHAMPERNOWN, Francis	John Miller	Deposition
1684, May 19	CHAMPERNOWN, Mary	Francis Champernown	Deed
1684, July 8	CHAMPERNOWN, Mary and Elizabeth Cutts	Francis Champernown	Deed
1680, July 8 1683, Sept. 5	CLARKE, Thaddeus	Elizabeth Harvy	Assignment
1679, Aug. 4	CLARKE, Thomas	Roger Playstead's estate, by Wm. Playstead for self and att'y for joint adm'rs	Deed
[No date.]	[CLOYCE, John]	John Webber	Deposition
1678, June 18	CONLEY, Abraham, estate of	Humphrey Chadborne Wm. Playstead	Deposition
	COOLE, Nicholas, see James Oare		
1685, June 24	CORBEN, Robert, heirs of	George Ingersall	Deposition
1684, Sept. 22 1684, Oct. 12	COSSONS, John, assigns of	Edward Stephens	Depositions
	COUCH, Joseph, see Roger Dearing		

Folio.	Description.
51	In the nature of a marriage settlement, between the obligor and Lucy Chadborne.
12	Vesting in Raynes and his heirs, disputed land at Braveboat harbor [in *Kittery*].
42	For £36 in full satisfaction of a note of Champernown's, by mesne transfers now property of deponent.
42	As to the transfers of the above note, which, becoming property of deponent, had been satisfied by Champernown; the paper now lost or in the hands of George Pearson.
71	Half of Champernowne's island in *Kittery*.
12	The other half of Champernowne's island in *Kittery* to Mary for life, remainder of said half to Elizabeth, reserving life estate to himself.
12	Of Thomas Brackett's bond, *q. v.*
9	Quitclaiming premises mortgaged to Playstead, and John Hull by John Wincoll, recorded at folio 8.
24	That he voyaged to Boston with Cloyce.
67	As to the bounds of Conley's lands at Sturgeon creek in *Kittery*.
43	As to Corben's occupation and possession of meadow [in *Falmouth*].
24	As to deed of Sir Ferdinando Gorges to Cossons, and his occupation of two islands called by his name in *Casco Bay*.

INDEX OF GRANTEES.

Date.	Grantee.	Grantor.	Instrument.
1683, Apr. 6	CRAFFTS, William	Arthur Beale	Deed
1678, Aug. 2	CRICKE, Edward	Thomas Haynes et ux.	Deed
1688, May 20	CROCKETT, Ephraim	Thomas Crocket's estate, by Ann Jefory adm'x	Deed
1695, July —	CROCKET, Ephraim, estate of	Thomas Crocket's estate, by Ann Jeofrey, adm'x	Deed
1689, Feb. 28	CROCKET, Joseph and Dennis Hicks	Benjamin Woodbridge	Deed
1682, June 12	CURTIS, Joseph	Thomas Withers	Deed
1682, Nov. 7	CURTIS, Joseph	Henry Bodg	Deed
1684, Nov. 12	CURTIS, Joseph	John Hoole et ux.	Deed
	CUTTS, Elizabeth, see Mary Champernown		
1686, July 22	CUTT, Mary	Richard Cutt	Deed
1684, Feb. 11	CUTT, Richard	Samuel Shrimpton et ux.	Deed
1696, Oct. 19	CUTT, Richard	Francis Nichols et ux.	Deed
1696, Oct. 19	CUTT, Richard	Francis Avant	Deed
169$\frac{4}{5}$, Jan. 18	CUTT, Richard	Joshua Crocket	Deed
1694, June 28	CUTT, Robert	Richard Cutt	Deed

INDEX OF GRANTEES.

Folio.	Description.
29	21 acres at Braveboat harbor, near the bridge, south of William Moore's land, as per town grant of and in *York*.
19	200 acres upland and 5 acres marsh called Barberry marsh at Maquoit [in *Casco Bay*].
154	All lands lying on Crocket's neck, bounded in part by Spruce creek in *Kittery*.
155	80 acres at the head of Braveboat harbor in *Kittery* near the bridge.
121	36 acres between Crocket's creek and Ashen brook swamp in *Kittery*.
25	80 acres east of and near the head of Spruce creek in *Kittery*.
25	5 acres bounded north by Eastern creek, east by a highway, and Wilson's and Hammon's land; also 5 acres at the Pudding-hole, all in *Kittery*.
38	135 acres near Spruce creek in *Kittery*, part bought of Thomas Withers, and part by town grant.
68	20 acres at Broad cove in Spruce creek in *Kittery*.
82	800 acres between Spruce creek and Crooked lane in *Kittery* levied from the estate of Robert Cutt.
131	2 acres, 6 acres and 60 acres by town grant; also 8 acres by town grant to Jonathan Orris; also Richard Smith's house lot near Fort Loyal, all in *Falmouth*.
156	10 acres called Crocket's plain; also assigning right to conveyance of 20 acres town grant to Joshua Crocket; all in *Kittery*.
157	20 acres at Crocket's plain in *Kittery*, between grantee's and Ephraim Crocket's land.
132	Half of the land on which he dwelt in *Kittery*.

Date.	Grantee.	Grantor.	Instrument.
1684, Nov. 16	DAGGETT, William et ux.	Arthur Wormestall	Deed
1681, May 15	DANIEL, Thomas	Thomas Ryce et ux.	Deed
1687, Dec. 19	DAVIS, Richard	James Emery	Deed
1661, June 1	DAVIS, Sylvanus	John Parker	Deed
1684, Nov. 30	DAVIS, Sylvanus	John Parker	Deed
1685, Nov. 23	DAVIS, Sylvanus	Samuel Webber et ux.	Deed
1686, May 8	DAVIS, Sylvanus	William Burrage et ux.	Deed
	DAVIS, Sylvanus, see George Ingersoll, jun.		
1685, Dec. 30	DEARING, Henry	Francis Hooke	Mortgage
1686, May 21	DEARING, Henry	John Parker, sen.	Levy on execution
1689, June 11	DEARING, Roger and Joseph Couch	Joan Amerideth	Deed
1686, Apr. 27	DENNET, Alexander	Edward Gilman Stephen Paul et ux.	Deed
1698, May 2	DENNET, John	Isaac Remich	Deed
1698, May 2	DENNET, John	Isaac Remich	Bond
	DENNET, John, see Isaac Remich		

Index of Grantees.

Folio.	Description.
27	7 acres upland, 4 acres salt meadow, also half undivided of land bought of Thomas Williams, all in *Saco*.
51	One half in common of an island in Piscataqua river, between Strawberry Bank and Thomas Withers's house, and by him conveyed to his two daughters.
88	10 acres out of a town grant of 1688, in *Kittery*.
33	Land on Kennebec river between two rivulets three-quarters of a mile apart, thence across to Casco bay.
34	In confirmation of the above, on west side of Kennebec river.
74	One half in common of a saw mill and 100 acres on Long creek in *Falmouth*.
62	6½ acres marsh at Nonesuch marshes in *Scarborough*.
133	House and land on Piscataqua river, adjoining land formerly Nicholas Shapleigh's, and of him bought, in *Kittery*, also chattels.
61	2¼ acres by the highway westerly from the meeting-house in *York*.
145	6 acres between Diggory Jeofery and Clement Dearing at the Stepping Stones; also 44 acres adjoining John Bray; all in *Kittery*. This purports also to be John Ameredith's deed, but he does not sign it.
143	20 acres in *Kittery*, adjoining grantee's, Ayer's and Hill's lands.
119	House with 77 acres in *Kittery*, as by deeds from his father Christian Remich, and by town grants.
120	Conditioned to warrant the titles to above conveyance.

INDEX OF GRANTEES.

Date.	Grantee.	Grantor.	Instrument.
1666, Dec. 4	DILL, Daniel	Rowland Young et ux.	Deed
168⅚, Jan. 6	DONELL, Thomas and Samuel Bragdon	Each other	Reference and award
169⅔, Jan. 5	DORMAN, Ephraim, sen.	Timothy Dorman	Deed
1683, June 2	DOWNING, Joshua	Nic. Shapleigh's estate by Alice Shapleigh ad'x	Deed
169⅜, Jan. 4	DOWNING, Joshua	Christian Remich	Deposition
169⅜, Jan. 4	DOWNING, Joshua	Richard Rogers	Deposition
1682, Sept. 8	DWIGHT, Timothy	Margaret Montegues's estate by Sam'l Snow, ex.	Mortgage
1683, Apr. 2	ELLDRIDG, John	Francis Littlefield sen.	Deed
1683, Apr. 7	ELLIETT, Robert	Nathan Bedford's estate	Commis'r's report
1686, Apr. 2	ELLIOT, Robert	Humphrey Spencer et ux.	Deed
1688, Feb. 18	ELLIOT, Robert	William Hilton	Deed
1698, Aug. 20	ELLIOT, Robert	Robert Bronsdon by John Watson, attorney	Assignment
1695, Dec. 18	ELLIOT, Robert	Robert Jordan	Deed
[1698] Aug. 23	ELLIOT, Robert	Nathanie Fryer	Deed

Index of Grantees. 73

Folio.	Description.
159	10 acres at Bass cove in *York*.
53	Determining dividing line between their plantations [in *York*].
106	500 acres in *Coxhall* on Mousam river, part of the Symonds purchase.
144	20 acres in *Kittery*, 4 acres south of the highway, adjoining Thomas Jones, 16 acres north of highway, adjoining grantor and the Bay land.
151	That Dennis Downing lived on and possessed the farm now possessed by Joshua [in *Kittery*].
151	That Dennis Downing lived on and possessed the farm now possessed by Joshua [in *Kittery*].
10	100 acres adjoining Morgan Howells, also 100 acres on Kennebunk river, and the commons; also 100 acres more at the Desert marshes, all in *Cape Porpoise*.
39	156 acres at Ogunquit river falls and 11¼ acres marsh, in *Wells*.
67	Allowing claim of £25 : 3 : 8¼.
149	Town grant of 50 acres and 10 acres of swamp on Wilcox's pond brook; also two fifths in common of the Further marsh [in *Berwick*].
158	Quitclaiming house and land on west side York river between Yeales and Trafton; also farm stock, in *York*.
140	Of Nathaniel Fryer's mortgage of Champernowne's island and chattels in *Kittery* to Bronsdon to secure £485.
87	Of all his remaining rights being 500 or 600 acres at Cape Elizabeth in *Falmouth*, also rights in common to marsh on Spurwink river.
142	All his lands [half of *Cape Elizabeth*, see Book III. 69] except small parcels conveyed. See Elliot's bond to reconvey, *post* fol. 161.

Date.	Grantee.	Grantor.	Instrument.
Recorded 169$\frac{9}{8}$, Mar. 24	ELLIOT, Robert	Humphrey Spencer et ux.	Deed
169$\frac{9}{8}$, Feb. 7	EMERY, Daniel	Israel Hodsden et ux.	Deed
169$\frac{9}{8}$, Feb. 17	EMERY, Daniel	Israel Hodsden et ux.	Deed
	EMERY, Daniel, see James Emery jun.		
1686, Mar. 25	EMERY, James	Nathan Lord, jr.	Deposition
1686, Mar. 25	EMERY, James, sen.	Thomas Abbett James Emery, jr.	Deposition
1686, Mar. 25	EMERY, James, sen.	Thomas Abbett Benoni Hodgden	Deposition
1686, Mar. 25	EMERY, James, sen.	Daniel Goodine [Goodwin], jr.	Deposition
1686, Mar. 30	EMERY, James, sen.	Daniel Stone	Deposition
	EMERY, James see John Wincoll		
169$\frac{9}{8}$, Mar. 1	EMERY, James, jun. and Daniel Emery Job Emery	James Emery, sr.	Deed
	EMERY, Job, see James Emery, jun.		
	ENDICOTT, John, see George Ingersoll, jun.		
1696, Nov. 16	ENGORSEL [Ingersoll] John	Elihu Gunnison	Deed
1675, Feb. 29	ETHERINGTON, Mary, Wm. Spencer, trustee of Patience Etherington	John Wincoll	Deed
	ETHERINGTON, Patience, see Mary Etherington		

Index of Grantees.

Folio.	Description.
103	30 acres at Newichewannock [in *Kittery*] bounded by lands of Daniel Goodwin, Capt. Wincoll, Moses Spencer and Eliakim Hutchinson.
98	12 acres bounded by Etherington, Gowen, Harris and Hodsden; also 50 acres near the Third hill, all in *Kittery*.
103	Re-record of the above.
56	As to John Roberts, junior's acknowledgment of the bounds between him and Emery.
55	Concerning Emery's possession of part of the "Fowling Marsh," in *Berwick*, and counter claim by John Roberts, jr.
55	As to location of fence between Emery's and John Roberts's land in *Berwick*.
56	As to controversy between Emery and John Roberts, jun., over marsh in *Berwick*.
56	As to controversy between Emery and John Roberts, jun., about right to cut hay on marsh claimed by Emery [in *Berwick*].
105	60 acres in *Kittery* [Berwick] between Rocky hill, Stony brook, and lands of Gooden, Nock and Plaisted, equally to each, but if Job default in payment, in halves to James and Daniel, reserving for seven years right to demand estate for life to grantor.
97	20 acres adjoining Richard Endle at Spruce creek in *Kittery*.
86	By way of marriage settlement, with remainder over to Patience, several tracts in *Kittery* aggregating 209 acres.

Index of Grantees.

Date.	Grantee.	Grantor.	Instrument.
1662, June 20	ETHERINGTON, Thomas et ux.	Thomas Spencer et ux.	Deed
1664, Oct. 20	ETHERINGTON, Thomas	John Gattinsby et ux.	Deed
	FABES, John, see Bryan Pendleton		
1697, Sept. 17	FERNALD, James	John Seward et ux.	Deed
1696, Nov. 30	FERNALD, Samuel	Richard Jose et ux.	Deed
1683, June 13	FERRIS, Aaron	Elihu Crockett	Deed
1683, Aug. 4	FERRIS, Aaron	Ephraim Crockett	Acknowledgment
1683, Aug. 4	FERRIS, Aaron	Ann Jeffery	Acknowledgment
1685, Aug. 12	FOLSAM [Foullsum], Peter	John Wadleigh et ux.	Deed
1685, Aug. 12	FOLSAM [Foullsum], Peter	Rob't Wadleigh, sen. et ux. John Wadleigh	Deed
	FORGISSON, Mary, see William Furbush		
1684, Dec. 8	FREATHY, James	John Davess	Deed
	FREATHY, John, see Samuel Freathy		
1683, Dec. 4	FREATHY, Samuel and John Freathy	William Freathy et ux.	Deed
169¾, Feb. 28	FRYER, Joshua	Nathaniel Fryer	Assignment
1674, Apr. 17	FRYER, Nathaniel	Henry Sayword	Mortgage

INDEX OF GRANTEES. 77

Folio.	Description.
84	12 acres, part of town grant of 200 acres in Unity parish, [*Kittery*].
85	12 acres in Unity parish [*Kittery*] conveyed grantor by Thomas Spencer.
110	20 acres in the Great cove below the Boiling rock in *Kittery*.
102	One half in common of town grant of 20 acres to Joseph Alcock in *Kittery*.
1	20 acres between Spruce creek and another creek, adjoining Joseph Crockett's, reserving a highway, in *Kittery*.
1	Quitclaim to above property.
1	Quitclaim to land in *Kittery* conveyed to grantee by Elihu Crocket, *q. v.*
63	One third part of a farm in *Wells* formerly his grandfather's John Wadleigh's, as by gift from his father Robert Wadleigh.
63	One sixth part of the farm of John Wadleigh in *Wells*.
30	12½ acres at Bass cove on the north east of the path to the marshes adjoining William Dixon in *York*.
5	Parts of his farm [in *York*] in severalty, part in common to be divided, reserving life estate to themselves.
82	Of Henry Sayword's mortgage of 370 acres on southwest side of York river in *York*.
82	350 acres upland and 20 acres swamp, on south west side of York river, as by town grant of and in *York*.

INDEX OF GRANTEES.

Date.	Grantee.	Grantor.	Instrument.
1679, July 14	FRYER, Nathaniel	Robert Jordan, jun.	Deed
1684, Oct. 29	FRYER, Nathaniel, sen.	John Parrett	Mortgage
1698, Aug. 24	FRYER, Nathaniel	Rob't Bronsdon by John Watson, attorney	Release
1698, Aug. 24	FRYER, Nathaniel	Robert Elliot	Bond
	FRYER, Nathaniel, see Samuel Shrympton		
	FROST, Charles, see Nicholas Frost's estate		
1682, May 29	FROST, Nicholas, estate of and Charles Frost	Stephen Jenkins Jabez Jenkins	Deposition
1680, Apr. 12	FURBUSH, William and Mary Forgisson	Each other	Reference and award
1689, July 13	FUZ, Allen	Robert Elliot	Deed
1695, June 11	FUZ, Allen	Robert Elliot	Deed
1662, June 25	GATTINSBY, John et ux.	Thomas Spencer et ux.	Deed
1681, July 12	GENDALL, Walter	Bartho. Gidney	Deed
	GILLISON, John, see Moses Abbet		
1684, July 17	GIDNEY, Bartholomew	Water Gendall	Deed
	GODINE, James, see Thomas Goddin		
1683, July 14	GODDIN, Thomas James Godine	Daniel Goddine [Goodwin], sr.	Deed

INDEX OF GRANTEES.

Folio.	Description.
141	One half in common of tract of land between the Long Sands and Great pond, at Cape Elizabeth [in *Falmouth*], also his rights to marsh on Spurwink river.
26	House, land, boats and appurtenances at Cape Elizabeth.
141	General discharge.
161	Conditioned to extend the time for the payment of a mortgage by Fryer, in case of obligor's prior death. See *ante* fol. 142.
67	As to bound marks of a parcel of land near the Cedars at Sturgeon creek, in *Kittery*.
35	Fixing division line between their home lots [in *Kittery*].
103	30 acres at Newichewannock in *Berwick*, conveyed to grantor by Humphrey Spencer et ux. *q. v.*
149	50 acres near Wilcock's pond; also two-fifths in common of the "further marsh," all in *Berwick*, conveyed to grantor by Humphrey Spencer et ux. *q. v.*
84	12 acres, part of town grant of 200 acres in Unity parish [*Kittery*].
75	The tract in *North Yarmouth* bought by Thomas Stephens of the Indians.
76	Quitclaim to lands [in *North Yarmouth* conveyed grantor by grantee, Book III. 96].
21	30 acres in *Berwick* bought of James Grant, with reservations.

Index of Grantees.

Date.	Grantee.	Grantor.	Instrument.
1667, Feb. 3	Gooch, James	Wm. Hammond et ux. Jona. Hammond	Deed
1696, June 16	Goodrich, Isaac	Samuel King	Deed
1643, July 18	Gorgeana, town of	Sir Ferdinando Gorges, by Thos. Gorges, dep.gov.	Deed
1686, Dec. 30	Gowell, Richard	Richard King et ux.	Deed
1697, Nov. 22	Gowell, Richard	John Hanscom's estate by Ann Hanscom, ad'x	Deed
	Gowen, John, see Nicholas Gowen		
169$\frac{8}{9}$, Feb. 27	Gowen, Nicholas and John Gowen *alias* Smith	Each other	Partition
1695, July —	Greenleafe, Enoch	John Morton et ux.	Deed
1695, June 15	Gunnison, Elihu	Samuel Cutt	Deed
1697, Apr. 2	Gunnison, Elihu	John Pickerin	Discharge
1684, June 2	Haley, Andrew et ux.	Gowen Wilson	Deed
1683, Dec. 3	Hammond, Joseph	William Goodhue, sen.	Power of attorney
169$\frac{4}{5}$, Feb. 8	Hammond, Joseph, sen.	Nathan Lord's estate by Martha Lord, adm'x	Deed
1661, Nov. 10	Hammond, William	Robert Nanney	Deed
1671, June 2	Harvy, Elizabeth	Thomas Brackett	Bond

Index of Grantees.

Folio.	Description.
128	Land and marsh in *Wells* conveyed by Robert Nanny, and by him bought of Mr. Cole.
88	34 acres at Mast cove on Piscataqua river, formerly his father William King's, by gift from his grandfather, William Palmer, and also by town grant, in *Kittery*.
46	Neck of land at the harbor's mouth, except Rev. Mr. Burdett's 20 acres; marsh at Braveboat harbor; all marsh and islands south of Gorgeana river; reserving the timber and right to set the fishermen by the shore.
158	3 acres upon Great cove, below Thomas Spinney's in *Kittery*.
159	20 acres by town grant of and in *Kittery*.
104	Of land in *Berwick* above the county road, near Rocky hill adjoining the brook from Broughton's swamp.
136	100 acres and meadow appurtenant, at Dunstan in *Scarborough*, bought of John Howell.
106	Three parcels aggregating 154 acres, at Goose cove in Spruce creek in *Kittery*.
107	Of the mortgage recorded at folio 107.
87	11 acres at Spruce creek, part of town grant by and in *Kittery*.
3	To take possession of and sell the land in *Kittery* mortgaged by William Oliver. See Book II. 149.
149	6 acres more or less of meadow, at Sturgeon creek in *Kittery*.
127	Tract 25 poles wide, between Main creek and Mussel ridge, in *Wells*.
12	For support and maintenance.

Index of Grantees.

Date.	Grantee.	Grantor.	Instrument.
	Hicks, Dennis, see Joseph Crocket		
1686, Sept. 18	Hill, John	Ambrose Berry	Deed
1693, Oct. 31	Hill, John	Robert Bronsdon [Brimsdon]	Assignment
1693, Oct. 31	Hill, John	Robert Bronsdon [Brimsdon]	Assignment
1693, Oct. 31	Hill, John	Robert Bronsdon [Brimsdon]	Assignment
	Hill, John, see Francis Backchouse		
1696, Oct. 19	Hill, Joseph	Samuel Miller et ux.	Deed
169$\frac{4}{5}$, Feb. 15	Hill, Joseph	Grace Banfield et ux.	Deed
169$\frac{5}{6}$, Mar. 6	Hill, Joseph	John Hill	Assignment
1680, May 12	Hinks, John	Margaret Jocelyn et ux.	Assignment
1669, Aug. 24	Hinxen[Hinkeson],Peter	Joshua Scottow	Deed
1668, Aug. 1	Hinkeson, Peter	Joshua Scottow	Deed
169$\frac{7}{8}$, Feb. 25	Holmes, Thomas, estate of	Walter Allin	Release
1685, Feb. 9	Hooke, Mary	Francis Hooke	Bill of sale
169$\frac{6}{7}$, Jan. 25	Hubbord, Philip	James Emery, sr. et ux.	Deed
1671, Apr. 6	Hull, John and Roger Playstead	John Wincoll	Mortgage

Index of Grantees.

Folio.	Description.
161	License to build and maintain two mill dams upon grantor's land, across Bulley's creek in *Saco*.
99	Of Richard Selly's mortgage of lands in *Saco* to Henry Kemble to secure £14.
99 100	Of Richard Selly's bond to Brimsdon to pay £30 : 15 : 2.
101	Of Richard Selly's mortgage of all his estate to Brimsdon, to secure the above bond.
90	30 acres and house formerly granted by and in *Kittery* to his father, Richard Miller.
91	Quitclaim of dower in land in *Kittery*, sold to Hill by Samuel Miller et ux. *q. v.*
102	Of the bonds and mortgages by Richard Zelly [Selly] assigned to assignor by Robert Brimsdon [Bronsdon], *q. v.*
69	Of Nathan Bedford's promissory note, *q. v.*
40	10 acres marsh near Pine tree creek in *Scarborough*.
40	23 acres upland at Black Point in *Scarborough*, with certain restrictions and quit rent reserved. Executed Aug. 9, 1676.
110	General discharge, and receipt for marriage portion of his wife Mary.
53	Of negroes, Thomas and Hannah.
96	40 acres on the main river in *Berwick*, between Dan'l Goodwin, jun., and John Plaisted, or Birchen point, reserving four rods square for a burying ground; also all right in the "Fowling marsh."
8	2 saw mills and appurtenances at Salmon falls in *Kittery*, with timber rights, &c.

Date.	Grantee.	Grantor.	Instrument.
1685, Nov. 11	HULL, John, estate of	John Broughton	Deed
1684, Jan. 20	HUNNIWELL, Richard	Sarah Jordan Robert Jordan	Deed
1694, Nov. 3	HUNNIWELL, Richard	Jos. Whinnick's estate, by Sarah Whinnick, ad'x	Deed
1684, Sept. 18	HUTCHINSON, Eliakim	Berwick parish	Bond
1687, Dec. 16	HUTCHINSON, Eliakim	Robert Tufton Mason	Deed
knowledged 1687, Mar. 12	HUTCHINSON, Eliakim	John Tufton	Release
	HUTCHINSON, Eliakim, see Samuel Shrympton		
	INGERSOLL, see Engorsel		
168¾, Mar. 18	INGERSOLL, George jun. and John Ingersoll John Phillips Sylvanus Davis John Endicott James Inglish	George Ingersoll et ux.	Deed
	INGERSOLL, John, see George Ingersoll, jun.		
	INGLISH, James, see George Ingersoll, jun.		
1678, Feb. 10	JENKINS, Jabez	Renold Jenkins	Deed

INDEX OF GRANTEES.

Folio.	Description.
53	Quitclaim to the eighth part of the two saw mills, &c., in *Berwick*, mortgaged Book III. 47.
80	10 acres of marsh on Black Point river in *Scarborough*.
80	46 acres on Black Point river and Bass creek in *Scarborough*.
5	To maintain Rev. John Emerson, or some other settled minister, or in default thereof to reconvey 10 acres land donated by Hutchinson.
151	500 acres on both sides Little Newichewannock river in *Kittery*, and parcels of marsh formerly granted by town of Kittery to Hutchinson, or George or Richard Leader, reserving an annual quit-rent.
153	Of all rights in land conveyed by his father Robert Tufton Mason, *q. v.*
72	One-half in common of grantor's part of Nonesuch meadow in *Scarborough*.
60	Two pieces of salt marsh on each side Sturgeon creek [in *Kittery*].

Date.	Grantee.	Grantor.	Inst
1684, Oct. 13	JENKINS, Jabez	Henry Pouning's [Pounding] est., by Elizabeth Pouning, adm'x Elizabeth Bridgham et ux. Sarah Pouning Daniel Pouning	Deed
1684, Oct. 13	JENKINS, Jabez	Henry Pouning's estate by Elizabeth Pouning, administratrix Elizabeth Bridgham et ux. Mary Pouning Sarah Pouning Daniel Pouning	Deed
169$\frac{5}{6}$, Feb. 6	JENKINS, Jabez	Alexander Forgisson et ux. Dan. Emery et ux. Elizabeth Gowen *alias* Smith	Deed
1679, Aug. 24	JOCELYN, Margaret	Nathan Bedford	Prom. note
1685, Apr. 5	JOHNSON, James	John Shapleigh	Deed
1685, June 23	JORDAN, Robert heirs or assigns of	John Smyth, sen.	Deposition
1684, May 23	JOY, Susanna et ux.	William Spencer	Deed
1691, June 13 1691, July 23 1692, Nov. 9	KANE, Nathaniel	John Shapleigh	Receipts(3)
1684, July 7	KELLY, Roger and James Blagdon	Humphrey Davie, by Wm. Goodhue, sen. and David Wilde, agents	Receipts(2)
1686, June 1	KELLY, Roger	Francis Wanewright	Deed

INDEX OF GRANTEES. 87

Folio.	Description.
27	6 acres as by town grant of and in *Kittery* between lands of John Whitte and Anthony Emery. Mary Pouning is named as a grantor, but does not sign.
28	By same description, evidently to cure defect of Mary's not signing the above.
97	11 acres adjoining the main river and Sturgeon creek; also 49 acres on Sturgeon creek near Bear cove in *Kittery*.
69	To pay £21 : 10.
57	One fourth in common of his saw mill and corn mill and appurtenances in *Kittery*.
41	That being marshal of the province, he levied execution in favor of Jordan upon a neck of land in *Saco*, as property of Richard Vines.
11	3½ acres by the highway to Hutchinson's mill in *Berwick*.
111	Together in full for land sold at Spruce creek [in *Kittery*].
13	For an anchor and cable.
64	House, land and appurtenances on Smuttynose island, *Isles of Shoals*.

Index of Grantees.

Date.	Grantee.	Grantor.	Instrument.
1698, July 23	KELLY, Roger	George Litten's estate, by Richard King, surviving exec'r Mary King et ux. Sarah Lary	Deed
1670, May 9	KEMBLE, Henry	Richard Selly	Bond
1670, Dec. 7	KEMBLE, Henry	Richard Selly	Mortgage
1696, June 17	KING, Samuel	Sarah King	Deed
1695, Jan. 14	KITTERY, town of	Town of York	Survey
1676, July 27	KNIGHT, Samuel	Richard Kirle	Deed
168¾, Mar. 18	LAMPRILL, Henry	Thomas Curtis	Deed
1671, Mar. 25	LEIGHTON, William, assigns of	William Everitt	Acknowledgment
1674, Nov. 23	LEIGHTON, William, assigns of	William Everitt's estate by Martha Lawd, ad'x	Acknowledgment
Recorded 1684, Mar. 14	LEIGHTON, William	Martha Lord et ux.	Acknowledgment
1674, May 13	[LEIGHTON, William]	Abraham Conley John Whitte	Deposition
1682, June 23	LEIGHTON, William	Martha Lord	Deposition
1683, June 23	LEIGHTON, William	Thomas Turner	Deposition
1683, June 23	LEIGHTON, William, assigns of	Renald Ginkens [Jenkins]	Deposition
1683, July 23	LEIGHTON, William	Thos. Hunscum	Deposition

INDEX OF GRANTEES. 89

Folio.	Description.
138	10 acres and house at Crooked Lane in *Kittery*.
99	To pay 10,000 feet of merchantable pine boards.
99	In form of a bond to secure £14, of house and land at Winter Harbor in *Saco*.
89	All title to her father William King's land in *Kitttery* by gift from William Palmer, and by town grant.
93	Of the dividing line between the towns.
72	6 acres, part of a town grant at Great cove in *Kittery*. In a postcript grantor attempts to revoke this conveyance.
7	10 acres fronting York river adjoining Bass cove and the road to Scotland in *York*.
5	Quitclaiming land in *Kittery* conveyed by Isaac Nash et ux. [Book 1. I. 75].
5	Quitclaiming the above property.
5	Quitclaiming the above property.
56	As to Renald Jenkins's purchase and occupation of six acres in *Kittery* [afterwards by mesne conveyances Leighton's].
56	As to her mother Margaret Everett's buying 6 acres in *Kittery*, of Renald Jenkins, and selling same to Leighton.
56	As to Dennis Downing's possession of 6 acres, afterward Leighton's in *Kittery*.
56	As to his purchase, occupation and sale of land in *Kittery* afterward by mesne conveyances William Leighton's.
57	As to location of fence between lands of Joshua Downing and Leighton in *Kittery*.

INDEX OF GRANTEES.

Date.	Grantee.	Grantor.	Instrument.
1685, Nov. 25	LEWIS, Peter	Jane Withers Elizab'th Withers	Deed
1683, Apr. 2	LITTLEFIELD, Francis, sr.	Joseph Cross et ux.	Deed
1685, July 9	LIVEINGSTOONE, Daniel and Joanna Liveingstone and children not named	Each other	Agreement
	LIVEINGSTONE, Joanna, and children not named, see Dan'l Liveingstoone		
1697, Apr. 20	LORD, Nathan	Sylvanus Nock et ux.	Deed
1662, Nov. 7	LORD, Nathan, sen.	John Neale	Deed
1684, Apr. 28	MACGOWEN, John	George Jeffray	Power of attorney
168$\frac{2}{3}$, Jan. 26	MARAUGH [Morrough], Dennis	George Munjoy's estate, by Mary Lawrence ad'x	Deed
1683, Oct. 16	MARTINE, Edward	Rowland Young et ux.	Deed
1684, May 15	MAYNE, John	John Cossons	Deposition
1684, June 9	MAYNE, John	Richard Carter	Deposition
1684, June 28	MAYNE, John	Massachusetts, by Thos. Danforth, president	Executive order
[No date]	MAYNE, John	Massachusetts, by Thos. Danforth, president	Executive order
1639, Mar. 18	MESSANT, Ann	George Burdett	Mortgage

INDEX OF GRANTEES.   91

Folio.	Description.
86	Lot 69 by 20 rods adjoining grantee's lot in *Kittery*.
38	Five parcels aggregating 176½ acres in *Wells*, most bordering Ogunquit river.
45	To unite in improving 40 acres land in *York;* after death of Joanna to be divided in halves between Daniel and three children not named.
109	18 acres near Rocky hill in *Berwick* adjoining lands of grantee, John Plaisted and Zachariah Emery, by gift from James Emery, Nock's father-in-law.
129	25 acres and house and 5 acres marsh, near White's marsh in *Kittery*.
9	General power.
35	50 acres at Ware creek in *Falmouth*, conveyed by Elizabeth Harvey to Thomas Brackett.
13	Dwelling house and appurtenances on Smuttynose island, *Isles of Shoals*.
11	As to Mayne's possession of marsh on Sysquissett creek [in *North Yarmouth*].
11	As to Mayne's possession of marsh in Sysquissett creek [in *North Yarmouth*].
28	Confirming to John Mayne, land possessed and improved by him at Casco, [in *North Yarmouth*.]
29	Re-record of the above.
20	Farm and stock [in *York*] to secure £112.

Index of Grantees.

Date.	Grantee.	Grantor.	Instrument.
1675, June 29	Mills, John	Henry Watts	Deposition
1679, July 29	Mills, John	George Tayler et ux.	Deed
1681, July 13	Mills, John	John Howell	Deposition
1681, July 25	Mills, John	George Tayler	Deposition
1685, July 25	Mills, John	Wm. Burrage	Deposition
168$\frac{2}{3}$, Mar. 20	Mills, John	Andrew Tayler [Taylour]	Release
168$\frac{2}{3}$, Mar. 20	Mills, John	Andrew Tayler	Deed
168$\frac{2}{3}$, Mar. 22	Mills, John	Andrew Tayler	Power of attorney
1664, July 18	Mills, Mary and her children not named	John Wadleigh	Deed
1683, April 16	Mills, Mary and her children not named	John Wadleigh's estate by Robert Wadleigh, adm'r	Deed
1685, Apr. 15	Moore, William	Francis Champernown	Deed
1684, Aug. 6	Mo(o)rey, Nicholas	Robert Gibbs's estate by Elizab'th Corwine, adm'x, by Jona. Corwine, agent	Power of attorney
1685, Feb. 2	Mo(o)rey, Nicholas	Margaret Mountegue's estate by Samuel Snow, executor	Deed

INDEX OF GRANTEES. 93

Folio.	Description.
43	As to Mills's possession and occupation of marsh on Nonesuch river [in *Scarborough*].
59	Plantation and island of marsh [in *Scarborough*].
43	As to Mills's occupancy of marsh by the river and path to Nonesuch [in *Scarborough*].
43	As to Mills's warning Anthony Libby not to cut hay on his marsh [in *Scarborough*].
43	As to Mills's possession of marsh [in *Scarborough*] and warning trespassers.
59	General discharge as heir to his father, George Tayler, and receipt of consideration for land sold.
59	Confirmation of land sold by his father George Tayler, *q. v.*; also 30 acres of meadow on Pigsty river, and elsewhere in Black Point [*Scarborough*].
60	To take possession of land sold by his father Geo. Tayler, *q. v.*
64	House lot and marsh on Webhannet river in *Wells*.
64	Confirmation of the above deed.
36	Quitclaim to two acres marsh bought by Moore of Ann Godfrey, northeast of Braveboat harbor [in *York*].
49	General power, with substitution.
61	100 acres formerly Griffin Montague's; also 50 acres, the Neck, formerly Morgan Howell's, in *Cape Porpoise*.

Index of Grantees.

Date.	Grantee.	Grantor.	Instrument.
1692, Mar. 26	MORRELL, John	Charles Adams	Deed
1696, Mar. 30	MORRELL, John	Temperance Adams	Deed
1696, Nov. 13	MORRELL, John	Charles Adams's estate, by Temperance Adams administratrix	Release
1696, Nov. 17	MORRELL, John, sen.	Town of Kittery	Survey
169$\frac{3}{3}$, Feb. 8	MORRELL, Nicholas	Richard Estis et ux.	Deed
1684, June 5	MOWLTON, Jeremiah and Joseph Mowlton	Thomas Mowlton et ux.	Conditional deed
1685, July 25	MOWLTON, Jeremiah and others	Robert Nanney's estate by Katherine Nanney, *alias* Nayler executrix, by Edward Rishworth attorney	Caution
1694, July 23	MOWLTON, Jeremiah	Ezekiel Rogers	Deed
1685, Apr. 10	MOWLTON, Joseph MOWLTON, Joseph see Jeremiah Mowlton	John Twisden Samuel Twisden Susanna Twisden	Deed
1684, June 5	MOWLTON, Thomas et ux.	Jere. Mowlton Joseph Mowlton	Agreement
1695, June 28	MUGRIDG, John	Richard Cutt	Deed
1668, Oct. 13	MUNJOY, George	Thomas Brackett	Deed
1670, July 21	MUNJOY, George	Mary Brackett	Deed
169$\frac{4}{5}$, Feb. 18	NOWELL, Peter	Joseph Banks	Deed

INDEX OF GRANTEES. 95

Folio.	Description.
92	Land in *Kittery* near Sturgeon creek, received as marriage portion of his wife, Temperance, from Philip Benmore and by him bought of James Emery.
92	Quitclaim of all her rights to property described above.
93	General discharge.
93	40 acres near the head of Sturgeon creek.
123	40 acres on Piscataqua river in *Kittery*, adjoining Alex. Dennet, as by deed from William Racklift.
60	All his estate real and personal in *York*, with reservations for support of self and wife.
43	Claiming title to Mr. Gorges's neck in *York*.
109	House and 31 acres in four parcels on York river, adjoining Eliakim Hutchinson and John Braun in *York*.
58	120 acres, as by town grant, on the country highway and the brook near Philip Adams's house lot, in *York*.
61	Accepting conditions of Thomas Mowlton's deed, *q. v.*
112	Land between Spruce creek, Broad cove, mill creek and Scriven's land in *Kittery*.
34	50 acres in *Falmouth* adjoining Ware creek.
35	Quitclaim to the above.
107	10 acres northeast of the river, between it and the highway, and lands of Daniel Dill and Henry Lamprill, in *York*.

Index of Grantees.

Date.	Grantee.	Grantor.	Instrument.
1695, Oct. 14	Nowell, Peter	Richard Coman	Deed
1684, Aug. 15	Oare, James Henry Brown Nicholas Coole	Nicholas Morey	Discharge
1684, July 15	Parker, John	Richard Wharton	Deed
1669, July 31	Pearson, George	Walter Barefoote	Assignment
1684, Jan. 3 1684, Feb. 16	Pearson, George	John Mayne Elizabeth Mayne	Deposition
1685, June 22	Pearson, George	Samuel Snow	Power of attorney
1685, —— 15	Pearson, George	Timothy Dwight	Letter
1685, Aug. 24	Pearson, George	Timothy Dwight	Power of attorney
1686, Mar. 15	Pendleton, Brian John Fabes	Francis Champernowne	Deed
	Penwill, John, see Samuel Shrympton		
1698, Apr. 4	Pepperrell, William	Edward Sergent	Deed
1698, July 18	Pepperrell, William	John Brawn et ux.	Deed
169$\frac{8}{9}$, Jan. 2	Pepperrell, William	Joseph Crocket et ux.	Deed
169$\frac{8}{9}$, Jan. 5	Pepperrell, William	Matthew Austine et ux.	Mortgage
	Phillips, John see George Ingersall, jun.		

Index of Grantees.

Folio.	Description.
108	10 acres northeast of York river above Bass cove, adjoining Freethee and Nowell in *York*.
61	Of claims growing out of the transactions at the mill at Mousam [in *Wells*].
17	Tract 6 miles in length between Casco bay and Kennebec adjoining Winnegance creek.
30	Of a bond of Francis Champernowne's to pay £40.
31	That 60 acres of land sold by Richard Bray to Pearson, adjoining deponent at Mayne's point [in *North Yarmouth*], had been occupied 35 years or more.
50	General and especially to manage property at *Cape Porpoise*.
50	About negotiations for purchase of land formerly Morgan Howell's at *Cape Porpoise*.
50	To collect debts, especially of Samuel Snow at *Cape Porpoise*.
94	Quitclaim to 100 acres at Sturgeon creek in *Kittery*, sold grantees by Francis Morgan et ux.
124	One half in common of 80 acres on the sea, of 15 acres of meadow, of 10 acres of meadow in two parcels, all at Winter Harbor and Little river in *Saco*.
130	Half an acre bounded by the sea and land of grantee in *Kittery*.
150	45 acres upland and meadow adjoining Jeofferys, Dearing, and the commons, as by town grants, in *Kittery*.
146	All his lands, formerly his father's, Matthew Austine, sen.'s, west of the new mill creek, adjoining the bridge in *York*.

Date.	Grantee.	Grantor.	Instrument.
1683, June 11	PICKERIN, John	Elihu Gunnison	Mortgage
1688, June 11	PICKERIN, John	Elihu Gunnison	Mortgage
169$\frac{8}{9}$, Feb. 22	PICKERIN, John, jr.	Robert Elleot	Deed
1699, Mar. 31	PLAISTED, James	John Davis	Deed
	PLAISTED, Roger, see John Hull		
1685, June 13	PREBLE, Joseph	Peter Weare John Twisden	Deposition
1674, Nov. 14	PRITCHETT, Jane and their son and daughter Richard Pritchett John Burrell	John Pritchett	Conditional deed
	PRITCHETT, Richard, see Jane Pritchett		
	PURRINGTON, John, see Samuel Shrympton		
1691, Nov. 5	RACKLIFF, John et ux.	Thomas Trafton	Deed
1681, Jan. 18	RAYNE, Joseph	William Furbush Thomas Rhodes	Prom. note
1684, July 8	RAYNES, Francis and Nathaniel Raynes	Alice Shapleigh	Deed
	RAYNES, Francis, see Nathaniel Raynes		
	RAYNES, Francis, see Francis Champernown		
1684, July 8	RAYNES, Nathaniel and Francis Raynes	Francis Raynes et ux.	Deed
1684, July 8	RAYNES, Nathaniel and Francis Raynes	Francis Champernowne	Deed

INDEX OF GRANTEES.

Folio.	Description.
6	House and land at Spruce creek, *Kittery*, and 4 acres more bought of William Adams.
107	Re-record of the above, made when the indorsed discharge was left for record.
121	Three parcels at Black point, *Scarborough*, on Nonesuch river.
154	Land at new mill creek between Thomas Moulton and Edward Rishworth [in *York*].
46	That 15 acres in *York*, originally William Johnson's, are now Joseph Preble's by mesne conveyances.
36	Lands and chattels at *Sagadahoc* to wife and to son and daughter in equal shares, except a neck of land to brother Richard, conditioned upon their joining him, or coming to look after the premises, otherwise all the premises to Burrell.
79	20 acres at Rogers cove in *York*.
6	Joint and several to pay £16:1:7.
20	Farm formerly Ann Godfrey's in *York*.
21	The farm they live on [in *York*], life estate to Nathaniel, remainder to Francis, reserving life estate to themselves.
21	Quitclaim to farm [at Braveboat harbor in *Kittery*], conveyed grantees by Capt. Francis Raynes.

Date.	Grantee.	Grantor.	Instrument.
	RAYNES, Nathaniel, see Francis Raynes		
1694, Mar. 30	REMICH, Isaac	Christian Remich	Deed
1694, June 20	REMICH, Isaac	Christian Remich	Deed
1694, June 20	REMICH, Isaac	Abraham Remich	Deed
1698, May 2	REMICH, Isaac and John Dennet	Christian Remich	Deed
1684, Nov. 4	RENDLE, Peter	John Renalds	Deed
1683, May 25 1683, June 20 1683, Nov. 13	RISHWORTH, Edward	John Cutt's estate by Reuben Hull, agent of John Cutt, executor	Receipts(3)
1683, Dec. 21	RISHWORTH, Edward	Town of York	Survey
	RISHWORTH, Edward, see Samuel Shrympton		
1687, May 25	ROGERS, Richard	James Gibbons	Deed
1697, Dec. 24	ROGERS, Richard, jr.	Richard Cutt et ux.	Deed
1683, Sept. 1	SANDERS, William	Town of Kittery	Survey
1684, May 26	SARGEANT, Edward	Pendleton Fletcher	Deed
1684, Oct. 17	SARGEANT, Edward	Dominicus Jordan et ux. David Trustrum	Deed
1695, July 1	SARGEANT, Edward	Ralph Trustrum's estate by Dominicus Jordan, administrator	Deed

Folio.	Description.
89	10 acres on the east side of Great cove in *Kittery*, being part of three town grants.
89	20 acres on the river in *Kittery* adjoining grantor, Spinney and Shapleigh.
90	Quitclaim to 20 acres in *Kittery* conveyed by Christian Remich to grantee, folio 89, *q. v.*
120	Quitclaim to the above two tracts releasing the entail.
29	100 acres, the former plantation of his father, William Renalds, 127 rods up the river from Peter Turbett's former plantation in *Cape Porpoise*.
30	Upon account.
28	74 acres as by town grant of April 22, 1661.
155	200 acres along the sea shore next Goosefair river in *Saco*.
157	30 acres called Crocket's plain in *Kittery*.
24	30 acres adjoining the commons, land of Francis Blachford and Captain Frost.
45	Land at Winter Harbor, *Saco*, formerly Simon Booth's.
44	House and lot adjoining John Sargeant and 5 acres marsh near Little river, in *Saco*.
94	100 acres and 25 acres meadow in two parcels at Winter Harbor in *Saco*.

INDEX OF GRANTEES.

Date.	Grantee.	Grantor.	Instrument.
1697, April 22	SARGEANT, Edward	John Taylor	Deed
1685, May 19	SARGEANT, John	John Giffard	Deed
1682, Nov. 3	SAWYER, William	John Smyth, sen. et ux.	Deed
1684, Aug. 11	SAWYER, William	John Wadleigh	Release
1685, Aug. 7	SAWYER, William	John Young et ux.	Deed
1685, Aug. 12	SAWYER, William	Rob't Wadleigh, sen., et ux. John Wadleigh	Deed
1680, Dec. 10	SAYWORD, John	Town of York	Conditional grant
1684, Dec. 3	SAYWORD, John	John Smith, sen.	Deed
168⅘, Mar. 24	SAYWORD, Jonathan	Benj. Whitney et ux.	Deed
	SAYWORD, Jonathan, see Mary Austine		
1673, Nov. 15	SCRIVINE, William	William Seely's estate by Elizabeth Seely, administratrix	Deed
1686, July 22	SCRIVINE, William	Richard Cutt	Deed
1683, Aug. 20	SHAPLEIGH, Alice and John Shapleigh	Each other	Arbitration and award
1684, July 10	SHAPLEIGH, Alice	Francis Raynes Nathaniel Raynes	Mortgage

Folio.	Description.
117	200 acres at Salmon falls; also three town grants aggregating 60 acres and 33 acres of swamp, formerly William Love's [in *Berwick*].
42	60 acres in two parcels and 6 acres meadow at Winter Harbor in *Saco*.
4	80 acres and 8 acres meadow in *Wells* at Little river, which came to his wife Mary from her father George Farrow.
48	Quitclaim to one third part of farm in *Wells*, conveyed by John Young et ux.
47	One third in common of a farm in *Wells*, conveyed by Robert Wadleigh, *q. v.*
45	One sixth part of the farm of John Wadleigh in *Wells*.
67	20 acres called the Bell marsh, 20 acres on Folly brook, and mill privilege, 20 acres and swamp below Cape Neddick pond, with timber rights, conditioned upon Sayword's building galleries and seats in the meeting house.
36	All interest in saw mill and 4 acres of land at Cape Neddick [in *York*].
37	House and 20 acres as by two town grants of and in *York*.
41	10 acres called Carle's point on the west side of Spruce creek in *Kittery*.
68	20 acres at Spruce creek, near the bridge in *Kittery*.
2	Choosing arbitrators to set out Mrs. Shapleigh's thirds in Major Nicholas Shapleigh's estate, with an inventory of the same.
24	Farm and buildings in *York*, where Ann Godfrey formerly dwelt, conveyed by Alice Shapleigh, folio 20.

Date.	Grantee.	Grantor.	Instrument.
1684, Sept. 6	SHAPLEIGH, Alice	Nicholas Shapleigh's estate	Commis'r's report
1684, Sept. 6	SHAPLEIGH, Alice	Nicholas Shapleigh's estate	Commis'r's report
1685, Nov. 10	SHAPLEIGH, Alice and John Shapleigh	Each other	Agreement & appraisal
1683, Feb. 5	SHAPLEIGH, John	Alice Shapleigh	Lease
1684, Mar. 19	SHAPLEIGH, John	Peter Coffin	Deposition
1684, Oct. 2	SHAPLEIGH, John	Thomas Kemble	Deposition
1685, April 3	SHAPLEIGH, John	Francis Smale, senior	Deposition
1691, May 12	SHAPLEIGH, John	Ursula Cutt	Letter
	SHAPLEIGH, John, see Alice Shapleigh		
1683, Feb. 6	SHAPLEIGH, Nicholas and other children of John Shapleigh	Alice Shapleigh	Bill of sale
1684, July 23	SHRYMPTON, Samuel and Eliakim Hutchinson John Purrington John Penwill Nathaniel Fryer Edward Rishworth	Nicholas Shapleigh's estate	Commis'r's report
1696, July 20	SMALL, Samuel	Mary Twisden	Deed
1696, Dec. 12	SMALL, Samuel	Petter Wittum et ux.	Deed
1695, Dec. 27	SMITH, James	John Harris, sen. et ux.	Deed

Index of Grantees.

Folio.	Description.
24	Assigning her as dower 253 acres adjoining the dwelling house; also 9 acres marsh at Sturgeon creek; also one third of two mills and chattels, all in *Kittery*.
26	Re-record of the preceding.
52	Dividing parts of Major Nicholas Shapleigh's estate, &c., and an appraisal thereof.
2	Of her third of the revenue of the saw mills at Spruce creek in *Kittery*.
41	That Nicholas Shapleigh stated John Shapleigh was his brother's son whom he had brought from his mother in England, and that John should be his heir.
41	As to Nicholas Shapleigh's intended disposition of his estate.
41	That he heard Major Nicholas Shapleigh say that he had brought John from his mother in England, and promised he should be heir to his whole estate, failing children, &c.
111	Agreeing to accept orders for £7:10, on account of Nathaniel Keen.
2	Of household stuff set out to her from the estate of Nicholas, her late husband.
26	Allowing several claims against the estate.
129	3 acres marsh on the west branch of York river, bought by Peter Twisden of Robert Edge, in *York*.
129	Messuage and 16 acres on south west side of Sturgeon creek in *Kittery*.
116	400 acres at *Coxhall* bought by grantor and others of Harlakenden Symonds.

Date.	Grantee.	Grantor.	Instrument.
168⅔, Feb. 3	SMITH, John and Mary Smith	Each other	Partition
	SMITH, Mary see John Smith		
1684, Aug. 1	SMYTH, John	John Smith, sen.	Conditional deed
1685, Apr. 21	SMYTH, John, jun.	John Smith, sen.	Receipt
1681, June 20	SNOW, Samuel	Morgan Howell's estate by Mary Booles, adm'x	Deed
1685, May 22	SPARKE, Thomas	Clement Swett	Deed
1695, June 11	SPENCER, Humphrey	Allen Fuz	Deed
1682, June 30	SPENCER, Moses	Patience Spencer	Deed
	SPINNEY, John see Thomas Spinney		
1696, Dec. 5	SPINNEY, Samuel	John Woodman	Deed
1694, Mar. 16	SPINNEY, Samuel	Thomas Hunscum	Deed
1694, Mar. 23	SPINNEY, Thomas and John Spinney	Each other	Lease and bond
1696, Nov. 2	STACKPOLE, James, sen.	Ephraim Joy	Deed
1692, Dec. 18	STAINFORD, John	John Honewell	Deed
1694, June 19	STAPLE, Peter	Abraham Remich et ux.	Deed
1694, Aug. 20	STAPLE, Peter, junior	Peter Staple	Conditional deed

Folio.	Description.
78	Of John Smyth, senior's real estate, setting off to Mary a parcel near Samuel Banks in *York*, she releasing to John all the other real estate.
19	Confirming former deed of land [in *York*] upon conditions and reservations.
32	For £30 : full consideration for land sold him.
48	50 acres upon that neck at *Cape Porpoise* formerly Howell's, and where his house stood.
38	House and 20 acres adjoining John Parrott's at Cape Elizabeth [in *Falmouth*].
103	30 acres at Newichewannock in *Berwick*, conveyed by grantee to Robert Elliot and by him to grantor, *q. v.*
7	What remained undivided of a 200 acre town grant, at Slut's corner; also 30 acres and half the meadow; also her third of Tom Tinker's and Great swamps [in *Berwick*].
95	20 acres, town grant of and in *Kittery*.
105	20 acres by town grant of and in *Kittery*.
112	Of all Thomas's estate in *Kittery*, conditioned upon John's managing upon halves during lives of Thomas and wife.
104	3¼ acres on the way to Hutchinson's saw mill in *Berwick*. See folio 11.
115	Honewell's neck at Winter Harbor in *Saco*.
128	30 acres in *Kittery*, adjoining Christian Remich, Spinney's Tetherly's and Rackley's lands.
113	80 acres, house and farm in *Kittery*, reserving 2 acres and al stock, conditioned upon grantee maintaining grantor and wife.

Index of Grantees.

Date.	Grantee.	Grantor.	Instrument.
1682, Nov. 8	STEPHENS, Amos	John Ryall	Deed
1684, Jan. 24	STORER, Joseph	Robert Gibbs's estate by Nicholas Moorey, attorney	Receipt
1684, Jan. 24	STORER, Joseph	Robert Gibbs's estate by Nicholas Moorey, attorney	Release
1696, June 16	STORER, Joseph	James Denmarke et ux.	Deed
169$\frac{3}{4}$, Mar. 10	TAYLOR, John	Samuel Willis	Deed
1694, Dec. 4	THOMPSON, Bartholomew	Miles Thompson et ux.	Deed
1682, May 17	TIDY, Robert	Town of Scarborough	Grant
1682, May 17	TIDY, Robert	Town of Scarborough	Grant
1695, Sept. 2	TOBEY, John and William Tobey	James Tobey, sr.	Conditional deed
1695, May 7	TOBEY, Stephen	James Tobey	Deed
169$\frac{5}{6}$, Jan. 13	TOBEY, Stephen	John Green's estate by Barnabas Wixon, administrator	Deed
	TOBEY, William, see John Tobey		
1674, Mar. 4	TUCKER, Francis	Robert Vickers Richard Bickham William Williams	Power of attorney
1691, June 5	TURFREY, George	Samuel Phillips et ux.	Deed

Index of Grantees.

Folio.	Description.
65	15 acres adjoining grantor and the river [in *North Yarmouth*].
49	In full of all accounts.
49	General discharge.
95	Marsh on Webhannet river adjoining grantee's in *Wells*.
117	200 acres and house at Salmon falls, on the river [in *Berwick*].
96	40 acres in *Berwick*, bought of Abraham Tilton.
69	6 acres by the highway from Black Point to Hunnewell's.
69	6 acres of swamp called the Beaver dam.
81	All his lands, except 4 acres to Stephen Tobey, and chattels in *Kittery* with exceptions, and conditioned for support, &c.
83	4 acres on the mast way, adjoining grantee's house in *Kittery*.
83	15 acres near Piscataqua river, in *Kittery*, at the cove above Frank's fort.
13	To collect debts of William Bickeham and others in New England.
134	One-fourth in common of saw-mill and tract of 16 square miles on Saco river, except 20 acres and timber sold out; also one quarter of Cow island, and one eighth Boniton's island, all in *Saco*.

INDEX OF GRANTEES.

Date.	Grantee.	Grantor.	Instrument.
1685, Apr. 10	TWISDEN, John and Susanna Twisden Samuel Twisden	Joseph Mowlton	Bond
1685, June 12	TWISDEN, John	Town of York	Survey
1685, June 12	TWISDEN, John	Town of York	Survey
	TWISDEN, Samuel, see John Twisden		
	TWISDEN, Susanna, see John Twisden		
1697, May 12	WADE, John	Jonathan Wade's estate by Jonathan Wade and Thomas Wade, executors	Power of attorney
1684, July 16	WAINWRIGHT, Francis	Richard Downs, sen.	Mortgage
1662, Oct. 6	WARREN, James	John Daves et ux.	Deed
1669, June 25	WELLS, Thomas	Nicholas Coole	Deed
167$\frac{3}{8}$, Feb. 18	WELLS, Thomas	Thomas Baston	Deed
1679, Aug. 29	WENTWORTH, John	Isaac Parker	Mortgage
1683, Jan. 10	WHARTON, Richard	Elizabeth Blany	Deed
1683, Jan. 10	WHARTON, Richard	Jane Elkine et ux.	Deed
1683, Jan. 10	WHARTON, Richard	Elizabeth Purchase	Deed
1683, Oct. 10	WHARTON, Richard	Eliezer Way	Deed
1683, Oct. 25	WHARTON, Richard	Thos. Purchase's estate by Elizabeth Blany, administratrix	Deed

Folio.	Description.
59	To secure payment of £180.
58	120 acres adjoining the brook, north east of Philip Adams's house lot.
59	Re-record of the above.
118	To collect debts due from estate of John Diamond of *Kittery*.
13	Tenement and outhouses, flakes and room, stage, shallop and appurtenances at Hog island, *Isles of Shoals*.
159	40 acres between grantor's marsh and the bridge in *York*.
12	Upland bought of Francis Littlefield, sen., and interest in grant of marsh in *Wells*, reserving family burying ground.
4	100 acres upland and 10 acres meadow at Merryland in *Wells*, bought of Francis Littlefield and Peter Cloyce.
21	Land and house bought of mortgagee [in *York*].
17	Quitclaim to the Way and Purchase patent in *Pejepscot*.
17	Quitclaim to the Way and Purchase patent in *Pejepscot*.
17	Quitclaim to the Way and Purchase patent in *Pejepscot*.
18	One half in common of the Way and Purchase patent of lands at *Pejepscot* and adjacent.
16	One half in common of the Way and Purchase patent of land. at Pejepscot and adjacent, reserving seven lots.

INDEX OF GRANTEES.

Date.	Grantee.	Grantor.	Instrument.
1683, Nov. 7 1684, July 25	WHARTON, Richard	General Court of Massachusetts	Order and survey
1684, July 7	WHARTON, Richard	Warumbee Darumkine Mihikermett Weeden Domhegon Numbanuett Nehonongassett Indian sagamores	Deed
1684, July 21	[WHARTON, Richard]	Thomas Haynes Joyce Haynes Sampson Penley	Deposition
1684, July 18	WHARTON, William	Elias White Edward Skinner	Deposition
1695, June 17	WHEELWRIGHT, John	Samuel Wheelwright et ux.	Deed
1698, June 9	WHEELWRIGHT, John	James Gooch et ux.	Deed
1694, July 6	WHEELWRIGHT, Samuel	Katherine Nanney *alias* Nayler	Deed
1685, June 26	WHITTE, Edmund	Massachusetts, by Thos. Danforth president	Executive order
1679, Nov. 25	WILLIAMS, Rowland	Thomas Withers	Deed
1684, July 20	WINCOLL, John and James Emery	John Thompson	Bond

INDEX OF GRANTEES. 113

Folio.	Description.
23	Confirming Wharton's former grant of 1000 acres, and report of surveyors appointed, that they had laid out 650 acres being the westerly half of Chebeague island, and 350 acres on the main land west of Maquoit, in *Casco Bay*.
15	Tract from Androscoggin falls 4 miles west, and so down to Maquoit, and by the Pejepscot river, and from the other side of Androscoggin falls, all the lands from the falls to Pejepscot and Merrymeeting bay to Kennebec and toward the Wilderness bounded by a southwest and northeast line to extend from Androscoggin uppermost falls to Kennebec river, and all the land from Maquoit to Pejepscot to Atkins bay in Kennebec river, also Mericoneag neck and Small Point harbor, and Sebascodegan island in Casco bay, and all islands in Kennebec and Pejepscot rivers and Merrymeeting bay.
19	That Francis Smale bought Sebascodegan island of the Indians for Major Nicholas Shapleigh.
19	That Richard Wharton delivered possession of Sebascodegan island in Casco bay to John Parker to the use of William Wharton.
126	One half in common of the tracts conveyed by Katherine Nanney, *q. v.*, in *Wells*.
125	Land adjoining the river; land adjoining Drake's island; also 12 acres marsh, all in *Wells*, formerly his father James Gooch's.
111	500 acres, except tract sold to William Hammond; also 30 acres marsh bought by her husband, Robert Nanney of Mr. Coole; also 165 acres and 15 acres marsh, bought by Robert of William Hammond; also 230 acres, bought by Robert of William Symonds, all in *Wells*.
46	Confirmation of title to Chebeague island in Casco bay, formerly granted by George Cleeve to Walter Merry.
5	Lot 75 poles long between lot of John Phillips, Nicholas Weeks and Enoch Houchings and Spruce creek in *Kittery*.
35	To save them harmless as administrators of estate of his father, William Tompson, and to protect town of Kittery from charges on account of his brother, James Tompson.

Index of Grantees.

Date.	Grantee.	Grantor.	Instrument.
	Wincoll, John, see Thomas Broughton		
1684, Dec. 22	Withers, Elizabeth	Thomas Withers et ux.	Bill of sale
1685, Apr. 22	Withers, Elizabeth	Jane Withers	Deed
1673, Mar. 14	Wittum, Peter	Abraham Conley	Deed
1686, Apr. 6	Wittum, Peter, jun.	William Wittum	Deed
1685, Mar. 18	Wittum, William	Peter Wittum et ux.	Deed
1682, May 18	Yeales, Timothy	William Hilton, sen.	Deed
1695, Jan. 14	York, town of	Town of Kittery	Survey
1675, Sept. 1	Young, John et ux.	Robert Wadleigh	Deed
1685, Aug. 25	Young, Rowland et ux.	Rowland Young, sen. et ux.	Deed
1682, Apr. 18	Young, Samuel	Rowland Young, sen. et ux.	Deed
1684, Feb. 11	Young, William	Benjamin Curtis	Deed

Folio.	Description.
35	Of cattle.
36	20 acres about the late Thomas Withers's dwelling house in *Kittery*, reserving life estate therein.
3	3½ acres 16 poles land between Conley's marsh and the highway in *Kittery*.
57	50 acres on Sturgeon creek, also 20 acres by town grant of and in *Kittery*.
57	One half in common of land at Tompson point in *Kittery*, purchased of Joseph Hammond.
43	One-half in common of Ingleby lot on west side of York river containing 100 acres: also half of Ingleby's meadow containing 3 acres, all in *York*.
93	Of the dividing line between the towns.
47	One third part of the farm in *Wells* formerly his father's, John Wadleigh's.
53	The former homestead of Robert Knight north of York river; also tract adjoining the above and Rob't Young, in *York*.
48	10 acres, part of town grant of and in *York*.
31	20 acres and house on southwest side of northwest branch of York river above the bridge, in *York*.

INDEX OF OTHER PERSONS.

Abbett, Abbott,
  Ensign, 56.
  John, 27.
  Richard, 94.
  Thomas, 23, 53, 114.
  Thomas, senior, 104.
Adams, Addams,
  Charles, 93.
  Christopher, 32.
  Margaret, 88.
  Mary, 88, 89, 147.
  Philip, 58, 59, 129.
  Temperance, 92, 93.
  William, 6, 32, 33, 107.
Addington, Isaac, 27, 28, 138, 153.
Alden, John, 135.
Alcock, Allcocke,
  Dorothy, 120.
  Job, 58, 59, 79, 83, 92, 98, 103, 105, 110, 120, 124, 129.
  John, 20, 129, 159.
  Joseph, 102.
Allard, Hugh, 64.
Alexander,
  Joseph, 79.
  Richard, 51.
Allen, Henry, 92.
Allene,
  Lewis, 49.
  Mary, 110.
  Robert, 27, 28.
Amerideth, 33, [see Meridies].
  John, 138, 145.
Andrews, James, 16, 23.
Appleton,
  Elizabeth, 118.
  John, 118, 144.
  Samuel, 3, 17.
Ardell, William, 153.
Atkines,
  Mathew, 9.
  Nathaniel, 128.
  Thomas, 36.

Atkinson, Theodore, 162.
Atwell, children of Benjamin, 37.
Austine,
  Mary, 66, 67.
  Matthew, 28, 66, 67, 68, 108, 116, 146.
  Matthew, senior, 66.
  Samuel, 49, 64, 111, 125, 126, 127.
  Sarah, 66.
  Sebellah, 66.
Avent, Francis, 157.
Axell, Humphrey, 32.
Ayers, Edward, 52, 98, 103, 143.

Backehouse, Francis, 61.
Bacon, William, 34.
Baker,
  Sarah, 72.
  Thomas, 106.
Ball, John, 119.
Bane, Lewis, 108.
Banefield, Christopher, 67, 91.
Banks, Bankes,
  Joseph, 108.
  Richard, 7, 58, 59, 61, 68, 159.
  Samuel, 78.
Barber, John, 47.
Barefoote, Walter, 41, 42.
Barrett,
  Elizabeth, 12.
  John, 11, 12, 64, 95.
Barter, Henry, 154.
Barton, Mary, 154.
Batson,
  Margery, 160.
  Stephen, 111, 126.
Battene, William, 40.
Beadle, Samuel, 49.
Beale,
  Ann *alias* Agnes, 29.
  Edward, 146.
Beane, Lewis, 46.

Index of Other Persons.

Beavis, Thomas, 100, 101.
Beeson, Thomas, 82.
Belcher,
  John, 98, 102.
  Samuel, 64.
Benmore,
  Philip, 92, [93].
  Temperance, 92.
Bennicke, Arthur, 41.
Benning, Henry, 23.
Berry, Ambrose, 10.
Bickeford, Thomas, 43.
Bickeham, William, 14.
Blachford, Francis, 24.
Blacklidge, *alias* Frethee, Mary, 108.
Blany,
  Elizabeth, 16, 17.
  John, 16, 17.
  Mr., 16.
  wife of, 16.
Blasdell, Ralph, 20.
Bodg, Henry, 38.
Bolls, Booles,
  Joseph, 12, 48, 128.
  Mary, 48, 62.
  Mis, 50.
Bonighton, Boniton,
  John, sen., 135.
  Mr., 22.
Booth,
  Robert, 42, 44, 45.
  Simon, 45, 94, 124.
  widow, 45.
Brackett,
  Anthony, 23, 41, 65.
  captain, 23.
  Thomas, 35
Bradstreet, S., 9, 10.
Bragdon,
  Arthur, 30, 48, 58, 59, 66.
  Arthur, sen., 66.
  Samuel, 51.
  Thomas, 58, 59.
Brawn, John, 7, 109.
Bray,
  Joan, 30.
  John, 134, 145.
  Richard, 31, 37.
  Richard, sen., 37.

Breadie, Bredy,
  John, 98, 103.
Breissan, Charles, 61.
Brimsdon, Robert, 102.
Broad, William, 103, 149.
Bronsdon, Joseph, 140.
Broosy, Mary, 12.
Broughton,
  George, 9, 55.
  John, 22, 55.
  Mr., 104.
Brown,
  Andrew, 59, 61.
  William, 17.
Bruken, Sarah, 86.
Bryar, Richard, 157.
Buckley, Peter, 9.
Burdett, George, 46.
Burnum, Job, 110.
Burredge, Burregh,
  William, 59, 69.
Burren, John, 40.
Burroughs, George, 12, 77.
Bush, John, 106.

Caldwell, Dillingem, 115.
Cally, Richard, 47.
Carle, Richard, 41.
Carmichael, see Chirmihill.
Carr, James, 60.
Carter, Richard, 81, [91].
Chadborne, Humphrey, 51.
Chamberlain, Richard, 41, 67.
Champernown,
  Francis, 2, 46, 139.
  Mary, 94.
Chillson, William, 115.
Chirmihill [Carmichael], John, 159.
Churchwood, Mary, 132.
Clarke,
  captain, 8.
  Daniel, 137.
  major, 30.
  Mr., 74.
  Nathaniel, 127.
  Thomas, 8, 9.
Cleaves, George, 41, 46.
Cloyce, Peter, 4.
Cobbett, Thomas, 142.

Cole, Coole, Cooly,
  Mr., 111, 126, 127, 128.
  Nicholas, 95.
Colebie, Thomas, 4.
Colton, William, 121.
Collier, Moses, jr., 10.
Convers, James, 99, 100, 101.
Cooke, Elisha, 50.
Coopper, John, 139.
Corban, Corben, 131.
  Robert, 43.
Corber, Thomas, 151.
Corwine, Curwine,
  Elizabeth, 49.
  Jonathan, 49, 106.
Cossons, 41.
  Isaac, 41.
  John, 11.
Couch, Joseph, 122.
Cowell,
  Mr., 6, 107.
  Joseph, 62.
Cranch, Elizabeth, 6.
Cranfield, Edward, 24.
Crocker, Johanna, 88.
Crocket,
  Ann, 155.
  Ephraim, 1, 6, 107, 157.
  Hugh, 154.
  Joseph, 1.
  Joshua, 154, 156.
  Thomas, 1, 121.
Cross, father of Joseph, 10.
Crown, Henry, 160.
Curtis,
  Benjamin, 4, 49.
  Thomas, 61.
Cutt,
  John, 9, 30, 106.
  Mary, 41, 68.
  Richard, 97.
  Robert, 32, 158.

Damforth, Danforth,
  Thomas, 9, 17, 18, 20, 28, 30, 41, 43, 47, 76.
Daniell, James, 48.
Daulton, Samuel, 47.
Davess, Davie, Davis, 66.
  Humphrey, 9, 36, 47.

  John, 2, 3, 6, 13, 21, 24, 36, 37, 41, 43, 45, 54, 61, 67, 68, 69, 72, 114, 140, 144, 158, 159.
  major, 2.
  Mary, 6.
  Sylvanus, 23, 73.
Davison, Nicholas, 118.
Dear, Thomas, 25.
Deareing,
  Clement, 145.
  John, 150.
  Roger, 25, 121, 122.
Delton, William, 43.
Denness, John, 10.
Dennet, Alexander, 123, 129.
Dill, Daniel 107.
Discoe, Drisco,
  John, 38, 39.
Dixon, William, 30, 47.
Donnell,
  Henry, 115.
  Samuel, 86, 93, 108, 110, 114, 116, 131, 146, 148.
Dorman,
  Ephraim, sen., 106.
  Mary, jun., 106.
Dow, Henry, 87.
Downeing,
  Dennis, 56, 151.
  Joshua, 56.
  Patience, 111.
Drinker, Edward, 27, 28.
Drowne, Leonard, 57.
Dudley, J., 153.
Dummer,
  Jeremiah, 112, 156.
  Shubael, 61, 115.
Dwight, Timothy, jr., 50.
Dyemont, Diamond, Deament,
  John, 32, 36, 86, 118.
  William, 33.
Dyer, Henry, 52.

Eastwick,
  Phesant, 91, 162.
  Sarah, 162.
Edge, Robert, 129.
Edmones, Robert, 36.
Eldredg, Thomas, 99.
Elliot, Ellet, Elliett,
  Mr., 67.

Nathaniel, 140, 141.
Robert, 31, 69, 94.
Ellingham, William, 79.
Ellkines, 40.
  Christopher, 40.
Emerson,
  James, 95.
  James, jr., 104.
  John, 23, 45.
Emery,
  Anthony, 27, 28, 93.
  Daniel, 104.
  James, 23, 35, 36, 53, 67, 92, 96, 109.
  Noah, 88.
  Zachariah, 88, 109.
Endell, Endle,
  Ephraim, 33.
  Michael, 33, 68, 112.
  Richard, 64, 97.
English, see Ingles.
Etherinton, Etherington, 98, 103.
  Thomas, 7, 84, 86.
Evans, Jonathan, 140.
Everell, Thomas, 32.
Everett,
  Andrew, 43.
  Margaret, Margery, 56.
  Martha, 56. See Martha Lord.
  William, 56.
Everey, John, 148.

Fabes, John, 65.
Farmer, Arthur, 134.
Farrow, George, 4.
Fernald,
  John, 110, 111, 119.
  William, 93, 131.
Felt, George, 16.
Fickett, Goodman, 69.
Fisher, Robert, 12.
Fletcher, Pendleton, 161.
Fluellin, sagamore, 106.
Folshum, Foullsam,
  John, 63, 64.
  Peter, 46.
Ford, Susanna, 81.
Forgisson, Forguson,
  Alexander, 104, 105.
  Daniel, 85.
Fox, Jabez, 9.

Foxwell,
  Philip, 31, 156.
  Sarah, 41.
Foy, James, 145.
Frees, James, 74.
Freethee *alias* Blacklidge, Mary, 108.
Frost,
  captain, 24, 67.
  Charles, 3, 9, 27, 30, 32, 35, 36, 50, 51, 53, 67, 81, 82, 83, 84, 91, 96, 97, 98, 102, 104, 109, 129, 130, 148.
  Charles, jr., 82, 98, 102.
  Nicholas, 67, 93.
  Philip, 31.
  William, 61, 135.
Fry, Adrian, 98.
Fryer,
  Joshua, 52.
  Nathaniel, 6, 26, 71, 149, 154, 158.
Fuller, Joseph, 144.
Furbush, William, 57.
Furnell, William, 32.

Gattensby, Gattinsby,
  John, 7, 84.
Gedney, Gidney, Gydney,
  Bartholomew, 4, 43, 115.
  Hannah, 75, 76.
  William, 77.
Gendall, see Gyndall.
Gibbons, James, 22.
Giffard, Margaret, 42.
Gillison, Nicholas, 55, 149.
Gillman, John, sen., 64.
Godfrey,
  Ann, 20, 36.
  Edward, 46.
  Mr., 43.
Godding, Gooden, Goodine, Gooding, Goodwin,
  Daniel, 7, 23, 55, 84, 86, 105, 150.
  Daniel, sen., 103.
  Daniel, jr., 96.
  George, 14.
Godsoe, William, 88, 89, 93, 95, 105, 112, 113, 147, 154, 156, 157, 159.

Index of Other Persons.

Goodhew, William, 13.
Gorges,
  Sir Ferdinando, 3, 24, 151, 152.
  Mr., 15, 43.
  Thomas, 3, 46.
Gouch, Gooch,
  James, 125.
  John, 11.
Goulding, Re., 20.
Gowell, Richard, 119.
Gowen,
  Mercy, 81.
  Nicholas, 51.
  William, 98, 103.
Gowen *alias* Smith, 104.
  William, 81, 35, 36, 57.
Grafford, Thomas, 153.
Grant,
  James, 21.
  Peter, 129.
Gray, George, 7, 55, 149.
Green,
  goodman, 55.
  Henry, 64.
  John, 72, 83.
  John, sen., 114.
  Richard, 83.
Greeneland, Henry, 30.
Greenham, 67.
Gyndall, Walter, 12, 37, 43, 59.

Haenen, Mr., 130.
Hall, Ralph, 64.
Haly, Deborah, 87.
Hammond,
  Francis, 10.
  Joseph, 24, 26, 52, 57, 60, 69, 79, 83, 91, 92, 94, 97, 109, 123, 147, 151, 158.
  Joseph, sen., 139.
  Joseph, jr., 92, 97, 109.
  Joseph, clerk, 128, 151.
  Joseph, register, 69, 79—162.
Hammonds,
  Jonathan, 11, 49, 61, 67, 95.
  William, 2, 3, 111, 126.
Hammons, Edmund, 25.
Hancock, John, 89, 108, 110, 114, 116, 146.
Hannah, a negress, 53.
Hannet, Edward, 18.

Harbert, James, 6, 67.
Hardy, Samuel, 4.
Harford, Thomas, 157.
Harker, John, 159.
Harmon, John, 53, 58, 59.
Hartwell, Thomas, 14.
Harris, Trustrum, 98, 103.
Harwood, Henry, 35, 65.
Hathorne, Hawthorne,
  John, 49, 76, 123.
Hatch, Samuel, 143.
Haynes, Heyns,
  William, 17, 35, 36.
Hayward, Haward,
  John, 9, 18, 20, 76.
Haywood, Robert, 155.
Heard,
  James, 129, 130.
  John, 149.
Henderson, William, 23.
Heskines, Nicholas, 68, 69, 101, 103, 104, 140, 141, 142, 149, 158.
Hill, Hills,
  Elizabeth, 1.
  John, 22, 136.
  Joseph, 91.
  Samuel, 143.
Hilliard, Benjamin, 77.
Hilton,
  Edward, 51.
  Richard, 113.
  Robert, 40, 61.
Hinckes, Hinkes,
  John, 33, 67, 68, 69, 107, 139, 141.
Hodsden, Hodgsden,
  Benoni, 25, 65, 86, 94, 96.
  Jeremiah, 98, 103.
  Joseph, 12.
Holicomb, John, 142.
Holms, Thomas, 30.
Holyoke, Elizur, 127.
Hooke,
  Francis, 1, 5, 6, 12, 21, 24, 25, 26, 29, 30, 35, 36, 55, 72, 88, 89, 90, 107, 111, 113, 123, 128, 132.
  Mary, 12, 88, 133.
  William, 20, 122.
Hoole,
  John, 25, Mr., 25.

Index of Other Persons. 121

Houchings, Enoch, 5.
Horewood, see Harwood.
Howe, John, 57.
Howell,
  John, 137.
  Morgan, 3, 50, 62.
  Prudence, 40.
Hoy, John, 31.
Hull, Reuben, 30.
Hunniwell, Honewell,
  goodman, 69.
  Richard, 69.
  Roger, 115.
Hunscom,
  Ann, 159.
  Thomas, 83.
Hutchinson,
  Eliakim, 9, 103.
  Elisha, 27, 28, 78, 127.
  Mr., 7, 11, 26, 109.

Indians, 19, 43, 75, 106.
  called heathen, 37. See Fluellin, Sagamores, Sosowen.
Ingersall, Ingerson,
  George, 12.
  George, sen., 41, 63.
  George, jun., 62.
Ingles, Inglish,
  James, 34, 73.

Jackeson,
  James, 19.
  John, 69.
Jaffray, Jaffrey,
  George, 91, 106, 160.
Jeffereys, Diggory, 1, 145, 150.
Jefory, Jeofrey,
  Ann, 154, 155.
Jenkins,
  Renald, 56.
  Stephen, 98, 103.
Joanes, Jones,
  Thomas, 56, 144.
Jocelyn, Joclein,
  Henry, 17, 23, 33, 40, 69.
Johnson,
  Francis, 144, 159.
  William, 46.
Johnston, Thomas, 99, 100, 101.

Jordan,
  Dominicus, 94, 124.
  Hannah, 94.
  Jeremiah, 81.
  John, 141.
  Robert, 43, 80, 142.
  Sarah, 142.

Kemble, Kymble,
  Henry, 102.
  Thomas, 33, 41, 99, 140.
  Thomas, sen., 99.
  Thomas, jun., 99.
Keen, Nathaniel, 111.
Keniston, Christopher, 107.
Key, John, 150.
King,
  Richard, 119, 138, 139.
  Samuel, 147.
  William, 88, 89, 147.
Knight, see Night,
  Ezekiel, 2, 128.
  Robert, 53.
  Samuel, 31.
  Sarah, 80.
Knill, Philip, 14.

Ladbrooke, widow, 45.
Lane, John, 13.
Lang, William, 13.
Lake, Thomas, 9.
Lamberd, Jonathan, 44.
Lamprill, Henry, 107.
Lary, John, 132, 138, 156.
Lawd, see Lord.
Lawrance,
  Mary, 35.
  Robert, 35.
Leach, James, 29.
Leader,
  George, 152.
  Richard, 152.
Leighton, Laiton, 73.
  John, 45.
  Katherine, 60.
Leverett, John, 9.
Lewes, Henry, 80.
Lewice, William, 6.
Lewis,
  George, 43.
  Susanna, 34.

Libby, Lybby,
    Anthony, 43.
    John, 40.
Lidston, Waymouth, 90.
Lincoot, John, 121.
Litten, Edward, 138.
Littlefield,
    Abigail, 125.
    Edmund, sen., 12.
    Francis, 4.
    Francis, sen., 12.
    James, sen., 38, 39.
    John, 12, 30, 39.
    John, sen., 39.
    Jonathan, 143.
Liveingstone, Livingstoun,
    Daniel, 31, 48, 159.
Lobdell, Joseph, 118.
Lord, Lawd,
    Abraham, 7.
    Martha, 5, 56, 149, 150.
    Nathan, 5, 56.
    Nathan, sen., 67.
    Samuel, 7.
Lott, Thomas, 69.
Love, William, 117.
Lyde, Edward, 33.
Lyn, Ephraim, 106.

Machanny, Mechenny,
    John, 40.
Maires, Benjamin, 127.
Manning, Daniel, 39.
Martine, William, 22.
Mason,
    John, 151, 152, 153.
    Robert, 6.
Masterson, Nathaniel, 61.
Mathews, Samuel, 13, 54.
Matton, Hubertus, 22.
Mavericke,
    Antipas, 79.
    Mr., 24, 26.
Maxell, Maxwell,
    Alexander, 45, 129.
Mayne,
    John, 32.
    Thomas, 44.
Maysterson, Nathaniel, 28.
Mendum,
    Jonathan, 35.

Robert, 87.
Meridies, Mr., 132. See Amerideth.
Merry, Walter, 46.
Messenger, Henry, 50.
Milborne, William, 112, 156.
Millard, Millerd,
    Samuel, 113.
Miller,
    John, 10, 61.
    Martha, 92.
    Mary, 91, 92.
    Richard, 90, 92.
    Samuel, 91.
Mills,
    Thomas, 63.
    children of Mary, not named, 64.
Mitton, Mittone,
    Mary, 34.
    Michael, 34.
    Nathaniel, 34.
Moody, Eliezer, 18, 42, 76, 125, 127, 136, 137.
Moore,
    Dorothy, 47.
    Richard, 40.
    Sarah, 158.
    William, 29, 159.
Moorey, Nicholas, 49, 50.
Morgan,
    Francis, 94, 106.
    Sarah, 94, 106.
Morgaridg, John, 68.
Morrall, Morrell,
    John, 27, 28, 98.
    Nicholas, 93.
Moulton, Thomas, 154.
Mountegue, Mowntegue, 50.
    Griffine, 10, 61, 62.
Munjoy, George, 12, 43.
Mussy,
    Benjamin, 36.
    Thomas, 10.

Nanny,
    Katherine, 43.
    Katherine *alias* Nayler, 126.
    Robert, 111, 126, 128.
    Samuel, 10, 50.
Nash,
    Isaac, 5.
    Margery, 5.

Index of Other Persons.   123

Nason, Richard, 7, 67, 84, 86' 149, 153
Nayler, *alias* Nanny, Katherine, 126.
Neale,
 Francis, 34, 35, 40.
 Francis, sen, 49.
Neal, Neail, Neaull,
 James, 96.
 John, 142.
Negus, Isaac. 148.
Negroes, not named, 2, 52. See Hannah, Thomas,
Nelson,
 Mary, 113.
 Matthew, 79.
 Samuel, 113.
Newgrove, John, 56.
Newmarch,
 John, 88, 158.
 John, jun, 132, 156.
 Thomas, 116.
Newysh, Jabesh, 50
Nicholls, Nicolls, Nicolle, 22, 67.
 Francis, 112, 132.
 John, 67
 mate, 67.
 Robert, 61.
Night, Bridget, 124.
Nock, Henry, 92.
Nocke, Sylvanus, 57, 93, 105.
Nowell, Samuel, 10, 12, 32, 50.

Odihorne, Philip, 13.
Oliver,
 Richard, 87.
 William, 3, 57.
Olliffe, Ralph, 14.
Oiriss, Jonathan, 131.

Packer, Thomas, 102, 121.
Page, Nicholas, 153.
Paine, Pane,
 John, 34, 73.
 Thomas, 45.
Palmer,
 John, 12.
 Mary, 5.
 Samuel, 155.
 William, 31, [88], 89, 102.

Parker, 11.
 John, 16, 19, 30.
 John, sen, 53.
 Margery, 33.
 Thomas, 34, 73.
Parrett, Parrott,
 John, 38, 142, 154.
Parsons, Richard, 142.
Partridge,
 John, 102, 160.
 Nehemiah, 67.
Paul, Stephen, 110.
Paulling, Mathew, 35, 65.
Pearson,
 Elizabeth, 112.
 George, 5, 23, 30, 39, 40, 41, 42, 43, 49, 59, 60.
Pecher, Samuel, 151.
Peckitt, Christopher, 40.
Pemberton, Thomas, 20.
Pendleton,
 Bryan, 45.
 major, 44
Penewell, Penuel, Penniwell, Pennuwell, Penwill,
 John, 24, 26, 30, 31, 36, 44, 53, 61, 68, 72, 114, 144, 146, 159.
 Joseph, 110.
 Walter, 45, 50, 94, 124.
 Sarah, 72
Penhallow, Samuel, 94, 106, 153.
Penny, Henry, 102.
Pepperrell, Peprell;
 Andrew, 151.
 William, 89, 94, 97, 112, 113, 132, 139, 145, 147, 154, 155, 156, 157, 158.
Phillips,
 Bridget, 20, 134, 135.
 John, 5, 32
 William, 134, 135
Phipps, Thomas, 120, 154.
Pickerin,
 John, 26, 52, 79, 94, 106, 121.
 John, jr, 107
Pike, Robert, 24, 62.
Place, Abraham, 66.
Plaisted, Playstead,
 Ichabod, 66, 150.
 James, 9, 23, 110.

Index of Other Persons.

John, 96, 105, 109, 110.
Mr., 117.
Roger, 9, 149.
William, 7, 9, 45.
Potter, Valentine, 72.
Powsland, Richard, 65.
Preble, Abraham, 28, 44, 53, 58, 59, 79, 108, 131.
Presby, Stephen, 134.
Price, captain, 65.
Pritchett, John, children of, not named, 36.
Prout, Timothy, 80, 99, 100, 101.
Purchase,
  Mr., 15.
  Thomas, 14, 16, 17, 18.
  Thomas, children of, 16.
  Thomas, jr., 17.
Purkis, George, 20.
Purrington,
  Elias, 47.
  John, 26, 57.

Rackliff, Racklift, Rackley, William, 79, 123, 128.
Randall, Richard, 44.
Randolph, Edward, 140.
Rawson, Edward, 23, 30.
Rayn, Joseph, 68, 69.
Rayns,
  Francis, 46.
  wife of Francis, 12.
Raynsford, Solomon, 62.
Redford, William, 82.
Reed, Sarah, 6, 107.
Remich, Remmich, 72.
  Christian, 83, 119, 128, 151.
  Isaac, 128.
  Jacob, 83, 90, 128, 158, 159.
  Joshua, 89, 90, 128.
  Lydia, 89.
Renalds,
  John, 10.
  William, 29.
Rice, Ryce,
  Mary, 36.
  Thomas, 119.
Richards,
  Daniel, 99, 100.
  John, 59, 60.
Rider, Thomas, 14.

Rigby,
  Alexander, 46.
  colonel, 41.
Rishford, error for Rishworth, q. v.
Rishworth,
  Edward, recorder, 1—67.
  Edward, 2, 4, 8, 11, 12, 13, 19, 21, 23, 24, 26, 27, 30, 31, 32, 35, 37, 42, 43, 45, 46, 48, 53, 55, 56, 57, 58, 59, 61, 63, 66, 67, 82, 86, 104, 109, 134, 148, 154, 159, 161.
  Mr., 50.
  Susanna, 82.
Roads, Thomas, 57.
Roanes, Hester, 43.
Roberts,
  John, sen., 35, 55, 56.
  John, jun., 55, 56.
  Thomas, sen., 35.
  William, 154.
Robinson,
  Francis, 40.
  James, 67.
  William, 33.
Rogers, Richard, 81, 91, 113.
Rolfe, Benjamin, 74.
Rudsby, John, 118.
Rule, John, 99.
Ryall,
  Elizabeth, 65.
  William, 65.

Sagamores of Androscoggin river, 14, 15, 16.
  Kennebec river, 14, 15, 16.
Sanders,
  John, 111, 126.
  lieutenant, 106.
  William, 57.
Sampson, Andrew, 69.
Sargent, Sargeant, Sergeant, Sergent,
  Edward, 44, 161.
  Elizabeth, 124.
  John, 27, 44, 45, 94, 124.
  Ruth, 27.
Sawyer, William, 64.
Sayward, Seaward, Sayword,
  Henry, 75.
  John, 8, 30, 31, 37, 58, 59, 66.

Index of Other Persons.

Mary, 8, 37.
Mary, jr., 32.
Samuel, 45.
Scottow,
  Joshua, 12, 22, 38, 81.
  Thomas, 23, 38, 74.
  Thomas, recorder, 67—69.
  Thomas, deputy register, 72—79.
Screven, Scriven,
  Samuel, 132, 156.
  William, 68, 112, 132.
Searle,
  Andrew, 84, 85, 86.
  John, 35.
  Mary, 35.
Seavy, William, 29.
Seawell, Sewell, Sewall,
  Samuel, 129.
  Stephen, 50, 51, 53.
Seely, Elizabeth, 41.
Selly, Richard, 102.
Shapleigh, 41.
  Alexander, 2.
  Alice, [133], 144.
  John, 2, 11, 51, 90, 93, 123, 130, 131.
  children of, not named, 2.
  major, 41, 67.
  Mr., 123.
  Mrs., 150.
  Nicholas, 15, 24, 41, 52, 56, 79, 133.
  Sarah, 111.
Sharpe,
  Elizabeth, 156.
  John, 22.
  Thomas, 69.
Shellden, William, 40.
Sheppard, John, 119.
Short, Clement, 86.
Shrympton, Samuel, 26.
Simmons, John, 90, 110.
Simpson, Sympson,
  Henry, 58, 59, 148.
Simson, John, 69.
Skillings, John, 62, 74, 75, 77.
Sloper, John, 158.
Smale,
  Francis, 19, 69.
  Samuel, 150.

Smith, Smyth,
  Edward, 46, 63, 64.
  Jacob, 139.
  James, 117.
  Joan, 19.
  John, 78.
  Nicholas, 57.
  Richard, 131.
Snell,
  George, 55.
  John, 120.
Snow,
  Samuel, 10, 61, 62.
  Sarah, 10, 61, 62.
Sosowen, sagamore, 106.
Sparke, Sparks,
  Thomas, 3, 142.
Spinney,
  James, 110, 113, 128.
  John, 110, 111.
  Margery, 112, 113.
  Mary, 113.
  Samuel, 90, 113, 128.
  Thomas, 72, 110, 111, 119, 158.
Spencer,
  George, 19.
  Humphrey, 7, 84, 85, 86, 149.
  Moses, 103.
  Thomas, 7, 11, 85, 86, 149.
  William, 22, 84, 85, 86, 104, 149.
Stacie, William, 145.
Stanion, Stanyan,
  Mary, 6, 107.
Stanly,
  Caleb, 117.
  Caleb, jr., 117.
  Sarah, 117.
Staple,
  Elizabeth, 113.
  Peter, 90, 91, 128.
Start,
  John, 23.
  William, 69.
Stevens,
  Agnes, 84.
  Caleb, 115.
  Thomas, 75.
Stoddard, Anthony, 99, 100, 101.
Stone, Stoone,
  Daniel, 56, 86, 96.

Stover, 78.
Styleman, Elias, 5, 26, 51, 69, 142.
Swaine, Roger, 154.
Symonds,
  Harlakenden, 106, 116.
  William, 30, 64, 111, 126, 128.

Tarr, Richard, 38.
Tavler, Taylor, Taylour,
  Edward, 66.
  George, 59, 60.
  James, 116.
  William, 185.
Tetherly,
  Gabriel, 119, 158.
  William, 128.
Thawits, [Thwaits],
  Alexander, 19.
Thomas, or Tom, a negro, 53, 133, 134.
Thomas. Nathaniel, 136.
Tilton, Abraham, 96.
Tobey,
  Isaac, 81.
  James, 81, 83.
  Mary, 81.
  Richard, 81.
  Stephen. 81.
Tompson, Tomson,
  Edward, 96.
  James, 35.
  John, 92, 159.
  William, 35, 98.
  William, children of, not named, 35.
Tozier, Richard, 65.
Trafton, Thomas, 93, 158.
Tredby, Nicholas, 65.
Treworgie, James, 105.
Trickey, Francis, 6, 107.
Trott, John, 2.
Trusedalle, Elizabeth, 137.
Trustrum, 104.
  Ralph, 42, 44, 124.
Tucker, Nicholas, 94, 134.
Turbett, Turbut,
  Peter, 29, 106.
Turfrey, George, 42.
Twisden,
  John, 37, 46, 67, 68, 159.
  Peter, 129.

Tyng,
  captain, 131.
  Edward, 9, 12, 14, 16, 18, 19, 23, 35, 42, 43, 61, 63, 65, 72, 74, 75.
  Elizabeth, 68.

Usher, John, 153.

Vahan [Vaughan], Mr., 30.
Veazie, George, 86.
Vines, Richard, 24, 42.
Vittrey, Edward, 142.

Wackum, John, 30.
Wade,
  Jonathan, 118.
  Thomas, 3, 116, 118.
Wadleigh,
  Henry, 48.
  John, 46, 47, 63, 64.
  Robert, 47, 48, 63.
Wakefield, John, 111, 126.
Waldern, Waldron,
  Richard, 84, 85.
Walters, Henry, 16.
Walton, Shadrach, 104, 149.
Wanewright,
  John, 13, 65.
  Simon, 13.
Ware,
  Joseph, 114, 116, 147.
  Peter, 115, see Weare.
Warren, James, jun., 104.
Watson, John, 140, 141.
Way,
  Eliezer, 16.
  George, 16, 17, 18.
Waymouth, Edward, 98, 103.
Weare,
  Elias, 148.
  Joseph, 45.
  Nathaniel, 118.
  Peter, 46, see Ware.
Webber,
  John, 78.
  Joseph, 75.
  Samuel, 78, 161.
Weekes, Nicholas, 5.
Welch, Philip, 114.
Wentworth, Ebenezer, 113.

Wharton, Richard, 19.
Wheelwright,
  John, 5, 39, 89, 111, 126.
  Samuel, 2, 5, 11, 12, 30, 39, 46, 49, 67, 69, 78, 89, 95, 126, 127, 128, 147.
Whinnicke,
  Joseph, 23.
  Sarah, 80.
White, Whitte,
  Elias, 18.
  John, 17, 27, 28, 138.
  Mary, 21.
  Richard, 36, 155.
  Sampson, 29.
Whitney, Benjamin, 159.
Wilde, 67.
  John, 13.
Williams,
  Henry, 32.
  Michael, 33.
  Thomas, 27, 42, 44.
Wilson, Willson,
  Joseph, 25, 97.
Winch, Samuel, 105.
Wincoll,
  captain, 88, 103, 154.
  John, 3, 5, 7, 9, 11, 22, 23, 24, 25, 26, 31, 35, 36, 38, 41, 44, 45, 55, 56, 60, 66, 67, 114, 149, 152, 157.

Winkley, Samuel, 155.
Wise, Thomas, 34.
Withers,
  Elizabeth, 5, 12, 51.
  Mary, 51.
  Thomas, 25, 36, 38, 51.
Wittum, Peter, 57.
Wixon, Barnabas, 83.
Wood, Judith, 144.
Woodberry, Priscilla, 78.
Woodman, John, 105, 118.
Woods, Richard, 46.
Wormewood, William, 7.
Wright, Mary, 78.

Yeales, Yealls,
  Timothy, 29, 53, 54, 55, 158, 159.
Yorke, John, 37.
Young,
  John, 46.
  Rowland, 114, 146.
  Sarah, 47.

Zelly, see Selly.

Surnames omitted,
  John, 40.
  Micum, 43.
  Robert, 128.
  Samuel, 124.

INDEX OF PLACES.

Alewife cove, Cape Elizabeth, Falmouth, 141.
Amesbury, Massachusetts, 4.
Andover, Massachusetts, 22.
Androscoggin falls, 15, 16.
Ambroscoggan, Andioscoggin river, 14, 15, 16.
　upper falls in, 15.
Ashing Swamp brook, Kittery, 121.
Atkins bay, Sagadahoc river, 15.

Backehouse's creek, Saco, 161.
Baker's spring, between York and ·Kittery, 93.
Barbadoes, island of, 53, 155.
Bare cove, Sturgeon creek, Kittery, 98.
Barnes point, Kittery, 132.
Barnstable county, Massachusetts, 83, 128.
Bass cove, York, 7, 30, 108, 159.
Bass cove brook, York, 67
Bass creek, Scarborough, 80.
Bay land, Kittery, 90, 144.
Bearberry marsh, North Yarmouth, 19.
Beaver Dam swamp, Scarborough, 69.
Beaver pond, Wells, 1.
Bell marsh, York, 67.
Berwick, 7, 11, 21, 23, 55, 56, 65, 92, 96, 104, 109, 110, 118. See Newgewanacke.
　Birchen point, 96.
　Broughton's swamp, 104.
　Daniel Stone's garrison house, 96
　Fowling marsh, 55, 96.
　Further marsh, 149
　Great mill works, 7.
　Great swamp, 7.
　Hutchinson's mill, 152, 153.
　Little river, 7.

Berwick, continued.
　Newgewanacke, great river, 50, 82, 103, 104, 149.
　little river, 152.
　parish of, 21, 23.
　Parker's marsh, 84.
Pipe-staff point, 153.
　Quamphegan, 8.
　Rocky hill, 104, 105, 109.
　Salmon falls, 8, 50, 86, 117.
　Slut's corner, 7.
　Tom Tinker's swamp, 7.
　Unity parish, 84, 85.
　Whitte's marsh, 55, 129.
　Wilcock's pond, 86, 149.
　York highway, 21.
Birchen point, Berwick, 96.
Black point, Scarborough, 22, 23, 38, 40, 59, 60, 61, 69, 80, 81, 121, 137.
　ferry, 22.
　plains, 23.
　river, 80.
Blue point, Scarborough, 31.
Boiling rock, Kittery, 110.
Boniton's island, Saco, 135.
Boston, Massachusetts, 8, 10, 13, 15, 16, 17, 18, 19, 22, 23, 24, 27, 28, 30, 31, 32, 33, 40, 41, 42, 46, 47, 48, 49, 50, 59, 60, 61, 65, 76, 77, 78, 80, 99, 100, 101, 102, 111, 112, 125, 126, 127, 133, 134, 136, 138, 139, 140, 141, 149, 151, 156, 161.
Boxford, Massachusetts, 106.
Braveboat harbor, York, 12, 29, 36, 46, 71.
　York and Kittery, 93.
　Kittery, 155.
Bristol, England, 13, 14.
　Corn street, 14.
Broadboat harbor, see Braveboat.
Broad cove, Kittery, 68, 112.

Index of Places.

Broughton's swamp, Berwick, 104.
Bulley's creek, Saco, 161.

Canoe point, Sagadahoc, 36.
Cape Elizabeth, Falmouth, 26, 38, 87, 141.
　cove, 26.
Cape Nuttacke or Neddick, York, 4, 19, 32, 36, 46, 54.
　river, 54.
Cape Porpoise, 1, 3, 10, 12, 29, 31, 48, 50, 61, 62, 160.
　commons, 10.
　Desert marshes, 10.
　Little river, 1.
　neck, 10, 48, 62.
　North river, 10, 29.
　stepping-stones, 1.
　river, 1, 29, 106, 160.
Carle's point, Spruce creek, Kittery, 41.
Casco, 12, 33. 44, 76, 77.
　for Falmouth, 34.
　for North Yarmouth, 28, 30, 75.
Casco bay, 14, 15, 16, 17, 19, 24, 31, 33, 34, 37, 44, 46, 62, 65, 72, 74, 77, 131.
　Chebeag island, 23, 46, 47, called Merry's island, 46, 47.
　Maquoit, 15, 19, 23.
　Middle creek, 1.
　Pogumqua river, 23.
　river, 74.
　Sebascodegan island, 15, 19.
　Small point harbor, 15.
Cedars, the, Kittery, 6, 7.
Champernown's island, Kittery, 12, 13, 71, 139, 140.
Charlestown, Massachusetts, 14.
Chebeag island, Casco bay, 23, 46, 47.
Clay brook, Wells, 143.
Clay pit, Nonesuch, Scarborough, 43.
Connecticut,
　Hartford, 18, 117.
　Middletown, 115.
Coole harbor, Kittery, 27, 28.
Cossons islands, called also Hog islands, Casco bay, 24.
Cow island, Saco, 135.

Coxhall, afterward Lyman, 106, 116. See Swansfield.
Crocket's creek, Kittery, 121.
　neck, 154.
　plain, 156, 157.
Crooked Lane, Kittery, 33, 138.
　marsh, Scarborough, 22.
Crosses point, Wells, 39.

Daniel's creek, Kittery, 79.
Daniel Stone's garrison house, Berwick, 96.
David's brook, Saco, 135.
Devon, county of, Maine, 46.
Devon, county of, England, 151.
Dorchester, county Dorset, England, 16, 18.
Dorset county, England, 18.
Dover, New Hampshire, 30, 55, 56, 65, 90, 92, 93, 109, 157.
Drake's island, Wells, 10, 11, 125.
Dunstance, Dunstan, Scarborough, 22, 137.

East York, county of, 36.
Eastern creek, Kittery, 25.
East Greenwich, England, 152.
Eastham, Massachusetts, 128.
England, 13, 16, 18, 41, 46, 47.
　Bristol, 13, 14.
　Devon county, 151.
　Dorchester, 16, 18.
　Dorset county, 18.
　East Greenwich, 152.
　Kent county, 152.
　London, 47.
　North Petherton, 14.
　Plymouth, 16, 17, 18, 151.
　Somerset county, 14.
　Westminster, 151.
Essex county, Massachusetts, 3, 4, 49, 64, 75, 106, 107, 108, 109, 116, 117, 118.
Exeter, New Hampshire, 45, 47, 63, 64, 143.
　Lamprill river, 41, 47.

Fall mill brook, York, 67.
Falmouth, 12, 16, 34, 44, 62, 72, 74, 77, 87, 131. Called Casco, 34.

130 INDEX OF PLACES.

Falmouth, continued.
  Alewife cove, Cape Elizabeth, 141
  Back cove, 34
  Cape Elizabeth, 26, 38, 87, 141.
  Fort Loyall, 131.
  George Lewis's marsh, 43.
  Great pond, Cape Elizabeth, 141
  Long creek, 74
  Long Sands, Cape Elizabeth, 141.
  neck, 34.
  Richmond's island, 141.
  Spurwink, 44, 80, 142.
  Ware creek, 34.
Fayal, 135.
Folly brook, York, 67.
Fort Loyall, Falmouth, 131.
Fowling marsh, Berwick, 55, 96.
Frank's fort, Kittery, 83.

Goose cove, Kittery, 106.
Goosefair river, Saco, 155.
Gorgeana, afterward York, 46
  harbor mouth, 46.
  neck, 46.
  pond, 46.
  river, 46.
  Sir Ferdinando Gorges's house, 46.
  Edward Godfrey's house, 45.
Gorges, Mr.'s point, York, 43.
Great cove, Kittery, 72, 89, 102, 110, 119, 158.
Great island, New Hampshire, 1, 6, 26, 82, 87, 103, 142, 149, 161.
Great mill works, Berwick, 7.
Great pond, Cape Elizabeth, Falmouth, 141.
Great swamp, Berwick, 7.
Greenham's gut, Kittery, 67.
Greenland, New Hampshire, 12.

Hampshire, New Hampshire, 24.
Hampton, New Hampshire, 57, 117.
Hartford, Connecticut, 18, 117.
Harwich, 73.
Hog island, Isles of Shoals, 13.
Hog islands, or Cossons islands, Casco bay, 24.
Honewell's neck, Saco, 115.

Hutchinson's mill, Berwick, 152, 153.

Ingleby's point, York, 46.
Ipswich, Massachusetts, 3, 4, 13, 65, 109, 115, 116, 118, 143, 144.
Islands not named,
  in Kennebec river, 15.
  in Merrymeeting bay, 15.
  in Pejepscot river, 15.
  in Piscataqua river, 51.
  at Scarborough, 59.
  in York river, 46
Isles of Shoals, 13, 26, 53, 64, 94, 129, 138
  the northernmost of the, 53.
  Hog island, 13.
  Smuttynose island, 13, 64.
  Star island, 13.

Jameco path, Scarborough, 121.

Kennebec, 16, 17, 19, 34, 73, 75.
  river, 14, 15, 16, 33, 34, 151.
  Salt marsh creek, 73.
  Stover's rock, 73.
Kennebunk, 29.
  river, 10, 29
Kent, county of, England, 152.
Kittery, 1, 3, 5, 6. 7, 8, 9, 11, 12, 20, 21, 23, 25, 26, 27, 28, 31, 32, 33, 35, 36, 38, 41, 50, 51, 52, 53, 55, 56, 57, 60, 65, 68, 71, 72, 79, 81, 83, 84, 86, 87, 88, 89, 90, 91, 92, 93, 94, 95, 97, 98, 102, 103, 105, 107, 110, 111, 112, 113, 117, 118, 119, 120, 121, 123, 124, 128, 129, 130, 131, 132, 133, 138, 143, 144, 145, 146, 147, 149, 150, 152, 154, 155, 156, 157, 158, 159.
  point, 133.
  Ashing [Ashen] brook swamp, 121.
  Baker's spring, 93.
  Barnes point, 132.
  Bay land, 90, 144.
  Boiling rock, 110.
  Braveboat harbor, 93, 155.
  Broad cove, 68, 112.
  Cedars, the, 67.

INDEX OF PLACES. 131

Kittery, continued.
  Champernown's island, 12, 13, 71, 139, 140.
  Coole harbor, 27, 28.
  Crocket's creek, 121.
    neck, 154.
    plain, 156, 157.
  Crooked lane, 33, 138.
  Daniel's creek, 79.
  Eastern creek, 25.
  Frank's fort, 83.
  Goose cove, 106.
  Great cove, 72, 89, 102, 110, 119, 158.
  Greenham's gut, 67.
  Kittery house, 24.
  Marsh cove, 106.
  Mast cove, 88.
  Mast way, 83.
  Mill creek, 112.
  Ministry land, 90.
  Pudding hole, 25.
  Spruce creek, 1, 2, 5, 6, 25, 33, 38, 41, 52, 57, 68, 87, 94, 97, 106, 107, 111, 112, 154.
    bridge, 68.
    Carle's point, 41.
    western creek of, 111.
    stepping stones, 145.
  Stony brook, 105.
  Sturgeon creek, 3, 24, 26, 57, 60, 67, 92, 93, 98, 129, 149.
    Bare cove, 98.
  Third hill, 98, 103.
  Tompson's point, 3, 57.

Lamprill river, [Exeter], N. H., 41, 47.
Little river, Berwick, 7.
  Cape Porpoise, 1.
  Saco, 44, 94.
  Wells, 4.
London, England, 47.
Long creek, Falmouth, 74.
Long sands, Cape Elizabeth, Falmouth, 141.
Lygonia, province of, 46.
Lyman, see Coxhall.
Lynn, Massachusetts, 16, 19.

Maine, Devon county, 46.

Maquoit, Casco bay, 15, 19, 23.
Marblehead, Massachusetts, 116.
Marsh cove, Kittery, 106.
Maryland, Wells, 4.
Massachusetts:
  Amesbury, 4.
  Andover, 22.
  Barnstable county, 83, 128.
  Boston, 8, 10, 13, 15, 16, 17, 18, 19, 22, 23, 24, 27, 28, 30, 31, 32, 33, 40, 41, 42, 46, 47, 48, 49, 50, 59, 60, 61, 65, 76, 77, 78, 80, 99, 100, 101, 102, 111, 112, 125, 126, 127, 133, 134, 136, 138, 139, 140, 141, 149, 151, 156, 161.
  Boxford, 106.
  Charlestown, 14.
  Eastham, 128.
  Essex county, 3, 4, 49, 64, 75, 106, 107, 108, 109, 116, 117, 118.
  Ipswich, 3, 4, 13, 65, 109, 115, 116, 118, 143, 144.
  Lynn, 16, 19.
  Marblehead, 116.
  Middlesex county, 55, 123.
  Newbury, 94, 117, 124.
  Norfolk county, 4, 47.
  Northam, 83.
  Salem, 49, 50, 75, 76, 77, 107, 108, 123.
  Suffolk county, 32, 48, 50, 60, 99, 100, 101, 111, 125, 134, 136, 138.
  Topsfield, 106.
  Watertown, 8, 55.
Mast cove, Kittery, 88.
Mayne's point, No. Yarmouth, 31.
Merriconeag [Harpswell], 15.
Merry's island, Chebeague island, Casco bay, 46, 47.
Merrymeeting bay, 15.
Middle creek, Cape Porpoise, 1.
Middlesex county, Massachusetts, 55, 123.
Middletown, Connecticut, 115.
Mill creek, Kittery, 112.
Ministry land, Kittery, 90.
Mooty brook, Scarborough, 80.
Mousam, Wells, 61.

Mousam *alias* Cape Porpoise river, Wells, 106.
Muddy marsh, York, 36.
Mussel ridge, Wells, 125, 127.

Nanney's creek, Wells, 125.
Newbury, Massachusetts, 94, 117, 124.
Newcastle, New Hampshire, 87, 104, 141, 142, 149, 158, 161.
New England, 9, 14.
Newgewanacke, Newchowanick, Nichewanick, Berwick, 50, 82, 103, 104, 149. See Berwick.
Newgewanacke great river, Berwick, 8, 23, 55, 65, 151, 152.
little river, 152.
New Hampshire,
  Dover, 30, 55, 56, 65, 90, 92, 93, 109, 157.
  Exeter, 45, 47, 63, 64, 148.
  Great island, 1, 6, 26, 82, 87, 103, 142, 149, 161.
  Greenland, 12.
  Hampton, 57, 117.
  Lamprill river, 41, 47.
  New Castle, 87, 104, 141, 142, 149, 158, 161.
  Portsmouth, 6, 9, 26, 31, 48, 51, 67, 69, 94, 98, 102, 103, 106, 107, 110, 111, 119, 120, 121, 141, 149, 154, 158, 160.
Nonesuch, Scarborough, 43.
  clay pit, 43.
  marshes, 62.
  meadow, 72.
  path to, 43.
  river or rivulet, 43, 62, 121, 160.
Norfolk county, Mass., 4, 47.
Norgunkiet river, see Ogunquit.
Northam, Massachusetts, 83.
North Petherton, county Somerset, England, 14.
North Yarmouth, 37, 41, 65, 75.
  called Casco, 28, 30, 75. See Wescustogo.
  Barberry marsh, 19.
  Cossons or Hog islands, 24.
  Mayne's point, 31.
  Ryall's river, [11], 37, 44, [65].
  Sysquissett creek, 11.

Ogunquit river, Wells, 39, 143.
  falls, 39
  marsh, 39

Parker's marsh, Berwick, 84.
Parker's neck, Saco, 115.
Pejepscot [Brunswick], 15, 16, 18.
  fort of, 16.
  river, 15.
Pemaquid, 69.
Pig-sty river, Black point, Scarborough, 60.
Pine tree creek, Scarborough, 40.
Pipe-staff point, Berwick, 153.
Piscataqua (a district), 11, 14, 61, 69, 92, 117, 130, 139.
  harbor, 23, 151.
Piscataqua, Piscataqua river, 3, 9, 11, 12, 24, 26, 30, 33, 51, 79, 82, 83, 88, 90, 91, 96, 98, 113, 117, 128, 129, 133, 138, 150.
  the long reach in, 91.
Plymouth, England, 16, 17, 18, 151
Pogomqua river, Casco bay, 23.
Portsmouth, New Hampshire, 6, 9, 26, 31, 48, 51, 67, 69, 94, 98, 102, 103, 106, 107, 110, 111, 119, 120, 121, 141, 149, 154, 158, 160.
  called Strawberry bank, 51.
Pudding hole, Kittery, 25.

Quamphegan, Berwick, 8.
Richmond's island, Falmouth, 141.
Rocky hill, Berwick, 104, 105, 109.
Rogers's cove, York, 79.
Ryall's river, North Yarmouth, [11], 37, 44, [65].
Saco, 22, 27, 41, 42, 43, 44, 45, 61, 94, 99, 102, 124, 155, 161.
  Backehouse's creek, 161.
  Boniton's island, 135.
  Bonighton, John's division, 22.
    old plantation, 22.
  Bulley's creek, 161.
  Cow island, 135.
  David's brook, 135.
  Gibbons, James's, second division, 22.
  Goosefair river, 155.
  Honewell's neck, 115.
  Little river, 44, 94.

Index of Places.

Saco, continued.
  main creek, 36.
  neck, 41, 42.
  Parker's neck, 115.
  sea wall, 45.
  Windmill hill, 115.
  Winter Harbor, 42, 43, 44, 45, 94, 99, 100, 101, 115, 124.
Saco river, 22, 100, 101, 106, 135.
  falls, 20.
Sagadahoc, 15, 36, 151.
  falls, 36.
  river, 151.
  Canoe point, 36.
Salem, Massachusetts, 49, 50, 75, 76, 77, 107, 108, 123.
Salmon falls, Berwick, 8, 50, 86, 117.
  river that runneth to, 86.
Scarborough, 22, 38, 40, 43, 61, 62, 69, 72, 80, 81, 121, 137, 160.
  Bass creek, 80.
  Beaver dam swamp, 69.
  Black point, 22, 23, 38, 40, 59, 60, 61, 69, 80, 121, 137.
    ferry, 22.
    plains, 23.
    river, 80.
  Blue point, 31.
  Crooked lane marsh, 22.
  Dunstance, Dunstan, 22, 137.
  first creek, 61.
  Jameco path, 121.
  meeting house, 69.
  Mooty brook, 80.
  Nonesuch, 43, 62, 72.
    river, 43, 62, 121, 160.
    river running up to Dunstance, 22.
    river, the, 61, 137.
  Pig-sty river, 60.
  Pine tree creek, 40.
Scotland, York, 7, 108.
Sebascodegan island, Casco bay, 15, 19.
Slut's corner, Berwick, 7.
Small's island, Sebascodegan island so called, 19.
Small point harbor, Casco bay, 15.
Smuttynose island, Isles of Shoals, 13, 64.

Somerset county, England, 14.
South Carolina, 120.
Spruce creek, Kittery, 1, 2, 5, 6, 25, 33, 38, 41, 52, 57, 68, 87, 94, 97, 106, 107, 111, 112, 154.
  bridge, 68.
  Carle's point, 41.
  western creek of, 111.
Spurwink, Falmouth, 44, 80, 142.
  river, 87, 142.
Star island, Isles of Shoals, 13.
Stepping stones, Kittery, 145.
Cape Neddick, York, 1.
Stony brook, Kittery, 105.
Stover's rock, Kennebec river, 73.
Strawberry bank, former name of Portsmouth, N. H., 51.
Sturgeon creek, Kittery, 3, 24, 26, 57, 60, 67, 92, 93, 98, 129, 149.
  Bare cove, 98.
Suffolk county, Massachusetts, 32, 48, 59, 60, 99, 100, 101, 111, 125, 134, 136, 138.
Swansfield, another name for Coxhall, 106.
Sysquisset creek, North Yarmouth, 11.

Third hill, Kittery, 98, 103.
Tompson's point, Kittery, 3, 57.
Tom Tinker's swamp, Berwick, 7.
Topsfield, Massachusetts, 106.

Unity parish, afterward Berwick, 84, 85.

Ware creek, Falmouth, 34.
Watertown, Massachusetts, 8, 55.
Webhannet river, Wells, 12, 47, 64, 95.
  alias great river, 95.
Wells, 1, 3, 4, 10, 12, 24, 30, 31, 38, 39, 45, 46, 47, 48, 49, 50, 61, 62, 63, 64, 85, 95, 99, 100, 101, 106, 111, 125, 126, 127, 128, 143.
  Beaver pond, 1.
  Clay brook, 143.
  Cross's point, 39.
  Drake's island, 10, 11, 125.
  Great plain, 128.
  Little river, 4, falls of, 4.

Wells, continued
　Main creek, 125, 127.
　Merryland, 4
　Mousam, 61.
　Mousam, or Cape Porpoise river, 106
　Mussel ridge, 125, 127.
　Nanney's creek, 125
　Ogunquit river. 39, 143.
　　falls, 39
　　marsh, 39.
　　sea wall, 12, 125.
　Webhannet river, 12, 47, 64, 95, called Great river, 95.
　　the river, 125
Wescustogo, Indian name of North Yarmouth, 19, 24, 37, 44.
Westminster, England, 151.
Whitte's marsh, Berwick, 55, 129.
Wilcock's pond, Berwick, 86, 149.
Windmill hill, Saco, 115.
Winnegance creek, Kennebec river, 17.
　carrying place, 34.
　marshes, 84, 73.
Winter harbor, Saco, 42, 43, 44, 45, 94, 99, 100, 101, 115, 124.

Yorkshire, 47, 140, 141.
　East York, 36.
York, town of, 7, 12, 19, 21, 23, 24, 28, 29, 30, 31, 32, 37, 42, 43,

York, continued
　45, 46, 47, 48, 50, 53, 58, 59, 60, 61, 66, 67, 78, 79, 82, 93, 107, 108, 109, 110, 114, 115, 128, 129, 146, 148, 154, 158, 159. See Gorgeana.
　Bass cove, 7, 30, 108, 159.
　　brook, 67.
　Bell marsh, 67.
　Braveboat harbor, 12, 29, 36, 46, 71, 93.
　bridge, 29, 31, 66, 146, 159.
　Cape Neddick, 4, 19, 32, 36, 46, 54.
　　river, 54.
　　stepping stones, 1.
　Fall mill brook, 67.
　Folly brook, 67.
　Gorges, Mr.'s, point, 43.
　Ingleby point, 43.
　marshes, 93.
　Meeting house creek, 114, 146.
　Muddy marsh, 36.
　New mill creek, 146, 154.
　　landing place, 154.
　pond, 93
　river, 7, 19, 31, 43, 46, 53, 78, 82, 107, 108, 109, 129, 148, 158, 159.
　　partings of, 148.
　Rogers cove, 79.
　Scotland, 7, 108.

GENERAL INDEX.

Accounts, 107.
  balance of, 49, 67.
  errors in, 9.
  stated, 2, 26, 67.
Acknowledgment:
  annual rents, 3, 17, 46, 47.
  days' work, 40.
  duties, 7.
  proprietor's rent, 58.
  quit rent, 47, 152.
  two dry cusk or cod fish, 17.
  to the king, 7, 152.
  to the lord proprietor, 7, 38, 145.
  yearly, 159.
Act of Massachusetts Gen'l Court for regulating townships and choice of town officers, 93.
Addition to a lot, 149.
Address, to the king, 24.
Administrators, 5, 9, 10, 16, 27, 28, 35, 41, 48, 49, 53, 80, 83, 91, 92, 93, 94, 118, 124, 138, 144, 149, 154, 155, 159.
Adverse possession, 37.
Agents. See Attorneys.
Agreements. See Contracts.
Agriculture. See Husbandry.
Allotment of land to new settlers, 41.
Anchors, 13, 26, 133.
Anchor-smith, 99.
Annuity, 111, 126.
Appeals, 43.
Apples, 52.
Appraisals, 26, 32, 40, 52, 61.
Appraisers, 26.
  sworn, 40.
Arabella, a fishing shallop, 133.
Assignments, 12, 30, 34, 35, 42, 43, 69, 82, 99, 100, 103, 104, 140, 149, 156.
Assistants, members of the governor's council in Massachusetts, 3,

Assistants, continued.
  4, 10, 14, 17, 20, 24, 27, 28, 32, 36, 42, 43, 49, 50, 59, 60, 62, 77, 78.
  of New Hampshire, 67.
Associates, Yorkshire magistrates, 3, 4, 5, 21, 34, 35, 40, 41, 43, 55, 56, 60, 67, 82.
Attachment, 41.
Attorneys, 3, 9, 13, 14, 16, 18, 19, 22, 30, 33, 35, 43, 44, 46, 47, 49, 53, 140, 141.
Award, 2, 35, 53. See Reference.

Bait, 141.
  right to procure reserved, 141.
Bait-house, 13.
Barns, 6, 20, 24, 26, 33, 52, 77, 79, 91, 104, 107, 109, 112, 113, 133, 147.
Bastard meadow, 11.
Bay land in Kittery, 90, 144.
Beaches conveyed, 18.
Beans, 52.
Bedding, 2, 81.
Beds, 2, 61, 81.
Berwick parish in the town of Kittery, 23. See Index of Places.
  commons, 55, 65, 86, 149.
  county road, 104.
  highways, 11, 86, 96.
  ministry lands, 23, 86.
  saw mills, 7, 8, 9, 11, 152.
  selectmen, 23.
  undivided lands, 117.
  grants recorded, see Index of Grantors under names following:
    Barnard, Joseph, 65.
    Broughton, John, 53.
    Elliot, Robert, 103, 149.
    Emery, James, 96, 105.
    Fuz, Allen, 103.
    Gattinsby, John, 85.

Berwick, continued.
  Goodwin, Daniel, 21.
  Gowen, Nicholas, 104.
  Joy, Ephraim, 104.
  Mason, Robert T., 151.
  Nock, Sylvanus, 109.
  Playstead, Roger's estate, 9.
  Spencer, Humphrey, 55, 103, 149.
    Patience, 7.
    Thomas, 84.
    William, 11.
  Taylor, John, 117.
  Thompson, Miles, 96.
  Tufton, John, 153.
  Willis, Samuel, 117.
  Wincoll, John, 8, 86.
  grants referred to:
    town(i e. Kittery) to Thomas Spencer, 7.
    to John Wincoll, 8.
    James Emery to Sylvanus Nock, 109.
    James Emery, sen. to James Emery, 96.
    James Grant to Daniel Goodwin, sen., 21.
    Benoni Hodgsden to Joseph Barnard, 65.
    Eliakim Hutchinson to John Emerson, 23.
    Thomas Spencer or his estate to Thomas Etherington, 7.
    to John Gattinsby, 7.
    to Daniel Goodine, 7.
    to Humphrey Spencer, 7.
    to William Spencer, 11.
    Abra Tilton to Miles Thompson, sen , 96.
Bills, 49, 107, 110.
  of sale, 35, 53.
Bipartite indentures, 52.
Blacksmith, 79, 99, 107, 108.
Bonds, 2, 8, 9, 12, 23, 30, 32, 35, 49, 59, 92, 100, 102, 111, 120, 126, 161.
  conditions of, broken, 12.
Book debts, 49, 107.
Bound stake, 90.
Bound trees, 67, 78. See Marked trees.

Brass vessels, 81.
Breaches, beaches, 135.
Brew-house, 24, 26.
Brick, 117.
Brick-layer, 93.
Brick-maker, 115.
Bridges, 29, 31, 66, 93, 146, 159.
Brunswick. See Pejepscot.
Burying grounds reserved, 12, 96.

Calendar, according to the account of England, 13.
Canting, caution, fustian, 67.
Captain, 2, 8, 9, 12, 20, 21, 23, 24, 25, 30, 35, 36, 40, 42, 50, 51, 53, 61, 65, 67, 72, 73, 82, 86, 88, 94, 99, 100, 101, 102, 103, 109, 110, 134, 151, 152, 154, 157, 159.
Cape Porpoise. See Index of Places.
  commons, 10.
  grants recorded, see Index of Grantors under names following:
    Batson, Stephen, 1.
    Bolles, Joseph, 3
    Ellet, Robert, 160.
    Howell, Morgan's estate, 48.
    Mountegue, Margaret's estate, 10, 61.
    Renalds, John, 29.
  grants referred to.
    town to Edmund Littlefield, Joseph Bolls, John Littlefield, Nicholas Coole, 12
    Mary Bolls to Samuel Snow, 62.
    Thomas Gorges to Morgan Howell, 3.
    Francis Littlefield, senior, to Nicholas Coole, 12.
Care and custody, 13.
Casco Bay See Index of Places
  grants referred to:
    Indians to Nicholas Shapleigh, 19.
    Walter Merry by mesne conveyances to Edmund White, 46.
    Alexander Rigby to Walter Merry, 46.

Casco Bay, continued.
   John Shapleigh to Richard Wharton, 15.
Carpenter, 3, 11, 27, 31, 61, 91, 96, 119, 120, 140, 160.
Cart-ways, 65, 73
Cattle. See Domestic Animals.
Cautions, caveats, 20.
Cellars, 24, 26.
Certain and uncertain, more or less, 10, 31.
Certificate of property taken for military use, 30.
Challenge, claim, 55.
Chamber, lodging, 24, 26
Charges, cost of, 2, 8, 113.
   town, 35.
Charter, of the province of Maine, 24.
Chests, 2.
Chief Justice of New Hampshire, Walter Barefoote, 41.
Chirurgeon, surgeon, 30.
Chimneys, 24, 26, 61.
Claims, 19, 43.
   against intestates' estate, 26.
   commissions to audit, 26.
Clearing meadow, 43.
Clerk, minister, 22
   of court, 151.
Clothes, wearing, 61.
   buttons, 67.
   hat, castor, 67, felt, 67.
Cloths, see
   broadcloth, 67.
   camlet, 67.
   canting, 67.
   canvas, 67.
   gympe, 67.
   kenten, 111
   kersey, 67.
   linen, 2, 81, 67.
   loceium, 67.
   nowels, 67.
   oniston, 67.
   searge, 86.
   silk, 67.
   tabby, 67
   woolen, 81.
Coality, commonalty, 46.

Commissioners, inferior magistrates in Yorkshire, 2, 5, 12, 40, 43, 59, 65, 73, 84, 85, 128.
   of Massachusetts, 99, 100, 101.
   of New Hampshire, 5, 47, 51, 142.
   Mr. Gorges's, 15.
   to superintend settlement of a town, 41.
   on intestate's estate, 61, 67, 69.
   appointed by courts, 23, 26
   by general assembly of Maine, 24, 26, 41.
Committee of the Boston militia, 30.
Commons, 10, 11, 24, 25, 42, 54, 55, 65, 67, 68, 98, 103, 119, 143, 149, 150.
Compass, 53.
Common law of England, cited, 12.
Conditions of sale, broken by grantee, 19.
   of a grant, 82.
Confirmation, 64
Connecticut, councillor of, 117.
Counows, canoes, 43, 56.
Consideration. See also under Pay.
   account for goods, 133
   affection and love, 7, 12, 19, 21, 22, 23, 27, 29, 34, 41, 48, 53, 60, 68, 71, 72, 73, 79, 81, 82, 84, 89, 96, 154
   annuity, 111, 126
   forfeiture of a bond, 101.
   labor on a farm, 19.
   land in exchange, 16, 57, 59.
   marriage portion, 47, 87.
   release of claims, 40
   saving harmless on a bond, 8
   support and maintenance, 12, 121.
   valuable, 13, 22, 29, 58, 61, 65, 89, 94, 102, 103, 154.
Contracts, 14, 45, 46, 56, 68, 161.
   agreements, 2, 12, 16, 37, 40, 50, 78, 80, 113, 161.
   marriage settlements, 51, 86.
Contribution toward building, &c., 104.
Coomes, coomb, a dry measure, four bushels, 35.

138   General Index.

Cooper, 7, 155, 157.
Cordwainer, 10, 48, 50, 61, 77, 115.
Corn, 2, 6.
  standing, 2, 6.
  growing, 40.
Corn and grist mills:
  at Kittery, 52, 57.
  at Saco, 45.
Council of Massachusetts, 30.
  councillors of, 90, 113, 115, 126, 127, 136, 147.
Council for New England, 16, 18, 151
Councillor of Connecticut, 117.
  of New Hampshire, 68, 69.
Country highway, 36.
Country's use, cow taken for, 30.
County road, 104.
Courts, 2, 85   See General Court
  executions, 32, 42, 61. See levy on.
  extent, 43
  judgment of, 32, 42, 43, 55, 61.
  license to sell real estate, 149.
  of appeals, 43
  of associates held at Wells, 61.
  of New Hampshire, 67.
  of pleas, 32, 43, 61.
  of quarter sessions, 18.
  of sessions, held at York, 128.
  held at Wells, 61.
    at York, 32.
  superior, held at Boston, 149.
Covenants:
  for further assurance, 12, 17, 18, 22, 54, 80, 108, 109, 112, 114, 115, 118, 119, 139, 146, 148, 153
  limited to seven years, 122.
  to reconvey, 23.
  to support a minister, 23.
Coverture, 53.
Coxhall. See Index of Places.
  grants recorded, see Index of Grantors under names following:
    Dorman, Timothy, 106.
    Harris, John, 116.
  grants referred to:
    Harlakenden Symonds to John Harris & als., 116.

Creditors of intestates, 61
Crows, iron, 57.
Cup-board cloth, 2.
Customs   See Manners and Customs.

Dams, 8, 52, 64, 74, 75, 135, 152, 161.
  beaver, 69.
Deeds:
  acknowledged before authority, 34.
  ante-dating of, 40
  called bills of sale, 21, 50, 58, 59 115.
  deferred, 155.
  Indian, 17.
  of gift, 6, 19, 88, 109.
Defeasance, 113
D.. headed, distracted, demented, 72.
Demands, 50.
Depositions. See Index of Grantors under names following:
  Abbett, Thomas, 55.
  Burrage, William, 43
  Carter, Richard, 11, 37.
  Chadborne, Humphrey, 67.
  Coffin, Peter, 41.
  Conley, Abraham, 56.
  Cossons, John, 11, 37.
  Donnell, Henry, 37.
  Emery, James, jr., 55.
  Ginkens [Jenkins], Renald, 56
  Goodwin, Daniel, jun., 56.
  Hammond, Jonathan, 61.
  Haynes, Joyce, 19
  Haynes, Thomas, 19.
  Hodgsden, Benoni, 55.
  Howell, John, 43.
  Howleman, John, 37.
  Hunscum, Thomas, 57.
  Ingersall, George, 43.
  Jenkins, Jabez, 67.
  Jenkins, Stephen, 67.
  Kemble, Thomas, 41.
  Leatherby, William, 37.
  Lord, Abraham, 114
  Lord, Martha, 56
  Lord, Nathan, 114.
  Lord, Nathan, jun, 56.

Depositions, continued.
  Mayne, Elizabeth, 31.
  Mayne, John, 31.
  Miller, John, 42.
  Penley, Sampson, 19.
  Playstead, William, 67.
  Remich, Christian, 151.
  Rogers, Richard, 151.
  Skinner, Edward, 19.
  Smale, Francis, 41.
  Smyth, John, 41.
  Stephens, Edward, 24.
  Stone, Daniel, 56.
  Tayler, George, 43.
  Turner, Thomas, 56.
  Twisden, John, 46.
  Watts, Henry, 43.
  Weare, Peter, 46.
  Webber, John, 24.
  White, Elias, 19.
  White, John, 56.
Deputy governor of Massachusetts, Thomas Danforth, 9.
  of the province of Maine, Thos. Gorges, 46.
Deputy marshal 61.
Deputy president of the province of Maine, John Davess, 13, 21, 36, 37, 41, 44, 54, 72, 140, 144.
  of the province of Lygonia (under Rigby), George Cleeve, 41, 46.
Discharge, release, 35, 107, 141.
Distraint, 40.
  growing corn excepted from, 40.
Ditch, a double, 61.
Divident, division, 21.
Dividing lines, 35.
Doctor, 154.
Dogs, iron, 57.
Domestic animals:
  bull, 81, 112.
  calves, 2, 52.
  cattle, 24, 36, 52, 61, 81, 110, 112, 140.
  cows, 2, 20, 30, 33, 35, 52, 61, 81, 112, 133, 140.
  creatures, 140.
  ewes, 52.
  heifers, 33, 35, 52, 81, 112.
  horses, 2, 113.

Domestic animals, continued.
  lambs, 52, 113.
  mares, 61, 81.
    breeding, 140.
  neat cattle, 23, 49, 113.
  oxen, 2, 33, 35, 81, 112, 140.
  sheep, 2, 23, 81, 112, 140.
  steers, 2, 20, 33, 35, 52, 81.
  swine, 2, 81, 140.
  yearlings, 2.
Domestic uses. See Domestic animals, Furniture, Garden.
  beef, 30.
  butter, 81, 113.
  brew-house, 24, 26.
  cheese, 81, 113.
  cider, 81, 113.
  coombs, 35.
  firewood, 21, 27, 52, 113.
  garden stuff, 113.
  loom, 66, 81.
  milk, 113.
  molasses, 69.
  provisions, 19.
  tackling, cotton, of a loom, 66.
  weaving, 66.
  woolen, on a loom, 81.
Dower, setting out of, 2, 24, 26.
  leased, 2.
  rights, 135.
Dowers, clerical error for donors, 53.
Draught, survey, plot, 31, 152.
Dwelling-room, 52, 81.

Egress, regress, &c., Right of way, q. v.
England, immigration from, John Shapleigh brought from, 41.
English, the first to settle at Kennebec, 17.
  improvement by at Sebascodegan island, 19.
Entailment, release of, 120.
Entry for condition broken, 26.
Esquire, 14, 17, 23, 30, 46, 51, 53, 75, 149, 153.
Estate, convey, 7, 57, 84.
Euon, yeoven, given, 7.
Execution, 61.
Executors, 10, 20, 30, 32, 43, 61, 64, 118.

140 GENERAL INDEX.

Falmouth. See Index of Places.
  selectmen, 74.
  town records, 131.
  grants recorded, see Index of Grantors under names following:
    Brackett, Mary, 35.
      Thomas, 34.
    Harvy, Elizabeth, 34.
    Harwood, Henry, 77.
    Jordan, Robert, 87.
      Robert, jun., 141.
    Morrough, Dennis, 74.
    Munjoy, George's estate, 35.
    Nichols, Francis, 131.
    Parrett, John, 26.
    Swett, Clement, 38.
    Webber, Samuel, 74.
  grants referred to:
    town to Dennis Morrough, 74.
      to Francis Nicholls, 131.
      to Jonathan Orris, 131.
      to Samuel Webber, 74.
    George Burroughs to Henry Harwood, 77.
    Nathaniel Fryer to John Hollicomb, 142.
      to John Parret, 142.
      to Thomas Sparks, 142.
      to Edward Vittery, 142.
    Elizabeth Harvy to Thomas Brackett, 12.
    Robert Jordan, to Robert Jordan, jun., 142.
    John Skillings, to George Burroughs, 77.
    Richard Smith to Fr. Nicholls, 131.
Families, number requisite to settle a town, 18.
Farm, 151.
Farm house, 46.
Feast of St. Michael, 69.
Fee simple, 18, 20, 38, 53, 75, 96, 116, 121, 133.
Fee tail, 23, 27, 79, 88, 120, 154.
Fences, 21, 23, 27, 28, 39, 40, 55, 56, 57, 61, 87, 96, 97, 117, 133, 145, 146.
Fencing, 19, 37, 48, 113.
Feofees in trust, trustees, 51.

Firewood, reserved, 21, 52, 113.
  grant of, 27.
Fish, 133. See under Pay and Prices.
Fisherman, 1, 13, 17, 26, 27, 29, 34, 38, 40, 42, 44, 46, 73, 80, 129, 143, 159.
Fishing and its uses, 141.
  bait, 141.
  bait-house, 13.
  encouragement of, 17.
  English fishery, 15.
  flakes, fishing, 13, 26, 64, 87.
  flakeroom, 13, 26, 87.
  kintolls, quintals, 111.
  liberty of, 16, 18, 33, 75, 135, 151, 152.
  liberty to build houses for fishermen, 46.
  right reserved by Indians, 15.
  salmon and sturgeon, 15.
  shallops, 13, 133.
  stages, 13, 26, 87.
  train vat, 64.
  winter voyage for, 133.
Flats, 18, 88, 94, 115, 124, 135.
Fodder, 52.
Foot-bridge, 64.
Fowling, liberty of, 16, 18, 33, 75, 135, 151, 152.
Freeholders of a town, 18, 131.
Fruit, gathering of, 52.
Furniture:
  bedding, 2, 81.
  beds, 2, 61, 81.
  brass vessels, 81.
  chests, 2.
  cupboard cloth, 2.
  household implements, 40.
  iron vessels, 81.
  moveables, chattels, 66.
  napkins, 2.
  pewter, 2, 81.
  pillow-bears, 2.
  platters, 61.
  sheets, cotton, 2.
    Dowless, 2.
  towels, 2.
  trunks, 2.
  wooden vessels, 81.

GENERAL INDEX. 141

Gardens, 19, 40, 52, 64, 75, 77, 91, 112, 117, 119, 123, 147.
plot, 24, 26.
Garrison, 96.
Gear, running of a mill, 8, 135.
General assembly of the province of Maine, 24, 26, 28, 29, 47, [93].
session of at York, 47.
General court of Massachusetts, 23, 93.
Generation, immediate family, 12.
Gentleman, 3, 5, 20, 30, 45, 46, 51, 63, 71, 109, 111, 112, 117, 126, 134, 157.
Gifts, 47, 114.
Glazier, 31.
Glover, 143.
Goldsmith, 10, 50.
Goodman, 32.
Governor, the, 93.
Governor of Massachusetts, Simon Bradstreet, 9, 10.
of New Hampshire, Edward Cranfield, 24.
Government under Alexander Rigby, 41.
Grain, English, 113.
Grants referred to. See Patents.
Grantors:
  Adams, William, 6, 107.
  Banks, Richard, 7.
  Benmore, [Philip], 93.
  Bolls, Mary, 62.
  Bonighton, John, 135.
  Booth, Simon, 45.
  Bush, John, 106.
  Cape Porpoise, town of, 12.
  Carle, Richard, 41.
  Champernown, Francis, 139.
  Cloyce, Peter, 4.
  Coole, Mr., 111, 126.
  Crocket, Joshua, 156.
  Cross, 10.
  Cutt, Robert's estate, 32.
  Edge, Robert, 129.
  Elkines, 40.
    Christopher, 40.
  Emery, Anthony, 93.
    James, 92, 96, 109.
  Endle, Richard, 64.
  Everett, Margaret, 56.

Grants referred to, continued.
  Falmouth, town of, 74, 131.
  Farrow, George, 4.
  Flewellin, 106.
  Fryer, Nathaniel, 39, 142.
  Ginkens [Jenkins], Renald, 56.
  Godfrey, Ann, 36.
  Gorges, Sir Ferdinando, 24, 152.
    Thomas, 3.
  Grant, James, 21.
  Green, Richard, 83.
  Hammond, Joseph, 57.
    William, 111, 126.
  Harvy, Elizabeth, 12.
  Hatch, Samuel, 143.
  Hodgsden, Benoni, 65.
  Howell, John, 137.
  Hutchinson, Eliakim, 23.
  Indians, 17, 75.
  Jocelyn, Henry, 23.
  Jordan, Robert, 142.
  Johnson, William, 46.
  King, Samuel, 147.
  Knight, Robert, 53.
    Samuel, 31.
  Kittery, town of, 8, 25, 27, 28, 38, 57, 84, 85, 86, 87, 88, 89, 90, 93, 95, 102, 105, 110, 117, 119, 138, 150, 152, 156, 159.
  Littlefield Francis, 4, 12.
  Lyn, Ephraim, 106.
  Massachusetts, 23.
  Mavericke, Antipas, 79.
  Maxell, Alexander, 129.
  Merry, Walter, 46.
  Morgan, Francis, 94, 106.
  Newgrove, John, 56.
  Oliver, William, 3.
  Palmer, William, 31, 88, 89.
  Phillips, William, 135.
  Purchase, Thomas, 15.
  Racklift, William, 123.
  Randall, Richard, 44.
  Remich, Christian, 119.
  Rigby, Alexander, 46.
  Rishworth, Edward, 109.
  Sanders, Lieutenant, 106.
  Sayword, Henry, 75.
  Scarborough, town of, 43, 121

Grants referred to, continued.
  Shapleigh, John, 15.
  Skillings, John, 77.
  Smyth, John, 19.
    Richard, 131.
  Sosowen, 106.
  Spencer, Thomas, 7, 11, 86.
    William, 86.
  Spinney, Thomas, 113.
  Stevens, Thomas, 75.
  Symonds, Harlakenden, 106, 116.
    William, 111, 126.
  Tilton, Abraham, 96.
  Turbet, Peter, 106.
  Veazie, George, 86.
  Vines, Richard, 41.
  Wadleigh, John, 63.
    Robert, 63, 64.
  Wells, town of, 38.
  Wentworth, John, 21.
  Wharton, Richard, 16.
  Wheelwright, John, 111, 126.
  White, John, 138.
  Withers, Thomas, 38, 51.
  Wittum, Peter, sen., 57.
    Peter, jun., 57.
  Woods, Richard, 46.
  York, town of, 7, 28, 29, 36, 37, 45, 46, 48, 66, 82, 93, 115, 159.
  Young, John, 46, 63.
  Young, Rowland, 53.
Grantees:
  Adams, Charles, 93.
  Alcock, Joseph, 102.
  Austine, Matthew, 66.
  Avant, Francis, 156.
  Barnard, Joseph, 65.
  Baston, Thomas, 4.
  Beale, Arthur, 29.
  Benmore, Philip, 92, 93.
  Bickford, Thomas, 43.
  Bodg, Henry, 25.
  Brackett, Thomas, 12.
  Bully, Joseph, 12.
  Burdett, George, 46.
  Burroughs, George, 77.
  Bush, John, 106.
  Coole, Nicholas, 12.
  Cossons, John, 24.

Grants referred to, continued.
  Crocket, Joseph, 150, 156.
  Cross, Joseph, 10, 38.
  Curtis, Thomas, 7.
  Cutt, John, 106.
  Davis, John, 159.
  Davis, 66.
  Donnell, Henry, 115.
  Dorman, Timothy, 106.
  Elleot, Robert, 121.
  Emery, Anthony, 93.
    James, 88, 96.
  Emerson, John, 23.
  Estis, Richard, 123.
  Etherington, Thomas, 7.
  Everett, Margery, 56.
    Martha, 56.
  Fabes, John, 94.
  Frost, Nicholas, 193.
    William, 135.
  Fryer, Nathaniel, 139.
  Gattensby, John, 7.
  Gidney Bartholomew, 75.
  Ginkens [Jenkins], Renald, 56.
  Glanfield, Peter, 31.
  Goodhue, William, 3.
  Goodine, Daniel, 7, 21.
  Goodridge, Isaac, 147.
  Green, John, 83.
  Gunnison, Elihu, 6, 107.
  Haenan, Mr., 135.
  Harker, John, 159.
  Harwood, Henry, 77.
  Harris, John, 116.
  Hincks, John, 139.
  Hinxen, Peter, 40.
  Holicomb, John, 142.
  Hoole, John, 138.
  Howell, Morgan, 3.
  Hunscum, John, 159.
    Thomas, 105.
  Hutchinson, Eliakim, 152.
  Jordan, Dominicus, 44.
    Robert, 41.
    Robert, jun., 142.
  King, William, 86, 88, 89.
  Kittery, town of, 93.
  Leader, George, 152.
    Richard, 152.
  Leighton, William, 5, 56.
  Litten, George, 138.

GENERAL INDEX. 143

Grants referred to, continued.
  Liveingstone, Daniel, 45.
  Littlefield, Edmund, 12.
    John, 12.
  Mason, John, 152.
  Merry, Walter, 46.
  Miller, Richard, 90.
    Samuel, 90.
  Moore, William, 159.
  Morrough, Dennis, 74.
  Morton, John, 137.
  Nanney, Robert, 111, 126.
  Neale, John, 36, 129.
  Nicholls, Francis, 131.
  Nock, Sylvanus, 109.
  Orris, Jonathan, 131.
  Parker, Isaac, 21.
    John, 17.
  Parret, John, 142.
  Pendleton, Bryan, 45, 94.
  Pennel, Joseph, 109.
  Phillips, William, 135.
  Pouning, Henry, 27, 28.
  Preble, Joseph, 46.
  Purchase heirs, 16.
  Redden, John, 43.
  Remich, Christian, 89.
    Isaac, 119.
  Rice, Mary, 51.
  Sanders, lieutenant, 106.
  Sawyer, William, 46, 64.
  Sayword, Henry, 75, 82.
  Scottow, Joshua, 23.
  Seely, William, 41.
  Shapleigh, Nicholas, 19, 79.
  Shrimpton, Samuel, 32.
  Simmons, John, 110.
  Smyth, John, 36.
    John, jun., 19.
  Snow, Samuel, 62.
  Sparks, Thomas, 142.
  Spencer, Humphrey, 7.
    William, 11.
  Spinney, John, 113.
  Stephens, Thomas, 75.
  Symonds, Harlakenden, 106.
  Thompson, Miles, 96.
  Turbet, Peter, 106.
  Twisden, Peter, 129.
  Vittery, Edward, 142.
  Wadleigh, John, 68.

Grants referred to, continued.
  Wadleigh, Robert, 68.
  Wanewright, Francis, 64.
  Webber, Samuel, 74.
  Wharton, Richard, 15, 23.
  White, Edmund, 46.
    John, 138.
  Whitney, Benjamin, 37.
  Wilson, Gowen, 87.
  Wincoll, John, 8, 86.
  Withers, Elizabeth, 51.
  Wittum, Peter, 57.
    Peter, jun., 57.
    William, 57.
  Woodman, John, 95.
  Woods, Richard, 46.
  Wormewood, William, 7.
  York, town of, 46, 93.
  Young, Robert, 53.
    Rowland, 48, 53, 159.
Grass, English, 52.
  thatch, 56.
Grist mills. See Corn mills.
Guardian, 86.
Gut, gully, 10, 37, 44, 67, 141.
Gympe, a silk twist edging, 67.

Half-deal, moiety, half part, 16, 141.
Hand-gun, musket, 35.
Havens, 151.
Hawking, liberty of, 33, 151, 152.
Hay, 2, 48, 52.
  cutting or mowing, 34, 43.
  fetching by canoes, 43.
  yard, 154.
Head-wears, 75, 135.
Heathen, Indians, 37, 52.
Heir, or heiress, by descent, 4, 5, 10, 12, 15, 16, 18, 27, 28, 29, 47, 58, 59, 60, 106, 125, 146.
  by devise, 3, 11, 41, 47, 80, 151, 152.
Heriots, 88.
Highways, 3, 4, 11, 21, 24, 25, 28, 35, 38, 39, 58, 59, 61, 86, 91, 93, 96, 107, 108, 114, 144, 156.
Home lots, 35, 88.
Homestall, homestead, 53.
Horse-cart, 40.
House-carpenter, 73.

Household implements, 40.
  stuff, see Furniture.
Houses, and appurtenances See Gardens, Messuages, Rights of way.
  addition to a lot, 149.
  brick, 117.
  cellars, 24, 26.
  chamber, lodging, 24, 26
  chimneys, 24, 26, 61.
  dwelling lot, 64.
    room, 52, 81.
  farm-house, 46.
  garrison, 96.
  hall, 24, 26.
  home lots, 35, 83.
  homestall, 53.
  kitchen 24, 26
  lean-to, 52, 64, 91, 112.
  linneys, lean-tos, 20.
  nails, 68
  parlor, 24.
  parsonage house, 64.
  repairs, 113
  timber, 108.
  well, 104
Hunting, right of reserved by Indians, 15.
  liberty of, 83, 135, 151, 152.
Husbandman, 19, 30, 44, 54, 106, 110, 130, 148 See Yeoman
Husband, to manage a farm, 113
Husbandry. See Domestic Animals, Fences, Orchards, Plantations, Rights of way.
  apples, 52.
  barns, 6, 20, 24, 26, 33, 52, 77, 79, 91, 104, 107, 109, 112, 113, 133, 147.
  bastard-meadow, 11.
  beans, 52
  cart-ways, 65, 73.
  clearing meadow, 43.
  corn, 2, 6, 40.
  cow-yard, 87
  ditch, 61.
  encouragement of, 17.
  farm, 151.
  farm-house, 46.
  fodder, 52.

Husbandry, continued.
  fruit gathering, 52.
  grain, English, 113.
  grass, English, 52.
    thatch, 56
  hay, 2, 34, 43, 52, 154.
  horse cart, 40
  implements of, 117.
  increase of stock, 112, 113.
  manure, to, 118.
  meadow land, 8.
  pasturage, 23, 40, 109.
  pease, 52.
  planting field, 6.
  plow stuff, 40
  quick stock, 40, 66.
  rails, 61.
  sheep-shed, 33.
  sled, 40.
  stables, 20, 77, 109
  stock of cattle, 2, 52, 61, 81, 112, 140.
  thatch, 55, -banks, 87, -creek, 56, 109, -grass, 56, 155.
  threshing, 61, 113.
  tools, 112.
  tools for, 112.
  unfenced land, 24, 26.
  wood, 90, 117.
  yoke of oxen, 35.

Indians, 43, 106.
Indian trader, 19.
Indian wars, 51, 52, 61.
Inhabitants, ancient, of Casco Bay, 19.
  English at Pejepscot, 15.
  of Kittery, 55.
  of York, 28.
  settled in the province of Maine, 28.
  to be received by commissioners appointed, 41.
Interest, at six per centum, 140, 161
Inventories, 2, 51.
Iron vessels, 81.
Iron work, of a mill, 57.
Isles of Shoals. See Index of Places.

Isles of Shoals, continued.
  grants recorded, see Index of Grantors under names following:
    Downs, Richard, 13.
    Wanewright, Francis, 64.
    Young, Rowland, 13.
  grant referred to:
    Richard Endle to Francis Wanewright, 64.
  Issue, failure of, 41.
  final determination, 12, 43, 49, 59.

Jail-keeper for the province, John Parker, 61.
Joiner, 96.
Joint note, 6, obligation, 9.
Joint tenants, 2, 13, 20, 41, 51, 60, 66, 81, 116, 134, 142.
Justices of the peace:
  Job Alcock, 79, 83, 92, 98, 103, 105, 110, 120, 124.
  John Davess, 6, 37, 43, 61.
  Samuel Donnell, 86, 108, 110, 114, 115, 131, 146, 148.
  Charles Frost, 9, 32, 51, 67, 81, 82, 83, 84, 91, 96, 97, 98, 102, 104, 109, 129, 130, 143.
  Joseph Hammond, 151.
  Francis Hooke, 1, 6, 12, 25, 26, 29, 30, 35, 36, 55, 72, 88, 89, 90, 107, 111, 113, 123, 128, 132.
  Henry Jocelyn, 17. Justice of the Quorum, 33.
  William Pepperrell, 89, 94, 97, 112, 113, 132, 139, 145, 147, 154, 155, 156, 157, 158.
  Ichabod Plaisted, 150.
  Abraham Preble, 79.
  Edward Rishworth, 2, 8, 11, 12, 13, 19, 21, 23, 24, 27, 30, 31, 35, 37, 42, 45, 46, 48, 53, 55, 57, 58, 59, 63, 66, 67, 86, 134, 159, 161.
  Joshua Scottow, 12, 22, 38, 81.
  Edward Tyng, 12, 16, 18, 19, 35, 42, 43, 61, 63, 65, 72, 74, 75.
  Samuel Wheelwright, 5, 11, 12, 39, 46, 49, 78, 89, 95, 127, 128, 147.

Justices of the peace, continued.
  John Wincoll, 7, 9, 11, 22, 25, 38, 44, 45, 55, 56, 66.
  of Massachusetts,
    Isaac Addington, 138.
    John Appleton, 118, 144.
    Jonathan Corwin, 106.
    Jeremiah Dummer, 112.
    John Fabes, 65.
    John Hathourn, 123.
    Elisha Hutchinson, 127.
    Timothy Prout, 80, 99, 100, 101.
    Edward Randolph, 140.
    Samuel Sewall, 129.
    Nathaniel Thomas, 136.
    Thomas Wade, 116.
  of New Hampshire,
    Thomas Atkinson, 162.
    Richard Chamberlain, 41.
    Henry Dow, 87.
    Nathaniel Fryer, 6, 149, 154, 158.
    Henry Greene, 64.
    Ralph Hall, 64.
    George Jaffrey, 91, 106, 160.
    Thomas Packer, 102, 121.
    Robert Wadleigh, 48, 63.
    Shadrach Walton, 104, 149.
    Nathaniel Weare, 118.
  of the sessions, 18.

Kennebec. See Index of Places.
  grants recorded, see Index of Grantors under names following:
    Parker, John, 33, 34, 73.
  grant referred to:
    Indians to John Parker, 17.
Kenten, Cantoon, fustian, 111.
Kilter, to put in order, 161.
King's fifth of gold and silver reserved, 152.
  ships, 152.
Kintolls, quintals, 111.
Kitchen, 24, 26.
Kittery. See Index of Places.
  commons, 11, 24, 25, 98, 103, 119, 150.
  corn mills, 52, 57.

Kittery, continued.
  highways, 3, 4, 11, 24, 25, 35, 91, 93, 144, 156.
  saw mills, 2, 24, 26, 52, 57.
  selectmen, 27, 28, 87, 93, 94, 102.
  town book, 27, 28, 90.
    clerk, 27, 28.
    line, 93.
    meeting, 117.
  town grants, 24, 93.
  other grants recorded. See Index of Grantors under names following:
    Adams, Charles, 92.
      Temperance, 92.
    Amerideth, Joan, 145.
    Avant, Francis, 156.
    Banfield, Grace, 91.
    Bodg, Henry, 25.
    Brawn, John, 130.
    Champernown, Francis, 12, 21, 36, 71. 94.
    Conley, Abraham, 3.
    Crockett, Elihu, 1.
      Ephraim, 1.
      Joseph, 150.
      Joshua, 157.
      Thomas's estate, 154, 155.
    Cutt, Richard, 68, 112, 132, 157.
      Samuel, 106.
    Emery, James, 88.
    Estis, Richard, 123.
    Everitt, William, 5.
    Forgisson, Alexander, 97.
    Fryer, Nathaniel, 139, 142.
    Gillman, Edward, 143.
    Glanfield, Peter, 31.
    Goodridge, Isaac, 147.
    Green, John's estate, 83.
    Gunnison, Elihu, 6, 97, 107.
    Hicks, Dennis 122.
    Hodsden, Israel, 98, 103.
    Hooke Francis, 133.
    Hoole, John, 38.
    Hunscum, John's estate, 159.
      Thomas, 105.
    Jeffery, Ann, 1.
    Jenkins, Renald, 60.
    Jose, Richard, 102.

Kittery, continued.
    King, Richard, 158.
      Samuel, 88.
      Sarah, 89.
    Kirle, Richard, 72.
    Litten, George's estate, 138.
    Lord, Nathan's estate, 149.
    Miller, Richard's estate, 91.
      Samuel, 90.
    Neale, John, 129.
    Pouning, Henry's estate, 27, 28.
    Remich, Abraham, 90, 128.
      Christian, 89, 120.
      Isaac, 119.
    Ryce, Thomas, 51.
    Seely, William's estate, 41.
    Seward, John, 110.
    Shapleigh, Alice, 2, 79.
      John, 57, 79.
      Nicholas's estate, 24, 144.
    Shrimpton, Samuel, 82.
    Spinney, Thomas, 112.
    Staple, Peter, 113.
    Tobey, James, 81, 83.
    Wilson, Gowen, 87.
    Withers, Jane, 86, 86.
      Thomas, 5, 11, 25.
    Wittum, Peter, 57, 129.
      William, 57.
    Woodbridge, Benjamin, 121.
    Woodman, John, 95.
  grants referred to:
    town to Joseph Alcock, 102.
    to Henry Bodg, 25.
    to Joseph Crocket, 150, 156.
    to Anthony Emery, 93.
    to James Emery, 88.
    to Nicholas Frost, 93.
    to John Hoole, 38.
    to John Hunscum, 159.
    to Thomas Hunscum, 105.
    to Eliakim Hutchinson, 152.
    to William King, 86, 88, 89.
    to George Leader, 152.
    to Richard Leader, 152.
    to William Love, 117.
    to Richard Miller, 90.
    to Samuel Miller, 90.
    to Henry Pouning, 27, 28.
    to Christian Remich, 89.

GENERAL INDEX. 147

Kittery, continued.
  town to Isaac Remich, 119.
    to John Simmons, 110.
    to Thomas Spencer, 84, 85.
    to John White, 138.
    to Gowen Wilson, 87
    to John Wincoll, 8, 86.
    to William Wittum, 57.
    to John Woodman, 95.
    to town of York, 93.
  William Adams to Elihu Gunnison, 6, 107
  [Philip] Benmore to Charles Adams, 93
  Richard Carle to William Seely, 41.
  Francis Champernown to Nathaniel Fryer, 39
  Joshua Crocket to Francis Avant, 156.
  Robert Cutt's estate to Samuel Shrimpton, 32
  Anthony Emery to [Philip] Benmore, 93.
  James Emery to Philip Benmore. 92.
  Margaret Everett to William Leighton, 56.
  Nath'l Fryer to John Hinks, 139
  Renald Ginkens to Margery Everett or Martha Everett, 56.
  Sir Ferdinando Gorges to John Mason, 152.
  Richard Green to John Green, 83.
  Joseph Hammond to Peter Wittum, 57.
  Eliakim Hutchinson to John Emerson, 23
  Samuel King to Isaac Goodridge, 147.
  Samuel Knight to Peter Glanfield, 31
  Ephraim Lyn to John Cutt, 106.
  Antipas Maverick to Nicholas Shapleigh, 79.
  Alexander Maxell to John Neale, 129.

Kittery, continued.
  Francis Morgan to Bryan Pendleton and John Fabes, 94.
  Francis Morgan to John Cutt, 106.
  Isaac Nash et ux to William Leighton, 5.
  John Newgrove to Renald Ginkens, 56.
  William Oliver to Wm. Goodhue, 3
  William Palmer to Peter Glanfield, 31
  William Palmer to William King, 88, 89.
  William Rucklift to Richard Estis, 129
  Christian Remich to Isaac Remich, 119
  Thomas Spencer to John Wincoll, 86
  William Spencer to John Wincoll, 86.
  Thomas Spinney to John Spinney, 113.
  George Veazie to John Wincoll, 86
  John White to George Litten, 138.
  Thos Withers to John Hoole, 38.
  Thomas Withers to Elizabeth Withers and Mary Rice, 51.
  Peter Wittum, sen. to Peter Wittum, jun., 57.
  Peter Wittum, jun to Wm. Wittum, 57.

Landing places, 21, 82, 154
Law, common, of England, cited, 12.
Laws of the Province cited, 22, 146.
  of Massachusetts, concerning land titles, cited, 29.
Lean-tos, 52, 64, 91, 112.
Leases, 2, 6, 52, 56, 112.
Legacies, 110, 134, 151.
Legal course, remedy at law, 59.
Letters:
  Ursula Cutt to [John] Shapleigh, 111.

Letters, continued.
   Timothy Dwight to [George] Pearson, 50.
   Maine, general assembly of to Gov. Edward Cranfield, 23.
Letters patent, 151.
Levy of execution, 32, 42, 43, 61
Liberties of the king's subjects in Maine to be secured by the general assembly, 24.
Lieutenant, 12, 39, 41, 106.
Life estates, 2, 12, 21, 41, 66, 79, 112, 113.
   limited to widowhood, 54, 113.
   reserved, 6, 13, 21, 57, 81, 86, 113.
Linen, 2, 81.
Linneys, lean-tos, 20.
Livery and seizin, 5, 16, 19, 33, 34, 46, 63, 89, 111, 134
   by a bottle of water, 16.
   by the horn, of cattle, 134.
   by turf and twig, 16, 33, 63, 134
   of a negro, 134.
Loggers, 61.
Log-swamps, 7.
Lord proprietor, judgment and execution against, 43
   of the province of Maine, 46, 47.
Lot-layers, 128.
Loume, loom, 66.
Lumbering and its uses. See Mills, Pay and Prices, under boards, pine boards, staves, timber, &c.
   crows, iron, 57.
   dogs, iron, 57.
   loggers, 61.
   log-swamps, 7
   rafting-place, 8.
Lygonia, province of, 41. 46.
   president, Alexander Rigby, 41.

Magistrate, 86.
Maine. See Lygonia, Pemaquid, Yorkshire.
   assembly, general, 23, 24, 26, 28, 29, 47, 93.
   charter of, 24.
   courts:
      of appeals, 43, 149.
      of associates, at Wells, 61.

Maine, continued.
   courts, held at York, 32.
     of pleas, 32, 43, 61.
     of quarter sessions, 18.
     of sessions, held at York, 128.
   laws of the province cited, 22, 146.
   lord proprietor of, 7, 38, 43, 47, 49, 145.
   militia, 30.
   orders, executive, 41.
     of the general assembly, 24, 26, 28, 29.
   magistrates and other officers. See Deputy governor, President, Deputy president, Assistants, Associates, Commissioners, Magistrate, Marshal, Deputy marshal, Notary public, Prothonotary, Register, Secretary, Treasurer, Clerk of court, Jail-keeper.
   records. See under Yorkshire.
   John Davess, deputy president, 13, 21, 36, 37, 41, 44, 54, 72, 140, 144.
   Thomas Danforth, president of, 17, 18, 28, 30, 41, 47, 76
   Thomas Gorges, deputy governor, 46.
Major, 15, 19, 20, 24, 26, 30, 41, 45, 51, 52, 67, 79, 114, 134, 144, 153.
Majority attained, 60.
Manners and customs. See Contracts, Domestic uses, Marriage settlements, Occupations, Partnerships, Pay, Prices, Support, Titles.
   allotment of land to new settlers, 41.
   annuity, 111, 126
   bound and marked trees, *q. v.*
   bridges
   burying-ground reserved, 12, 96.
   country's use, 30.
   creditors of intestate, 61.
   feast of St. Michael, 69.
   fowling, hawking, hunting, *q. v.*
   garrison, 96.
   labor, 50.

GENERAL INDEX.   149

Manners and customs, continued.
  liberties, 24.
  majority, 60.
  meeting houses, 61, 68, 69.
  rates, taxes, 7, 43, 113, 151
Manure, a farm, 113.
Mariner, 11, 14, 29, 51, 65, 83, 85, 99, 100, 125, 161.
Marked trees, 1, 10, 23, 24, 25, 26, 28, 34, 37, 38, 40, 44, 54, 65, 67, 68, 93, 102, 103, 109, 127, 145, 150, 156.
  bound trees, 34.
Marriage, provision restricting, 36.
  portion, 47, 78, 86, 91, 110, 111, 126, 160.
Marshal of the province, John Smyth, 41, 42
  Nathaniel Masterson, 61.
Massachusetts. See Assistants and Justices.
  Simon Bradstreet, governor, 9, 10.
  Thomas Danforth, deputy governor, 9.
  Edward Rawson, secretary, 23, 30.
  act of general court, 23, 93.
  commissioners of, 99, 100, 101.
  council of, 30.
  councillors of, 90, 113, 115, 126, 127, 136, 147.
  court records, 23.
  general court, 23, 93.
  laws of, concerning land titles, 29
  record book of notary public for, 9, 20.
  orders of general court, 23.
  superior court at Boston, 149.
Masts reserved for the King's ships, 152
Mast-way, 83.
Mayor, 14, 46.
Mayor and coality [commonalty], 46.
Meeting houses, 61, 68, 69.
  banisters, benches, galleries, seats, stairs, 68.
  gallery for men, 68, women, 68.

Merchant, 3, 6, 9, 14, 15, 16, 17, 18, 23, 26, 30, 32, 42, 47, 49, 50, 51, 82, 87, 94, 99, 100, 101, 102, 108, 127, 130, 139, 140, 141, 146, 149, 150, 151, 158, 161.
Messuages, 13, 41.
Militia, 30.
  committee of, 30.
  certificate of seizure of property for military use, 30.
Miles, English, 15.
Milk, cow's, 52
Mills. See Corn mills, Lumbering, Saw mills, Timber, Water courses
  dams, 8, 52, 64, 74, 75, 135, 152, 161.
  gear, 8, 135.
  head-weirs, 75, 135.
  implements, 57.
  iron-work, 57.
  landing places, 21, 82, 154.
  privileges, 47, 64, 67, 122.
  produce of, 2.
  rent, 2, 9.
  piling places, 64
  saws, 57.
  slabs, 56.
  utensils, 8.
  yard-room, 8.
Mill-wright, 5, 57, 82.
Minerals, 15, 16, 18, 19, 39, 62, 116, 139, 151, 152.
Mines, 15, 16, 18, 19, 39, 62, 106, 116, 139, 151, 152.
Ministers, 9, 23, 46, 64, 118, 121. See Clerk.
  settlement of, 23.
Ministry lands, 23, 86, 90, to be reserved, 41.
Minority, 86, 92.
Mis, Mrs, 2, 12, 20, 21, 24, 26, 30, 35, 36, 41, 49, 52, 62, 69, 112, 135, 144, 145, 150.
Mistress, 88, 147.
Money, lent, 26.
Mooring-places, 13, 26.
Mortgages, 50, 53, 75, 77, 82, 99, 102, 107, 132, 139, 146, 117, 158.
  foreclosure of, 75.
  pleadable in court, 147.

150 GENERAL INDEX.

Motto on a seal, 14.
Moveables, chattels, 66.
Mowing, 34, 43.
Mr., 2, 3, 5, 7, 9, 11, 12, 14, 15, 16, 17, 18, 19, 22, 23, 24, 25, 26, 28, 30, 31, 34, 35, 36, 38, 39, 40, 41, 42, 43, 46, 49, 50, 51, 56, 57, 61, 62, 64, 65, 69, 71, 72, 74, 79, 94, 96, 99, 102, 104, 106, 107, 109, 111, 112, 114, 115, 116, 117, 118, 123, 126, 127, 128, 129, 131, 132, 135, 139, 140, 141, 142, 144, 145, 146, 148, 157.
Muniments of title, 50, 137.
Musket, 35.

Nails, 68.
Napkins, 2.
Negroes, 2, 52, 53, 133.
New Hampshire. See Justices.
  chief justice of, Walter Barefoote, 41.
  commissioners of, 5, 47, 51, 142.
  councillors of, 68, 69.
  governor, Edward Cranfield, 24.
  officers of the province of, 23.
  president, John Cutt, 106.
    John Hincks, 107, 141.
  tolls levied on Maine vessels, 23.
North Yarmouth. See Index of Places.
  orders for settlement of, 41.
  grants recorded, see Index of Grantors under names following:
    Bray, Richard, 44.
    Drake, Thomas, 32.
    Gendall, Walter, 76.
    Gidney, Bartholomew, 75.
    Haynes, Thomas, 19.
    Maine, province of, 28, 29, 46.
    Ryall, John, 65.
  grants referred to:
    Sir Ferdinando Gorges to John Cossons, 24.
    Indians to Thomas Stephens, 75.
    Henry Sayword to Bartholomew Gidney, 75.
    Thomas Stephens to Bartholomew Gidney, 75.

North Yarmouth, continued.
  Thomas Stephens to Henry Sayword, 75.
Notary public, 9, 13, 14, 18, 20.
  record book of, for Massachusetts, 9, 20.
Nowels, noyles, shoddy woolen cloth, 67.

Occupation and possession, 4, 11, 12, 14, 16, 19, 23, 24, 31, 34, 37, 43, 55, 73, 74, 80, 82, 115, 126, 151.
Occupations:
  anchor smith, 99.
  blacksmith, 79, 99, 107, 108.
  brick-layer, 98.
  brick-maker, 115.
  carpenter, 3, 11, 27, 31, 61, 91, 96, 119, 120, 149, 160.
  chirurgeon, surgeon, 30.
  clerk, minister, 22.
  clerk of court, 151.
  cooper, 7, 155, 157.
  cordwainer, 10, 48, 50, 61, 77, 115.
  doctor, 154.
  fisherman, 1, 13, 17, 26, 27, 29, 34, 38, 40, 42, 44, 46, 73, 80, 129, 143, 159.
  glazier, 31.
  glover, 143.
  goldsmith, 10, 50.
  house carpenter, 73.
  husbandman, 19, 30, 44, 54, 106, 110, 130, 148.
  Indian trader, 19.
  jail keeper, 61.
  joiner, 96.
  loggers, 61.
  lot layers, 128.
  mariner, 11, 14, 29, 51, 65, 83, 85, 99, 100, 125, 161.
  merchant, 3, 6, 9, 14, 15, 16, 17, 18, 23, 26, 30, 32, 42, 47, 49, 50, 51, 82, 87, 94, 99, 100, 101, 102, 103, 127, 130, 139, 140, 141, 146, 149, 150, 151, 158, 161.
  mill-wright, 5, 57, 82.
  minister, 9, 23, 46, 64, 118, 121.

General Index.   151

Occupations, continued.
  planter, 3, 4, 7, 12, 19, 21, 45, 63, 84, 85, 88, 91, 93, 149, 150, 155.
  saddler, 156.
  sailor, 146.
  sawyer, 61.
  scrivener, 160.
  seaman, 14, 51, 59. 60.
  servant, 18, 30, 66, 76.
  ship-wright, 54, 83, 97, 102, 105, 110, 145, 157, 158.
  shop-keeper, 27, 28.
  smith. 154.
  surveyor, 24, 88, 90, 93, 128, 149.
  tailor, 19, 31, 87, 108, 115.
  tanner, 77.
  victualler, 134.
  vintner, 94, 117, 124.
  weaver, 66, 114, 115, 146, 148.
  yeoman, 8, 10, 11, 14, 22, 31, 32, 38, 39, 51, 58, 60, 68, 74, 75, 80, 81, 87, 88, 89, 95, 100, 101, 109, 112, 113, 117, 125, 126, 131, 136, 147, 156, 159.
Oniston, Honiton, 67.
Option to purchase, 161.
Orchards, 6, 19, 24, 26, 52, 61, 66, 75, 77, 79, 87, 91, 104, 109, 112, 117, 119, 123, 124, 130, 137, 138, 147.
Orchard trees, 130.
Orders, 30, 47, 159.
  of court, 52, 144.
  of general assembly of Maine, 24, 26, 28, 29.
  of general court of Massachusetts, 28.
Overplus, surplus, 134.

Parish of Berwick, 65.
Parlor, 24.
Parsonage house, 64.
Partitions, 22, 45, 104, 116.
Partnerships, 72, 116, 161.
Pasturage, 23, 40, 109.
Patents:
  Council for New England, 151.
  Lewis and Bonighton's and divisions thereof, 22.
  Scottow's, 40.

Patents, continued.
  Sir Ferdinando Gorges, 151.
  Way and Purchase, 14, 16, 17, 18.
Pay. See also under Consideration.
  beaver (spring), 6.
  beef, 30.
  boards, 111, 153.
  butter, 81, 113.
  cash, 67.
  cheese, 81, 113.
  cider, 81, 113.
  corn, 32, 81.
    English, 113.
    Indian, 57, 69, 86, 113.
  cows, 80.
  current money of New England, 10, 16, 18, 24, 27, 28, 31, 32, 42, 65, 68, 77, 78, 94, 97, 101, 102, 104, 107, 108, 109, 111, 117, 120, 124, 125, 126, 130, 133, 135, 136, 138, 139, 140, 144, 146, 147, 149, 150, 152, 156, 158, 161.
  current pay of New England, 1, 4, 26, 30, 39, 41, 51, 54, 61, 69, 81.
  domestic animals, 113.
  equivalent to money, 11, 52, 67, 92.
  fish, 6, 67, 107.
    codfish, 13, 30, 31.
    cusk, 17.
    dry codfish, 13, 17, 26, 64.
    merchantable, 26, 31, 111.
    refuge, refuse, 31.
  fruit, 113.
  garden-stuff, 113.
  goods, 6, 7, 12, 59, 92, 107, 134.
  lawful, 30.
  merchantable, 66, 92.
  milk, 113.
  molasses, 69.
  money, 7, 11, 59, 61, 62, 81, 88, 89, 92, 95, 105, 106, 111, 115, 128, 132, 142, 146, 147, 154, 157, 158, 159, 160.
    current, 19, 20, 37.
    lawful, 20, 44, 83, 87, 92, 96, 100, 102, 109, 110, 114, 115, 119, 129, 148.

Pay, continued.
  oxen, 80.
  pine boards, 2, 8, 30, 37, 52, 82, 99, 102.
  pipe staves, 3.
    hogshead, 21.
    merchantable, 21, 31.
    red oak, 21.
    white, 21.
  produce of a plantation, 81, 113.
  provisions, 19.
  serge, 86.
  silver, 43, 86, 111.
  speties, specie, like kind, 26.
  swine, 59, 113.
  wool, 113.
  work, 32.
Pease, green, 52
Pejepscot, afterward Brunswick. See Index of Places.
  grants recorded, see Index of Grantors, under the names following:
    Blany, Elizabeth, 17.
    Elkine, Jane, 17.
    Massachusetts, 23.
    Purchase, Elizabeth, 17.
      Thomas's estate, 17
    Warumbee, 15.
    Way, Eleazer, 18.
    Wharton, Richard, 17.
  grants referred to:
    Massachusetts to Rich'd Wharton, 23
    Thomas Purchase to Inhabitants at, 15.
    John Shapleigh to Richard Wharton, 15
    Richard Wharton to Purchase heirs, 16.
Pemaquid, Thomas Sharp commander at, 69.
Penelope, a fishing shallop, 133.
Petitions, 23, 24, 28, 29.
  address to the king, 24.
Pewter [ware], 2, 81.
Pileing places, 64.
Pillow-bears, 2.
Plantations, 22, 29, 32, 44, 53, 59, 113, 151, 158.

Planter, 3, 4, 7, 12, 19, 21, 45, 68, 84, 85, 88, 91, 93, 149, 150, 155.
Planting, 19, 31.
  field, 6.
  grounds, 27.
    ancient Indian, reserved, 15.
  on halves, 19.
Plat, survey, 152.
Platters, 61
Plough-stuff, timber for, 40.
Portion, marriage, 27, 34.
Powers of attorney, 3, 9, 13, 18, 33, 34, 49, 50, 60, 118, 140, 141.
Precious stones, 151, 152.
President of the court of appeals, Thomas Danforth, 43
  of the province of Maine, Thos. Danforth, 17, 18, 28, 30, 41, 47, 76.
  of the province of New Hampshire, John Cutt 106, John Hinckes, 107, 114.
Prices:
  beaver [spring], 6.
  boards, 26
  broadcloth, per yard, 67.
  buttons, by the gross, 67.
  silk, 67.
  calf, 52.
  camlet, 67.
  canting, fustian, 67.
  canvas, 67
  cattle, neat, per head, 113.
  cattle, pastured, 40.
  cod lines, per dozen, 67.
  cows, 30, 35, 52.
  day's work, 40.
  fish, 67.
  gimp, 67.
  hall cloth, 57.
  hat, castor, 67.
    felt, 67.
  heifers, 52.
  hogshead, head, 67.
  Honiton lace, 67.
  horse, 2
  kenten, fustian, 111.
  kersey cloth, 67.
  lambs, 52.
  land, per acre, 56.

GENERAL INDEX. 153

Prices, continued.
  linen, blue, 67.
  locerum, lockram, a coarse linen, 67.
  mackerel, per barrel, 67.
  molasses, per hogshead, 67.
  nowels, 67.
  oakum, 67.
  pease, 67.
  pine boards, 8.
  pipe staves, red oak, 21, 26.
    white, 21.
  pork, 67.
  refuse fish, 67.
  salt, per hogshead, 67.
  serge, 67.
  sheep, 52.
  silk, skeins, 67.
  steers, 52, 56.
  tabby, taffety, 67.
  trees, felled, 40.
Produce of a farm, 113.
Proclamation set up, by way of notice to creditors, 61.
Promissory note, 42, 99.
Prothonotary, 67.

Quick stock, 40, 66.
Quit-rent, 47, 152, 153.

Rafting-place, 8.
Rafts of canoes, 56.
Rails, 61.
Rates, taxes, 113, 151.
Receipts, 13, 30, 31, 32, 35, 42, 49, 50, 59, 61, 69, 86, 99, 111, 126, 134, 136, 159.
Re-entry for condition broken, 24.
References, 2, 12, 18, 25.
Referring, recorder's error for reserving, 21.
Refuse, option, 65.
Registers, or Recorders,
  Edward Rishworth, 1—67.
  Thomas Scottow, 67—78.
  Joseph Hammond, 69, 79—162.
Releases, 19, 35, 50, 90, 91, 93, 106, 110.
Remainders, 2, 12, 13, 36, 41, 86.

Rents, 2, 9, 40, 52, 57, 81, 111, 126, 152, 153.
  payable in produce, 113.
Repairs, liberty to make, 24.
  to house, 113.
Reports, by commissioners, committee, &c., 23.
Reservations, 1, 6, 12, 15, 21, 28, 40, 44, 46, 52, 57, 61, 63, 64, 67, 81, 105, 107, 113, 126, 132, 135, 139, 142, 146, 153.
Residuary legatee, 41.
Restrictions, 141.
  as to alienation, 40.
  as to felling timber, 40.
  as to grazing cattle, 40.
Return to assessors of taxable estate, 43.
Reverend Mr., 77.
Reversions, 40, 47, 65, 68, 79, 111, 137.
Revocation of a deed, 72.
Rights of way, 4, 8, 24, 26, 28, 40, 54, 59, 65, 87, 90, 104, 121, 135, 141.
Roads, cables, 133.
Run, of water, 61, 67, 78, 114.
Ryall, real, a Spanish silver coin, 12½ cents.

Saco. See Index of Places.
  Andover men settling at, 22.
  commons, 42.
  grist mill, 45.
  saw mills, 20, 42, 161.
  grants recorded, see Index of Grantors under names following:
    Berry, Ambrose, 161.
    Bonighton, John, 22.
    Fletcher, Pendleton, 45.
    Gibbons, James, 22, 155.
    Giffard, John, 42.
    Honewell, John, 115.
    Jordan, Dominicus, 44.
    Phillips, Samuel, 134.
    Selly, Richard, 99, 101.
    Sergent, Edward, 124.
    Trustrum, Ralph's estate, 94.
    Wormestall, Arthur, 27, 43.

Saco, continued.
　grants referred to:
　　John Bonighton to William Phillips, 135.
　　Simon Booth to Bryan Pendleton, 45.
　　William Phillips to William Frost, 135.
　　to Mr. Haenan, 135.
　　Richard Randall, by mesne conveyances to Dominicus Jordan, 44.
　　Richard Vines to Robert Jordan, 41.
Saddle of a rock, 73.
Saddler, 136.
Sagadahoc.
　grant recorded, see Index of Grantors under Pritchett, John, 36.
Sagamores, of the Androscoggin and Kennebec, 14, 15, 16.
Sailor, 146.
Salmon, 15.
Saw-mills, at Berwick, 7, 8, 11, 152.
　at Falmouth, 72, 74.
　at Kittery, 2, 24, 26, 52, 57.
　at Saco, 20, 42, 135, 161.
　at Wells, 61.
　at York, 36, 54, 66.
Sawyers, 61.
Scarborough. See Index of Places.
　highway, 69.
　selectmen, 69.
　town clerk, 69.
　　records, 69, 121.
　town grants, 69.
　other grants recorded, see Index of Grantors under names following:
　　Burrage, William, 62.
　　Elleot, Robert, 121.
　　Ingersall, George, 72.
　　Jordan, Sarah, 80.
　　Morton, John, 136.
　　Scottow, Joshua, 22, 23, 40, 61.
　　Tayler, Andrew, 59.
　　　George, 59.
　　Whinnick, Joseph's estate, 80.

Scarborough, continued.
　grants referred to:
　　town to Thomas Bickford, 43.
　　to Robert Elliot, 121.
　　Christopher Ellkines to Peter Hinxen, 40.
　　Christopher's father to Peter Hinxen, 40.
　　John Howell to John Morton, 137.
　　Henry Jocelyn to Joshua Scottow, 23.
Scrivener, 160.
Seals, official, of notary public, 14.
　of mayor of a city, 14.
　common, of council for New England, 151.
　great of England, 151.
Seamen, 14, 51, 59, 60.
Secretary of the general assembly of the province of Maine, Edward Rishworth, 24.
　of Massachusetts, Edward Rawson, 23, 30.
Selectmen, to be chosen by a majority of inhabitants, 18.
　of Berwick, 23.
　of Falmouth, 74.
　of Kittery, 27, 28, 87, 93, 94, 102.
　of Scarborough, 69.
　of York, 28, 30, 37, 46, 48, 58, 59, 67, 93.
Sergeant-at-law, 46.
Servant, 18, 30, 66, 76.
Shallop, a fishing boat, 13.
Sheep-shed, 33.
Sheets, cotton, 2.
　Dowless, a coarse linen, 2.
Shipwright, 54, 83, 97, 102, 105, 110, 145, 157, 158.
Shop, 13, -keeper, 27, 28.
Slabs, 56.
Sled, 40.
Smith, 154.
Springs, 73, 93, 111, 116.
Stables, 20, 77, 109.
Stages, fishing, 13, 26, 87.
Stepping stones, 145.
Stock of cattle, 2, 52, 61, 81, 112, 140.

Sturgeon, 15.
Successors, 151.
Support and maintenance, 12, 61, 66, 113, 121.
Surveys, 61, 63, 88.
Surveyors, 24, 88, 90, 93, 128, 149.
Surviving heir, 106.
Survivor, 59, 113.

Tackling, cotton, of a loom, 66.
Tackle, of a vessel, 13.
Tailor, 19, 31, 37, 108, 115.
Tanner, 77.
Taxes, 7, 43.
   country, 7.
   town, 7, 151.
Tenants in common, 7, 10, 17, 18, 27, 43, 47, 57, 63, 71, 75, 124, 132, 141, 149, 159.
Tenure, as of the manor of East Greenwich, 152.
   by free and common soccage, 152.
   by knight's service, 152.
   in capite, 152.
Thatch, 55.
   banks, 87.
   creek, 56, 109.
   grass, 56, 155.
Thirds, dower, q. v.
Threshing, 61, 113.
Timber, grants of, 7, 8, 15, 19, 27, 33, 37, 38, 39, 57, 58, 63, 65, 67, 73, 74, 81, 89, 105, 117, 123, 139, 144, 150, 152.
   building, 23, 40.
   fencing, 40.
   for plow stuff, 40.
   house, 108.
   leased, 52.
   pines, right to cut, 23.
   reserved, 46, 105, 135.
      for masts, 152.
Titles:
   captain, 2, 8, 9, 12, 20, 21, 23, 24, 25, 30, 35, 36, 40, 42, 50, 51, 53, 61, 65, 67, 72, 73, 82, 86, 88, 94, 99, 100, 101, 102, 103, 109, 110, 134, 151, 152, 154, 157, 159.
   doctor, 154.

Titles, continued.
   esquire, 14, 17, 23, 30, 46, 51, 53, 75, 149, 153.
   gentleman, 3, 5, 20, 30, 45, 46, 51, 63, 71, 109, 111, 112, 117, 126, 134, 157.
   goodman, 32.
   lieutenant, 12, 39, 41, 106.
   major, 15, 19, 20, 24, 26, 28, 34, 37, 38, 40, 44, 54, 65, 67, 68, 93, 102, 103, 109, 127, 145, 150, 156.
   Mis, Mrs., 2, 12, 20, 21, 24, 26, 30, 35, 36, 41, 49, 52, 62, 69, 112, 135, 144, 145, 150.
   mistress, 88, 147.
   Mr., 2, 3, 5, 7, 9, 11, 12, 14, 15, 16, 17, 18, 19, 22, 23, 24, 25, 26, 28, 30, 31, 34, 35, 36, 38, 39, 40, 41, 42, 43, 46, 49, 50, 51, 56, 57, 61, 62, 64, 65, 69, 71, 72, 74, 79, 94, 96, 99, 102, 104, 106, 107, 109, 111, 112, 114, 115, 116, 117, 118, 123, 126, 127, 128, 129, 131, 132, 135, 139, 140, 141, 142, 144, 145, 146, 148, 157.
   Reverend Mr., 77.
Tolls levied on Maine vessels entering Piscataqua, by New Hampshire, 23.
Tools, for husbandry, 112.
Towels, 2.
Town, an English, proposed to be settled opposite Brunswick, 15.
   on the site of Bath, 18.
   at North Yarmouth, 41.
   bounds of, to be new marked every three years, 93.
   free holders of, 18.
   meetings, 117.
   officers, act regulating choice of, 193.
   provision to be made for eighty families in, 41.
   regulation of the affairs of, 18.
Trade, grant of town lot as an inducement for a special, 41.
Traine fat, oil vat, 64.
Treasurer of York county, Samuel Wheelwright, 30.

Trunks, 2.
Trustees, 19, 51, 86.

Unfenced land, 24, 26.

Vantage, upwards of, 52.
Verbal agreement for sale of land, 80.
Vessels, 23.
　anchors, 13, 26, 133.
　appurtenances, 13.
　Arabella, a fishing shallop, 133.
　boat, 13, 26.
　cables, 13,
　canoes, 43, 56.
　compass, 53.
　furniture, 26.
　grappers, grapnels, 13.
　masts, 13.
　mooring-cable, 13, 26.
　　places, 13, 26.
　oars, 13.
　Penelope, a fishing shallop, 133.
　porridge-pot, 13.
　roads, cables, 133.
　sails, 133.
　shallop, a fishing boat, 13, 133.
　spars, 25.
　standing part, 13.
　tackle, 13.
　yards, 13.
　obstruction of, entering Newgewannacke river, 23.
　tolls levied on, by New Hampshire, 23.
　voyages, 24, 133.
Victualler, 134.
Village, 137.
Vintner, 94, 117, 124.
Voyage from Wells to Boston, 24.
　winter, for fishing, 133.

War, Indian, 15, 16, 43.
Water courses, 116, 124, 133, 135, 150 and elsewhere.
Weaver, 66, 114, 115, 146, 148.
Weaving, art of, 66.
Well, 104.
Wells. See Index of Places.
　commons, 143.

Wells, continued.
　highways, 38, 39.
　saw mill, 61.
　town lot, 47.
　grants recorded, see Index of Grantors under names following:
　　Baston, Thomas, 4.
　　Coole, Nicholas, 12.
　　Cross, Joseph, 10, 38.
　　Denmarke, James, 95.
　　Gooch, James, 125.
　　Hammond, William, 128.
　　Littlefield, Francis, 39.
　　Nanney, Katherine, 111.
　　　Robert, 127.
　　Ridden, John, 143.
　　Smyth, John, 4.
　　Wadleigh, John, 48, 63, 64.
　　　Robert, 45, 47, 63.
　　Wheelwright, Samuel, 126.
　　Young, John, 47.
　grants referred to:
　　town to Joseph Cross, 38.
　　Peter Cloyce to Thomas Baston, 4.
　　Coole to Robert Nanney, 111, 126.
　　Cross to Joseph Cross, 10.
　　Geo. Farrow to Mary Smyth, 4.
　　Samuel Hatch to John Redden, 143.
　　William Hammond to Robert Nanney, 111, 126.
　　Francis Littlefield to Thomas Baston, 4.
　　William Symonds to Robert Nanney, 111, 126.
　　John Wadleigh to Rob't Wadleigh, 63.
　　Robert Wadleigh to William Sawyer, 64.
　　to John Wadleigh, 63.
　　John Wheelwright to Robert Nanney, 111, 126.
　　John Young to William Sawyer, 46.
Wharves, 135.
Widowhood, estate limited to, 54.
Widow's thirds, or dower right, 52.

Wills referred to:
Matthew Austine (not allowed), 66.
Lucy Chadbourne *alias* Wills, 51.
John Cutt, 30.
Davis, 66.
Morgan Howell, 3.
John Hull, 53.
Margaret Mountegue, 10, 62.
Bryan Pendleton, 45.
William Phillips, 134.
Nicholas Shapleigh, 41.
Thomas Spencer, 11.
Thomas Wade, 118.
John Wadleigh, 47, 64.
Thomas Withers, 36.
Wood, 90, 117.
  privilege of storing, 13.
Wooden vessels, 81.
Woolen, on a loom, 66, cloths, 81.

Yards, 24, 26, 52, 75, 104.
Yeoman, 8, 10, 11, 14, 22, 31, 32, 38, 39, 51, 58, 60, 68, 74, 75, 80, 81, 87, 88, 89, 95, 100, 101, 109, 112, 113, 117, 125, 126, 131, 136, 147, 156, 157. See Husbandman.
Yoke of oxen, 35.
York. See Index of Places.
  commons, 54, 67, 68.
  highways, 28, 46, 58, 59, 61, 107, 108, 114.
  meeting house, 61, 68.
  mills, 36, 54, 66.
  records, 7, 48, 58, 59.
  selectmen, 28, 30, 37, 46, 48, 58, 59, 67, 93.
  town clerk, 58.
    land reserved, 67.
    line, 93.
    meeting, 48.
  town grants, 28, 58, 59, 67, 93.
  other grants recorded, see Index of Grantors under names following:
    Austine, Matthew, 114. 146.
    Banks, Joseph, 107.
    Beale, Arthur, 29.
    Burdett, George, 20.
    Coman, Richard, 108.

York, continued.
  Curtis, Benjamin, 31.
  Curtis, Thomas, 7.
  Davess, John, 30, 154, 159.
  Dixon, James, 47.
  Freathy, William, 5.
  Gooch, Benjamin, 115.
  Gorges, Sir Ferdinando, 46.
  Hilton, William, 43, 148, 158.
  Liveingstone, Daniel, 45.
  Mowlton, Thomas, 60.
  Parker, Isaac, 21.
    John, 61.
  Raynes, Francis, 21, 24.
  Rogers, Ezekiel, 109.
  Sayword, Henry, 82.
  Shapleigh, Alice, 20.
  Smyth, John, 19, 36, 54, 78.
  Trafton, Thomas, 79.
  Twisden, John, 58.
    Mary, 129.
  Weare, Joseph, 146.
  Whitney, Benjamin, 37.
  Young, Rowland, 48, 53, 159.
grants referred to:
  town to Matthew Austine, 66.
  to Arthur Beale, 29.
  to George Burdett, 46.
  to Thomas Curtis, 7.
  to Henry Donnell, 115.
  to John Davis, 159.
  to Davis, 66.
  to John Harker, 159.
  to town of Kittery, 93.
  to William Johnson, 46.
  to Daniel Liveingstone et ux., 45.
  to William Moore, 159.
  to Henry Sayword, 82.
  to John Smyth, 36.
  to Benjamin Whitney, 37.
  to Rowland Young, 48, 159.
Richard Banks to William Wormewood, 7.
Robert Edge to Peter Twisden, 129.
Ann Godfrey to Wm. Moore, 36.
William Johnson to town of York, 46.
  to Richard Woods, 46.

York, continued.
    Robert Knight to Rowland Young et ux., 53.
    Edward Rishworth to Job Allcocke, 109.
    Ezekiel Rogers to Joseph Penuel, 109.
    John Smyth to John Smyth, jun., 19.
    John Wentworth to Isaac Parker, 21.

York, continued.
    Rich'd Woods to Jós. Preble, 46.
    Rowland Young to Robert Young, 53.

Yorkshire,
    court records of, 32.
    records of, 5, 17, 20, 23, 47, 96, 140, 141.
    treasurer of, 30.
    treasury of, 30.

CPSIA information can be obtained
at www.ICGtesting.com
Printed in the USA
LVHW081948070521
686793LV00002B/81

9 781344 730495